DEFENSE TRANSPORTATION: ALGORITHMS, MODELS, AND APPLICATIONS FOR THE 21ST CENTURY

DEFENSE TRANSPORTATION: ALGORITHMS, MODELS, AND APPLICATIONS FOR THE 21ST CENTURY

Editors

ROBERT T. BRIGANTIC, LT. COL., USAF
Air Force Institute of Technology
Department of Operational Sciences (AFIT/ENS)
2950 Hobson Way
Wright Patterson AFB, OH 45433-7765, U.S.A.

JEAN M. MAHAN
Northrop Grumman Information Technology Government Solutions
United States Transportation Command (USTRANSCOM)
TCJ5-AS
Joint Analytical Support Program
Scott AFB, IL 62225, U.S.A.

Reprinted from Mathematical and Computer Modelling, Volume 39, No. 6-8, 2004

2004

ELSEVIER

Amsterdam - Boston - Heidelberg - London - New York - Oxford - Paris - San Diego - San Francisco
Singapore - Sydney - Tokyo

'IER B.V.
ırgerhartstraat 25
›x 211, 1000 AE
·dam, The Netherlands

ELSEVIER Inc.
525 B Street, Suite 1900
San Diego, CA 92101-4495
USA

ELSEVIER Ltd
The Boulevard, Langford Lane
Kidlington, Oxford OX5 1GB
UK

ELSEVIER Ltd
84 Theobalds Road
London WC1X 8RR
UK

dition 2004

y of Congress Cataloging in Publication Data
log record is available from the Library of Congress.

Library Cataloguing in Publication Data
logue record is available from the British Library.

SBN 10: 0 080 44405 9
SBN 13: 9780080444055

nted from Mathematical and Computer Modelling, Volume 39, No. 6-8, 2004
sferred to digital printing, 2007
ed and bound by CPI Antony Rowe, Eastbourne

CONTENTS

Available online at www.sciencedirect.com
SCIENCE DIRECT
Mathematical and Computer Modelling 39 (2004) vii
MATHEMATICAL AND COMPUTER MODELLING
www.elsevier.com/locate/mcm

Preface

As this special edition goes to press, our nation is engaged in the final phases of Operation Iraqi Freedom (OIF). However, our mission is far from over. The United States Transportation Command remains fully engaged supporting operations in Iraq, the continuing war on terrorism, and the global peacetime and contingency requirements of our nation's warfighters. With few exceptions, the military forces and their equipment engaged around the world are transported by the Defense Transportation System (DTS). The ships, planes, trains, and trucks, of the DTS, operated by our superb military, civilian, and commercial team are vital to our success now and in the future.

The composition and employment of today's transportation systems have their foundations in superb, thorough studies and analyses. Such studies and analyses, for example, delineated the need to modernize our strategic airlift fleet with the C-17 Globemaster III and acquire additional "large medium-speed roll-on roll-off" ships (LMSRs), both of which proved so effective in recent operations. Agile, capable, and reliable forces are key to future force projection and sustainment. We demonstrated significantly improved delivery rates of equipment and supplies by air and sea for Operation Iraqi Freedom compared to Operation Desert Storm. These trends are certainly in the right direction—they must continue to meet our increasingly dynamic world.

In this 21st Century, new mobility studies and analyses will be conducted to assess the transportation feasibility of proposed peacetime operations, war plans, and other concepts of operation in support of our nation's National Security Strategy. The *algorithms, models, and applications* presented in this special issue will play a significant role in that effort and will facilitate quality decision support tools needed by our nation's senior leadership to plan for, secure, and execute billions of dollars in transportation resources required in the defense of the country.

Your work is extremely important. My personal thanks to all the contributors in this special issue, and the many military, civilian, and commercial analysts and modelers throughout the DoD who contribute to our nation's warfighting success and the mission of the United States Transportation Command. You make it happen!

John W. Handy
General, USAF

doi:10.1016/j.mcm.2004.02.024

Typeset by $\mathcal{A}\mathcal{M}\mathcal{S}$-TEX

Available online at www.sciencedirect.com
SCIENCE DIRECT®
ELSEVIER
Mathematical and Computer Modelling 39 (2004) ix–x
MATHEMATICAL AND COMPUTER MODELLING
www.elsevier.com/locate/mcm

Introduction and Dedication

This special issue of *Mathematical and Computer Modelling* contains a collection of manuscripts that addresses algorithms, models, and applications related to the Defense Transportation System (DTS). DTS research topics can be both highly specialized (e.g., aerial refueling tanker crew scheduling algorithms) and broad (e.g., models that simultaneously allocate and assign transportation airlift and sealift resources to move military cargo and passengers from the "Fort to the Foxhole"). Accordingly, we received a wide variety of papers for consideration, papers from government and industry defense transportation analysts, as well as papers from tenured professors and graduate students from civilian and military universities.

With this special issue's focus on the Defense Transportation System, we felt it was important to include papers that present DTS models and applications that have recently been used in analysis efforts supporting key transportation procurement and operational decisions. We believe inclusion of these papers contributes to the overall intent of this special issue to publicize and disseminate DTS research and analysis efforts.

We grouped the papers into three general sections according to the title of this special issue. The first section on algorithms, contains eight papers that are theoretical in nature or contain new techniques that relate to DTS processes. A sampling of the papers contained in this section deals with group theoretic "tabu" search techniques, shortest path sailing distance algorithms, and strategic airlift model validation methods. The second section, contains eight papers on various transportation models used throughout the DoD and transportation industry, as well as some newly developed transportation modeling methods that may eventually find their way into larger scale transportation models. A review of the major strategic mobility models is also contained in this section. The third section contains six papers on various transportation applications that have been used to support various DTS studies and analyses. This section also contains a diverse set of topics, with articles ranging from a paper on North Atlantic Treaty Organization (NATO) strategic lift requirements to an analysis paper on theater reception, staging, onward movement, and integration.

Despite the relatively large number of papers in this special issue and their diverse nature, we must point out that this special issue only scratches the surface on all of the algorithms, models, and methods in use today throughout the DTS. The analysis problems presented by the DTS are often extremely complex and challenging to address. Because the DTS constitutes the biggest and best transportation company in the world, there will always be a demand for talented and motivated transportation professionals such as those who have contributed to this special issue.

We would like to thank Professor Ervin Y. Rodin for inviting us to be guest editors for this special issue on Defense Transportation. It has been a unique and rewarding experience for both of us. We acknowledge and thank everyone who participated in the successful outcome of this journal by either submitting and/or reviewing candidate manuscripts. Lastly, in the aftermath of September 11, 2001 and with the on-going War on Terrorism, we dedicate this special issue to the men and woman of the United States Armed Forces who are currently serving on foreign soil

doi:10.1016/j.mcm.2004.02.005
Typeset by $\mathcal{A}_{\mathcal{M}}\mathcal{S}$-TEX

and placing their lives on the line for our freedom. We trust that solid transportation analyses will continue to contribute to their success and safe return home. Godspeed!

Robert Brigantic
Jean Mahan
Guest Editors

Available online at www.sciencedirect.com

SCIENCE DIRECT®

Mathematical and Computer Modelling 39 (2004) 581–598

MATHEMATICAL AND COMPUTER MODELLING

www.elsevier.com/locate/mcm

Continuous Management of Airlift and Tanker Resources: A Constraint-Based Approach

S. F. SMITH
Carnegie Mellon University, 5000 Forbes Avenue
Pittsburgh, PA 15213, U.S.A.
sfs@cs.cmu.edu

M. A. BECKER
Kestrel Institute, 362 Hillview Avenue
Palo Alto, CA 94304, U.S.A.
becker@kestrel.edu

L. A. KRAMER
Carnegie Mellon University, 5000 Forbes Avenue
Pittsburgh, PA 15213, U.S.A.
lkramer@cs.cmu.edu

Abstract—Efficient allocation of aircraft and aircrews to transportation missions is an important priority at the USAF Air Mobility Command (AMC), where airlift demand must increasingly be met with less capacity and at lower cost. In addition to presenting a formidable optimization problem, the AMC resource management problem is complicated by the fact that it is situated in a continuously executing environment. Mission requests are received (and must be acted upon) incrementally, and, once allocation decisions have been communicated to the executing agents, subsequent opportunities for optimizing resource usage must be balanced against the cost of solution change. In this paper, we describe the technical approach taken to this problem in the AMC barrel allocator, a scheduling tool developed to address this problem and provide support for day-to-day allocation and management of AMC resources. The system utilizes incremental and configurable constraint-based search procedures to provide a range of automated and semi-automated scheduling capabilities. Most basically, the system provides an efficient solution to the fleet scheduling problem. More importantly to continuous operations, it also provides techniques for selectively reoptimizing to accommodate higher priority missions while minimizing disruption to most previously scheduled missions, and for selectively "merging" previously planned missions to minimize nonproductive flying time. In situations where all mission requirements cannot be met, the system can generate and compare alternative constraint relaxation options. The barrel allocator technology is currently transitioning into operational use within AMC's Tanker/Airlift Control Center (TACC). A version of the barrel allocator supporting airlift allocation was first incorporated as an experimental module of the AMC's Consolidated Air Mobility Planning System (CAMPS) in September 2000. In May 2003, a new tanker allocation module is scheduled for initial operational release to users as part of CAMPS Release 5.4.

Keywords—Continuous scheduling, Constraint-based search, Configurable scheduling, Frameworks.

The research reported in this article was sponsored in part by the Department of Defense Advanced Research Projects Agency and the U.S. Air Force Research Laboratory under Contracts F30602-97-2-0227 and F30602-96-D-0058, by the USAF Air Mobility Command under Subcontract 10382000 to Northrop-Grumman Information Technology, and by the Robotics Institute at Carnegie Mellon University.

0895-7177/04/$ - see front matter Typeset by $\mathcal{A}\mathcal{M}\mathcal{S}$-TEX
doi:10.1016/j.mcm.2004.02.001

Many individuals have contributed to the development and deployment of the AMC allocator software system. The authors would like to thank S. Buchman, M. Burstein, C. Collins, D. Crimm, C. Dearth, B. Gloyer, D. Hildum, O. Lassila, D. Lemmermann, G. Pelton, L. Resnor, M. Shieh, S. Torma, R. Thornton, C. Whittenburg, and Joe Zhou.

1. INTRODUCTION

Efficient utilization of transportation resources is central to the effectiveness of operations at the USAF Air Mobility Command (AMC). In normal day-to-day operations, airlift demand must increasingly be met with less capacity and at lower cost. In crisis situations, rapid, large-scale deployment is crucial to overall military success. The allocation of aircraft and aircrews to airlift and tanker missions is a challenging problem. Several thousand missions are typically flown worldwide on a weekly basis, involving several hundreds of aircraft and comparable numbers of air crews. Individual missions impose a myriad of temporal constraints on their execution, and these constraints must be reconciled with resource availability and usage constraints (e.g., crew duty day restrictions and scheduled return dates, aircraft speed, range, and capacity) to find feasible assignments. Generally, there are many more mission requests than can be accommodated by available assets in any given time frame, and hence, an ability to optimize resource usage contributes directly to reduced reliance on higher-cost, commercial transportation assets.

Like many practical planning and scheduling problems, resource management at AMC is further complicated by the fact that it is situated in a continuous planning and execution environment. New mission requests of varying priority enter the system every day, and the current schedule is constantly evolving. Since taskings are incrementally communicated to the executing air wings, new requirements must be integrated into the current schedule without wholesale disruption to previous assignments. Likewise, the dynamics of execution regularly force changes to planned activities. Aircraft break down, airports become unavailable due to weather, missions become delayed due to diplomatic clearance problems, etc., and all such events can warrant reassessment of previous allocation decisions. In such execution-driven rescheduling contexts, it is similarly important to remain sensitive to solution stability concerns.

A third distinguishing aspect of the AMC allocation problem is the need for flexible accommodation of and integration with human decision-making. Given the scale and complexity of the AMC environment, there will always be user knowledge that is outside of system models and hence it must always be possible for the user to over-ride, constrain, bias, or otherwise direct system problem solving processes. While problem scale necessitates automation, effective problem solving also requires flexible user intervention.

These problem requirements are at direct odds with the design of most current transportation planning and scheduling tools. Current tools tend to be organized as black-box, batch-oriented solution generators which, when invoked, re-solve the problem from scratch. This presents three fundamental problems. First, there is no memory of solutions from one run to the next, and small changes in inputs can lead to large changes in outputs. Hence, they are difficult to control and use in circumstances where localized change is necessary or advantageous. Second, the computational cost of batch-oriented solution procedures makes it difficult for planning to keep pace with execution in dynamic (or higher tempo) circumstances, forcing the traditional disconnect between these two processes. Finally, in user-driven (and mixed-initiative) problem solving contexts, the "specify and solve" pattern of user-interaction promoted by batch-oriented solvers is inherently inefficient.

In this paper, we describe an alternative approach implemented in the AMC allocator, a tool for day-to-day allocation of aircraft and aircrews to airlift and tanker missions. In contrast to the above-mentioned tools, the AMC allocator is designed specifically for continuous operations, and provides a range of automated and semi-automated capabilities for allocating resources to missions against the backdrop of a pre-existing airlift schedule. Underlying the AMC allocator is a novel constraint-based search approach to transportation scheduling. This approach is *incremental* by nature, and this characteristic is key to the allocator's effectiveness as a continuous planning tool. The incrementality of the approach provides a direct basis for localizing and controlling solution change. It also enables real-time response to user rescheduling directives. The AMC allocator has been positively evaluated by AMC personnel and is currently transitioning into operational use within the Tanker Airlift Control Center (TACC) at AMC. It was first embedded as an experimental component of AMC's Consolidated Air Mobility Planning System (CAMPS) in 2000, and an enhanced tanker allocation module is scheduled for operational release in May 2003.

The remainder of the paper is organized as follows. In Section 2, we summarize the allocation problem faced by AMC. In Section 3, we contrast identified problem requirements with traditional solution approaches, and consider the advantages of incremental, constraint-based search models as a basis for a more suitable approach. The solution framework developed within the AMC allocator is then described in Section 4. We first review basic representational assumptions and solution generation procedures, along with the functional capabilities they give rise to. We then discuss some layered solution optimization capabilities. In Section 5, we summarize the history of the AMC allocator project and indicate the current status of the work. Finally, in Section 6, we indicate the current directions of our research and development efforts.

2. THE AMC BARREL MASTER ALLOCATION PROBLEM

The overall mission planning, scheduling and execution process in the TACC at AMC is depicted in Figure 1. Customer requirements flow into several distinct planning offices which respond by generating *missions*. A mission typically involves the movement of cargo and/or personnel, and each planning office generates air missions of a specific type. The channel planning office, for example, is responsible for planning channel missions, which correspond closely to the types of routes flown by commercial airlines; these missions are established and revised periodically, and then flown repeatedly at regular (e.g., daily or weekly) intervals. Special assignment airlift missions (SAAMs) planned by the SAAM planning office, alternatively, correspond more to chartered air flights. In this case, custom itineraries are generated to satisfy the customer's movement requirements, and the customer's requirements constitute the sole focus of the mission. The missions associated with Presidential travel are SAAM missions. Other offices are concerned with generating missions that address other types of requirements, such as contingency operations, exercises, and training. Different types of missions create different types of resource

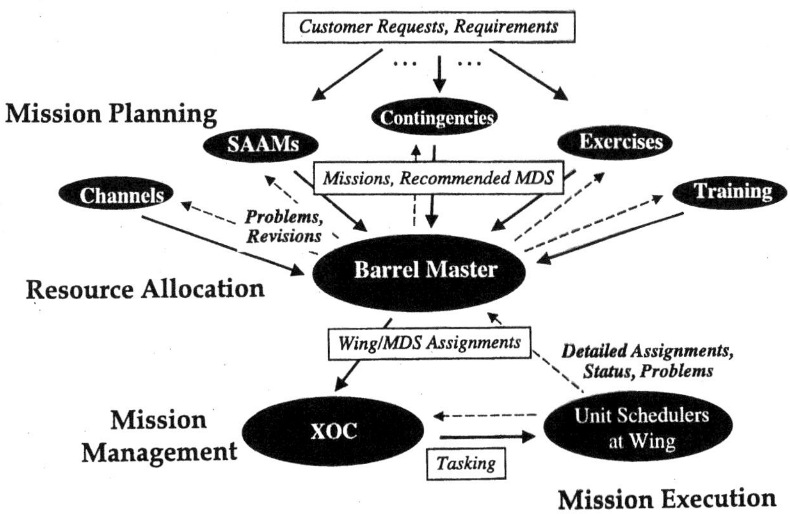

Figure 1. The AMC planning and execution environment.

requirements, but all planned missions specify an itinerary, a priority, a particular type of aircraft (technically referred to as the model development series or MDS type) to be used, a preferred USAF unit (or *wing*) assignment and a time period, represented as a pair of dates, in which the mission should be executed.

All generated missions flow into the "barrel master" office (or barrel for short) for allocation of necessary resources. The barrel is the office within the TACC that has total visibility of AMC assets. Based on mission specific constraints and current resource availability, the barrel determines which missions will be supportable and for those that are, which air wing(s) will be tasked to fly them. Within the barrel master office, the resource allocation and management problem is distributed among multiple barrel masters. Each barrel manages the aircraft and crews of a particular set of air wings, determined by aircraft type and geographic location. An air *wing* consists of a set of aircraft (and corresponding crews) of the same type stationed at a particular USAF base. For example, McGuire Air Force base has a wing of C141s and a wing of KC135s. Currently, the "west strat" barrel is responsible for all west coast C141, C5, and C17 wings, the "east strat" barrel is responsible for all east coast C141, C5, and C17 wings, the "tanker barrel" is responsible for all tanker wings (i.e., KC135s and KC10s) and so on.

At present, all barrels track available aircraft and aircrew capacity at various wings, and taskings of missions to specific wings are made on this notional basis. The individual air wing has responsibility for determining the actual aircraft tail and air crew(s) that will fly a given assigned mission.[1] The resource assignment for any planned mission is managed by the barrel until the 24 hours before execution point, at which time the mission is "pushed" to the execution office (XOC) for plan review and execution management. As problems arise during the execution of missions, this information flows back to the barrel, and may necessitate either reassignment of specific assets or revision to previously planned missions.

In allocating resources to a given mission, the barrel must confirm that all constraints associated with its planned itinerary can be satisfied. A mission's itinerary is the sequence of stops or airports the aircraft should visit during the execution of the mission. We refer to the flight between two successive stops as a *mission leg* (or *leg* for short). Each leg has an origin airport, the point of embarkation (POE), and a destination airport, the point of debarkation (POD). Each leg is followed (or preceded) by a certain ground time. During the period the aircraft is on the ground, a number of activities, or *ground events*, can occur: for example, loading and offloading of cargo, refueling, crew rest, crew change. The time period specified in the mission request should be at least as large as the time required by the aircraft to fly between all intermediate stops in the itinerary plus the required ground time at each airport. To feasibly support the mission, a sufficient number of aircraft and aircrews of the specified MDS type must be available during this entire period. The earliest date the mission can start is called the *available to load date* (ALD) and the latest date the mission should finish is called the *latest arrival date* (LAD). The length of this interval should be at least as large as the total duration of the mission.

Aircraft availability and aircrew availability are defined for each wing on a daily basis. Each wing has a total number of aircraft of a particular type and a corresponding total number of aircrews. Considering that some planes are undergoing maintenance and the wing also has some need for training and local missions, the wing will make a subset of its total aircraft and crews available for tasking to AMC missions. Each day, each wing will provide a certain number of *contract* aircraft and crews that can be allocated by the barrel. The remaining wing assets, designated as *fenced* aircraft and aircrews, are reserved for local wing use and are beyond the jurisdiction of the barrel.

[1]Plans call for this assumption to change and for the barrel to begin to track and allocate actual tails, as AMC's "state of the world" initiative increases the visibility of execution data to planning processes.

The allocation problem just outlined is similar to the classically defined *fleet assignment problem*: given a schedule of flights defining the departure and arrival times for each flight leg, the fleet assignment problem is the problem of deciding which flight equipment, or fleet, should be assigned to each flight segment [1,2]. For commercial airlines, the standard objective is to maximize revenues minus operating costs. The barrel master, alternatively, generally tries to maximize the total sum of priorities: s/he will try to assign the maximum number of high priority missions, and will generally only consider assigning lower priority missions after all higher priority ones have been assigned.

Most traditional solutions to the fleet assignment problem assign fleets to individual flight segments. The barrel master, alternatively, is concerned with assigning fleets to a sequence of segments or *strings*. A *string* is a sequence of connected flight segments that begins and ends at possibly different maintenance stations [3]. By default, an AMC mission itinerary is planned as a string that starts and ends at the same location (i.e., a round trip). Strings that start and end at the same station are usually referred as *aircraft rotations*. If possible, the barrel would consider, and sometimes even prefer, using the same rotation for more than one mission. The difficulty in combining missions is in identifying and sorting out the opportunities for potential combinations among thousands of missions in the database.

The barrel master responsible for refueling assets, the tanker barrel, has a somewhat different allocation problem. In this case, the starting point is an *air refueling event*, which identifies one or more receiver missions, a cumulative fuel requirement, a refueling location (or track), and a rendezvous time. Considering the availability of tanker assets at various wings within range of the target refueling constraint, together with the fuel carrying capacities and burn rates of available aircraft types, one or more tanker missions are generated, sourced to a specific wing (or wings), and linked to the originating air refueling event.

In current practice, the allocation process carried out within the barrel master office is a mostly manual process. In her/his daily activities, each barrel master utilizes an electronic *commitment matrix*, which tracks available aircraft and aircrew capacity of different wings over time and records those missions already allocated. As new missions are received from various planning offices, the barrel consults this matrix and tries to allocate resources which satisfy mission requirements. If all requirements can be satisfied, the wing assignment is made and this commitment is communicated back to the mission planner. In those cases where there are insufficient resources available to support a particular set of missions, the barrel will consider more disruptive allocation alternatives. For example, s/he may consider using resources already allocated to lower priority missions, s/he may consider using resources provided by a wing other than the planner's preference, s/he may consider delaying the mission, and so on. Once one or more acceptable options are found, the barrel communicates these possibilities back to the relevant planner and a solution that would best satisfy all sides is negotiated. A mission may also be determined to be unsupportable, in which case this information is communicated back to the planner. In general, resource assignment is performed one mission at a time with little automation. Capabilities for generating more sophisticated allocation alternatives (e.g., involving mission combination) are quite limited, and generally such optimizations are not considered. In crisis situations where time pressure is greater, the lack of automated decision aids has increasing ramifications; high priority missions get accomplished, but at the expense of inordinate numbers of routine missions and at very high cost.

3. INCREMENTAL CONSTRAINT-BASED SEARCH MODELS

The continuous, dynamic nature of the barrel master's allocation problem restricts the appropriateness of various automated planning and scheduling techniques. For example, classical fleet assignment solution procedures present several practical difficulties. First, they operate as black-box solution generators, and, as such, provide no ability to control solution change over time. Second, by virtue of their "re-solve from scratch" design, it can be difficult for these techniques to keep pace with execution events as tempo increases. In commercial airline settings, these shortcomings are not that important, since the set of routes to be flown tends to be rather stable (e.g., changing only month to month), and scheduling is more of a periodic activity aimed at establishing assignments for the next period. However, in the AMC environment, short notice (SAAM) missions mix with longer term (channel) mission sets to create dynamically changing demand patterns over time. This requires more attention to advance commitment, and since new orders must be "recut" each time a mission is retasked, there is pragmatic utility to minimizing disruption to scheduled missions when responding to new mission requests. Moreover, the higher time pressure associated with crisis situations puts increased emphasis on computationally efficient scheduling and allocation processes. In these contexts, automated techniques that integrate flexibly and gracefully with user decision processes is an important additional necessity.

Constraint-based search models provide a general approach to scheduling that is well matched to the requirements of the barrel allocator's allocation problem. Constraint-based scheduling models combine principles of constraint programming and heuristic search in the formulation and solution of scheduling problems (e.g., [4–6]). Figure 2 shows the basic framework, which consists of three main components. In the center is an *active database*, which contains a representation of the current solution. As scheduling decisions are posted to or retracted from this database, a set of *constraint propagation* routines are triggered. Propagation computes the consequences of any change for related scheduling decisions, possibly winnowing (or enlarging) the set of feasible values for other decision variables or detecting a constraint conflict (which signifies an infeasible state). The other two principal components of a constraint-based scheduling model are commitment and retraction strategies/heuristics, which respectively guide the search process in moving forward (e.g., allocating resources or assigning start and end times to an as yet unassigned mission) or moving backward (e.g., unassigning a previously assigned mission) in the underlying search space. By configuring commitment and retraction heuristics with different search control mechanisms and search space assumptions, it is possible to define a range of both constructive (i.e., global search) and repair-based (i.e., local search) scheduling methods.

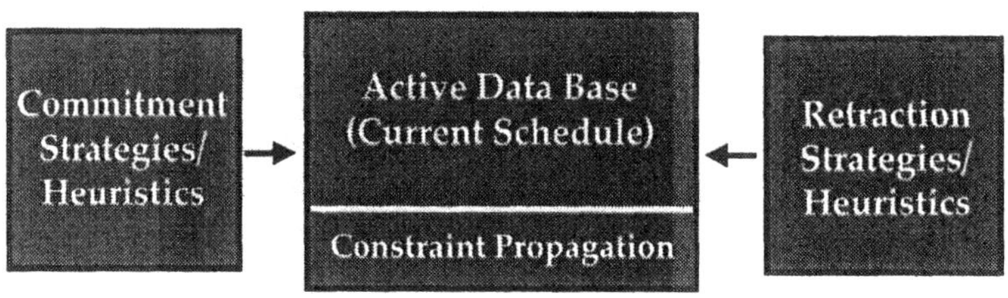

Figure 2. Constraint-based scheduling models.

Constraint-based scheduling models are attractive in the current context for several basic reasons.

INCREMENTALITY. By definition, constraint-based scheduling models are incremental decision-making procedures. As such, they provide a direct basis for managing solution change over time, and for minimizing undue disruption to the current schedule as new demands (missions) are accommodated.

GENERALITY. Constraint-based models have been shown to operate efficiently under quite general representational assumptions. Simple temporal problem (STP) constraint networks [7], for example, allow expression of a diverse range of relative and metric temporal constraints, while providing efficient incremental propagation algorithms. Similarly rich representations of resource constraints are also possible.

CONFIGURABILITY. Constraint-based search procedures are also quite compositional by nature and these models tend to be easily reconfigured to accommodate new constraints and objectives [4]. In the case of the AMC allocator described below, this property is used to provide selective constraint relaxation capabilities in situations where all constraints cannot be simultaneously satisfied.

4. THE AMC ALLOCATOR

As just suggested, an incremental, constraint-based scheduling model provides the core basis for the functionality provided by the AMC allocator, a software tool designed to address the AMC barrel master allocation problem. Most basically, this model is used to define an efficient solution to a dynamic, string-based variant of the fleet assignment problem. More importantly, from the standpoint of continuous operations, it is also used to define techniques for selectively re-optimizing to accommodate higher priority missions while minimizing disruption to most previously scheduled missions, and for selectively "merging" previously planned missions to minimize nonproductive flying time. Finally, it is used to generate and compare alternative constraint relaxation options.

The AMC allocator has been developed using the ozone scheduling framework [4,8], a shell for constructing constraint-based scheduling applications. Ozone consists of three major components:

(1) a library of modeling primitives for constructing scheduling domain models,
(2) an underlying constraint-based search architecture (an elaborated version of the basic model in Figure 2), and
(3) a library of scheduling and rescheduling methods (encoding various commitment and retraction strategies/heuristics).

Through instantiation of an *abstract domain model* with modeling primitives that match the characteristics of a given application domain, and selection of one or more basic scheduling methods, it is possible to quickly obtain an executable model, and allow development effort to quickly focus on the customizations of the model and the scheduling methods necessary to obtain high performance. The ozone application framework consolidates the results of application building experiences in a wide range of complex scheduling domains.

The AMC allocator itself currently provides two core sets of functionality to the AMC barrel master: *resource allocation* and *mission combination*. Separate modules are provided for airlift allocation and tanker allocation, respectively, owing to differences in the nature of these two allocation problems as currently structured within the barrel master office. In all cases, functionality may be utilized in a more or less automated fashion, ranging from a fully manual mode where the system does little more than decision bookkeeping, to a semiautomatic mode, where the system generates alternative options and previews their impact, to a completely automatic mode, where the system determines the best decisions based on user-specified preferences. The system may also be invoked in an extended optimize mode, in which case the underlying incremental search process that is performed is broadened. All of these capabilities are provided within a graphical, spreadsheet-like user interface, designed to emphasize the real-time responsiveness of the system's scheduling and allocation procedures.

In the following sections, we describe the representations and search procedures underlying the AMC allocator in more detail. The configurability of these search procedures is considered in further depth in [9]. Other mixed-initiative aspects of the approach are emphasized in [10].

4.1. Representational Assumptions

Within the AMC allocator, missions are represented as hierarchical task (or activity) networks. A mission expands into a network of more detailed flight segments and ground activities. Flight segments correspond to individual legs of the mission's itinerary; ground activities model such activities as crew rest periods and aircraft preparation tasks. Each constituent activity has a *start time* and an *end time*, and is linked via precedence constraints to other mission activities. The duration of an activity is a function of its type. For example, the duration of a flight activity depends on resource speed and the distance traveled from its *origin* to its *destination*.[2] For many ground events, durations are specified as fixed constants. The duration of an aggregate activity (e.g., a mission) is the duration of its subnetwork.

A mission specifies requirements for resource capacity for its entire duration. In the case of airlift missions, some number of aircraft and aircrews of a particular type are specified. In the case of air refueling (or tanker) missions, there is often flexibility with respect to type of refueling aircraft, and the required numbers of aircraft and aircrews are derived from fuel offload requirements and fuel carrying capacity limits. A mission also has associated temporal restrictions on when it can execute. In the case of an airlift mission, execution is constrained by its "available to load date" (ALD) and its "latest arrival date" (LAD). Tanker missions, alternatively, must synchronize to arrive at the refueling point at the designated "air refueling control time" (ARCT).

Aircraft and aircrews are modeled at an aggregate wing level. A wing designates a co-located set of aircraft and aircrews of a particular type. It specifies a particular geographic *location*, a pool (or fleet) of aircraft and a pool of aircrews. A given pool of aircraft or aircrews has a *total capacity*, with each unit of capacity representing one aircraft or aircrew. The total capacity of a resource pool is partitioned into two subsets: *contract* capacity, representing the capacity that has been budgeted to AMC and is available for allocation, and *fenced* capacity, representing the aircraft that have been held back for the wing's local use. The contract and fenced capacity of a wing can vary over time, and resource availability will become further restricted as capacity is assigned to specific missions over time. The available capacity of a resource pool is thus represented as a sequence of *capacity intervals*, each recording the total, contract, fenced and available capacity over the interval spanned by its start and end time. As missions are assigned to wings (or de-assigned) during the allocation process, the affected portion (along the time line) of their available capacity representations is updated to reflect the reserving (or freeing up) of required aircraft and aircrew capacity. Thus resource capacity is represented and allocated over continuous time, at some level of temporal granularity.

The output of the AMC allocator (i.e., the current schedule) is a set of assignments of the form *(mission, wing, start-time, end-time)*, indicating that *wing* will perform *mission* over the interval from *start-time* to *end-time*. To be feasible, such an assignment must satisfy the following constraints.

WING CAPACITY CONSTRAINTS. The cumulative resource requirements of all missions assigned to *wing* over the interval from *start-time* to *end-time* must not exceed the number of contract aircraft or aircrews available at *wing* for any t, *start-time* $\leq t \leq$ *end-time*.

RESOURCE GROUND TIME CONSTRAINTS. The assigned interval from *start-time* to *end-time* must account for aircraft onload, offload, and minimum time-on-ground requirements. Each of these constraints is specified as a function of aircraft type.

FLIGHT DURATION CONSTRAINTS. The assigned interval from *start-time* to *end-time* must account for cumulative flight time requirements, including necessary positioning and depositioning flight segments.

AIRCRAFT RANGE CONSTRAINTS. Any given flight segment inserted into *mission's* itinerary as a consequence of assigning *wing* must cover a distance less than the flying range of the assigned aircraft type. In general, the creation of positioning flights, depositioning flights and/or bridging legs (from offload of one mission to onload of the next) may be implied by a given wing assignment.

CREW DUTY DAY CONSTRAINTS. Depending on positioning/depositioning considerations and the crew type required by *mission*—basic or augmented—it may be necessary to insert crew rest

[2]Currently, distances are computed based on great circle route.

periods at appropriate intermediate points of the mission to enforce crew duty day restrictions. The assigned interval from *start-time* to *end-time* must account for this additional constraint as well.

MISSION TIMING CONSTRAINTS. Finally, *start-time* and *end-time* must be consistent with all timing constraints on the execution of *mission*. In the case of an airlift mission, the start of the first cargo carrying flight segment must be $\geq$ *mission's* ALD, and the end of the last cargo carrying leg must be $\leq$ *mission's* LAD. For tanker missions, the end time of the positioning flight must $=$ *mission's* ARCT.

Given the oversubscribed nature of the barrel master allocation problem, it is not always possible to satisfy mission time constraints with existing available lift capacity, and those missions that cannot be feasibly scheduled at any point are designated as unassignable. In such situations, the user may choose to analyze and compare options that involve relaxation of various constraints. Currently, the following relaxed formulations may be solved to generate such options.

PRIORITY-BASED PREEMPTION. Every mission has a predefined priority that establishes its intrinsic importance. Under a priority-based preemption formulation, an unassignable mission may obtain its required resource capacity by preempting (or bumping) one or more previously assigned, lower-priority missions. If this occurs, the set of preempted missions is then rescheduled in succession and may, in turn, find alternative resource assignments at the expense of still lower priority missions. At quiescence, any remaining unassigned missions become unsupportable and are added to the current set of unassignable missions. When operating under this formulation, additional constraints can be added by the user to exert greater control of the extent of solution change. A *mission locking* mechanism allows any specific mission assignment to be designated as unalterable. A *freeze interval*, specifying a period of time in advance of execution within which preemption is not allowed, can also be imposed.

RESOURCE OVERALLOCATION. Under this formulation, the aircraft and aircrew contract capacity constraints are considered relaxable. Since the numbers of contract aircraft and aircrews are typically smaller than the total number of assets possessed by the wing, the user may choose to go over the published contract levels of a given wing. This happens with a fair amount of frequency. It generally reflects private knowledge that the barrel master may have about wing assets or agreement on the part of the wing to use fenced aircraft.

MISSION DELAY. Under this formulation, the mission's LAD constraint (in the case of airlift) or ARCT constraint (in the case of refueling) is considered relaxable. The user may consider the option of delaying the current mission until necessary resources are available. If delay seems like a potentially viable alternative, then this information can be suggested to the mission planner.

ALTERNATIVE MDS. Under this formulation, the requirement that the mission use the airframe (or MDS) type designed by the mission planner is relaxed, and alternative aircraft types can be considered as a means of accommodating the mission. Due to differences in carrying capacities of different aircraft, the numbers of aircraft and crews required to support a mission may vary across aircraft type as well. As with mission delay, potentially viable options can be communicated back to the mission planner as suggestions.

COMPOSITE MISSION CONSTRAINT RELAXATIONS. Formulations that permit simultaneous relaxation along multiple dimensions (e.g., mission delay and priority-based preemption, mission delay, and overallocation) are also possible.

MISSION COMBINATION. By default, missions are flown as round trips from a particular home base. If the origin and/or destination do not coincide with this base, then positioning and/or depositioning flight segments are added into the mission itinerary. In mission combination mode, the requirement that each mission be flown as a round trip is relaxed, and opportunities to exploit nonproductive flying time by "recycling" an aircraft directly from the destination (offload) of one mission to the origin (onload) of the next are sought. Mission combination can provide a direct option for supporting an otherwise unassignable mission. It can also provide a basis for compressing the resource requirements of a set of previously assigned missions and reclaiming resource capacity for other use.

Below, we outline solution procedures for these various problem formulations.

4.2. Allocation of Airlift Assets

The central function supported by the allocator is that of assigning planned missions to wings over time. In typical mode of operation, there is an existing set of assignments (i.e., the current schedule) in place, and the problem is one of determining assignments for sets of newly planned missions in the presence of this backdrop. Figure 3 graphically depicts the basic search procedure used to make the wing/time assignment for a single mission.

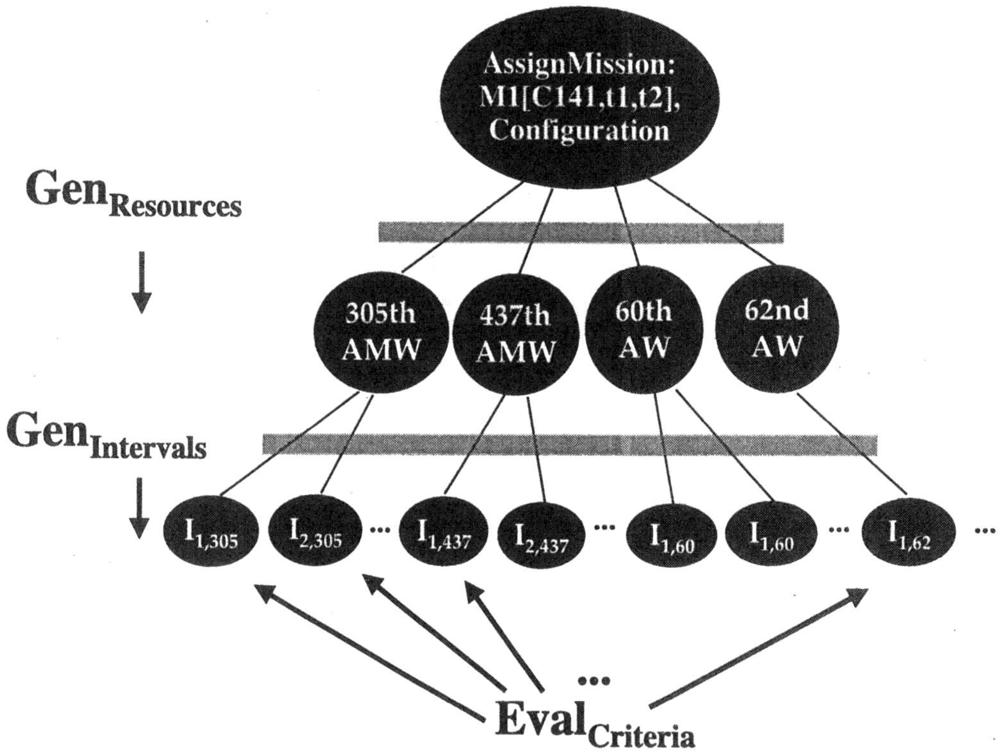

Figure 3. Basic search procedure for resource allocation. This example assumes that mission $M1$ requires C141 aircraft with earliest pickup at $t1$ and latest delivery by $t2$ and that C141s can be provided by either the 305th Air Mobility Wing (AMW), the 437th AMW, the 60th Air Wing (AW) or the 62nd AW.

The search procedure proceeds in 3 basic steps:

1. a set of candidate resources (wings) is generated,
2. for each candidate wing, a set of possible allocation intervals is generated, and
3. each ⟨wing, allocation interval⟩ pair is evaluated and the highest ranked candidate is selected.

As implied by Figure 3, a full instantiation of the `AssignMission` search procedure is obtained by specifying three components: a search operator for generating candidate resources (referred to generically as $\text{Gen}_{\text{Resources}}$), a search operator for generating candidate allocation intervals (generically called $\text{Gen}_{\text{Intervals}}$), and an evaluation metric ($\text{Eval}_{\text{Criterion}}$) for ranking alternatives. By parameterizing the procedure to operate with different sets of operators and evaluation criteria, resource assignments can be generated and evaluated under a range of different constraint relaxation assumptions.

In the most basic case, `AssignMission` is configured to search only for feasible assignments, i.e., ⟨`wing, allocation interval`⟩ pairs that are consistent with the time and resource requirements specified by the mission and are also compatible with the assignments of previously scheduled missions. This *feasible* configuration of `AssignMission` is obtained by incorporation of the triple $\langle \mathrm{Gen}_{\mathrm{RequestedRes}}, \mathrm{Gen}_{\mathrm{FeasibleInts}}, \mathrm{Eval}_{\mathrm{MinFlyingTime}} \rangle$. Here, $\mathrm{Gen}_{\mathrm{RequestedRes}}$ generates candidate wings consistent with aircraft type requested by the mission. Likewise, $\mathrm{Gen}_{\mathrm{FeasibleInts}}$ scans a candidate wing's aircraft and aircrew capacity profiles for allocation intervals

(1) with sufficient amounts of available capacity to support mission requirements,
(2) with a duration greater than or equal to the time required to accomplish the mission (a function of mission itinerary, aircraft speed, wing's home base location, crew rest requirements, and other constraints on duration identified in Section 4.1, and
(3) with start and end times that satisfies the mission's earliest onload time and latest offload time constraints.

Candidates are differentiated on the basis of total flying time and the candidate assignment that minimizes this metric is selected.

By selectively substituting different search operators and/or evaluation criteria, `AssignMission` can alternatively be used to find assignments under various relaxed problem assumptions identified in Section 4.1. For some types of constraints, relaxation simply implies the consideration of a different discrete set of options. For example, substitution of $\mathrm{Gen}_{\mathrm{AlternativeRes}}$ for $\mathrm{Gen}_{\mathrm{RequestedRes}}$ results in generation of assignments that consider types of aircraft other than the type requested by the mission planner. For other classes of constraints, however, relaxation is more continuous in nature, and in substituting a search operator that assumes constraints can be relaxed, the search must also be biased to promote their satisfaction to the extent possible.

By varying the operator used to generate allocation intervals and the evaluation metric used to prioritize candidate solutions, a number of useful `AssignMission` configurations are defined.

DELAY. *Incorporation of the triple* $\langle \mathrm{Gen}_{\mathrm{RequestedRes}}, \mathrm{Gen}_{\mathrm{DelayInts}}, \mathrm{Eval}_{\mathrm{MinTardiness}} \rangle$ *yields an assignment procedure which assumes that mission deadlines can be relaxed if necessary.* $\mathrm{Gen}_{\mathrm{DelayInts}}$ *uses the same mechanism used by* $\mathrm{Gen}_{\mathrm{FeasibleInts}}$ *but considers a larger portion of the candidate wing's aircraft and crew capacity profiles, and* $\mathrm{Eval}_{\mathrm{MinTardiness}}$ *ensures that the mission deadline will be relaxed to the minimum extent possible.*

In this configuration and others, advantage can be taken of the relationship between search operator and evaluation criterion to effectively constrain the number of candidate solutions generated. For example, by scanning forward in time through the capacity profiles of required resources, the first interval with available capacity found will be the one that minimizes delay for that resource. If this approach is taken, only one interval need be generated for each candidate resource. In other configurations (e.g., the preemption case below), where there is no such dominance condition for constrained solution generation, more ad-hoc heuristic cutoffs can be used.

OVERALLOCATION. *The triple* $\langle \mathrm{Gen}_{\mathrm{RequestedRes}}, \mathrm{Gen}_{\mathrm{OverInts}}, \mathrm{Eval}_{\mathrm{MinOverUsage}} \rangle$ *defines an assignment procedure where capacity constraints are relaxable.* $\mathrm{Gen}_{\mathrm{OverInts}}$ *scans the capacity profile of a candidate wing, but generates allocation intervals that extend above the wing's "contracted" level (i.e., dipping into its locally reserved or "fenced" pool of aircraft capacity).* $\mathrm{Eval}_{\mathrm{MinOverUsage}}$ *promotes selection of the generated allocation interval that minimizes the level of overallocation.*

In this case, maximal intervals at different levels of overallocation can be efficiently generated via linear scans of the capacity profiles of the two required resources, and subsequently pruned to minimize the temporal extent of overallocation.

PRIORITY-BASED PREEMPTION. *A configuration which assumes that some number of previously made assignments can be relaxed (or disrupted) is defined by the triple* $\langle \mathrm{Gen}_{\mathrm{RequestedRes}}, \mathrm{Gen}_{\mathrm{BumpInts}}, \mathrm{Eval}_{\mathrm{MinDisruption}} \rangle$. *This configuration implements a form of preemption, based on mission priority. In scanning a candidate wing's capacity profile,* $\text{Gen}_{\text{BumpInts}}$ *considers capacity currently allocated to lower priority missions as available for assignment, and generates allocation intervals based on this assumption.* $\text{Eval}_{\text{MinDisruption}}$ *promotes allocation intervals that disrupt the fewest missions and those with the lowest priority. This minimizes the cascading effect (since any mission that is preempted by a higher priority mission is recursively rescheduled using the same procedure).*

Given the combinatorial number of allocation intervals that can be generated via a complete capacity profile scanning procedure ($O(c^f)$ where c is the capacity of the resource and f is the duration of capacity profile fragments), our current implementation utilizes a linear, heuristic sampling strategy compatible with $\text{Eval}_{\text{MinDisruption}}$. *Briefly, allocation intervals are generated by single forward scan through the required resources' capacity profiles over the time interval where capacity is required. At each time point encountered during the scan, the set of preemptable missions is computed. If nonempty, the current allocation interval is extended by*

(1) *computing the subset of preemptable missions of lowest priority, and*
(2) *selecting the mission in this subset that maximally extends the current interval; if there are no preemptable missions, the current allocation interval is ended (and retained if of sufficient duration), and the scan continues at the start point of the next preemptable mission.*[3]

COMPOSITE RELAXATIONS. *Components of the above base configurations can also be composed to define configurations of* `AssignMission` *where multiple constraints are simultaneously relaxed.*

`AssignMission` (in any of the configurations described above) can be applied to any selected set of missions via the `AssignMissions` procedure given in Figure 4. Within this constraint satisfaction problem solving (CSP) style search procedure, the *sort-order* parameter determines the overall variable-ordering strategy (i.e., the order in which missions are selected for assignment). In the current implementation, mission priority (first) and latest delivery date (second) are used as a heuristic basis for prioritizing unassigned missions. Input missions are sorted on this basis (within `SelectMission`) and `AssignMission` is then sequentially applied to each to allocate required resources (using whichever of the above configurations has been designated).

In cases where a given mission has no feasible assignments (i.e., `AssignMission(M, feasible)` is applied and returns no solution), an exploration of possible relaxation options can be conducted through repeated application of `AssignMission` in different configurations.

```
AssignMissions(UnassignedMissions, configuration, sort-order)
    While UnassignedMissions ≠ ∅ Do
        M ← SelectMission(UnassignedMissions, sort-order)
        UnassignedMissions ← UnassignedMissions − {M}
        If AssignMission (M, confirmation)
            Then Status_M ← assigned
            Else Status_M ← unassignable
    EndWhile
End
```

Figure 4. Overall mission scheduling procedure.

In the current implementation, this procedure is used in what-if mode to generate alternative options, and the user performs the evaluation and selection. Figure 5 shows a sample output as displayed within the allocator's "Compare Options" interface.

[3]An alternative heuristic strategy, which attempts to find preemptable missions that best match target "resource area" requirements, is described in [11]. Though somewhat more costly computationally, this approach has been found to be considerably less disruptive than the above strategy, and we plan to incorporate it as an option in a future allocator release.

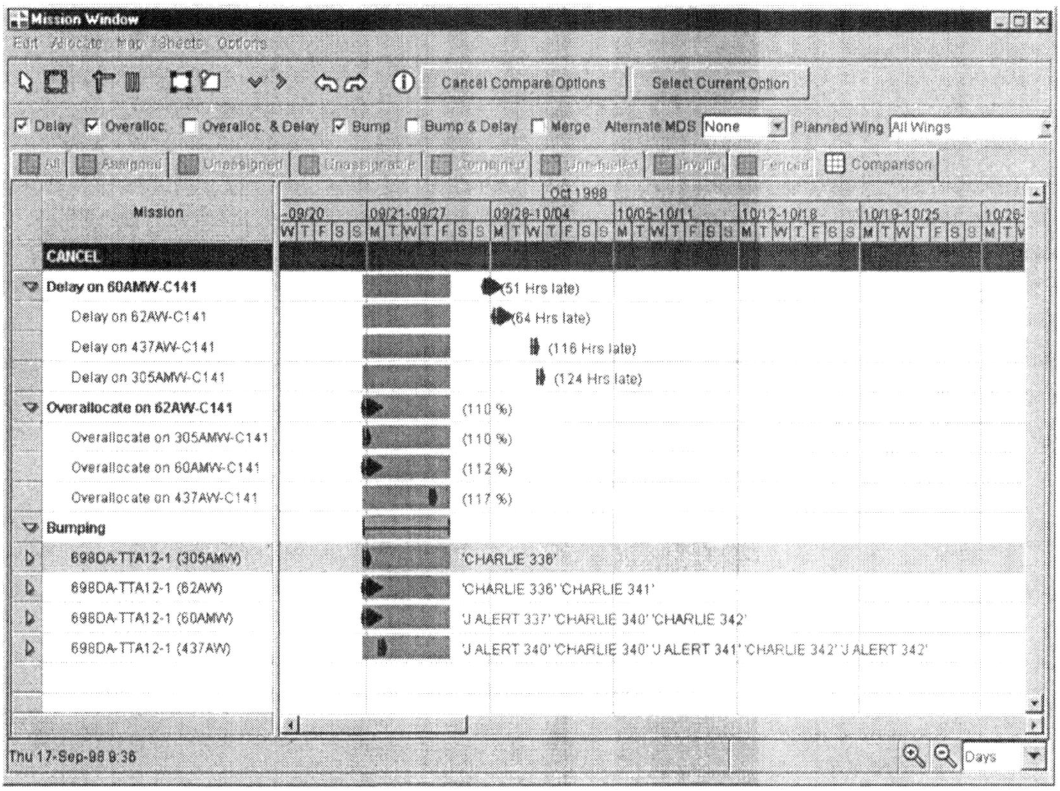

Figure 5. Generating options for an unassignable mission.

4.3. Allocation of Air Refeuling Missions

The process of allocating wings to refueling or "tanker" missions is similar to that used for assignment of airlift missions, but requires an important extension. Tanker missions are generated and sourced to satisfy an *air refueling (AR) request*, which minimally calls for a specified amount of fuel to be delivered to a particular rendezvous point at a particular time. The number of tanker missions required to satisfy a given AR request will be a function of the fuel required and the fuel capacity of aircraft allocated, and hence, may not be specified in advance. The AR request may also specify a particular aircraft type and possibly a preferred wing assignment, which is referred to as a specific tanker request.

Given these distinctions, the tanker allocation process must incorporate an additional mission planning function. The extended `AssignRequest` procedure is given in Figure 6. In this proce-

---

AssignRequest($AR, configuration$)
    While $RequiredFuel_{AR} > 0$ **Do**
        $M \leftarrow$ GenerateNewTankerMission(AR)
        If `AssignMission`($M, configuration$)
            Then $RequiredFuel_{AR} \leftarrow RequiredFuel_{AR} - FuelCapacity_M$
            Else $Status_{AR} \leftarrow$ `unassignable`; **Return**
    EndWhile
    $Status_{AR} \leftarrow$ `assigned`
End

Figure 6. Air refueling AssignRequest procedure.

dure, a mission generation and assignment loop is iterated until either the fuel requirement has been satisfied or it is determined that the AR request is unsupportable. As indicated, the full range of AssignMission configurations available for airlift allocation are equally applicable in the air refueling allocation context.

4.4. Mission Combination

A second core function provided by the barrel allocator is mission combination. This capability is defined by coupling the basic `AssignMission` procedure with a procedure for generating possible mission pairings.

More specifically, the process of merging a given mission M with another existing mission proceeds in three basic steps.

STEP 1. GENERATE A SET OF POSSIBLE COMPOSITE MISSIONS. In this step, all possible composite missions involving M are generated. For any pair of missions (M_1,M_2), there are two potential pairings: one in which mission M_2 flies after the end of mission M_1's last leg; and one in which mission M_1 flies after mission M_2. A possible combination is one which

(1) satisfies the conjunction of constraints established by spatial and temporal restrictions, and
(2) satisfies user-imposed limits on acceptable candidates; the user may specify three additional constraints on acceptance:
   - a minimal percentage reduction in total duration of the combined mission,
   - a maximum layover time between missions, and
   - a maximum distance between the destination of the first mission and the origin of the second.

The output of this step can be seen as the set of all notional composite missions $\bar{M}$ resulting from concatenation of possible combination pairs (M_1,M_2).

STEP 2. GENERATE SET OF FEASIBLE COMPOSITE MISSIONS. In this step, `AssignMission` is applied to each candidate $\bar{M}$ identified in Step 1 to determine the set of composite missions that are resource feasible (i.e., there is available resource capacity to support the composite mission over its entire duration). Although currently only *feasible* allocations are considered, any of the relaxed `AssignMission` configurations could also be used.

STEP 3. SELECTION OF BEST CANDIDATE. Once all feasible combinations have been determined, the candidate providing the largest overall reduction in airplane flying time is selected.

Figure 7 summarizes the mission combination procedure. Note that although `CombineMission` performs only pairwise merging of missions, the combination of larger numbers of missions can be accomplished by recursively applying the algorithm to composite missions.

CombineMission$(M, MaxLayover, MaxDistance, ReqReduction)$
    $PossibleCombinations \leftarrow \emptyset$
    For each mission pair $(M_1, M_2) : (M_1 \vee M_2 = M) \wedge (M_1 \neq M_2)$ **Do**
        $\bar{M} \leftarrow$ GenerateCompositeMission(M_1, M_2) $\quad ; \bar{M} = M_1 + M_{1,2} + M_2$
        If ConstraintsSatisfied$(\bar{M}, MaxLayover, MaxDistance, ReqReduction)$
            Then $PossibleCombinations \leftarrow PossibleCombinations \cup \{\bar{M}\}$
        EndFor
        $Candidates \leftarrow \emptyset$
        For each $\bar{M} \in PossibleCombinations$ **Do**
            If `AssignMission`$(\bar{M},$ `feasible`$)$ **Then** $Candidates \leftarrow Candidates \cup \{\bar{M}\}$
        EndFor
        SelectCandidate$(Candidates, Eval_{MaxTripRed})$
    End

Figure 7. Mission combination procedure.

4.5. Incremental Optimization

The above-described procedures are designed to flexibly support a continuous, interactive resource management process. New missions are integrated incrementally as problem constraints permit, and in circumstances where missions cannot be feasibly accommodated, a range of constraint relaxation and solution change options can be explored to find acceptable compromises and increase the number of supportable missions. In operation, the system provides an efficient, mixed-initiative decision-making environment—a two week interval of missions extracted from the current AMC database (approximately 1000 missions, 5000 flights) is scheduled from scratch in less than five seconds on a Pentium 4, 1 GHz machine. More typical incremental planning and scheduling actions are executed in real-time.

This efficiency is gained principally through reliance on search heuristics, and within the core allocator procedures, automated solution generation is strongly biased by mission priority. This coincides well with AMC business practice, but can also sometimes result in missed opportunities to support additional lower priority missions.

To compensate for such circumstances, we have been exploring the development and use of incremental optimization procedures, which can be applied at extended computational cost when decision time constraints permit. One simple example provided within the current allocator release is a "resource usage compression" capability, which applies the basic mission combination procedure discussed above to the entire set of missions allocated to a wing (or set of wings) over some interval, to identify opportunities for more efficient recycling of assets and to reclaim resource capacity for additional tasking.

Another incremental optimization procedure we have recently developed attempts to incorporate additional missions by temporarily de-emphasizing mission priority as a preemption criterion and exploring other feasible ⟨resource, allocation interval⟩ assignments for selected higher priority missions [11]. One consequence of the priority-based allocation bias of the core `AssignMissions` procedure is that some (higher priority) missions with greater scheduling flexibility may be assigned before other (lower priority) missions with less scheduling flexibility; and this possibility can lead to suboptimal greedy commitments that leave lower priority missions unassignable. The `MissionSwap` procedure (see Figure 8) is designed to provide a framework for locally rearranging assignments to take better advantage of the collective scheduling flexibility associated with a given set of competing missions. It proceeds by retracting some number of currently assigned missions, which frees up capacity sufficient to enable insertion of the (previously unassignable) input mission. `MissionSwap` is then recursively called for each retracted missions that cannot be immediately assigned elsewhere (by a subsequent call to `AssignMission`), with the additional constraint that once a mission has been reassigned via a swap move, it is "protected" from further retraction.[4] In our current implementation, the results of MissionSwap are incorporated conditionally; if the procedure bottoms out with feasible reassignments for all retracted missions, then the results are accepted as a new improved solution. Alternatively, if all retracted missions cannot be feasibly reassigned, then the solution is restored to its prior state and the original input mission is returned to "unassignable" status".

Central to the effectiveness of this swapping procedure is the heuristic employed to select which mission or missions to retract in a given conflict situation. Conceptually, one would like to retact the mission (or missions) that possess the greatest potential for reassignment. One simple estimate of this potential is the scheduling flexibility provided by a mission's feasible execution window. More precisely, we define the flexibility of a given mission m as

$$\text{Flex}_m = \frac{\sum_{r \in R_m} \text{alloc-dur}_{r,m}}{(\text{lft}_m - \text{est}_m) \times |R_m|},$$

[4]It should also be noted that since this and other incremental optimization procedures utilize the same underlying search infrastructure, additional constraints can always be introduced to prohibit the system from changing specific allocation decisions if greater control over solution change is required.

```
MissionSwap(M, ProtectedMissions)
        ConflictSet ← ComputeCapacityConflicts (M)
        Retracted ← RetractMissions (ConflictSet, ProtectedMissions)
        if Retracted = ∅  then Return (∅)   ; no possibility to assign M
        ProtectedMissions ← ProtectedMissions ∪ {M}
        AssignMission (M, feasible)
        AssignMissions (Retracted, feasible, least-flexible-first)
        For each (i ∈ Retracted ∧ status_i = unassignable) do
            ProtectedMissions ← MissionSwap(i, Protected)
            if ProtectedMissions = ∅ then  Return (∅)     ; unable to reassign i
        EndFor
        Return (ProtectedMissions)     ; success
End
```

Figure 8. Mission swap procedure.

where R_m is the set of alternative resources (i.e., wings) that could support m, alloc-dur$_{r,m}$ is the duration that resource r would require to perform m, est$_m$ is the earliest start time of m, and lft$_m$ is the latest finish time of m. This measure of scheduling flexibility gives rise to the following retraction heuristic:

$$\text{MaxFlex} = i \in C : \text{Flex}_i \leq \text{Flex}_j, \qquad \forall j \neq i,$$

where C is a set of conflicting missions in the ConflictSet$_u$ for some unassignable task u. This MaxFlex heuristic drives the `RetractMissions` step of `MissionSwap`.

Preliminary experimental analysis of the performance of the `MissionSwap` procedure on representative AMC mission data at different levels of resource contention has indicated an ability to substantially improve the airlift schedules initially produced by `AssignMissions` in certain circumstances. As well, the MaxFlex heuristic has been shown to consistently outperform several, more complex "contention-based" retraction heuristics at a fraction of the computational cost. The reader is referred to [12] for a complete description of this incremental optimization procedure and for full details of these initial performance results. Our current work is investigating the performance/cost tradeoffs associated with variants of `MissionSwap` that carry out additional search when initial retraction choices do not pan out. We anticipate full incorporation of this capability in a future allocator release.

A final longer-term approach to incremental optimization that we have been exploring involves the use of randomization to boost the performance of search heuristics [13,14]. This work assumes an iterative sampling approach, where solutions (schedules) are generated repeatedly through nondeterministic application of base search heuristics. The key idea is to bias the degree of randomness to the level of discrimination provided by the heuristic in different decision contexts; when the heuristic clearly favors one choice over others, choose more deterministically, and vice versa when the heuristic is less informing choose more randomly. These techniques have yielded strong performance on classical scheduling problems but have not yet been extended to deal with the full range of constraints in the barrel master allocation problem.

5. PROJECT HISTORY AND STATUS

The AMC allocator was developed initially under sponsorship of the joint Department of Defense Advanced Research Projects Agency/USAF Research Laboratory (DARPA/AFRL) Planning Initiative Program. Following early success within this core technology development program in the area of constraint-based planning and scheduling, we were put in contact with AMC in hopes of identifying potential avenues for future technology transition. The AMC barrel master allocation problem was selected as an initial application focus, and several successively more sophisticated allocator prototypes were developed over the following two years. Following positive evaluation by AMC personnel in 1999, a decision was made to transition the allocator technology into operations within the TACC. In April 2000, project sponsorship shifted from DARPA/AFRL to AMC, with research and development work continuing under subcontract to Northrop Grumman Information Technology (NGIT), the prime contractor of AMC's operational Consolidated Mobility Planning System (CAMPS). This collaboration with NGIT is ongoing.

A version of the allocator supporting airlift allocation was first incorporated as a module of CAMPS for user testing and experimental evaluation in September 2000. In this preliminary insertion, where the goal was to gain experience and build user acceptance, provisions were made to shadow the operational CAMPS business process rather than directly manipulate the data in the CAMPS database. In retrospect, this decision turned out to be ill-advised, since users essentially had to do "double work" to make use of the new technology. Nonetheless, considerable insight was gained regarding how to better insert the allocator technology into current CAMPS business processes. Following this feedback, and a programmatic decision to refocus on the tanker barrel's problem and processes, an enhanced AR (air refueling) allocator module was developed and integrated into CAMPS. In May 2003, this version of the allocator is scheduled for initial operational release as part of CAMPS Release 5.4. At this point, tanker barrels will commence training for actual operational use.

6. SUMMARY AND CURRENT DIRECTIONS

In this paper, we have described the incremental, constraint-based scheduling model that underlies the design of the AMC allocator. The model is particularly well suited to the continuous nature of the AMC barrel master allocation problem, where newly planned missions must be integrated into an evolving global schedule on an ongoing basis. In this environment, it is important to manage solution change, as it can be unproductive and costly to continually redirect various executing agents. The incremental scheduling and allocation procedures provided by the allocator directly address this issue. When possible, they allow new missions to be incorporated without change to previous allocation decisions. In situations where nondisruptive allocation is not possible, the procedures support generation of multiple change options and promote selective, controlled manipulation of previous allocation decisions. These capabilities are provided in a real-time, interactive decision-support framework.

Our current research aims at broadening the scope and applicability of the allocator functionality. One major thrust aims at integration with "state of the world" information updates. Although current application of the technology within the barrel master office aims primarily at supporting the AMC mission planning process in advance of execution, the incremental scheduling and allocation capabilities provided by the allocator are equally applicable in the context of execution management, where unexpected events (e.g., aircraft failures, base closures) often necessitate reassessment of current plans. Furthermore, there is increasing momentum within AMC and the TACC toward tighter integration and information flow between planning and execution offices, which can be expected to provide the basis for more execution-driven planning and allocation processes. Our work here is focusing on

(1) techniques for reconciling actual execution status with expectations contained in the current schedule and recognizing the need for change,
(2) tools for visualizing current replanning problems and opportunities, and
(3) strategies and heuristics for responding to unexpected execution events.

A second thrust of our current research is on expanding the core search procedures to incorporate a larger and more diverse set of mission planning and scheduling constraints. In some cases, these model extensions correspond directly to the additional types of constraints that come into play in closing the loop with execution. Others relate to a desire to explore the applicability our current incremental constraint-based search approach to upstream mission planning problems.

REFERENCES

1. L.W. Clarke, C.A. Hane, E.L. Johnson and G.L. Nemhauser, Maintenance and crew considerations in fleet assignment, *Transportation Science* **30**, 249–260, (1996).
2. R.A. Rushmeier and S.A. Knotogiorgis, Advances in the optimization of airline fleet assignment, *Transportation Science* **31** (2), 159–169, (May, 1997).
3. C. Barnhart, N.L. Boland, L.W. Clarke, E.L. Johnson, G.L. Nemhauser and R.G. Shenoi, Flight string models for aircraft fleeting and routing, *Transportation Science* **32** (3), 208–220, (August, 1998).
4. S.F. Smith, O. Lassila and M.A. Becker, Configurable, mixed-initiative systems for planning and scheduling, In *Advanced Planning Technology*, (Edited by A. Tate), AAAI Press, Menlo Park, (1996).
5. C. Cheng and S.F. Smith, Applying constraint satisfaction techniques to job shop scheduling, *Scheduling: Theory and Practice* Special Issue of *Annals of Operations Research* **70**, 327–357, (1997).
6. P. Baptiste, C. LePape and W. Nuijten, *Constraint-Based Scheduling: Applying Constraint Programming to Scheduling Problems*, Kluwer Academic, Boston, MA, (2001).
7. R. Dechter, I. Meiri and J. Pearl, Temporal constraint networks, *Artificial Intelligence* **49** (1), 61–96, (May, 1991).
8. M.A. Becker, Reconfigurable architectures for mixed-initiative planning and scheduling, Ph.D. Thesis, Graduate School of Industrial Administration and The Robotics Institute, Carnegie Mellon University, Pittsburgh, PA, (July, 1998).
9. M.A. Becker and S.F. Smith, Mixed-initiative resource management: The AMC barrel allocator, In *Proceedings of the Fifth International Conference on Artificial Intelligence Planning and Scheduling (AIPS-00)*, pp. 32–41, The AAAI Press, Breckenridge CO, (April, 2000).
10. L. Kramer and S.F. Smith, Optimizing for change: Mixed-initiative resource management with the AMC barrel allocator, In *Proceedings of the 3rd International Workshop on Planning and Scheduling for Space*, Houston, TX, (October, 2002).
11. Q. Zhou and S.F. Smith, A priority-based pre-emption algorithm for incremental scheduling with cumulative resources, Technical Report CMU-RI-TR-02-11, Robotics Institute, Carnegie Mellon University, (June, 2002).
12. L. Kramer and S.F. Smith, Maximizing flexibility: A retraction heuristic for oversubscribed scheduling problems, In *Proceedings 18th International Joint Conference on Artificial Intelligence*, Acapulco, Mexico, Springer-Verlag, (August, 2003).
13. A. Cesta, A. Oddi and S.F. Smith, A constraint-based method for project scheduling with time windows, *Journal of Heuristics* **8** (1), 109–136, (2002).
14. V. Cicirello and S.F. Smith, Amplification of search performance through randomization of heuristics, In *Proceedings of the 8th International Conference on Principles and Practice of Constraint Programming*, pp. 124–137, Springer Verlag, Ithica, NY, (September, 2002).

Available online at www.sciencedirect.com
SCIENCE DIRECT
Mathematical and Computer Modelling 39 (2004) 599–616
MATHEMATICAL AND COMPUTER MODELLING
www.elsevier.com/locate/mcm

Solving the Theater Distribution Vehicle Routing and Scheduling Problem using Group Theoretic Tabu Search

J. R. CRINO AND J. T. MOORE
Department of Operational Sciences, Graduate School of Engineering and Management
Air Force Institute of Technology, AFIT/ENS, Building 640, 2950 Hobson Way
Wright-Patterson AFB, OH 45433-7765, U.S.A.

J. W. BARNES
Graduate Program in Operations Research and Industrial Engineering
The University of Texas at Austin, Austin, TX 78712, U.S.A.

W. P. NANRY
Army Quadrennial Defense Review Office
Office of The Army G8, Pentagon, Washington, DC, U.S.A.

Abstract—The military "theater distribution vehicle routing and scheduling problem" (TDVRSP) is associated with determining superior allocations of required flows of personnel and materiel within a defined geographic area of operation. A theater distribution system is comprised of facilities, installations, methods, and procedures designed to receive, store, maintain, distribute, and control the flow of materiel between exogenous inflows to that system and distribution to end-user activities and units within the theater. An automated system that can integrate multimodal transportation assets to improve logistics support at all levels has been characterized as a major priority and immediate need for the U.S. military services.

This paper describes both the conceptual context, based in a flexible group theoretic tabu search (GTTS) framework, and the software implementation of a robust, efficient, and effective prescriptive generalized theater distribution methodology. This methodology evaluates and prescribes the routing and scheduling of multimodal theater transportation assets at the *individual asset operational level* to provide economically efficient time-definite delivery of cargo to customers.

Keywords—Vehicle routing, Scheduling, Theater distribution, Tabu search, Group theory, Group theoretic tabu search, Symmetric group.

1. INTRODUCTION

In the last decade, serious shortcomings during military operations such as *Desert Shield/Desert Storm* and *Allied Force* dramatically illustrated the need for logistical process improvement [1,2]. As a result, the creation of a methodology that integrates multimodal transportation assets to more efficiently and effectively plan and execute logistics support within a theater has become a major priority and immediate need among the military services [2].

0895-7177/04/$ - see front matter Typeset by $\mathcal{A}\mathcal{M}\mathcal{S}$-TEX
doi:10.1016/j.mcm.2004.02.002

Achieving superior logistical efficiency mandates that the military discard the outmoded "just-in-case inventory" approach (with its extremely costly long-term stockpiles of materiel [3], and move to a rapid and reliable transportation process that provides time-definite delivery to customers. Responding to this requirement, the United States Air Force (USAF) initiated the development of an automated theater distribution management system (TDMS) which enables logistics planners to react to rapidly developing contingency operations common to the expeditionary USAF [2]. The USAF also plans to develop a scalable model that meets the other services' theater distribution modeling requirements.

Theater distribution is the flow of personnel and materiel within the theater to meet the geographic combatant commander's intent [4]. (A theater is a geographical location outside the continental United States for which a commander of a unified command is assigned military responsibility [5].)

A theater distribution system is comprised of facilities, installations, methods, and procedures designed to receive, store, maintain, distribute, and control the flow of materiel between exogenous inflows to that system and distribution to end-user activities and units within the theater [6]. Such a distribution system may be efficiently represented by a *network* where the associated physical components are categorized as nodes, modes, and routes.

This paper describes a deterministic methodology that, for the *first time*, provides vehicle routing and scheduling of multimodal theater transportation assets at the *individual asset operational level* to provide economically efficient, time-definite delivery of cargo to customers for generalized theater distribution problems. The model has been shown to be robust, flexible, and capable of solving a hierarchy of TDVRSP problems (theater distribution vehicle routing and scheduling problems) [7]. Group theoretic tabu search (GTTS) was the underlying framework utilized in the development of this methodology and several significant new abstract algebraic concepts were brought to light during the associated research.

2. LITERATURE REVIEW

All current theater distribution models used by the military are simulation models. Among such models are the enhanced logistics intratheater support tool (ELIST), transportation resource assessment network simulator (TRANS), and the mobility analysis support system (MASS). While these models assist in the understanding of distribution networks, none fulfill the defined requirements for theater distribution planning [8]. These requirements include prescribing routing and scheduling plans that optimize the utilization of theater assets while satisfying customer demand and time requirements.

One way to meet the stated requirements is to model the theater distribution problem as a vehicle routing and scheduling problem (VRSP) and use deterministic methods to solve the problem. VRSPs have been attacked using both optimization methods and heuristic methods. Classical optimization methods that find and verify an optimal solution require unacceptably large computation effort and time for practical sized problems. In addition, data describing a practical TDVRSP instance will be imprecise. Pristine optimal solutions based on such inputs will typically be inapplicable to the practical scenario. While modern metaheuristic search methods do not guarantee an optimal solution, they have been shown to find excellent robust solutions for real-world problems with dramatically less time and effort, usually within a real-time planning horizon. Such robust solutions, appropriate to a wide spectrum of TDVRSP instances, are highly preferred by theater distribution movement planners. Additionally, a theater distribution plan is often not a static document. Unforeseen events can entail modifications to the initial plan requiring planners to respond in a short time horizon.

A well-established heuristic method for solving VRSPs is tabu search (TS) [9]. A recent survey conclusively showed that TS outperforms other heuristics in finding solutions to established VRSP benchmark problems [10]. TS has successfully solved other military applications addressing a number of vehicle routing, scheduling, and assignment problems [7,11–19].

In a groundbreaking dissertation, Colletti pioneered the association of group theory with metaheuristics when he identified the symmetric group on n-letters, S_n, as a natural setting for solving permutation and ordering problems with metaheuristic techniques [20]. Wiley [17] was the first to apply GTTS. Other related research efforts include [21–24].

3. PROBLEM STATEMENT

A TDVRSP methodology should provide military planners with a tool that provides economically efficient vehicle routing and scheduling plans that achieve time-definite delivery of requested cargo to customers. As detailed below, modeling requirements for the TDVRSP extend well beyond those of the typical VRSP.

Within a typical theater, there are multimodal vehicles with differing characteristics such as cruising speed, capacity, cruising length, fixed and variable costs, route type (air, ground, water), and service times. Vehicle modeling requirements include the ability to make one or more trips during the planning horizon, the ability to perform direct delivery from outside the theater, and the ability to refuel at customer locations. Scheduling considerations include vehicle availability, service times, load times, and unload times. All vehicles operate from a depot or a hub.

Theater distribution network nodes are depots, hubs, and customers. Depots, aerial ports of debarkation (APODs), and seaports of debarkation (SPODs) are the supply nodes. The hubs, or support areas (SAs) which occur at corps (CSA), division (DSA), and brigade (BSA) levels, are transshipment nodes, which receive, store, and distribute cargo. Customers are sink nodes that receive cargo. All nodes have time window constraints, fuel storage capacity, and maximum on the ground (MOG) constraints. Hubs have cargo storage constraints and customers have cargo demand requirements and time-definite delivery requirements.

A TDVRSP has three types of time window constraints: early time-definite delivery (ETDD), time-definite delivery (TDD), and multiple time windows for nondeparture and nonarrival times (MTW). An ETDD stringently defines a customer service starting time but does not constrain vehicle arrival or departure times. A TDD defines when a customer service must be complete but does not constrain service occurrence, or vehicle arrival and departure times. MTWs restrict vehicle arrival and departure at a node but do not stipulate when vehicles are loaded or offloaded.

There are two types of maximum on the ground (MOG) constraints. A working MOG limits the number of vehicles that can simultaneously service a customer. A parking MOG limits the number of vehicles parked at a customer location.

The TDVRSP has a tiered distribution architecture. The first-order tier contains the depots and customers/hubs served by the depots. Middle tiers consist of hubs that service customers/hubs. The last-order tier consists of end customers served by a hub. Each tier is a self-contained distribution network. However, they are not independent of each other. Lower-ordered tiers are dependent on higher-ordered tiers. For example, the hubs in a lower-ordered tier receive logistics as a customer within a higher-ordered tier. Once a hub receives its cargo supply, it can then distribute the cargo to its customers.

Figure 1 presents an example of a TDVRSP. There are four tiers within this network: Tier 0 is the APOD with Customers (1,2,CSA); Tier 1 is the CSA hub with Customers (DSA1, DSA2, 3); Tier 2 is the DSA1 hub with Customers (BSA3, BSA4, and 5); and Tier 3 is the DSA2 hub with Customers (BSA1, BSA2, and 4). Note that, unlike a classical network hierarchy, both Tiers 2 and 3 derive from Tier 1.

Hubs distribute cargo after it is received and processed. Cargo, characterized by the amount delivered and time of delivery, is processed and prepared for delivery to its next customer. Cargo is either loaded directly onto available vehicles or stored for later delivery.

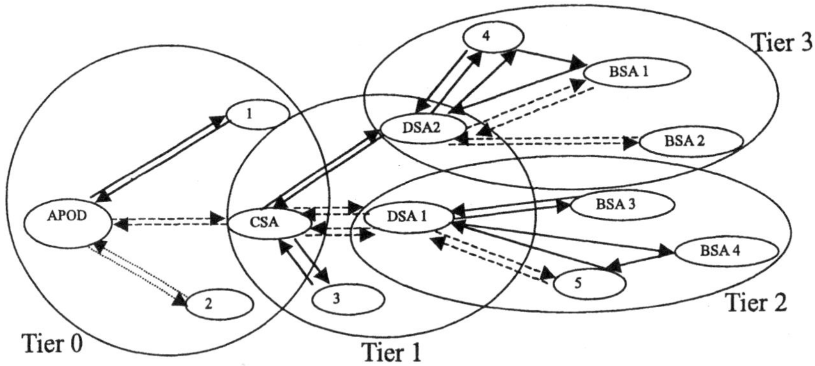

Figure 1. Example TDVVRSP.

The TDVRSP primary objectives are to minimize unmet customer demand (demand shortfall), late deliveries (TDD shortfall), vehicle fixed costs, and vehicle variable costs. Late delivery times are weighted by the amount of demand delivered late. A fixed cost is charged for each vehicle used in the solution and variable vehicle costs are associated with vehicle travel.

4. TDVRSP SOLUTION METHODOLOGY

GTTS has been used successfully to attack several difficult combinatorial optimization problems [7,14,17,19]. Crino shows that GTTS provides an efficient and effective means to find quality TDVRSP solutions. This section provides algebraic foundations, a description of how the TDVRSP is represented in the GTTS framework, and a description of the GTTS methodology employed.

4.1. Algebraic Foundations

Abstract groups are simply explained as sets of objects, together with a method of combining its elements that is subject to a few simple rules [25].

A *semigroup* is a nonempty set G together with a fixed binary operation $\oplus$ that satisfies the following conditions.

1. $x \oplus y \in G, \forall x, y \in G$; the operation is closed.
2. $(x \oplus y) \oplus z = x \oplus (y \oplus z) \forall x, y, z \in G$; the operation is associative.

A *group* is a semigroup that satisfies the additional conditions.

1. $\exists ! \ e \in G \ni \forall x \in G, \ e \oplus x = x \oplus e = x$; there exists a unique identity.
2. For each $x \in G$, $\exists ! \ x^{-1} \in G \ni x^{-1} \oplus x = x \oplus x^{-1} = e$; there exists a unique inverse. Groups have some elementary properties that are used in this research. These properties, presented as a theorem with a proof in [26], are presented below.

1. For $x, y \in G$, if $x \oplus y = e$, then $x = y^{-1}$ and $y = x^{-1}$.
2. $(x \oplus y)^{-1} = y^{-1} \oplus x^{-1} \forall x, y \in G$.
3. $(x^{-1})^{-1} = x \forall x \in G$.
4. For $x, y, z \in G$, if $z \oplus x = z \oplus y$, then $x = y$ and if $x \oplus z = y \oplus z$, then $x = y$.

A *permutation of Set A* is a function from A into A, which is both one to one, and onto [27].

The *symmetric group on n-letters*, S_n, is the group of all permutations of Set A if A is the finite set $\{1, 2, 3, \ldots, n\}$ [27].

Since the TDVRSP is fundamentally a combinatorial optimization problem involving the partitioning and ordering of letters, S_n provides a natural setting for structuring the problem.

There are two different notations for S_n, the standard form and cyclic form. The standard form notation is a $2 \times n$ array that represents a one-to-one and onto function whose domain (top row) and image (bottom row) are the integers $\{1, 2, \ldots, n\}$ [20]. Let elements $\pi \in S_n$ be permutations. The notation is the following array.

$$\begin{matrix} 1 & 2 & 3 & 4 & 5 & \ldots & n \\ \pi(1) & \pi(2) & \pi(3) & \pi(4) & \pi(5) & \ldots & \pi(n) \end{matrix}$$

The cyclic form notation is a streamlined notation of S_n. Given $i \in \{1, 2, \ldots, n\}$, $p \in \mathbf{N}$, and $\pi^p(i) = i$, the first cycle is represented as

$$\left(i, \pi(i), \pi^2(i), \ldots, \pi^{p-1}(i)\right).$$

Equivalently, the cycle (i, j, k, l) means π sends i to j, j to k, k to l, and l back to i. The process continues by picking an element not in the cycle containing i and iterating the process until all members of $\{1, 2, \ldots, n\}$ have been used. A cycle of length k is a cycle containing k elements [28]. Cycles with only one element are called unit cycles, where unit cycles can be implied and dropped from cyclic notation. Examples of the standard form permutation and cyclic form permutation are presented below [28].

If $\pi \in S_5$ is given by

$$\pi(1) = 2, \qquad \pi(2) = 3, \qquad \pi(3) = 1, \qquad \pi(4) = 4, \qquad \pi(5) = 5,$$

then the standard form is

$$\pi = \begin{pmatrix} x \\ \pi(x) \end{pmatrix} = \begin{pmatrix} 1 & 2 & 3 & 4 & 5 \\ 2 & 3 & 1 & 4 & 5 \end{pmatrix}$$

and the cyclic form is $\pi = (1, 2, 3)(4)(5)$ or $\pi = (1, 2, 3)$. The length of the first cycle is 3 and the unit cycles are (4) and (5).

The binary operation for S_n is function composition. The product of two permutations, $\pi \oplus \sigma$, is composition. Given x$\in$ S$_n$, then $(\pi \oplus \sigma)(x) = \sigma(\pi(x))$.

For example, let

$$\pi = \begin{pmatrix} x \\ \pi(x) \end{pmatrix} = \begin{pmatrix} 1 & 2 & 3 & 4 & 5 \\ 2 & 3 & 1 & 4 & 5 \end{pmatrix} \quad \text{and} \quad \sigma = \begin{pmatrix} x \\ \sigma(x) \end{pmatrix} = \begin{pmatrix} 1 & 2 & 3 & 4 & 5 \\ 4 & 3 & 1 & 2 & 5 \end{pmatrix},$$

then

$$\pi \oplus \sigma = \begin{pmatrix} 1 & 2 & 3 & 4 & 5 \\ 2 & 3 & 1 & 4 & 5 \end{pmatrix} \begin{pmatrix} 1 & 2 & 3 & 4 & 5 \\ 4 & 3 & 1 & 2 & 5 \end{pmatrix} = \begin{pmatrix} 1 & 2 & 3 & 4 & 5 \\ 3 & 1 & 4 & 2 & 5 \end{pmatrix}.$$

An operation used throughout this research as a means to execute TS moves is conjugation. Conjugation provides a relabeling of permutation letters while maintaining the original cyclic structure.

Conjugation is an operation, denoted $x = y^k$, where $x = k^{-1} \oplus y \oplus k$ for some $x, y, k \in G$ where G is a group.

An example of conjugation as applied in TS is the operation between two permutations where one represents an incumbent solution, $x =$ (1,3,2)(4)(5), and the other a two-letter swap move, $k =$ (2,4). Conjugating x by k results in the solution $x^k = k^{-1} \oplus x \oplus k =$ (1,3,4)(2)(5), where the cyclic structure is maintained and only letters in the conjugator permutation are moved.

Group theory provides for the partitioning of groups into conjugacy classes, group actions, and orbits. In general, any abstract group G inherently self-partitions into mutually exclusive and exhaustive conjugacy classes.

A conjugacy class, CClass $(G, g) = \{g^h : h \in G\}$, is the set of all elements $\{h^{-1} \oplus g \oplus h : h \in G\}$ for $g \in G$.

Another feature of group theory that partitions S$_n$ solution spaces are group actions and orbits. Given an abstract group G and a set X, a *group action*, denoted $_GX$ defines how G-elements operate upon X-elements to create X-elements [20].

For $g \in$ G and $x \in$ X, let x^g denote the unique X-element that satisfies

- $x^e = x, \forall x \in X$ (e is the G-identity),
- $\forall g, h \in G$ and $x \in X$, $(x^g)^h = x^{gh}$.

The "conjugation-like" notation $x^g \in X$ denotes the result of $g \in G$ acting upon $x \in X$. The user defines G and the result of x^g must be closed on X.

Let G be a group and X be a nonempty set. For $x \in X$, an orbit is the set of all elements in X to which x can be moved by $g \in G$, i.e., $x^G \equiv \{x^g : g \in G\}$. A group action inherently partitions X into *orbits.*

The *orbit* of $x \in X$ is x^G and denotes the G-orbit of x, Orbit (G, x). Since any two orbits of ${}_GX$ either coincide or are disjoint, orbits of a group action partition X. If X is a conjugacy class in S_n, orbits will exhaustively and exclusively partition the conjugacy classes [20].

Specifically for this research, the set X is a CClass (S_n, x) which comprises the solution space of the TDVRSP. The group G is a user-defined subgroup of S_n that moves solution letters. The G-orbit of $x \in X$ defines a TS move neighborhood of x. A particular x^g defines a move neighbor of x. Each orbit is the neighborhood of any one of its permutations, and the members of an orbit share the same neighborhood [20].

4.2. Using $\mathbf{S}_n$ to Represent the TDVRSP

Applying GTTS to the TDVRSP requires that solutions be represented as elements of S_n. For a TDVRSP solution, each cyclic factor in the solution's disjoint cyclic structure represents a vehicle trip. For $p = (1,4,5)(2,3) \in S_5$, (1,4,5) represents the following tour: $1 \to 4 \to 5 \to 1$. For the TDVRSP, the first letter in the tour represents a vehicle. Subsequent letters represent the customers serviced by that vehicle. In this example, a vehicle leaves a depot/hub and services two customers before returning back to the depot/hub. A unit cycle represents either a vehicle letter not leaving the depot/hub or a customer letter not serviced. Permutations having a single factor represent TDVRSP solutions having one tour. Permutations with k factors represent k vehicles conducting at most k tours. The k vehicles could be from the same depot/hub or different depot/hubs depending on the vehicle location data.

In group theoretic notation, let C and V be the disjoint customer and vehicle letter-sets, respectively, where $|V| < |C|$, and let X be the permutations in $S(C \cup V)$ whose factors each contain a sole V-letter. The *first position* of any cycle in X contains the cycle's single V-letter, and the factors of $x \in X$ are arranged in ascending V-letter order, thus implying lexicographic ordering.

In a TDVRSP problem, vehicles can make multiple trips and customers can receive multiple services within a time period. A letter is allocated for each vehicle trip and each customer service. Letters are assigned sequentially for each vehicle or customer. For example, if Vehicle A has the potential to make three trips, three letters are assigned to Vehicle A's trips. If Customer D has the potential to receive two services, two letters are assigned. Table 1 shows a letter assignment to Vehicles A, B, and C and Customers A, B, and C. Vehicle A has the potential for three trips, Vehicle B can make two trips, and Vehicle C can make four trips. Customer A has the potential for servicing two times, Customer B can be serviced three times, and customer C may be serviced only once.

The network representation of Table 1's TDVRSP solution is presented in Figure 2. For the solution tour, vehicle trips occur in numerical order but customer services do not necessarily occur in numerical order. The solution is (1,10)(2,11,13)(4,12)(6,15) where there are five unused vehicle trips and one unused customer service letter.

Figure 3 presents another example of a TDVRSP solution. The hubs in this TDVRSP require a letter assignment scheme based on the tier levels within the distribution structure. The highest tiers are the depots and the customers they serve. The second highest tiers are the customers served by the hubs in the highest order. The third highest tiers are the customers serviced by the hubs in the second order. This hierarchical structure is replicated until all nodes are considered. Letter assignments are first given to the highest tier's vehicles. Subsequent assignment of vehicle letters moves to the next highest tier. This continues until vehicles for the lowest tier are assigned letters. Next, an identical procedure is followed for the assignment of customer letters.

Table 1. S_n letter assignment example.

	Number of Trips/Services	Assigned Letters
Vehicle A	3	1,2,3
Vehicle B	2	4,5
Vehicle C	4	6,7,8,9
Customer A	2	10,11
Customer B	3	12,13,14
Customer C	1	15

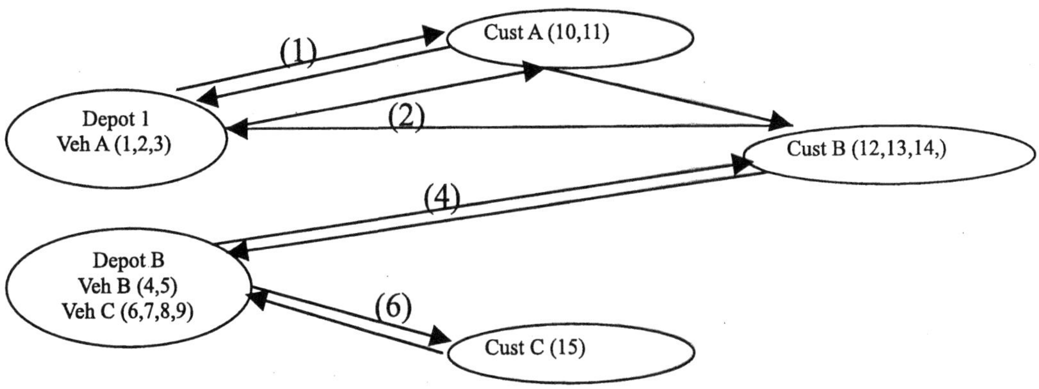

Figure 2. TDVRSP solution tour example.

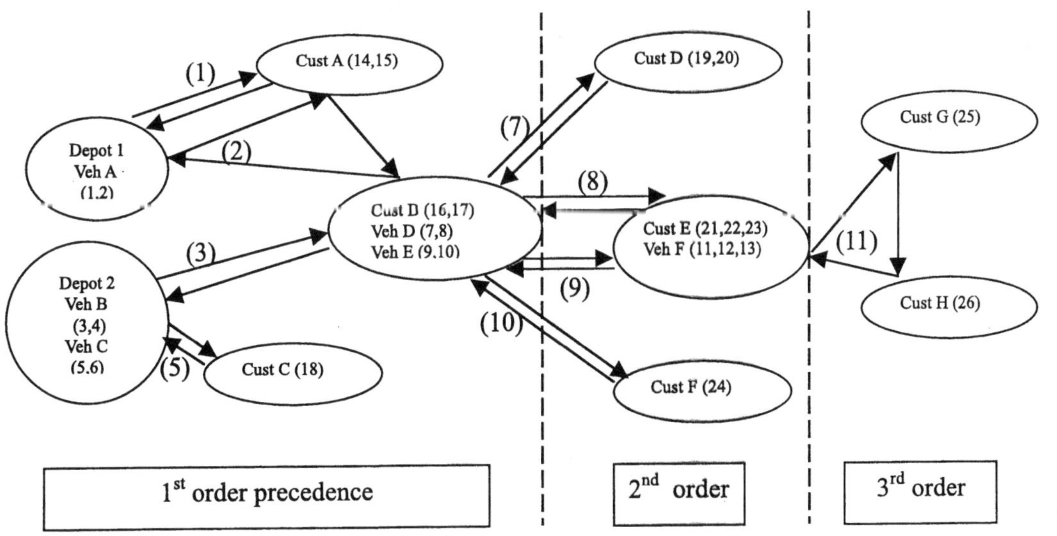

Figure 3. Solution tour with hubs example.

The solution given in Figure 3 is (1,14)(2,15,16)(3,17)(5,18)(7,19)(8,21)(9,22)(10,24)(11,25,26). The implied unit cycles (4), (6), (12), and (13) are unused vehicle trip letters and unit cycles (20) and (23) are unused customer service letters.

In addition to yielding an efficient and effective solution methodology for the TDVRSP, the research documented here also provided *significant* advances in the development of GTTS as applied to vehicle routing and scheduling problems. These GTTS advances, described in detail in [7], included, for the *first* time, the formulation of move neighborhoods defined using groups to generate orbits. These orbits were used as a means to efficiently search the solution space. They eliminated cycling, prevented solution reevaluation, and avoided entrapment in local optima. This methodology prevents the search from being trapped in a subset of the solution space topology and eliminates the need for a restart mechanism. This technique allowed exhaustive nonrepetitive search of each partition and, by placing a utilized orbit on an orbit tabu list, prevented reevaluation.

A unique solution space partition hierarchy was developed using the symmetric group on n-letters. Conjugacy classes, cyclic form structures, orbital planes, and orbits were defined that partition the solution space. Solution space partitions were exploited in the diversification and intensification process. In addition, neighborhoods were constructed to intelligently traverse the partitions and enable a potential search of the entire space. Group move neighborhoods steered the search between different orbits. Swap move neighborhoods traversed the search between different orbital planes. Insert and extraction move neighborhoods moved the search to different conjugacy classes and cyclic form structures.

Orbital planes were defined and used as a primary search mechanism of the GTTS. Orbital planes are orbits partitioned by orbits. They provide a more atomic partitioning of the solution space permitting partial or exhaustive search. Using orbital planes is a highly efficient special case of Colletti's [20] orbital transversal method because the search may reexamine an orbit (orbital plane) without reevaluating solutions within the orbit (orbital plane).

4.3. TDVRSP Modeling Assumptions

It is a recognized fact that no "real-world" problem's inherent complexities can be captured in a usable model of manageable size. For this reason, while preserving the methodology's capability for practical planning purposes, a number of assumptions have been incorporated into the GTTS representation of the TDVRSP. The primary assumptions are listed below.

1. Sufficient supplies of required materiel are available at Time 0 at all depot locations.
2. All cargo is aggregated into a single commodity and vehicle capacity restrictions are enforced.
3. All airfields accommodate all aircraft types
4. Each aircraft or ground vehicle type uses the same loading and unloading materiel handling equipment, personnel, and docking space for assessing working MOG constraints.
5. Unloading and loading requirements are independent of customer and load conditions.
6. Vehicle travel costs are independent of load weight.
7. Working MOG constraints are constant for each customer and depot.
8. Vehicles depart from and return to the same depot/hub.
9. All hubs have no supplies of materiel in storage at Time 0.
10. Vehicles wait to depart hubs with full loads, unless customer demands require less than a full load.
11. Customers within the same tier are serviced exclusively from a single hub.
12. For a hub, working MOGs that unload vehicles are independent of working MOGs that load vehicles.

4.4. An Overview of GTTS

In this section, the GTTS architecture [29] used to solve the TDVRSP is presented. Figure 4 graphically depicts this architecture which is partitioned into a pre-TS phase and the TS phase. Figure 4 pictures the major components of each procedure within each phase. Due to space limitations, only an overview of the GTTS for the TDVRSP can be presented here. (The reader *desiring greater detail*, including algorithmic and code implementation is referred to [7] which may be requested from J. T. Moore (`james.moore@afit.edu`).)

4.4.1. The pre-TS phase

The pre-TS phase achieves the following:

(1) sets parameter values and assimilates a text file containing the customer and vehicle specifications for the current problem to be solved,

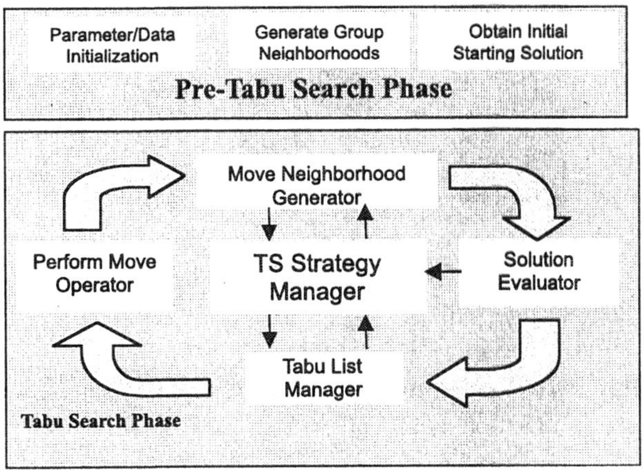

Figure 4. Group theoretic tabu search architecture.

(2) generates the group neighborhoods, and
(3) creates and evaluates an initial solution.

Generation of the group neighborhoods partitions the customer service letters C into disjoint subsets C_i, $i = 1, 2, \ldots, n$, where different customers are represented in each C_i. The process then generates the mutually exclusive groups, $G_i = S(C_i)$, the symmetric group on the letters in C_i. The G_i are stored within the *move neighborhood generator* for future use as move neighborhoods.

A greedy assignment heuristic creates the initial solution by assigning prioritized customers to vehicles that best meet their demands. Customers are assigned priority ratings using the following equation:

$$\text{CustomerPriorityRating} = \frac{\text{custDist}}{\text{avgDist}} * \sum_{i=1}^{n} \left[\text{custDemand}_i * (\text{periodLength}/TDD_i)\,(n-i)\right],$$

where

$$\begin{aligned} i &= \text{TDD requirement index per customer},\\ n &= \text{number of TDD requirements per customer},\\ TDD_i &= \text{customer TDD requirement for index } i,\\ \text{custDist} &= \text{distance of customer to nearest depot/hub},\\ \text{avgDist} &= \text{average distance of all customers to their nearest depot},\\ \text{custDemand}_i &= \text{customer demand},\\ \text{periodLength} &= \text{total model time period}. \end{aligned}$$

Vehicles are ordered based on the ratio of their capacity and average trip time.

$$\text{VehCapPerAvgTripTime} = \text{vehCap}/(2^{*}\text{avgDist}/\text{speed} + \text{loadTime}+\text{unloadTime}+\text{servTime}),$$

where

$$\begin{aligned} \text{vehCap} &= \text{vehicle capacity},\\ \text{speed} &= \text{vehicle cruising speed},\\ \text{loadTime} &= \text{time to load a vehicle},\\ \text{unloadTime} &= \text{time to unload a vehicle},\\ \text{servTime} &= \text{time to service a vehicle}. \end{aligned}$$

Once created, the initial solution, or first *incumbent solution*, is evaluated according to an objective function that assesses the demand filled shortfall, TDD shortfall, fixed costs, variable costs, and other penalties.

4.4.2. The TS phase

Running until a termination criterion is satisfied, each iteration of the TS phase passes through five major components; *move neighborhood generator, solution evaluator, TS strategy manager, tabu list manager*, and *perform move operator*. An iteration begins by generating and applying a move neighborhood to the incumbent solution and ends when the *perform move operator* creates a new incumbent solution.

The *move neighborhood generator* creates and applies move neighborhoods to the incumbent solution. Move neighborhoods are generated and employed based on solution attributes and data collection. The types of move neighborhoods generated are

- *intraorbital plane mutually exclusive group action neighborhood,*
- *interorbital plane swap move neighborhood,*
- *fill demand insert move neighborhood,*
- *interconjugacy class insert move neighborhood,*
- *interconjugacy class extraction move neighborhood.*

The *intraorbital plane mutually exclusive group neighborhood* is a collection of move neighborhoods generated by mutually exclusive groups created in the pre-TS phase. They are the primary search mechanism used by the TS strategy during normal search cycles. The *interorbital plane swap move neighborhood* is a collection of two-letter swap moves, where each letter is from a disjoint set of customer letters, C_i, $i = 1, 2, \ldots, n$. This neighborhood provides move combinations not offered by the group neighborhoods. The *fill demand insert move neighborhood* is a collection of moves that reduce the demand shortfall. The *interconjugacy class insert move neighborhood* consists of *intercycle insert moves* that diversify the search by moving to a new conjugacy class. This neighborhood also uses solution attributes to create moves that potentially decrease the solutions' demand shortfall or TDD shortfall. Finally, the *interconjugacy class extraction move neighborhood* consists of extraction moves that diversify the search by moving into new conjugacy classes. This neighborhood extracts customer letters from cycles in order to reduce fixed and variable costs. It is specifically called when excess customer letters reside in cycles and when the *TS strategy manager* dictates implementing super diversification measures.

Working closely with the *tabu list manager*, the *solution evaluator* determines the objective function value for each p-neighbor, q, where $q = (p \oplus \text{move}, p^{\text{move}})\, \forall\, \text{move} \in$ MoveNeighborhood. The goal of this process is to find the best nontabu q to replace the incumbent solution p. The *solution evaluator* has four main components: the permutation preprocessor, the vehicle loader/scheduler heuristic, the objective function evaluator, and the solution comparison method. The *solution evaluator* iterates through the four components for all q.

The permutation preprocessor simply transforms the incumbent solution's permutation representation into that of a defined neighboring solution. The vehicle loader/scheduler heuristic determines the vehicle loads and delivery schedules by using constraint-programming techniques to determine the loads and schedules for each vehicle. A vehicle is loaded to its specified capacity unless no more supply exists at the depot/hub or the customers in the tour do not demand a full load. The amounts of supply customers receive are determined by one of two options. The first option, until the vehicle is empty, provides a customer with his total demand based on the trip order. The second option equally splits the vehicle load between all customers in the trip. If a customer does not demand its share, then its share is distributed equally among the remaining customers. Vehicle schedules are determined based on travel times, service times, time constraints, and working MOG constraints. A vehicle schedule begins at its available time and is influenced thereafter by such things as customer time and MOG constraints along its trip.

The final results provided by the vehicle loader/scheduler heuristic's are complete details for each customer regarding each servicing vehicle's visit and complete details for each vehicle used including timing and routing information, and customers served on each vehicle trip. (The vehicle loader/scheduler heuristic clearly does not guarantee that the optimal use of vehicles is found for

```
Obtain initial solution & initialize parameters
p = Incumbent solution = initial solution
WHILE iteration_count <= MaxLoops, do:
        Increment iteration_count
        Select MoveNeighborhood
                a. If super diversification counter ≥ superDiversifyTolerance and
                   diversifyingCounter ≤ superDiversifyMoves
                        i. Select interconjugacy class extraction move neighborhood
                b. Else If worsening move counter ≤ worseningMoveTolerance or
                   constant move counter ≤ constantMoveTolerance
                        i. Select next sequential group neighborhood, or
                        ii. Select swap move neighborhood at end of group sequence
                        iii. If strictly intensifying in an orbital plane, do not include step ii.
                c. Else If intensificationOn = true
                        Select swap move neighborhood
                d. Else (select and generate a diversification move neighborhood)
                        i. If solution demand shortfall > 0
                                Select fill demand move neighborhood
                        ii. Else If unnecessary vehicle trips > 1 or customer services > 2
                                Select interconjugacy class extraction move neighborhood
                        iii. Else If TDD shortfall > 0
                                1. Select interconjugacy class extraction move
                                   neighborhood, or (alternate)
                                2. Select interconjugacy class insert move neighborhood
                        iv. Else
                                Select interorbital plane swap move neighborhood
        Evaluate q = p ⊕ move or q = p^move ∀ move ∈ MoveNeighborhood.
        Select best q based on objective function values and tabu status.
        Register evaluated orbit, conjugacy class, and/or move in tabu list
        Perform p⊕ move or p^move and generate a new incumbent solution, p
        Determine TS type, normal or intensification
                e. If TS counter = iterations,
                        i. Begin intensification search process
                        ii. Set p = an elite list permutation
                        iii. IntensificationOn = true
                f. Else If intensification TS counter = intensificationIterations,
                        i. Begin normal TS process
                        ii. Set intensificationOn = false.
End while
End
```

Figure 5. An outline pseudocode of the GTTS TDVRSP algorithm.

the neighborhood solution being investigated. Fortunately, this heuristic performed sufficiently well for the overall GTTS algorithm to provide excellent solutions to the overall optimization problem.)

As stated earlier, the objective function evaluator measures demand shortfall, time-definite delivery (TDD) shortfall, fixed costs, variable costs, and penalty costs. Penalty costs include parking MOG violations and hub storage capacity violations.

The *tabu list manager* uses the *orbit* and *move* lists to interact with the *solution evaluator* to prevent cycling within the TS process. The orbit list tracks traversed orbits and the move list tracks recent diversification moves. Both lists allow an element's tabu status to be determined and changed.

The *TS strategy manager* determines whether to continue with normal TS processes, to intensify or to diversify the search. Decisions are based on collected search data and search parameters. Intensification occurs in conjugacy classes that generate good solutions. Diversification, in a normal or "super" form, occurs when the search process needs to explore different conjugacy classes. Normal diversification imparts a new search direction towards a different solution space partition. Super diversification departs the current local search areas where moves tend to be unimproving.

Figure 5 presents an outline pseudocode of the GTTS algorithm.

5. A DETAILED TDVRSP EXAMPLE WITH COMPUTATIONAL RESULTS

Prior to the research documented here, no benchmark problems existed for the TDVRSP. Crino [7] used valid experimental design methodology to construct a set of 39 problems that effectively test the robustness of the GTTS TDVRSP algorithm. The problems are composed of three TDVRSP types: the Air Force multiple trips multiple services (MTMS) without hub, the joint MTMS without hub, and the joint MTMS with hub and other defining constraints. The 39 problems were further categorized by problem size (small, medium, and large), delivery restriction density (low, medium, and high), and demand to capacity ratio (low, medium, and high).

Figure 6 presents Crino's benchmark problem 37, one of the large Joint MTMS problems with hub and other defining constraints. Only customers 0, 1, 2, and 3 can accommodate Air Force cargo aircraft and all aircraft are located at the APOD. Table 2 gives the tier structure for the MTMS with hub instance. Tables 3–5 display data for the 31 customers whose demands range

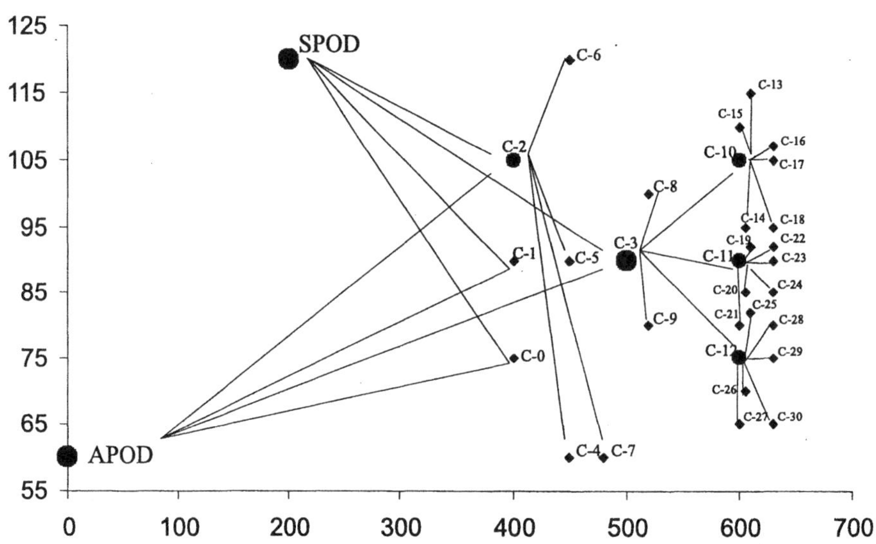

Figure 6. TDVRSP depot, hub, and customer locations.

Table 2. TDVRSP tier structure.

Tier	Supply Source	Customers
0	APOD, SPOD	C-0, C-1, C-2, C-3
1	C-2	C-4, C-5, C-6, C-7
2	C-3	C-8, C-9, C-10, C-11, C-12
3	C-10	C-13, C-14, C-15, C-16, C-17, C-18
4	C-11	C-19, C-20, C-21, C-22, C-23, C-24
5	C-12	C-25, C-26, C-27, C-28, C-29, C-30

from 65 to 1800 tons. The working and parking MOGs vary in size from 1–3 for the working MOG-for-aircraft (MOGA) and MOG-for-ground-vehicles (MOGG) and 2 – 6 for the parking MOGA. The APOD is restricted to a working MOGA = 6 and the SPOD has a working MOGG = 8. Some customers have ETDD constraints > 0 and some have time windows that restrict arrival and departure times. Table 4 presents TDD requirements for the customers with more than one TDD. Table 5 displays time windows for the APOD and Customer 2, which restrict aircraft arrival and departure within those windows.

Table 3. TDVRSP customer data.

Cust.	Location Coordinates		Demand	wMOGA	wMOGG	pMOGA
0	400	75	300	1	3	2
1	400	90	300	2	3	4
2	400	105	800	3	3	6
3	500	90	1800	3	3	6
4	450	60	200	0	2	0
5	450	90	200	0	2	0
6	450	120	200	0	1	0
7	480	60	200	0	1	0
8	520	100	75	0	1	0
9	520	80	75	0	2	0
10	600	105	550	0	3	0
11	600	90	550	0	3	0
12	600	75	550	0	3	0
13	610	115	65	0	1	0
14	605	95	70	0	2	0
15	600	110	70	0	2	0
16	630	107	115	0	3	0
17	630	105	115	0	3	0
18	630	95	115	0	3	0
19	610	92	65	0	1	0
20	605	85	70	0	2	0
21	600	80	70	0	3	0
22	630	92	115	0	1	0
23	630	90	115	0	3	0
24	630	85	115	0	3	0
25	610	82	65	0	1	0
26	605	70	70	0	2	0
27	600	65	70	0	3	0
28	630	80	115	0	2	0
29	630	75	115	0	3	0
30	630	65	115	0	3	0

Table 3. (cont.)

Cust.	eTDD	TDD	Hub	Tier	Prior	Storage	ACfuel	Gfuel
0	0	96	0	0	1	0	0	200
1	0	96	0	0	1	0	0	200
2	0	96	1	0	1	200	2000	400
3	0	96	2	0	1	300	8000	500
4	0	96	0	1	1	0	0	200
5	0	96	0	1	1	0	0	200
6	36	96	0	1	1	0	0	200
7	24	96	0	1	1	0	0	200
8	0	48	0	2	1	0	0	50
9	0	72	0	2	1	0	0	50
10	0	96	3	2	1	0	0	200
11	0	96	4	2	1	0	0	200
12	0	96	5	2	1	0	0	200
13	0	24	0	3	1	0	0	50
14	0	36	0	3	1	0	0	50
15	0	72	0	3	1	0	0	50
16	0	30	0	3	1	0	0	50
17	0	66	0	3	1	0	0	50
18	0	96	0	3	1	0	0	50
19	24	70	0	4	1	0	0	50
20	24	96	0	4	1	0	0	50
21	24	96	0	4	1	0	0	50
22	24	96	0	4	1	0	0	50
23	24	36	0	4	1	0	0	50
24	24	90	0	4	1	0	0	50
25	48	96	0	5	1	0	0	50
26	48	96	0	5	1	0	0	50
27	48	96	0	5	1	0	0	50
28	48	72	0	5	1	0	0	50
29	48	96	0	5	1	0	0	50
30	48	72	0	5	1	0	0	50

An example of the vehicle data is displayed in Table 6. There are a total of 90 vehicles. There are two aircraft types and five ground vehicle types. The aircraft closely resemble the C-17 and C-130 cargo aircraft. The ground vehicles represent heavy and medium fleet assets. The capacity is in tons, speed is in miles per hour, and service, load, and unload times are in hours. Available time is in hours relative to the model start time and the cruise lengths are in miles.

The summary problem results are given in Table 7. Examples of detailed vehicle loads, schedules, and customer deliveries are displayed in Tables 8 and 9. Due to route length constraints,

Table 4. Customers with multiple TDD requirements.

Cust.	Cummulative Demand	ETDD	TDD
0	69	0	36
0	142	0	60
0	219	0	84
0	300	0	96
1	70	0	36
1	150	0	60
1	215	0	84
1	300	0	96
4	90	0	36
4	200	0	96
5	110	0	60
5	200	0	96
7	80	24	60
7	200	24	96

Table 5. Customer time windows.

Cust.	AC-time windows		G-time windows	
APOD	24	30	0	0
APOD	48	54	0	0
APOD	72	78	0	0
2	24	30	0	0
2	48	54	0	0
2	72	78	0	0

Table 6. Vehicle data.

Veh. Type	Capacity	Speed	Fixed Cost	Var. Cost.	Cruise Length	Service Time	Load Time	Unload Time
A	85	470	10	.05	9000	2	4	2
A	12	330	2	.02	3000	1	2	1
G	28	45	1	.01	300	2	3	1
G	16	60	1	.01	300	1	2	1

Table 7. Evaluation summary.

Total Demand Shortfall	0.0
Sum TDD Shortfall (weighted)	3.41
Fixed Cost	106.5
Variable Cost	112.98
Storage Constraint Penalty	3.0
MOG Parking Penalty	0.0
Total cost	**225.88**

Table 8. Vehicle schedule example.

Vehicle	Cust/Dep	Arr. Time	Start Off/Onload	End Off/Onload	Depart	Delivery
4		0	0	4	4	
4	3	5.07	5.07	7.07	7.07	85
4		8.13	10.13	14.13	14.13	
4	3	15.2	15.2	17.2	17.2	85
4		18.26	20.26	24.26	30	
4	3	31.07	31.07	33.07	33.07	85
4		34.13	36.13	40.13	40.13	
4	3	41.2	41.2	43.2	43.2	85
4		44.26	46.26	50.26	54	
4	3	55.07	55.07	57.07	57.07	85
4		58.13	60.13	64.13	64.13	
4	3	65.2	65.2	67.2	67.2	56

Table 9. Customer delivery example.

Customer	Vehicle	Delivery Amount	Arr.	Offload	Dep.
6	39	4	22.98	36	37
6	34	28	27.32	37	38
6	38	4	31.87	38	39
6	37	8	37.79	39	40
6	39	4	41.26	41.26	42.26
6	34	28	44.59	44.59	45.59
6	36	12	59.83	59.83	60.83
6	33	28	61.15	61.15	62.15
6	35	16	64.49	64.49	65.49
6	36	12	64.77	65.49	66.49
6	37	8	65.74	66.49	67.49
6	38	4	65.78	67.49	68.49
6	33	28	68.74	68.74	69.74
6	35	16	69.44	69.74	70.74

Table 10. Example solutions.

Demand Shortfall	TDD Shortfall	Fixed Cost	Variable Cost	Total Cost	Time	Iteration
0.0	9.02	108.0	113.91	251.94	11.5	145
0.0	4.71	107.5	113.43	230.64	24.5	290
0.0	3.41	106.5	112.98	225.88	62.75	709

some vehicles refueled at customer locations to have enough fuel to return to their depot/hub. Customers 0, 1, and 2 provided 178.6, 146.3, and 384.3 gallons of fuel to ground vehicles.

The total run time for 1,000 iterations was 110 minutes, where the best solution was found at iteration 709 (62.8 minutes). However, competitive satisfactory solutions, where all customer

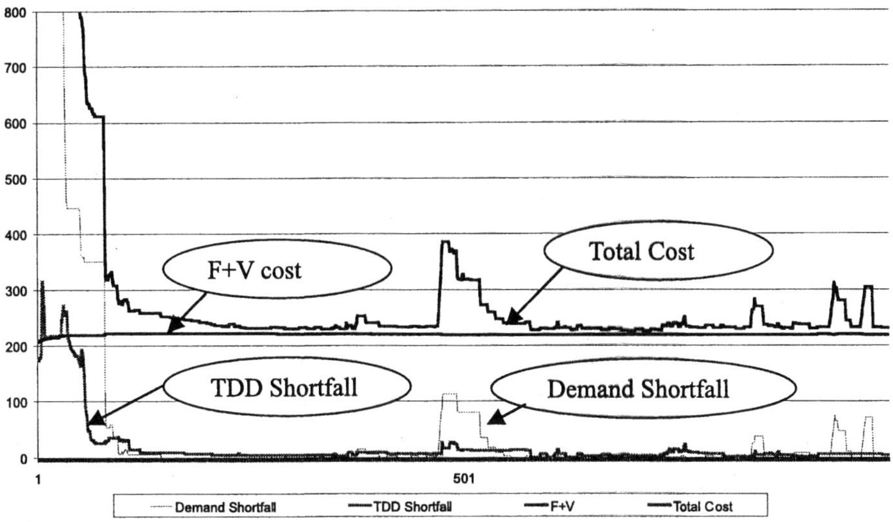

Figure 7. TDVRSP Objective function values.

demands were satisfied, were found much earlier in the search process. Two such solutions are documented in Table 10.

Problem 37's results are indicative of the timely, effective, and robust results provided by the GTTS approach for all 39 benchmark problems. The GTTS method has clearly displayed its ability to solve the multiple objective TDVRSP problem.

Figure 7 displays the TS objective function values for each of the 1,000 iterations. The chart evidences a "healthy" TS search process that moves through different areas of the solution space as reflected by the variation of the objective function values.

6. CONCLUDING REMARKS

The development of an automated solution methodology to the TDVRSP problem has been characterized as a major priority and immediate need for the U.S. military services.

This paper documents groundbreaking new theoretical results based in a flexible group theoretic tabu search (GTTS) framework and presents a powerful software implementation of those results. This marriage of theory and application has resulted in a robust, efficient, and effective generalized theater distribution methodology. This methodology evaluates and determines the routing and scheduling of multimodal theater transportation assets at the *individual asset operational level* to provide economically efficient time-definite delivery of cargo to customers.

Many software programs are available that "perform" theater distribution modeling. However, all but the technique presented in this paper are simulation models and simulations cannot prescribe highly effective, near optimal routes and schedules for all vehicular transport assets. Therefore, this model is the *first* of its kind to offer this functionality.

In a recent study funded by HQ USAF [30], a number of recommendations were made to the Air Force on types of models that could support an automated theater distribution management system. The purpose of the system is to "optimize" the entire theater distribution system, from the number of bases and vehicles, down to the vehicle routes and schedules. They concluded that vehicle routing and scheduling was very difficult to optimize, and development of an optimization approach is considered a high-risk methodology. Therefore, they proposed a low risk method using simulation. Unfortunately, they lose the functional requirements of prescribing detailed vehicular routes and schedules when using simulation. The HQ USAF study [30] validates the importance and magnitude of this research. What was regarded as *too difficult* has been successfully *created and developed* in this research.

REFERENCES

1. P.G. Kaminski, The revolution in defense logistics, In *Keynote Address of the USAD for Acquisition and Technology*, Alexandria, VA, (October 1995).
2. Position paper on the theater distribution management system (TDMS) initiative, Headquarters, United States Air Force, Washington, DC, (May 2000).
3. D. Schrady, Combatant logistics command and control for the joint force commander, Navy Report, (1999).
4. Department of the Chairman of the Joint Chiefs of Staff, Joint tactics, techniques, and procedures for joint theater distribution, Joint Publication 4-01.4. Washington, CJCS, (August 2000).
5. Department of the Chairman of the Joint Chiefs of Staff, Joint tactics, techniques, and procedures for movement control, Joint Publication 4-01.3, Washington, CJCS, (June 1996).
6. Department of the Chairman of the Joint Chiefs of Staff, Department of Defense dictionary of military and associated terms, Joint Publication 1-02, Washington, CJCS,, (September 1993).
7. J.R. Crino, A group theoretic tabu search methodology for solving theater distribution vehicle routing and scheduling problems, Ph.D. Dissertation, AFIT, (2002).
8. Synergy, Theater distribution management system requirements and feasibility study, (2002).
9. F. Glover and M. Laguna, *Tabu Search*, Kluwer Academic, Boston, MA, (1997).
10. G. Laporte, M. Gendreau, J.Y. Potvin and F. Semet, Classical and modern heuristics for the vehicle routing problem, *International Transactions in Operational Research* **7** (4/5), 285–300, (2000).
11. D.M. Ryer, Implementation of the metaheuristic tabu search in route selection for mobility analysis support system, Master's Thesis, Air Force Institute of Technology, (1999).
12. K.P. O'Rourke, Dynamic unmanned aerial vehicle (UAV) routing with a Java-encoded reactive tabu search metaheuristic, Master's Thesis, Air Force Institute of Technology, (1999).
13. C.A. Cullenbine, A tabu search approach to the weapons assignment model, Master's Thesis, Air Force Institute of Technology, (2000).
14. S.N. Hall, A group theoretic tabu search approach to the traveling salesman problem, Master's Thesis, Air Force Institute of Technology, (2000).
15. K.M. Calhoun, R.F. Deckro, J.T. Moore, J.W. Chrissis and J.C. Van Hove, Planning and replanning in project and production scheduling, *Omega* **30** (3), 155–170, (2002).
16. G.W. Kinney, A hybrid jump search and tabu search metaheuristic for the unmanned aerial vehicle (UAV) routing problem, Master's Thesis, Air Force Institute of Technology, (2000).
17. V.D. Wiley, The aerial refueling problem—A doctoral dissertation proposal, The University of Texas at Austin, (2000).
18. D.T. Brown, Routing unmanned aerial vehicles while considering general restricted operating zones, Master's Thesis, Air Force Institute of Technology, (2001).
19. T. Combs, A combined adaptive tabu seaarch and set partitioning approach for the crew scheduling problem with an air tanker crew application, Ph.D. Dissertation, AFIT, (June 2002).
20. B.W. Colletti, Group theory and metaheuristics, Ph.D. Dissertation, The University of Texas at Austin, (1999).
21. J.W. Barnes, B. Colletti and D.L. Neuway, Using group theory and transition matrices for conjugative move disciplines in multiple TSPs with known solution structure, *European Journal of Operational Research* **138**, (2002).
22. B.W. Colletti and J.W. Barnes, Using group theory to efficiently compute move values for routing problems, working paper (1999).
23. B.W. Colletti, J.W. Barnes and S. Dokov, A note on characterizing the k-OPT neighborhood via group theory, *Journal of Heuristics* **5**, (1999).
24. S.K. Jones, A highly effective and efficient method for neighborhood evaluation in metaheuristic search, Master's Thesis, University of Texas at Austin (2002).
25. B. Baumslag and B. Chandlerv, *Group Theory: Schaum's Outline Series*, McGraw-Hill, (1968).
26. T. Barnard and H. Neill, *Mathematical Groups*, Cox and Wyman, Berkshire, (1996).
27. J.B. Fraleigh, *A First Course in Abstract Algebra*, Addison-Wesley, Reading MA, (1976).
28. B.E. Sagan, *The Symmetric Group*, Wadsworth and Brooks/Cole, Pacific Grove, (1991).
29. R.W. Harder, A jump search enhanced reactive tabu search in a universal vehicle router appied to routing unmanned aerial vehicles, Master's Thesis, Air Force Institute of Technology, (2000).
30. HQ USAF/ILA, Theater distribution management system requirements and feasibility study, (January 2002).

Available online at www.sciencedirect.com
SCIENCE DIRECT
Mathematical and Computer Modelling 39 (2004) 617–640
MATHEMATICAL AND COMPUTER MODELLING
www.elsevier.com/locate/mcm

Solving the Aerial Fleet Refueling Problem using Group Theoretic Tabu Search

J. W. BARNES
Graduate Program in Operations Research and Industrial Engineering
The University of Texas at Austin
Austin, TX 78712, U.S.A.

V. D. WILEY AND J. T. MOORE
Department of Operational Sciences, Graduate School of Engineering and Management
Air Force Institute of Technology
AFIT/ENS, Bldg. 641, 2950 Hobson Way
Wright-Patterson AFB, OH 45433-7765, U.S.A.

D. M. RYER
HQ AMC/XPY
402 Scott Drive, Unit 3L3
Scott AFB, IL 62225-5307, U.S.A.

Abstract—The aerial fleet refueling problem (AFRP) is concerned with the efficient and effective use of a heterogeneous set of tanker (refueling) aircraft, located at diverse geographical locations, in the required operations associated with the deployment of a diverse fleet of military aircraft to a foreign theater of activity. Typically, the "receiving" aircraft must traverse great distances over large bodies of water and/or over other inhospitable environs where no ground based refueling resources exist. Lacking the ability to complete their flights without refueling, each receiving aircraft must be serviced one or more times during their deployment flights by means of in-flight refueling provided by one of the available tanker aircraft. The receiving aircraft, aggregated into receiver groups (RGs) that fly together, have stipulated departure and destination bases and each RG's arrival time is bounded by a stated desired earliest and latest time. The excellence of a suggested solution to this very challenging decision making problem is measured relative to a rigorously defined hierarchical multicriteria objective function.

This paper describes how the AFRP for the Air Mobility Command (AMC), Scott Air Force Base, IL, is efficiently solved using group theoretic tabu search (GTTS). GTTS uses the symmetric group on n letters (S_n) and applies it to this problem using the Java™ language.

Keywords—Aerial refueling, Military logistics, Tabu search, Group theory, Group theoretic tabu search, Symmetric group.

1. INTRODUCTION

Air refueling, the in-flight transfer of fuel between tanker and receiver aircraft, provides rapid response, increased range, and extended airborne operations for all aircraft. The capability to perform air refueling makes the United States (U.S.) the dominant air power in the world today. This capability, coupled with the ability to efficiently employ air refueling assets, is essential for

0895-7177/04/$ - see front matter Typeset by AMS-TEX
doi:10.1016/j.mcm.2004.02.003

the U.S. to maintain this dominance [1]. The Air Mobility Command (AMC) of the United States Air Force (USAF) is responsible for determining the use of the U.S. tanker fleet to meet the air refueling needs of the Air Force, Navy, Marines, U.S. allies, and coalition partners. As part of this responsibility, AMC plans, schedules, tasks, and executes operations involving the use of its forces. Part of AMC's planning encompasses the intertheater movement of forces from the U.S. to areas around the globe. This "deployment" of forces and its accompanied air refueling requirement is known as the aerial fleet refueling problem (AFRP).

As the agency responsible for air refueling, AMC addresses many questions involving the allocation and use of tankers. During Operations Desert Shield and Desert Storm, approximately 400 tankers offloaded over 1.2 billion pounds of fuel to over 80,000 aircraft while flying over 30,000 sorties and logging over 140,000 hours of flight time [2]. The many planning scenarios, like Desert Shield/Desert Storm, that must be considered create complex sets of questions whose answers demand the use of powerful analytical tools. Among these tools are the combined mating and ranging planning system (CMARPS), the quick-look tool (QLT), and the tanker assignment planning (TAP) tool.

CMARPS is a computer program that helps analyze, plan, and schedule deployment of tankers and receiver aircraft in support of immediate and anticipated military operations. Unfortunately, this tool can take many weeks if not months to produce meaningful results. The QLT is a simple spreadsheet model used for determining gross tanker capabilities for supporting deployments. The TAP tool is a spreadsheet model used for assigning tankers to refueling points. The simplicity of the QLT and TAP tool makes them incapable of addressing the problem in required levels of detail. AMC possesses a compelling need for a tool that will provide the detailed analysis of CMARPS within a planning horizon comparable to that required by the QLT. Given a deployment scenario, examples of overview questions that require answers are as follows.

- How many tankers are required to meet the air refueling requirements?
- How quickly can all the receivers be deployed to their final destinations?
- How far do the tankers and receiver aircraft have to travel?
- How much fuel is burned by both tankers and receiver aircraft?

In order to meaningfully answer upper level questions like these, as well as more probing questions relating to the efficiency of planning operations, a great many detailed operational aspects must be addressed.

2. PROBLEM STATEMENT

We assume that the following information is given:

- a known set of tankers and their associated original beddown (starting) bases;
- a known set of receiver aircraft, each with an initial departure base and a final destination base, where one or more receiver aircraft are aggregated to form receiver groups (RGs) (each RG has a stipulated desired earliest arrival time and latest arrival time);
- a known set of RG starting and ending bases and tanker beddown bases;
- a known set of flight characteristics for each aircraft including flight speed, altitude, take-off weight, fuel capacity, and fuel-burn rates;
- a known set of tanker specific characteristics including fuel-offload capacity and fuel-offload rates.

Figure 1 pictures an example of a scenario with two tankers and two RGs where the RGs' flight paths are displayed. Waypoints (WPTs) define the physical locations and start times where each refueling of an RG will take place. In Figure 1, each RG has two WPTs (circles) scheduled before arrival at a common destination base. The pentagons labeled T1 and T2 represent the beddown bases of Tankers 1 and 2.

For a given deployment, the following decisions compose the solution to the AFRP:

- the waypoints (WPTs),

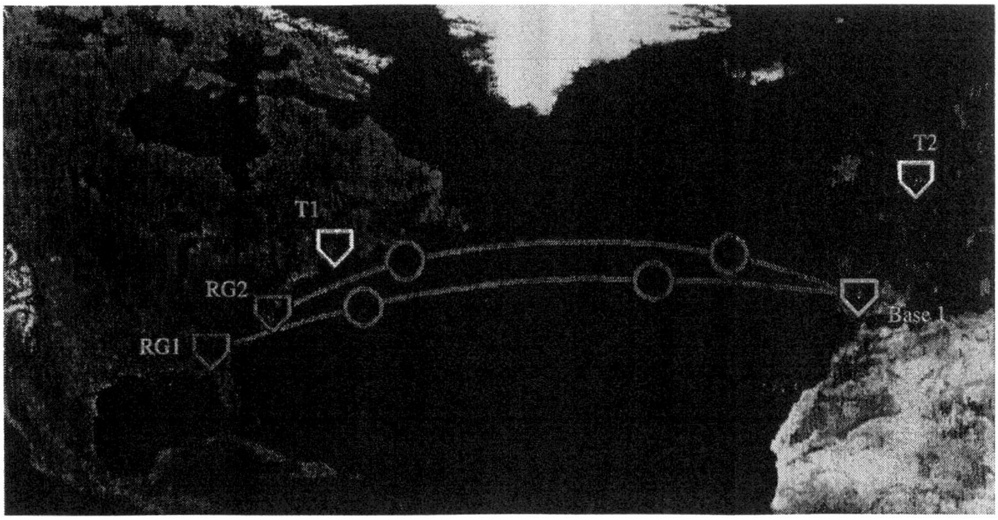

Figure 1. A small scenario.

- the tanker(s) that will serve each WPT,
- how much fuel the assigned tanker(s) should deliver to a WPT.

To this end, this paper will demonstrate how S_n will be used to represent the assignment of tankers to WPTs as well as the specific order that the WPTs will be visited (see Section 4). The amount of fuel delivered is a function of the RG, the fuel it has used since last receiving fuel, and how much fuel it needs to arrive at its final destination.

We further assume that the decision maker has the authority to

(a) stipulate the departure times of all RGs and tankers, and
(b) to require both tankers and RGs to "orbit" at specified locations to satisfy WPT requirements in terms of timing and location.

These two assumptions allow an AFRP solution to satisfy a number of constraints while exhibiting a number of desirable qualities to include deconflicting schedules and reducing the number of tankers required.

Given these assumptions, this paper concentrates on determining the "best" assignment and ordering of WPTs with tankers while generating a flyable schedule for the tankers and RGs alike.

The determination of "best" is influenced by a large number of factors. Among these factors are feasibility related criteria such as providing the required amount of fuel at each WPT and respecting the precedence relationships along an RG's flight path. Other factors include optimality related criteria such as the number of tankers used, the distance flown by the tankers, and the arrival time of RGs at their destinations.

The AFRP objective function, as implemented in this research, is multicriterial and hierarchical. The hierarchical ordering of the associated criteria is subject to redefinition in accordance with perceived mission priorities. For the purposes of this research, the following criteria, in the order given, define the specific hierarchical objective function addressed.

Minimize:

1. the number of unescorted RGs requiring escort between WPTs,
2. the number of WPTs not serviced by a tanker,
3. the number of WPTs serviced out of order for an RG's flight path,
4. the amount of required fuel not available,
5. the amount of time spent by RGs and tankers in "orbit" at WPTs,
6. the amount of RG late arrival time, i.e., where one or more RGs arrive later than a desired latest time,
7. the number of tankers used,

8. the amount of tanker mission time required,
9. the total distance flown by tankers,
10. the amount of fuel used by tankers,
11. the amount of fuel offloaded by tankers,
12. the amount of fuel used by RGs.

For any pair of solutions, superiority is determined by strict hierarchical criteria comparison starting at Index 1 and traversing through increasing indices. At any index, a lower criterion value (bounded below by zero) implies a better solution and the comparison process is stopped. Two solutions are equivalent only if all 12 criteria are equivalent.

When Criteria 1–4 exceed zero, the solution is not feasible because of policy violation or failure of aircraft to complete their required flights. Criteria 5–12 were determined by Ryer of the Studies and Analysis Division of AMC.

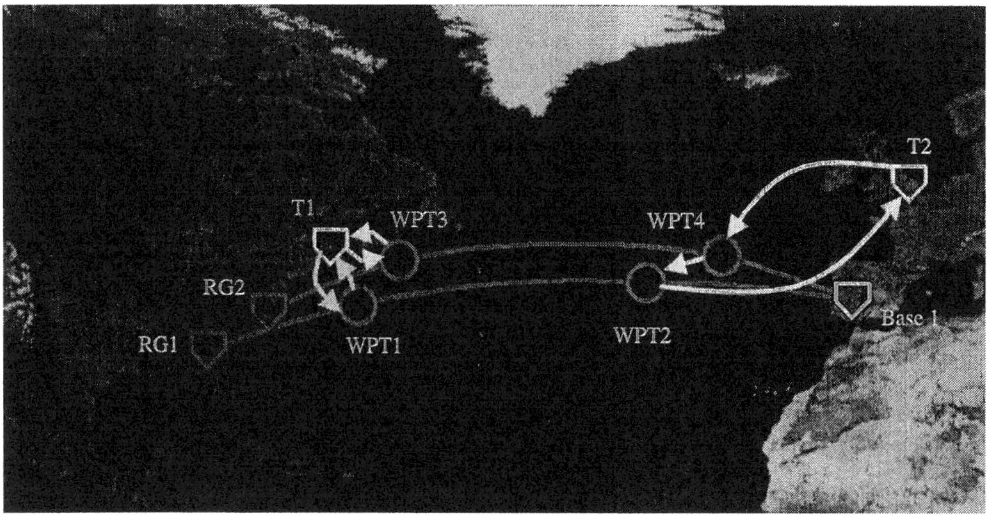

Figure 2. A specific AFRP solution.

Figure 2 displays a specific solution to the scenario of Figure 1. Using the cyclic notation of S_n (see Section 4), this solution would be (T1,WPT3,T1,WPT1)(T2,WPT4,WPT2). In this solution, the first tanker, T1, services RG2 at WPT3 and returns to its beddown base, denoted T1. It then continues operations by flying to WPT1, servicing RG1, and then returning once again to its beddown base. The second tanker, T2, services RG2 at WPT4, then flies to WPT2 and services RG1 before returning to its beddown base. In this solution, the assignment of tankers to WPTs influences the timing of other physical activities including the departure time of each RG and the initial and subsequent departure times of the tankers during their service to the deployment.

Thus, the solution to the AFRP is composed of a complex set of interrelated decisions involving time, space, and amounts of fuel. Usually, the effect of changing any individual decision will "ripple" through the AFRP structure forcing multiple associated changes in the solution.

One consideration not taken into account in the example of Figure 2, is that fighter aircraft require continuous escort (deployment support) while flying over large bodies of water. The added consideration of deployment support further restricts the assignment of tankers to WPTs by forcing a tanker to follow a RG along segments of the RG's flight path. Tankers that provide escort typically do not immediately return to their original base. Instead, they often continue escort duties until passing the receivers on to another available tanker or proceeding to another enroute base.

Figure 3 provides an example of RG1 and RG2 being escorted during part of their flight to Base 1. T1 escorts RG1 from WPT1 to WPT2 and lands at Base 1 while T2 escorts RG2 from

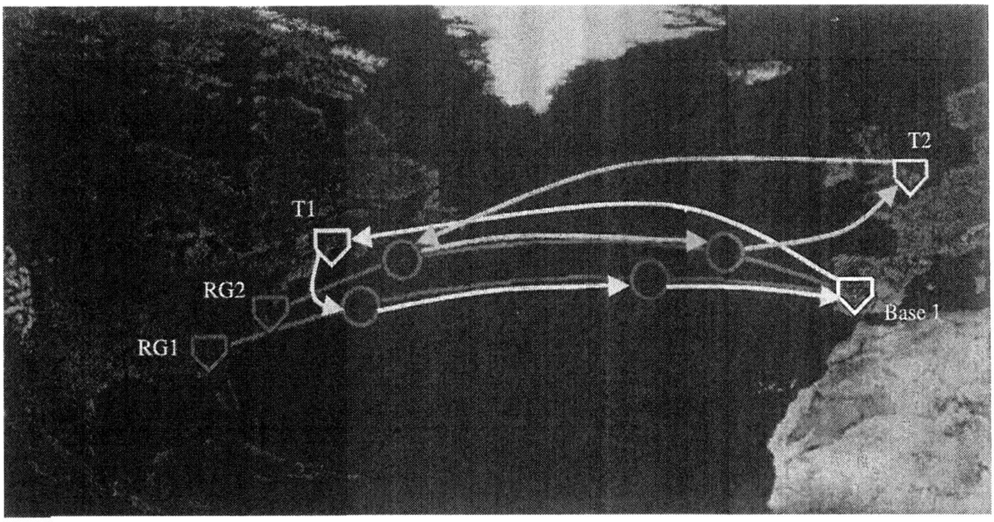

Figure 3. RG escort example.

WPT3 to WPT4 and then returns to its beddown base. In this example, T1 is serviced at Base 1 and then returns to its beddown base. In other scenarios, T1 could have been refueled at Base 1 and continued to service the deployment without returning to its beddown base.

The AFRP solution is constrained by a large number of limiting factors. The safety of the crews and aircraft associated with the deployment is dominant, i.e., no tanker or receiver aircraft should have to divert from its flight path due to lack of fuel. Many other constraints must also be satisfied. For example, a tanker has limited fuel capacity and its crew has flight duration restrictions which affect the crew-tanker ability to travel long distances and to provide fuel. Certain bases have limited capacity for resident aircraft (known as *maximum on ground* or MOG). In the scenarios considered in this research, the important constraint of MOG was not a consideration, but could be addressed in future analysis. A tanker requires time to fly between any two locations and time to perform midair refueling. Hence, all tanker WPT assignments must be limited to those where the tanker is physically capable of being present at the specified WPT time.

The AFRP is unique, complicated, and extremely difficult to model and solve when viewed in its full practical context. As is discussed in [3], the AFRP can be related to other classical combinatorial optimization problems by relaxing specific constraints or by fixing selected decision variables. Perhaps the most closely associated classical problem is a variation of the multivehicle, multidepot vehicle routing problem (VRP).

In the AFRP, we have finite-capacity heterogeneous vehicles located at multiple depots (with route length/route duration upper bounds) that are required to deliver product to customers (such deliveries require a finite-service time). In the notation of Carlton [4], the AFRP is a variation of problem type $\alpha = (\text{MV}\bar{\text{H}}, \text{MD}, \text{VRP}, \text{RL})$ which is known to be NP-hard [5].

However, there are several additional considerations present in the AFRP that are not present in problem α. These are as follows.

1. In problem α, the customers' locations are fixed in space, requiring only that the customers be partitioned among the vehicles and that each vehicle's customers be ordered for service. Further, the amount of product to be delivered to each customer is a known amount and there is a single delivery to any customer. Finally, the route length restriction is given only in terms of a total travel distance that may not be exceeded. Problem α has no explicit accounting for the timing of events.

   As in problem α, we must stipulate the responsible vehicle (tanker) and the ordering of any delivery. In addition, for all RGs, we must also stipulate the spatial location (longitude, latitude, and altitude in three-dimensional space) and start time of each fuel

delivery and the number of possibly multiple deliveries and the amount of product (fuel) to be provided in each delivery.
2. All customers must be supplied with fuel in a timely manner that will assure that no receiving aircraft has its available fuel fall below a prespecified "minimal reserve".
3. Directly associated with the WPT decisions are the decisions on the takeoff time of each RG and the possibly multiple takeoff times of each tanker.

If we desired to solve the AFRP by forcing it to be equivalent to problem α, all considerations of event timing must be relaxed; the spatial location and fuel requirement of each WPT must be fixed known constants; and each WPT becomes equivalent to a separate customer in the problem α formulation.

Problem α may be brought closer, in some respects, to the AFRP through the inclusion of a "time window" constraint on each of the WPTs, i.e., the stipulation of an earliest and latest time that refueling can begin at each WPT (customer).

The stipulation of time windows on the WPT refuelings would reintroduce some of the time based considerations, i.e., time ordered precedence relations between events, but would still require the spatial location and fuel requirement of each WPT to be fixed known constants.

The primary objective of the research documented in this paper was to develop methods for producing an "ensemble" of excellent solutions to any instance of the AFRP. To achieve this objective, a group theoretic tabu search (GTTS) approach was used. Our GTTS makes use of adaptive tabu search [6,7] to dynamically update the memory structures, promote diversification, and remove the need to empirically "tune" a static tabu tenure. GTTS represents a solution to the AFRP as an element from the symmetric group on n letters, S_n [8], and creates move neighborhoods that can be represented by S_n acting under conjugation or multiplication upon itself. To address the issue of reusability and portability, the GTTS approach was implemented using the Java^{TM} programming language. Our implementation makes extensive use of Wiley's [3] Java^{TM} class library for S_n. Secondary research goals were to investigate the effects of selecting different move neighborhoods both from a static and dynamic context.

How these goals were accomplished is discussed in detail in the remainder of this paper.

3. LITERATURE REVIEW

CMARPS was originally built in 1982 and has continued to evolve to its present form. It is currently maintained for AMC by the Northrop Grumman company. CMARPS is a deterministic computer planning system that assists analysts and warplanners in developing and scheduling the deployment of tankers and receivers during peacetime, crisis, contingency, and wartime operations. Unfortunately, because of the great number of scenarios, as well as their formidable size that must be explicitly constructed, this tool can take several analysts many weeks to produce meaningful results. An extremely large multivolume user's manual is available only in hard copy and provides no detail on the methodology employed by CMARPS.

While CMARPS can assist in providing extensive, detailed, and accurate data for predicting receiver and tanker aircraft mission requirements, CMARPS marked complexities make quick and effective use difficult even for highly experienced users. The limitations of CMARPS caused several later studies that attempted to improve on these shortcomings.

With the aforementioned problems and time limits associated with CMARPS, AMC has been sponsoring research into aerial refueling for years. Initial attempts include [9,10]. Yamani's research was limited to

(a) consideration of RGs where only one WPT was required, and
(b) consideration of single aircraft that required two WPTs.

Hostler [10] allowed a tanker to refuel at most two WPTs and ignored the travel distance and fuel consumption limitations associated with the tankers.

More recent research includes [11,12]. Russina and Ruthsatz's QLT attempted to provide a more responsive program than CMARPS. The goals of this spreadsheet tool were to quickly estimate the number of tankers needed for a deployment and then determine how quickly that deployment could be achieved. The QLT incorporated several simplifying assumptions. Among these were

(a) constant flight speeds for all aircraft,
(b) the refueling tanker must provide any required escort duties,
(c) all tankers were identical,
(d) only one tanker could be assigned to a WPT (regardless of fuel requirements),
(e) each tanker must return to its home base after a single refueling, and
(f) the locations of all WPTs and the amount of fuel required at the WPT are assumed to be known constants and are part of the input data.

The most limiting assumption in the QLT was that, when escort was not required, all tankers were assumed to take the same constant amount of time to travel to a WPT, complete refueling, and return to homebase. Thus, the QLT did not explicitly take into account the very important limitations of actual tanker travel and tanker fuel use. Useful for determining initial estimates, the QLT is incapable of addressing the problem in required levels of detail.

The work of Capehart [12] extends the QLT through the use of a tabu search (TS) approach [7] within the TAP tool. Capehart [12] models the AFRP as an assignment problem [13] with time windows. This formulation makes a number of simplifying assumptions which limit the solutions it produces. Among these limiting assumptions are:

(a) a tanker providing fuel to a RG requiring escort must escort the RG to the next WPT,
(b) each tanker must return to its home base after a single refueling,
(c) light aircraft are escorted over their entire flight, not just when over large bodies of water,
(d) the approach does not explicitly account for tanker reuse, but rather corrects time conflicts involving any individual tanker using a penalty structure, and
(e) the locations of all WPTs and the amount of fuel required at the WPT are calculated based on a percentage of the full capacity of the RG.

The GTTS method described below possesses none of the above limitations. The next section provides a brief overview of how group theory and in particular, S_n, are incorporated into GTTS. The reader familiar with these topics may find this section superfluous.

4. ALGEBRAIC CONCEPTS

A *group* is made up of any set of objects and an operation acting on this set which satisfies the properties of *closure, associativity, identity, and invertibility* (g^{-1} is the inverse of group element g). Well-known examples of groups include integers under addition, positive real numbers under multiplication, and $n \times n$ invertible matrices under matrix multiplication. Another group of particular interest is the symmetric group on n-letters (S_n).

S_n is the group of permutations of the set $\{1, 2, \ldots, n\}$ of integers from 1 to n [14]. Specific elements of S_n may be represented in the long or cyclic form. The long form appears as a matrix with two rows and n columns. The first row represents the index position of a letter within the permutation. The second row represents the letter located at the index position of the first row. The cyclic form appears as a set of cycles delineated by parentheses. Here is the same permutation taken from S_6: first in the long form and then in the cyclic form[1]:

$$\begin{pmatrix} 1 & 2 & 3 & 4 & 5 & 6 \\ 3 & 6 & 5 & 4 & 1 & 2 \end{pmatrix} \leftrightarrow (1,3,5)(2,6)(4) \equiv (1,3,5)(2,6)$$

Figure 4. Permutation representations.

[1] "Unit" cycles, i.e., (4), are customarily dropped from the cyclic representation.

Permutations are composed of cycles and an m-cycle has m letters. A two-cycle is also called a transposition and an n-cycle is a permutation with a single cycle containing all the letters of S_n (equivalent to a 1-TSP tour). Every permutation is a unique product of disjoint cycles, i.e., cycles sharing no common cities. The number of cycles and the cycle sizes define the permutation's cycle structure. The cycles partition the letters of S_n into mutually exclusive sets. The placement of letters within each cycle determines the ordering. Thus, S_n provides a means to represent any partitioning and ordering problem solution.

The AFRP will make use of S_n's ability to represent any partitioning and ordering problem by specifically assigning tankers and WPTs to cycles. Each cycle will then represent the assignment of WPTs to a single tanker and the specific order that these WPTs will be visited.

The operation associated with the collection of permutations of the set $\{1, 2, \ldots, n\}$ satisfying the conditions necessary for a group is *function composition*. This research uses multiplication and conjugation as forms of function composition.

Multiplication and conjugation of S_n will be used extensively by the AFRP as the means to assign WPTs to tankers and order the WPTs.

4.1. Multiplication

Let $p = (1,3,5)(2,6)$, the permutation from the above example. Let $q = (4,6,5)$, be another permutation. The product pq is the composite function (multiplication) produced by applying p and then q, i.e., for letter x, $xpq = (xp)q$. If the letter of interest is 3, then $3pq = (3p)q = 5q = 4$, and so under pq, 3 is mapped into 4. Permutation multiplication is not commutative since $3qp = (3q)p = 3p = 5$, and therefore, $pq \neq qp$. Since a permutation represents a 1 to 1 mapping from the letters $\{1, \ldots, n\}$ onto itself, multiplication is associative and closed. The inverse of a permutation reverses each cycle, i.e., $(1,3,5)^{-1} = (1,5,3)$, and the identity permutation maps each letter into itself, i.e., is composed of n unit cycles. Thus, the four properties of a group are satisfied and the set of all $n!$ permutations under multiplication is S_n.

4.2. Conjugation

Conjugation is a special form of multiplication that takes the form $q^{-1}pq$. Conjugation also satisfies the properties of an operation acting upon a set necessary for a group. Conjugation has the additional quality of maintaining the current cyclic structure of the permutation being acted upon, i.e., p. This quality allows the number of letters assigned to a cycle to remain constant while reassigning and reordering letters within the cycles.

4.3. Examples

Using the permutation p, if one wanted to move letter "5" from its current position and place it in between letters "2" and "6" then, using multiplication as defined in Section 4.1 and denoted by $*$, the following operation would be performed: $p*(1,6,5) = (1,3,5)(2,6)*(1,6,5) = (1,3)(2,5,6)$.

Likewise, if one wanted to rearrange the assignment and ordering of such that letter "3" occupied the position currently held by letter "6" and that "6" was placed after letter "5", then, using conjugation as defined in Section 4.2 and denoted by $\hat{}$, the following operation would be performed: $p\,\hat{}\,(3,5,6) = (1,3,5)(2,6)\,\hat{}\,(3,5,6) = (1,5,6)(2,3)$.

S_n is particularly important in group theory since all groups can be isomorphically mapped into S_n. Hence, group theory can be thought of as the "algebra of permutations". For further insights, see [15–19].

This concludes the short review of the mathematical background needed for the remainder of this paper. The next section presents a detailed discussion of the implementation of the adaptive GTTS methodology that was developed to solve the AFRP.

5. IMPLEMENTATION OF THE GTTS FOR THE AFRP

Our implementation of GTTS for the AFRP is written in the Java[TM] language and makes extensive use of the object-oriented view of that language. Wiley [3] presents a detailed discussion of object-oriented programming and we have found this perspective to be very beneficial in our implementation.

In order to effectively construct a GTTS for the AFRP, five primary types of *implementation* objects are defined and used:

(1) locations,
(2) aircraft,
(3) RGs,
(4) tankers, and
(5) nodes.

These objects store detailed information beyond the partitioning and ordering captured by S_n. The connection between S_n and these objects occurs through a mapping of node labels to the integer set. Based on the placement of these node labels (a permutation of S_n), the information, described in the following paragraphs, associated with tankers, RGs, and nodes will be determined. For example, in Figure 4, the permutation could be mapped by labels to the following solution: two tankers (letters "1" and "2") have been assigned to three WPTs (letters "3", "5", and "6", respectively). The first tanker ("1") will serve its two assigned WPTs in order of placement of labels within its cycle, i.e., services letter "3" then letter "5". Given this ordering, the timing and scheduling of activities will be determined.

A solution of the AFRP requires detailed information about

(1) the physical locations of bases and WPTs,
(2) the flight characteristics of aircraft,
(3) the assignment of aircraft to RGs and the stipulation of the flight path that a RG will follow, and
(4) the number of tankers available for refueling activities and their associated beddown bases.

In addition, information about the actual AFRP solution is stored in the tanker and RG objects. This is accomplished in the following ways. (Information not germane to a particular object is left blank.)

Locations (bases, WPTs)

(a) unique ID,
(b) code name,
(c) coordinates,
(d) MOG,
(e) whether over open water.

(After all location objects are created, a symmetric distance matrix is generated using the "great circle" distances associated with every pair of locations [12].)

Aircraft (light receivers, heavy receivers, tankers)

(a) unique ID,
(b) airframe type (light, heavy, tanker),
(c) nominal true air speed,
(d) total fuel capacity,
(e) fuel burn characteristics (required fuel reserve, nominal take-off fuel, nominal fuel flow coefficient, nominal altitude, empty weight, and nominal load weight).

Receiver groups

(a) unique ID,
(b) total fuel upload requirement,
(c) list of aircraft IDs in the RG (determines escort requirement),
(d) flight path information (start and end base IDs, RG flight characteristics, earliest departure time (EDT) and latest departure time (LDT)),
(e) RG solution attributes,
  (e1) list of flight path WPT nodes,
  (e2) arrival, service, and departure times at each WPT node,
  (e3) amount of fuel burned between WPT nodes,
  (e4) amount of fuel required to completely refuel each member of the RG,
  (e5) start and finish times.

Tankers

(a) unique ID,
(b) offload capacity,
(c) tanker solution attributes (blank unless tanker used),
  (c1) WPT nodes served and associated times (arrival, service, and departure),
  (c2) fuel burned and fuel offloaded for each WPT served, and
  (c3) tanker start and finish times for deployment.

Nodes (tanker, WPT, RTB[2])

(a) a unique ID (implies node type),
(b) spatial location and fuel requirement,
(c) RG assigned,
(d) precedence relations with other nodes,
(e) whether linked to another node for escort duty,
(f) tanker assigned,
(g) the fuel demand.

Since the node objects are used to represent disparate entities, some additional remarks are appropriate. A tanker node uses only Field (a). Creating a feasible solution (where no tanker runs out of fuel), may require some of the tankers to return one or more times to a base capable of tanker maintenance and refueling. At such a base, completion of these operations allows the tanker to continue servicing WPTs. To allow for this, tanker return to base (RTB) nodes are created for each active tanker base (as needed). RTB nodes are distinguished by zero fuel demand (from a tanker) and the lack of an assigned RG. Created only if needed, an RTB node will possess a unique ID (Field (a)), its spatial location (Field (b)) will correspond to the associated refueling base, and the tanker ID of the associated tanker will occupy Field (f). (All other fields are blank for an RTB node.)

A WPT node uses all seven fields. Field (d) will contain the information to assure that WPT nodes are visited in precedence (temporal) order along the RG's flight path. If a consecutive pair of WPT nodes within an RG's flight path are both over water and the RG has escort requirements, Field (e) will indicate that the flight "leg" between the WPT pair requires escort by a tanker. Field (f) remains blank until a tanker is assigned to the WPT node as part of a generated solution to the AFRP. Field (g) will contain the RG's fuel demand at that WPT.

In solving a particular AFRP, the tanker nodes are generated first and are sequentially assigned indices starting at index 0. The WPT nodes are then created in the ascending order by RG ID

[2]Return to base (RTB).

and then by ascending order of associated WPT IDs within the RG flight path. For each WPT, its WPT nodes are indexed sequentially starting with the next available index. For every WPT along each RG's flight path, either 1, 2, or 3 WPT nodes are generated.

Only one WPT node is required if both of the following conditions hold true.

(a) The RG's fuel demand at that WPT can be satisfied by a single tanker.

(b) The RG does not require an escort to its next WPT.

Two WPT nodes are required if either of the following two sets of conditions are true.

(a) The RG's fuel demand at that WPT requires multiple tankers and the RG does not require an escort to its next WPT.

(b) The RG's fuel demand at that WPT can be satisfied by a single tanker and the RG requires an escort to its next WPT.

If Condition (a) holds, the WPT is represented by two WPT nodes where each is assigned one-half of the original WPT's fuel demand. With this representation, a different tanker can be assigned to each WPT node, jointly satisfying the total WPT demand.[3]

If Condition (b) holds, the WPT is represented by two WPT nodes. The first node is assigned all of the WPT demand and the other is assigned a demand of zero. These WPT node creations and assignments are made so that one tanker can perform the refueling function at the WPT and, if appropriate, another tanker can perform the escort duty to the next WPT. (The escorting tanker will provide the refueling function at the next WPT in the RG's flight path.)

Three WPT nodes are required if the RG's fuel demand at that WPT requires multiple tankers and the RG requires escort to the next WPT. In this case, two of the three WPT nodes serve to allow the required refueling by two different tankers and it is possible that another tanker will assume the escort duty to the next WPT by being assigned to the third WPT node. When the WPT nodes are created, the fuel burned between a RG's adjacent WPTs is calculated and becomes the fuel demand for the latter WPT.

RTB nodes are generated as needed and are assigned the next available index.

Once the AFRP node objects have been created, they are used in the GTTS implementation using the openTS framework of Harder [20]. As explained in detail in [3], Harder's framework requires the creation of the following objects: solutions, moves, neighborhoods, objective function, tabu list, and aspiration criteria. In this paper, we assume that the reader is familiar with classical tabu search techniques as described in [7]. Harder's framework provides the mechanism for implementing the TS process as illustrated in Figure 5. A description of open TS is provided at `http://oss.software.ibm.com/developerworks/opensource/coin/OpenTS/`.

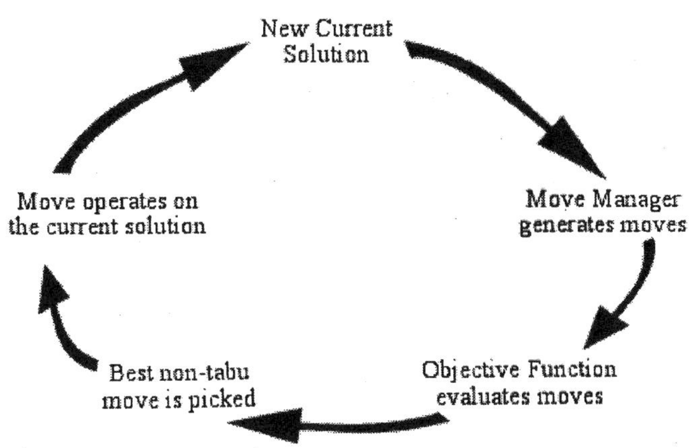

Figure 5. An iteration under the OpenTS architecture.

[3]In this paper, two tankers could feasibly meet all of the demand at any WPT. This had the benefit of limiting the cardinality of the solution space by restricting the number of tankers that had to visit a WPT to at most two (without escorts). This assumption is consistent with the deployment scenarios considered herein.

A solution in our AFRP GTTS approach is represented by a permutation, $s \in S_n$, where n is the cardinality of the set of node objects defined for the current instance of the AFRP being solved. Each letter in a solution, s, corresponds to the index of a AFRP node object and each solution is stored as a symmetric group object as defined by Wiley's Symmetric Group Class Library [3]. An in depth description of the symmetric group class and the accompanying abstract group class is presented in [3]. A java archive file, "jar", with the executable code and the associated Java^{TM} documentation is available at `http://www.me.utexas.edu/~orie/techrep.html`.

Each solution, s, embodies methods for creating moves, for performing conjugation and multiplication of elements of S_n and the current tanker assignments are implied in the solution's cyclic structure and the node indexing scheme described above. For example, the cycle, (0,15,16,17), would be interpreted as "Tanker 0 flies to (services) AFRP Nodes 15, 16, and 17 and then returns home". All other tanker assignments are also represented with additional cycles. Indeed, all cycles in a solution will contain a single tanker node, which, by convention, will be placed in the first position of each cycle in the permutation representation.

Since S_n acts upon itself, all AFRP moves are also represented as permutations in S_n and move permutations act directly on solution permutations to produce different AFRP solutions. At each iteration, a defined neighborhood of eligible moves is evaluated. The neighborhoods generated by the AFRP are move-based neighborhoods rather than the more traditional solution-based neighborhoods. A solution-based neighborhood considers solutions reachable by one move. Rather than storing solutions, the moves that transform the current solution to a neighboring solution may be stored. Since function composition in S_n is a bijection of the set $\{1, 2, \ldots, n\}$ onto itself, the move neighborhoods for the AFRP are composed of permutations in S_n and the move-based neighborhood is a natural extension of this concept.

After a candidate list [7] of moves is stipulated, the solution resulting from each move is evaluated relative the hierarchical objective function. This evaluation automatically performs any operations required to deconflict the schedules of the tankers and RGs in the new solution. Any solution that is the best solution found so far (within the current iteration), causes a check on the tabu status of the associated move. If the move is not tabu, that move is stored as the iteration's current best move found. Once the best available move is selected, that move is implemented and recorded within the tabu structure and the TS procedure begins a new iteration.

When an aspiration criterion is used, a move satisfying the associated criterion will be accepted regardless of its tabu status. An aspiration criterion object allows the definition of a criterion for any particular solution/move combination. The most common aspiration criterion used states that when a new solution is found that is superior to any found earlier in the search, the new solution is accepted regardless of its tabu status.

6. SOLUTION METHODOLOGY

We now discuss some specific procedures and concepts unique to the GTTS and the AFRP:

(a) construction of the initial solution,
(b) dynamic AFRP move neighborhoods,
(c) AFRP move evaluation criteria,
(d) tabu memory structures used, and
(e) consistent WPT generation.

6.1. Construction of the Initial Solution

For the current discussion, we assume that the WPT locations for all RGs have been supplied by an external source. This case prevails under previous AFRP solution techniques. (We present an adaptive tabu search approach for the WPT location problem later in the discussion.)

The initial solution created for the AFRP assigns all WPT nodes to the first tanker (Tanker 0). Usually this will produce a highly infeasible solution (i.e., the tanker's capacity will be exceeded).

If a problem had 15 tankers and 32 WPT nodes, the initial solution would be $(0,15,16,17,\ldots,44,45,46)$. To overcome this infeasibility, the *tanker insert* (TKI) move neighborhood is used to insert unused tankers into the current employed tanker's WPT node assignments. In addition to reducing any infeasibility, the insertion point is strongly influenced by the requirement that some RGs must be escorted over open water. For the generation of TKI moves, the tankers are placed in a "pool" for each beddown base. If a beddown base has unassigned tankers in its pool, then one of the unassigned tankers is selected. For each selected tanker, moves that insert the selected tanker into the current solution are generated. Available insertion points start before the second waypoint node assigned to any tanker and continue up to before that tankers last waypoint node. An example of a TKI move, given the above initial solution, is "insert Tanker 5 in front of Node 25". Using permutation postmultiplication, this move is represented by (0,5,25).

Performing multiplication, $(0,15,16,\ldots,24,25,26,\ldots,46) * (0,5,25)$, yields $(0,15,16,\ldots,24)$ $(5,25,26,\ldots,46)$. Now Tanker 0 is assigned Nodes 15–24 and Tanker 5 is assigned Nodes 25–46.

Placement of the remaining tankers continues until there are no available tankers or until a feasible solution is obtained. For example, if there were 14 required escort arcs between the 32 WPTs, the 15 tankers might be assigned to the WPTs yielding the following initial solution:

$$(0,15)(1,16,17)(2,18,19)(3,20,21)(4,22,23,24)(5,25,26)(6,27,28)(7,43,44)(8,29,30)(9,45,46)$$
$$(10,31,32,33,34)(11,35,36)(12,37,38)(13,39,40,41,42),$$

where 14 tankers are used before TKI moves are no longer used.

For every iteration where the TKI move neighborhood is used, a TKI move will be generated for each WPT node and tanker base with available tankers combination for a total of |WPT nodes| * |tanker bases| moves.

The choice of the above approach was motivated by two benefits:

(1) the approach is easy to implement, and
(2) the associated move evaluation process drives the initial solution towards excellent solutions while feasibility is simultaneously being achieved.

6.2. Dynamic AFRP Move Neighborhoods

Once the initial TKI moves have performed their function, additional move types are invoked based on the current search status and solution. The move types discussed below were determined by both historical successes with the VRP [4] and by the need to develop new move types that would exploit the specific structure of the AFRP. These move neighborhoods include:

(1) return to base inserts (RTBI),
(2) restricted inserts (RI),
(3) escort pair inserts (EPI),
(4) return to base deletes (RTBD),
(5) tanker swaps (TKS),
(6) restricted swaps (RS), and
(7) return to base swaps (RTBS).

Each move neighborhood creates a set of eligible moves to be evaluated and all use permutation postmultiplication. Postmultiplication allows the search to investigate AFRP solutions from different conjugacy classes in S_n, where a conjugacy class represents the number of tankers and their assigned WPTs within the current AFRP solution. In the following sections, each move neighborhood cited above is described with the conditions that cause them to be invoked.

Return To Base Insert Moves (RTBI). After the TKI strategy is complete, the solution may still be infeasible, primarily due to a lack of tanker capacity. After the initial solution is achieved, the RTBI neighborhood is invoked whenever the current solution is infeasible. An RTBI move can be used to reduce infeasible fuel shortage at the cost of delaying one or more RGs, i.e., the tanker is unavailable until it has been refueled and allowed to reenter service.

The RTBI neighborhood is implemented by making available an RTB node for each active tanker base in the deployment scenario. These RTB nodes may be inserted within each of the current tankers' assignments. Available insertion points start at the first waypoint node assigned to a tanker within the solution and continue until after the last waypoint node. Suppose an RTB node is placed in Tanker 4's assignment before Node 24 for the solution

$$(0,15)(1,16,17)(2,18,19)(3,20,21)(4,22,23,24)(5,25,26)(6,27,28)(7,43,44)(8,29,30)$$
$$(9,45,46)(10,31,32,33,34)(11,35,36)(12,37,38)(13,39,40,41,42).$$

The move that will accomplish this is (24,49). The only affected cycle in this solution contains Tanker 4, so only changes in that cycle need to be shown. (This convention of showing only the affected cycles will be followed throughout the rest of this paper.) Performing this move yields $(4,22,23,24)*(24,49) = (4,22,23,49,24)$. Tanker 4 is now allowed to return to base, after servicing Nodes 22 and 23, for refueling and ancillary operations before completing its assignment by servicing Node 24.

For every iteration where the RTBI move neighborhood is used, an RTBI move will be generated for each node (WPTs and tankers) that is part of the current solution and tanker base combination for a total of |WPT nodes + active tanker nodes| * |tanker bases| moves.

RESTRICTED INSERT MOVES (RI). Following initial solution construction, the RI neighborhood is invoked at each iteration of the search and allows an individual node to be inserted in a different position in its cycle or to be inserted in another tanker's cycle. An RI move can either reorder a tanker's assignment or change the partitioning of the letters among the tankers. The "restriction" on this type of move limits the allowable "distance" that a letter can be moved within the current permutation solution representation. "Distance" is defined as the number of positions a letter may move from its current position either to the left or right. For the results presented in this paper, the distance was set at five positions. This parameter setting and similar parameter settings discussed below were found through empirical experimentation for the example problems studied.

Consider the following two RI example moves. First, we insert a node within its current cycle, i.e., "insert Node 24 in front of Node 22 within Tanker 4's current assignment". The move and changes in Tanker 4's assignment are achieved by $(4,22,23,24)*(4,22,24) = (4,24,22,23)$.

Next, we insert a node into another tanker's cycle., i.e., "insert Node 24 from Tanker 4's assignment in front of Node 25 in Tanker 5's assignment". The move and changes in the tankers' assignments are: $(4,22,23,24)(5,25,26)*(4,25,24) = (4,22,23)(5,24,25,26)$.

For every iteration where the RI move neighborhood is used, an RI move will be generated for every node (WPTs and RTBs) and position combination within five places, left or right, of the node. This will produce a total of |WPT nodes + RTB nodes| * (Distance * 2) moves.

ESCORT PAIR INSERT MOVES (EPI). After the initial solution construction, the EPI neighborhood is invoked for each iteration of the search. The EPI neighborhood inserts the two nodes associated with an escort arc. (An escort arc connects the last node of an earlier WPT to the first node of the adjacent WPT later in the path of a RG requiring escort. In any feasible solution, this pair of nodes must be adjacent and in the correct temporal order.)

Consider the following two clarifying examples. First, we "insert the pair (31,32) after Node 34 in Tanker 10's assignment". The move and changes in Tanker 10's assignment are $(10,31,32,33,34) * (10,31,33) = (10,33,34,31,32)$.

Second, we "insert the pair (31,32) after Node 46 in Tanker 9's assignment". The move and changes in the tankers' assignments are

$$(9,45,46)(10,31,32,33,34)*(9,31,33) = (9,45,46,31,32)(10,33,34).$$

This reassigns the escort arc duty from Tanker 10 to Tanker 9.

For every iteration where the EPI move neighborhood is used, an EPI will be generated for each escort pair and position combination within five places, left or right, of the node. This will produce a total of $|\text{escort pairs}| * (\text{Distance} * 2)$ moves.

Both the RI and EPI neighborhoods can be viewed as variants of the traditional k-OrOpt move.

RETURN TO BASE DELETE MOVES (RTBD). RTBI moves help the search progress towards feasibility while increasing the number of nodes being used in the solution. Once the number of letters reaches 1.5 times the original number of nodes, the RTBD move neighborhood is invoked. This neighborhood is used to remove any extra, i.e., nonbeneficial, RTB nodes from the solution.

An illustrative example of an RTBD move is "remove the return to base Node 49 from Tanker 4's assignment".

The move and change in Tanker 4's assignment is: $(4, 22, 23, 49, 24) * (24, 49) = (4, 22, 23, 24)$.

For every iteration where the RTBD move neighborhood is used, an RTBD move will be generated for each RTB node in the current solution for a total of $|\text{active RTB nodes}|$ moves.

TANKER SWAP MOVES (TKS). In addition to the RTBD neighborhood, the TKS neighborhood is invoked when the number of nodes in the solution has grown to 1.5 times the original number. This neighborhood allows idle tankers to be exchanged with active tankers (from different bases) to reduce travel and fuel usage. For each beddown base that has unassigned tankers in its tanker pool, a move that exchanges an assigned tanker from a different beddown base within the current solution is generated.

An example of a TKS move is "swap Tanker 14 for Tanker 10". The move and changes in the solution are $(10, 31, 32, 33, 34) * (10, 14, 31) = (14, 31, 32, 33, 34)$.

Additionally, the TKS neighborhood allows an idle tanker to be exchanged with an active tanker that has been relocated to the idle tanker's beddown base. This may occur in two ways:

(1) a tanker may relocate, provide service, and then return to an active tanker base (which differs from the relocation base and beddown bases), and
(2) the tanker relocates, provides service, and then returns to the relocation base.

An example of the first case is "swap idle Tanker 10 for active Tanker 7". Tanker 7 has relocated to Tanker 10's beddown base prior to servicing WPTs. After servicing Nodes 36 and 37, Tanker 7 relocates to another active tanker base. If the original assignment for Tanker 7 is (7,67,35,36,65) (idle Tanker 10's assignment is (10)), the move and change is $(7, 67, 35, 36, 65) * (7, 10, 35, 67) = (10, 35, 36, 65)$. Note that RTB Node 67 also has been removed from activity.

An example of the second case is "swap idle Tanker 5 for active Tanker 13". Tanker 13 has relocated to Tanker 5's beddown base, provided service, and then returned to Tanker 5's beddown base. Suppose the original assignment for Tanker 13 is (13,51,41,42,57). The move and changes are $(13, 51, 41, 42, 57) * (5, 41, 51, 13, 57) = (5, 41, 42)$ and two RTB Nodes, 51 and 57, have been removed.

For every iteration where the TKS move neighborhood is used, a TKS move will be generated for each tanker in the current solution and tanker base combination for a total of $|\text{active tankers}| * |\text{tanker bases}|$ moves. Additionally, a TKS move will be generated for each active relocated tanker and tanker base combination for a total of $|\text{relocated active tankers}| * |\text{tanker bases}|$ moves. In total, $|\text{active tankers} + \text{relocated active tankers}| * |\text{tanker bases}|$ moves are generated.

RESTRICTED SWAP MOVES (RS). During the search, if a specified number of iterations have passed (20 iterations for the results of this paper) without a new best solution being identified, the RS neighborhood is invoked. RS moves allow an individual node within a tanker's assignment to be swapped either with a node in its cycle or with a node in another tanker's cycle. This maintains the current cardinality of the partitioning of the letters amongst the tankers. The "restriction" of this neighborhood limits the allowable distance (five positions for this paper) that any letter can be moved.

An example of an RS move where we swap a letter with another in its current cycle is "swap Node 31 for Node 34 in Tanker 10's assignment". The move and changes of Tanker 10's assignment is $(10, 31, 32, 33, 34) * (10, 32)(31, 34) = (10, 34, 32, 33, 31)$.

An example of swapping one tanker's node with another tanker's node is "swap Node 34 from Tanker 10's assignment with Node 24 of Tanker 4's assignment". This yields

$$(4, 22, 23, 24)(10, 31, 32, 33, 34) * (4, 10)(24, 34) = (4, 22, 23, 34)(10, 31, 32, 33, 24).$$

For every iteration where the RS move neighborhood is used, an RS move will be generated for each node (WPTs and RTBs) and position combination within five places, left or right, of the node. This will produce a total of |WPT nodes + RTB nodes| * (Distance * 2) moves.

RETURN TO BASE SWAP MOVES (RTBS). Like the RS neighborhood, the RTBS neighborhood is invoked when a specified number of iterations (20 for this paper) have passed without a new best solution being identified. This neighborhood allows the RTB nodes to be exchanged with other RTB nodes. This allows the solution to adjust the locations of the return to base nodes to fit the current set of tanker assignments. For each beddown base, an RTB node is available. For each selected RTB node, a move that exchanges an RTB node from a different beddown base within the current solution is generated.

An example of an RTBS move is "swap Node 48 for Node 56 in Tanker 13's assignment". If Tanker 13's assignment was (13,34,48), the move and change in Tanker 13's assignment is $(13, 34, 48) * (13, 48, 56) = (13, 34, 56)$.

For every iteration where the RTBS move neighborhood is used, an RTBS move will be generated for each RTB node and tanker base combination for a total of |active RTB nodes| * |tanker bases|.

6.3. Move Evaluations

AFRP move evaluations determine, first and most importantly, whether a move yields a feasible solution and, second, whether a move yields a superior solution. We discuss below, first, a number of feasibility conditions that effect the hierarchical move evaluations for the AFRP. Any violations of these conditions are noted and counted, one at a time, during the hierarchical evaluation of an AFRP solution. Item (d) does not appear in the hierarchical list presented in Section 2. Its presence here is due strictly to algorithmic concerns in the implementation of the GTTS.

(a) UNESCORTED ARCS. If a RG requires escort, all escort legs of its flight path must be accompanied by a tanker. Each escort arc must be represented as adjacent nodes within a tanker assignment. The number of unescorted arcs is returned for the purpose of objective function evaluation.

(b) UNCOVERED RG DEMAND. For every RG, a set of WPTs with fuel demands are generated. Within the current tankers' assignments, feasibility requires that the entire set of WPT fuel demands be covered. During the tabu search process, it is possible to have solutions that leave some WPT fuel demands uncovered. The number of uncovered WPT fuel demands is returned.

(c) MISORDERED TANKER SERVICES. For every tanker assignment, the order of service for the assigned WPT fuel demands is extremely important. A tanker cannot first provide service to a RG at a WPT that is farther along the RG's flight path and later service a WPT earlier along the same flight path. The number of misordered WPT fuel demands is returned.

(d) BAD TANKER ASSIGNMENTS. As the tabu search progresses, there are a number of items that logically should not occur. These items include:

(a) "tanker base hopping" (adjacent RTB nodes),
(b) two tankers within a single cycle in the AFRP solution representation, and
(c) a tanker providing repeat servicing to the same RG.

Tanker base hopping occurs during the search when return to base nodes become adjacent to one another within a tanker's assignment. This has the effect of repositioning the tanker from one location to another without providing any useful service. The number of adjacent return to base nodes is recorded.

During the search, a tanker may be assigned within another tanker's route. For the purposes of this model, a tanker must either be providing service or receiving service as part of a RG, but not both. The number of tankers assigned within another tanker's route is recorded.

A tanker providing repeat servicing captures the condition that a tanker could be assigned to provide service to a specific RG, return to an active tanker base, and then provide service to the same RG. This pattern is considered undesirable since a tanker, when it returns to an active tanker base, must remain at that base for a minimum amount of service time (four hours for this research). During this service, the RG is continuing along its flight path and, more than likely, cannot be feasibly serviced again by the same tanker. The number of tanker repeat servicings is recorded.

The sum of the three items is returned.

(e) INFEASIBLE FUEL USAGE. If any tanker or any RG attempts to use more fuel than is available to it in an AFRP solution, the total amount of such infeasible "phantom" fuel used is returned.

In addition to feasibility, Criteria (f)–(m) of the AFRP objective function effect the move evaluation.

(f) "ORBIT" TIMES. During the search, scheduled times for a tanker's arrival to an assigned WPT may not coincide with the RG's arrival at that WPT. When this occurs, either the tanker must "orbit" (fly in circles) until the RG arrives or vice versa. In either case, the total amount of time spent in "orbit" by all tankers and RGs is returned.

(g) RG LATE ARRIVAL. It is not always possible for all RGs to reach their final destinations by their desired latest times. The sum of all RG late arrival times is returned.

(h) TANKERS USED. The actual number of tankers assigned to one or more RG WPTs is returned.

(i) TANKER MISSION TIME. The total of all tanker usage times, end of mission time minus start of mission time, is returned.

(j) TANKER DISTANCE FLOWN. The sum of all tanker distances flown in the solution is returned.

(k) TANKER FUEL USAGE. The sum of all the fuel consumed by tankers in the solution is returned.

(l) TANKER FUEL DELIVERED. The sum of all fuel delivered to RGs in the solution is returned.

(m) RG FUEL USAGE. The sum of all the fuel used by RGs in the current solution is returned.

6.4. Tabu Memory Structure

Part of the power of tabu search is achieved by using the solution and/or move history. The memory structure used in GTTS stores attributes of the moves that have been previously selected and changes the length of the "short term memory" (tabu tenure) using an adaptive procedure. Move attributes are stored in a square matrix of dimension n, the number of solution nodes. As moves are implemented, the letters of the move are recorded in the matrix. For each letter of the move, the row index is the letter, the column index is the image of the letter (the "next" letter in the cyclic context of the move), and the value placed in the matrix is the current iteration plus the current tabu tenure. Suppose $n = 3$. At iteration zero, the tabu matrix would be as (a) in Figure 6. A tabu tenure of 7 and a move of (1,2,3) yields, at iteration 1, the tabu matrix (b) in Figure 6.

$$\begin{bmatrix} 0 & 0 & 0 \\ 0 & 0 & 0 \\ 0 & 0 & 0 \end{bmatrix} \qquad \begin{bmatrix} 0 & 7 & 0 \\ 0 & 0 & 7 \\ 7 & 0 & 0 \end{bmatrix}$$

(a) (b)

Figure 6. Tabu memory structure.

For future iterations, any move that contains one or more of the letter-to-image-of-letter (row-to-column) combinations with nonzero entries in the tabu matrix will be considered tabu.

Whenever the value of n changes, the tabu matrix is automatically redimensioned and the current tabu structure is preserved.

As the search progresses, the tabu tenure is adaptively modified based on the status of the current solution [6,21]. If the current solution is the best solution found so far, the tabu tenure is reset to a specified default value (seven for this paper). If the current solution is a better move than the last, but not the best solution so far, the tabu tenure remains at its current value. If the current solution is not better than the previous move, the tabu tenure is increased by one.

6.5. An Iteration in the GTTS

A GTTS iteration begins relative to the current solution. Based on the characteristics of this solution and the current status of the tabu search, move-based neighborhoods are generated. At any point in the search, one or more of the neighborhoods described in Section 6.2 is invoked. Their union forms the composite search neighborhood for the current iteration.

Once the generation of moves is completed, the evaluation of these moves begins. A move's value is the difference between the current solution and the solution created by the move. Initially, the first move evaluated is considered the best move found. All other moves are compared against the current best move found by using the hierarchical objective function described earlier.

Items (a)–(d) listed in Section 6.3 require only the specific partitioning and ordering of the waypoint nodes to the tankers as contained in the S_n representation. Each of these may be evaluated without the determination of the specific timing of events.

The remaining items in Section 6.3 require the computation of specific timing of events for evaluation. Once the timing of events is determined, the evaluations of each of the hierarchical objectives is straightforward; therefore, the remainder of this section concentrates on the determination of the timing of events for a particular move being applied to the current solution.

The determination of the timing of events occurs through the application of the following three steps.

1. Determine each RG's flight path times regardless of tanker assignments.
2. Determine each tanker's route times regardless of assigned RG times.
3. Deconflict schedules determined in Steps 1 and 2.

The first step takes each individual RG and, based on its EDT with no delays, determines the arrival, service, and departure times at each waypoint node along its flight path as well as its destination arrival time. Similarly, the second step takes each individual tanker and, with no delays, determines the arrival, service, and departure times at each of its assigned waypoint nodes.

The third and final step in determining the timing of events for a solution deconflicts the schedules created in the first two steps through an iterative approach. This iterative approach involves two primary stages. The first stage considers each RG and determines the largest difference between its arrival at any waypoint node and the arrival of the tanker assigned to that waypoint node. For each RG whose largest difference is positive, the starting time of the RG is adjusted by the amount of this largest difference. The second stage considers each tanker and its associated route assignment. The difference between the tanker arrival at its first waypoint node and the associated RG arrival is determined. The tanker's schedule is adjusted to ensure that it either arrives at the same time as the RG or "orbits" until the RG arrives. Once the first waypoint node in the tanker's assignment is deconflicted, the procedure continues with the next waypoint node in its assignment. This iterative approach continues until all nodes within the tanker's assignment have been deconflicted. When all tankers have been deconflicted, Step 3 repeats. This iterative process continues until no conflicts are found or until ten iterations of Step 3 have been completed. If ten iterations are reached, the current candidate move is removed from consideration.

The choice of placing all "orbit" time in the tanker schedules is based on the capacity of the airframes that comprise the RGs, particularly fighters. For smaller aircraft, their fuel capacity minimizes their allowable orbit times. With the timing of events determined, the remaining objectives are evaluated. Once the best move is determined by the objective function, it is placed within the tabu structure. After this placement, the best move selected is implemented on the current solution, creating the next solution to be used in the tabu search iterative process.

6.6. Consistent WPT Generation

The above description of the GTTS assumed that the RG WPTs were provided by an external source and were consistent, i.e., feasible (flyable) solutions could be found when those WPTs were used. Of course, externally supplied WPTs are not necessarily consistent. To account for this possibility, a modified form of the GTTS, the GTTS preprocessor (GTTSP), has been developed to determine consistent WPTs for a single RG's flight path. GTTSP is also an adaptive tabu search method developed specifically to find consistent active WPT node sets for a single RG. Reasons for using the GTTSP include:

(a) no externally supplied WPTs are available,
(b) the provided WPTs are untested, and
(c) a comparison of the supplied WPTs against the GTTSP WPTs is desired.

GTTSP requires the use of a set of candidate WPTs (nominally 100 nautical miles (NM) apart) throughout the selected RG's flight path. From this set of candidate WPTs, a subset is selected as "active". This active subset of WPTs defines the actual WPTs for the RG's flight path in the AFRP to be solved by the GTTS.

The active subset of WPTs is selected based on objectives identical to those for the GTTS and imposes the same tanker resource configuration that is used by the GTTS on the AFRP. The application of the GTTSP differs depending on whether an RG requires escort.

For the no escort case, each candidate WPT is associated with a single candidate WPT node. Once the set of WPT nodes are available, an initial WPT node selection set for the individual RG is constructed by first selecting the "midway" WPT node along the RG flight path. If the number of candidate WPTs is odd, the midway WPT is uniquely determined. If the number of candidate WPTs is even, the midway WPT is taken to be the earliest WPT of the two midway WPTs. The amount of fuel required at this active WPT node is computed to be equal to the RG fuel used to reach the midway WPT node's location. Depending on the consistency of this initial WPT node selection, one of two moves is employed.

A preprocessor TKI (PTKI) move neighborhood is used if the WPT node set is inconsistent. Three conditions can cause such an inconsistency.

(a) No tanker can fly to the midway point, provide service to the RG, and then return to its original beddown base without running out of fuel.
(b) The RG cannot fly to the midway WPT node without running out of fuel.
(c) The RG cannot fly from the midway WPT node to its destination base without running out of fuel.

If any of these conditions exist, then a PTKI move adds a WPT node to the current active set, assigns a tanker to that node, and checks for consistency. If the active WPT node set is still inconsistent, the PTKI move neighborhood is employed again. In this manner, the PTKI neighborhood determines the cardinality of the active node set. Once a feasible solution is found, the preprocessor WPT node adjacent swap (PAS) neighborhood is employed.

PAS moves serve to iteratively improve upon the consistent "active" node set. It achieves this by taking each "active" node and generating a move that replaces it with either its predecessor or successor along the flight path. For example, if the consistent solution is (0,50)(6,75), then (0,49)(6,75), (0,51)(6,75), (0,50)(6,74), and (0,50)(6,76) are reachable in a single PAS move. The best active WPT node set found by iteratively applying the PAS neighborhood within the GTTSP then serves to define the flight path WPTs for the RG in the AFRP.

Now suppose that escort is required for a RG. If a WPT is not located over open water, then a single candidate WPT node is generated. If a WPT node is located over open water and the adjacent WPT farther along the flight path is also over open water, then two candidate WPT nodes are generated. The *escort range* is a single contiguous interval starting at the first WPT escort node and ending at the last WPT escort node.

The initial solution is constructed as (tanker ID, first WPT node ID, last WPT node ID), i.e., the tanker flies to the first WPT node, provides service to the RG, escorts the RG to the last WPT node, provides service to the RG, and then returns to its beddown base. The fuel requirements at each of these "active" WPT nodes are determined by the GTTSP and, depending on consistency, either PTKI and/or PAS moves are employed until consistency is achieved. This process, which is very similar to the no escort required case, is discussed in detail in [3].

7. EXAMPLE RESULTS

Wiley [3] presents results for a small example with three RGs and 18 tankers, for a benchmark example with nine RGs and 60 tankers and for a "typical middle east deployment" with 99 aircraft in 26 RGs serviced by 120 tankers.

The small example, depicting a fictitious deployment from the continental U.S. to Saudi Arabia, was solved to enhance understanding of the complex interactions embodied in the solution to any AFRP and to clarify how such a solution may be presented to a prospective user of the GTTS solution. The details on the RGs are given in Table 1 for an assumed deployment start designated as time 0 (zero).

Table 1. Departure and destinations information.

RG ID	AC Type	No. AC	Origin	Destination	EDT	RDT
0	F15	6	KLFI - Langley AFB, VA	OERY - Riyadh AB	8	40
1	F15	6	KLFI - Langley AFB, VA	OERY - Riyadh AB	0	40
2	F117	6	KHMN - Holloman AFB, NM	OEDR - King Abdul Aziz AB	0	40

The RGs may be serviced by any of 18 KC-135R tankers located at KBGR (six tankers—Bangor IA, ME), EGUN (six tankers—Mildenhall AB, UK), KGSB (three tankers—Seymour-Johnson AFB, NC), and PAEI (three tankers—Eielson AFB, AK). The scenario for this small deployment is pictured in Figure 7 where the tanker and RG departure bases are presented as pentagons and the RG flight paths are shown as WPTs and destination bases (circles) connected by lines. The results pictured in Figures 8 and 9 are based on applying the GTTS on an AMD Athlon 950 Mhz machine. The best results were achieved at iteration 369 (in about 25 minutes) of a 30 minute run where 430 iterations were completed. Figure 8 shows how the number of tankers used (left vertical axis) and the hours of orbit delay time at WPTs (right vertical axis) changed during the iterations (horizontal axis) of the search procedure.

Figure 9 presents the best solution found from a "temporal assignment" viewpoint. As may be observed, 12 of the 18 tankers are employed in refueling and escort activities over the 40 hour time horizon of the deployment. In addition, each RG's and tanker's activities can be observed,

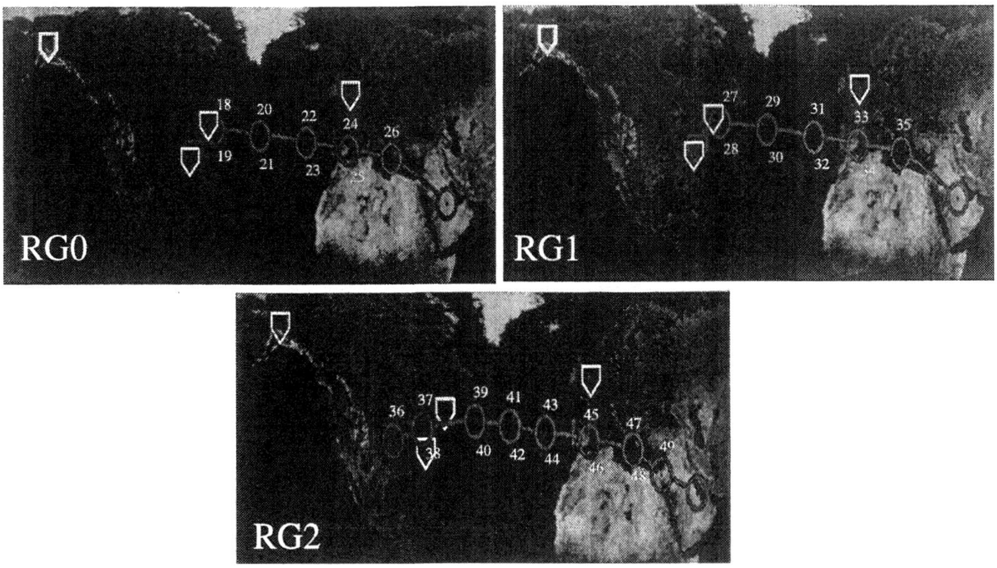

Figure 7. Scenario for small deployment.

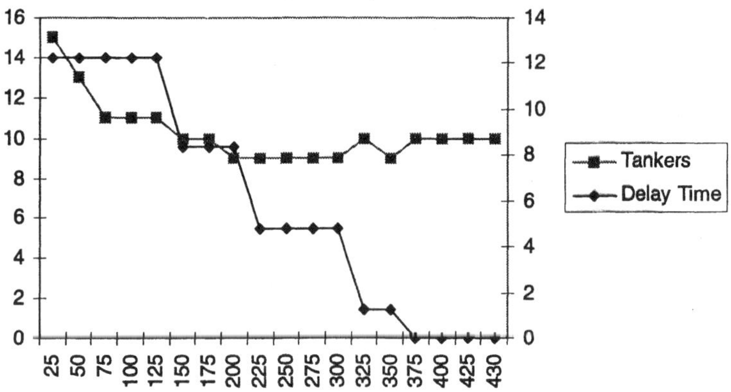

Figure 8. Solution snapshot plot.

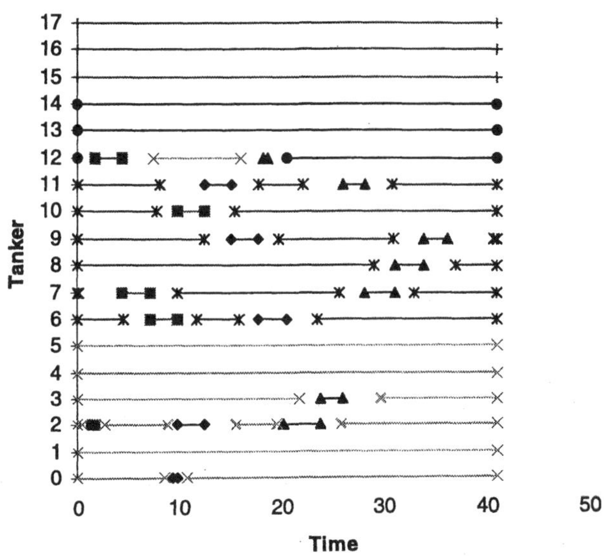

Figure 9. Tanker assignments for a small deployment.

in *detail*, from a careful examination of Figure 9. For example, Tanker 6, based at EGUN, is idle until Hour 4 when it flies to a WPT to provide service to RG1 between Hours 7 and 10; it returns to EGUN, takes off at Hour 15 and provides service to RG0 and then returns to EGUN for the remainder of the deployment. Similarly, RG2's activities can be determined. RG2 takes-off in time to meet Tanker 2 for service, beginning at the Atlantic coast at Hour 20. It is subsequently serviced by Tankers 2,3,7–9,11. After service by Tanker 9, RG2 completes its flight to OEDR.

The benchmark problem was studied to provide a comparison of the TAP tool to the GTTS method. The TAP tool was run six *times* for 90 minutes (with different static tabu tenures) on an Intel Pentium II 350 Mhz machine (a total of nine *hours*). Using the same problem structure and assumptions as those embodied in the TAP tool, the GTTS was run *once* for 30 minutes on an Athlon 950 Mhz machine. The best results from the six TAP tool runs yields a composite solution using 24 tankers traveling 215,204 miles with the latest RG arrival requiring 69.1 hours. The best solution from the single GTTS run used 23 tankers, flying 106,227 miles, with the latest RG arriving at 69.2 hours. Thus, the GTTS used one fewer tankers, less than half the tanker fuel consumption, with only one-tenth of an hour added to the latest RG arrival time.

The typical middle east deployment scenario was constructed with the aid of AMC to provide information on GTTS performance on an AFRP of practical size. The best solution, found in two hours and 16 minutes, employed 95 tankers flying 326,968 miles and allowed the latest RG to arrive in 55 hours. The tanker assignments in this solution were obtained at the *detailed asset operational level* (individual tankers or receivers) and yield excellent assignments in terms of such metrics as minimizing tanker usage, tanker travel, and total deployment time. In general, depending on the desire of the user, Wiley's AFRP method can provide either a single "best" solution to a particular problem or, as indicated in Figure 6, a set of robust, comparable solutions to a problem instance. The fact that the best previous method, CMARPS, requires several analysts weeks, and occasionally months, to achieve a single feasible solution strongly underscores the power that GTTS methods bring to the solution of USAF logistics problems. Thus, with this new tool, analysts and decision makers not only can have the flexibility and added insight provided by multiple solutions, they also can make critical decisions in a tremendously shortened planning horizon.

8. CONCLUSIONS AND DIRECTIONS FOR FUTURE WORK

This research has yielded three major contributions:

(1) a reusable, portable code for implementing and applying group theory to P | O combinatorial problems,
(2) a demonstration of the effectiveness of using dynamic search methodologies has been shown for the AFRP, and
(3) the development of a very effective solution methodology for the AFRP.

Future work could be addressed at both improving the scope and efficiency of Wiley's [3] Java™ class library for S_n. In addition, the efficiency of the GTTS code could be improved both in the construction of the initial solution and in the algorithmic implementation of the search technique. The current GTTS uses an adaptive approach to adjusting the tabu tenure; the more powerful reactive approach of Battiti and Tecchiolli [22] could possibly yield significant improvements in the solution methodology. An investigation of more sophisticated tabu memory structures also might be beneficial.

Further, the AFRP is just one of a myriad of problems being addressed by AMC. Other important AMC problems are associated with

(a) refueling needs in intratheater employment,
(b) once tanker schedules have been determined, assigning aircrews to the tankers,
(c) assigning the aircrews for RGs.

In addition to USAF logistics problems, the GTTS, or just the symmetric group class, can be applied to any problem where the partitioning and ordering of elements is important. Colletti [15] describes the use of the S_n for representing the m-TSP. As the GTTS has demonstrated, far more complicated problems can be solved using S_n as the basic representation of solutions and for constructing varied move neighborhoods.

These move neighborhoods can be compactly represented using the group actions of multiplication and conjugation. Any k-OrOpt move can be represented by three letters from S_n combined with right-multiplication. The first of the three letters represent the beginning of the k-length pattern, the second represents the letter immediately following the end of the k-length pattern, and the third letter represents the letter to insertion point of the k-length pattern. Any m-letter rearrangement move can be represented by m-letters from S_n combined with conjugation. An excellent discussion of these rearrangement moves can be found in [15]. In fact, S_n facilitates the construction of very complex move neighborhoods in a compact representation through the use of conjugation and multiplication as described and demonstrated in [3,23,24].

In conclusion, the computational results reported here indicate that the GTTS is efficient and effective, providing excellent results with no tuning. The procedures are sufficiently robust to embrace variants of the basic AFRP with modified objectives and constraints. Future researchers should be able to build on the foundation provided by this GTTS application to the AFRP to construct highly effective approaches to other combinatorial optimization problems.

REFERENCES

1. AFDD 2-6.2, Air refueling: Air Force doctrine document 2-6.2, Part of *Joint Publication 3-17, Joint Tactics, Techniques, and Procedures for Air Mobility Operations*, (1999).
2. Gulf War Air Power Survey, *Logistics and Support, Volume III*, Washington, D.C., (1993).
3. V.D. Wiley, The aerial fleet refueling problem, Ph.D. Dissertation, The University of Texas, (2001).
4. W.B. Carlton, A tabu search to the general vehicle routing problem, Ph.D. Thesis, University of Texas, Austin, TX, (1995).
5. M. Gendreau, G. Laporte and G. Potvin, *Vehicle Routing: Modern Heuristics*, Chapter 9, pp. 311–336, John Wiley & Sons, Chichester, (1997).
6. M. Dell'Amico and M. Trubian, Applying tabu search to the job-shop scheduling problem, *Annals of Operations Research* **41**, 231–252, (1993).
7. F. Glover and M. Laguna, *Tabu Search*, Kluwer Academic, Boston, MA, (1997).
8. I.M. Isaacs, *Algebra*, Brooks/Cole Publishing, Pacific Grove, CA, (1994).
9. A.A. Yamani, Analysis of an air transportation system, Ph.D. Thesis, University of Florida, (1986).
10. H. Hostler, Air refueling tanker scheduling, Master's Thesis, Air Force Institute of Technology, Wright-Patterson AFB, OH, (1987).
11. B. Russina and B. Ruthsatz, The quick look tool for tanker deployment, Technical Report, Center for Optimization and Semantic Control, St. Louis, MO, (1999).
12. S.R. Capehart, A tabu search metaheuristic for the air refueling tanker assignment problem, Master's Thesis, Air Force Institute of Technology, Wright-Patterson AFB, OH, (2000).
13. H. Kuhn, The Hungarian method for the assignment problem, *Naval Res. Logistics Quart.* **2**, 83–97, (1955).
14. M. Artin, *Algebra*, Prentice Hall, Englewood Cliffs, NJ, (1991).
15. B.W. Colletti, Group theory and metaheuristics, Ph.D. Thesis, The University of Texas, Austin, TX, (1999).
16. B. Colletti, J. Barnes and S. Dokov, A note on characterizing the K-OPT neighborhood via group theory, *Journal of Heuristics* **5**, 51–55, (1999).
17. B.W. Colletti and J.W. Barnes, Linearity in the traveling salesman problem, *Appl. Math. Lett.* **13** (3), 27–32, (2000).
18. B. Colletti and J.W. Barnes, Local search structure in the symmetric traveling salesperson problem under a general class of rearrangement neighborhoods, *Appl. Math. Lett.* **14** (1), 105–108, (2001).
19. J.W. Barnes, B. Colletti and D. Neuway, Using group theory and transition matrices to study a class of metaheuristic neighborhoods, *European Journal of Operational Research* **138**, 531–544, (2002).
20. R.W. Harder, A jump search enhanced reactive tabu search in a universal vehicle router applied to routing unmanned aerial vehicles, Master's Thesis, Air Force Institute of Technology, Wright-Patterson AFB, OH, (2000).
21. J.B. Chambers, Classical and flexible job shop scheduling by tabu search, Ph.D. Thesis, The University of Texas at Austin, (1996).
22. R. Battiti and G. Tecchiolli, The reactive tabu search, ORSA, *Journal on Computing* **6** (2), 126–140, (1994).
23. T. Combs, A group theoretic tabu search approach to tanker crew scheduling, Technical Report AFIT/DS/ENS/02, Air Force Institute of Technology, (2001).

24. J.R. Crino, A group theoretic tabu search methodology for solving the theater distribution vehicle routing and scheduling problem, Ph.D. Dissertation, Air Force Institute of Technology, (2002).

Available online at www.sciencedirect.com
SCIENCE DIRECT
Mathematical and Computer Modelling 39 (2004) 641–647
MATHEMATICAL AND COMPUTER MODELLING
www.elsevier.com/locate/mcm

An Algorithm for Finding the Shortest Sailing Distance from Any Maritime Navigable Point to a Designated Port

E. R. BEEKER
The MITRE Corporation
7515 Colshire Drive
McClean, VA 22102, U.S.A.
ebeeker@mitre.org

Abstract—Many simulations and deployment analyses use networks to evaluate ship paths at sea. Ships are constrained to travel along links between specified nodes. When ships may need to change their destination while at sea, the network path can deviate significantly from an actual shortest path. Additionally, when it is desired to initialize simulation data from actual ship positions, ships must move to a node to use the network. By triangulating open navigable water areas, a shortest path from all points at sea to selected ports can be calculated. A Delaunay triangulation of the open areas can be calculated in $O(n \log n)$. Using the Delaunay triangulation, the shortest path triangulation from a point (port) can be calculated in $O(nk)$ where n is the number of points specifying the sea-land border and k is the number of islands. The resulting data can provide distance from any point on the sea surface to the port in $O(1)$ time when the triangle containing the point is known, or in $O(n/2)$ if the triangle must be determined.

Keywords—Deployment, Strategic sealift, Delaunay triangulation on a sphere, Shortest path.

1. INTRODUCTION

For many years, the primary method for representing ship movement in computer models has been taken from the SAIL model. The SAIL model consists of a set of nodes, arcs, and lines. Ship routes are represented as arcs between nodes. The Maritime domain (oceans, seas, canals, rivers, straights) are represented as a network. In the SAIL network, there is a node every 15° of latitude and longitude. There are additional nodes to represent critical locations, such as the Straights of Gibraltar, the Panama Canal, and Horn of Africa. Although the arcs between the nodes are great circle routes, and therefore, shortest paths on the surface of the Earth, the approximations using the nodes are not. Long routes are broken into smaller segments, and while each segment is a shortest path, the overall route deviates significantly from a shortest path. Figure 1 shows a portion of the SAIL network (solid lines) between New York and Gibraltar along with the actual shortest path (dashed line). The path selected on the SAIL network would be along the bottom solid lines. When used in a simulation, the path of a ship will deviate from the shortest path and

0895-7177/04/$ - see front matter Typeset by $\mathcal{A}_{\mathcal{M}}\mathcal{S}$-TEX
doi:10.1016/j.mcm.2004.02.004

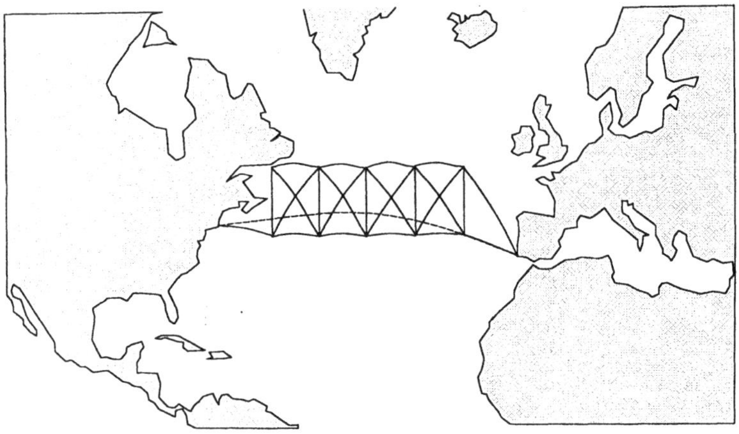

Figure 1.

the distance calculation will be in error. To overcome this, the SAIL network adds long routes across the oceans, for example from the Panama Canal to the Straights of Gibraltar. These added arcs bypass the oceanic nodes to yield a true shortest path. The SAIL set of lines is used to represent land. The model is initialized by connecting ports to the network and placing ships on the network. Ports are connected by finding the nearest node to the port's position that is not separated by a line and adding a link from the port to the node. Ships are placed by finding the closest node to each ship position that is not separated by a line and having the ship sail to the node. Because ships initially travel to the closest node, they may not be traveling towards their next port. After a beginning period, ships are confined to the network and so no more anomalies enter the ship simulation. However, the restriction of ships to the network limits the flexibility of the simulation. If a simulation wanted to change the destination of a ship at sea, perhaps because a canal was closed, the ship would have to continue to the next node before changing course. If the ship were on one of the long arcs, this could take it thousands of miles out of its way.

The area based ship model solves these problems by dividing the ocean into areas such that the next point on the shortest path to a port is the same for all the points in the area. This is illustrated in Figure 2, showing the Mediterranean Sea. A ship anywhere in the vertically shaded area can travel directly to Naples. Figure 3 shows two areas for Gibraltar. Any ship in the vertically shaded area can travel directly to Gibraltar. A ship anywhere in the horizontally shaded area must first travel to Point A and then to Gibraltar. For every possible destination, the area-based ship model divides the navigable waterways into a set of regions. Each region is a regular polygon and it is represented as a set of triangles for computational purposes. All of

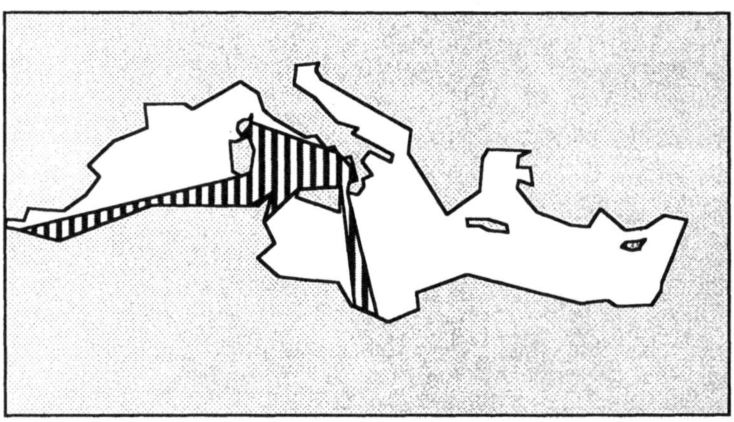

Figure 2.

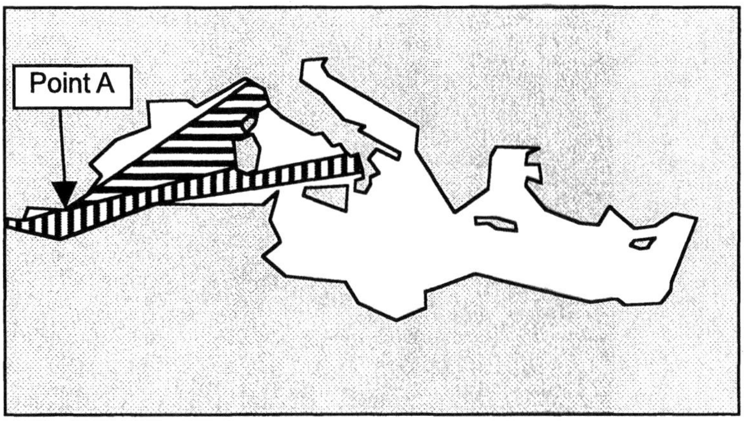

Figure 3.

the triangles that form a region have the same next point on the shortest path to a destination. By determining the triangle containing a ship's position, the shortest path to a destination is determined. No matter where the ship is, it can find the shortest path from its current position to a destination. The ship never backtracks or continues to a node that is not on the great circle shortest path to its destination. The triangulation is combined with a network algorithm for line-oriented routes, such as the Saint Lawrence Seaway, and the Panama and Suez Canals to provide complete coverage of sea routes. The following sections describe the procedures used to build the triangulation.

2. DELAUNAY TRIANGULATION

The shortest path algorithm depends upon a Delaunay triangulation. A set of points can be triangulated in a number of different ways. A Delaunay triangulation has several features that make it desirable. Delaunay triangles connect nearest neighbors. Also, a Delaunay triangulation makes the minimum angle of a triangle, as large as possible. In a sense, the triangles are as fat as possible so that the ratio of length of sides to area is as small as possible. A Delaunay triangulation can be considered a normalized triangulation for a set of points and is unique with an exception to be described.

The test for a Delauney triangulation uses the circumscribing circle defined by the three vertices of a triangle. In a Delaunay triangulation, no other points lie within the circle. Four points can be triangulated in two ways. Figure 4 shows four points in a non-Delaunay triangulation, since Point D lies within the circle defined by Points ABC. The triangulation can be turned into a Delaunay triangulation by "flipping" the shared side (AC) to the other option (BD). Figure 5 shows the same points in a valid Delaunay triangulation. If four points form a square, then two triangulations exist using either of the diagonals of the square, as shown in Figure 6. With this exception, a Delaunay triangulation is unique for a set of points. Some authors call a set of points that contain squares, degenerate, and will move one of the points to eliminate the condition. In this application the diagonal can be chosen arbitrarily.

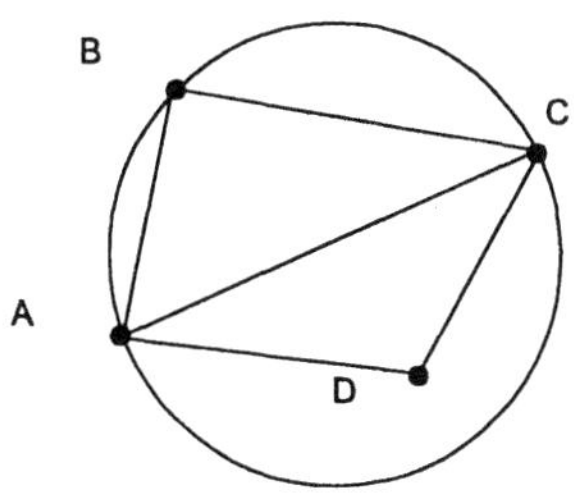

Figure 4.

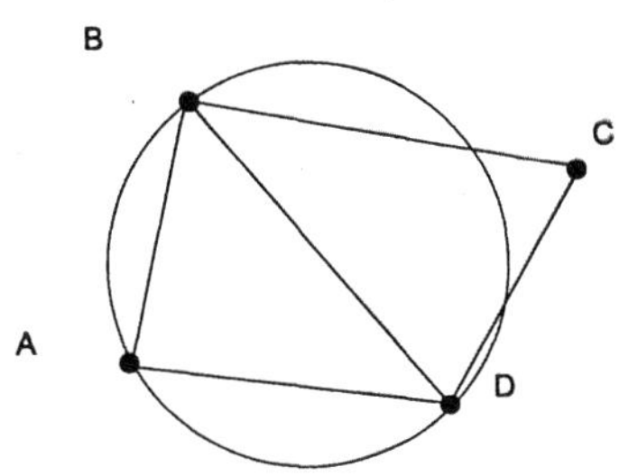

Figure 5.

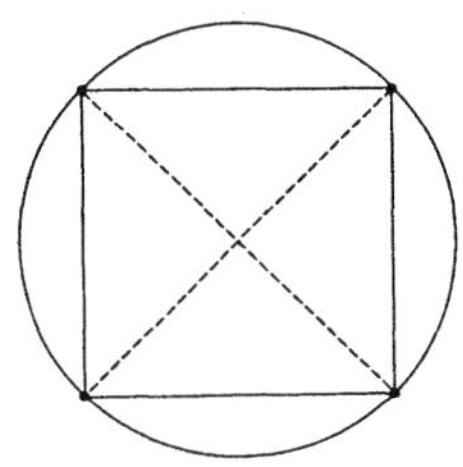

Figure 6.

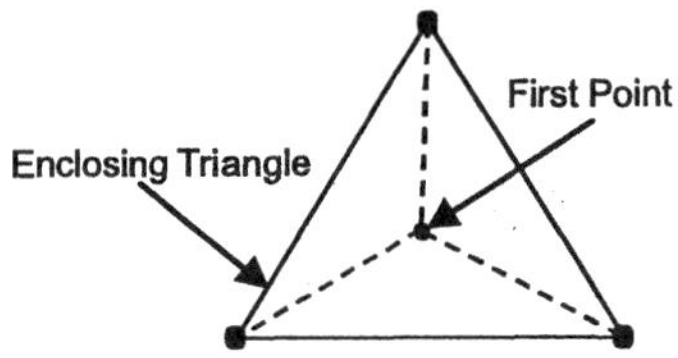

Figure 7.

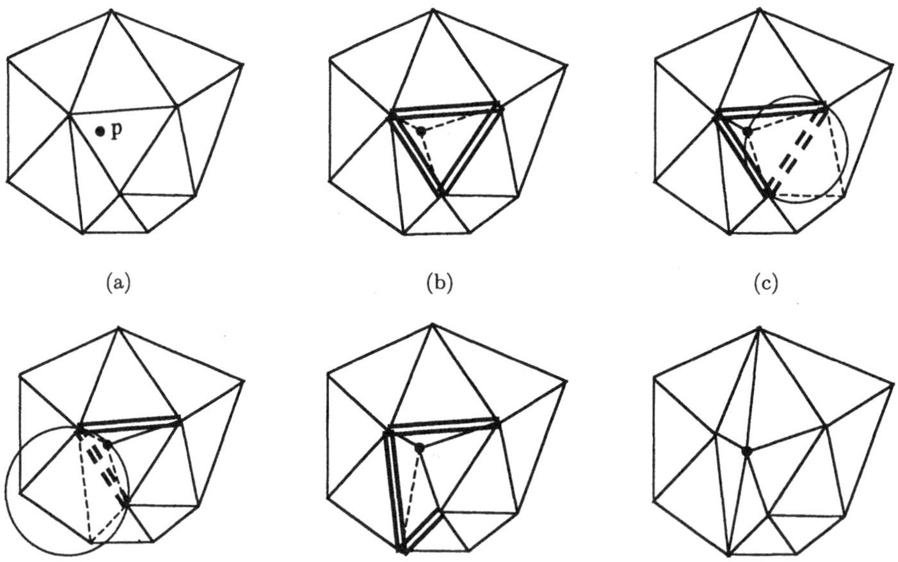

(a) (b) (c)

(d) (e) (f)

Figure 8.

This application uses an insertion algorithm to form the Delaunay triangulation, adapted from Shewchuck's triangle program [1]. In the plane, first an enclosing triangle is created that is guaranteed to contain all of the points in the input set. Then, each point is added, one at a time. Figure 7 shows the enclosing triangle and the first point. When a point is added, it is attached to the vertices of the enclosing triangle. Then each of the newly formed triangles is tested for the Delaunay condition. The triangulation is adjusted to maintain the Delaunay condition. After all the points are added, the enclosing triangle can be deleted, leaving the input point set in a valid Delaunay triangulation.

The process of adding a point and adjusting the triangulation is shown in Figure 8. In Figure 8a, the existing triangulation meets the Delaunay condition when Point P is added. Point P is connected to the vertices of the triangle that contains P as shown in Figure 8b. The three new triangles whose bases are the edges of the enclosing triangle and have the Point P as apex must be tested for the Delaunay condition. The bases, shown with a double line in Figure 8b, are added to a list of sides to be checked. Figure 8c shows the test of the first side, which is successful. The second test, shown in Figure 8d is unsuccessful. Therefore, the base of the test triangle is an incorrect edge. It is flipped by replacing it with the diagonal that crosses it as shown in Figure 8e. When it is flipped, the attached two sides of the triangles just formed are added to the list for testing. The algorithm continues testing and flipping diagonals until all of the marked edges are tested with no more changes. In practice, the swaps die out quickly. Figure 8f shows the final triangulation after adding Point P.

3. PARTITIONING THE POLYGON

The Delaunay triangulation is used for traversing the nodes of the polygon. The following description is adapted from Storer [2]. Figure 9 shows a polygon without obstacles. The al-

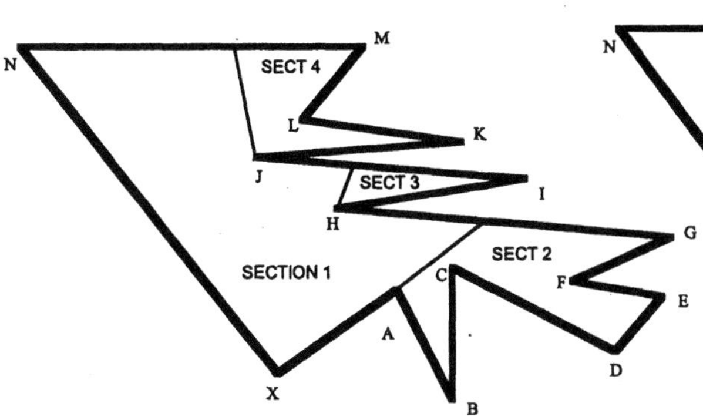

Figure 9.

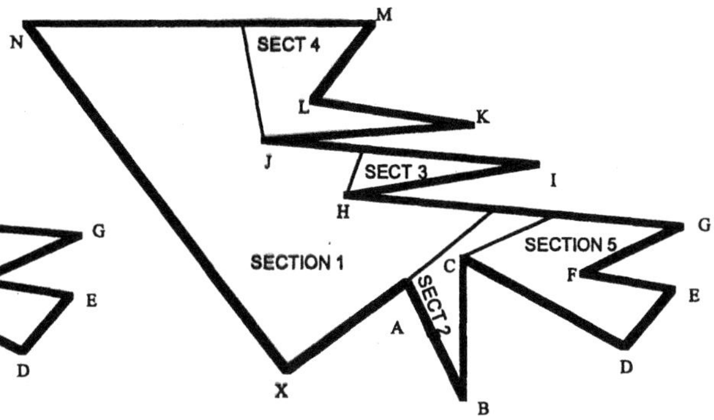

Figure 10.

gorithm begins from a source Point X and partitions the polygon into the section that can be directly reached from the source point, and other sections that must go through an intermediate point. The other sections will be partitioned recursively until there are no more sections to be partitioned. The basic algorithm begins by examining the first point counter-clockwise along the boundary of the polygon (Point A). As the angle at A is more than 180°, the X-A edge is extended until it strikes a boundary edge, dividing the polygon into two sections. The right section (Section 2) will be saved for partitioning from Point A. Partitioning of the left section continues until the polygon has been partitioned into four pieces. All of Section 1 has a direct path to X. Any point in Section 2 must go through Point A to reach Point X. Any point in Section 3 must go through Point H and any point in Section 4 must go through Point J. After partitioning from Point X, Section 2 can be further partitioned using Point A as the origin. This creates Section 5, as shown in Figure 10. The shortest path from Section 5 must go through Point C then Point A.

A similar approach can be taken for obstacles, with the proviso that an area behind an obstacle may be reached more than one way, and the first way may not be the shortest. If not, then the triangulation must be changed. If a triangle behind an obstacle can be reached from two directions, then it should be split. The boundary generally is a series of quadratic curves, as seen in Figure 11. In the ship sailing model, the quadratic curves are replaced by straight edges, as the error is negligible for this use. Another alternative would be to keep the next point for both triangles in each triangle. Then a simple test could determine whether it would be shorter to go to one or the other next point.

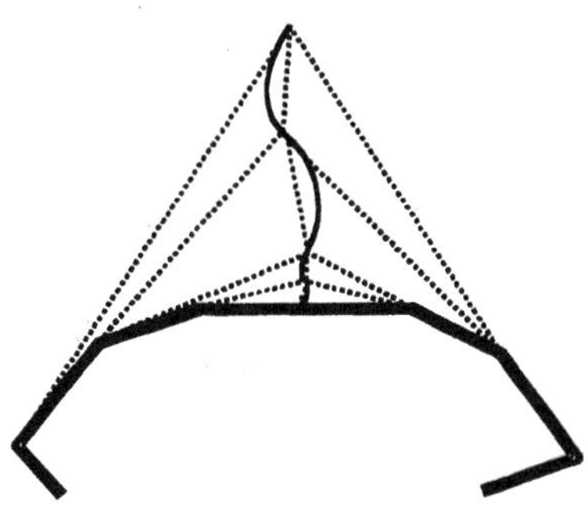

Figure 11.

4. PRIMITIVES

There are two basic primitives used to create the Delaunay triangulation: the test for counterclockwise and the test for in-circle. In a plane, the test for counterclockwise is straight-forward. Given two vectors **<u>AB</u>** and **<u>AC</u>**, the cross product of the two vectors is positive when **<u>AC</u>** is counterclockwise to **<u>AB</u>** and negative if **<u>AC</u>** is clockwise to **<u>AB</u>**. If **<u>AB</u>** and **<u>AC</u>** are collinear,

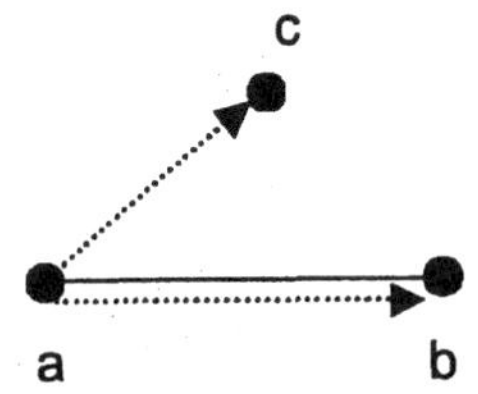

Figure 12.

$$\begin{vmatrix} b_x - a_x & b_y - a_y \\ c_x - a_x & c_y - a_y \end{vmatrix}$$

Figure 13.

then the cross product is zero. The cross product can be evaluated by finding the determinant of the matrix in Figure 13.

In three-space, the vector product of three vectors gives the volume of a parallelepiped and the sign shows their orientation as seen from the vector origination point as shown in Figure 14. Using Earth centric coordinates, the vector product can be calculated by the determinant as shown in Figure 15.

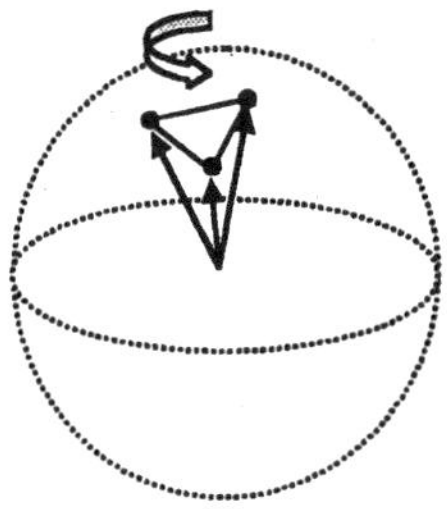

Figure 14.

$$\begin{vmatrix} a_x & a_y & a_z \\ b_x & b_y & b_z \\ c_x & c_y & c_z \end{vmatrix}$$

Figure 15.

The in-circle test in a plane is illustrated in Figure 16. It can be performed by taking the determinant of the matrix in Figure 17. Again, a positive determinant means the point under test is inside the circle, a negative determinant means the point is outside of the circle, and zero indicates the point is on the circle.

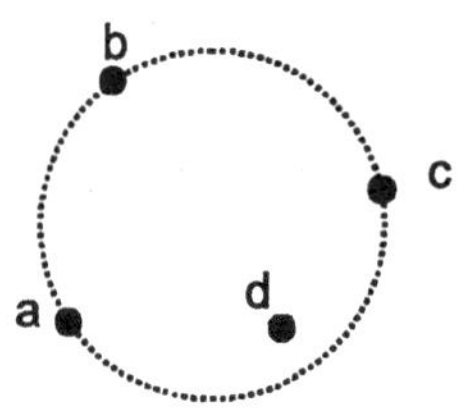

Figure 16.

$$\begin{vmatrix} a_x & a_y & a_x^2 + a_y^2 & 1 \\ b_x & b_y & b_x^2 + b_y^2 & 1 \\ c_x & c_y & c_x^2 + c_y^2 & 1 \\ d_x & d_y & d_x^2 + d_y^2 & 1 \end{vmatrix}$$

Figure 17.

The spherical in-circle test reuses the spherical counterclockwise test. As shown in Figure 18, the three vertices of the triangle establish a plane in three-dimensional space. Because the point under test must be on the surface of the sphere, it is sufficient to determine if the point under test is on the same side of the plane established by the three vertices as the center of the Earth. If Point D in Figure 18 is on the same side of the plane as the Earth center, then it is outside of the circle established by the vertices. If the point under test is on the other side of the plane from the Earth's center, then the point is in the circle. If the point under test is on the plane, then it is on the circle established by the vertices. The test is the same as the counterclockwise test, except using the point under test as the origin of the vectors. The test consists of calculating the determinant shown in Figure 19.

Each of the primitives can be calculated by taking a determinant. However, the exact value of the determinant is not required, only the sign. In general, the sign of the determinant can be calculated more quickly than the value [3].

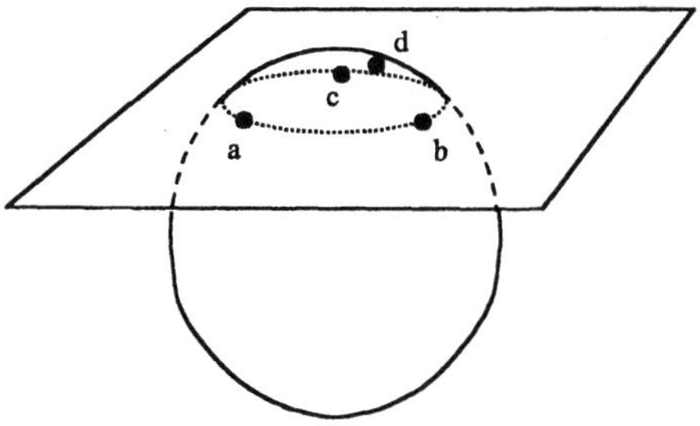

Figure 18.

$$\begin{vmatrix} a_x - d_x & a_y - d_y & a_z - d_z \\ b_x - d_x & b_y - d_y & b_z - d_z \\ c_x - d_x & c_y - d_y & c_z - d_z \end{vmatrix}$$

Figure 19.

5. LOCATING THE ENCLOSING TRIANGLE

Locating the triangle containing an arbitrary point takes $O(n/2)$ time. On a sphere, select an initial triangle with vertices less than 180° from the point. Select one of the edges of the triangle and test whether the point is potentially in the triangle using the counterclockwise test. If this test shows the point is outside of the triangle, then move to the adjacent triangle and continue testing. When a successful test is performed, check the next edge of the triangle. If the point is outside of it, then move to the adjacent triangle and continue testing. If it is inside the this edge, then we have determined the point is between two of the sides. Eventually, the point must be between two edges. Test the point against the third side. If it is inside, then we have located the triangle and we are finished. If not, move to the triangle opposite the last tested edge and continue testing.

6. CONCLUSION

The area-based sea routing has been implemented in the strategic deployment portion of the Joint Warfare System, a simulation used to provide force structure analysis and course of action analysis for the Office of the Secretary of Defense and the major combatant commands. For this use, the triangulation is calculated the first time a port is used as a destination and then saved for later use. The algorithm is being evaluated for use in the naval engagement simulation by triangulating smaller areas such as seas and gulfs.

After partitioning the maritime areas, each triangle and each point has an exit point that is the next point on the shortest path to the desired port. After arriving at the first point, from then on travel is along edges of triangles. Because the triangles can be precalculated, the next point is always a single look-up. During execution, the only calculation is to find the triangle that contains the ship. Once the ship is placed, the entire route can be found by tracing next points. As the total distance is known at each point, it is not necessary to have the whole route to calculate sailing time, only the distance to the next point.

Because the route segments (triangle edges) are great circle arcs, the routes are actual shortest paths, unlike the SAIL network. Additionally, there are no nodes between turn points, so the number of nodes on a route is less with the network-based system. Finally, it is simple to determine a shortest path to any port for a ship at sea, making it easy to change destinations.

REFERENCES

1. J. Shewchuck, Triangle: A two-dimensional quality mesh generator and delaunay triangulator, `http://www.cs.cmu.edu/~quake/triangle.html`.
2. J. Storer and J. Reif, Shortest paths in the plane with polygonal obstacles, *Journal ACM* **41** (5), 982–1012, (1994).
3. J. Shewchuck, Adaptive precision floating point arithmetic and fast robust geometric predicates. Technical Report CMU-CS-96-140, School of Computer Science, Carnegie Mellon University, Pittsburgh, PA. (1996).

Available online at www.sciencedirect.com
SCIENCE @ DIRECT®
Mathematical and Computer Modelling 39 (2004) 649–656
MATHEMATICAL AND COMPUTER MODELLING
www.elsevier.com/locate/mcm

The Algebra of Airlift

R. T. BRIGANTIC
United States Transportation Command
Strategy, Plans, Policy and Programs Directorate
508 Scott Dr., Bldg. 1900, Scott AFB, IL 62225, U.S.A.
robert.brigantic@hq.transcom.mil

D. MERRILL
HQ Air Mobility Command, Studies and Analysis Division
402 Scott Drive, Unit 3L3 Scott AFB, IL 62225, U.S.A.
dave.merrill@scott.af.mil

Abstract—This paper describes fundamental algebraic relationships that characterize the movement of cargo and passengers via strategic aircraft that comprise an air mobility system. In particular, we present formulae for computing the number of airlift missions required to deliver a given force a given distance; relationships for estimating the throughput or average daily tons that can be delivered to a particular airfield based on that airfield's operating characteristics; and formulae for estimating the force total closure time based on airlift fleet parameters and the intended operational scenario. We also provide a methodology to compute million ton-miles per day (MTMs/D), a common metric for conducting air mobility analyses and force structure capacity assessments.

Keywords—Air mobility, Airlift, Capability, Capacity, Closure time, Number of missions, Throughput, Ton-miles per day, Tons per day.

1. INTRODUCTION

Many of today's defense transportation system (DTS) models and algorithms that deal with strategic airlift make use of fundamental algebraic relationships that characterize the movement of cargo and passengers. With these relationships and appropriate input planning factors, one can compute a variety of important force closure metrics that are vital to assess the transportation feasibility of proposed peacetime operations, war plans, and other concepts of operation. For instance, this paper will show how to compute the metric million ton-miles per day (MTM/D), a measure of unconstrained airlift capacity. The Department of Defense Mobility Requirements Study 2005 (MRS-05) established a total strategic airlift requirement of 54.5 MTM/D to meet the warfighting requirements that formed the basis of this study [1]. This number is based on combining the capacity contributions from the C-5 Galaxy, the C-17 Globemaster III, the KC-10 Extender, and civilian aircraft. Based on their quantities and respective performance parameters, the 54.5 MTM/D number is arrived at by simple summation of the individual MTM/D contributions of these different aircraft types. The 54.5 MTM/D number is currently the foundation for programming and budgeting decisions for strategic airlift acquisition. As the world and associated enemy threats have significantly changed since the completion of MRS-05, new scenarios

0895-7177/04/$ - see front matter Typeset by $\mathcal{A}_\mathcal{M}\mathcal{S}$-TEX
doi:10.1016/j.mcm.2004.02.006

and associated strategic airlift requirements are now under study throughout the United States Transportation Command (USTRANSCOM) and the rest of the Department of Defense.

The formulae presented herein are based on a simple strategic airlift cycle. Figure 1 depicts a notional such cycle. This cycle consists of a strategic airlift aircraft departing its home station or origin airfield (e.g., a C-17 Globemaster assigned to Charleston Air Force Base (AFB)); stopping at a specified on-load airfield or aerial port of embarkation (APOE) (e.g., Pope AFB); stopping for gas and/or replacement crews at an en route airfield (e.g., Naval Air Station (NAS) Rota, Spain); stopping at a specified off-load destination (e.g., Kuwait City International Airport); returning through the original en route airfield for gas and/or replacement crews or alternatively through a separate recovery airfield (e.g., NAS Sigonella, Italy); and then finally stopping at the on-load airfield to begin another cycle.

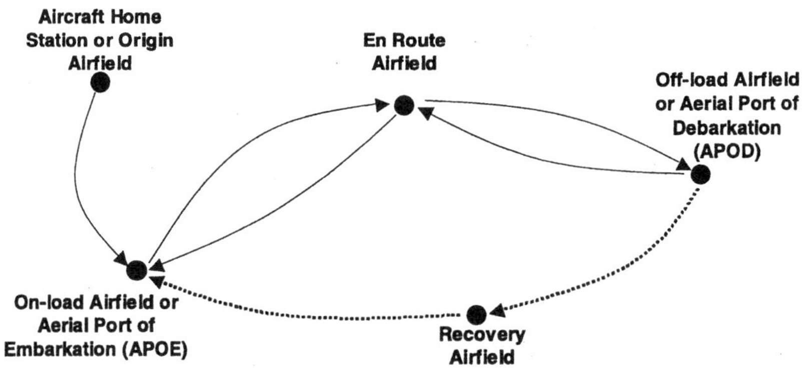

Figure 1. Simple strategic airlift cycle.

2. EQUATIONS

Equations are listed in an order that allows the results of early equations to be used in subsequent calculations. Where appropriate, units are indicated in [ ] brackets. We start with the number of cargo missions required to deliver a certain amount of tonnage, cargo requirement, and the number of PAX missions (PAX is short for passengers) required to deliver a certain amount of personnel PAX requirement.

$$\text{number of cargo missions} = \frac{\text{cargo requirement}}{\text{average payload}}, \tag{1}$$

where average payload is the average or planning factor payload for each type of aircraft to be used. If a mix of aircraft type is to be utilized, a weighted average payload can be used based on the appropriate number of each type of aircraft.

$$\text{number of PAX missions} = \frac{\text{PAX requirement} - \text{PAX on cargo missions}}{\text{PAX capability per PAX mission}}, \tag{2}$$

where PAX on cargo missions is the number of passenger seats available on each cargo mission multiplied by the number of cargo missions. PAX capability per PAX mission is the number of passengers that can be transported by passenger aircraft under the Civil Reserve Airlift Fleet (CRAF) program, such as a Boeing 747 [2]. With this, the total missions required for a certain operation is given by

$$\text{total missions required} = \text{number of cargo missions} + \text{number of PAX missions}. \tag{3}$$

Next, we calculate the round trip flying time (RTFT) for a given strategic airlift cycle. RTFT is computed as

$$\text{RTFT} = \frac{\text{leg dist}_1}{\text{block speed}_1} + \frac{\text{leg dist}_2}{\text{block speed}_2} + \cdots + \frac{\text{leg dist}_n}{\text{block speed}_n}\ [\text{hrs}], \tag{4}$$

where dist is short for distance and the subscripts indicate each of the n legs of the cycle from origin to off-load and back again to the on-load. For simplicity, the origin to on-load leg is often dropped or ignored from this equation. The block speed for each leg is equal to the leg distance divided by the total elapsed time, from aircraft brake release on takeoff to block-in (i.e., parking) after landing. From this, the average block speed for a cycle is computed as

$$\text{average block speed} = \frac{\text{round trip distance}}{\text{RTFT}}\ [\text{nm/hr}], \tag{5}$$

where round trip distance is the sum of the leg distances.

We calculate the total ground time (TGT) for a complete strategic airlift cycle as

$$\begin{aligned}\text{TGT} &= \text{on-load time}\\ &+ \{(\text{en route time}) \times (\text{number of en route stops in cycle})\} + \text{off-load time}\ [\text{hrs}],\end{aligned} \tag{6}$$

where ground times at the on-load, en route, and off-load stops are typically provided via Air Force Pamphlet 10-1403, Air Mobility Planning Factors [3].

Finally, with equations (4) and (6), we can compute the total strategic airlift cycle time as

$$\text{cycle time} = \text{RTFT} + \text{TGT}\ [\text{hrs}]. \tag{7}$$

Next, we compute a series of intervals—the station interval, the aircraft allocation interval, the flying hour capability interval, and the crew stage interval. In turn, this will allow us to determine a closure estimate based on the limiting one of these intervals. We start by computing the station interval, which is an estimate of how many aircraft can be processed per hour on average at a single airfield. Specifically, we compute the Station Interval as

$$\text{station interval} = \frac{\text{station ground time}}{\text{station capability}}\ [\text{hrs}], \tag{8a}$$

where station ground time is the expected ground time for a given type of operation at the station being examined (e.g., the planned ground time for servicing at an en route airfield). The planned ground time for each aircraft type is the expected value measured from block-in to takeoff, and includes parking and servicing times. AFPAM 10-1403 contains planning factor ground times for on-load, en route, and off-load operations for different types of mobility aircraft. Station capability should be expressed in terms of numbers of aircraft a station is capable of handling during the planned ground time at that station. For example, the planned en route ground time for a C-5 Galaxy is three hours and 15 minutes. If an airfield can only process a total of two C-5s in three hours and 15 minutes, then the station capability would be two. The station interval would then be one hour and 38 minutes (or 1.625 hours). This means one could expect to see a C-5 take-off (and land) approximately every 1.625 hours. We note that station capability may be limited by ramp space (i.e., number of parking spaces), maintenance services, material handling equipment, refueling services, net weight restrictions, other facility limitations, or command and control constraints. Station capability will be the most restrictive of these factors.

The aircraft allocation interval, a measure of average timing between aircraft cycles, is computed as

$$\text{aircraft allocation interval} = \frac{\text{cycle time}}{\text{allocated aircraft}}\ [\text{hrs}], \tag{8b}$$

where allocated aircraft is the number of aircraft of a certain type one has access to for a given operation. If the cycle time is 20 hours and the number of aircraft we have access to is ten, then the aircraft allocation interval would be two hours, meaning we would expect to see an aircraft begin a new cycle about every two hours.

The flying hour capability interval, a measure the aircraft launch rate to meet the expected daily flying hour rate for a given number of aircraft, is computed as

$$\text{flying hour capability interval} = \frac{\text{RTFT} \times 24}{\text{objective ute rate} \times \text{allocated aircraft}} \text{ [hrs]}, \tag{8c}$$

where objective ute rate (ute is short for utilization) will be described later by equation (22). For now, consider the objective ute rate as the average number of hours aircraft of a certain type can be expected to fly per day. For example, if the round trip flying time is 12 hours, the objective ute rate is 18 hours, and the allocated aircraft is ten, then the flying hour capability interval would be 1.6 hours.

The stage crew interval, a measure of how often fresh or rested crews are available at a given airfield, is computed next. After flying a certain number of hours, an aircraft crew is required to rest a mandatory number of hours and/or be replaced by a fresh crew before moving the aircraft on to its next destination. When replacement crews are used, we compute the stage crew interval as

$$\text{stage crew interval} = \frac{\text{crew rest period} - \text{aircraft ground time}}{\text{number of stage crews}} \text{ [hrs]}, \tag{8d}$$

where crew rest period is the mandatory number of rest hours, aircraft ground time is an average measure of how long an aircraft of a given type remains on the ground for processing at a given airfield, and the number of stage crews is the expected number of rested crews to be placed at a given airfield. If the crew rest period is 12 hours, aircraft ground time is three hours and 15 minutes, and number of stage crews is four, the stage crew interval would be 2.188 hours, meaning a rested crew would be ready every two hours and 11 minutes to move an aircraft on to its next destination.

We can now compute the flow interval, which is simply the maximum of the four intervals defined above. The flow interval tells us on average how often we can expect to start a new strategic airlift cycle.

$$\text{flow interval} = \max\{(8a),(8b),(8c),(8d)\} \text{ [hrs]}. \tag{9}$$

Ideally, we would like the flow interval to be the aircraft allocation interval as this means no other constraints other than the number of aircraft available are being imposed. For the example data provided above, the flow interval would be $\max\{1.625, 2, 1.6, 2.188\} = 2.188$ hours (the stage crew interval). By increasing the number of stage crews to six, the stage crew interval would become 1.458 hours and the flow interval would then be $\max\{1.625, 2, 1.6, 1.458\}$ = two hours (the aircraft allocation interval). At this point, the only way to reduce the flow interval further would be to increase the number of allocated aircraft.

Finally, with the flow interval, we can compute an estimate of closure time as

$$\text{closure} = \frac{(\text{missions required} - 1) \times (\text{flow interval}) + \text{one way en route time}}{24} \text{ [days]}, \tag{10}$$

where the one way en route time is the total time for an aircraft mission to go from the on-load to the destination. If a total of 50 missions were required, the flow interval is two hours, and the one way en route time is 12 hours, then a closure estimate would be 4.583 days. This equation of course can be used to compute the flow interval needed to meet a specified closure time.

Now we consider a commonly used term in dealing with air mobility operations, maximum on the ground (MOG). MOG is either defined as parking MOG (the maximum number of aircraft of a given type that can be parked at a given airfield) or working MOG (the maximum number of aircraft of a given type that can be simultaneously processed, or worked, within a specified ground time at a given airfield). For the remainder of this paper, we assume we are using the definition of working MOG. In this case, one way to compute MOG is

$$\text{MOG} = \frac{\text{limiting ground time}}{\text{flow interval}}, \tag{11}$$

where the limiting ground time is the longest planned stop in the cycle. Typically, the limiting ground time will be defined by ground events required at the on-load location. Limiting ground time presumes a continuous flow of aircraft without pronounced delays for aircraft breaks, non-scheduled maintenance, or ground delays due to other factors (crews, air traffic, weather, etc.).

As mentioned above, we can compute the flow interval needed to meet a specified closure time. In turn, this can be used to compute the number of required aircraft (assuming this is the limiting interval) to meet this closure requirement. In this case, the required aircraft is computed as

$$\text{required aircraft} = \frac{\text{cycle time}}{\text{flow interval}}. \tag{12}$$

Using our example numbers, if we desire to reduce the closure time from 4.583 days to four days, the required flow interval (or the aircraft allocation interval) would need to be 1.714 hours. In turn, the required aircraft would need to be increased from 10 to 11.67 (rounded to 12).

Next, we compute another common mobility metric tons per day delivered from the origin to the destination. Tons per day, most often reported in short tons (i.e., 2,000 pounds) per day or STons/D is computed as

$$\text{tons per day} = \frac{\text{average payload} \times 24 \times \text{required aircraft}}{\text{cycle time}} \ [\text{STons/D}]. \tag{13}$$

Again, back to our example numbers, using a C-5 average payload of 61.3 STons, 12 required aircraft, and a cycle time of 20 hours, we would estimate that approximately 882.7 STons/D could be delivered.

If our flow should happen to be constrained by available rested crews, we can compute the number of stage crews needed at each airfield as follows

$$\text{number of stage crews needed} = \frac{\text{crew rest time} - \text{aircraft ground time}}{\text{flow interval}}. \tag{14}$$

Note that the number of stage crews does not need to be any greater than that necessary to have the stage crew interval equal to the aircraft allocation interval since there would not be enough aircraft for them to fly in this case.

We can estimate the total crews required for a proposed air mobility operation as

$$\begin{aligned}\text{total crews required} &= (\text{number of stage crews needed}) \\ &\quad \times (\text{stages in cycle}) + \text{required aircraft}.\end{aligned} \tag{15}$$

We can estimate the crew ratio required (i.e., the ratio of crews to aircraft) for a given operation as

$$\text{crew ratio required} = \frac{\text{total crews required}}{\text{crew availability} \times \text{required aircraft}}, \tag{16}$$

where crew availability is a percentage of crews who remain available to fly after discounting those unavailable due to various circumstances (e.g., crews are on leave, unqualified status, etc.). Normally, this number is between 0.86 and 0.92[1]. In more general terms, Air Mobility Command defines the crew ratio for a particular aircraft fleet as the total number of aircraft crews for that aircraft type divided by the total number of aircraft available for mission operations. The full computation of crew ratio for Air Mobility Command is beyond the scope of this paper, but involves the inclusion of guard and reserve call-up schedules, crew augmentation levels, crew duty

[1] Crew availability estimates based on 1994 survey polling of all Air Mobility Airlift Wings for a consecutive 30-day period of operations. Each unit monitored the categories of normal leave, emergency leave, nonflying temporary duty, school attendance, duty not including flying, illness, staff responsibilities, mission and aircraft qualification levels, fenced training, and disciplinary grounding factors to establish crew availability statistics.

day limitations, 30-day and 90-day flying hour limits and waivers, and scenario stage/recovery policies[2].

We now return to a more in-depth discussion on aircraft utilization or ute rate. The ute rate of an aircraft fleet is computed as

$$\text{ute rate} = \frac{\text{RTFT} \times 24}{\text{flow interval} \times \text{allocated aircraft}} \text{ [hrs/day]}. \tag{17}$$

For a round trip flying time of 12 hours, a flow interval of two hours, and ten allocated aircraft, we would expect an average utilization rate for an aircraft to be 14.4 hours. We note that the ute rate provided by equation (17) should be used if the objective ute rate in equation (8c) was not the limiting constraint on flow interval. In this case, this ute rate will be less than the objective ute rate. Another commonly used expression for the maximum theoretical ute rate is (RTFT × 24)/cycle time. This ute rate is appropriate if the aircraft allocation interval in equation (8b) is the limiting constraint on flow.

Assuming allocated aircraft ≥ required aircraft, we compute the average aircraft on station (i.e., on the ground) at an airfield by the following expression:

$$\text{average aircraft on station} = \frac{\text{required aircraft} \times \text{aircraft ground time}}{\text{cycle time}}. \tag{18}$$

For ten allocated aircraft, an aircraft ground time of 3.25 hours, and a cycle time of 20 hours, an airfield would have an average of 1.625 aircraft on the ground at any given time.

Another useful metric is the aircraft productivity factor. Productivity factor is computed as

$$\text{productivity factor} = \frac{\text{one way en route flying time}}{\text{RTFT} + \text{origin to on-load flying time}}, \tag{19}$$

where the one way en route flying time is the flying time only from the on-load to the off-load destination and the origin to on-load flying time is the flying time from the aircraft's origin (home station) to the on-load airfield. Based on this, the productivity factor is less than or equal to 0.5, meaning that a strategic airlift aircraft is often flying back to the on-load airfield without a payload.

With this, we can now compute a common metric used throughout the transportation industry—that is, million ton miles per day (MTM/D) . For an airlift operation, million ton miles per day is computed as

$$\begin{aligned}\text{million ton miles per day} &= \text{average block speed} \times \text{ute rate} \times \text{productivity factor} \\ &\times \text{average payload} \times \text{allocated aircraft}/1,000,000 \text{ [MTMs/D]}.\end{aligned} \tag{20}$$

When computing the MTM/D capability of an entire fleet of a certain aircraft type, instead of using the formula for ute rate provided earlier by equation (17), the objective ute rate is used and PMAI (described below) is used in place of allocated aircraft. To determine the objective ute rate, we need first need to compute the scenario use rate as

$$\text{scenario use rate} = \frac{\text{scenario flying time} \times 24}{\text{scenario flying time} + \text{TGT}} \text{ [hrs/day]}, \tag{21}$$

where scenario flying time is the same as RTFT given by equation (4). The objective ute rate is then computed as follows:

$$\begin{aligned}&\text{objective ute rate} \\ &= \frac{(\text{PMAI} \times \text{MC rate} - \text{JCS withholds}) \times \text{scenario use rate} + (\text{JCS withholds} \times 4)}{\text{PMAI}} \text{ [hrs/day]},\end{aligned} \tag{22}$$

[2]Air Mobility Command crew ratio calculation method used by the AMC Studies and Analysis Division (AMC/A59). Contact coauthor D. Merrill for literature relating to crew ratio computations and models used to facilitate crew planning at Air Mobility Command.

where (PMAI is short for primary mission aerospace vehicle inventory) is a measure of how many aircraft of a certain type are authorized for conducting mission operations, MC rate is given below, and JCS withholds are determined from the scenario specific operations documents (JCS withholds represent the number of aircraft that must be set aside from the PMAI number for other possible uses). A useful formula for PMAI is

$$\text{PMAI} = \text{TAI} - \text{BAI} - \text{TF}, \tag{23}$$

where TAI (short for total active inventory) is the total number of aircraft of a certain type owned by the Air Force, BAI (short for backup aerospace vehicle inventory) is the number of aircraft that are planned for depot maintenance, and TF (short for training force) is the number of aircraft possessed by the Air Education and Training Command (AETC) that are used for training aircrews [4]. As an example, the Air Force currently owns 126 C-5 Galaxy aircraft (TAI = 126). Of these, 16 are routinely programmed for depot maintenance (BAI = 16) and six are used for training (TF = 6). Therefore, PMAI = 126 − 16 − 6 = 104, meaning that 104 C-5s are authorized for mission operations (but they are all not necessarily operational because of reliability issues which we discuss next).

For a given aircraft type, the logistics mission capable rate, MC rate, is computed by

$$\text{MC rate} = \frac{\text{possessed hours} - \text{NMC hours}}{\text{possessed hours}}, \tag{24}$$

where possessed hours is the total number of hours aircraft were in PMAI status (which is equivalent to the total number of hours aircraft were not in BAI or TF status) and NMC hours is the total number of not mission capable (i.e., a disabled or broken aircraft) hours. That is,

$$\text{NMC hours} = \text{possessed hours} - \text{FMC hours} + \text{PMC hours}, \tag{25}$$

where FMC hours is the total number of fully mission capable (i.e., an aircraft has no maintenance deficiencies which prevent it from flying all of its intended missions) hours and PMC hours is the total number of partially mission capable (i.e., an aircraft has some maintenance deficiencies, but it can still fly some subset of intended missions) [5].

The U.S. Air Force's Air Mobility Command Directorate of Logistics (AMC/LG) routinely tracks and reports MC rate for all of the AMC aircraft types. With these data and the subsequent computation of objective use rate, the metric million ton miles per day can be computed for different strategic airlift fleets. As noted in the introduction, the total MTM/D capability of combined fleets is obtained by simple summation of the individual contributions of the different aircraft types.

There will always be a difference between what Air Mobility Command programs to achieve and actual performance. Typically, any given air mobility fleet of aircraft is annually under-funded in crews, spares, maintenance manpower, and support resources like material handling equipment. As a result, actual MC rates and subsequent dependent ute rates will seldom match those used for planning purposes. The programmed MC rates for each weapon system are goals published in operational requirements documents (ORDs) that reflect the objective values the Air Force hopes to achieve based on current technologies and expected performance when fully funded and resourced. To highlight the distinction, the following table provides an example of programmed MC rates versus actual recent performance for some selected strategic airlift aircraft [6].

Table 1. Programmed and actual MC rates.

Weapon System	Programmed MC Rate	Actual MC rate
C-17	90.0 %	85.1 %
C-5	75.0 %	68.9 %
KC-10	93.0 %	80.9 %

3. CONCLUSIONS

This paper describes fundamental algebraic relationships that characterize the movement of cargo and passengers by strategic airlift aircraft. With these relationships and appropriate input planning factors, one can compute a variety of important force closure metrics that are vital to assess the transportation feasibility of proposed peacetime operations, war plans, and other concepts of operation. Indeed, these relationships are often the basis for conducting quick look assessments as requested by commander's considering potential operations, conducting what-if future program analyses, and modeling that incorporates deterministic and/or stochastic discrete event simulation. Ultimately, these relationships underpin approved U.S. war plans and defense procurement decisions for billions of dollars worth of strategic airlift resources.

With this said, a closing point is needed to underscore the real world complexities of the global air mobility system. The assumed simple strategic airlift cycles behind this airlift algebra imply perfect scheduling, an assumption that is difficult to achieve in the real world. A myriad of factors and uncontrollable variables within the global air mobility "system-of-systems" cause friction and related constraints on actual throughput and closure metrics. Therefore, one should recognize that the results of the algebra presented herein might tend to overestimate true mobility capability. For this reason, algebra alone is seldom used in major mobility studies. Rather, as alluded to above, transportation analyst will also make use of simulation models that incorporate the algebraic relationships presented in this paper, but as impacted by random events such as broken aircraft, competition for limited resources such as fuel, material handling equipment, or personnel, adverse weather conditions, and the like. Indeed, these are just a few of the reasons for the development of the various transportation models that are discussed in this special issue.

REFERENCES

1. Mobility Requirements Study 2005, Office of the Secretary of Defense, Program Analysis and Evaluation, OSD(PA&E), (2000).
2. USTRANSCOM Handbook 24-2, *Understanding the Defense Transportation System*, United States Transportation Command, (2000).
3. Air Force Pamphlet 10-1403, *Air Mobility Planning Factors*, U.S. Air Force (1998)..
4. Air Force Instruction 16-402, *Aerospace Vehicle Programming, Assignment, Distribution, Accounting, and Termination*, U.S. Air Force (1997).
5. AMC Instruction 21-101, Air Mobility Command Supplement 1, *Aerospace Equipment Maintenance Management*, U.S. Air Force (2003).
6. Health of the Force Rates: March 2002–February 2003, HQ AMC/LGXI, `https://amclg.scott.af.mil/hof/docs/hofrates.pdf`, (March 12, 2003).

Available online at www.sciencedirect.com
SCIENCE DIRECT
Mathematical and Computer Modelling 39 (2004) 657–675
MATHEMATICAL AND COMPUTER MODELLING
www.elsevier.com/locate/mcm

Using Low-Dimensional Patterns in Optimizing Simulators: An Illustration for the Military Airlift Problem

W. B. POWELL, TONGQIANG TONY WU AND H. P. SIMAO
Department of Operations Research and Financial Engineering
Princeton University, Princeton, NJ 08544, U.S.A.

A. WHISMAN
Air Mobility Command
Scott Air Force Base, IL 62225-5307, U.S.A.

Abstract—Optimization models are sometimes promoted because they provide "optimal" solutions as defined by a cost model. Simulation models, by contrast, are guided by rules that are specified by experts in operations. While these may seem heuristic in nature, they often reflect issues that are difficult to capture in a cost-based objective function. "Optimizing simulators" combine the intelligence of optimization with the flexibility of simulation in the handling of system dynamics, but still suffer from the limitation that the behavior is entirely determined by a cost model. In this paper, we show how a cost-based model can be guided through a set of low-dimensional patterns which are essentially simple rules determined by a domain expert. Patterns are incorporated through a penalty term, scaled by a coefficient that controls that tradeoff between minimizing costs and minimizing the difference between model behavior and the exogenous patterns.

Keywords—Military airlift, Optimizing simulator, Pattern matching, Proximal point algorithm.

The analysis group at the Air Mobility Command has long used simulation to assist with the analysis of different operational scenarios to determine the effects of changes in airbases, the size and mix of the fleet and a variety of operational policies. The most significant effort has evolved around MASS (and its replacement, AMOS), which captures a wide range of operational issues. MASS simulates the flows of cargo aircraft moving a set of requirements (loads of freight and passengers) that are designed to meet a particular scenario. The requirements are characterized by an origin, destination, weight, time of availability and other descriptors that capture the nature of what is being moved (passengers or freight, and a measure of how much freight is oversized, requiring the largest cargo aircraft). The requirements are specified in a "time-phased force deployment dataset" or TPFDD, which is prepared by analysis groups familiar with the needs of a scenario.

As an analysis methodology, MASS/AMOS offers the flexibility to incorporate the complex dynamics of these systems and the ability to explicitly control the behavior of the system through

This research was supported in part by Grant AFOSR-F49620-93-1-0098 from the Air Force Office of Scientific Research.
We also appreciate the detailed comments of a conscientious reviewer.

0895-7177/04/$ - see front matter Typeset by $\mathcal{A}_{\mathcal{M}}\mathcal{S}$-TEX
doi:10.1016/j.mcm.2004.02.007

the specification of the rules used to manage the aircraft. At the same time, these models struggle with the challenge of juggling multiple aircraft; instead, they resort to simple rules to reduce the dimensionality of the problem. Simulation has been criticized by optimization specialists in the academic community because the behavior is not "optimal", but also by the practitioner community for the noise inherent in the behavior of even deterministic simulations, which complicates the analysis of small changes in rules and inputs.

A development effort focusing on the use of optimization models to model the airlift flow problem has paralleled the development of simulation models. The military airlift model (MOM), described in [1], is one of the earliest published efforts focusing on the airlift problem. Reference [2] compares several optimization formulations of the airlift problem. Thruput, developed by Yost [3], captures the specifics of airlift operations in a static model. Thruput II extended this model to a dynamic formulation, described in [4]. A similar model was developed at Rand called CONOP (concept of operations) which contained several important features. For this reason, the Naval Postgraduate School and the Rand Corporation merged the two models into NRMO (NPS/Rand mobility optimizer). The most comprehensive model to date in this line of research is described in [5]. Optimization offers the theoretical appeal of providing "optimal" solutions. Also, small changes in the input data tend to produce small, and reasonable, changes in the objective function. For example, if aircraft are added to an optimization model that minimizes total delay, adding an aircraft will result in a reduction in total delay (or at least, it will not increase). This is not guaranteed by simulation models.

Optimization, however, suffers from some significant limitations. Perhaps the most apparent is the difficulty in modeling complex operational problems in a realistic way. Optimization algorithms require that the dynamics of the system be expressed in the form of systems of linear equations. The inability to incorporate uncertainty is also an issue, complicating, for example, the modeling of aircraft failures and their effect on airbase capacity. More problematic is the difficulty in modeling the evolution of the system over time. For example, the capacity of an airbase may depend on the detailed modeling of how aircraft on the ground are parked, maintained, refueled, loaded, and unloaded.

We have overcome some of the limitations of simulation by using the concept of an *optimizing simulator*. This technology is a form of intelligent simulation. Instead of using one large math program (as would be used in a pure optimization approach), we solve sequences of smaller math programs in an iterative fashion. We step through time just as any (discrete time) simulator would do, allowing us to apply classical simulation strategies to capture complex system dynamics. However, we solve sequences of small optimization problems (covering one time period at a time) just as an optimization model would. As a result, the behavior of our system is guided by a cost function rather than rules, which govern the dynamics of many simulation models.

Our use of sequences of optimization problems exposes us to an often overlooked weakness of all optimization models. It is often the case that we assume that the solution of an optimization model is "optimal" because it has provided the lowest possible costs. In fact, the true quality of our solution depends on the cost function, which is typically a mixture of hard and soft costs. We may, for example, have a hard estimate of the cost of flying an aircraft for one hour, but we struggle with the "cost" of landing a military aircraft at an unfriendly airbase, or one which has limited maintenance abilities, or which does not have a reliable supply of fuel. People in operations may "prefer" to use certain routes due to potential weather problems or problems with flying over or around nations which are not comfortable with U.S. military overflights.

The modeling of complex operational problems face a host of such soft issues which may be difficult to quantify. Optimization models handle these by introducing soft penalties (costs for penalizing activities which we allow, but do not like) and bonuses (for activities we want to encourage). But it is often the case that the resulting model produces behaviors that a knowledgeable expert "does not like". This problem does not arise in settings such as a research environment, but it is a major issue in a setting where an expert can analyze and criticize the results.

Simulators avoid the need to use soft costs because decisions are made through a set of rules. The value of rule-based logic is that the analyst has direct control over the behavior of the system. If the model makes decisions that the analyst does not like, he has only to change the rules. An optimization modeler, on the other hand, has to adjust the costs, rerun the model, and hope that the change produces the desired results. Practitioners who have experienced the challenge of actually implementing a model are well familiar with this problem.

Simulation practitioners, especially those working in the area of transportation and logistics, also struggle with the limitation of rule-based systems. The biggest challenge is juggling multiple resources. For example, we may need to find an aircraft to move a requirement from New Jersey to Europe. The closest available aircraft may be in Ohio, but that aircraft is better suited for another requirement also leaving from Ohio. Trading off the competing demands on resources, especially when those demands arise over time, can be especially difficult in a simulator (but quite easy for an optimization model).

In this paper, we build on the work of Marar and Powell [6] to propose a merger of the strengths of simulation and optimization. We retain what is fundamentally an optimization-based framework, which is to say that we will be minimizing costs. But we will allow the user to express desirable rules that communicate what an expert feels are desirable behaviors. For computational reasons, these rules are restricted to be of a relatively simple form which consist only of the attributes of the decision of a particular type of resource, and the decision being applied to the resource. In practice, the rules are aggregations of the attribute/decision pair, and hence, we refer to these as low-dimensional patterns. For example, a cost model might assign a C-17 in England to a requirement that requires landing in Saudi Arabia. But the base in Saudi Arabia may not have proper maintenance facilities to handle a C-17 failure. The proper answer of an optimization expert is that the cost of such a breakdown has to be added to flows of C-17s going into Saudi Arabia, but estimating these costs can be very time consuming. In addition, we are generally not aware of these issues until the simulation is up and running, with results being examined by a knowledgeable expert. At this point, it becomes important to get the model to "behave properly" as quickly as possible. It is useful to be able to simply state (through a data file): "avoid sending C-17s into Saudi Arabia". This rule is purely a function of the aircraft being affected. We would not be able to handle a rule of the form "do not send a C-17 to Saudi Arabia if there is already another C-17 located there" since this reflects the status of two different aircraft. We also note that our policy of avoiding C-17s in Saudi Arabia is a function of a subset of all the attributes of this aircraft. If there is more than one air base in Saudi Arabia, then the pattern is also an aggregation on the decision itself.

We allow the user to guide the behavior of the model by creating files which capture these low-dimensional patterns. These are then incorporated into the objective using a penalty function known as a proximal point term, which penalizes deviations from these user specified patterns. By restricting our rules to low-dimensional patterns, we ensure that the rules are relatively simple, which also implies that there will not be too many of them. As a byproduct, the rules will not be detailed enough to guide the simulator in a realistic way. For this, we depend on the fact that the optimization model can specify a complete set of behaviors. However, it is our presumption that if we depended solely on the cost model, we would ignore important issues that are otherwise hard to quantify.

The paper is organized as follows. Section 1 gives an overview of the basic principles of an optimizing simulator. Section 2 introduces the concept of low-dimensional patterns and illustrates their role in the military airlift problem. Section 3 extends this concept by introducing the powerful concept of hierarchical patterns, which allows patterns to be described at different levels of aggregation. Then, Section 4 presents an algorithm for incorporating static patterns (patterns that are not indexed by time) into a dynamic model, where the challenge is to solve the model in a time-staged manner and obtain a solution that reasonably matches a set of patterns. Finally, Section 5 illustrates the technique in the context of the military airlift problem.

1. THE OPTIMIZING SIMULATOR CONCEPT

Central to our presentation is the use of a concept we call an "optimizing simulator". This approach to modeling combines concepts from simulation, which involves stepping through time solving sequences of decision problems, with optimization, which requires the use of a cost-based objective function to guide model behavior. Of particular importance is our representation of the flows of "resources". The model might assign a particular C-17 to a particular airbase in Saudi Arabia, whereas a pattern might indicate that C-17s should not be used in the Middle East. Patterns are typically specified at a more aggregate level than how they are modeled, and we have to be able to work with different levels of aggregation at the same time.

It is useful to start with a classical linear programming formulation of our problem, which might look like (in matrix form)

$$\min_{x \in \mathcal{X}} \sum_{t \in \mathcal{T}} c_t(x_t) \tag{1}$$

$$\text{subject to: } A_t x_t - B_{t-1} x_{t-1} = \hat{R}_t, \tag{2}$$

$$D_t x_t \le u_t, \tag{3}$$

$$x_t \ge 0. \tag{4}$$

In this formulation, matrices A_t and B_t capture the interaction of the system between time periods, D_t represents coupling constraints (which would be needed to represent the limit on the number of aircraft needed to move a requirement), u_t is the upper bound on flows (which could be the size of a requirement, or limits on flows through airbases), and $\hat{R}_t$ models the arrival of new resources to be managed. x_t is the decision vector (which may be continuous, discrete or mixed), and $c_t(x_t)$ is a one period cost function to be minimized. $\mathcal{T} = \{0, 1, \ldots, T-1\}$ is the set of discrete time points over which our system is defined.

Our interest is in problems that exhibit a natural state variable. For this purpose, replace equation (2) with the equations

$$A_t x_t - R_t = \hat{R}_t, \tag{5}$$

$$R_t - B_{t-1} x_{t-1} = 0, \tag{6}$$

R_t plays the role of a "resource" state variable, where we model both aircraft and the requirements as "resources" (think of these as objects being managed). Our modeling of resources is critical to our ability to represent patterns. We first note that in any operational problem there are different classes of resources. In our modeling paradigm (based on [7]), a resource class is any object that constrains the system. In a basic model of the airlift flow problem, there would be two classes: the aircraft, and the requirements representing the freight and passengers that have to be moved. Thus, we would represent our resource classes using

$\mathcal{C}^R$ = set of resource classes
= (aircraft, requirements).

A resource in class $c \in \mathcal{C}^R$ is characterized by a vector of attributes. These are modeled using

a = the attribute vector of a resource being managed;
$\mathcal{A}^c$ = the space of possible resource attribute vectors for a resource in class $c \in \mathcal{C}^R$;
R^c_{ta} = the number of resources with attribute $a \in \mathcal{A}^c$ at time t, before new arrivals have been added to the system (that is, R^c_{ta} excludes arrivals in time period t);
$R^c_t = (R^c_{ta})_{a \in \mathcal{A}^c}$.

For notational compactness, we suppress the reference to the resource class unless we need it explicitly. The arrival of new resources (these can be aircraft or requirements) are modeled using

$\hat{R}_{ta}$ = the number of new arrivals in time period t, which we assume can be acted on in time period t;

$\hat{R}_t = (\hat{R}_{ta})_{a \in \mathcal{A}}$.

We act on resources using decisions. There may be different classes of decisions, which we denote using

$\mathcal{C}^D$ = the set of decision classes.

Examples of decision classes are: pick up a requirement, move (with or without a requirement), be refueled, be repaired. Each decision class will typically consist of a set of elements, so we denote

$\mathcal{D}^c$ = the set of decisions within class $c \in \mathcal{C}^D$.

For the military airlift problem, the decision classes would be

$\mathcal{D}^R$ = the decisions to pick up a requirement, each element of $\mathcal{D}^R$ is a particular requirement;

$\mathcal{D}^M$ = the decision to move an aircraft, where each element of $\mathcal{D}^M$ would be an airbase we can move to, the aircraft may be loaded or empty (being loaded simply changes the attributes of the aircraft being moved);

$\mathcal{D}^F$ = the decision to refuel an aircraft (typically an on-ground activity, but this could represent the decision to move to a mid-air refueling point);

$\mathcal{D}^P$ = the decision to repair an aircraft, there might be different degrees of "repair" which would make up the elements of $\mathcal{D}^P$.

We generally model a special decision, denoted d^ϕ, which represents the decision to "do nothing". Doing nothing depends on the state of the attribute. An on-ground aircraft would simply sit, while a flying aircraft (if we choose to model the state of the aircraft in the air) would simply continue flying. If an aircraft has just unloaded at a distant location, the "do nothing" decision might be modeled as the decision to return to a particular airbase (when there are effectively no other options).

We let

$$\mathcal{D} = \mathcal{D}^R \cup \mathcal{D}^M \cup \mathcal{D}^F \cup \mathcal{D}^P \cup d^\phi$$

be the set of all possible types of decisions (where again we have dropped the reference to the resource class for compactness). This set is typically modeled as being dependent on the attributes of the resource to which the decisions are being applied. For this purpose, we often write

$\mathcal{D}_a$ = the set of decisions for a resource with attribute a.

The set $\mathcal{D}_a$ represents the *types* of decisions we can make. We next define the decisions that we actually make using

x_{tad} = the number of resources with attribute a to which we apply decision d at time t;

$x_t = (x_{tad})_{d \in \mathcal{D}_a a \in \mathcal{A}}$.

We let $\mathcal{X}_t$ be the feasible region for x_t, where the constraints typically consist of flow conservation, and upper bounds on flows that capture airbase capacity due to storage, maintenance, refueling, loading, and unloading. Flow conservation implies that the vector of flows must satisfy

$$\sum_{d \in \mathcal{D}_a} x_{tad} = R_{ta} + \hat{R}_{ta}. \tag{7}$$

To develop an objective function, we then define

c_{tad} = the cost of assigning decision d to resources with attribute a at time t;
$c_t = (c_{tad})_{d \in \mathcal{D}_a, a \in \mathcal{A}}$.

We assume a linear cost function, which allows us to write

$C_t(x_t)$ = the total cost of decision vector x_t at time t;
$= c_t x_t$.

We next face the challenge of determining how to make the decision x_t. We represent this problem through a decision function

X_t^π = the decision function, which produces a vector of decisions x_t at time t;
Π = the family of functions (or *policies*) for making decisions, where $X_t^\pi, \pi \in \Pi$ is a member of this family.

There are two major classes of decision functions: rule-based and cost-based. Rule-based functions are almost always based purely on the resource vector R_t, a class that we refer to as myopic policies. Cost-based functions can be further divided into subclasses based on the information available to the decision function. We can generally represent a cost-based decision function using

$$X_t^\pi = \arg\min_{x \in \mathcal{X}_t} C_t^\pi(x),$$

where $C_t^\pi(x)$ is any approximate cost function for time period t. Since an approximate cost function determines a policy, we index the approximate cost functions by $\pi \in \Pi$.

To properly specify a policy, we have to clearly define the information that is available when a decision is made. Although the airlift flow problem is typically modeled using a deterministic dataset, the simulation assumes that we do not know anything about a new requirement until the time it has to depart. For our purposes, we will assume that the only new information is in the form of new "resources" (which may be new aircraft entering the system or new requirements becoming available). Other forms of information might be updates in travel times due to weather conditions or delays through airbases due to equipment failures.

For our purposes, there are three important classes of cost-based decision functions that have been used. These are defined by

Π^M = the class of myopic policies, which do not use any information from the future;
Π^{RH} = the class of rolling horizon policies, which combine what we know at time t with forecasts of future activities (in practice, these are typically *point forecasts*);
Π^{DP} = the class of policies based on dynamic programming, which use a forecast of the value of putting the system in a particular state in the future.

Myopic policies can be represented simply using:

$$X_t^\pi = \arg\min_{x_t \in \mathcal{X}_t} c_t x_t.$$

There are three interesting classes of myopic policy, which we depict graphically in Figure 1. The first is one that uses a rule to pick a single requirement (for example, the first one that needs to be moved) and then uses a different rule to pick a particular aircraft, and then tests the feasibility of the assignment (by simulating the route and making sure there is sufficient capacity at the intermediate airbases to handle the assignment). This is roughly what is being coded into the new AMOS simulator which replaces the older MASS simulator. A more sophisticated policy would choose a single requirement, and then enumerate a list of eligible aircraft and choose the "best" one based on minimizing some cost criterion. This is trivial from an algorithmic perspective, but requires the major transition from a rule-based decision function to a cost-based one. Such a step introduces two complications: first is the design of a cost function, and second is the need to enumerate a set of options and evaluate all of them. The current AMOS (or MASS) simulator requires running a simulation of a flight in order to check the feasibility of assigning an aircraft to a requirement. Repeating this exercise over a set of aircraft would be computationally demanding, and strategies would need to be devised to manage this efficiently (we could, for example, use an optimistic approximation that assumes that there is no congestion, and then check the feasibility of the optimal route from this assignment).

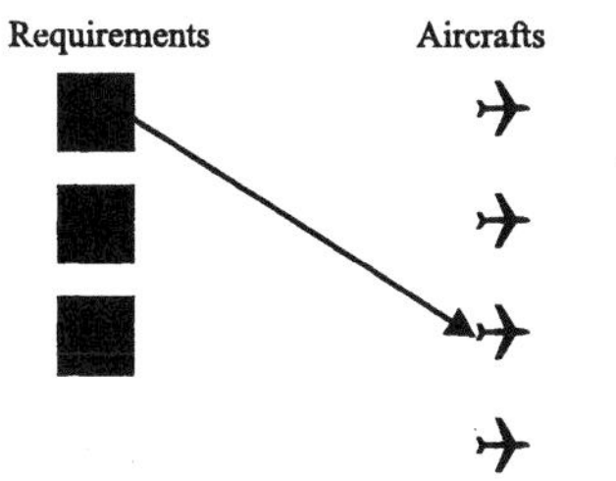

(a) Myopic Policy 1. Illustrates a rule which picks one aircraft and one requirement.

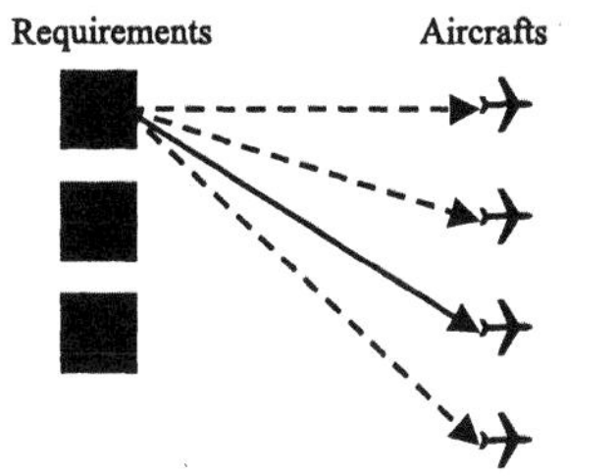

(b) Myopic Policy 2. Illustrates picking one requirement and selecting the best aircraft from a set.

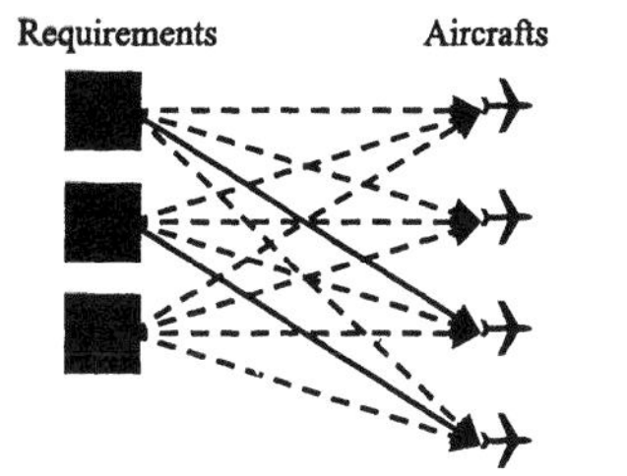

(c) Myopic Policy 3. Illustrates choosing the best assignment of aircraft and requirements from sets of each.

Figure 1. Rule-based and myopic cost-based policies

A third myopic policy would enumerate a set of aircraft and a set of requirements, and consider all possible combinations using an optimization algorithm (the resulting problem is a relatively small network problem). Such a model absolutely requires the development of a fast cost approximation for each possible assignment.

Rolling horizon policies use forecasts of activities at time $t' > t$, using information available at time t. For such models, we let

$x_{tt'}$ = flows that are assigned in time period t to be implemented at time period $t' \geq t$, flows where $t' > t$ are referred to as *plans* and would not be implemented;

$c_{tt'}$ = the cost of executing decision $x_{tt'}$ using the information we have at time t.

As an illustration, we may wish to assign an aircraft to a route where we have an estimate of the flying time at the time the aircraft actually departs. We may then wish to simulate a weather problem that arises en route, which may produce a delay in the flight. This is a case where $c_{t't'}$ would be higher than $c_{tt'}$ for $t < t'$.

Rolling horizon procedures can be represented compactly using formulations of the form

$$X_t^\pi = \arg \min_{x_t \in \mathcal{X}_t} \sum_{t' \geq t} c_{tt'} x_{tt'},$$

where $x_t \in \mathcal{X}_t$ means $x_{tt'} \in \mathcal{X}_{tt'}$. We would say that $x_{tt'}$ is the vector of decisions made in time period t to be implemented at time t'. Decisions $x_{tt'}$ where $t' > t$ represent *plans* which may be changed in future time periods.

Finally, we may use policies based on the dynamic programming principle of optimality. Following methods outlined in [8,9], we can make decisions by solving problems of the general form

$$X_t^{\pi}\left(R_t+\hat{R}_t\right)=\arg\min_{x_t\in\mathcal{X}_t} c_t x_t+\hat{V}_{t+1}^{\pi}\left(R_{t+1}\left(x_t\right)\right), \tag{8}$$

where $\hat{V}_{t+1}^{\pi}(R_{t+1}(x_t))$ is a conveniently chosen approximation that approximates the value of making a decision x_t that puts the system in state $R_{t+1}(x_t)$ in the future. For example, we may use a linear approximation of the form

$$\hat{V}_{t+1}^{\pi}\left(R_{t+1}\left(x_t\right)\right)=\sum_{a\in\mathcal{A}}\hat{v}_{t+1,a}R_{t+1,a}\left(x_t\right). \tag{9}$$

Another class is separable nonlinear (typically piecewise linear) functions of the form

$$\hat{V}_{t+1}^{\pi}\left(R_{t+1}\left(x_t\right)\right)=\sum_{a\in\mathcal{A}}\hat{V}_{t+1,a}\left(R_{t+1,a}\left(x_t\right)\right).$$

The policies in the set Π^{DP} would represent different types of approximations for $\hat{V}_{t+1}^{\pi}(R_{t+1}(x_t))$.

Godfrey and Powell [8] and Powell and Topaloglu [9] have shown that piecewise linear, separable approximations can produce near optimal solutions for deterministic problems, with solutions that are significantly better than myopic or rolling horizon solutions for stochastic problems. Spivey and Powell [10] show that linear approximations can work very well in the context of dynamic assignment problems which involve assigning resources to tasks over time.

The important point here is that policies that are based on stepping through time, using only information available at that time, can produce very high quality solutions that are competitive with commercial solvers on deterministic versions. The larger issue, which is the focus of this paper, is that these supposedly "optimal" solutions are only as good as the cost functions which are being used.

2. INCORPORATING EXPERT KNOWLEDGE THROUGH LOW-DIMENSIONAL PATTERNS

In practical applications, it is virtually always the case that an expert in the operational application disagrees with some (perhaps many) of the decisions made by the model. Sometimes we can claim that the model is smarter than the expert, but in the vast majority of instances with which we are familiar, the expert simply knows something about the problem that the modeler did not realize. It would be nice to say that we are going to take everything into account before we start the model, but this is both impractical and unrealistic. Models are built with a reasonable understanding of the problem, and invariably important issues are left out. As a result, a knowledgeable expert can look at the results and provide constructive, reasoned criticism of some of the decisions made by the model.

The response of optimization modelers is that they have to include these new issues by adjusting costs and modifying constraints. In the context of very complex operations such as military airlift, some factors can be especially difficult to quantify. For example, it may be hard, but not impossible, to repair certain aircraft types at some airbases. Working out the real cost of these repairs may be impractical. Instead, a user may be satisfied if the frequency of these aircraft at these airbases is sufficiently small (but not necessarily zero). It may be acceptable to use certain aircraft configurations to carry passengers, but the practice is discouraged because it requires making changes to the aircraft. In principle it is possible to work out these costs, but this can be very time consuming. The response more often is to simply add an artificial penalty, which the modeler then has to play with to obtain desired behaviors.

A major practical difficulty from a modeler's perspective is that the interaction with experts tends to come in the later stages of the development of a simulator, at a time when the model is nearing completion. There simply is not time to begin a significant engineering effort to estimate costs, especially when someone simply "knows" what the answer is supposed to look like.

Simulation models overcome this limitation by allowing the modeler to simply adjust the rules. There are two limitations inherent in this approach. First, rules in simulators tend to be hard. For example, it is easy to ensure that a C-17 is *never* assigned to an airbase that does not have the repair facilities. In practice, real operations may sometimes have to take undesirable steps. Cost models have an easier time putting penalties on undesirable activities to discourage, but not entirely prevent, actions which may incur high costs. It is for this reason that we refer to these guidelines as *patterns* rather than rules (which carry the connotation of being hard and fast).

The second limitation is that simulation models struggle with the high dimensionality of the problems that arise in transportation. For example, consider the problem of writing a rule to find the best assignment of three different aircraft to three different requirements. The number of combinations of even a small problem becomes quite large. It is not surprising, then, that airlift simulators work with one aircraft at a time (the original MASS simulator works with one aircraft at a time, trying to find a feasible requirement to move, while the new AMOS simulator works with one requirement at a time).

We have found that in practice, expert knowledge tends to arise in the form of very low-dimensional patterns. We have never encountered an instance where an expert has complained about how we juggled multiple resources. Instead, the complaints are more of the form "why did you make that type of decision with that type of resource". Such patterns can be expressed in terms of aggregated state/action pairs, where the state is limited to the attributes of a single resource. Since the attribute vector of a resource can become quite complex in real applications, aggregating on the attribute vector becomes very important.

Just as attribute vectors can be aggregated, decisions can be aggregated as well. A detailed decision would be to assign an aircraft to a *particular* requirement which might consist of the destination, total weight, number of passengers, amount of outsized cargo, and the time at which the cargo has to be delivered (in an actual operational problem, there may be even more attributes). However, an expert might say "try not to assign this type of aircraft to requirements with passengers" which would represent an aggregation not only on the attributes of the resource but also on the decision.

Needless to say, patterns come in different forms, each communicating a different issue. We might have patterns of the form "do not assign this type of aircraft to airbases in this region" (for maintenance reasons); "do not assign large aircraft to this route" (headwinds produce high fuel consumption); "do not assign aircraft in one location to requirements which have to be picked up in another location" (requires flying around restricted airspaces); "avoid assigning aircraft which are configured purely for freight to requirements which include passengers" (requires reconfiguring the aircraft for passengers).

To capture these patterns, we define

$\mathcal{P}$ = a collection of different patterns.

A pattern can always be expressed as an aggregation on an attribute or a decision. We represent these aggregation functions as

G_a^p = aggregation function for pattern $p \in \mathcal{P}$ that is applied to the attribute vector a;
G_d^p = aggregation function for pattern $p \in \mathcal{P}$ that is applied to the decision d.

The aggregation functions can be used to create aggregations of the attribute space $\mathcal{A}$ and the decision set $\mathcal{D}$. We let

$$\mathcal{A}^p = \{G_a^p(a) \mid a \in \mathcal{A}\},$$
$$\mathcal{D}_a^p = \{G_d^p(d) \mid d \in \mathcal{D}_a\}.$$

We refer to each class of aggregation as a *pattern* because each expresses a different behavior. A special case is when the patterns represent a hierarchical set of aggregations, which we discuss in Section 3.

Below, we use the notation $\bar{a}$ to refer to an aggregated attribute vector, since generally we do not need to specify the specific pattern. Similarly, a decision $\bar{d}$ is an aggregated decision. The combination $(\bar{a}, \bar{d})$ represents an aggregated state action pair, obtained using $(G^p_a(a), G^p_d(d))$ for pattern $p \in \mathcal{P}$. Our patterns are typically not hard rules, but are more of the flavor of "try to do something" or "try not to do something". We formalize this concept by specifying our patterns in the form of fractions

$\hat{\rho}^p_{\bar{a}\bar{d}}$ = the fraction of time that resources with attribute $G^p_a(a) = \bar{a}$ are acted on using decision $G^p_d(d) = \bar{d}$.

We assume that $\hat{\rho}^p_{\bar{a}\bar{d}} = 0$ means "never take this action" while $\hat{\rho}^p_{\bar{a}\bar{d}} = 1$ means "you must take this action". For patterns between zero and one, we want an algorithm that will produce the decision $\bar{d}$ a fraction $\hat{\rho}^p_{\bar{a}\bar{d}}$ of the time for resources with the aggregated attribute vector $\bar{a}$. It is unlikely that we can match a given pattern exactly (in fact, different pattern classes may conflict with each other), but it does provide a means for guiding the model.

To determine how well our current solution matches a pattern, we have to express our vector of flows x_t at an aggregated level. Let

$$\begin{aligned} \bar{x}^p_{t\bar{a}\bar{d}} &= G^p(x_t) \\ &= \sum_{\forall a \in \mathcal{A}} \sum_{\forall d \in \mathcal{D}_a} x_{tad} I_{\{G^p_a(a)=\bar{a}\}} I_{\{G^p_d(d)=\bar{d}\}}, \end{aligned} \tag{10}$$

where $I_X = 1$ if X is true. Since the vector of aggregated model flows $\bar{x}^p_t$ (where $\bar{x}^p_t = (\bar{x}^p_{t\bar{a}\bar{d}})_{\bar{a}\in\mathcal{A}^p, \bar{d}\in\mathcal{D}^p_{\bar{a}}}$) must satisfy flow conservation (equation (7)), we can also write the aggregated form of R_t using

$$\bar{R}^p_{t\bar{a}} = \sum_{\forall \bar{d} \in \mathcal{D}^p_{\bar{a}}} \bar{x}^p_{t\bar{a}\bar{d}}. \tag{11}$$

Furthermore, we can express model flow over the entire simulation horizon through the model flow fraction defined as

$$\bar{\rho}^p_{\bar{a}\bar{d}}(x_t) = \frac{\sum_{t'=1}^{t-1} \bar{x}^p_{t'\bar{a}\bar{d}} + \bar{x}^p_{t\bar{a}\bar{d}} + \sum_{t'=t+1}^{T} \bar{x}^p_{t'\bar{a}\bar{d}}}{\bar{R}^p_{\bar{a}}(x_t)}, \qquad \forall \bar{a} \in \mathcal{A}^p, \quad \forall \bar{d} \in \mathcal{D}^p_{\bar{a}}, \tag{12}$$

where

$$\bar{R}^p_{\bar{a}}(x_t) = \sum_{t'=1}^{t-1} \bar{R}^p_{t'\bar{a}} + \bar{R}^p_{t\bar{a}} + \sum_{t'=t+1}^{T} \bar{R}^p_{t'\bar{a}}. \tag{13}$$

If we wish our flows to follow the exogenous pattern $\hat{\rho}^p_{\bar{a}\bar{d}}$ then we would like the model flow fraction $\bar{\rho}^p_{\bar{a}\bar{d}}(x_t)$ to be as close as possible to $\hat{\rho}^p_{\bar{a}\bar{d}}$.

We incorporate patterns into our cost model using a *proximal point term* of the form

$$X^\pi_t = \arg\min_{x_t \in \mathcal{X}_t} c_t x_t + \sum_{p\in\mathcal{P}} \sum_{\bar{a}\in\mathcal{A}^p} \sum_{\bar{d}\in\mathcal{D}^p_{\bar{a}}} \theta^p_{\bar{a}\bar{d}} \bar{R}^p_{\bar{a}}(x_t) \left(\bar{\rho}^p_{\bar{a}\bar{d}}(x_t) - \hat{\rho}^p_{\bar{a}\bar{d}}\right)^2. \tag{14}$$

As $\theta^p_{\bar{a}\bar{d}}$ increases, the model is given a greater emphasis on trying to match its own flows $\bar{\rho}^p_{\bar{a}\bar{d}}(x_t)$ with the flows that would be predicted by the pattern, $\hat{\rho}^p_{\bar{a}\bar{d}}$. This leaves open the question of how $\theta^p_{\bar{a}\bar{d}}$ should be set. In practice, we are not going to get a perfect match between model flows and pattern flows. We might use a single parameter θ, instead of one that depends on each type of pattern and attribute-vector/decision combination, producing the model

$$X_t^\pi = \arg\min_{x_t \in \mathcal{X}_t} c_t x_t + \theta \sum_{p\in\mathcal{P}} \sum_{\bar{a}\in\mathcal{A}^p} \sum_{\bar{d}\in\mathcal{D}_{\bar{a}}^p} \bar{R}_{\bar{a}}^p(x_t) \left(\bar{\rho}_{\bar{a}\bar{d}}^p(x_t) - \hat{\rho}_{\bar{a}\bar{d}}^p\right)^2. \tag{15}$$

Now, we set θ so that it appears to be striking a good balance between our engineering cost function and our "expert". As θ is increased, the cost function will also increase as the model works to match the patterns. The tradeoff between minimizing our cost function (which we claim is inherently imperfect) and matching patterns (which themselves are imperfect because they do not capture all the information required to fully determine the behavior of the system) is inherently subjective.

3. HIERARCHICAL PATTERN REPRESENTATION

An important special case arises when the patterns constitute a hierarchical set of aggregations, with each pattern representing an aggregation of a lower level pattern. Hierarchical patterns arise when we wish to guide the model with a very specific behavior, but where we are also interested in guiding the model along more general statements of the same behavior. When we have hierarchical patterns we will observe the property that $a^{(p+1)} = G_a^{p+1}(a) \in \mathcal{A}^{p+1} \subset \mathcal{A}^p$.

To illustrate, assume that our attribute vector consists of the elements

$$a = (a_{\text{location}}, a_{\text{type}}, a_{\text{fuel}}, a_{\text{load\_weight}}, a_{\text{final\_dest}}, a_{\text{maintenance}}).$$

An elementary decision might be

$$d = (d_{\text{destination}}, d_{\text{requirement}}).$$

We might have a state/action pair (a, d) which consists of

$$\begin{aligned}(a,d) = \{a = (&a_{\text{location}} = \text{England}, a_{\text{type}} = \text{C-17}, a_{\text{fuel}} = 1200\,\text{lbs.}, a_{\text{load\_weight}} \\ &= 45,000\,\text{lbs}, a_{\text{final\_dest}} = \text{Seoul}, a_{\text{maintenance}} = \text{Status 4}), \\ d = (&d_{\text{destination}} = \text{Saudi Arabia}, d_{\text{requirement}} = \text{ORGDEST1234})\}.\end{aligned}$$

If a model implements (a, d), which is to say that it acts on an aircraft with the above attribute vector a using the above decision d, it is entirely possible that an expert will object on some basis. For example, the lack of appropriate maintenance facilities for C-17s in Saudi Arabia may make this an undesirable combination for loaded aircraft (since these presumably need to move in a timely manner). To express this behavior, we might use the aggregation

$$\begin{aligned}G^1(a,d) = \{a = (&a_{\text{location}} = \text{—}, a_{\text{type}} = \text{C-17}, a_{\text{fuel}} = \text{—}, a_{\text{load\_status}} \\ &= \text{loaded}, a_{\text{final\_dest}} = \text{Seoul}, a_{\text{maintenance}} = \text{—}), \\ d = (&d_{\text{destination}} = \text{Saudi Arabia}, d_{\text{requirement}} = \text{ORGDEST1234})\},\end{aligned}$$

where a_{location} = "—" represents an aggregation on the attribute "location".

Note that we have replaced $a_{\text{load\_weight}} = 45,000\,\text{lbs.}$ with the new attribute $a_{\text{load\_status}}$ = "loaded". Clearly $a_{\text{load\_status}}$ is an aggregation of $a_{\text{load\_weight}}$, but this sort of aggregation implies that $\mathcal{A}^{g+1}$ is not necessarily a subset of $\mathcal{A}^p$. Since it may be convenient to have the property $\mathcal{A}^{g+1} \subset \mathcal{A}^p$, we can handle aggregations such as $G^1(a_{\text{load\_weight}}) \to a_{\text{load\_status}}$ by appending the attribute $a_{\text{load\_status}}$ to the original attribute vector

$$\begin{aligned}(a,d) = \{a = (&a_{\text{location}} = \text{England}, a_{\text{type}} = \text{C-17}, a_{\text{fuel}} = 1200\,\text{lbs.}, a_{\text{load\_weight}} = 45{,}000\,\text{lbs.}, \\ &a_{\text{load\_status}} = \text{loaded}, a_{\text{final\_dest}} = \text{Seoul}, a_{\text{maintenance}} = \text{Status 4}), \\ d = (&d_{\text{destination}} = \text{Saudi Arabia}, d_{\text{requirement}} = \text{ORGDEST1234})\}.\end{aligned}$$

Then, we can write our aggregated attribute by simply aggregating over the attribute $a_{\text{load\_weight}}$. Using this construction, we may assume without loss of generality that $\mathcal{A}^{g+1} \subset \mathcal{A}^p$.

Continuing our example, our expert may say that while it is particularly bad to have a loaded C-17 come into Saudi Arabia, it is undesirable to have C-17s in general in Saudi Arabia (for the same reason). In fact, the problem may extend to the entire set of airbases in that region. We would express such a pattern using

$$G^2(a,d) = \{a = (a_{\text{location}} = \text{—}, a_{\text{type}} = \text{C-17}, a_{\text{fuel}} = \text{—}, a_{\text{load\_weight}} = \text{—}, a_{\text{load\_status}} = \text{—}, a_{\text{final\_dest}} = \text{—}, a_{\text{maintenance}} = \text{—}), d = (d_{\text{destination}} = \text{Middle East}, d_{\text{requirement}} = \text{—})\}.$$

$\hat{\rho}^p_{\bar{a}\bar{d}}$ gives the fraction of time that we would want to match the pattern $(\bar{a}, \bar{d})$ at aggregation level p. However, it is likely that the degree to which we would want to match a pattern $\hat{\rho}^p_{ad}$ would depend on the level of aggregation. More aggregate patterns can be viewed as more general statements of behavior, and we may be more willing to accept deviations than we would with a more detailed instruction. We can handle this by using a weight θ^p that depends only on the level of aggregation, producing a decision function of the form

$$X_t^\pi = \arg\min_{x_t \in \mathcal{X}_t} c_t x_t + \sum_{p \in \mathcal{P}} \theta^p \sum_{\bar{a} \in \mathcal{A}^p} \sum_{\bar{d} \in \mathcal{D}^p_{\bar{a}}} \bar{R}^p_{\bar{a}}(x_t) \left(\bar{\rho}^p_{\bar{a}\bar{d}}(x_t) - \hat{\rho}^p_{\bar{a}\bar{d}}\right)^2. \tag{16}$$

Just as θ in equation (15) might be a user specified parameter (the analyst can play with different settings to find what appears to be an appropriate balance), the same approach could be used with a pattern specific weight θ^p. We would expect that $\theta^0 > \theta^1 > \cdots$, and we might specify a simple relationship such as $\theta^{g+1} = \gamma\theta^p$, where $\gamma \leq 1$ indicates how much less important a more aggregate pattern is than a more detailed one. With such a structure, we only have to choose θ^0 and γ.

An attraction of low-dimensional patterns is that they are quite easy to express in a simple data layout. Table 1 illustrates a set of patterns for a three-dimensional resource attribute vector and a two-dimensional decision (the location the plane should go to, and the route it should follow getting there). The last column expresses the desired fraction of time that the pattern should be matched. Rows 1–4 are a hierarchical set of patterns, each representing an aggregation of the one before. Pattern 1 says that 30% of loaded C-17s in location L123 should be set to location M2345 using Route A. The second pattern states that 40% of all loaded C-17s should go to M2345, regardless of the origin location of the aircraft or the route chosen. The third pattern drops the attribute of being loaded, and the fourth pattern applies this pattern to all airbases in Region M. Pattern 5 says that all aircraft in location L123 should go to Region M regardless of the attributes of the aircraft.

Table 1. Patterns at different levels of aggregation.

Attribute Vector				Decision		Pattern Fraction
Pattern	Location	Type	Loaded/Empty	Destination	Route	
1	L123	C-17	loaded	M2345	A	0.30
2	—	C-17	loaded	M2345	—	0.40
3	—	C-17	—	M2345	—	0.50
4	—	C-17	—	M	—	0.35
5	L123	—	—	M	—	1.00

It is, of course, possible to specify patterns that are inconsistent. This does not actually create a problem, since we do not provide any guarantee that we will match a pattern (although the results may look somewhat odd). In actual applications, there will typically be different classes of patterns, where each may have its own hierarchical representation. For example, one class of patterns may be focused on maintenance issues, another will have more to do with aircraft size and the routes being used (because of wind problems), while a third will attempt to keep certain aircraft types moving certain types of requirements (such as those involving passengers).

4. AN ALGORITHM FOR PATTERNS

Our algorithm for incorporating patterns is based on the work of Marar and Powell [11]. The main challenge in matching a pattern is that we are solving a problem over time, but our patterns are expressed as averages over time. This means that in any one time period, we are not going to exactly match a pattern, but we would like to approximately match a pattern if we look at the activities over the entire simulation. Earlier, we had defined $\hat{\rho}^p_{\bar{a}\bar{d}}$ as the pattern, given the aggregation level $G^p = (G^p_a, G^p_d)$, which specifies the fraction of time that resources with attribute vector $G^p_a(a) = \bar{a}$ are acted on with decision $G^p_d(d) = \bar{d}$. We then have to compare this to the fraction of time that the model is making the same type of decision for the same type of resource. Throughout this section, we let $\bar{a}$ and $\bar{d}$ represent the attribute and decision at some level of aggregation (we suppress the p index and the *bars* from the flow variables for simplicity). Let $\rho_{\bar{a}\bar{d}}(x_t)$ be the *pattern flows* from the model, defined by equation (12), and $R_{\bar{a}}(x_t)$ be the total number of resources with attribute $\bar{a}$ over the entire horizon, given by equation (13). For notational simplicity, we assume that the pattern flows $R_{\bar{a}}(x_t)\hat{\rho}_{\bar{a}\bar{d}}$ and the model flows $x_{\bar{a}\bar{d}}$ are represented at the same level of aggregation.

We next define a *pattern metric* which gives the distance between the exogenous patterns and the model pattern flows

$$H(\rho(x_t), \hat{\rho}) = \sum_{\bar{a}\in\mathcal{A}^p} \sum_{\bar{d}\in\mathcal{D}^p_{\bar{a}}} R_{\bar{a}}(x_t)\left(\rho_{\bar{a}\bar{d}}(x_t) - \hat{\rho}_{\bar{a}\bar{d}}\right)^2. \tag{17}$$

We sometimes refer to $H(\rho(x_t), \hat{\rho})$ as the *happiness function* since the closer we match the user specified pattern, the "happier" he is.

Substituting our pattern metric into the modified objective function (15) gives us

$$x^*_t(\theta) = \arg\min_{x_t\in\mathcal{X}_t} c_t x_t + \theta H(\rho(x_t), \hat{\rho}).$$

We are generally unable to solve this problem, so we use instead sequences of approximations of the pattern metric, which for the moment we can write as

$$x^n_t(\theta) = \arg\min_{x_t\in\mathcal{X}_t} c_t x_t + \theta \hat{H}^{n-1}\left(\rho^{n-1}(x_t), \hat{\rho}\right).$$

The proximal term complicates our problem because it is defined in terms of totals over the entire horizon, and is also normally written at some level of aggregation. Instead of solving the original problem, we solve sequences of approximations at each time period. An especially appealing approximation, due to its simplicity, would be to solve sequences of linear approximations of the form

$$x^n_t(\theta) = \arg\min_{x_t\in\mathcal{X}_t} c_t x_t + \theta h\left(\rho^{n-1}(x_t)\right), \tag{18}$$

where $h(\rho^{n-1}(x_t))$ is the gradient of the pattern metric using the flows from iteration $n-1$. The gradient is given simply by

$$\begin{aligned} h^n_{\bar{a}\bar{d}}(\rho) &= \left.\frac{\partial H}{\partial \rho_{\bar{a}\bar{d}}}\right|_{\rho_{\bar{a}\bar{d}}=\rho^n_{\bar{a}\bar{d}}}, \qquad \forall \bar{a}\in\mathcal{A},\ \forall \bar{d}\in\mathcal{D}_{\bar{a}}, \\ &= 2R^n_{\bar{a}}\left(\rho^n_{\bar{a}\bar{d}} - \hat{\rho}_{\bar{a}\bar{d}}\right), \qquad \forall \bar{a}\in\mathcal{A},\ \forall \bar{d}\in\mathcal{D}_{\bar{a}}. \end{aligned} \tag{19}$$

The problem with using a linear approximation as in equation (18) is that it will generally be unstable. It basically adds a higher cost to each decision which is used more frequently than what is specified in the exogenous pattern ρ, and adds a negative cost when a decision is underutilized. Normally we would introduce a smoothing step of the form

$$x^n = (1-\alpha^n)x^{n-1} + \alpha^n \hat{x}^n,$$

where $\hat{x}^n$ is the solution to equation (18). Smoothing, however, destroys integrality.

A convergent algorithm can be obtained by using the following strategy. First, we have to keep track of how far we are deviating from the historical patterns as we step through time. When we are solving the subproblem at time t in iteration n, we construct our gradient by using our solution $x^n_{t'}(\theta)$ for $t' < t$, and $x^{n-1}_{t'}(\theta)$ for $t' \geq t$. This is known as a Gauss-Seidel strategy. Then, we solve a separable quadratic programming problem that is particularly easy to work with. We begin our presentation by first developing the gradient using the Gauss-Seidel methodology. Let

$$\tilde{R}^n_{\bar{a}}(t) = \sum_{t'=1}^{t-1} \sum_{d \in \mathcal{D}_{\bar{a}}} x^n_{t'\bar{a}\bar{d}} + \sum_{t'=t}^{T} \sum_{\bar{d} \in \mathcal{D}_{\bar{a}}} x^{n-1}_{t'\bar{a}\bar{d}}$$

and

$$\tilde{\rho}^n_{\bar{a}\bar{d}}(t) = \sum_{t'=1}^{t-1} \left(\frac{x^n_{t'\bar{a}\bar{d}}}{\tilde{R}^n_{\bar{a}}(t)} \right) + \sum_{t'=t}^{T} \left(\frac{x^{n-1}_{t'\bar{a}\bar{d}}}{\tilde{R}^n_{\bar{a}}(t)} \right), \qquad \forall \bar{a} \in \mathcal{A}, \quad \forall \bar{d} \in \mathcal{D}_{\bar{a}}, \quad \forall t \in \{1, 2, \ldots, T\}. \tag{20}$$

$\tilde{\rho}^n_{\bar{a}\bar{d}}(t)$ is computed using the solution from iteration n for time periods before t, and the solution from iteration $n-1$ for later time periods. The Gauss-Seidel version of the gradient is now

$$\tilde{h}^n_{\bar{a}\bar{d}}(t) = 2\tilde{R}^n_{\bar{a}}(t) \left(\tilde{\rho}^n_{\bar{a}\bar{d}}(t) - \rho_{\bar{a}\bar{d}} \right), \qquad \forall \bar{a} \in \mathcal{A}, \quad \forall \bar{d} \in \mathcal{D}_{\bar{a}}, \quad \forall t \in \{1, 2, \ldots, T\}. \tag{21}$$

Our algorithm proceeds by iteratively solving subproblems of the form

$$x^n_t(\theta) = \arg\min \sum_{a \in \mathcal{A}} \sum_{d \in \mathcal{D}_a} c_{tad} x_{tad} + \sum_{\bar{a} \in \mathcal{A}} \left(\frac{\theta}{\tilde{R}^n_{\bar{a}}(t)} \sum_{\bar{d} \in \mathcal{D}_{\bar{a}}} \int_0^{x_{t\bar{a}\bar{d}}} \left[\tilde{h}^n_{\bar{a}\bar{d}}(t) + 2\left(u - x^{n-1}_{t\bar{a}\bar{d}}\right) \right] du \right). \tag{22}$$

Note that the first term on the right-hand side is defined over the disaggregate attribute and decision spaces, while the pattern term is aggregated (hence, the use of $\bar{a}$ and $\bar{d}$ in this term). The algorithm progresses by stepping forward through time. At the end of each forward pass, we start the process over again with the new solution. The proximal term in equation (22) is separable, and as a result does not significantly complicate the original term. For integer problems, we would replace the nonlinear term in (22) with a piecewise linear approximation of the same function. The resulting problem can be easily solved using standard commercial linear programming solvers. We can also easily handle aggregation. The proximal term in (22) can be defined in terms of the total aggregated flow for a particular pattern.

5. A NUMERICAL ILLUSTRATION

Low-dimensional patterns represent a very simple way of controlling the behavior of an optimizing simulator. We illustrate this ability using a simple example. We have an optimizing simulator running on an unclassified dataset for a military airlift problem. The problem is to manage six aircraft types (C-5A, C-5B, C-17, C-141B, KC-10A, and NBC) to move a set of requirements. The requirements represent what are typically large movements of freight (often requiring a number of aircraft) to a destination in a theatre of operations. Moving a requirement involves being assigned to a route which will bring the aircraft through a series of intermediate airbases for refueling and maintenance. One of the biggest operational challenges of these aircraft is that their probability of a failure of sufficient severity to prevent a timely takeoff ranges between 10 and 25%. A failure can result in a delay or even require an off-loading of the freight to another aircraft.

Since full maintenance capabilities do not exist for all aircraft types at all airbases, there may be a desire to control the behavior of a simulation in terms of the number of aircraft who are allowed to use pass through a particular airbase (or region). The problem cannot be posed as a strict rule (e.g., "never use a C-5 in Saudi Arabia") because an airbase without proper maintenance capabilities for a C-5 can, in fact, handle a C-5, but a failure may involve flying in parts and technical support. Traditional optimization modeling requires determining a cost for these activities, but this can be quite difficult to handle. An analyst may be satisfied as long as the percentage of movements through an airbase using C-5s is less than a certain tolerance.

It is also possible that we want to encourage a behavior. An airbase may be particularly well suited to handle C-17s, and we may want to encourage a high percentage of these movements. It is important to realize, however, that it may not be possible to match a pattern, especially when we want to encourage more of an activity. For example, it may be simply impossible to require that 80% of the movements through a region be with C-17s, simply because there are not enough of them.

A pattern is expressed at a level of aggregation on the attribute-decision combination (a, d). In our simulation, we are managing two resource classes

$$\mathcal{C}^R = (\text{aircraft (A)}, \text{requirements (R)}).$$

The attributes of an aircraft are given by

$$a^A = (\text{type}, \text{loaded/empty}, \text{current location}, \text{load attributes}).$$

The attributes of a requirement are given by

$$a^R = (\text{origin}, \text{destination}, \text{weight characteristics}, \text{available time}, \text{due time at destination}).$$

Our decision classes are

$$\mathcal{C}^D = (\text{assign to a requirement (R)}, \text{Move to a location (M)}, \text{Hold (H)}).$$

The decision sets are then

$$\begin{aligned}
\mathcal{D}^R &= \text{the set of requirements;}\\
\mathcal{D}^M &= \text{the set of airbases, a "move" decision can be loaded or empty, and the move will be}\\
&\quad\ \text{to the next airbase on a route (not necessarily the final destination of the requirement);}\\
\mathcal{D}^H &= d^\phi \text{ (the "do nothing" option)}.
\end{aligned}$$

For our illustration, we are going to focus on patterns that are related to aircraft and move decisions. We could work at a number of different levels of aggregation, but since our focus is on the problem of handling a type of aircraft at certain locations, we are going to use the function

$$G_a\left(a^A\right) = (\text{aircraft type}).$$

The move decision will normally be expressed at the level of an airbase (e.g., "move to LERT"). However, we are going to assume that our problem with maintenance actually applies to all the airbases in a region, expressed by the first letter of an airbase. Specifically, we are going to use patterns to control our use of C-5A and C-5B aircraft in Region L, which represents airbases in Spain, France, and Italy. This parameter is expressed as the single scalar $\rho_{\bar{a}\bar{d}}$ where $\bar{a} =$ (C-5A or C-5B) and $\bar{d} =$ (Region L).

A full description of our optimizing simulator can be found in [12]. The simulator uses an optimization model to assign multiple aircraft to multiple requirements over a 16 day time interval. Each time period is equivalent to four hours. As a result, there are 96 time periods in the simulation horizon. The system uses the approximate dynamic programming formulation given in equation (8) with linear value function approximations as given in equation (9). The cost function is a simple engineering cost calculation based on distance ("MOG" constraints which capture airbase congestion were not considered in this set of experiments).

We first ran the simulator without patterns and found that 9.5% of the movements of aircraft C-5A and C-5B were to Region L. To illustrate how the logic works with pattern matching turned on, we ran the simulator using $\rho_{\bar{a}\bar{d}} = 0.2$. Also, for illustration purposes, we set θ to a very large number (in our case, 10,000) so that we would try to match the pattern exactly (if possible).

The results are shown in Figure 2, which gives two measures. We let

$$\tilde{\rho}^n_{t\bar{a}\bar{d}} = \frac{x^n_{t\bar{a}\bar{d}}}{R^n_{t\bar{a}}}$$

be the *instantaneous* pattern flows at time t during iteration n of the algorithm. $\bar{\rho}^n_{\bar{a}\bar{d}}(t)$, given by equation (20), is the *average* pattern flow when we are at time t in iteration n (which means we are using decisions from iteration $n-1$ for time periods later than t). Since we are only interested in matching patterns on average over time, it can happen that we do too much of an activity early in a simulation, then less of it later in the simulation in order to come out with the overall average. We show this in Figure 2 where we see that we are actually matching the pattern at the end of the first iteration, but early in the simulation we are doing less of the activity, and compensating by doing more as the simulation progresses. In the second iteration, we encourage the activity through the gradient, and the result is that we are actually doing too much of the activity earlier in the simulation, and compensating later. In the third iteration, the pattern matching is more consistent throughout the simulation.

Our ability to match a pattern after even a single iteration, especially one that is expressed at such a high level of aggregation, is quite useful. It implies that this logic could be integrated into a cost-based version of an airlift simulation (which does not use value functions) with virtually no additional effort. Of course, additional iterations are needed to improve the overall quality of the solution.

We cannot always match an exogenous pattern. Figure 3 shows $\bar{\rho}^3_{\bar{a}\bar{d}}(T)$ at the end of the third simulation, as a function of the desired pattern. We are simply not able to produce a solution where more than about 30% of the aircraft are C-17s. This behavior reflects the mix of aircraft and the needs of the requirements.

In practice, it is simply not the case that we will want to precisely match an exogenous pattern. If we have some level of confidence in our cost function, then we will generally be willing to accept

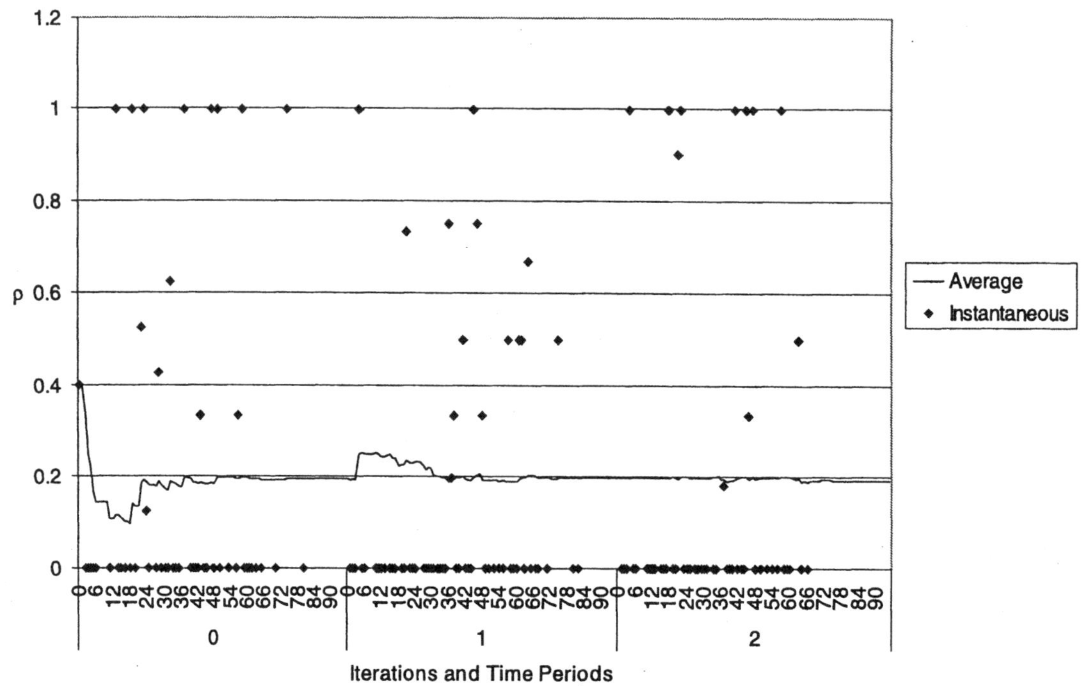

Figure 2. Average vs. instantaneous pattern flows.

a deviation from a pattern to obtain a lower cost. This can be achieved by using a lower value of θ. Figure 4 gives $\tilde{\rho}^3_{\bar{a}\bar{d}}(T)$ as a function of θ, illustrating this intuitive tradeoff. The problem is: what should θ be set to? Unfortunately, there is not a scientific answer to this question. The whole point of using the patterns is to achieve a behavior that reflects expert knowledge, so only an expert can judge whether the solution appears to be acceptable.

To illustrate the use of patterns graphically, we ran a simulation to illustrate our ability to limit the flows of C-5As through the airbase EGVA in England, something we might want to do to reflect our inability to properly maintain a particular aircraft type at a particular airbase. Figure 5 shows just the flows of C-5As through EGVA in our base case (with no patterns). Figure 6 shows the same flows when we specify a pattern that limits the use of C-5As on flights that

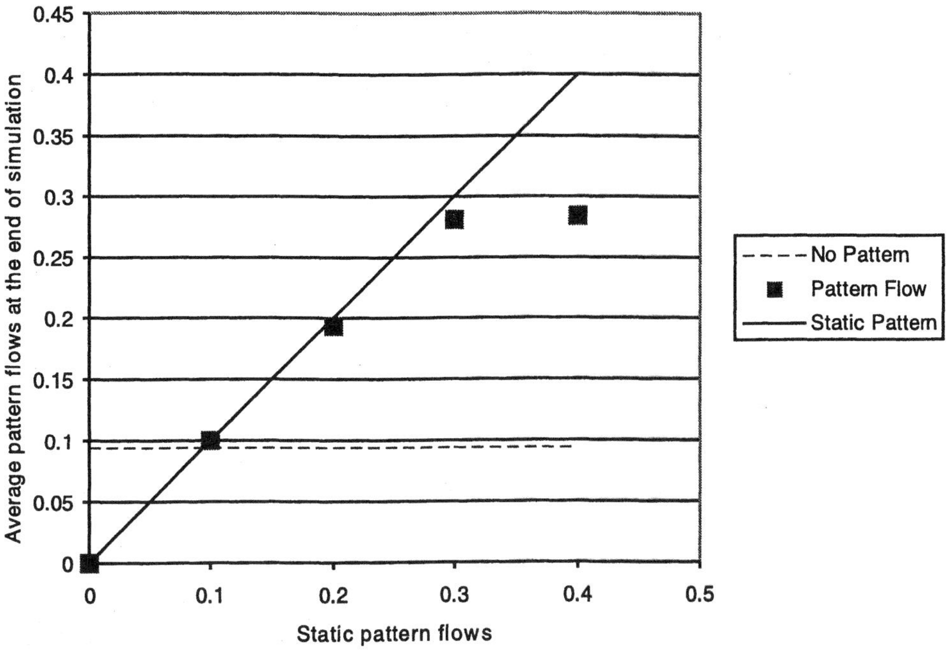

Figure 3. Different pattern flows.

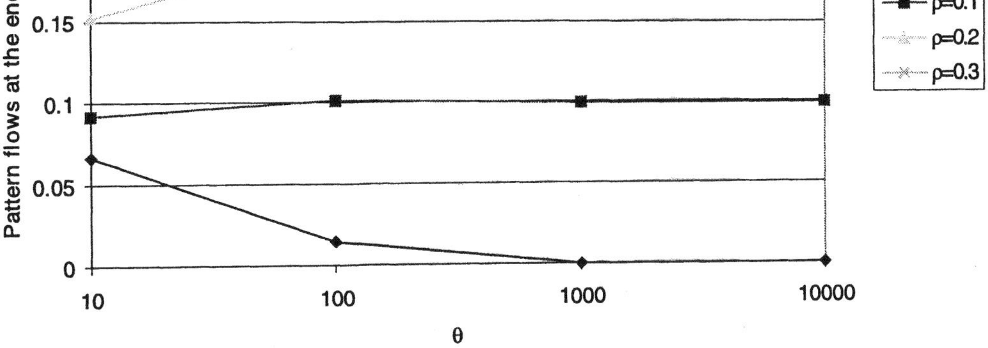

Figure 4. Pattern flows vs. θ.

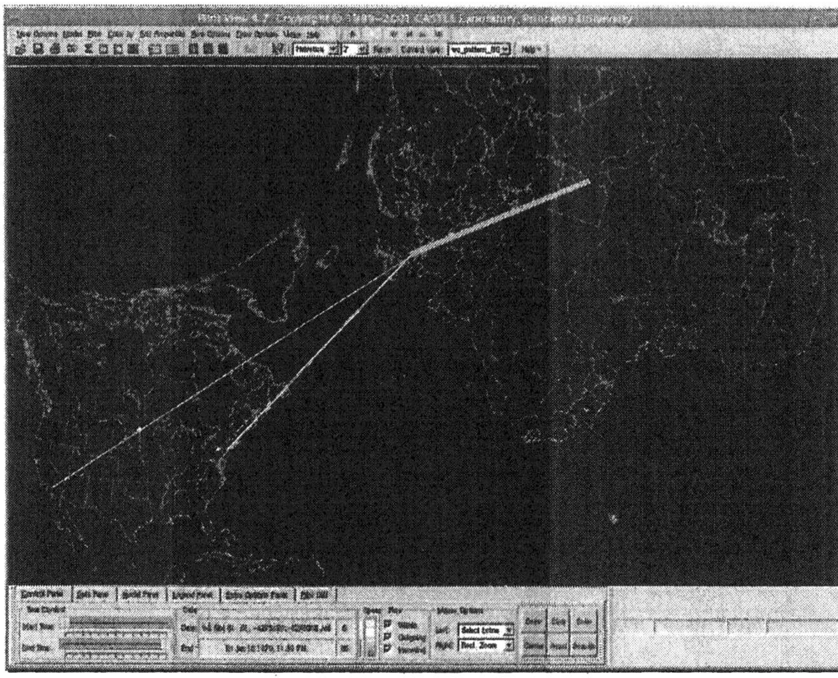

Figure 5. The flow of C-5As to EGVA in England without restriction. C-5As comprise 10.2% of the total flow.

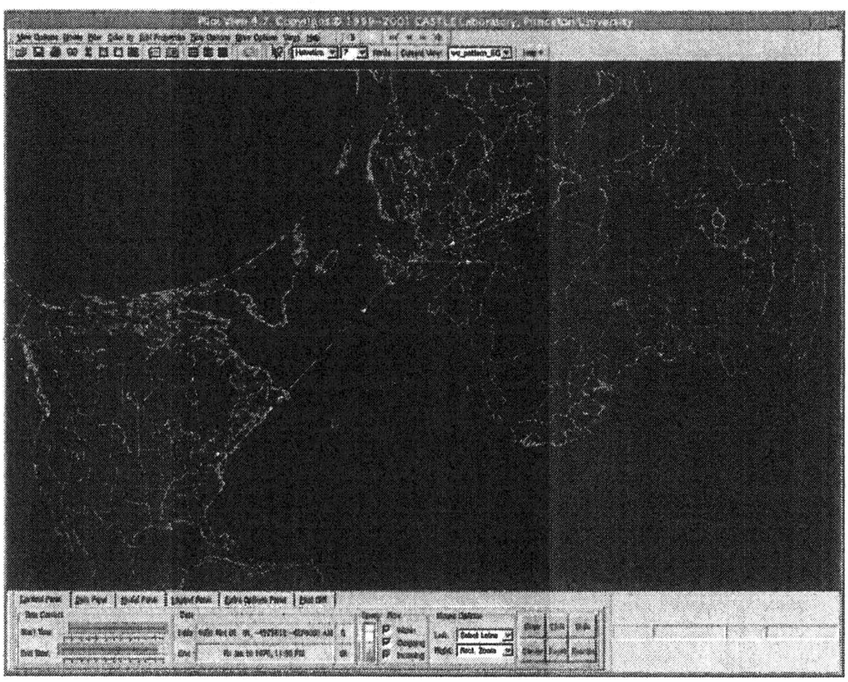

Figure 6. The flow of C-5A to EGVA with a 2% static pattern and $\theta = 10000$. The flows of C-5As are substantially reduced compared to the base case.

pass through EGVA to less than 5% of the total. Such a pattern reduces, but does not entirely eliminate, the use of this type of aircraft on that route.

6. CONCLUSIONS

This paper proposes a method that combines the ability of math programming models to handle high-dimensional problems using a cost function, with the flexibility of simulation models whose behavior can be adjusted by modifying the rules for making decisions. We introduce the use of a penalty term that seeks to minimize the difference between the decisions made by a model and a set of rules that must be expressed in terms of low-dimensional patterns that must be a function of the attribute of the resource being affected, and the decision being made. In addition, it is common that these rules be expressed in terms of the attribute-decision pair at some level of aggregation. This has the benefit of keeping rules simple, but does restrict our ability to use this logic to provide fine control.

The patterns can be expressed at different levels of aggregation in external data files which are easy to edit. This gives users the ability to manipulate the behavior of the model without changing code.

An algorithm is outlined which pushes the solution toward the exogenous patterns. Using a Gauss-Seidel strategy, the simulator adjusts its behavior as it progresses through the simulation. Our example shows that we can match a pattern after a single iteration, but we get a more consistent behavior after as few as two or three iterations. This result is very encouraging, although additional experimentation is needed.

REFERENCES

1. V. Wing, R.E. Rice, R. Sherwood and R.E. Rosenthal, Determining the optimal mobility mix, Technical Report, Force Design Division, The Pentagon, Washington, DC, (1991).
2. M.G. Mattock, J.F. Schank, J.P. Stucker and J. Rothenberg, New capabilities for strategic mobility analysis using mathematical programming, Technical Report, Rand Corporation, (1995).
3. K.A. Yost, The thruput strategic airlift flow optimization model, Technical Report, Air Force Studies and Analyses Agency, The Pentagon, Washington, DC, (1994).
4. R. Rosenthal, D. Morton, S. Baker, T. Lim, D. Fuller, D. Goggins, A. Toy, Y. Turker, D. Horton and D. Briand, Application and extension of the Thruput II optimization model for airlift mobility, *Military Operations Research* **3** (2), 55–74, (1997).
5. S. Baker, D. Morton, R. Rosenthal and L. Williams, Optimizing military airlift, *Operations Research* **50** (4), 582–602, (2002).
6. A. Marar and W.B. Powell, Capturing incomplete information in resource allocation problems through patterns, Technical Report, Princeton University, Department of Operations Research and Financial Engineering, (2002).
7. W.B. Powell, J.A. Shapiro and H.P. Simão, A representational paradigm for dynamic resource transformation problems, In *Annals of Operations Research*, (Edited by R.F.C. Coullard and J.H. Owens), pp. 231–279, J.C. Baltzer AG, (2001).
8. G. Godfrey and W.B. Powell, An adaptive, dynamic programming algorithm for stochastic resource allocation problems I: Single period travel times, *Transportation Science* **36** (1), 21–39, (2002).
9. W.B. Powell and H. Topaloglu, Stochastic programming in transportation and logistics, In *Handbook in Operations Research and Management Science, Volume on Stochastic Programming*, (Edited by A. Ruszczynski and A. Shapiro), North-Holland, Amsterdam (to appear).
10. M.Z. Spivey and W.B. Powell, The dynamic assignment problem, Technical Report CL-00-03, Department of Operations Research and Financial Engineering, Princeton University, (2000).
11. A. Marar and W.B. Powell, Using static flow patterns in time-staged resource allocation problems, Technical Report, Princeton University, Department of Operations Research and Financial Engineering, (2002).
12. W.B. Powell, T.T. Wu and A. Whisman, Using low-dimensional patterns in optimizing simulators: An illustration for the airlift mobility problem, In *Defense Transportation Algorithms, Models, and Applications for the 21st Century* , Special Issue of *Mathl. Comput. Modelling*, (this issue).

Available online at www.sciencedirect.com
SCIENCE DIRECT®
Mathematical and Computer Modelling 39 (2004) 677–696
MATHEMATICAL AND COMPUTER MODELLING
www.elsevier.com/locate/mcm

The Covalidation of Dissimilarly Structured Strategic Airlift Models

S. A. WRIGHT
Department of Mathematical Sciences
United States Military Academy
646 Swift Road
West Point, NY 10996-1905, U.S.A.
Sam.Wright@usma.edu

K. W. BAUER, JR.
Department of Operational Sciences
Graduate School of Engineering and Management
Air Force Institute of Technology
2950 P Street
Wright-Patterson AFB, OH 45433-7765, U.S.A.
Kenneth.Bauer@afit.edu

M. E. OXLEY
Department of Mathematics and Statistics
Graduate School of Engineering and Management
Air Force Institute of Technology
2950 P Street
Wright-Patterson AFB, OH 45433-7765, U.S.A.
Mark.Oxley@afit.edu

Abstract—A methodology is presented which allows comparison between models constructed under different modeling paradigms. Consider two models that exist to study different aspects of the same system, specifically Air Mobility Command's strategic airlift system. One model simulates a fleet of aircraft moving a given combination of cargo and passengers from an onload point to an offload point. The second model is a linear program that optimizes aircraft and route selection given cargo and passenger requirements in order to minimize late and nondeliveries. Further, the optimization model represents a more aggregated view of the airlift system than does the simulation. The two models do not have immediately comparable input or output structures, which complicates comparisons between the two models. We develop a methodology that structures this comparison and use it to compare the two large-scale models described above. Further, our technique has the fortunate byproduct of improving the fidelity of the models through a series of iterative refinements of the input to each model based on the output of the other. Models that compare favorably with regard to our methodology are deemed covalid models.

Keywords—Airlift model, Model comparison, Simulation, Optimization, Validation.

INTRODUCTION

Mathematical models provide representations of real-world systems. These representations may

0895-7177/04/$ - see front matter Typeset by $\mathcal{AMS}$-TEX
doi:10.1016/j.mcm.2004.02.008

take many forms: simulation, optimization, and regression, to name a few. Each model requires an input set, employs some set of rules and relations, and returns a set of dependent variable(s) as output. Inputs consist of input variables that can be observed directly in the real-world system (such as the amount of a resource), and input parameters that cannot be directly observed (such as a service rate or an efficiency factor). It is possible that a real-world system has more than one model that may be employed to characterize some unique aspect of the system. For instance, a system that consists of implementing a schedule of events of variable duration could be modeled as a simulation in order to determine the (distribution of) total time required to complete the schedule. Such a model is descriptive in nature and could be used to forecast resource or personnel requirements. Alternately, an optimization model may be created in order to determine the shortest length of time in which the schedule may be implemented. This model optimizes some aspect of the system and could be used to study policy changes, such as improvement of the schedule driving the simulation model. Either model (or both) may be valid representations of the real-world system in question, and both, assuming their validity, should give results appropriate for their respective purposes.

In order for models to be useful, they should approximate the real-world system to the degree to which they are designed, a degree that varies with each system and its associated models. Model validation is defined as "substantiating that the model, within its domain of applicability, behaves with satisfactory accuracy consistent with the study objectives" [1]. There is a myriad of techniques available to assess the validity of simulation models, and many of these techniques may be applied to more general classes of models [1–3]. These techniques include both objective and subjective tests that may assess the validity of a model's assumptions, structure, execution, or output performance. Depending on the study, different aspects of model validation may be of paramount importance. Here, we focus on models' output performances.

There is a large body of literature related to determining the output validity of a model for which real-world data can be obtained (see [1; 4, pp. 314–322], for examples). However, it is often the case that the system being represented cannot be sampled in order to make comparisons. In such a case, a method of model output validation is not as obvious. Sargent recommends the comparison of simulations to other validated simulations, as well as the comparison of simple simulations to known analytic results in cases of nonobservable systems [2]. The use of similarly structured models (specifically, simulations) also has been proposed to assist in establishing model credibility [5]. Kleijnen suggests that if relevant data are unattainable, a sensitivity analysis may be performed with the results compared against a system expert's judgment [6].

In this research, we propose a method of *covalidation* in which models, either similarly (e.g., simulation and simulation) or dissimilarly structured (e.g., optimization and simulation), representing the same real-world system (perhaps for which output data are unattainable), may be compared. We define *covalidation* as the process of comparing models, mindful of each model's domain of applicability, with the object of relative substantiation. Further, if one of the models has been independently validated with respect to the real-world system it represents, models that are covalid relative to that model may be considered *valid by association*.

We summarize our methodology using Figure 1, general methodology. The major blocks in the figure encapsulate the most basic interpretation of our method.

(1) Models are created.
(2) An attempt is made to use the outputs of the models to improve the inputs of the other models (a method we call "output/input crossflow").
(3) The models' inputs and outputs are analyzed to determine their closeness to each other and/or reality. A poor comparison between the models or with reality leads the modeler to modify the models and return to the output/input crossflow.

On a more specific level, we refine the steps as follows.

(1a) Candidate models are built to represent, as closely as possible for dissimilarly structured

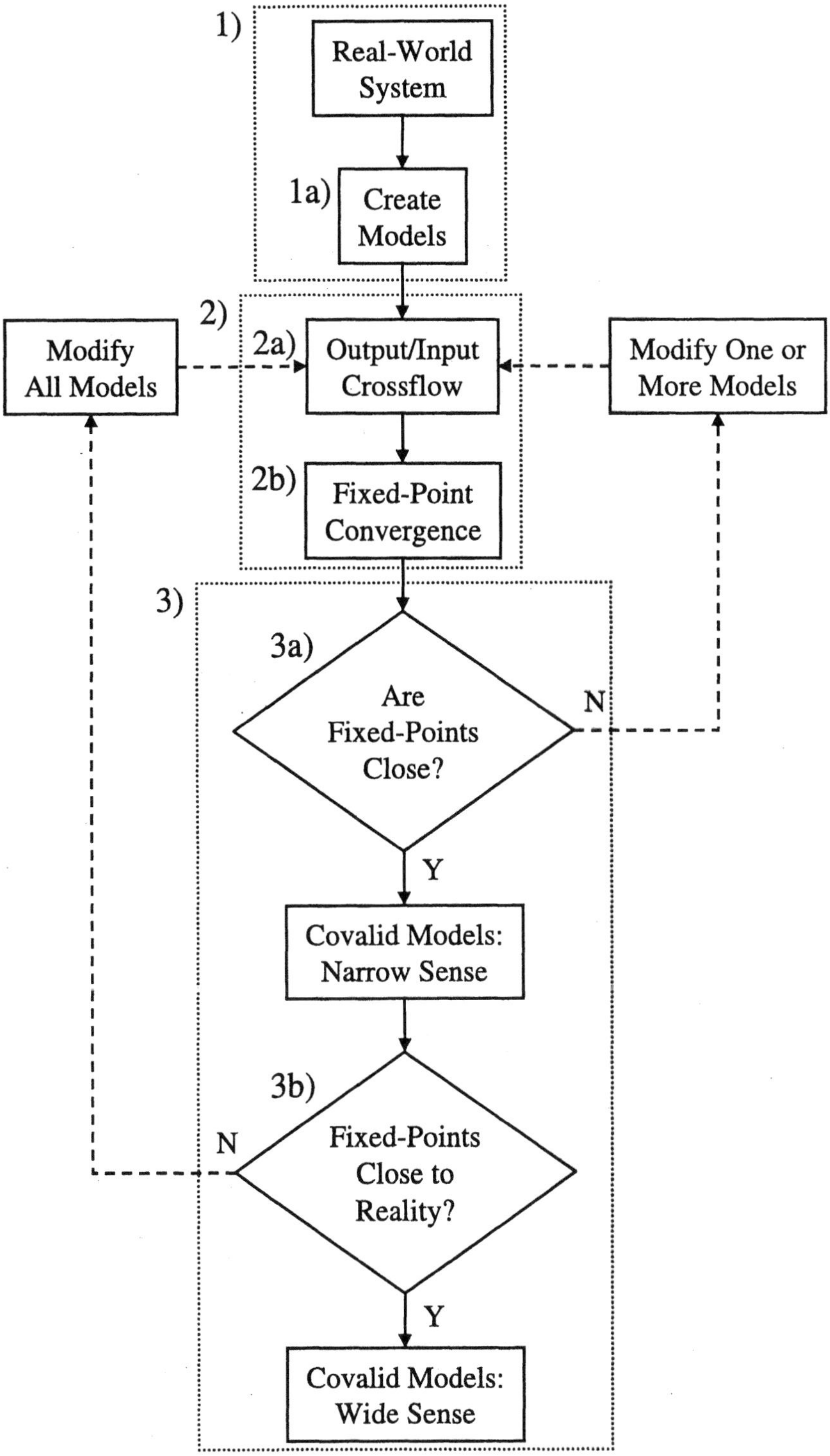

Figure 1. General methodology.

models, the same real-world system.

(2a) Strengths of each model are exploited through an informational crossflow. This crossflow utilizes knowledge and insights cultivated from the performance of each model with the goal of improving the performance of the other model(s) in an iterative scheme.

(2b) The result of the crossflow is a convergence of input and output values (for each model) to a fixed point that is considered to represent the intended modeling situation most closely for each model.

(3a) An evaluation of the closeness of the respective fixed points occurs. This closeness represents the degree of commonality of function that exists amongst the models. If this closeness is low, some or all of the models are not representing the same situation and require modification (and returning to Step (2a) above).

(3b) A determination is made concerning the covalidity of the models.

The closeness between models indicates the level of covalidity between models we term narrow-sense covalidity. Mutual closeness to the real-world system (if such a comparison is possible) indicates wide-sense covalidity. If models are covalid in the narrow sense, but not the wide sense, the models do not adequately represent the real-world system, and all require modification (and returning to Step (2a) above). Further, it may be the case that no real-world data exists, yet one of the models has been validated by means other than output comparison, or has been simply accepted by acclamation (accredited). Models that are narrow-sense covalid with such a model may be considered valid (accredited) by association.

This research provides significant contributions to the general field of mathematical modeling. An original paradigm is established for the construction, improvement, and validation of models. Within this framework, the original notion of the covalidation of models is detailed. First, an iterative method is devised that seeks the improvement of the inputs to each model considered. Second, a method of gradient analysis is devised which allows the direct comparison of the models. Finally, we demonstrate the entire process on two large-scale, real-world models in use by the United States Air Force Air Mobility Command.

The rest of this paper is organized as follows. First, we provide a background to the specific application which motivated the requirement for this research. The next sections describe the methods used: first, an iterative technique designed to exploit the crossflow of information between dissimilarly structured models; then, a gradient analysis approach to model comparison. Following these sections, the methodology is employed using two strategic airlift models currently in use, followed by our concluding thoughts.

MOTIVATION

The ultimate goal of this research is to provide a methodology by which two or more large-scale models that model the same real-world system may be compared and contrasted. Comparing two models of this type provided the impetus for this research. One model is a large-scale discrete event simulation model that enjoys a relatively high level of acceptance. The other is a large-scale linear programming model designed to optimize the same general system modeled by the simulation.

The simulation model is used by the Air Mobility Command (AMC) of the United States Air Force and is known as the mobility analysis support system (MASS). The simulation core of MASS, known as the airlift flow module (AFM), simulates the movement of detailed cargo requirements through the airlift system based on the availability of aircraft, air routes, and air base infrastructure and resources. The simulation is deterministic in its mission planning while mission execution is stochastic. For a detailed synopsis of AFM, refer to the AMC studies and analysis flight (AMCSAF) point paper prepared for the Congressional Budget Office [7].

The other model is a large-scale optimization model developed jointly by the Naval Postgraduate School (NPS) and the Rand Corporation known as the NPS/Rand mobility optimizer (NRMO) [8]. NRMO models the strategic airlift system as a multiperiod, multicommodity network-based linear program (LP) with many side constraints. Use of the model is intended to provide insight into mobility problems such as fleet and infrastructure adequacy, and the identification of system bottlenecks.

NRMO's minimization objective function is the weighted sum of three subobjectives that seek to minimize the nondelivery of cargo, the lateness of cargo deliveries, and the penalty for performing certain undesirable actions (such as deadheading crews). First, a large relative weight is attached to the nondelivery of cargo. Next, in relative importance is minimizing the lateness of cargo deliveries. Finally, a third, relatively small weight is applied to minimizing the penalty for performing undesirable actions. The weights applied to each subobjective are subjective, but they are generally ordered such that weight for nondelivery is far greater than the weight for late delivery that, in turn, is far greater than the weight of the (negative) bonus.

The two models have many differences as well as similarities. One similarity is that both model strategic airlift and provide certain common outputs, such as the amount of cargo delivered. A major difference is that NRMO optimizes the airlift schedule while AFM schedules flights based on the availability of aircraft and a prioritized list of routes. Another major difference is that AFM models most event durations as random variables while NRMO employs mean values. Also, while AFM provides a detailed look at many aspects of the airlift system, NRMO represents a more aggregate view of the airlift system.

The AFM simulation has long been in use by the AMC studies and analysis flight (AMCSAF), and though a formal validation has not been accomplished, its results are generally accepted as valid. One obstacle to a traditional, output-based validation of either model is that there is no way to collect real-world data from a strategic airlift system due to the infrequency of actual large-scale conflicts. Desire by AMCSAF to have some basis for the use of the NRMO optimization model has provided a motive for comparing and contrasting the two models. Baker *et al.* [8] provide a comparison of the two models' performance in general terms. Here, we provide not only metrics with which to characterize the differences between the models, but also a method that aims to utilize the different natures of the models in order to improve each model's performance.

OUTPUT/INPUT CROSSFLOW

We employ an iterative method in which selected inputs as well as outputs from the models may converge. The purpose of this iterative scheme is to effect a crossflow of information between the outputs and the inputs of the models, as described in Figure 1, Step 2. That is, one model's output (or a function of that output) is supplied as input to the other model. For instance, NRMO provides as output the optimal selection of aircraft routes, while AFM accepts as input the frequency of route usage. On the other hand, AFM provides output that can be translated to the efficiency of parking space use, an input parameter required by NRMO.

In dealing with dissimilarly structured models, the differences between the models must be carefully examined and exploited. Typically, dissimilarly structured models not only have different input (including both variable and parameter) sets, but they could also have different levels of aggregation as well as different capabilities in terms of modeling the actual system. In order to make a reasonable assessment of the models' covalidity, however, these differences must be examined.

Structurally different models commonly employ different levels of data aggregation. For instance, the AFM simulation models the strategic airlift system to a high level of fidelity in terms of its level of detail compared to the NRMO optimization model. When comparing such models, each model's designed level of aggregation should be maintained. In other words, the fidelity of models should not be compromised for the sake of "fair comparison". For example, optimistic optimization results could prove to be the result of unwarranted aggregation, since it may be the case that the unrealistic divisibility of aircraft or units of cargo in the optimization results in more cargo movement than is actually possible. Further, by maintaining the appropriate levels of aggregation in each model, the covalidation process may also provide information on the appropriateness of such aggregation.

Whether to use the different modeling capabilities inherent in each model should be carefully considered on a case-by-case basis before model comparison is performed. In general, the "extra" capabilities of one model compared to the other model should be switched off, if possible. For example, since NRMO can effectively model aerial refueling aircraft operations while AFM cannot, the NRMO capability should be turned off during the comparison. If this is not possible, selection of the input variables or parameters should be such that the capability exercises no significant effect.

An exception to this rule occurs when inherent differences in the modeling paradigms used allow one model to adequately model a system aspect while the other cannot. A simple example of this is that NRMO does not model the variability inherent in many airlift processes, relying instead on mean values, while AFM models the random distributions of such variables. This difference in capabilities accounts for a fundamental difference between the two models, one for which comparisons in terms of covalidation are desired.

A difficult area is ensuring a rough parity in inputs between the two models, particularly models of different types or models that operate at different aggregation levels. Even when a particular input feeds both models, if the level of aggregation for this input is different between the two models, special care must be taken to ensure equitable representation.

After all else has been accomplished in order to ensure the models are executing the same scenario, it is likely, due to the differing natures of the modeling paradigms used, that the models will not yield the same result in terms of some common output. This is expected since, for instance, one model creates a schedule based strictly on the placement of required cargo movements on the TPFDD while the other model optimizes this schedule in order to maximize the movement of the cargo. A possible solution to this problem involves taking what is learned from the execution of one model and using it to improve the execution of the other. For this effort, we propose adapting certain outputs of each model for use as inputs to the other. Given the different world-views inherent in the models, it seems reasonable to assume that lessons learned from the output of one model may be used to improve the use of the other model. It is desired to select outputs of each model that can serve as inputs to the other. In general, it is not clear that finding such outputs to crossflow is possible. However, since optimization models provide the "best solution" while simulation models can provide estimates of system parameters, it seems reasonable that information could be meaningfully exchanged between these particular model types.

An iterative scheme is presented that demonstrates the crossflow of outputs to inputs between two models, Model i and Model j. The application is described in Figure 2, output/input crossflow iterative method. In the figure, the superscript n denotes the current iteration number. Each model has an input set: X_i and X_j are the complete input sets required for each model. X_{ji} and X_{ij} are subsets of X_i and X_j, respectively, that represent the input derived from or modified in reaction to the other model's output (i.e., from the output of Model j to the input of Model i, or vice versa; $X_{ji} = f_{ji}\ (Y_{ji})$). For the first model execution, some (subjective) nominal values are placed on these inputs that, during later iterations, will be derived from the output of the other model. Likewise, Y_i (or Y_j), is the complete output set from Model i (or Model j) and Y_{ij} (or Y_{ji}) is a subset of Y_i (or Y_j) that contains output which is utilized by the other model (output from the simulation to be used as input to the optimization or vice versa). The output subset used by the other model is "filtered" appropriately through the f_{ij} and f_{ji} feedback functions to make it usable as input for the other model. This filtering can be realized as a direct mathematical relationship or reflected as changes in policy or by adding model constraints.

At each iteration, a check is made to determine if the stopping criterion has been met. This criterion can be that a model's input has converged. Alternatively, successive iterations may indicate that a point of diminishing returns has been reached with this process. Either way, the final iteration inputs (denoted by "*") are deemed those which are as close to each other as possible, and they are used as the experimental design center for the ensuing model comparison.

In Figure 2,

n	is the iteration number

Model i Input/Output

X_i	is input to Model M_i
$X_{ji} = f_{ji}(Y_{ji})$	is input to Model M_i that is derived from output of Model M_j
Y_i	is output of Model M_i
$Y_{ij} \subseteq Y_i$	is output from Model M_i that is to be used as input to Model M_j

Model j Input/Output

X_j	is input to Model M_j
$X_{ij} = f_{ij}(Y_{ij})$	is input to Model M_j that is derived from output of Model M_i
Y_j	is output of Model M_j
$Y_{ji} \subseteq Y_j$	is output from Model M_j that is to be used as input to Model M_i

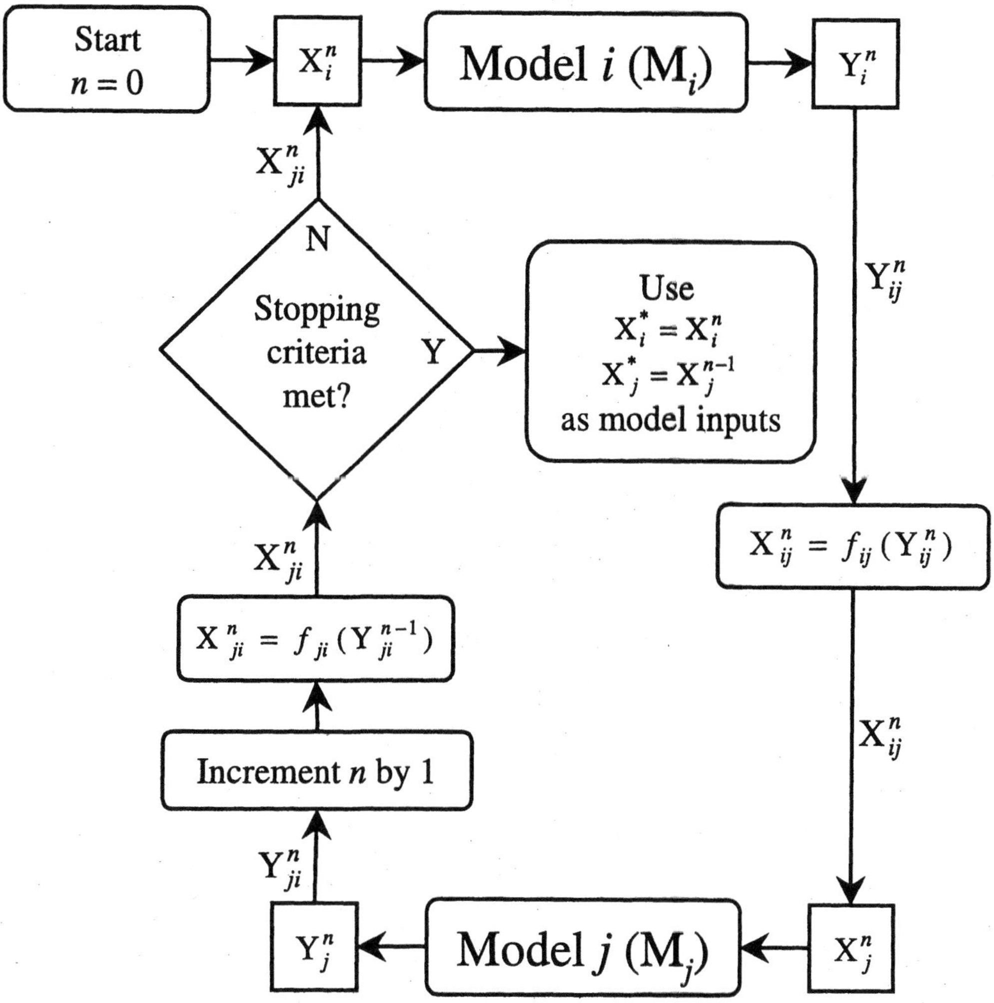

Figure 2. Output/input crossflow iterative method.

The information provided by the output/input links is used in an iterative fashion aimed at improving both models. This iterative scheme results in convergence to a fixed point of inputs and outputs (which may not be identical for each model). The input fixed points should represent a state where the models represent similar situations. The output fixed points can provide the first indication of whether the models are performing analogously. Wright [9] provides both the underlying framework upon which this method is based and shows that it is possible to create feedback functions that will guarantee the convergence of each model's inputs and outputs through this method.

Prior to developing the particulars of model comparison, a summary of the steps taken to achieve a crossflow of information is offered (see Figure 1, Step 2). First, the input/output structures of the models are carefully studied and appropriate adjustments are made due to the differences in level of detail and capability. Next, output/input links are determined which will allow for a potentially meaningful crossflow of information. Finally, the information provided by these links is used in an iterative fashion aimed at improving both models. Convergence of these inputs should indicate a state where the models, as closely as possible, represent the same scenario. Further, convergence in the model's outputs provides the first indication that the models are performing similarly. A detailed output comparison is examined in the following section.

GRADIENT ANALYSIS

In this section, we develop a means for assessing the "closeness" of the models, as described in Figure 1, Step 3. In the limit of the iterative method, we have fixed points (the converged outputs) from each model that may be compared. Rather than simply relying on this comparison made at a point, we propose estimating the gradient of each model relative to selected inputs and comparing these vectors. Linear regression metamodels constructed across a small experimental design of relevant input variables provide a convenient means of effecting this comparison. Both models are executed (during the iterative scheme) at the same basic input settings. The final input settings from the iterative scheme become the center point of an experimental design aimed at estimating the local gradients of each model. A comparison of these gradient estimates indicates whether the models respond in a similar fashion to perturbations in the selected inputs.

The method we develop allows comparison between both the relative closeness of average model outputs and estimates of gradients of the models representing the sensitivity of a selected output to a set of common inputs. Using this method, we are able to investigate both the relative predictive values of the metamodels (through the output comparison) as well as compare the metamodels' abilities to provide description of the physical system (through comparison of local gradients). The method is summarized in two parts. The first is the creation of an experimental design, and the second requires the comparison of the resulting metamodels.

The experimental design chosen for this study is based on the desire to evaluate the sensitivities of a single output to changes in key inputs. The choice of design depends on the study. The number of model executions to be performed is limited by the size of the models, the number of input factors to be varied, the desired design resolution, and the number of replications to be made at each design point (to reduce the output variability of simulations) [10].

The result of the iterative scheme is a fixed point of the models' inputs. This fixed point provides the input element to each model (to include parameters and variables) which corresponds as nearly as possible to the inputs and outputs (as applicable) of the opposing model. This input establishes the center point for the experimental design. It is significant that the convergence that results from the iterative scheme is valid only for the design point upon which the scheme was performed. We are assuming that the perturbations used in the experimental design are small enough so that the effect of using the same fixed points across the entire design is insignificant.

Since exercising the technique across a wide experimental design may yield convergence to greatly different sets of specific model inputs, the iterative method would require repetition at each design point. For instance, a large change in the number of available aircraft (or any resource) may significantly affect optimal routing (one of the crossflow variables). For this reason and since one of the goals is gradient approximation at the center design point, we assume that design points are very close to one another (approximately plus or minus 10%) and that the potential differences in fixed points are unimportant. The desired closeness of the design points creates a trade-off with the number of runs required for a model with output variability (such as a simulation) so that a statistically significant difference may be seen between the design points.

We recognize that there are a number of methods available for comparing the result of the experimental design. The method we employ takes advantage of the difference between the optimization and the simulation model. This method considers that the resulting gradient direction found by each model should be similar. As such, the angle between the gradient vectors created by each metamodel should be relatively small.

Box and Draper [10] describe the computation of a confidence region around the coefficients of a linear regression that we employ here. A confidence region shaped as a hypercone is constructed about the gradient vector of the simulation metamodel (chosen since there will likely be more variability in this metamodel). The following equation is used to determine the angle about the determined gradient vector the confidence region extends.

$$\sin\theta = \left\{ \frac{(k-1)\, s_b^2 F_\alpha\,(k-1, \nu_b)}{\sum_{i=1}^{k} b_i^2} \right\}^{1/2} . \tag{1}$$

In the equation, θ is the angle the confidence region extends from the estimated gradient vector, k is the number of variables estimated, b is the set of coefficients, s_b is the standard error of the set of coefficients, and v_b is the number of degrees of freedom on which s_b is based.

If the gradient vector of the optimization model lies in the constructed hypercone, we may not declare that a difference exists between the two gradient vectors. The closeness of the mean values of the metamodels should also be considered, however, before making a determination as to the two models covalidity.

RESULTS

This section documents the performance of the covalidation methodology on the actual AFM and NRMO models at two distinct scenarios. We developed a scenario and translated it into two sets of inputs, one for each model. Further, a second scenario (as well as applicable input sets) was created from the first in order to provide an indication of covalidation at more than a single input point. Each scenario was exercised using the method of output/input crossflow until a sequence of input values appeared to converge. Then, each scenario was used as the center of a 2^6 plus center point experimental design for gradient comparison.

This section is organized much as the basic modeling paradigm presented in Figure 1. The first section corresponds to Block 1 in Figure 1; the basic scenario developed by modelers at AMCSAF is summarized. The following section, representing Block 2 in Figure 1, presents the setup of the output/input crossflow with respect to two distinct feedback functions. The next section covers the experimental design used to conduct the gradient analysis applied to the result from the output/input crossflow application (Block 3 in Figure 1). The results from the actual performance of the output/input crossflow method are presented in the sequent section, followed by a section concerning the actual performance of the gradient analysis where we also discuss the covalidation decision.

The Scenarios

The notional scenario used for this research uses a fleet of 160 military aircraft mixed among C-5s, C-17s, and C-141s, plus several wide body passenger (wbp) aircraft from the Civil Reserve Air Fleet (CRAF). These aircraft are used to fly some 26,000 short tons (STons) of cargo and 35,700 passengers from five onload bases (primarily McGuire and Charleston Air Force Bases (AFB) for the military aircraft and John F. Kennedy (JFK) International Airport for the CRAF) to six offload bases (mainly Bahrain, Dhahran, and King Abdul Aziz International Airports in Saudi Arabia) over a 20-day period. Each cargo mission from the continental United States (CONUS) is flown either direct to its destination, or through one of four en route bases in Europe, specifically Mildenhall, England; Ramstein, Germany; and Moron and Rota, Spain (the passenger carrying CRAF aircraft use separate civil airports in Europe as their en route stops).

The scenario contains delivery requirements through the 20th day after the start of the scenario, but we only collect data for the first 15 days, so that statistics may be drawn from the initial surge of cargo requirements into the theater, while not implying that cargo requirements end after 15 days. The cargo requirements are mixed among bulk (palletized) cargo, oversized cargo (cargo that will not fit on a pallet, but will fit on a C-130, C-141, or larger aircraft), and out-sized cargo (cargo that will not fit on a C-130 or C-141 aircraft, but will fit on a C-5 or C-17 aircraft).

The initial aircraft fleet is a combination of 60 C-5 aircraft, 50 C-17 aircraft, 50 C-141 aircraft, and 25 wide body passenger CRAF aircraft. These aircraft are first available for missions on the first two days of the scenario. In AFM, the initial location of the military aircraft is specified as either McGuire or Charleston AFB, and the 25 CRAF aircraft begin at JFK International Airport. In NRMO, the initial location of aircraft is not specified, and the model operates such that the aircraft are initially located where they are first required.

The infrastructure available at the various bases used in the AFM and NRMO models are for the most part implicitly assumed in the values of the input variable "MOG" (maximum on ground). This MOG value (often referred to as "working MOG") is intended to provide a measure of the maximum number of aircraft a base can support in terms of runway usage, taxiing, parking, loading, unloading, and refueling during a designated period of time. One important base function that is explicitly modeled, however, is the daily total fuel available at the base (as opposed to the number of fuel trucks or fuel pumps available, which is included in MOG). Depending on assumptions of the availability of resources, each base is given either a particular value for its MOG and fuel, or a value that indicates the resource is unconstrained. Infrastructure at bases in the United States is considered unconstrained. This assumption implies that both MOG and fuel at CONUS bases are unlimited. Bases in Saudi Arabia are considered to have unlimited fuel, but limited MOG. The en route bases in Europe have both limited fuel and MOG.

The modified scenario, used to provide a look at covalidation at a second point, was created using the base scenario as a starting point. The delivery requirements were then increased by 50% to create a total requirement of 39,000 short tons of cargo and 53,500 passengers delivered. Other than the delivery requirements, the scenarios are identical. However, this does not imply that the iterative method converges to the same fixed point. For reference, the scenarios are referred to as the "small scenario" and the "big scenario."

Iterative Method of Output/Input Crossflow

The performance of the iterative method on two or more models is highly dependent upon the choice of feedback functions used in the iterations. We examined the input of each model to determine parameters (in NRMO) whose values had little justification and variables (in AFM) that could benefit from the optimizing nature of a linear program (LP). In addition to determining input parameters and variables that could be improved upon, we needed to find parameters and variables that could be derived from the opposing model's output. Clearly, the determination of suitable crossflow feedback functions is an activity best accomplished by experts who have an in-depth understanding of the models in question and can effectively hypothesize what types of feedback functions hold promise for model improvement. The crossflows between AFM and NRMO deemed the most significant include the mix of military aircraft type, which may be derived from NRMO, and the MOG efficiency parameter in NRMO, which may be derived from AFM output.

MIX OF MILITARY AIRCRAFT. The initial fleet of military aircraft utilized in the scenario consisted of 60 C-5s, 50 C-17s, and 50 C-141s. AFM utilizes these allocated aircraft as they become available, without determining whether a particular aircraft is the best choice to transport a particular cargo requirement or not. All aircraft are, therefore, used in approximately the same proportions as their availability and utilization (ute) rates allow. (The ute rate dictates a percentage of flying time which a particular aircraft type may not exceed when averaged over a model specified period of time.)

This method of scheduling aircraft for missions has proven historically not to be optimal. For instance, AMCSAF conducted a study where the addition of an aircraft type (without the removal of any other aircraft) actually reduced throughput during a scenario, presumably because the new aircraft type was not as efficient as the aircraft already included in the study.

Therefore, altering the mix of aircraft available to an AFM study might similarly alter the throughput. An optimal aircraft mix is not necessarily what the NRMO model provides, however. NRMO starts its run with an initial mix of aircraft, just as AFM. However, NRMO is free to use (or not use) each aircraft in any way it deems appropriate for the movement of cargo. It may be implied that this method of aircraft use suggests a more efficient aircraft mix than is found by using the aircraft in the proportions in which they are provided. Therefore, we determine the percentage of all military missions that each military aircraft type fly as output from NRMO. Then, assuming the total size of the military fleet used (160 aircraft) remains constant, we determine a new number of each military aircraft used by AFM with equation (2). For $i = \{$C-5, C-17, C-141$\}$,

$$\text{Planes}_i^{\text{new}} = \min\left(\text{round}\left(\frac{\text{Msn}_i}{\text{TotalMsn}} \times \text{TotalAC}\right), \text{Avail}_i\right). \tag{2}$$

In equation (2), $\text{Planes}_i^{\text{new}}$ is the number of aircraft Type i to be used as AFM input during the next iteration; Msn_i is the number of missions performed by aircraft Type i during the first 15 days of the scenario (from NRMO); TotalMsn is the total number of missions performed by all military aircraft types during the first 15 days of the scenario (from NRMO); TotalAC is the total number of aircraft available in the inventory (160 in this scenario); and Avail_i is the maximum number of aircraft Type i available for use. The min function simply takes the least of the two arguments, but the round function used is somewhat different than a typical round function. Since there are three aircraft types and the sum of the $\text{Planes}_i^{\text{new}}$ must be TotalAC, the round function rounds the two aircraft types closest to an integer to that integer, while the remaining $\text{Planes}_i^{\text{new}}$ is evaluated such that the sum of all $\text{Planes}_i^{\text{new}}$ equals TotalAC.

Note that if one of the military aircraft types, C-17 for instance, returns $\text{Planes}_{\text{C-17}}^{\text{new}} = \text{Avail}_{C-17}$, equation (2) is not sufficient to evaluate the other aircraft types since the total number of aircraft must remain constant at TotalAC. In this case, the other aircraft types must use equation (3) to evaluate the new number of that aircraft type to be employed in the next iteration. We leave open the possibility of more than one aircraft type equaling its maximum number available, though this may not be possible because of the Avail_i constants. For $k = \{k \in i \ni \text{Planes}_k^{\text{new}} = \text{Avail}_k\}$, $j = i - k$,

$$\text{Planes}_j^{\text{new}} = \text{round}\left(\frac{\text{Msn}_j}{\text{TotalMsn} - \sum_k \text{Msn}_k} \times \left(\text{TotalAC} - \sum_k \text{Planes}_k^{\text{new}}\right)\right). \tag{3}$$

Wright describes the validity of the necessary assumptions required to take advantage of the output/input crossflow method which include that the feedback function's input set be compact and that the feedback function itself is continuous, notably that we consider the function continuous when clearly, its output is integer [9]. The argument suggests that we may contrive the "rounding" function to look continuous, where, in a one-dimensional example, the "steps" of the function which maps real numbers to their closest integers are actually not steps and have derivatives at the step points that are less than infinity.

In considering the performance of the experimental design on the AFM and NRMO models, we realized that use of the preceding mix of military aircraft feedback function would result in breaking one of this method's fundamental assumptions that inputs for each model be as analogous as possible. The problem is that while we modify the AFM input with the number of each type of military plane each iteration, the NRMO input of the number of each type of military aircraft remains constant. Therefore, we also feed the same mix of military aircraft values back to the NRMO model.

MOG EFFICIENCY. The function used to feedback AFM output to NRMO input is the MOG efficiency of the three primary offload bases. MOG efficiency in NRMO is a measure of how efficiently we anticipate a particular base is able to utilize its MOG. This number is an attempt to compensate for the fact that parking spaces, fuel trucks and stations, material handling equipment (MHE), taxiways, etc., cannot be optimally scheduled and utilized in real-life operations. NRMO runs are generally devised so that this MOG efficiency value is 0.68 for all bases (though the model is capable of separate MOG efficiency values for each base). This value may or may not provide a reasonable estimate of the inefficiencies of working MOG on average, but it almost certainly does not accurately reflect the inefficiencies experienced by every base, as these inefficiencies are likely to differ from base to base.

Deriving the MOG efficiency feedback function from AFM output to NRMO input is not a straightforward task, however, and the actual function is open to some debate. In fact, many forms of this feedback function were considered. Some of the AFM outputs available which could be considered useful in the creation of such a feedback function include the minimum, average, and maximum numbers of aircraft which are present at each base and the numbers of daily landings and takeoffs that occur at each base. Also of use is the input of the amount of MOG available at each base.

The AFM to NRMO MOG efficiency feedback function we selected uses the average number of aircraft on the ground divided by the average (over the days of the study) of the maximum number of aircraft on the ground (for each day). Of course, the average for any given day cannot be greater than the maximum for that day, so the averaging of each over the length of the simulation cannot produce a MOG efficiency of greater than 1.0. Since AFM may, at times, place more aircraft on the ground at a base than is feasible, it is considered that this MOG efficiency function (given in the following equation) may well indicate the actual MOG efficiency for a base.

$$\text{MOGEffavgmax}_j^{\text{new}} = \frac{\text{Avgplanes}_j}{\sum_{d=0}^{\text{days}} \text{Maxplanes}_{j,d} \Big/ \text{days}}.$$

In equation (4), $\text{MOGEffavgmax}_j^{\text{new}}$ is the MOG efficiency of Base j to be used as NRMO input during the next iteration ("avgmax" denotes that we take the *average* number of aircraft divided by the average of the daily *maximum* number of aircraft at the base, and the term may be used to refer to this feedback function); Avgplanes_j is the average number of planes at Base j over the course of the scenario (from AFM); *days* is the number of days considered in the scenario; and $\text{Maxplanes}_{j,d}$ is the maximum number of aircraft on the ground at Base j on Day d (from AFM).

The assumptions of compactness and continuity in the feedback function cause no problems in this case. The MOG efficiency is limited to real values between 0.0 and 1.0 (inclusive), and the feedback function is clearly continuous.

The flow of the output/input crossflow method model is depicted in Figure 3.

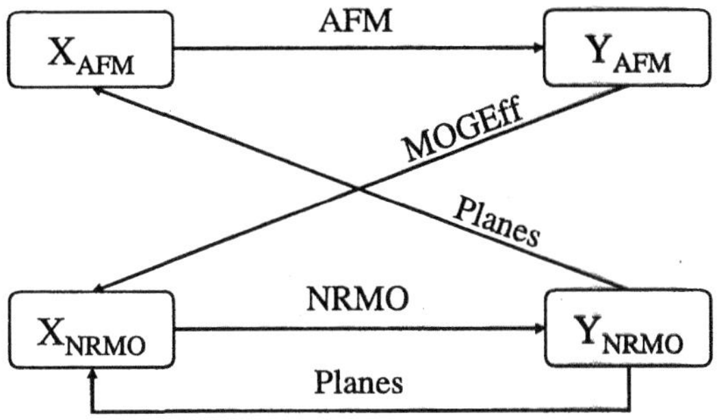

Figure 3. Feedback relationship between AFM and NRMO.

Experimental Design

Recall that we wish to construct metamodels across a small experimental design of relevant input variables to provide a convenient means of effecting a rational comparison of the models. We constructed two experimental designs; one around the input point of convergence corresponding to the small scenario and one around the input point of convergence of the big scenario. An important factor to realize is that each input variable we wish to use as a factor in the experimental design must be present as an input variable into each model.

First, we varied the number of military aircraft available for use. Regardless of the breakdown of C-17, C-5, and C-141 aircraft arrived at during the iterative procedure, the total size of the military fleet is 160 aircraft. We varied the size of this total fleet by as much as 10% by varying the number of C-5 and C-17 aircraft by eight aircraft each from the base case (as described later, the iterative method drove the number of C-141 aircraft to zero, so we did not vary this input variable from that value).

The other variables we used as factors in the experimental design are the fuel available to military aircraft at the four en route bases. The base amount of fuel at these en route bases is 800,000 gallons per day available at each Mildenhall (International Civil Aviation Organization (ICAO) identifier EGUN), Ramstein (EDAR), and Moron (LEMO), and 250,000 gallons per day available at Rota (LERT). The total amount of fuel available per day at the en route bases, then, is 2,650,000 gallons. Using a method similar to the varying of aircraft, we wish to vary the amount of total fuel available by some small relative amount; we selected a change representing just under 10% of the total fuel available; 249,000 gallons per day.

With six factors to vary, a full-factorial design yields a total requirement of 2^6, or 64, design points. Including the center point in the design, each experimental design (the small and big scenarios) consists of 65 design points, which are run on the AFM and NRMO models for comparison. We run 30 replications of the AFM model at each design point to narrow the confidence region established by the created metamodel.

Performance Results—Output/Input Crossflow

This section examines the actual performance of the output/input crossflow method on the AFM and NRMO models with respect to the small and big scenarios.

SMALL SCENARIO. Table 1 shows the input convergence through iterations of the output/input crossflow method performed on the small scenario. In the table, the inputs to NRMO are again labeled with ICAO identifiers, where OBBI represents Bahrain, OEDR is Dhahran, and OEJN refers to King Abdul Aziz. The initial inputs are displayed as Iteration 1. As shown, the number of C-141s goes to zero. This event is not unexpected since the C-17 and C-5 may carry much more cargo each mission than the C-141. The C-17 hauls over twice the average load of the C-141 (45 STons versus 19 STons) while occupying (to the degree that the models are concerned) the same amount of MOG. The C-5 requires roughly twice the MOG as the C-141 (and C-17), while

Table 1. Feedback values: small scenario.

To	AFM/NRMO			NRMO		
Feedback	Planes			MOG Efficiency		
Iteration	C-17	C-5	C-141	OBBI	OEDR	OEJN
1	50	60	50	0.680	0.680	0.680
2	37	104	19	0.634	0.577	0.650
3	56	104	0	0.734	0.438	0.571
4	56	104	0	0.725	0.215	0.602
5	56	104	0	0.725	0.215	0.602

Table 2. Output convergence: small scenario.

Iteration	Total STons/day		AFM is __% Greater than NRMO			
	AFM	NRMO	Bulk	Over	Out	Total
1	1634.2	1280.0	28.2%	30.4%	20.1%	27.7%
2	1625.9	1338.9	23.1%	18.2%	27.3%	21.4%
3	1616.3	1355.1	23.3%	15.3%	23.3%	19.3%
4	1616.3	1403.7	5.4%	17.6%	28.9%	15.1%
5	1616.3	1403.7	5.4%	17.6%	28.9%	15.1%

carrying an average load over three times that of a C-141 (61.3 STons versus 19 STons). Since in NRMO a small bonus is awarded to the objective function for using as few aircraft as possible (i.e., remaining at home station), the most efficient aircraft are used first. In fact, as shown in the table, no C-141s are recommended to move the requirement. Further, C-5 aircraft are preferred to C-17s because, while they use more MOG per short ton of cargo, the requirement is relatively undemanding to move, even while using the added MOG. The number of C-5s, in fact, is driven to the maximum number available ($\text{Avail}_{\text{C-5}}$). Notice that with the number of aircraft stabilizing so quickly, the MOG efficiency is forced to stabilize quickly as well, and the convergence occurs in only five iterations.

Table 2 displays the output convergence during the small scenario. Of note is the improvement of the models' outputs with respect to each other, ending with total throughput only 15% from each other.

BIG SCENARIO. The big scenario differs from the small scenario only in the size of the requirements in the TPFDD. Each tonnage in the small scenario TPFDD is multiplied by 1.5 to obtain the tonnage for the big scenario. The big scenario application of the output/input crossflow method again uses the MOG efficiency feedback function, equation (4), from the AFM to the NRMO model, and the NRMO model supplies the result of the mix of military aircraft feedback function, equations (2) and (3), to both AFM and NRMO. Table 3 shows the convergence of the dynamic inputs.

The number of C-141s used is again (as in the small scenario) driven to zero. In this application, however, C-17s are preferred to C-5 aircraft. The number of C-17s required is pushed to its maximum ($\text{Avail}_{\text{C-17}} = 102$) because the C-17 delivers cargo more efficiently in terms of MOG use than does the C-5, and the big scenario is demanding enough to require conservation of MOG by the models for the cargo to be moved.

Table 4 lists the total throughput of each model as well as the relative difference between AFM and NRMO for each throughput category (output convergence). A point of interest in the table is that the relative difference between the models, while starting small (10.9%) in Iteration 1, grows to 18.6% by the final iteration. This is due to AFM having use of more efficient aircraft which it flies continually without consideration of whether the requirement is satisfied or not. The only

Table 3. Feedback values: big scenario.

To	AFM/NRMO			NRMO		
Feedback	Planes			MOG Efficiency		
Iteration	C-17	C-5	C-141	OBBI	OEDR	OEJN
1	50	60	50	0.680	0.680	0.680
2	76	29	55	0.516	0.568	0.651
3	102	41	17	0.413	0.471	0.599
4	102	53	5	0.464	0.370	0.670
5	102	57	1	0.516	0.286	0.698
6	102	58	0	0.537	0.251	0.710
7	102	58	0	0.533	0.244	0.708
8	102	58	0	0.533	0.244	0.708

Table 4. Output convergence: big scenario.

Iterations	Total STons/day		AFM is ___% greater than NRMO			
	AFM	NRMO	Bulk	Over	Out	Total
1	2085.4	1879.8	7.5%	5.9%	36.6%	10.9%
2	2038.6	1954.6	4.1%	7.3%	−2.9%	4.3%
3	2269.4	1982.7	11.8%	17.5%	11.3%	14.5%
4	2329.2	1983.7	16.6%	18.9%	15.0%	17.4%
5	2361.2	1980.0	16.9%	20.4%	20.6%	19.3%
6	2371.0	1991.2	15.6%	21.6%	19.2%	19.1%
7	2371.0	1999.2	20.7%	14.4%	26.9%	18.6%
8	2371.0	1999.2	20.7%	14.4%	26.9%	18.6%

condition needed for AFM to attempt to move the next requirement in the TPFDD is that the requirement is available to load, as specified by its available-to-load date (ALD). NRMO, on the other hand, is also using the more efficient aircraft, and in fact is able to deliver about 6% more cargo in the last iteration than the first, but NRMO does not let itself deliver cargo early unless it would improve its objective function. NRMO opts instead to allow aircraft to remain at home station and obtain the small bonus for doing so.

Figure 4 graphically displays the convergence of the three throughput categories. The fact that the requirement is large enough to at least somewhat stress the airlift system, combined with the fact that the most efficient aircraft are allowed to be used, results in more dynamic fluctuations than seen for the small scenario. These factors also allowed the total throughput for each model

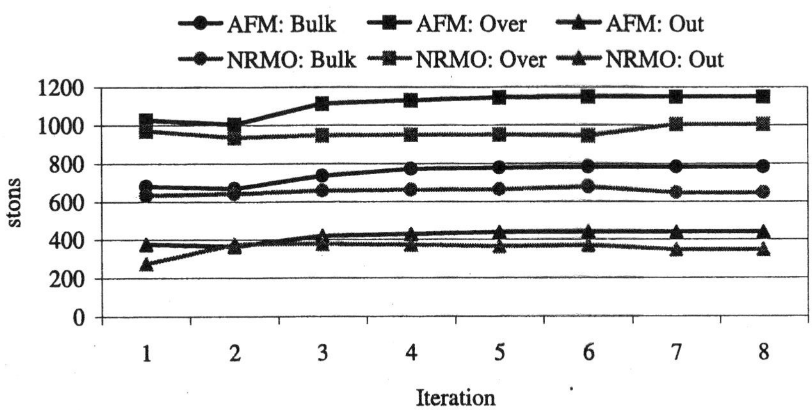

Figure 4. Output convergence: big scenario.

to increase with the iteration; the final AFM throughput growing almost 14% from the first to the last iteration, and the final NRMO throughput growing over 6%.

Performance Results—Gradient Analysis

This section examines the performance of the design of experiments on the AFM and NRMO models with respect to the small and big scenarios. The input values from the final iteration of each output/input crossflow are used as the center point of each design. We run each experiment as described previously. Recall that the factors we vary to create this experimental design include the number of C-5 and C-17 aircraft and the amount of fuel available at each of the four en route bases, Ramstein, Germany; Mildenhall, England; Moron, Spain; and Rota, Spain. Thirty replications are run at each point in the AFM model to reduce variation. Of course, we run the NRMO model only once per design point since successive runs yield identical results. The constructed metamodels use the output total throughput as the dependent variable since it is a high-level response of greatest concern to decision makers. If the models compare favorably using this output, other responses may be analyzed to determine the extent of covalidity. However, if the models do not compare favorably using this high-level response, a strong claim may be made that the models are not covalid for the scenarios under observation. The first section details the experimental design performed on the small scenario, and the next section describes the experimental design applied to the big scenario.

SMALL SCENARIO. The AFM model is run 30 times and NRMO is run once at each of the 65 design points. The initial regression metamodel is constructed using all six factors plus all two-way interactions. A lack of significance in the interaction terms combined with a lack of agreement of which interaction terms were significant led to dropping all the interactions and dealing only with the main factors. In this way, the metamodels for the AFM and NRMO models are readily comparable.

Table 5 lists a few statistics concerning the resulting metamodels for AFM and NRMO, built with regard to total throughput. The mean total throughput of the AFM model is 17.5% higher than that of the NRMO model, roughly as expected given the result of the output/input crossflow method (see Table 2).

The only significant factors in the AFM metamodel are the aircraft (C-5 and C-17) and the fuel at LEMO (Moron). In the NRMO model, the number of C-5s is the only clearly significant factor, and the number of C-17s is marginally significant at the $\alpha = 0.10$ level. That the aircraft factors could both be considered significant in each model is favorable to the consideration of the models' covalidity for this scenario until it is noticed that the signs of the coefficients do not agree for the C-5 factor. Of course, one would expect all coefficient signs to be positive since an increase in any of the factor levels means an increase in resources available to deliver cargo. Specifically, the coefficients may be interpreted as the change in the total short tons delivered per day due to an increase in the factor level by approximately 10% (eight aircraft for the aircraft factors, 62,250 gallons of fuel for each of the base fuel factors). That the signs on the AFM coefficients are not all positive, then, is a matter to look into more closely.

In the small scenario, movement requirements are not demanding for either model. AFM delivers requirements using the first available aircraft searching for the first available cargo requirement and carrying it using the first available route. Therefore, if the model has delivered all required cargo by the appropriate date, the model will still search for the next available piece of cargo and deliver it, effectively getting ahead on its required deliveries. The AFM model, however, can only pick-up cargo for delivery on or after the cargo available-to-load date (ALD). If AFM is picking up all or most of its cargo on the ALD, adding resources (or taking away resources to the extent that the model can still pick up all the cargo on the ALD) will not affect throughput. This is the case for the AFM model operating on the small scenario. The delivery requirement is easily handled regardless of small perturbations made to the resource levels studied, and the

Table 5. Small scenario total throughput metamodel results.

		AFM	NRMO
Coefficient	Mean	1616.4	1375.6
	C-5	−0.4	16.2
	C-17	0.9	2.5
	EDAR	−0.1	0.0
	EGUN	0.1	−0.3
	LEMO	0.5	−0.7
	LERT	0.1	2.0
P-Value	Mean	0.000	0.000
	C-5	0.013	0.000
	C-17	0.000	0.101
	EDAR	0.589	1.000
	EGUN	0.671	0.859
	LEMO	0.001	0.629
	LERT	0.736	0.187
Coefficient Standard Error		0.149	1.481
MSR		381.0	2918.9
MSE		42.6	140.3
F*		8.94	20.80
F* Significance		0.0	0.0
R^2		0.027	0.683

small coefficients are due to both random variation of the responses and nuances in the complex simulation model. A look at the R^2 value indicates that the fitted model does not explain a significant portion of the variation of the responses, further demonstrating that the AFM regression metamodel is inadequate to explain changes in total throughput due to incremental changes in the factors of interest.

The NRMO regression metamodel displays, as the AFM metamodel, that the fuel at the en route bases is not a significant factor when considering this small scenario. The significance of the C-5 factor, however, allows the fitted NRMO metamodel to explain much more of the response variation than the AFM metamodel. The relatively large value for this factor is explained by the efficiency of the C-5 compared to the C-17 when fuel and MOG are not (tightly) constrained, as in the small scenario.

BIG SCENARIO. The big scenario is analyzed just as the small scenario. Again, 30 replications at each design point are run for the AFM design of experiments, and we construct the metamodels for total throughput using only the main effects in order to develop a linear gradient estimate.

Table 6 displays the characteristics of the AFM and NRMO metamodels created for the big scenario. The first point to note is that both metamodels account for a much larger percentage of the variations of the response, as indicated by the R^2 values, than in the small scenario. This is due to the fact that the scenario's increased size means that the models can no longer easily move the entire requirement in an environment that appears unconstrained. In particular, in the AFM metamodel, it is clear that the fuel available at the en route bases is becoming a constraint, considering the large coefficients of these factors. Interestingly, the NRMO model (delivering about 15% less cargo due to reasons discussed previously) seems to be on the edge of this fuel constraint, with only the fuel at Rota, Spain providing a significant factor. However, this is the

Table 6. Big Scenario total throughput metamodel results.

		AFM	NRMO
Coefficient	Mean	2341.4	1980.8
	C-5	2.3	16.2
	C-17	13.3	12.2
	EDAR	28.4	0.0
	EGUN	23.3	0.9
	LEMO	34.0	0.8
	LERT	34.1	12.9
P-Value	Mean	0.000	0.000
	C-5	0.009	0.000
	C-17	0.000	0.000
	EDAR	0.000	1.000
	EGUN	0.000	0.154
	LEMO	0.000	0.196
	LERT	0.000	0.000
Coefficient Standard Error		0.904	0.614
MSR		1231511.4	6199.8
MSE		1567.7	24.1
F*		785.55	257.15
F* Significance		0.0	0.0
R^2		0.708	0.964

base we would expect to notice the fuel constraint first since the initial amount of fuel available at Rota is less than at the other en route bases (250,000 gallons per day versus 800,000 gallons per day), while the amount we vary the fuel remains constant (62,250 gallons per day) regardless of the base.

In this big scenario, it is clear that AFM is unable to pick up the requirements on the ALD as in the small scenario. This is evidenced by the increased magnitude and significance of the coefficients. A comparison of the NRMO coefficients shows that the big scenario is more demanding, as well. The exception here is that fuel at the first three en route bases in the NRMO metamodel still has little significance in regards to throughput.

Therefore, whereas in the small scenario the metamodels are of limited significance, the big scenario metamodels appear much more conducive for comparison. In the following section, we discuss the comparison of the metamodels and allude to the implications of covalidity between the models.

MODEL COMPARISON. The method we consider to assist in the determination of models' covalidity tests whether one of the metamodel's gradient vectors can be found within the confidence region (hypercone) of the other metamodel's gradient vector. Of course, this method tests only the similarity of the gradient vectors and should be accompanied by an examination of the differences between the mean response values (unless an application is solely concerned with the sensitivity of the response to the inputs).

We treat the small scenario comparison first. Of course, the difference between the mean values for the total throughput output of the two metamodels is statistically nonzero, so we concentrate here on the analysis of the gradient values. The angle between the gradient vector and the extent of the confidence hypercone has been described by equation (1). We construct a 95% confidence

Table 7. Gradient comparison summary.

Scenario	Angle Between Gradients	95% Confidence Region Angle	
		AFM	NRMO
Small	103.04°	27.05°	17.96°
Big	62.61°	2.78°	5.03°

hypercone about the AFM small scenario metamodel gradient vector and determine that the confidence hypercone extends 27.05 degrees from the gradient vector. The angle between the AFM and NRMO metamodel gradient vectors is determined by the taking the arc cosine of the dot product of the vectors divided by the product of the magnitudes of the vectors. We calculate the angle between the gradient vectors to be 103.04 degrees. This angle being larger than a right angle implies that at least one factor's coefficient is of opposite sign from one model to the other. We noted this phenomena in the discussion of the small scenario's C-5 factor. The gradient comparison results are summarized in Table 7.

We acknowledge that there is a degree of latitude when making the determination as to whether models are covalid or not. For instance, determining the F statistic in equation (1) to a different level of significance would give a different angle to test the gradient vectors against (finding a 99% confidence region for the small scenario results in an angle that extends 32.1 degrees from the AFM metamodel gradient vector). No confidence region may extend beyond 90 degrees from the gradient vector, however, since the angle is found by taking an arc sine. So we may clearly state that these metamodels are not close enough in terms of response or gradients developed with respect to inputs of interest to claim that the AFM and NRMO models are covalid at the input point identified as the small scenario.

Next, we examine the big scenario. Again, the difference between the mean total throughput values for the metamodels created for the big scenario is so great that the means cannot be considered equal. The angle between the gradient vector of the AFM model's metamodel and the extent of its 95% confidence region hypercone is only 2.78 degrees. The angle between the AFM and NRMO metamodel gradient vectors is found to be 62.6 degrees.

Obviously, the NRMO metamodel gradient vector does not exist inside the confidence region of the AFM metamodel's gradient vector. We also consider whether a confidence region constructed around the NRMO metamodel gradient vector would overlap the AFM metamodel gradient vector confidence region. The confidence region created around the NRMO metamodel gradient vector extends 5.03 degrees from the vector. Therefore, the 95% confidence regions for the two metamodels' gradient vectors do not overlap.

Though we cannot claim that the AFM and NRMO models compare favorably enough at the small or big scenarios to warrant the claim that they are covalid, some consolation may be taken in the fact that the coefficients from the big scenario's metamodels all agree in sign. This information may be used by system experts to claim some limited level of covalidity between the models at the big scenario, particularly since the signs of the gradient coefficients all agree with expectations, namely that an increase in resources will yield an increase in total throughput. Also, the fact that for the big scenario gradient vectors are closer than in the small scenario could lead experts to consider that an even larger, more constrained scenario may produce closer gradient vectors. This consideration could lead to the creation of such a scenario, and possibly a gradient analysis performed at this new scenario would yield more favorable results.

CONCLUSION

We have devised a method that allows for comparisons between models under different modeling paradigms. We began with the description of a general modeling paradigm, particularly applicable when multiple models are created to represent the same system. The paradigm serves as a framework for the developed methodology. Our proposal is to use two or more models in concert in order to improve the performance of each. The output/input crossflow method is developed to generate this model improvement. Through the use of the output/input crossflow method, we hope to arrive at models that are as close as possible in terms of their inputs and outputs. We then develop a method to characterize the difference not only in the model outputs, but also in the models' sensitivities to input variations. The end result is a characterization of the models' covalidity. We apply the developed methods to two large-scale models used by AMCSAF to analyze the strategic airlift system; AFM, a simulation model, and NRMO, an optimization model.

We have effectively established an original paradigm regarding the construction, improvement, and validation of models that represent real-world systems. This paradigm describes the translation of real-world systems to the modeling world, the way in which models (and the real-world system) may be enhanced based on the findings of the other models (or of the system itself), and methods of determining the correctness of the models, both in relation to each other and to the real-world system they attempt to characterize.

We also hope to have instilled a sense that, instead of considering two models created for the same real-world system as rivals, they may at times be considered allies. Developing multiple perspectives of the same divisive topic tends to create a clarity in the consideration of the topic. In the same way, multiple models developed for the same system can create a better understanding of the system that leads to improvements in both models. By realizing these improvements, the hope is to decrease the impact that assumptions have on the models.

Finally, the comparison of models with the real world has long been known to lead to increased faith and trust in models. We argue that the comparison of models with each other leads to faith and trust that the models are mimicking the real world in the same way. This covalidity in the narrow sense may be expanded to a covalidity in the wide sense if the models also compare favorably with the real-world system. The important note here is that models should have some benchmark of comparison if they are to be used in rigorous analysis, and if the real-world system upon which they are based is not available for that use, another model can serve as a reasonable proxy. The extent of these models' believability relies on this comparison.

REFERENCES

1. O. Balci, Validation, verification, and testing techniques throughout the life cycle of a simulation study, *Annals of Operations Research* **53**, 121–173, (1994).
2. R.G. Sargent, Verifying and validating simulation models, In *Proceedings of the 1996 Winter Simulation Conference,* Coronado, CA, pp. 55–64, (1996).
3. R.G. Sargent, Some subjective validation methods using graphical displays of data, pp. 345–351, In *Proceedings of the 1996 Winter Simulation Conference,* Coronado, CA, (1996).
4. A.M. Law and W.D. Kelton, *Simulation Modeling & Analysis*, Second Edition, McGraw-Hill, New York, (1991).
5. D.A. Diener, H.R. Hicks and L.L. Long, Comparison of models: Ex post facto validation/acceptance, In *Proceedings of the 1992 Winter Simulation Conference,* Arlington, VA, pp. 1095–1103, (1992).
6. J.P.C. Kleijnen, Verification and validation of simulation models, *European Journal of Operations Research* **82**, 145–162, (1995).
7. D.L. Merrill, Analyst, air mobility command studies and analysis flight, Point paper on the Mobility Analysis Support System prepared for Congressional Budget Office analysts, Air Mobility Command, Scott AFB, IL, (27 October 1993).
8. S.F. Baker, D.P. Morton, R.E. Rosenthal and L.M. Williams, Optimizing military airlift, *Operations Research* **50** (4), 582–602, (2002).
9. S.A. Wright, Covalidation of dissimilarly structured models, Ph.D. Dissertation, AFIT/DS/ENS/00-02, School of Engineering and Management, Air Force Institute of Technology (AU), Wright-Patterson AFB, OH, (March 2001).
10. G.E.P. Box and N.R. Draper, *Empirical Model-Building and Response Surfaces*, John Wiley & Sons, New York, (1987).

Available online at www.sciencedirect.com
SCIENCE DIRECT•
Mathematical and Computer Modelling 39 (2004) 697–714
MATHEMATICAL AND COMPUTER MODELLING
www.elsevier.com/locate/mcm

Large-Scale Optimization Planning Methods for the Distribution of United States Army Munitions

S. J. CLARK
United States Air Force Materiel Command, Management Sciences Division
4375 Chidlaw Road, Room B204, Wright-Patterson AFB, OH 45431, U.S.A.
steven.clark@wpafb.af.mil

C. BARNHART
Massachusetts Institute of Technology
77 Massachusetts Avenue, Bldg. E40-149
Cambridge, MA 02139, U.S.A.
cbarnhar@mit.edu

S. E. KOLITZ
The Charles Stark Draper Laboratory, Inc.
555 Technology Square, Cambridge, MA 02139, U.S.A.
kolitz@draper.com

Abstract—Coordinating the distribution of ammunition and scheduling strategic transportation resources during military contingency operations is a complex process. This paper presents a large-scale optimization-based planning method that uses column generation to schedule the movement of ammunition and transportation resources through a time-space network representation of the distribution system. The optimization-based planner is initialized using a feasible solution generated by a heuristic planning method. Both the optimization-based planner and the heuristic planner generate plans with improved ship utilization and delivery tardiness values as compared to plans generated using current planning techniques. In addition, the heuristic planner is implemented within a closed-loop planning and control framework, and is used to generate plans on a rolling horizon basis.

Keywords—Ammunition, Sealift, Distribution, Scheduling, Large-scale, Optimization.

1. INTRODUCTION

Distribution, as defined by the Joint Chiefs of Staff, is the "operational process of synchronizing all elements of the logistic system to deliver the right things to the right place at the right time" in support of a combatant commander [1]. To reach warfighters in the field, materiel must travel through an extensive network of processing facilities and transportation links. The processing facilities include depots, ports, and in-theater staging areas interconnected by multiple commercial and military transportation resources including railcars, trucks, barges, ocean-going cargo ships, and cargo aircraft.

This material is based upon work prepared as a Draper Fellow at the Massachusetts Institute of Technology, and was sponsored by the Logistics Integration Agency.

0895-7177/04/$ - see front matter © 2004 Elsevier Ltd. All rights reserved. Typeset by AMS-TEX
doi:10.1016/j.mcm.2004.02.009

Previous ship routing and scheduling research has focused on variants of decomposition and heuristic techniques. Christiansen [2], as well as Rana and Vickson [3], use a decomposition approach to create ship schedules for a fleet of ships over a finite-planning horizon. Their models do not, however, address the detailed scheduling of cargo items, but instead focus on meeting the aggregate demand at a series of ports over the planning horizon. Heuristics, such as those developed by Ronen [4] are also prevalent in the literature and are often based on partial enumeration, marginal analysis, or more sophisticated techniques such as tabu search. A number of "human-in-the-loop" approaches such as Nulty and Ratliff [5] or Boffer *et al.* [6] have also been developed to augment the solutions of an optimization or heuristic model with the knowledge and experience of a human planner.

This paper focuses on one segment of the overall military logistics system. In particular, an optimization-based, real-time planning, and control methodology is developed and applied to the wholesale distribution of containerized, follow-on sustainment ammunition. During wartime, this type of ammunition flows from war reserve stockpiles in the continental United States (CONUS) to military units in overseas theaters of operations. This segment was selected because the ammunition distribution network is somewhat separated from the rest of the logistics network, yet it has many of the attributes that make these types of planning problems so complex.

Responsibility for the management of ammunition items is assigned to Operations Support Command (OSC) at Rock Island Arsenal in Illinois, a subordinate command of U.S. Army Materiel Command (AMC). In 1995, OSC was assigned the role of the Single Manager for Conventional Ammunition (SMCA) for the Department of Defense. The SMCA mission was created in an attempt to consolidate the wholesale ammunition logistics functions of the different service branches including production, storage, maintenance, and transportation.

OSC controls a number of CONUS depot facilities that maintain and store ammunition items. Each depot facility is comprised of two main areas: storage areas (usually referred to as bunkers or magazines) and transshipment pads. The storage structures are typically dispersed over many acres in order to limit the amount of damage that would result from an accidental explosion. During contingency operations, ammunition items are removed from the storage structures and consolidated into containerized shipments called strategic configured loads. A strategic configured load consists of a predetermined mix of ammunition items that is transported as a single unit and is tailored to support a particular unit type or weapons system [7]. For example, a strategic configured load might include the quantity and mix of ammunition that is required to support an M1-A1 Abrams tank for several weeks.

Once the ammunition items are consolidated into strategic configured loads, they are placed inside standard 20-foot shipping containers. These containers queue at the transshipment pads until they are transported to CONUS ports of embarkation (POEs) by either commercial truck or rail.

There are three POEs that are capable of handling the unique requirements of ammunition items. As of October 1999, all three ports are controlled by the Military Traffic Management Command (MTMC), a component command of U.S. Transportation Command (USTRANSCOM). At the POEs, the containers holding the ammunition items are transferred onboard large cargo ships, which transport the items to ports of debarkation (PODs) in or near the theater of operations.

Each POE is comprised of three main processing areas. The first area is used to receive ammunition items arriving from the depots by either trucks or railcars. The second area includes all of the temporary storage pads where ammunition items are placed after being unloaded off inbound conveyances. The final processing area includes all of the berths that are used when loading the containerized ammunition items onboard ships.

The ports of debarkation (PODs) typically belong to a host nation in the neighboring region of a contingency operation. Because of the diversity of regions where a contingency can occur, the type and level of sophistication of PODs can vary greatly. Each POD facility must be capable of unloading arriving ships, storing ammunition items, and loading the transportation resources used to move the ammunition items from the POD to in-theater locations.

2. NETWORK REPRESENTATION

In order to apply analytical planning tools, the ammunition distribution system is represented within the computer as a time-space network, G, comprised of a set of nodes, N, and directed arcs, A. Time-space networks have been used in other scheduling applications where information about the movement of goods is important, as well as the timing of the movements (see [8–10], for examples). Representing the distribution system as a network of nodes and directed arcs allows us to use specialized algorithms such as shortest path and maximum flow algorithms that exploit the network's underlying structural properties.

A two-step process is used to create a time-space network. First, a static network representation of the distribution system is created using nodes and directed arcs. To accomplish this, the subfacilities of each depot, port of embarkation, and port of debarkation are represented as nodes in the graph. For example, a depot is represented as two subfacilities: a storage area and an outbound staging area. Directed arcs are then used to connect the subfacilities. Each directed arc is known as a *processing arc* and corresponds to a different ammunition processing activity such as loading, unloading, or transporting.

The set of directed arcs that connect the internal subfacilities of a depot, port of embarkation, or port of debarkation are used to model the flow of ammunition items within these facilities. Similarly, the set of directed arcs that connect depot subfacilities to port of embarkation subfacilities and port of embarkation subfacilities to port of debarkation subfacilities are used to model the flow between facilities. It is possible for multiple directed arcs to exist between subfacilities if more than one type of transportation resource is available (e.g., both truck and rail transportation). A sample static network is shown in Figure 1.

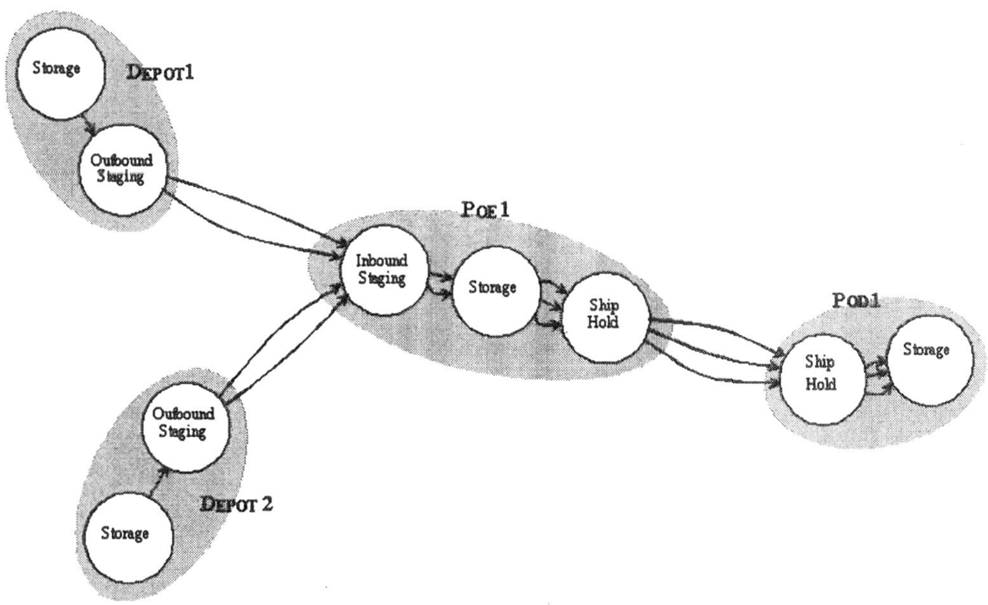

Figure 1. Static network representation.

The second step in creating the time-space network is replicating the static network representation over a finite-planning horizon. Each node in the time-space network that is created by replicating a node in the original static graph corresponds to the same subfacility. However, each node represents the subfacility at a different time period over the planning horizon. As a result, it is possible to reference each node by a unique ordered pair (i, t). The first element, i, is the node's spatial index and the second element, t, is the node's temporal index.

In a time-space network representation, directed arcs are included between nodes to represent the possible movement of items in both the spatial and temporal dimensions. In order to model the duration of processing activities, processing arcs can connect nodes with different temporal indices. The difference between the spatial index of an arc's starting and ending node is used to represent movement from one subfacility to another. Similarly, the difference between the temporal index of an arc's starting and ending node is used to represent the duration of the processing activity that the arc represents. Because a node exists for each discrete time period in the planning horizon, the duration of each processing activity must also take on a discrete value. It is assumed that loading and unloading activities within a facility require one time period. Transportation activities between subfacilities depend on the mode and the distances traveled, but require at least one time period.

In addition to modeling the movement of ammunition items between subfacilities, the time-space network representation allows us to model the inventory level of ammunition items at each subfacility over time. For example, an ammunition item might remain at a depot's storage facility for multiple time periods. This type of movement is modeled by adding directed arcs called *inventory arcs* to the time-space network. Inventory arcs connect nodes with the same spatial index, but temporal indices that differ by a single time period. Ammunition items can remain at a particular subfacility for multiple discrete time periods by flowing over multiple inventory arcs.

Unlike processing arcs, inventory arcs are not always directed forward in the temporal dimension of the time-space network. A special type of inventory arc, known as a *late arc*, is added between each node in the time-space network corresponding to the storage subfacility at each POD facility. The temporal index of each late arc's starting node is one discrete time period greater than the temporal index of its ending node.

It is assumed that all ammunition items are sourced from depot storage facilities and are demanded at POD storage subfacilities. The addition of late arcs allow us to capture the flow of ammunition items that arrive late to each POD storage subfacility with respect to the ammunition item's required delivery date (RDD). In order to satisfy the demand for each ammunition item that arrives late, the ammunition items must be able to flow "backwards" in the time-space network with respect to the temporal dimension. The number of late arcs that a particular ammunition item must use between the discrete time period it arrives at a POD storage facility node and the time period corresponding to the ammunition item's RDD is the amount of time that the ammunition item is tardy. While the flow on these arcs has no physical meaning in the real-world distribution system, they allow planning algorithms to keep track of which items are late, and by how many discrete time periods. This information is useful, for example, when attempting to create a distribution plan that minimizes the total system-wide tardiness.

Two ordered pairs are used to reference each processing and inventory arc in the time-space network. Some arcs also include an index that specifies the type of transportation resource associated with the processing or inventory activity that the arc represents. The first-ordered pair specifies the directed arc's starting node, while the second-ordered pair specifies its ending node. The transportation resource index is only included when it is applicable to the processing activity or inventory activity that the directed arc represents. For example the directed arc $\{(m,t),(n,t'),r\}$ begins at node (m,t) ends at node (n,t') and uses transportation resource r. For simplicity, this paper also uses the notation (i,j) to represent an arc $\{(m,t),(n,t'),r\}$ where i is the starting node, j is the ending node, and the resource type r is implied.

A cost value and capacity value are associated with each arc in the time-space network. The cost value on each arc specifies the contribution to some objective function that is incurred for each unit of ammunition that uses the directed arc. The capacity of a directed arc is defined as the limit on the total amount of flow that may traverse the arc. The capacity value corresponds to either a physical limit, or a maximum throughput constraint on the number of ammunition items that the processing activity or storage activity associated with each arc can support. For example, the capacity of an inventory arc equals the physical capacity of the storage area, while the capacity of loading or unloading processing arcs equals the quantity of ammunition items that may be processed during one discrete time period.

2.1. Modeling Ship Movements Using the Time-Space Network

In addition to providing a framework to model the movement of ammunition items through the distribution system, the time-space network is also used to model the movement of the ships. Ships are resources that must be present during certain processing and inventory activities. For example, ships are used to transport ammunition items from POEs to PODs. The presence of a ship provides physical capacity for the storage or movement of ammunition items. In the time-space network, this corresponds to allocating capacity on the directed arcs associated with the processing and inventory activities that require a ship. The capacity of these directed arcs in the absence of a ship's presence is zero.

Like ammunition items, ships flow through the time-space network using directed arcs. The movement may be in the temporal dimension only (e.g., if the ship is berthed at a POE or POD facility), or both the temporal and spatial dimension (e.g., if the ship is sailing between facilities). For the movement to be continuous over the entire planning horizon, additional directed arcs known as *salvage arcs* must be added to the time-space network from each POD to each POE. The difference between the temporal indices of each salvage arc's ending node and each directed arc's starting node corresponds to the discrete travel time for each ship between the two facilities.

Because feasible ship movements only correspond to a subset of arcs in the time-space network, the overall time-space network may be divided into two disjoint subsets. The first subset, known as the *fixed portion* of the time-space network, includes those directed arcs whose capacity does not depend on the presence of a ship to allocate capacity in order for ammunition items to flow from one node to another. The remaining processing and inventory arcs form a subset whose capacity does depend on the presence of a ship. In other words, ammunition items may not flow on a particular directed arc unless a ship is also present to provide capacity. This subset of arcs, A^d, is referred to as the *design portion* of the time-space network.

2.2. Ammunition and Ship Schedule Representations

The planning algorithms presented in this paper use the time-space network representation of the distribution system to produce schedules for both ammunition items and ships. Schedules are different from routes, with routes being a subset of schedules. Routes are only concerned with the spatial movements of ammunition items or ships from one subfacility to another, not the timing of the movements.

Ammunition item schedules specify a continuous sequence of subfacilities visited by an ammunition item from its source subfacility to its destination subfacility. The ship schedules generated by the algorithms must support the movement of ammunition items as they travel from POE facilities to POD facilities. Like ammunition item schedules, a ship schedule specifies a continuous sequence of POE and POD subfacilities visited by a ship, as well as the timing of the ship's movements.

Both ammunition item schedules and ship schedules are subject to a variety of constraints. For example, the schedule for an ammunition item must adhere to capacity constraints within and between each subfacility, as well as the transit and processing times associated with each processing activity. In addition, the schedules must specify the transportation mode or resource used for each activity, when applicable.

With respect to the time-space network, generating an ammunition item schedule corresponds to finding a path of directed arcs through the time-space network, called an ammunition path. An ammunition path, P_A, is a continuous sequence of directed arcs from the ammunition item's source node to its destination node in the time-space network.

Each path's source node is located at a depot, while each path's destination node is located at a POD. The ammunition item's ready-to-load date (RLD) at the depot and RDD at the POD determine the temporal indices of the ammunition item's source node and its destination node, respectively. Ammunition items that use a particular ammunition path are said to *flow* on the path and utilize capacity on each of the directed arcs included in the path.

Similar to an ammunition path, a ship schedule corresponds to the movement of a ship through the time-space network and, as a result, also corresponds to a path of directed arcs. A ship path, P_S, is a continuous sequence of directed arcs, $(i, j) \in A^d$, that corresponds to a set of feasible movements for a ship through the time-space network.

Unlike ammunition items, which utilize capacity, a ship flowing over a ship path allocates capacity to the directed arcs included in the ship path. Ships also allocate capacity to other processing arcs associated with the ship path including arcs that represent loading and unloading activities.

3. OPTIMIZATION-BASED MODEL FORMULATION

This section describes the development of an optimization-based model that is used to schedule the movement of ammunition items and the ships used to transport them. The formulation can be classified as a network design problem, with an embedded multicommodity flow problem involving the flow of nonhomogeneous commodities (i.e., different containerized strategic configured loads) through the time-space network. It is a network design problem because the capacities of the arcs included in the design portion of the time-space network are a function of ship scheduling decisions, which are determined by solving the optimization model.

The optimization model formulation is based upon Dantzig-Wolfe decomposition. Instead of a single, large optimization formulation, a separate planning problem is created for each ammunition commodity type (i.e., each type of strategic configured load) and ship fleet type. Each subproblem uses optimization techniques to generate paths through the time-space network. Once these paths are generated, another optimization model, known as the *master problem* is solved to determine the best subset of paths.

We use an iterative solution procedure in which new paths are generated in solving each subproblem, and added to the master problem at each iteration. After the new paths are generated, the master problem is re-solved. Dual price information from the resulting solution is used as input to each subproblem, providing information about the level of congestion on each arc in the time-space network. This information is used in solving the subproblems to influence the ammunition and ship paths generated for inclusion in the master problem during the next iteration of the solution procedure. This iterative process continues until the master problem's dual price information indicates that the global optimal solution has been discovered or some other stopping criteria, such as an iteration limit or time limit, has been reached.

The remainder of this section outlines the decomposition strategy and details the development of the master problem formulation, as well as each ammunition and ship scheduling subproblem.

3.1. Master Problem Optimization Formulation

The master problem solution specifies the quantity of ammunition that should flow along each ammunition path and the number of ships that should flow along each ship path. It also provides dual price information to the ammunition and ship scheduling subproblem to assist them with generating new paths for the master problem to optimize over during subsequent iterations.

The columns in the master problem's constraint matrix correspond to paths through the time-space network for ammunition items and ships. Binary coefficients within the column are used to indicate the arcs used by each path. The objective function coefficient for each path is determined by the number of late arcs that the path uses to deliver ammunition items to the time and place that they are demanded.

To solve the subproblems using an efficient shortest path algorithm, the master problem must consist entirely of bundle constraints. Bundle constraints limit the aggregate flow across all ammunition paths that use a particular directed arc in the time-space network. Unfortunately, bundle constraints are not always sufficient to model network design problems. For example, in order to avoid a situation where different ship paths jointly cover an ammunition path, but no single ship path independently covers the ammunition path, the nodes and arcs in the design portion of the time space network must be replicated for each ship. For scenarios with a large number of ships, the size of the time-space network quickly becomes intractable. Instead, an alternative formulation based on *composites* is presented.

Composites are used to aggregate multiple scheduling decisions into a single decision for both ammunition items and ships. *Ammunition path composites* are used to aggregate ammunition scheduling decisions. An ammunition path composite, $\bar{P}_A$, is a set of directed arcs that form a path through the design portion of the time-space network and includes a single ship loading arc, a single ship transport arc, and a single ship unloading arc. To control the number of ammunition path composites that are considered, maximum berth times, B_{POE} and B_{POD}, are specified for each POE and POD, respectively.

The composite $\bar{P}_A$ aggregates all of the activities required for an ammunition item to flow through the design portion of the time-space network. Furthermore, each ammunition path composite has an associated ammunition path composite arc. The start node, i, of ammunition path composite arc (i, j) associated with ammunition path composite $\bar{P}_A$ is the starting node of the unique loading arc in and the ending node, j, is the ending node of the unique unloading arc in $\bar{P}_A$.

By formulating the master level planner with a constraint for each ammunition path composite arc, all of the constraints become bundle constraints and correspond directly to individual arcs (including composite arcs). This results in a master problem formulation where column generation techniques may be used and efficient shortest path algorithms can be used to solve the subproblems.

Parameters and Sets

Y	the set of ship fleet types
K	the set of ammunition commodity types
R	the set of CONUS transportation resource types
POE	set of all port of embarkation facilities
POD	set of all port of debarkation facilities
T	set of all discrete time periods in the planning horizon
N	set of all nodes (i, t) in the time-space network
A	set of all arcs (j, k, r) in the time-space network where $j, k \in N$ and $r \in R$
A^d	set of all design arcs in the time-space network
P_A^k	set of all feasible directed ammunition paths for commodity $k = 1, 2, \ldots, \|K\|$
P_S^y	set of all feasible directed ship paths for ship fleet type $y = 1, 2, \ldots, \|Y\|$
$C_{\bar{P}_A}$	set of all feasible ammunition path composites $\bar{P}_A$
c_{ij}^k	cost of arc $(i, j) \in A$ for commodity $k \in K$
c_{ij}^y	cost of arc $(i, j) \in A^d$ for ship fleet type $y \in Y$
$c_k(P_A)$	cost of ammunition path P_A for commodity type $k \in K$
$c_y(P_S)$	cost of ship path P_S for ship fleet type $y \in Y$
$\tilde{H}_y$	hold capacity of a ship from ship fleet type $y \in Y$
b_{ij}	capacity of arc $(i, j) \in A$
d_k	aggregate demand for commodity type $k \in K$ over the planning horizon
F_y	number of ships in fleet type $y \in Y$

Decision Variables

$f(P_A)$	flow of ammunition items of a particular commodity type on ammunition path P_A
$f(P_S)$	flow of ships of a particular fleet type on ship path P_S

INDICATOR VARIABLES

$$\alpha_{ij}(P_A) = \begin{cases} 1, & \text{if ammunition path } P_A \text{ includes arc } (i,j) \in A, \\ 0, & \text{otherwise.} \end{cases}$$

$$\beta_{ij}(P_S) = \begin{cases} 1, & \text{if ship path } P_S \text{ covers arc } (i,j) \in A^d, \\ 0, & \text{otherwise.} \end{cases}$$

$$\mu_{\bar{P}_A}(P_A) = \begin{cases} 1, & \text{if ammunition path } P_A \text{ uses the arcs in path composite } \bar{P}_A, \\ 0, & \text{otherwise.} \end{cases}$$

$$\upsilon_{\bar{P}_A}(P_S) = \begin{cases} 1, & \text{if ship path } P_S \text{ covers the arcs in path composite } \bar{P}_A, \\ 0, & \text{otherwise.} \end{cases}$$

MASTER LEVEL PLANNER FORMULATION

$$\min \sum_{k=1}^{|K|} \sum_{P_A \in P_A^k} c_k(P_A) f(P_A) + \sum_{y=1}^{|Y|} \sum_{P_S \in P_S^y} c_y(P_S) f(P_S), \tag{1}$$

$$\text{subject to} \sum_{P_A \in P_A^k} f(P_A) = d_k, \qquad \forall k = 1,2,\ldots,|K| \; [\sigma_k]. \tag{2}$$

$$\sum_{P_S \in P_S^y} f(P_S) \le F_y, \qquad \forall y = 1,2,\ldots,|Y| \; [\sigma_n]. \tag{3}$$

$$\sum_{k=1}^{|K|} \sum_{P_A \in P_A^k} \alpha_{ij}(P_A) f(P_A) \le b_{ij}, \qquad \forall (i,j) \in A \; [\phi_{ij}]. \tag{4}$$

$$\sum_{k=1}^{|K|} \sum_{P_A \in P_A^k} \alpha_{ij}(P_A) f(P_A) \le \sum_{y=1}^{|Y|} \sum_{P_S \in P_S^y} \beta_{ij}(P_S) \tilde{H}_y f(P_S), \qquad \forall (i,j) \in A^d \; [\gamma_{ij}]. \tag{5}$$

$$\sum_{k=1}^{|K|} \sum_{P_A \in P_A^k} \mu_c(P_A) f(P_A) \le \sum_{y=1}^{|Y|} \sum_{P_S \in P_S^y} \upsilon_c(P_S) \tilde{H}_y f(P_S), \qquad \forall c \in C_{\bar{P}_A} \; [\pi_c]. \tag{6}$$

$$f(P_A) \ge 0, \qquad \forall k = 1,2,\ldots,|K| \text{ and } P_A \in P_A^k. \tag{7}$$

$$f(P_S) \in Z^+, \qquad \forall y = 1,2,\ldots,|Y| \text{ and } P_S \in P_S^y. \tag{8}$$

The objective of the formulation is to minimize the tardiness of ammunition items past their RDD. A cost is also placed on ship schedules in order to penalize underutilization. Constraints (2) and (3) enforce demand requirements and fleet size limitations, respectively, while constraints (4) and (5) enforce bundle capacity restrictions. Constraints (6) state that for ammunition items of a particular commodity type to flow on any path P_A that uses path composite $\bar{P}_A$, some ship path must cover $\bar{P}_A$. A ship path, P_S, covers an ammunition path composite, $\bar{P}_A$, if $(i,j) \in (\bar{P}_A \cap P_S)$, $\forall (i,j) \in \bar{P}_A$. Finally, the values enclosed in square brackets alongside constraints (2) through (6) are the dual variables.

Because the number of all possible ammunition paths and ship paths can be extremely large, the column generation process is started with a subset of all possible columns and rows. Columns are added as ammunition paths and ship paths are generated by the subproblems. Likewise, rows corresponding to constraint (6) are added to the restricted master problem during the course of the column generation routine if a new ammunition path or ship path is generated that uses a path composite whose associated row is not already included.

Once no additional columns with negative reduced cost are found or an alternative stopping criteria is satisfied, an integer solution is obtained by using a heuristic method described by

Barnhart *et al.* [11]. This method uses column generation to solve the LP-relaxation of the root node of the branch-and-bound tree. Once a solution to the LP-relaxation of the root node is found, a standard branch-and-bound algorithm is used to find an integer solution. This heuristic procedure does not guarantee an optimal integer solution, but is generally much simpler to implement than a branch-and-price algorithm.

3.2. Ammunition Item Scheduling Subproblem Formulation

The ammunition item scheduling subproblem uses dual price information from the master problem (shown in brackets) to find an ammunition path, $P_A \in P_A^k$, for each commodity k through the time-space network that minimizes the following objective function with decision variables $\alpha_{ij}(P_A)$ and μ_c:

$$\min_{P_A \in P_A^k} z_k = \sum_{(i,j)\in A} \alpha_{ij}(P_A)\left(c_{ij}^k - \phi_{ij} - \gamma_{ij}\right) - \sum_{c\in C_{\bar{P}_A}} \mu_c \pi_c - \sigma_k. \tag{9}$$

At the optimum, the value z_k corresponds to the reduced cost value of the ammunition path with the most negative reduced cost. Because σ_k is a constant, it may be omitted from the objective function without affecting the value of the decision variables at the optimum. Furthermore, because the set of all directed arcs in the time space network are partitioned into two disjoint sets, $(i,j) \in A^d$ and $(i,j) \notin A^d$, the commodity subproblem objective function may be written as

$$\min_{P_A \in P_A^k} z_k = \sum_{(i,j)\notin A^d} \alpha_{ij}(P_A)\left(c_{ij}^k - \phi_{ij} - \gamma_{ij}\right) + \left[\sum_{(i,j)\in A^d} \alpha_{ij}(P_A)\left(c_{ij}^k - \phi_{ij} - \gamma_{ij}\right) - \sum_{c\in C_{\bar{P}_A}} \mu_c \pi_c - \sigma_k\right]. \tag{10}$$

The first summation corresponds to the directed arcs in the ammunition path that are not included in the set of design arcs in the time-space network, whereas the second set of summations (in brackets) is exclusively associated with the directed arcs in the set of design arcs and ammunition path composites. Using the fact that each ammunition path composite, $\bar{P}_A$, is uniquely defined by a single loading arc $l \in A^d$, a single ship transport arc $s \in A^d$, and a single unloading arc $u \in A^d$, the objective function may be rewritten as

$$\min_{P_A \in P_A^k} z_k = \sum_{(i,j)\notin A^d} \alpha_{ij}(P_A)\left(c_{ij}^k - \phi_{ij} - \gamma_{ij}\right) + \left[\sum_{c\in C_{\bar{P}_A}} \sum_{(i,j)\in c} \mu_c\left(c_{ij}^k - \phi_{ij} - \gamma_{ij}\right) - \sum_{c\in C_{\bar{P}_A}} \mu_c \pi_c\right] \tag{11}$$

$$= \sum_{(i,j)\notin A^d} \alpha_{ij}(P_A)\left(c_{ij}^k - \phi_{ij} - \gamma_{ij}\right) + \left[\sum_{c\in C_{\bar{P}_A}} \mu_c \left(\sum_{(i,j)\in c}\left(c_{ij}^k - \phi_{ij} - \gamma_{ij}\right) - \pi_c\right)\right]. \tag{12}$$

The solution to this minimization problem corresponds to an ammunition path with the minimum reduced cost and is found using a shortest path algorithm. To accomplish this, a new time-space network, G^k, is created for each subproblem corresponding to commodity type k. Each arc associated with a directed arc $(i,j) \notin A^d$ in the original time-space network, G, is assigned a modified cost of $(c_{ij}^k - \phi_{ij} - \gamma_{ij})$. In addition, all arcs in the design portion of G are removed and replaced in G^k by ammunition path composite arcs for each ammunition path composite, $\bar{P}_A$, with a cost equal to $\sum_{(i,j)\in \bar{P}_A}(c_{ij}^k - \phi_{ij} - \gamma_{ij}) - \pi_{\bar{P}_A}$.

This optimization problem is solved in $O(m)$ time using a modified version of the topological search shortest path algorithm found in [12], where m is the number of arcs. If $(z_k' - \sigma_k) < 0$ the ammunition path generated by the shortest path algorithm has negative reduced cost and is added as a column to the constraint matrix of the master problem.

3.3. Ship Scheduling Subproblem Formulation

Like the ammunition scheduling subproblems, each ship scheduling subproblem uses dual price information from the master problem to generate ship paths through the time-space network. The objective of the ship scheduling subproblem for fleet type f with decision variables $\beta_{ij}(P_S)$ and υ_c is

$$\min_{P_S \in P_S^y} z_y = \sum_{(i,j)\in A^d} \beta_{ij}(P_S)\left(c_{ij}^y - \tilde{H}_y \gamma_{ij}\right) + \sum_{c \in C_{\bar{P}_A}} \upsilon_c \pi_c - \sigma_y. \tag{13}$$

The time-space network must be transformed so that a shortest path algorithm can be used to solve this optimization problem. The transformation uses two concepts: *ammunition path composite dominance* and *ship path composites*. An ammunition path composite, $\bar{P}_A^1 = \{l_1, s_1, u_1\}$, dominates another ammunition path composite, $\bar{P}_A^2 = \{l_2, s_2, u_2\}$, if the start time of arc l_1 is no later than the start time of l_2, the end time of arc u_1 is no earlier than the end time of arc u_2, and both ammunition path composites share the same ship transport arc (i.e., $s_1 = s_2$). If we define

$D_{\text{path}}^{\bar{P}_A}$ set of all ammunition path composites dominated by ammunition path composite $\bar{P}_A$,

then a ship path that covers some path composite $\bar{P}_A$ also covers all other path composites $c \in D_{\text{path}}^{\bar{P}_A}$.

A ship path composite, $\bar{P}_S$, is a set of ammunition path composites. For each ammunition path composite $\bar{P}_A \in \bar{P}_S$, $\bar{P}_S$ includes all other path composites $c \in D_{\text{path}}^{\bar{P}_A}$. A ship path composite also has a starting and an ending time. The starting time of the ship path composite $\bar{P}_S$ is equal to the start time of the earliest loading edge of all ammunition path composites in $\bar{P}_S$ while the ending time of is equal to the end time of the latest unloading arc of all path composites in $\bar{P}_S$.

Finding a new ship schedule through the time-space network corresponds to finding a feasible sequence of ship path composites. If we define

- $D_{\text{path}}^{\bar{P}_S}$ set of all ammunition path composites dominated by ship path composite $\bar{P}_S$
- $D_{\text{arc}}^{\bar{P}_S}$ set of all arcs dominated by ship path composite $\bar{P}_S$
- $\delta_{\bar{P}_S}^{P_S}$ indicator variable that equals 1 if ship path P_S covers ship path composite $\bar{P}_S$ and 0 otherwise
- $C_{\bar{P}_S}$ set of all feasible ship path composites $\bar{P}_S$

then the objective of the subproblem with decision variable $\delta_{\bar{P}_S}^{P_S}$ is

$$\min_{P_S \in P_S^y} z_y = \sum_{c \in C_{\bar{P}_S}} \delta_{\bar{P}_S}^{P_S} \left(\sum_{(i,j)\in D_{\text{arc}}^c} \left(c_{ij}^y + \tilde{H}_y \gamma_{ij}\right) + \sum_{q \in D_{\text{path}}^c} \tilde{H}_y \pi_q \right) - \sigma_y. \tag{14}$$

The minimum z_y is obtained by selecting a feasible sequence of ship path composites with the least aggregate cost. The contribution of each ship path composite, $\bar{P}_S$, to the objective function depends on the modified costs of all the arcs that $\bar{P}_S$ dominates, as well as the cost of all the ammunition path composites that $\bar{P}_S$ dominates.

Determining a feasible sequence of ship path composites that minimizes z_y is accomplished by solving a shortest path problem in a modified network, G'. To create the modified network, a node is created for every possible ship path composite in addition to a single source and sink node. A directed arc is added from the source node to every ship path composite node and from every ship path composite node to the sink node. Next, an outgoing directed arc is added from each ship path composite node $\bar{P}_S^1$ to every other ship path composite node $\bar{P}_S^2$ where it is feasible for a ship to sail from the ending location of ship path composite $\bar{P}_S^1$ to the starting location of ship path composite $\bar{P}_S^2$ in an amount of time equal to the difference between their ending and starting times, respectively. The cost of the directed incoming arcs to each ship path composite node is equal to the ship path composite's corresponding summation term in (14). For the node corresponding to composite ship path $\bar{P}_S$ this cost is equal to

$$c'_{ij} = \sum_{(i,j)\in D^{\bar{P}_S}_{\text{arc}}} \left(c^y_{ij} + \tilde{H}_y \gamma_{ij}\right) + \sum_{q\in D^{\bar{P}_S}_{\text{path}}} \tilde{H}_y \pi_q, \qquad \forall (i,j) \in \{\text{incoming arcs to } j\}. \tag{15}$$

Because G' consists of a node for each possible ship path composite, the size of this modified network can be extremely large. A final transformation drastically decreases the size of the network. The reformulation requires that we consider ship path composites as directed arcs rather than nodes. Similar to ammunition path composites, each ship path composite has a corresponding arc known as a *ship path composite arc*. A ship path composite arc, (i,j), corresponding to ship path composite $\bar{P}_S$ is an arc such that the start node i is the starting node of the earliest loading arc in $D^{\bar{P}_S}_{\text{arc}}$ and j is the ending node of the latest unloading arc in $D^{\bar{P}_S}_{\text{arc}}$.

The transformation requires the construction of a new subproblem network, G^y. A node representing each POE and POD is created for each time period in the planning horizon. Forward directed arcs are added to connect the nodes at each POE and POD from time period t to period $t+1$. Finally, ship path composite arcs are added from each POE to each POD with a cost equal to the value of c'_{ij} in (15).

Once the subproblem graph is constructed, a standard topological search algorithm such as an $O(m)$ reaching algorithm (see [12] for details) may be used to find the shortest path because the network is completely acyclic. If $(z'_y - \sigma_y) < 0$, the generated ship path has a negative reduced cost and is added as a column to the master problem.

4. HEURISTIC PLANNER FORMULATION

This section describes a heuristic planning algorithm that finds ammunition paths for each ammunition item through the time-space network. It also schedules ships to carry the flow of ammunition on the directed arcs included in the design portion of the time-space network. The primary intent of the heuristic procedure is to obtain "good" feasible solutions quickly that can either be used as stand-alone solutions or to initialize the optimization planner.

The heuristic planner consolidates ammunition items traveling to a common POD facility into *shiploads*. The planner then finds ammunition paths through the time-space network for all of the ammunition items contained within each shipload. These paths use specific ship *schedule segments* that carry the flow of ammunition items through the design portion of the time-space network. Schedule segments allocate physical capacity provided by a ship for loading, unloading, and transporting each shipload and are assigned to a specific ship from a homogeneous fleet.

The supply of ammunition items at the depots is related to the demand for ammunition items at the PODs through *ammunition requests*. An ammunition request specifies the quantity, priority, origin depot, destination POD, RLD at the depot, and RDD at the POD for a particular type

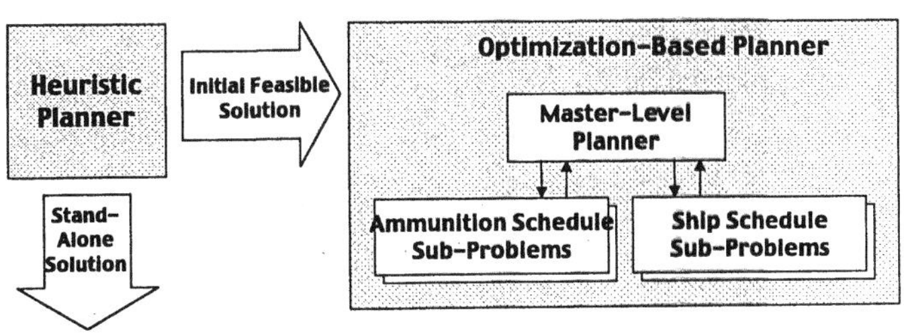

Figure 2. Heuristic planning algorithm.

of ammunition. The shipload generation algorithm begins by sorting the list of ammunition requests by increasing RDD. Once this is accomplished, the algorithm starts at the beginning of the sorted list and sequentially adds ammunition from each request until a shipload is formed. The quantity of ammunition items included in each shipload is constrained from above by the capacity of a ship and the cumulative unloading capacity at the shipload's destination POD over a total of B_{POD} time periods. If sufficient capacity is available and if sufficient demand exists at a POD, the heuristic planner also attempts to add an amount of ammunition to each shipload equal to a user-specified utilization target, UtilTarget, multiplied by the capacity of a ship. This process repeats until all of the ammunition items in each ammunition request from the ammunition request list are assigned to a shipload.

Once a list of shiploads has been created, the planning algorithm searches for a set of ammunition paths through the time-space network to carry the ammunition items in each shipload from their source depots to their destination POD. The heuristic planner begins by sorting the list of shiploads by increasing weighted RDD value. The weighted RDD value of a shipload is an average of the RDD values of all the ammunition items in the shipload weighted by the priority and quantity of the ammunition items contained in the shipload.

Shiploads are processed sequentially starting with the first shipload in the sorted list. Shiploads with earlier weighted RDDs are processed first using the heuristic rule that the items required first should be processed first. The shiploads that are processed early in the planning horizon consume capacity on arcs in the time-space network, thereby limiting the capacity available for shiploads processed later in the list. However, it is always feasible to process a shipload by scheduling it to be transported from a POE to a POD later in the planning horizon (assuming a sufficiently long planning horizon).

Because each ammunition item has a fixed origin depot and a fixed destination POD, the objective of the heuristic planner is to schedule a ship at the earliest possible time such that all ammunition items in the shipload are able to make it onboard the ship. Ideally, a ship should be scheduled at the earliest possible time in order to minimize the collective tardiness of the shipload. In the process of scheduling the ship, however, the heuristic planner must honor the capacity constraints of the time-space network and other requirements, such as delivery windows and constraints on the availability of ship resources.

To determine the best schedule segment for a shipload, the algorithm first finds the best candidate schedule segment originating from each POE facility. This involves determining when the candidate schedule segment should begin and how many days should be allotted to load and unload the ship carrying the shipload. Once the best candidate schedule segment is determined from each POE facility, the best candidate schedule segment is selected from across all POE facilities.

The heuristic computes a maximum loading and unloading time for each shipload based on the ports' throughput capacity and the number of ammunition items in the shipload. Shiploads might not be able to load and unload in the times allowed if other ships are also trying to load or unload at the same time. If this occurs, the heuristic planner will seek a later time period to start the candidate schedule segment.

Once the loading and unloading times are set, the algorithm determines the earliest possible time period to start each candidate schedule segment from each POE facility subject to the following conditions: at least one ship must be available to cover the candidate schedule segment; ammunition items in the shipload must arrive at their destination POD no earlier than $MaxEarly$ days before their RDD; and enough capacity must be available throughout the entire network to ensure that all ammunition items in the shipload can travel from their origin depots to their destination POD.

Verifying the third condition is the most challenging computationally, and is only checked if the first two conditions are satisfied. To ensure that it is possible for each ammunition item in the shipload to make it onboard a ship assigned to the candidate schedule segment, a set of ammunition paths that use the candidate schedule segment are generated for each ammunition item in the shipload. The availability of capacity through the time-space network is verified by successively using a breadth-first search algorithm to find ammunition paths for all of the ammunition items in the shipload. As ammunition paths are found, ammunition items from the same ammunition request are augmented over each ammunition path until either the capacity of some directed arc along the path is completely utilized, or all of the ammunition items from the ammunition request are augmented. This process is repeated for each ammunition item in the shipload.

If it is possible to augment all of the ammunition items in the shipload, then the candidate schedule segment is feasible. Furthermore, the paths generated in the process of checking the availability of capacity through the time-space network constitute a feasible set of ammunition paths for the shipload. If sufficient capacity is not available to augment all the ammunition items, the starting time period of the candidate schedule segment is incremented by one and the process repeats until a feasible candidate schedule segment is found.

Once the best schedule segment is determined for each POE facility, the best schedule segment is determined across all POEs. Selecting the best POE is a function of not only the structural properties of the time-space network (transportation times, etc.), but also the capacity available in the time-space network. This is done by comparing the actual arrival date of each candidate schedule segment at each POD to the ideal arrival date of the shipload, EarliestArrivalDate. The EarliestArrivalDate of a shipload is equal to the earliest RDD of all ammunition items in the shipload minus a MaxEarly parameter. MaxEarly is used to specify the maximum number of time periods an ammunition item may arrive before its RDD. The candidate schedule segment with the minimum deviation from this ideal is selected as the schedule segment to implement.

After determining the best candidate schedule segment across all POEs, a specific ship is assigned to cover the candidate schedule segment. The heuristic planner selects the ship with the minimum amount of slack between the time period that the ship last became available and the starting time period of the candidate schedule segment. This rule is used so that ships available early in the planning horizon are not unnecessarily used when it is possible that other, unprocessed shiploads might be able to use them in future iterations within the planning phase. The heuristic planner also checks to ensure that enough time is allowed for a ship to sail from the end of its last assigned schedule segment to the starting POE of the candidate schedule segment. It must also ensure that a ship is never assigned to a candidate schedule segment that forces it to be in two locations at the same time.

Once a ship has been assigned to the candidate schedule segment, the final step in processing a shipload is to augment flow over the set of ammunition paths discovered during the process of selecting the best candidate schedule segment. After the ammunition items in the shipload have been augmented over each ammunition path, the capacity of the directed arcs in each ammunition path is updated to reflect their remaining residual capacity. This process is similar to those used by augmenting path maximum flow algorithms such as the labeling algorithm described in [12].

The process described above is repeated for each shipload in the shipload list until a path is found for each ammunition item. When complete, the set of ammunition and ship paths constitutes a feasible, but not necessarily optimal distribution plan for the user-defined scenario.

5. PLANNING WITH A ROLLING HORIZON

This section presents a modified version of the heuristic planner that is applicable to planning with a rolling horizon. When planning during actual contingency operations, the state of the distribution system evolves in real time and generally is not known *a priori*. For example, planners might only have knowledge about requisitions for ammunition items a few weeks in advance, rather than hundreds of days. To cope with this situation, a closed-loop planning and control system must be able to incorporate this new information and modify the current plan with a new plan on a rolling horizon basis.

Planning with a rolling horizon is a method to generate new plans for a system whose state is continuously evolving over time. Each time replanning occurs, the planning algorithm generates a *new plan* that is spliced into the *current plan* such that the transition from the current plan to the new plan is seamless. For example, in the ammunition distribution problem, the transition from the current plan to the new plan must ensure the continuous movement, both physically and temporally, of ammunition items and ships through the distribution system.

Each plan generated by the planning algorithm has an associated *start date* and includes schedules for ammunition items and ships over a finite amount of time known as the *plan horizon.* To generate a new plan, the planning algorithm uses information about the *current state* of the system at the current time to forecast the *splice state* of the system at the new plan's start date. The new plan's start date is also known as the *splice point*, and the difference in time between the splice point and the current time is referred to as the *replanning window.* If replanning is instantaneous (i.e., the replanning window is zero), the current state and the splice state are identical. If the replanning window is nonzero and, if the current state of the system does not match the forecasted splice state, local fixes must be used to ensure that the transition from the current plan to the new plan occurs seamlessly.

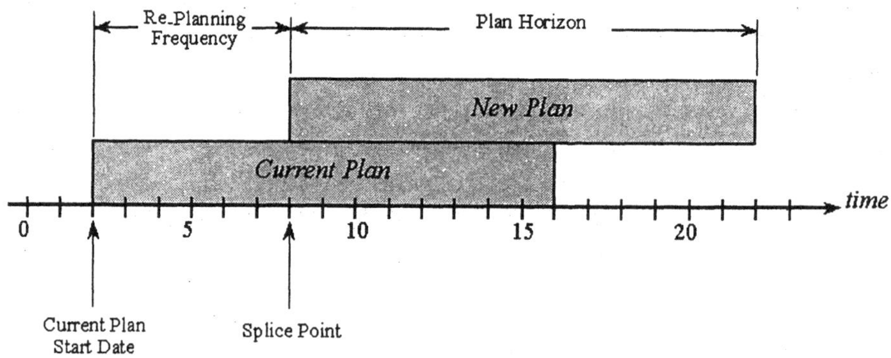

Figure 3. Rolling horizon planning.

In addition to using the forecasted splice state of the system, the planning algorithm uses forecast information from the splice point forward over the plan horizon. For the ammunition distribution problem, the forecast information includes things such as projected ammunition requisitions, or an anticipated change in a facility's processing capacity.

The scheduled rate at which new plans are generated is known as the *replanning frequency*. The replanning frequency is the amount of time between the starting times of consecutive replanning activities. To ensure that a current plan always exists, the replanning frequency must be less than or equal to the plan horizon minus the replanning window. Replanning may be initiated because new information becomes available that requires replanning, or because a certain amount of time has passed and a new plan is required to ensure plan coverage.

To operate in this type of planning environment, the heuristic planner discussed in the previous section must be modified. This is because it is no longer valid to assume that all ammunition items originate at depot storage subfacilities at the beginning of the planning horizon. When planning with a rolling horizon, some ammunition items might be in-transit and, as a result, can originate at locations other than depot storage subfacility when replanning is initiated.

Despite the fact that ammunition items can originate at any location within the distribution system, the core processing logic of the original heuristic planner is still applicable. The modified heuristic planner finds paths from the nodes in the time-space network corresponding to each ammunition item's spatial and temporal starting position to the node corresponding to its destination POD facility and RDD.

The challenge associated with using the modified heuristic planner to plan with a rolling horizon is guaranteeing the existence of a feasible distribution plan. When all ammunition items originate at the depot facilities, a feasible solution is guaranteed by exploiting the fact that it is always possible to find a feasible solution by processing shiploads of ammunition items at later time periods, assuming a sufficiently long planning horizon. This is not the case, however, when ammunition items can originate anywhere. To guarantee a feasible solution, the modified heuristic planner processes ammunition items with the least amount of scheduling flexibility first. This corresponds to processing the ammunition items furthest along in the distribution system first. For example, an ammunition item onboard a ship waiting to be unloaded at a POD has much less scheduling flexibility, both spatially, as well as temporally, than an ammunition item that has not departed its source depot. Thus, the ammunition item onboard the ship is processed first.

6. RESULTS

This section compares a plan generated by the current planning technique to the plans generated by the optimization and heuristic planners. It also investigates the performance of the modified heuristic planner in a rolling-horizon planning environment as a function of the forecast horizon used and choice of replanning frequency.

6.1. Optimization Planner and Heuristic Planner Versus the Current Method

The results in this section were generated using a 200 day planning scenario with 13 depot facilities, seven POE facilities, 17 POD facilities, both truck and rail CONUS transportation resources, 175 ships from a homogenous fleet, and a single commodity type. The scenario inputs were derived from the time phased force deployment data (TPFDD) of a real-world deliberate planning scenario that were generated using the current deliberate planning process. This process uses a combination of experienced human planners and decision support tools such as the Joint Flow Analysis System for Transportation (JFAST) and the Ammunition Distribution System (ADS).

Table 1 shows a comparison across planning methods for a similar level of tardiness. To generate the results in Table 1, the heuristic's *UtilTarget* parameter and the optimization planner's $c_v(P_S)$ parameter were varied until a cumulative tardiness value similar to that of the current method was produced. Also, the optimization planner was initialized using the solution generated by the heuristic planner.

As Table 1 shows, both the heuristic planner and optimization planner generate plans with better ship utilization values for similar cumulative tardiness values. Although the heuristic uses the same number of ships as the current method, its ship utilization value is higher because the total number of voyages made by the ships is less.

Table 1 also shows that the percent of ammunition items that are late in the plans generated by the heuristic planner and optimization planner are greater than the percent in the current

Table 1. Results for similar cumulative tardiness case.

Metric	Current Process	Heuristic Planner	Optimization Planner
Ship Utilization	41.4%	54.9%	63.0%
Cumulative Tardiness ($\times 1,000,000$)	5278.7	5278.2	5273.3
Number of Ships Used	175	175	162
% Early or On Time	88.63%	85.76%	85.99%
% Late	11.37%	14.24%	14.01%
Plan Generation Time	Unavailable	701 sec.	3642 sec.

method's plan, the ammunition items are late a smaller number of total time periods. Furthermore, the maximum amount that any ammunition item is late is relatively constant across all three planning methods. This results because some of the items have RLDs that are much later than their RDDs. Given this constraint, it is impossible for the ammunition items to arrive any earlier.

Table 2 shows a comparison for a similar level of ship utilization. To generate these results, the heuristic's *UtilTarget* parameter was set at 0.05 and the optimization planner's $c_y(P_S)$ parameter was set at zero in an attempt to produce a ship utilization value as low as the current method's. As the table shows, both the heuristic planner and optimization planner generate plans with better cumulative tardiness values. Similar to the results in Table 1, the percent of ammunition items that arrive late compared to their RDDs is greater in the plans generated by the heuristic and optimization planner, but the ammunition items are late a smaller number of total time periods.

Table 2. Results for similar ship utilization case.

Metric	Current Process	Heuristic Planner	Optimization Planner
Ship Utilization	41.4%	52.2%	49.9%
Cumulative Tardiness ($\times 1,000,000$)	5278.7	5260.0	5201.8
Number of Ships Used	175	175	175
% Early or On Time	88.63%	85.47%	86.56%
% Late	11.37%	14.53%	13.44%
Plan Generation Time	Unavailable	711 sec.	2409 sec.

6.2. Rolling-Horizon Results Using the Modified Heuristic Planner

The results and analysis in this section explore the effects of planning with a rolling horizon. To investigate the effect of varying forecast horizon length, the forecast horizon was varied between 20 and 50 time periods while the replanning frequency was fixed at 20 time periods. Also, the ship utilization target parameter, UtilTarget, was set at 0.1 and the maximum number of periods a ship could berth at a POE or POD was set at one time period. The cumulative tardiness as a function of time is shown in Figure 4. The cumulative tardiness values in the figure correspond to the actual cumulative tardiness incurred over time, not the anticipated cumulative tardiness derived from the plans.

The cumulative tardiness value with *perfect information* is also shown in Figure 4. Perfect information implies all demand is known with certainty over the entire planning horizon. As the figure shows, plans generated using the modified heuristic planner for forecast horizons of 40 or 50 periods have cumulative tardiness values nearly as good as a plan generated with perfect information. On the other hand, plans generated with forecast horizons less than 30 periods have significantly worse cumulative tardiness values.

One reason for the rapid decay in cumulative tardiness performance with short forecast horizons is the long lead-time required for ammunition items to travel from their origin depots to their destination PODs. For example, with the scenario data used for the experiments in this section, the average amount of time required for an ammunition item to travel from a depot facility to a POD facility using the quickest path and without delay due to congestion effects is approximately 20 time periods, while the maximum is 31 time periods. Thus, with longer forecast horizons, the modified heuristic planner is better able to anticipate future requests for ammunition and schedule their movements through the distribution system, as opposed to reactively processing ammunition items that have no chance of arriving on time.

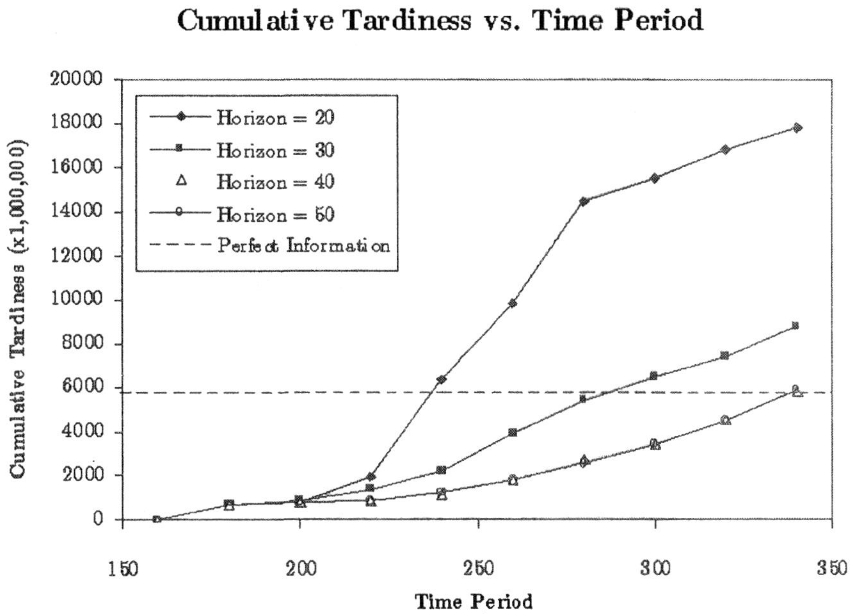

Figure 4. Cumulative tardiness as a function of forecast horizon.

To investigate the effect of varying replanning frequency, the replanning frequency was varied between 20 and 50 time periods while the forecast horizon was fixed at 50 time periods. The ship utilization parameter, *UtilTarget*, was set at 0.5, and the maximum number of periods a ship could berth at a POE or POD was set at one time period. The cumulative tardiness as a function of time is shown in Figure 5. Like the previous experiment, the cumulative tardiness values correspond to the actual cumulative tardiness incurred over time.

Figure 5 illustrates the value of frequent replanning. Replanning frequencies of every 20 or 30 time periods result in plans with cumulative tardiness values nearly as small as a plan generated with perfect information. On the other hand, plans generated less frequently result in significantly worse cumulative tardiness values.

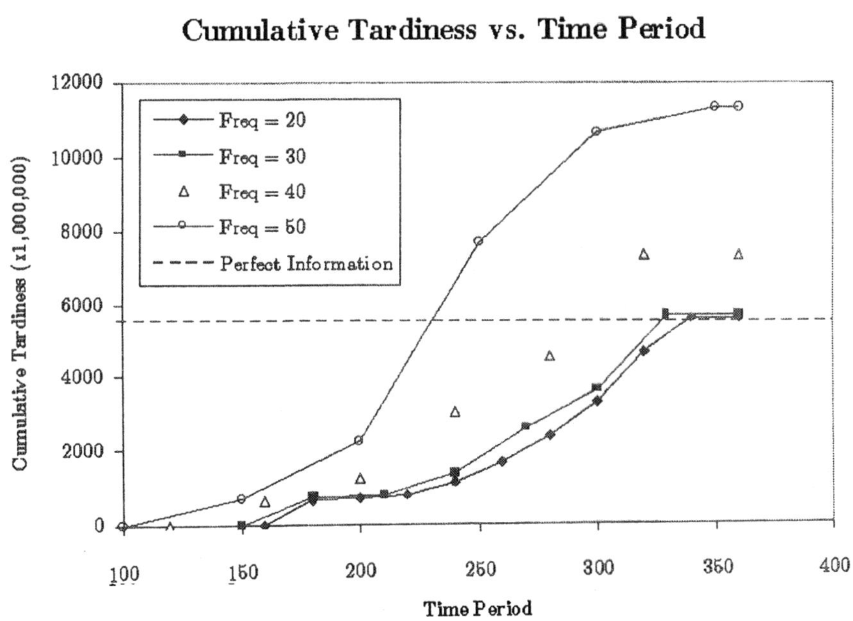

Figure 5. Cumulative tardiness as a function of replanning frequency.

When replanning is conducted more frequently for a given forecast horizon length, information about future ammunition requests is incorporated more frequently and the planning and control system is better able to adapt to the changing environment.

7. SUMMARY

The development of planning algorithms is an important first step towards implementing a closed-loop planning and control approach for the distribution of contingency munitions. This paper described two such algorithms: an optimization planner and a heuristic planner. Both methods produce plans with better tardiness and ship utilization values compared to a plan generated using current planning techniques. Furthermore, a modified version of the heuristic was used to demonstrate that good plans can be generated even in situations where there is frequent replanning and limited forecasting horizons. This is extremely important in an environment as dynamic as war.

REFERENCES

1. Joint Publication 4-0, *Doctrine for Logistic Support of Joint Operations*, Joint Chiefs of Staff, Washington D.C., (April 2000).
2. M. Christiansen, Decomposition of a combined inventory and time constrained ship routing problem, *Transportation Science* **33** (1), 3–16, (February 1999).
3. K. Rana and R. Vickson, Routing container ships using Lagrangean relaxation and decomposition, *Transportation Science* **25** (3), 201–214, (August 1991).
4. D. Ronen, Short-term scheduling of vessels for shipping bulk or semi-bulk commodities originating in a single area, *Operations Research* **34** (1), 164–173, (January/February 1986).
5. W. Nulty and H. Ratliff, Interactive optimization methodology for fleet scheduling, *Naval Research Logistics* **38** (5), 669–677, (1991).
6. T. Boffey, E. Edmond, A. Hinxman and C. Pursglove, Two approaches to scheduling container ships with an application to the North Atlantic route, *Journal of the Operational Research Socitey* **30** (5), 413–425, (1979).
7. Army Field Manual 63-2, Division Support Command, Armored, Infantry and Mechanized Infantry Divisions, (1991).
8. A. Levin, Scheduling and fleet routing models for transportation systems, *Transportation Science* **5**, 233–255, (August 1971).
9. M. Florian, G. Bushell, J. Ferland, G. Guerin and L. Nastansky, The engine scheduling problem in a railway network, *Infor.* **14** (2), 121–138, (June 1976).
10. W. Powell, Optimization models and algorithms: An emerging technology for the motor carrier industry, *IEEE Transactions on Vehicular Technology* **40** (1), 68–80, (1991).
11. C. Barnhart, E. Johnson, G. Nemhauser, M. Savelsbergh and P. Vance, Branch-and-price: Column generation for huge integer programs, *Operations Research* **46** (3), 316–329, (May/June 1998).
12. R. Ahuja, T. Magnanti and J. Orlin, *Network Flows: Theory, Algorithms, and Applications*, Prentice Hall, Upper Saddle River, NJ, (1993).

Available online at www.sciencedirect.com
SCIENCE @ DIRECT•
ELSEVIER
Mathematical and Computer Modelling 39 (2004) 715–731
MATHEMATICAL AND COMPUTER MODELLING
www.elsevier.com/locate/mcm

PORTSIM 5: Modeling from a Seaport Level

D. L. HOWARD*, M. J. BRAGEN, J. F. BURKE, JR. AND R. J. LOVE
Decision and Information Sciences Division, Argonne National Laboratory
9700 S Cass Avenue, Argonne, IL 60439, U.S.A.
<dhoward><bragen><jay><love>@anl.gov

Abstract—This paper describes PORTSIM 5, a discrete-event seaport simulation model. Specifically, we discuss the developmental efforts and existing system limitations that have led up to the current efforts being undertaken by the Military Traffic Management Command Transportation Engineering Agency and Argonne National Laboratory. PORTSIM 5 builds on the knowledge and expertise gained from two preceding port simulation models, PORTSIM 4.3 and CPORTS 1.4, and incorporates a set of rules and conventions to address the issue of resource competition. We will provide a brief description of the preceding models and illustrate their individual shortcomings. The paper will go on to describe PORTSIM 5 and the three main areas it models, port areas of operation, port processes, and port resources. Port resource allocation methods will also be addressed. In PORTSIM 5, the graphical user interface (GUI) has been decoupled from the simulation. Here we provide a short section on the GUI and illustrate with sample screens and output. Finally, future enhancements are suggested. © 2004 Elsevier Ltd. All rights reserved.

Keywords—Port, Seaport, Modeling, Simulation, Logistics, Transportation, Military, Mobility, Infrastructure.

1. INTRODUCTION

Accurate, dependable computer modeling of seaport operations has been a priority of the military logistics community in recent years. Because an ability to simulate seaport operations provides military logistics analysts with the detailed information necessary to plan efficient deployments, a high level of effort has been dedicated to simulating flows of cargo and equipment through both ports of embarkation and ports of debarkation. Until now, the tasks of modeling these movements have been undertaken independently, with Argonne National Laboratory (ANL) developing the port of embarkation (POE) model, PORTSIM, and the Virginia Modeling, Analysis and Simulation Center (VMASC) developing the port of debarkation (POD) model, CPORTS.

The POE and POD modeling efforts have focused on simulating one-way traffic through a port, modeling from an isolated perspective. There was a conscious decision made to model the seaport

The submitted manuscript has been created by the University of Chicago as Operator of Argonne National Laboratory ("Argonne") under Contract No. W-31-109-ENG-38 with the U.S. Department of Energy. The U.S. Government retains for itself, and others acting on its behalf, a paid-up, nonexclusive, irrevocable worldwide license in said article to reproduce, prepare derivative works, distribute copies to the public, and perform publicly and display publicly, by or on behalf of the Government.
Argonne National Laboratory's work was supported by the Military Traffic Management Command Transportation Engineering Agency, Department of Defense under interagency agreement, through U.S. Department of Energy contract W-31-109-Eng-38.
*Author to whom all correspondence should be addressed.

0895-7177/04/$ - see front matter © 2004 Elsevier Ltd. All rights reserved. Typeset by $\mathcal{A}_{\mathcal{M}}\mathcal{S}$-TEX
doi:10.1016/j.mcm.2004.02.010

as a dedicated system, allocating all available resources to the selected operation, either POE or POD. While this modeling approach provided an accurate analysis, it soon became apparent that the core of the port operations problem lay in modeling port processes from a bidirectional port-level rather than the previous one-way assumption. By implementing a port-level design, a more accurate representation of resource and infrastructure constraints could be achieved. The level of detail acquired previously by focusing on each type of operation, either POE or POD, became an invaluable foundation for the next phase of development, the port-level model. PORTSIM 5 is being developed at ANL as such a model.

The challenge of modeling concurrent port processes lies in dealing with the issue of resource constraints. Competition for and availability of common resources can impact throughput dramatically, and decreases in throughput can have a substantive negative impact on a deployment mission. While PORTSIM 4.3 and CPORTS 1.4 address resource constraints from their individual perspectives, PORTSIM 5 addresses those challenges by integrating embarkation and debarkation processes and implementing a set of rules and conventions that assign precedence and priorities to competing resources. The result is a more accurate port simulation model that affords better overall data on throughput capabilities.

This paper describes the evolution and subsequent shortcomings of the seaport modeling efforts undertaken by ANL and VMASC and the current challenges being met at Argonne in developing a port-level model that accurately simulates the system and measures throughput while addressing the resource constraints that tax the system. Finally, we take a look at high-level architecture (HLA) requirements and future enhancements that advance beyond port infrastructure and processes to exogenous variables that can directly impact the simulation.

2. PORTSIM 4—MODELING THE PORT OF EMBARKATION (POE)

PORTSIM began as an Argonne proposal to the Military Traffic Management Command Transportation Engineering Agency (MTMCTEA) in the fall of 1993 as a response to the military's growing need to simulate movement through seaports. Equation-based programs were already in use letting analysts calculate throughput. One such program is the port operational performance simulator (POPS)—"a deterministic throughput calculator computer program that allows seaport analysts to quickly determine seaport throughput capabilities on an aggregate level" [1]. Both Argonne and the MTMCTEA saw a need for a more detailed model that relied on discrete-event simulation theory. Argonne began working on such a model in 1994 and continued to revise and refine the model based on MTMCTEA requirements and guidance through the fall of 2001.

PORTSIM 4 continues to be supported by Argonne, and Version 4.3 is currently in use at the MTMCTEA. PORTSIM 4.3 is a discrete-event simulation that facilitates the analysis of movement of military-unit equipment through seaports worldwide and allows for detailed infrastructure analyses. It assists planners in comparing and selecting ports by determining their throughput capabilities and their utilization of critical resources [2]. It is primarily used to determine a port's ability to deploy units of various sizes—for example, the length of time it takes to deploy an armored cavalry division through the port, given a specified allocation of port resources. It can also be used to identify ports for which additional infrastructure (newly constructed or leased from the port) can speed the process of deployment. For example, if additional rail spurs are added for offloading, the force may close ten hours earlier. PORTSIM 4.3 has recently been used to develop contingency deployment plans for classified real-world scenarios.

The POE model looks at reception, staging, and ship loading. Reception models the means and resources required to move cargo through a port's entry points, including gates, which accept highway transports, and interchange yards, which accept railway transports. Staging models the methods and resources needed to inspect cargo and queue it for ship loading. Ship loading models the methods and resources required to call forward cargo to a berth and load it onto a ship.

While used successfully and extensively for port throughput analyses (its original purpose), PORTSIM 4.3 suffers from several shortcomings that hamper the military analyst's ability to analyze force deployments. Though PORTSIM models individual pieces of cargo and can provide detailed information about that cargo, the closure profiles can only be analyzed for the entire force. Closure profiles for subsets of the force cannot be taken literally due to the model's shortcomings. Among these shortcomings are the following.

- Lack of unit integrity for ship loading—equipment may be spread across multiple ships without planning to account for the ships final destinations.
- Equipment is loaded on a first-in, first-out basis without regard for the required delivery date at the destination.
- Port resource and infrastructure utilization information is captured at the beginning of each simulated hour rather than on a continual basis leading to inaccurate representation of the actual utilization.
- Not all port resource and infrastructure utilization information is saved at the end of a simulation run.
- Helicopter processes are not sufficiently detailed. In 4.3 these processes were added primarily so that the model could account for space consumption on the ships.
- The graphical user interface and the simulation are tightly coupled resulting in long run times. This can limit the number of "what-if" cases that the analyst can run when a quick turn-around analysis is required.
- The set of reports and graphs is fixed and does not provide the capability to view results for user-defined subsets of the data. The saved output cannot be processed to provide this information either.

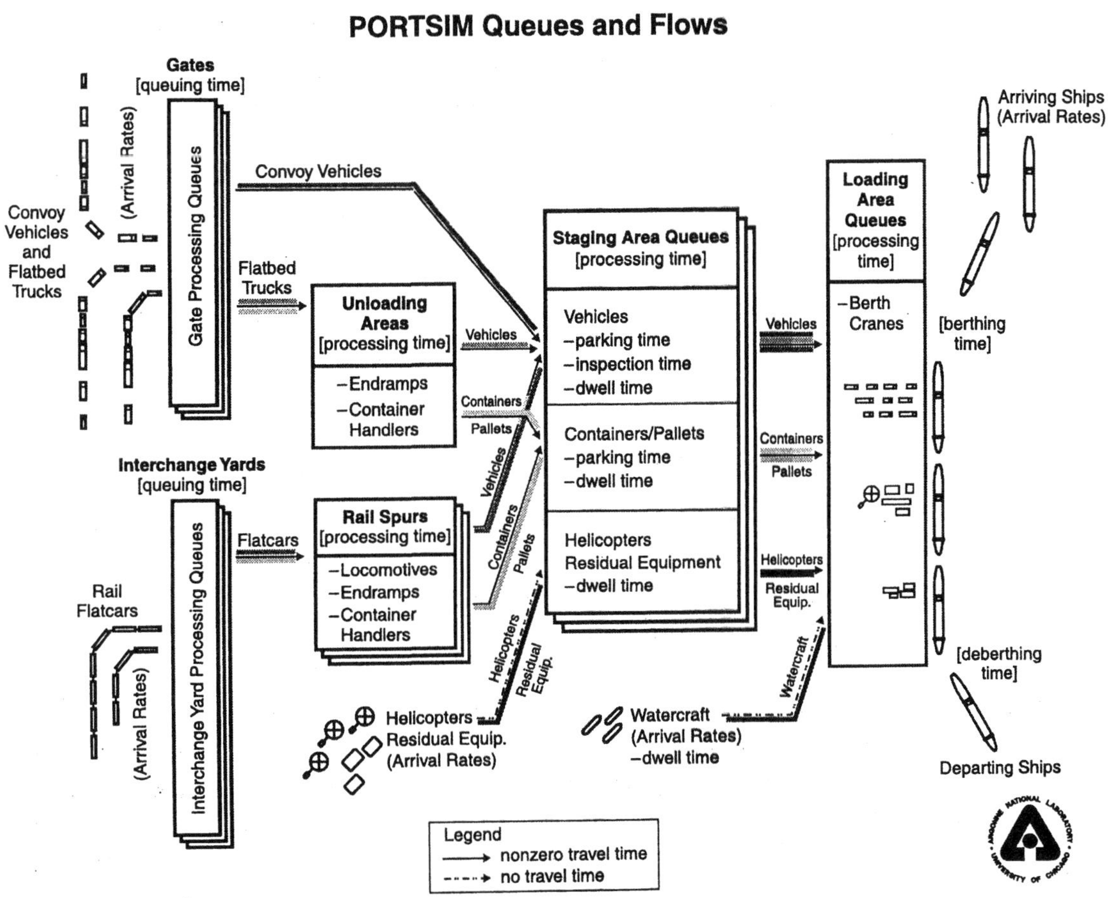

Figure 1. PORTSIM 4.3 models flows of cargo through ports of embarkation.

- The representation of the port requires that all port infrastructure be physically located within the port boundaries. For large U.S. ports, this can be a reasonable assumption. However, for smaller foreign ports, this may not be accurate and the model provides no means to simulate port areas, such as staging, outside the boundaries of the port.
- Travel times between port areas were specified simply as averages rather than individual travel times for each area to area route.

Figure 1 depicts the flow of cargo through a POE.

3. CPORTS 1.4—MODELING THE PORT OF DEBARKATION (POD)

The CPORTS 1.4 POD model follows cargo as it arrives on a ship at a berth and performs an analysis similar to that of a POE model, but looks at berth, anchorage, staging, loading area, call forward area, gate area, and interchange yard area objects. The POD model tracks cargo items as they are offloaded from a ship and make their way through a port, finally exiting the port either under their own power (wheeled vehicles, helicopters, and watercraft) or upon highway or rail transport (tracked vehicles, containers, etc.). A major contribution to the port modeling process in CPORTS 1.4 is the ability to reconfigure the port during the simulation. CPORTS 1.4 supports programmed events that allow the user to specify changes in data at specific times during the simulation. Many scenario parameters can be affected by these events, including process times, port area capacities and routing. Currently, these programmed events would be calculated externally and specified in the scenario input file. The CPORTS model also has been extensively used in the analysis of and planning for military deployments.

VMASC was contracted by MTMCTEA to develop a port of debarkation (POD) version of the PORTSIM model. Among their requirements was the need to address the shortcomings that were present in the POE version of PORTSIM. The result of their efforts is CPORTS 1.4. CPORTS 1.4 successfully overcame the issues of unit integrity, ship-loading order, helicopter processing, GUI-simulation coupling, reporting and graphing, port reconfiguration, and travel time specification. However, the issue of port resource and infrastructure utilization data remains. To increase the performance of the simulation, a conscious decision not to capture this data was made. Rather, the data could be inferred from the information stored at the end of the simulation run. However, wait times for resources and infrastructure could be lost in this process. In addition, new shortcomings were introduced in CPORTS 1.4. Among these were the following.

- Virtual port areas are defined for which the accounting of space utilization is not totally complete.
- Only one anchorage is supported.
- For each type of helicopter processing area, only one type is supported.
- Only a single staging area/gate association can be made (i.e., exiting the port from a specific staging area requires the use of only one specific gate—no optional routing is allowed).
- The GUI is cumbersome to use. (Note: the GUI was developed with the understanding that it would be completely rewritten.)

Figure 2 depicts the flow of cargo through a POD.

In addition to the shortcomings of each model listed above, useful enhancements were made individually to the models as their development continued in parallel to address the needs of the different user communities. Most important among these are the ability to change process times and various other model parameters during a CPORTS simulation run (data specified prior to run time) and the greater flexibility PORTSIM 4.3 offers in the assigning of ships to berths.

These two models could be used independently to analyze a single port that serves both embarking and debarking forces provided that there was no overlap in time frames as information

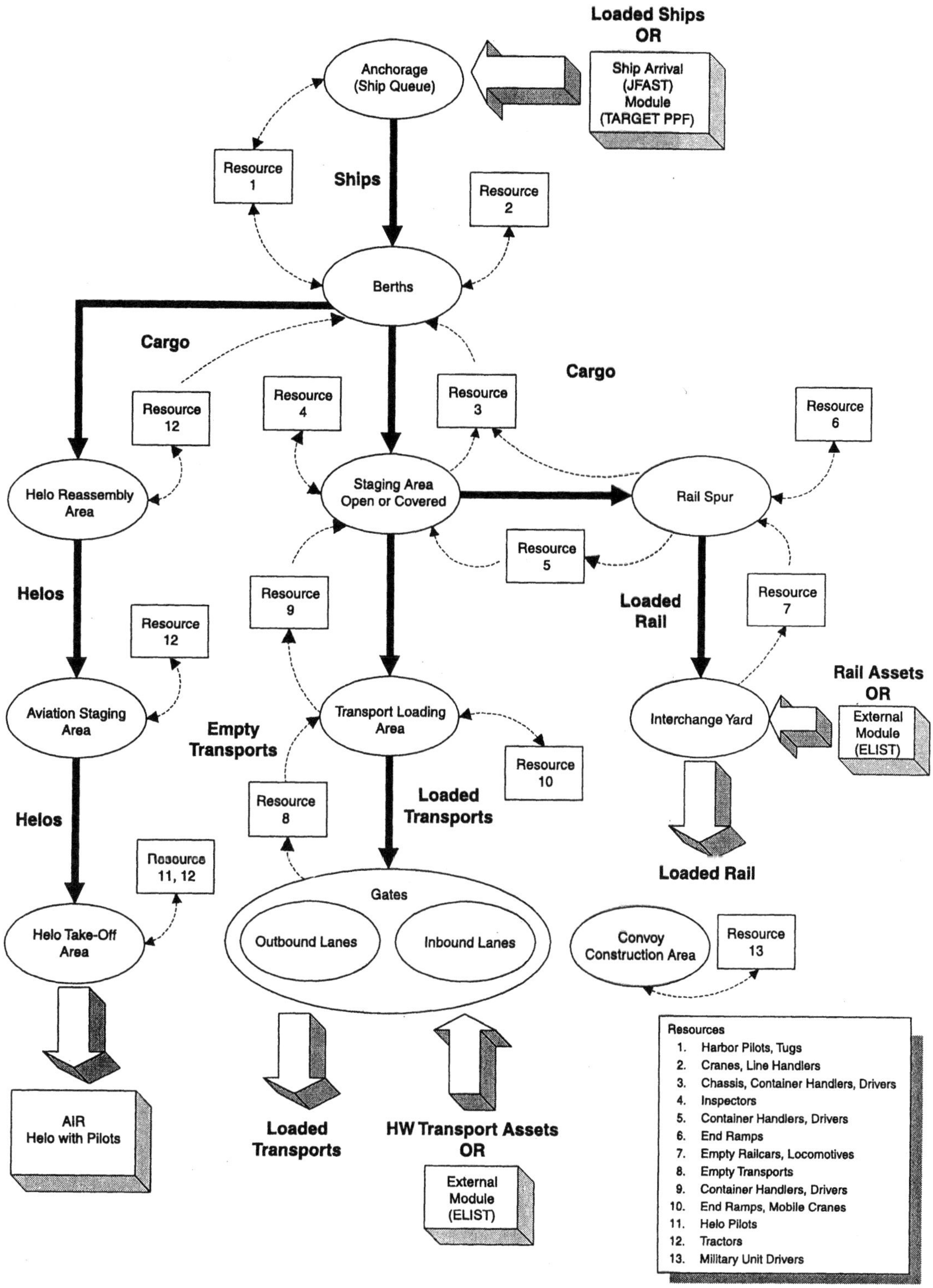

Figure 2. CPORTS models flows of cargo through port of debarkation [2].

cannot be shared between the two models. Even in the best of situations, there would be inconsistencies in the level of information that could be reported from the simulations. A decision was made to merge the two models in an effort to provide the analysts with a port model that could simulate embarking and debarking forces in a common environment and capture the subtle implications of port resources and infrastructure sharing.

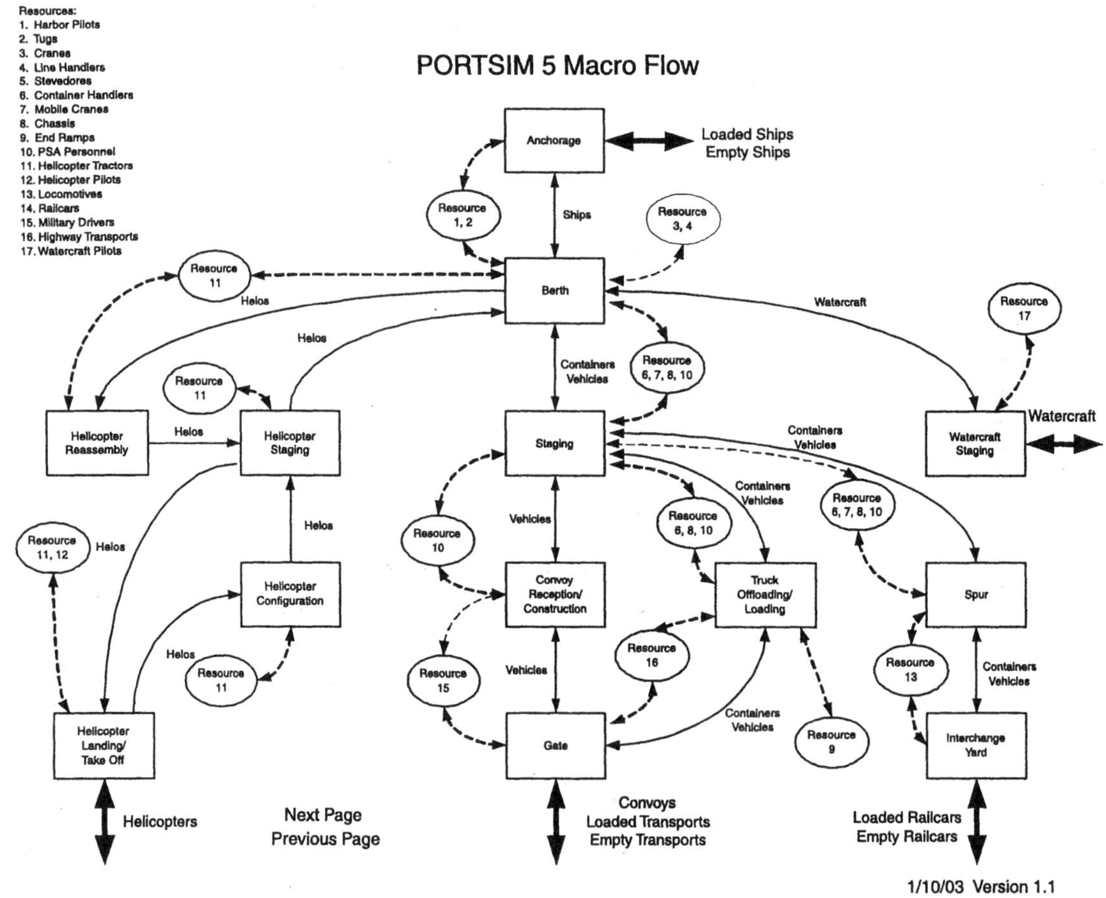

Figure 3. PORTSIM 5 macro flow.

While the POE and POD models are an invaluable foundation for seaport simulation, there still exists a need to model a seaport as one entity, rather than as two separate components, while taking advantage of the work already done on the POE and POD sides. Work on PORTSIM 5 began in earnest at Argonne in the fall of 2001 under direct guidance from the MTMCTEA. The beta version of PORTSIM 5 was delivered on April 30, 2003. The challenge is to make full use of the knowledge gained in developing the component pieces while merging them into a model that will accurately simulate real-life seaport trafficking. In looking at the problem from a port perspective, the model will simulate simultaneous inbound and outbound traffic for the first time.

PORTSIM 5 blends the features of CPORTS 1.4 and PORTSIM 4.3 into a single model that alleviates the shortcomings of the individual models, applies the enhancements to the opposite model, and allows the user to simulate POD-only, POE-only, and concurrent operations.

Figure 3 depicts cargo flow through a combined POE/POD port.

PORTSIM 5 is designed to model the significant areas of operation, processes, and resources at a port. It is being implemented in MODSIM III, an object-oriented simulation language developed by CACI. The model uses the MTMCTEA GIS ACCESS database for its source of port infrastructure.

4.1. Areas of Operation

Each port can have six different types of physical port areas: anchorages, berths, spurs, gates, interchange yards, and staging areas. The staging areas are divided into a number of virtual areas: convoy processing, truck processing, container staging, vehicle staging, helicopter landing, helicopter processing, helicopter landing and takeoff, and watercraft. These virtual areas are treated as rectangular areas of a specified size and consume space within the staging area in which they are located. Though the source of data is a GIS database, no spatial data on the port areas is extracted.

The equipment that is processed by the port is defined by the time phased force deployment data (TPFDD). A TPFDD is the joint operation planning and execution system database portion of an operation plan; it contains time-phased force data, non-unit-related cargo and personnel data, and movement data for the operation plan, including:

(a) in-place units;
(b) units to be deployed to support the operation plan with a priority indicating the desired sequence for their arrival at the port of debarkation;
(c) routing of forces to be deployed;
(d) movement data associated with deploying forces;
(e) estimates of nonunit-related cargo and personnel movements to be conducted concurrently with the deployment of forces;
(f) estimate of transportation requirements that must be fulfilled by common-user lift resources as well as those requirements that can be fulfilled by assigned or attached transportation resources [4].

A TPFDD is "expanded" to Level 6 detail (individual cargo items) by software developed at MTMCTEA [5]. These records contain the data on the type of cargo, the physical size and weight of each item, when they are scheduled to arrive at the port, the transport on which they arrive, if not self-propelled, and when they are required to be at their final destination and the ship on/from which they are to be loaded/offloaded.

The port area set object hierarchy is provided in Figure 4.

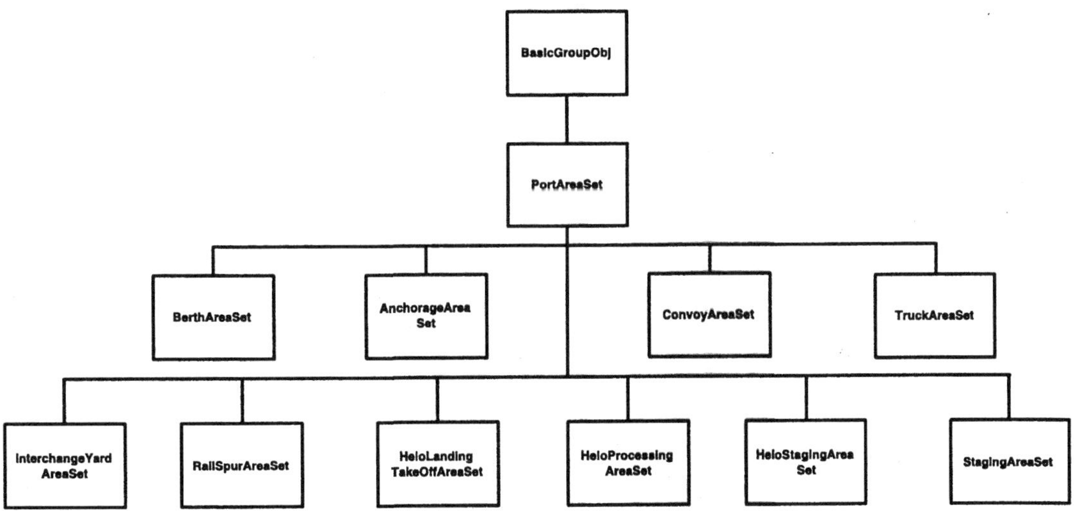

Figure 4. Port area set object hierarchy.

For each distinct type of port area, there is one port area set object instantiated. These objects contain the attributes that are common across all port areas of the same type. The process time distribution associated with a specific process is used by all port areas of the appropriate type. For example, the vehicle staging inspection time, stored in the StagingAreaSet object, will be referenced by all defined vehicle staging areas at the port. The model does not allow for area-specific process times. These objects also contain a list of all defined port areas of the appropriate type. The logic that determines which of the physical areas will be accessed during the simulation is contained in these objects.

Figure 5 depicts the port area objects that model a specific physical area in the port.

There is one object of the appropriate type instantiated for each physical port area that is defined as being available for military use. These objects serve as the "containers" in which

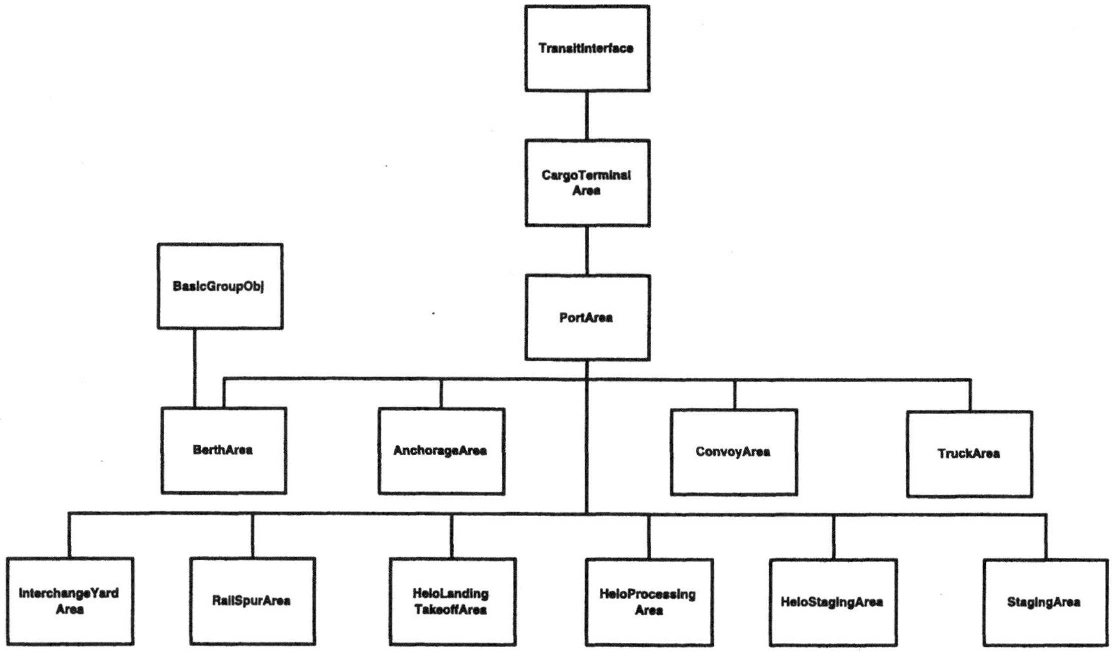

Figure 5. Port area objects.

cargo items are processed and stored as the simulation executes.

4.2. Processes

A total of 88 processes are included in the simulation. These processes effect a state change for the individual cargo item being processed, the port area(s) in which it is being processed, and any resources that may be acting upon it. Each process is assigned a process time distribution to specify the time required to complete the process. Six distribution types supported by MODSIM III are made available to the user for each process. They are: triangular, exponential, uniform, normal, gamma, and beta distributions.

The cargo type, its physical characteristics, its transport, and the port configuration will define the ordered set of steps through which each cargo item must go. Some of these steps represent actual processes for which a time distribution is specified by the user and some are requests for resources or infrastructure to be assigned to the cargo. For example, a container arriving on a flatbed truck that will be handled with a CHE will always go through this defined set of steps processes. Steps annotated with a "*" indicate a process for which a process distribution time will be assigned and those annotated with a "#" indicate a step during which an undetermined amount of time can elapse waiting for port resources or infrastructure. Those steps without an annotation either occur instantaneously or spawn off a new time consuming activity for which time is accounted elsewhere.

1. Arrive at the port.
2. Assign a truck offloading area and wait for available space #.
3. Assign a container staging area and wait for available space #.
4. Assign a gate and lane and enter gate queue #.
5. Enter gate, be processed and pass through the gate *.
6. Transit to a truck offloading area *.
7. Enter truck offloading area and consume space.
8. Request and wait for port support activity (PSA) personnel #.
9. Complete the receipt process *.
10. Release PSA personnel.

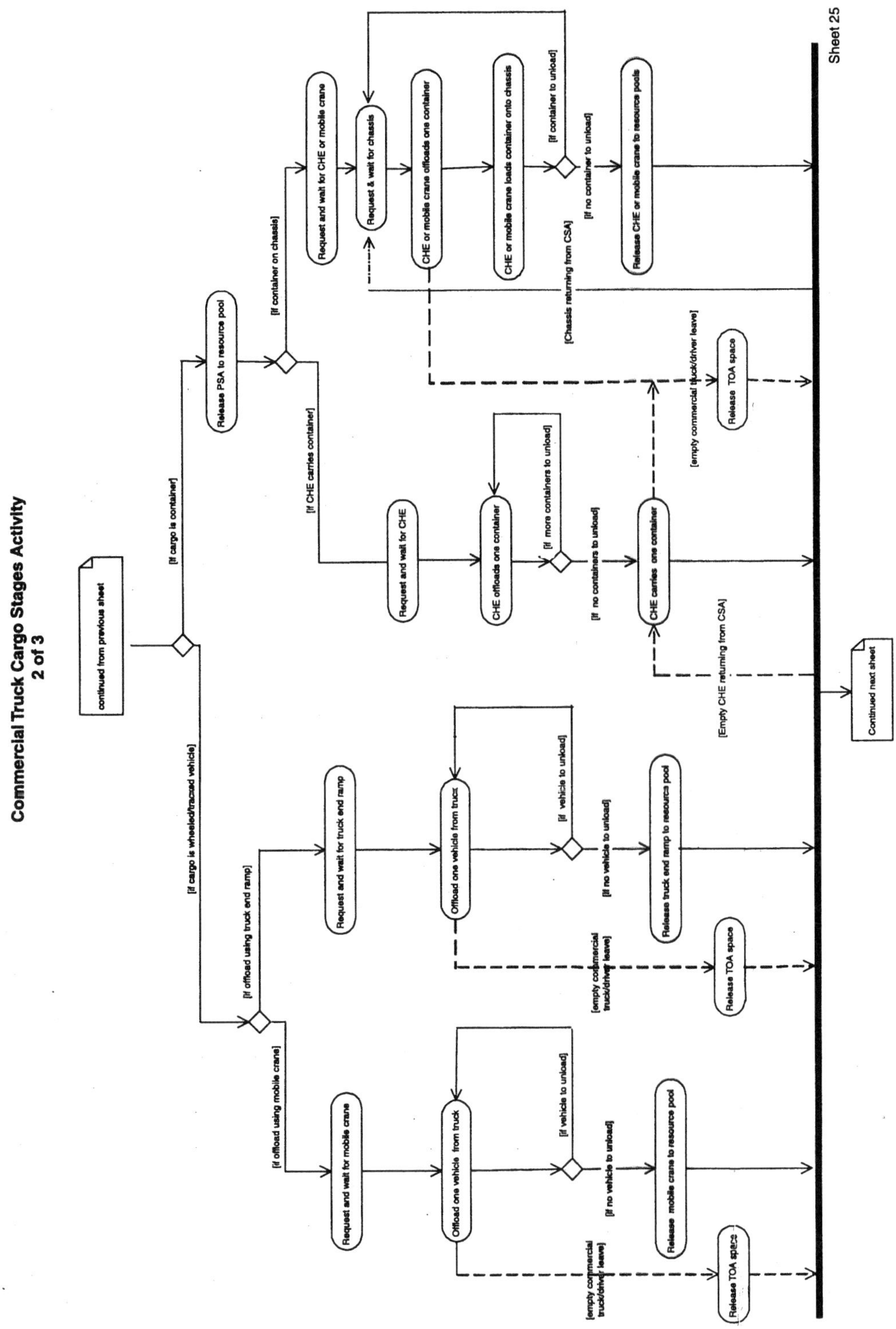

Figure 6. Commercial truck cargo stages activity.

11. Request and wait for CHE #.
12. Offload container from truck *.
13. Release truck to exit port.
14. Transit to container staging area *.
15. Enter container staging area and consume space.
16. Park the container *.
17. Release the CHE.
18. Request and wait for PSA personnel #.
19. Complete the inspection process *.
20. Release PSA personnel.
21. Wait for the specified dwell time to elapse *.
22. Wait to be called forward to the berth #.
23. Request and wait for CHE #.
24. Transit to the berth *.
25. Offload container onto berth *.
26. Wait for berth crane #.
27. Be loaded onto the ship *.
28. Complete the lashing process on the ship *.

Figure 6 is a portion of the activity diagram that defines the commercial truck cargo stages activity.

The 28 steps listed above for containers on flatbeds processed with CHE would be distributed across a number of these activity diagrams.

The variability in the time required to process this piece of cargo will be affected by the availability of the port infrastructure (gate, truck offloading area, container staging area, berth) and the availability of port resources to support the activities (mobile crane or CHE, inspector, chassis, berth crane) as this piece of cargo competes against all other cargo items at the port being processed.

4.3 Resources

During the systematic analysis of PORTSIM 4.3 to verify its proper implementation, parameter sweeps for port resources would occasionally show counterintuitive results. The allocation of additional resources would sometimes lead to degraded port performance. It was discovered that the simplistic first-come, first-served approach to allocation of port resources often resulted in a feast or famine scenario. Some operations received all the resources requested while others would receive only a fraction of the resources requested. The total amount of work accomplished in the simulated port in a given time with the same amount of resources could actually fluctuate with different allocation schemes. However, the design of PORTSIM 4.3 was not sufficiently flexible to facilitate the implementation of alternate strategies. As a result, "what-if" scenarios to implement different allocation schemes were time consuming to implement and were impractical at best. The discovery of the potential negative impacts of an allocation scheme made it clear that the manual integration of results from a POE simulation run and a POD simulation run could not simply be accepted as accurate (especially when the allocation of resources is not specifically reported). The added complexity of additional port operations (POE and POD) competing for the limited resources needed an automated solution rather than a manual one. As a result, the need for an integrated port model became even more apparent.

The allocation scheme anomalies also pointed out that the model must allow for multiple allocation schemes to be implemented. At a real world port, a resource manager with years of experience, knowledge of port priorities, and knowledge of future workloads would rely on this experience and knowledge in making decisions. A simplistic approach would not be sufficient. PORTSIM 5 will have the flexibility to support multiple allocation schemes. Some schemes under consideration are the following:

- first-come, first-served global resource pools;
- first-come, first-served separate POE and POD resource pools;
- workload-based allocation smoothing;
- POE vs. POD priority schemes;
- port operation (train unloading vs. ship loading) priority schemes.

Allowing multiple allocation schemes and making the low-level allocation data available for analysis will help ensure that model results are not influenced by any modeling artifacts.

A total of 17 resource types are modeled in the simulation. These include transports that bring cargo into or out of the port (ships, trucks, locomotives, railcars), resources that move cargo within the port proper (tugs, helicopter tractors, chassis, CHE), equipment that loads/offloads cargo onto/from transports (truck end ramps, mobile cranes, berth cranes) and people (PSA personnel, harbor pilots, helicopter pilots, unit drivers, line handlers, and stevedores). Note that some resources such as container handling equipment (CHE) can serve multiple purposes: transport cargo within the port and load/unload cargo.

Resource pools are either defined for a specific port area type or are defined as global port resources. An example of each are line handlers at the berth and PSA personnel, respectively. A resource pool can either be shared by both POE and POD operations, or it can be allocated specifically to only one type of operation (and thus, two such resource pools must be defined if both POE and POD operations take place at the port area(s)). Depending on the options selected, the total number of resource pools supported during a simulation run can vary from 15 to 30. The request for a resource from a pool will wait until the total number of resources that has been requested can be supplied. Currently, all but helicopter tractors are allocated on a first-come, first-served basis. Helicopter tractors are distributed based on a priority system. Since the loading and offloading of helicopters is a time consuming process, the model will assign a higher priority to requests for a tractor that will keep the loading/offloading process moving while it will allow requests for a tractor to move a helicopter from reassembly to staging to delay.

4.4 INTERFACE

This section provides a brief description of the GUI for PORTSIM 5 and provides a few screen captures to show the general structure of the GUI and the steps that would be required to define and run a simulation. The GUI for PORTSIM 5 is written in Visual Basic 6.0. The steps to define a scenario and run a simulation are as follows:

- select a port and terminal;
- select type of port operation: (POE, POD, concurrent);
- for each of the port areas, enter attribute, resource, and process data as required;
- build routes between the various port areas and specify transit times;
- select the POE and/or POD force to move through the port;
- run the simulation.

Figure 7 is a screen capture of the top level configuration screen from which the user can access all scenario definition screens.

Figures 8–10 show attribute, resource and process time screens for anchorages.

On this screen, the user specifies whether the anchorage is to be used for: POE-only, POD-only, or concurrent operations, which of the available anchorages can be utilized, the types of ships that this anchorage can accept, and finally, the capacity of the anchorage.

On this screen, the user would specify whether the resources pools supporting the anchorage will be shared by POE and POD operations, the sizes of the tug and harbor pilot pools, and the number of tugs that would be assigned to each ship as it is moved to and from the berth.

On this screen, the user specifies the types of distributions that will be made available to the user and the process times distributions associated with the anchorage areas. The default

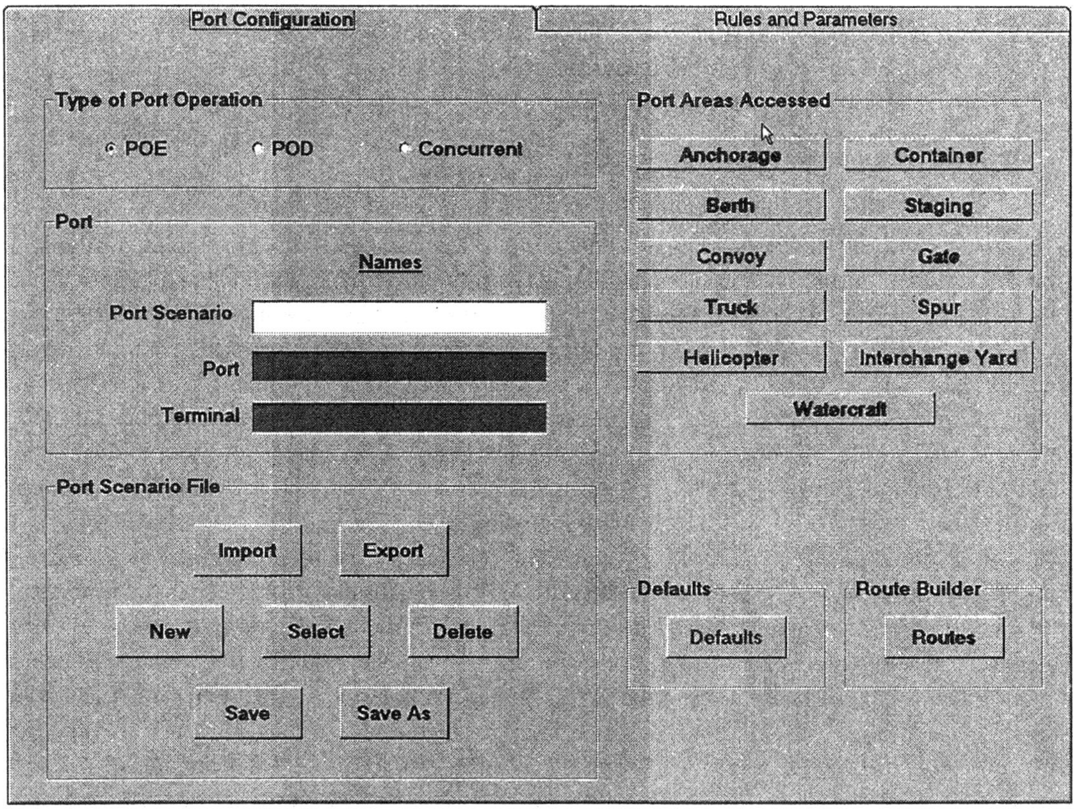

Figure 7. Port configuration screen.

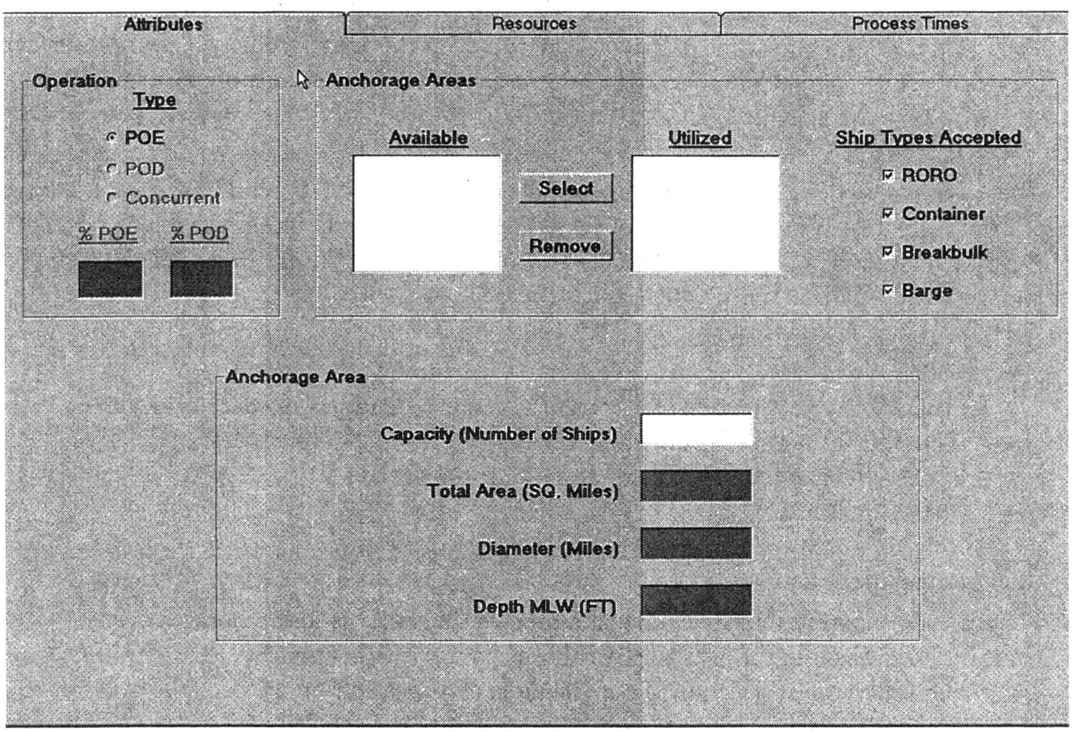

Figure 8. Anchorage attributes screen.

distributions limits the user to the default distribution type that has been assigned to this process. In this example, both process time distribution types would be triangular. By clicking on the advanced radio button, the user has access to all six distribution types supported by the model.

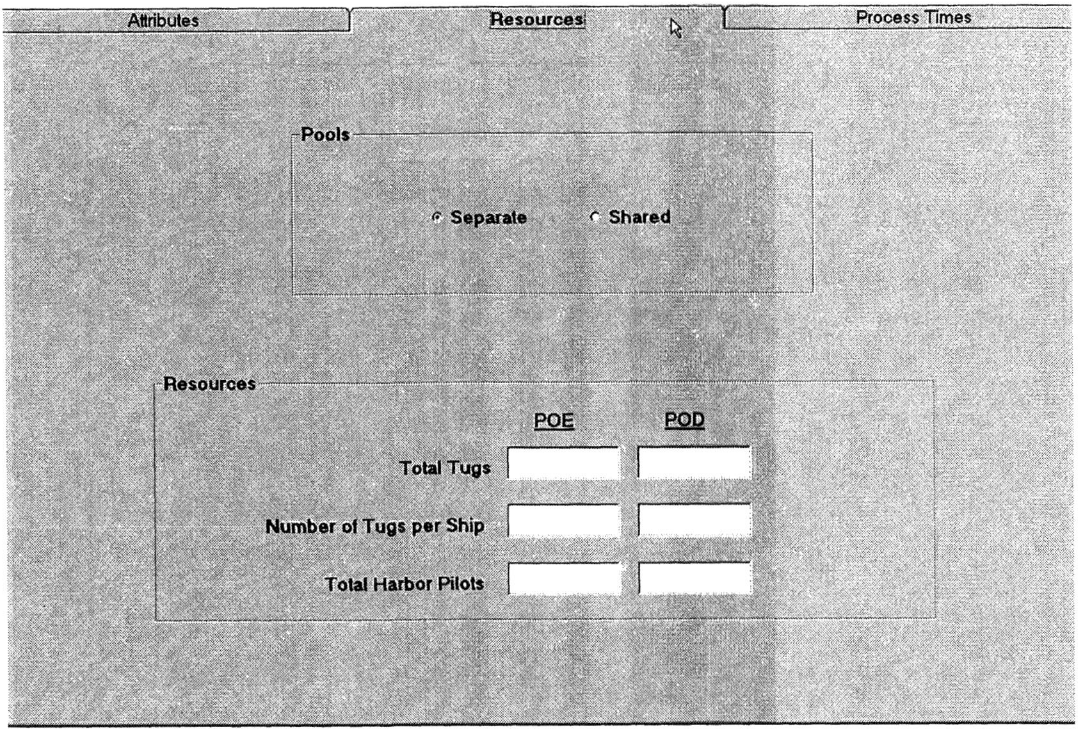

Figure 9. Anchorage resources screen.

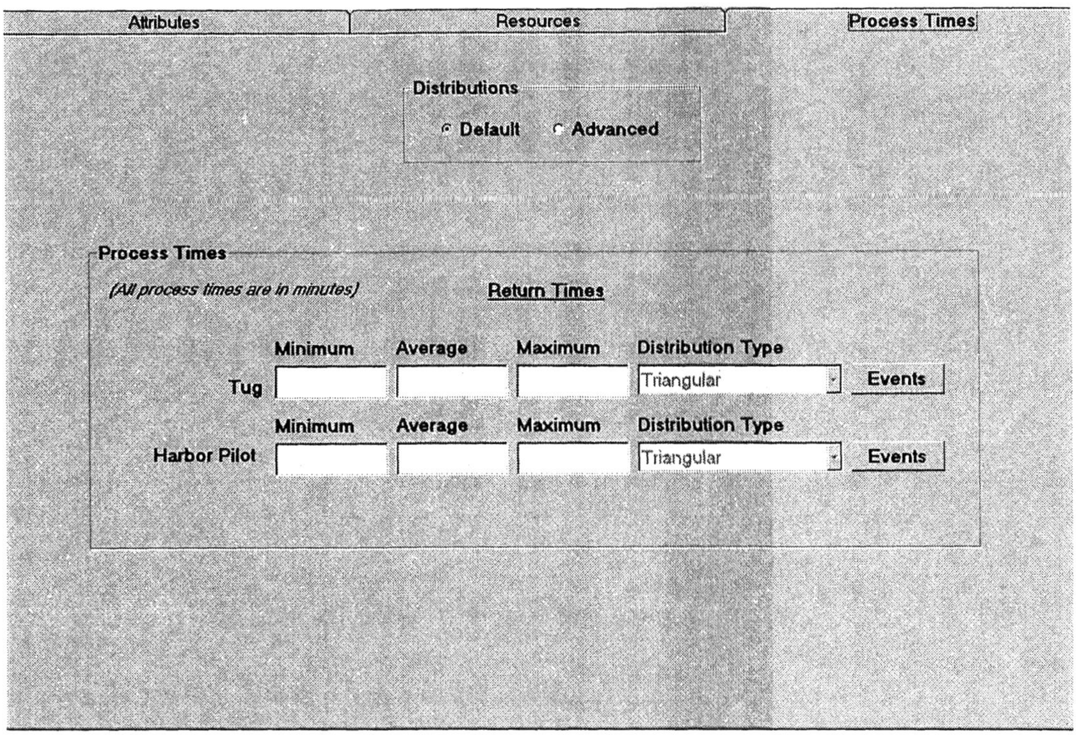

Figure 10. Anchorage process times screen.

This next section describes some of the outputs that PORTSIM 5 will generate. These three examples are prototyped graphs and reports.

Figure 11 is a clearance profile graph that depicts the progress of the cargo items as they are processed through the port on their way to being loaded onto a ship. The left-most portion of

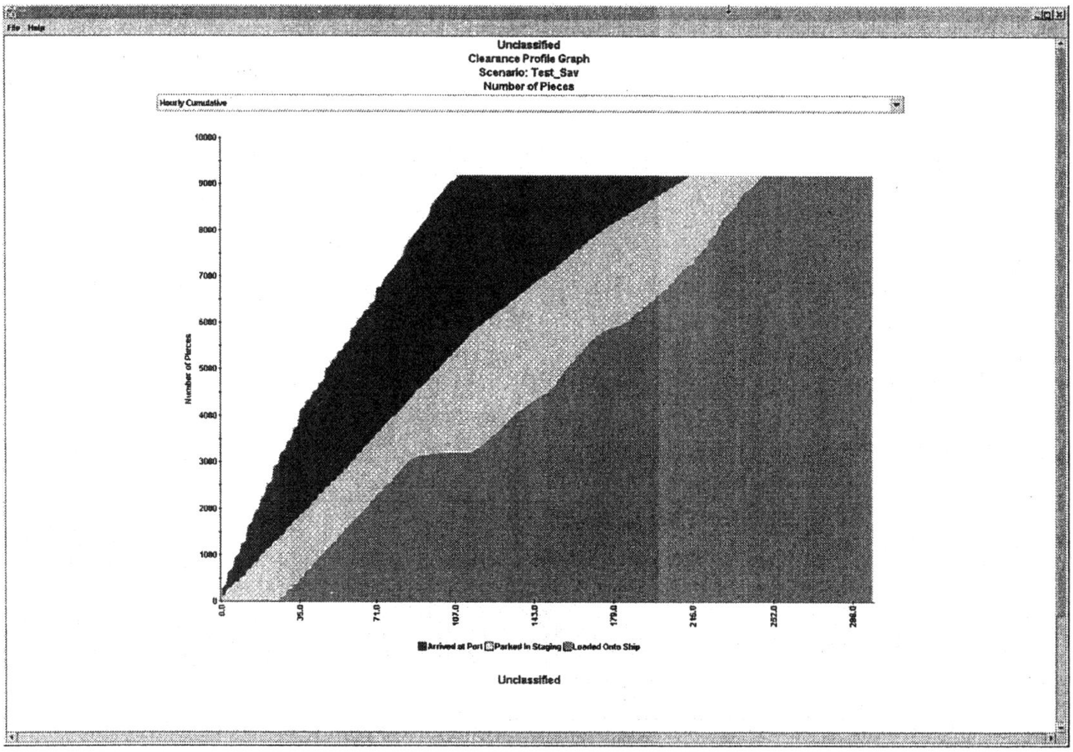

Figure 11. Clearance profile graph.

the graph shows the cumulative total of the cargo arriving at the port. The center portion of the graph shows the cumulative total of cargo items that are parked in staging and ready to be loaded onto a ship. The difference in the slopes of the two portions indicates that the cargo items are arriving faster than they can be processed through to their ready-to-load state. From this graph, however, the user cannot determine if this condition is causing backlogs at various locations within the port. Finally, the right-most portion of the graph shows the cumulative total of cargo items that have been loaded onto a ship. This graph primarily shows how long a deployment would take to clear the port.

Figure 12 is a cargo report that shows the simulated time of major state changes for each individual cargo item: arrival at the port, cleared through the gate, parked in staging, available to load, and loaded onto a ship. This report can indicate that there may be insufficient port resources and/or infrastructure made available for use in the simulation. For example, significant time durations between arrival at port and cleared through gate can indicate insufficient gate allocation to the military operation (or inappropriately quick arrival of cargo at the port).

Figure 13 is a staging area utilization graph that depicts the hourly utilization of staging space. This graph can be used to determine if sufficient resources have been allocated for the deployment. A graph showing the achievement of 100% utilization of a resource cannot be interpreted as a necessarily good or bad situation. 100% utilization can indicate that an optimized allocation has been met. Or it can indicate that not enough resources have been allocated and the progress of the whole system is being slowed. Or the situation could exist that there is too much of a resource and that removing some of the resource will not affect the final outcome.

The ultimate goal for PORTSIM 5 is for it to become a key player in a transportation command (TRANSCOM) federation that will model end-to-end mobilization and deployment operations. The HLA data flows for the federation are enumerated below.

- ELIST will flow forces from the fort to the POE and supply arrival information of all cargo and transports via HLA to PORTSIM.

File Help

Unclassified

Fri Mar 07 15:06:26 CST 2003

Scenario Name: Test_Sav

PORTSIM Detailed Cargo Report

SRC UIC	Unit Index	LIN ID	LIN	Nomenclature	Time Arrived At Port	Time Cleared Gate	Time Parked In Staging	Time Available To Load	Time Loaded	Loading Time (Mins)	Ship Loaded Onto
01302A000		ARM2001EQ00000014	C32887	CLEANER STM TLR MTD	0:00:00	0:00:05	0:00:12	1:00:34	1:02:17	0.84	Algol
01302A000		ARM2001EQ00000015	G42170	GEN SET DED TRL MTD	0:00:00	0:00:09	0:00:15	1:00:40	1:02:18	1.11	Algol
01302A000		ARM2001EQ00000007	L28351	KITCHEN FIELD TLR MTD	0:00:00	0:00:14	0:00:22	1:00:43	1:02:20	1.39	Algol
01302A000		ARM2001VE00000009	T07679	TRK UTIL, HVY HMMWV	0:00:00	0:00:18	0:00:26	1:00:56	1:02:27	3.03	Algol
01302A000		ARM2001VE00000002	T60081	TRK CARGO LMTV W/EQP	0:00:00	0:00:22	0:00:29	1:00:57	1:02:31	3.81	Algol
01302A000		ARM2001VE00000003	T60081	TRK CARGO LMTV W/EQP	0:00:00	0:00:26	0:00:32	1:00:55	1:02:24	4.18	Algol
01302A000		ARM2001VE00000001	T60149	TRK CARGO: LMTV W/EQU	0:00:00	0:00:30	0:00:38	1:01:07	1:02:35	4.16	Algol
01302A000		ARM2001VE00000010	T61494	TRK UTIL CRG/TRP CARR	0:00:00	0:00:34	0:00:40	1:01:09	1:02:43	3.56	Algol
01302A000		ARM2001VE00000011	T61494	TRK UTIL CRG/TRP CARR	0:00:00	0:00:38	0:00:45	1:01:08	1:02:39	3.26	Algol
01302A000		ARM2001VE00000012	T61494	TRK UTIL CRG/TRP CARR	0:00:00	0:00:42	0:00:48	1:01:16	1:02:50	4.41	Algol
01302A000		ARM2001VE00000013	T61494	TRK UTIL CRG/TRP CARR	0:00:00	0:00:47	0:00:54	1:01:19	1:02:54	3.75	Algol
01302A000		ARM2001VE00000014	T61494	TRK UTIL CRG/TRP CARR	0:00:00	0:00:50	0:00:57	1:01:24	1:03:04	2.93	Algol
01302A000		ARM2001VE00000015	T61494	TRK UTIL CRG/TRP CARR	0:00:00	0:00:54	0:01:00	1:01:28	1:03:08	3.82	Algol
01302A000		ARM2001VE00000016	T61494	TRK UTIL CRG/TRP CARR	0:00:00	0:00:58	0:01:04	1:01:29	1:03:14	3.90	Algol
01302A000		ARM2001VE00000017	T61494	TRK UTIL CRG/TRP CARR	0:00:00	0:01:02	0:01:10	1:01:31	1:03:18	3.35	Algol
01302A000		ARM2001VE00000018	T61494	TRK UTIL CRG/TRP CARR	0:00:00	0:01:05	0:01:12	1:01:33	1:03:22	4.35	Algol
01302A000		ARM2001VE00000019	T61494	TRK UTIL CRG/TRP CARR	0:00:00	0:01:09	0:01:15	1:01:37	1:03:27	3.89	Algol
01302A000		ARM2001VE00000020	T61494	TRK UTIL CRG/TRP CARR	0:00:00	0:01:13	0:01:19	1:01:44	1:03:32	2.60	Algol
01302A000		ARM2001VE00000021	T61494	TRK UTIL CRG/TRP CARR	0:00:00	0:01:16	0:01:23	1:01:47	1:03:36	4.47	Algol
01302A000		ARM2001VE00000022	T61494	TRK UTIL CRG/TRP CARR	0:00:00	0:01:19	0:01:26	1:01:48	1:03:40	3.84	Algol
01302A000		ARM2001VE00000023	T61494	TRK UTIL CRG/TRP CARR	0:00:00	0:01:22	0:01:28	1:01:55	1:03:27	2.71	Altair
01302A000		ARM2001VE00000024	T61494	TRK UTIL CRG/TRP CARR	0:00:00	0:01:26	0:01:33	1:01:54	1:03:26	2.86	Altair
01302A000		ARM2001VE00000025	T61494	TRK UTIL CRG/TRP CARR	0:00:00	0:01:30	0:01:36	1:02:07	1:03:35	4.42	Altair
01302A000		ARM2001VE00000026	T61494	TRK UTIL CRG/TRP CARR	0:00:00	0:01:35	0:01:41	1:02:07	1:03:38	2.73	Altair
01302A000		ARM2001VE00000027	T61494	TRK UTIL CRG/TRP CARR	0:00:00	0:01:39	0:01:46	1:02:16	1:03:42	2.97	Altair
01302A000		ARM2001EQ00000002	T61630	TRK UTIL EXPANDED CAP	0:00:00	0:01:43	0:01:49	1:02:18	1:03:45	2.92	Altair
01302A000		ARM2001EQ00000003	T61630	TRK UTIL EXPANDED CAP	0:00:00	0:01:47	0:01:55	1:02:21	1:03:50	3.37	Algol
01302A000		ARM2001EQ00000004	T61630	TRK UTIL EXPANDED CAP	0:00:00	0:01:51	0:01:57	1:02:21	1:03:53	3.18	Algol
01302A000		ARM2001EQ00000005	T61630	TRK UTIL EXPANDED CAP	0:00:00	0:01:56	0:02:03	1:02:31	1:04:09	3.44	Algol
01302A000		ARM2001EQ00000006	T61630	TRK UTIL EXPANDED CAP	0:00:00	0:01:59	0:02:05	1:02:31	1:04:06	3.79	Algol
01305A200		ARM2001EQ00000109	H30616	HELICOPTER INT&ELEC	0:00:00	NA	0:00:00	0:00:00	1:04:27	138.66	Algol
05335L000		ARM 1EQ00001427	B31098	BRDG ARMD VEH LCHR	0:00:00	NA	0:00:00	0:00:00	5:18:49	215.06	Capella
01305A200		ARM2001EQ00000110	H30616	HELICOPTER INT&ELEC	0:00:00	NA	0:00:00	0:00:00	1:05:32	141.31	Altair
05335L000		ARM 1EQ00001428	B31098	BRDG ARMD VEH LCHR	0:00:00	NA	0:00:00	0:00:00	5:19:40	222.50	Bellatrix
01305A200		ARM2001EQ00000111	H30616	HELICOPTER INT&ELEC	0:00:05	NA	0:00:05	0:00:05	1:06:36	161.31	Antares
05335L000		ARM 1EQ00001429	B31098	BRDG ARMD VEH LCHR	0:00:05	NA	0:00:05	0:00:05	5:22:10	200.39	Capella
01305A200		ARM2001EQ00000085	H32361	HELICOPTER UTILITY	0:00:10	NA	0:00:10	0:00:10	1:07:19	171.60	Algol

Unclassified

Figure 12. Cargo report.

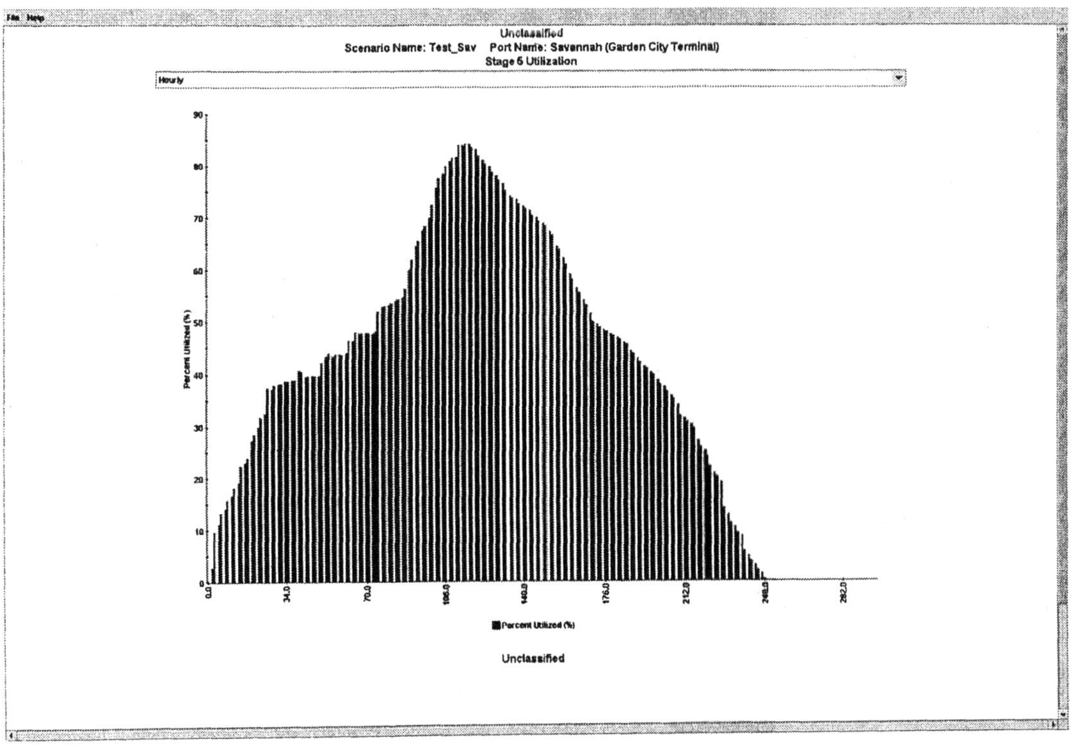

Figure 13. Staging area utilization graph.

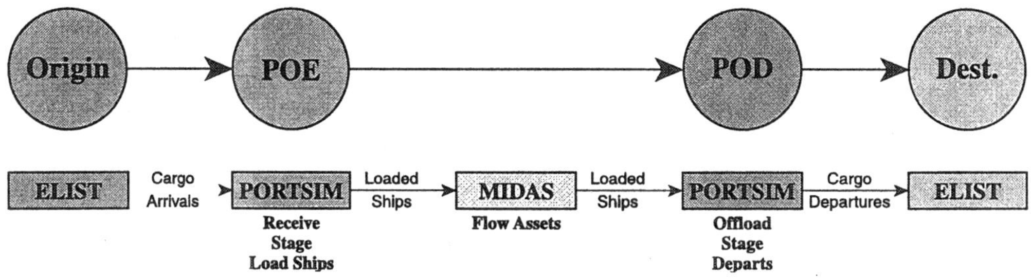

Figure 14. TRANSCOM federation overview.

- Using this information, PORTSIM will load the cargo onto the ships.
- The loaded ships will then be passed via HLA to MIDAS.
- MIDAS will move the ships along the strategic leg to the POD.
- MIDAS will feed this information via HLA to PORTSIM.
- PORTSIM will offload cargo from the ship and feed ELIST with cargo departure information via HLA.

Future enhancements will allow PORTSIM 5 to use these data feeds for virtually all scenario parameters.

Other goals and applications for PORTSIM 5 and beyond could include chemical and biological terrorism, weather impacts and labor unrest. For example, a chemical attack would constrain the availability of port areas, due to contamination cleanup time, and downgrade the overall labor resource as a function of the required protective measurements that need to be employed in such a situation. Overall port throughput would be expected to diminish. The estimated changes to system parameters could be computed external to the model and passed in via HLA.

The value of PORTSIM to the military has been ongoing and well documented. Much of PORTSIM's real world application is classified. Two general applications were "port workload" and "port regional readiness" studies done for the U.S. Army. PORTSIM also lends itself well to commercial port operations and could easily be adapted to model nonmilitary processes. For example, the modeling infrastructure could be used to represent grain loading and offloading or bulk loading of coal. A cost component could be developed to further enhance the model's appeal to the nonmilitary community.

The addition of spatial representation would further enhance the model, allowing port-specific data on travel times, distances and road capacities to impact the throughput and rate of closure. PORTSIM could also be enhanced to take advantage of the 2D and 3D visualization work currently under development at Argonne. Visualization provides an animated, graphical representation of a scenario run and gives a fast, accurate picture of cargo flow, highlighting bottlenecks, and underutilization of resources within the port.

5. CONCLUSION

The ability to accurately simulate throughput at a seaport remains a high priority for today's military. PORTSIM 5 builds on the existing body of work that has already been done in the logistics community and enhances the overall accuracy and dependability by modeling at the port level. Port-level modeling integrates POE and POD processes and provides for the system resource constraints that occur when simultaneous operations are necessary. PORTSIM 5 uses a set of conventions to handle resource allocation and improves the overall accuracy of throughput analysis.

REFERENCES

1. MTMCTEA, `http:///www.tea.army.mil/tools/pops.htm`.
2. M. Nevins, C. Macal and J. Joines, A discrete event simulation model for seaport operations, In *Proceedings of the 1995 Summer Computer Simulation Conference*, Ottawa, Ontario, Canada, 1995, (1996).

3. VMASC, http://www.vmasc.odu.edu/portsim/CPorts_Process_Model_frame.htm.
4. Joint Deployment Training Center, http://www.jdtc.transcom.mil/DeploymentGlossary/terms%20q-t.htm#T.
5. PortSim Port of Debarkation (POD) PreProcess User Manual and System Guide, Military Traffic Management Command Transportation Engineering Agency, Newport News, Virginia (November 16, 2001).

Available online at www.sciencedirect.com

SCIENCE @ DIRECT®

ELSEVIER

Mathematical and Computer Modelling 39 (2004) 733–744

MATHEMATICAL AND COMPUTER MODELLING

www.elsevier.com/locate/mcm

Modelling Force Deployments from Army Installations using the Transportation System Capability (TRANSCAP) Model: A Standardized Approach

J. F. BURKE, JR.*, R. J. LOVE AND C. M. MACAL
Argonne National Laboratory
9700 S. Cass Ave, Bldg. 900
Argonne, IL 60439, U.S.A.
<jay><love><macal>@anl.gov

Abstract—Argonne National Laboratory (Argonne) developed the transportation system capability (TRANSCAP) model to simulate the deployment of forces from Army bases, in collaboration with and under the sponsorship of the Military Transportation Management Command Transportation Engineering Agency (MTMCTEA). TRANSCAP's design separates its pre- and post-processing modules (developed in Java) from its simulation module (developed in MODSIM III®). This paper describes TRANSCAP's modelling approach, emphasizing Argonne's highly detailed, object-oriented, multilanguage software design principles. Fundamental to these design principles is TRANSCAP's implementation of an improved method for standardizing the transmission of simulated data to output analysis tools and the implementation of three Army deployment/redeployment community standards, all of which are in the final phases of community acceptance. The first is the extensive hierarchy and object representation for transport simulations (EXHORT), which is a reusable, object-oriented deployment simulation source code framework of classes. The second and third are algorithms for rail deployment operations at a military base.

Keywords—Deployment, Transportation, Discrete-event simulation, Army standards, Standardization, Object-oriented analysis, Object-oriented design.

1. INTRODUCTION

Logistics and mobility have become increasingly important in our rapidly changing world. Since September 11, 2001, it has become even more critical to move soldiers and supplies with limited resources in support of the war on terrorism. During a military deployment, both personnel and

---

The submitted manuscript has been created by the University of Chicago as Operator of Argonne National Laboratory ("Argonne") under Contract No. W-31-109-ENG-38 with the U.S. Department of Energy. The U.S. Government retains for itself, and others acting on its behalf, a paid-up, nonexclusive, irrevocable worldwide license in said article to reproduce, prepare derivative works, distribute copies to the public, and perform publicly and display publicly, by or on behalf of the Government.
This work was supported under a military interdepartmental purchase request from the U.S. Department of Defense, MTMCTEA, through the U.S. Department of Energy contract W-31-109-ENG-109. The authors wish to acknowledge the support of our program managers of MTMCTEA. The authors also thank members of Argonne's Information and Publishing Division for their editorial assistance.
*Author to whom all correspondence should be addressed.

0895-7177/04/$ - see front matter Typeset by $\mathcal{A}\mathcal{M}\mathcal{S}$-TEX
doi:10.1016/j.mcm.2004.02.011

equipment are transported from a fort to a tactical assembly area (the logistics and mobility phase) and then to their final destination—the forward line of troops (the war-fighting phase). With so many active deployments in recent years, there has been little opportunity to practice and test experimental ideas, which would not be under realistic circumstances in any case. In these recent active deployments, the Army has had ample time to deploy its forces. However, rapid deployments to suddenly erupting world hot spots remain in the mission statements of many of our most important fighting forces. As a result, simulation continues to be an important tool in preparing for the constraints and complexities of deployments.

To address this issue, Argonne National Laboratory (Argonne), in collaboration with the Military Traffic Management Command Transportation Engineering Agency (MTMCTEA) and others, is developing simulations that may be used to analyze, plan, train for, and execute the transportation portion (part of the logistics and mobility phase) of military deployments. New simulation models and technologies are a good investment because simulating deployment scenarios on a computer is more efficient and cost-effective than testing them in the real world. The transportation system capability (TRANSCAP) model simulates the first step of a military deployment after mobilization, the loading operations at any Army installation, from power project platforms the Army's biggest and best developed home forts, to the smallest support installations in the continental United States. Specifically, the model simulates installation transportation operations, computes the time-phased outloading capability, and identifies system and infrastructure constraints and installation-specific force departure profiles.

This paper describes TRANSCAP's modelling approach, both with regard to the simulation code and the other critical pieces that make for a functioning application. At the heart of the design of the simulation code are classes with fields and methods specific to Army installations, as part of its implementation of a reusable deployment simulation framework of classes [1]. This framework, called the extensive hierarchy and object representation for transport simulations (EXHORT), was created as part of the design for TRANSCAP and has been successfully reused in the coastal integrated throughput model (CITM), another MTMCTEA and Argonne deployment simulation, thus proving the general utility of the design, since CITM and TRANSCAP simulate radically different processes. The other modules of TRANSCAP were designed to use other Army deployment community standards, and were organized into distinct modules operating as a cooperative cluster. This layer of abstraction allowed us to reap the benefits of modern software design strategies.

2. MODELLING APPROACH

TRANSCAP was written at the highest possible level of detail in data and process. Its processes were also written in an object-oriented programming language to foster the greatest amount of modularity and potential for reuse for future simulation projects.

The following paragraphs describe the three types of low-level data that TRANSCAP uses: transportation assets and cargo, infrastructure, and resource. Transportation and cargo data are at the maximum level of detail, Level 6, which means that details are available for each piece of cargo and each transport vehicle. These are each configured for their particular mode of movement, rather than being an aggregated data description based on tonnage or category. Infrastructure data is the most detailed type of data concerning the quantity and measurements of existing infrastructure. For example, rather than using an aggregate capacity for all marshaling areas or rail yards, the model uses specific square footage and tangent spur-length data for each. Resource data include information about existing facility resources such as the quantity and location of truck loading ramps, rail end ramps, inspectors, mechanics, and tie-down crews [2].

This highly detailed data drove the design of the simulation. In deployment simulations, there are also two types of processes—infrastructure utilization (movement) and resource utilization (a specific activity). In TRANSCAP, because of the detail of the data, these processes are modelled at a high level of detail. Processes simulating infrastructure utilization are based on the actual distances that are traversed in the infrastructure, rather than on aggregate stochastic distributions. Resource processes performed on transportation assets and cargo are associated with individual resources, and each individual resource is represented as an object. Again, there are no unknown actors performing aggregate processing on unknown entities. Each resource is assigned a specific responsibility and a specific service time, instead of representing multiple processes with a general rate. The design of the simulation is explained in detail in Section 4.

The highly detailed data also drove the design of the application. High resolution typically creates a large quantity of data to be handled between modules of the application, and between applications in a federation. Details of these design issues are explained in Sections 5 and 6.

3. IMPLEMENTING THE COMPONENT MODULES IN DIFFERENT LANGUAGES

TRANSCAP comprises four categories of component modules: preprocessing, simulation, postprocessing, and interprocess communication.

- The modules of the preprocessing category include the installation, force, and scenario manager and the scenario report manager. These preprocessing modules manage data input, create the installation, select the installation, specify pieces for deployment, identify the method of deployment (e.g., convoy), and specify deployment characteristics (e.g., the method used to form the convoy groups). Most of these tasks are encapsulated in the user interface, which also can be thought of as a component module.
- The simulation category contains the heart of TRANSCAP, the discrete-event simulation module.
- The modules of the postprocessing category handle the reporting, presentation, animation, and analysis of simulation results and the export of results to other simulation models.
- The module of the interprocess communication (IPC) category enables interaction between the pre- and post-processing modules and the simulation module.

Due to its portability across the multiple platforms employed by Army analysts, Java was the natural choice for the main programming language for all of these component modules. However, we decided to implement the actual discrete-event simulation in CACI MODSIM III® programming language, a language that is designed for the special needs of discrete-event programming,

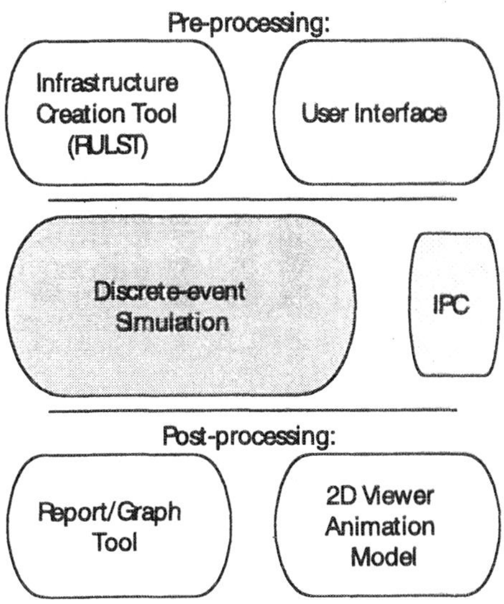

Figure 1.

and which is a much more suitable tool for this type of programming than Java was during the years of the development of this model.

4. SOFTWARE DESIGN OF THE DISCRETE EVENT SIMULATION

This section describes the layered approach taken in designing the discrete-event simulation. EXHORT, a reusable deployment simulation class framework, is subclassed under the template method design pattern, thus creating another class framework encapsulating Army installation specifics. This additional class framework provides the building blocks from which military processes are encapsulated.

4.1. The EXHORT Framework

EXHORT consists of two hierarchies that together constitute a standard and consistent class attribute representation and behavior that could be used directly by a large set of deployment simulations. The hierarchies are unusual in that they provide for a class factoring detailed enough to be a document from a design workflow, rather than merely an aggregate document from an analysis workflow. To encapsulate the characteristics of multiple deployment simulations written at different levels of aggregation, the class abstractions in EXHORT needed to be presented as a design workflow document, rather than as an analysis workflow document, which is more typical of object modeling in the larger community. This greater detail was incorporated because we decided that these classes were "key abstractions" and are well suited for use in new federations of simulations where reusability and intercommunication for new simulations are important [3].

The two EXHORT hierarchies will allow many deployment simulations to use the same set of underlying class data and will significantly reduce the effort needed to integrate simulations that analyze the defense transportation system. The first hierarchy, the transportation class hierarchy

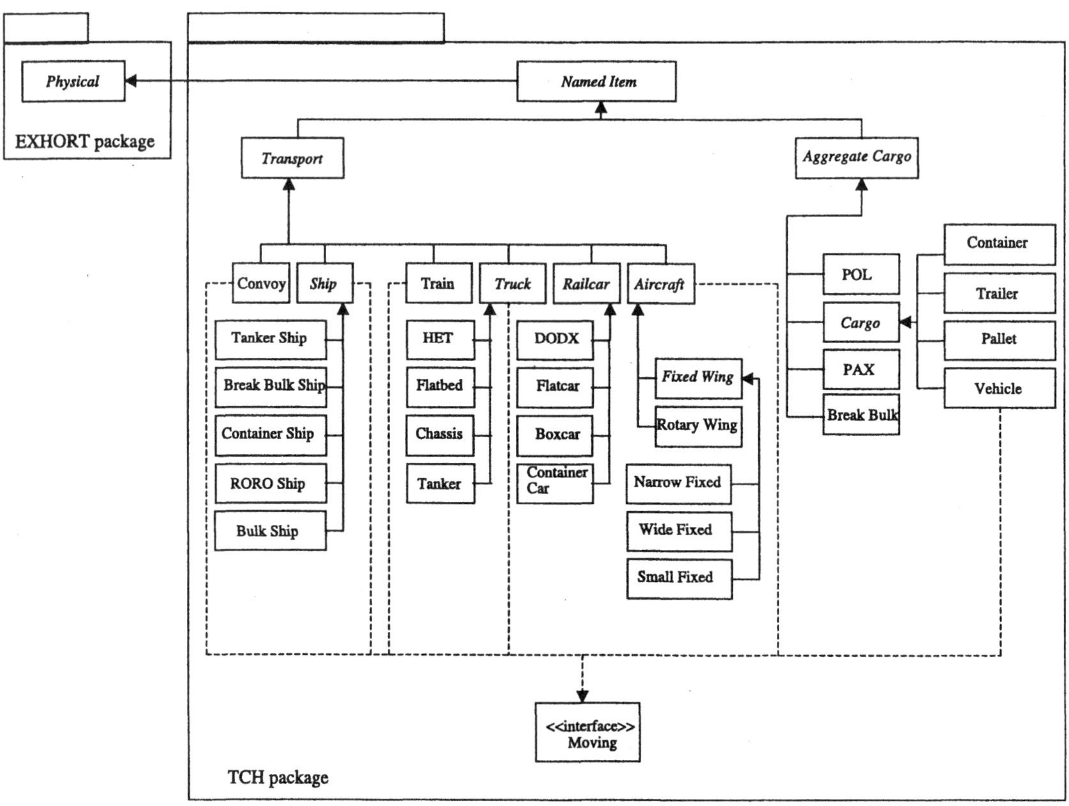

Figure 2. Transportation class hierarchy.

(TCH), encapsulates commercial transportation assets and military cargo. This hierarchy is the Army Modeling and Simulation Office (AMSO) deployment/redeployment community standard SRD 00068 in AMSO's Army standard repository (ASTARS), at `http://www.msrr.army.mil/astars` [3].

The second hierarchy is the infrastructure class hierarchy (ICH), which deals with locations where activities are performed and with the physical infrastructure, such as a motor pool at a fort or a berth at a port. These areas contain the resources needed to support deployment (e.g., ramps, rough-terrain container handlers, cranes, and forklifts). Both hierarchies are needed to describe major portions of the defense transportation system. The goal was to define EXHORT so it could provide a standardized code structure for object-oriented deployment simulations to ensure meaningful data exchanges. A report on the ICH was also submitted to AMSO's deployment/redeployment community for acceptance in the ASTARS repository [3].

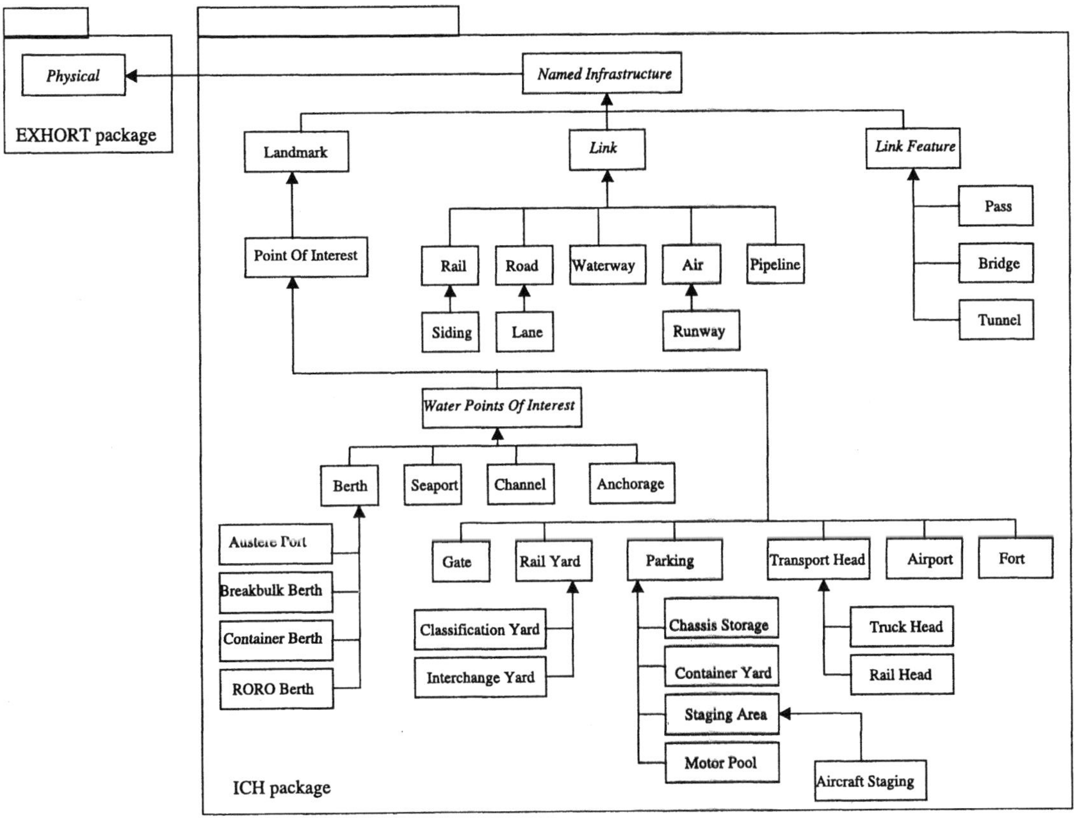

Figure 3. Infrastructure class hierarchy.

4.2. Army Installation-Specific Subclasses of the EXHORT Framework

EXHORT was extended for TRANSCAP to develop military fort-specific subclasses containing logic for specific interactions between clients, servers, and areas. In sum, these subclasses form a new class framework composed of specific "business logic" of military fort deployment that overrides certain generic deployment simulation logic, as needed. An example of how the template method design pattern is implemented to create this new framework of classes is a vehicle being loaded onto a railcar. In the reusable framework, the interaction between clients and servers is implemented as a resource holding a piece of cargo in place for a stochastic process time and then updating the vehicle's current status field when completed. No additional processing is done to the client or the server during the service period. However, when a vehicle (i.e., a client) interacts with a rail end ramp (i.e., a resource) with the goal of loading that vehicle onto the next available position on a train of railcars, the code that chooses a process time stochastically needs to be overridden. The new code (that overrides the old code) will choose a process time on the basis of the length of the railcars and spanners over which the vehicle must drive. In this way, the generic interaction between a client and a server, which is found in the reusable deployment simulation, is subclassed for a specific situation at a fort [2].

4.3. Building Military Processes

The EXHORT framework, which is the kernel of the TRANSCAP discrete-event simulation, was subclassed to create interactions specific to an Army installation deployment simulation. This new class framework inherits and, when appropriate, overrides EXHORT attributes and interactions. This new Army installation-specific framework consists of components that are the building blocks of TRANSCAP's discrete-event simulation processes. The ten processes created from these building blocks include:

- simulation initialization,
- vehicle generation,
- vehicle processing,
- transport loading,
- container movement,
- truck transport asset generation,
- truck transport asset processing,
- train generation,
- train processing,
- call forward locomotive processing.

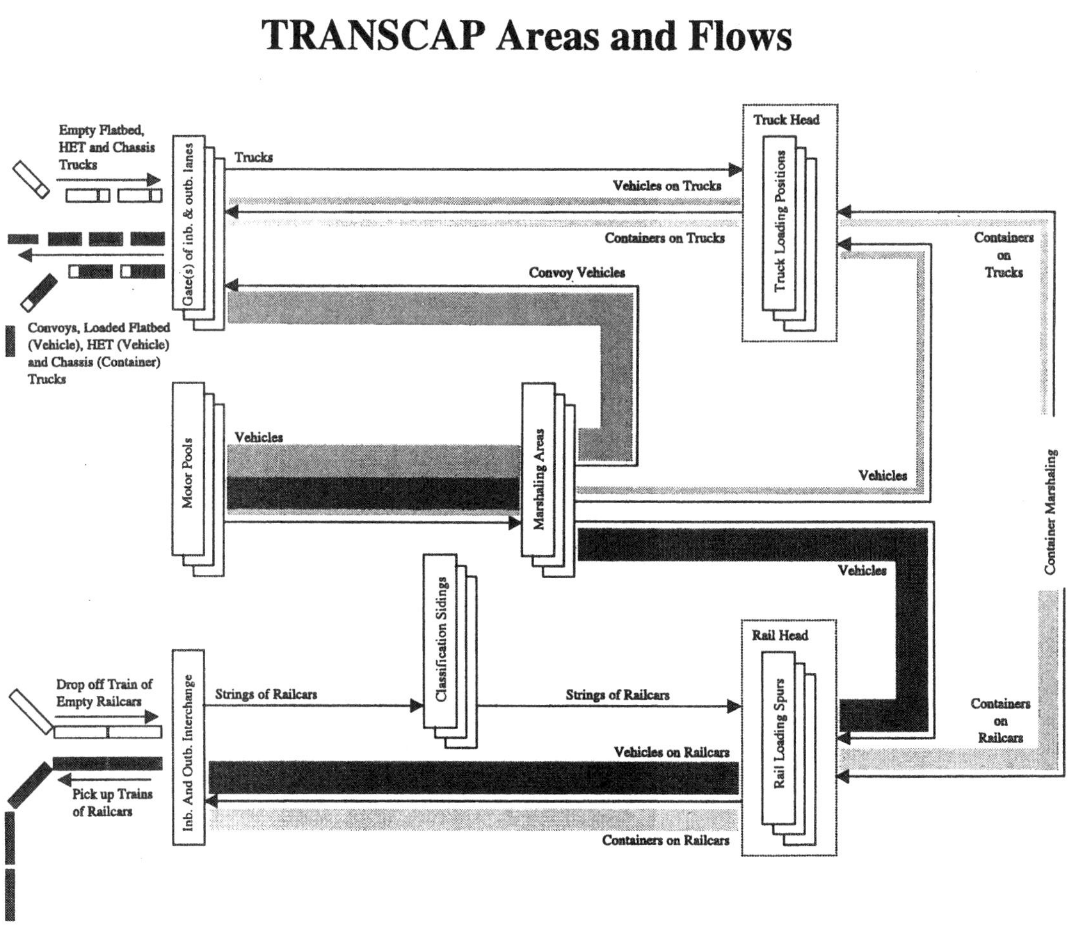

Figure 4.

As with EXHORT, these ten processes that comprise an Army installation class framework can be reused by any deployment simulation that requires any of these Army installation processes. The transport loading and train processing processes were designed in the greatest detail. As such, they were also accepted in AMSO's deployment/redeployment community (SRD 00199) for acceptance in the ASTARS repository [2,4].

When simulating, these military processes execute in parallel to produce a scenario of cargo flows through an Army fort, as pictured in Figure 4. Military vehicles are assigned (by the user or an input source) to leave the fort by convoy, by highway on a truck, or by rail. These vehicles start at their home motor pool and begin by moving to a marshaling area for various inspections and repairs, and then onto a gate (if leaving by convoy) or to the appropriate loading area. Containers start at a container marshaling area, and are called forward to an appropriate loading area. (Container preparation is currently not modeled.) Truck transport assets start with gate processing, followed by a movement to a truck loading position, where they wait to be loaded. Loaded trucks then return to their original gate with cargo. A train of railcars, dropped off by a commercial carrier, start with interchange siding processing, followed by a movement to classification sidings, where they are sorted. At these sidings, strings of railcars are called forward to loading spurs, based on cargo ready for loading at that simulation time. Loaded railcars are then taken back to an interchange siding before being removed from the installation by a commercial carrier.

5. ARCHITECTURE OF COMPONENT MODULES

A kind of cluster architecture is used for TRANSCAP's component modules. Instead of one monolithic simulation model that also handles all preprocessing, postprocessing, and communication between these processes, TRANSCAP's capabilities have been separated into distinct modules and arranged as a cooperative cluster (see Figure 1) [4]. This provides a layer of abstraction that allows each module to

(1) focus on its own tasks,
(2) be written in a language that is appropriate for its tasks,
(3) be developed independently, and
(4) more easily take advantage of a multiple processor or a distributed computing environment.

Further, other models can then more easily reuse TRANSCAP's modules, and vice versa. In fact, reuse is already being achieved with several modules; other simulations also use the RULST (route and landmark selection tool) infrastructure creation tool, the report/graph tool, and the 2D viewer animation model.

With this type of architecture, however, the data exchanged between modules tends to increase in volume, so standardizing the data mapping becomes more important. This data exchange becomes the interface between the modules, as well as between TRANSCAP and other models. The format of this data becomes vital when multiple models and modules read some of the same data files.

6. STANDARDIZATION BETWEEN MODULES

As the interface between modules and models, data exchange can benefit greatly from standardization. By standardizing the format of a data file, the data becomes easier to understand. By leveraging standard tools (e.g., APIs, XML), the development of software code is alleviated. In both cases, it becomes much easier to share the data and reuse file formats, processes, components, and code. To various degrees, TRANSCAP takes advantage of both standardized data file formats and tools, and more standardization efforts are planned for the future.

The data files used by TRANSCAP, standardized or not, are shown in Figure 5, as well as how they flow through the model.

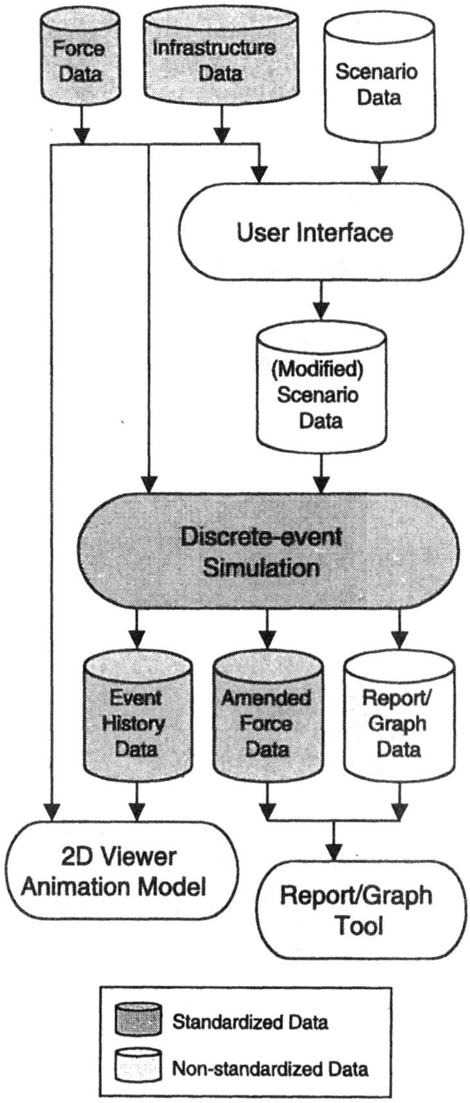

Figure 5. Data file flow.

6.1. Force Data

Standardization of force data is critical among deployment simulations that will be participating in the same federation. Both infrastructure and scenario data are within the boundaries of what TRANSCAP is responsible for simulating, and do not necessarily need to be reusable across applications. However, the actual cargo items that make up the deploying forces must be passed between the various applications that simulate the different legs of a deployment. Therefore, multiple deployment applications will be using the same data, and should use the same data sources. As such, TRANSCAP reuses a standard force profile database to determine which cargo objects will be simulated. A standard file format for a subset of that information is then reused among TRANSCAP's modules and between TRANSCAP and other models.

MTMCTEA and Argonne also collaborated to create the expanded TPFDD editor (ETEdit) and the theater-level analysis, replanning, and graphical extension toolbox (TARGET) force database systems to convert the nearly universal, aggregated time phased force deployment data (TPFDD) into highly detailed Level 6 data. TRANSCAP and the other highly detailed deployment simulations then use this converted data, via standard, unclassified type unit characteristics (TUCHA) force templates. The end data produced for TRANSCAP describes each piece of cargo (e.g., wheeled or tracked vehicles, trailers, and stuffed containers) of each unit (TRANSCAP requires that data be specified at the company and small battalion level) located at a particular military fort, as well as a TARGET-optimized deployment mode (e.g., leaving the fort by road in a convoy, loaded on a truck transport, or loaded on a train). Different data sets are produced for different deployment mode optimizations, with the same cargo in the same units.

6.2. Infrastructure Data

The infrastructure data was designed to be independent of the simulation models that use them. They encapsulate data about the physical structures of Army forts, seaports, and airports, such as landmarks and the road, rail, sea, and air routes between them, including their geographic location. RULST is a graphical map-based model that facilitates the identification and creation of this data. It also provides a way to add logical data on top of the physical data, such as the availability and direction of routes. Any number of specific instances of these installations can then be saved as a standardized set of infrastructure files.

Since the infrastructure database itself was designed with the needs of various deployment simulations in mind, it was also submitted and accepted (SRD 00152) by the AMSO deployment/redeployment community as a standard database for the community. A common infrastructure database allows deployment simulations to use an identical set of underlying infrastructure data. This significantly reduces the effort required for both maintaining the common infrastructure data and integrating the defense transportation simulations for analysis. A relational database is chosen as the proposed standard because it is virtually a *de facto* standard in the larger community, and therefore, is able to support the greatest possible number of deployment simulations. By using more recent database design concepts, such as object-oriented databases, it would be a more difficult fit for older and perhaps non-object-oriented simulations. The goal is to provide a standardized infrastructure database for deployment simulations as a way to ensure meaningful data exchanges between all models in the deployment community [5].

For the infrastructure database, an area of interest is called a landmark. A landmark might be a structure (e.g., gate) or an area of land (e.g., staging area); that is, a landmark is any place where activities occur. Attributes are defined for each landmark that uniquely identify it throughout the entire database, which may contain multiple facilities. Identification attributes are common to all infrastructure tables. For the gate, only one attribute needs to be obtained to determine how many vehicles can be processed simultaneously—the number of inbound lanes. For the staging area, only one attribute needs to be obtained to determine if there is sufficient space to park arriving vehicles—the total available area. Some of the attributes of landmarks required by deployment simulations are not built into the infrastructure database, since they do not pertain to physical and spatial infrastructure [5].

Deployment simulations consistently use certain types of infrastructure data, such as the lengths and positions of a road and rail network, or the distances between two significant facilities (i.e., forts and ports) or landmarks (e.g., parking lots, call forward lines in front of a loading ramp, spurs, or gates—locations used during a deployment). The data requirements supporting deployment simulations extend beyond the physical and spatial infrastructure of the facility. Types of equipment, such as truck end ramps or wharf cranes, are used for facility operations. The physical and spatial attributes of such equipment are available and incorporated into the database; the resource-oriented attributes (e.g., the number of minutes per inspector per inspection) are not [5].

The standardization of these sets of infrastructure files allows RULST to provide data for several of our models. TRANSCAP uses sets of files that describe Army forts. Our port simulation (PORTSIM) model uses those that describe seaports. Our enhanced logistics intratheater support tool (ELIST) uses those that describe the networks of routes between forts, seaports, and airports. TRANSCAP's 2D viewer animation module also uses the same set of files to graphically play back the event output generated by the simulation module [6]. Further, partially because of this standardization, the report/graph tool module may also be redesigned to take advantage of these sets.

6.3. Scenario Data

A scenario file encapsulates all of the data that TRANSCAP needs to simulate a specific scenario. It includes a pointer to a force file; a small amount of infrastructure data that has been extracted from a set of infrastructure files; and fort-specific deployment data, which includes resource-oriented attributes. The user interface module reads in the scenario data, populating the many windows, and allowing the data to be viewed, edited, and saved in new scenario files. The user interface also directs the simulation module to run a scenario by telling it which scenario file to read.

Infrastructure data extraction is performed due to the small amount of data that had been used within the simulation in the past. As TRANSCAP has developed, however, the simulation has used more of the infrastructure data. Further, planned enhancements regarding how the simulation handles traffic will require even more of the data. Thus, a pointer to a set of infrastructure files will likely replace the extracted data.

6.4. Event History and Report/Graph Data

The beginning, end, or instantaneous completion of an interaction between an object with a lineage from the TCH (e.g., cargo and transportation assets) and a resource object (e.g., cranes, truck and rail end ramps, locomotives, inspectors) at an ICH object (e.g., a staging area, a rail spur) during a TRANSCAP run is called an event. TRANSCAP writes all of these events to an event history database. An event can be conceived of as a database join of information about a client (from the TCH) with a server at an area (from the ICH) at a simulated time. As such, an event record consists of a simulated event, a simulated time, and several keys to the force, infrastructure, and scenario databases.

The simulation module typically generates hundreds of thousands of events while simulating a given scenario. These results must be output in a way that allows for analysis and presentation, as well as for other modules/models to input the data. Early in TRANSCAP's development, various reports and graphs were the only desired output. So the results as a whole were not saved, but data was aggregated into several files, each one formatted specifically to support a different report or graph. As development continued through its planned phases, the simulation grew more detailed, analysis requirements increased, and more analytical tools were added (specifically, more reports and graphs and new 2D and 3D animation models). This presented a problem; the simulation module should be focused on simulating the deployment scenarios and outputting the results, not on supporting multiple postprocessors.

To solve this problem, the event history was designed as a standard output format for all of the simulation's results, effectively abstracting the postprocessor support. It shields the simulation from dealing with postprocessor changes or additions, while still providing those postprocessors with the required data.

The event history consists of the entire event data created by a simulated scenario, with a header section added to the beginning. The header contains scenario-level data and meta-data about the event data. The scenario-level data includes pointers to the force and infrastructure files that were used to simulate the scenario, further leveraging those standard files. The event history can be written into an Access database or as a fixed-column, comma-delimited text file, which is a format that can be read by almost any program. Java programs can read fixed-column formats quickly, and many spreadsheet and database programs can read comma-delimited formatted data. A database is obviously a standard tool; its event data could be analyzed directly, and would still be available to Java programs.

Investigations have been made into serializing the events as Java objects, and using XML as the file format. Serializing Java event objects would require the definition of a standard event class, which could possibly be used by other Java programs, and would improve event history I/O dramatically. However, it would make analysis more difficult for non-Java programs and tools, such as spreadsheets and databases.

Using XML, a standard data format, would allow TRANSCAP to take advantage of a great variety of existing XML tools, with more on the way. Java programs could use existing XML-handling APIs, and many spreadsheets and databases can now input XML files. Further, as a self-describing format, making changes in the structure or contents of the event history data would be much less likely to require changes in the programs that output or input the data. This should reduce the development time of these programs. For these reasons, the event history is headed for XML.

The 2D viewer animation module extracts the output data that it needs from this one file, as well as the pointers to where it can find the associated force and infrastructure files. The report/graph tool is being reconfigured to get its data from this one file, instead of many report- or graph-specific files. Spreadsheets and databases can also be used to perform systematic analysis of the simulation.

7. CONCLUSION

TRANSCAP is a significant part of the military deployment community's plan to create an HLA federation of deployment simulations. Already, the community has begun work on linking AMP, MIDAS, and ELIST into a federation. TRANSCAP has a strong connection to ELIST in design, implementation, and data sources. With ELIST as the CONUS (continental United States) model in the AMP federation, TRANSCAP could be used by ELIST as a more focused fort simulation in a running federation [6]. The end goal is a complex, predictive planning tool simulating the entire deployment process. TRANSCAP can also be used independently by civilian installation transportation officers and military division transportation officers for planning a particular installation's deployment. TRANSCAP's architecture was designed to take advantage of the benefits of standardized, reusable deployment simulation classes and installation components and the independent nature of its major processes. Its pre- and post-processing component modules have been separated from the discrete-event simulation to simplify both design and development, which are facilitated by the use of standardized classes and file formats. TRANSCAP's potential for reuse is enhanced by having and sharing well-defined modules and implementing three AMSO deployment community standards: EXHORT, the infrastructure data standard, and the rail loading and switching algorithm. This approach has resulted in a richer, more dynamic simulation model.

REFERENCES

1. J.F. Burke, C.M. Macal, M.R. Nevins, C.N. VanGroningen, D.L. Howard and J. Jackson, Standardization of transportation classes for object-oriented deployment simulations, In *Proceedings of the Simulation Interoperability Standards Organization 1999 Fall Simulation Interoperability Workshop*, Orlando, FL, pp. 1142–1152, (1999).
2. J.F. Burke, R.J. Love, C.M. Macal, D.L. Howard and J. Jackson, Modeling force deployment from army installations using the transportation system capability (TRANSCAP) model, In *Proceedings of the 2001 Summer Computer Simulation Conference*, Orlando, FL, pp. 663–668, (2001).
3. J.F. Burke, C.N. VanGroningen, M.J. Bragen and C.M. Macal, Adding the infrastructure class hierarchy to the EXHORT framework for object-oriented deployment simulations, In *Proceedings of the Simulation Interoperability Standards Organization 2002 Fall Simulation Interoperability Workshop*, Orlando, FL, (2002).
4. R.J. Love, J.F. Burke, C.M. Macal, D.L. Howard and J. Jackson, The transportation system capability model (TRANSCAP): A mixed language development approach for an army deployment simulation, In *Proceedings of the 2001 Summer Computer Simulation Conference*, Orlando, FL, pp. 669–674, (2001).
5. M.J. Bragen, J.F. Burke, W.H. Horsthemke, D.L. Howard, J. Jackson, R.J. Love, C.M. Macal, C.N. VanGroningen and M.A. Widing, Standardizing infrastructure data for deployment simulations, Report prepared

for MTMCTEA and presented to the Army Modeling and Simulation Office as part of the Army Model Improvement Plan, (1999); Available at `http://www.msrr.army.mil/astars`.

6. R.J. Love, W.H. Horsthemke, J.F. Burke and C.M. Macal, Spatio-temporal animation of an army logistics simulation, the transportation system capability (TRANSCAP) model, In *Proceedings of the 2001 Summer Computer Simulation Conference*, Orlando, FL, pp. 332–337, (2001).

ELSEVIER

Available online at www.sciencedirect.com
SCIENCE DIRECT•

Mathematical and Computer Modelling 39 (2004) 745–758

MATHEMATICAL AND COMPUTER MODELLING

www.elsevier.com/locate/mcm

Airfield Simulation with Optimization via Decomposition

T. W. CUSICK
7730 Carondelet Ave., Suite 303
Clayton, MO 63105, U.S.A.
travisc@iqtech.com

Abstract—The United States Transportation Command (USTRANSCOM) is responsible for managing our Air Force's capability to move personnel, equipment, and cargo during wartime and peacetime from any origin to any destination within its global system of airfields. The analysis groups of USTRANSCOM and the Air Mobility Command (AMC) employ sophisticated computer models and simulations to help them better understand the capabilities and limitations of the many types of resources making up this complex transportation system. This study describes the development and use of the computer model that analyzes the complex activities that occur at a military airfield in order to assess the airfield's ability to support many types of aircraft missions. It also outlines the optimizing of complex hybrid systems using a method of decomposition that allows for the use of classical methods to improve the performance of the airfield system. Previously known as the Base Resource and Capabilities Estimator (BRACE), the model and computer simulation are now referred to as the Airfield Simulation Tool (AST). BRACE/AST is used by the Air Force on a daily basis to analyze the capabilities of their many airfields throughout the world and has been used to support several major policy and infrastructure enhancement studies.

Keywords—Transportation, Airfield capacity, Simulation, Optimization, Hybrid systems, Logistics.

1. INTRODUCTION

One of the major focuses of the analysis conducted at the Air Mobility Command (AMC) is to help the Air Force to be prepared for a major cargo moving operation to any point on the globe. The systems they must model include the fleet of many types of aircraft, the mix of home-base locations for the aircraft, the possible flying routes around the globe, the personnel and support requirements, the capacities and capabilities of the many airfields around the globe, and the maintenance infrastructure at various regions. Due to the extremely complex, nonlinear, and stochastic nature of the transportation system, the analysts have had limited success using optimization techniques to study and improve the performance of the system. They have turned instead to simulations to analyze current capabilities of the system and to plan for possible future contingencies that require relocating vast amounts of personnel, supplies, and equipment.

For many years, the AMC has been using a simulation model known as MASS, or Mobility Analysis Support System, to provide schedules for cargo and aircraft in support of such opera-

0895-7177/04/$ - see front matter Typeset by $\mathcal{A}_{\mathcal{M}}\mathcal{S}$-TEX
doi:10.1016/j.mcm.2004.02.012

tions. MASS does an adequate job of addressing the constraints associated with the Air Force's fleet of aircraft, pool of aircrews, and set of flying routes. However, it does not accurately capture the capacities of the airfields used in the global system in the face of dynamic load requirements. In addition to the BRACE simulation, the Air Force currently uses the airfield capacity tool ACE (Airfield Capability Estimator) developed by the RAND corporation. ACE is a mathematical spreadsheet model developed with Microsoft Excel and Visual Basic for Applications. ACE calculates the maximum capacity of each service type and uses the results to indicate an upper bound to the capacity of an airfield.

The capability of an airfield to handle aircraft is often referred to as the airfield's maximum on ground, or MOG, value. Because of the dynamics of an actual airfield and differing service needs of the aircraft using that airfield, using a hard number for MOG does not give an accurate account of the airfield's true capacity. To remedy this shortcoming, the airfield simulation called BRACE was developed for use by the Air Force to determine the capability of airfields to handle dynamic loads over time. By testing the schedule produced by the global model, BRACE can establish whether the schedule is feasible from the perspective of each of the airfields used in the schedule. Likewise, it can identify lightly used airfields and slack resources in the system that could be better utilized in a different location. The BRACE simulation has also been used as the main analysis tool in several studies to help the Air Force budget and prepare for future infrastructure changes and improvements. In addition to being used to analyze the capability of military airfields around the globe, BRACE has been used to support several large studies by Air Force analysts as well as by private industry. There are currently no other tools available to the Air Mobility Command that simulate the capabilities of an airfield with the precision that BRACE allows.

The airfield systems that are used by the Air Force and that are simulated by BRACE are very complex in nature. In order to provide all of the services required by the aircraft and crews, each airfield possesses many different types of resources that must be managed and controlled in order for the airfield to succeed. The different types of resources must interact with each other and with the aircraft using the airfield, while following set policies that help insure safety and efficiency. Together, the airfield, the airfield's resources, and the aircraft receiving service make up a complex, hybrid transportation system. Because a hybrid system contains within it both continuous and discrete dynamics, its parameters cannot be optimized using classical optimization techniques.

In order to attempt to improve the performance of the complex hybrid system that makes up an airfield, a decomposition method is used. The large hybrid system is decomposed into smaller subsystems that can be robustly modeled and optimized using proven methods. Once optimized, the subsystems are rejoined to create a complete system that possesses the improved or optimized characteristics of the subsystems. This decomposition method is applied to the airfield systems simulated with BRACE in order to improve many of the parameters as well as the overall performance of the systems.

2. BRACE SIMULATION

The Base Resource Allocation and Capabilities Estimator (BRACE) is an object-oriented program that simulates the important ground activities at a strategic airfield (Figure 1). The equipment and activities deemed important to characterizing the capabilities and limitations of airport resources are modeled as well as the aircraft and cargo flow in and out of the facility. Real time and statistical data is gathered to assess the degree to which the airfield accomplishes a desired aircraft movement. The resources and associated activities are simulated in an object-oriented architecture. The behavior of different mechanical resources are modeled independently as well as their interactions with the other resources and the customers, the aircraft, cargo, and passengers.

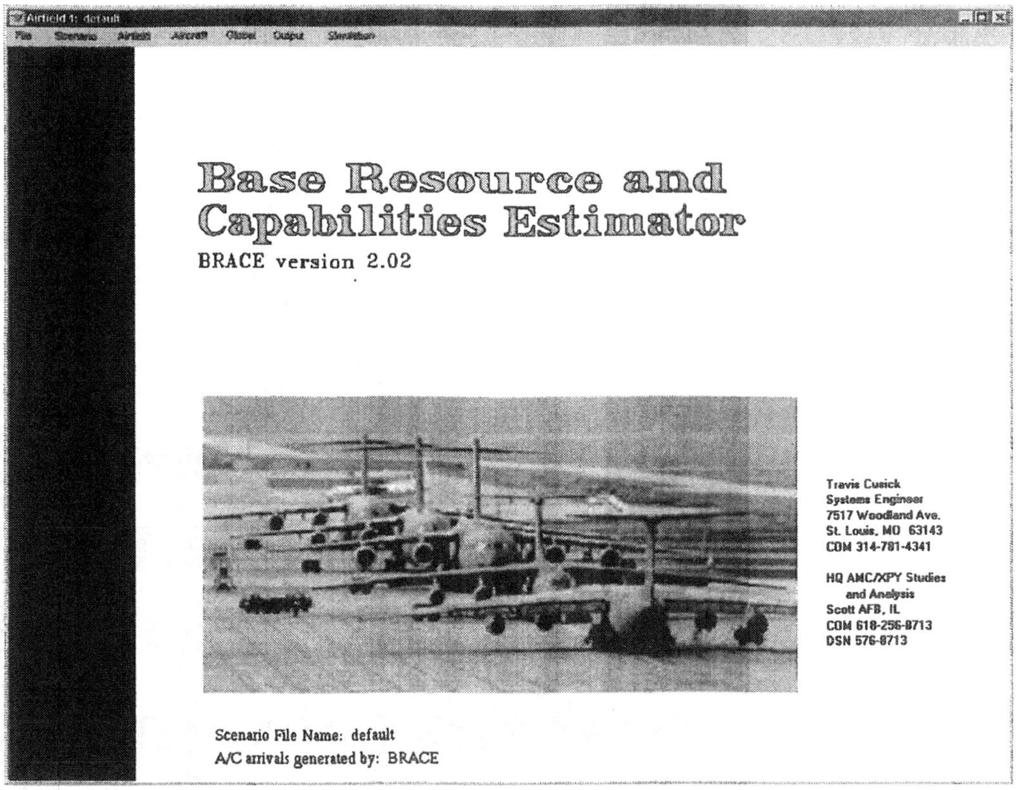

Figure 1. BRACE simulation.

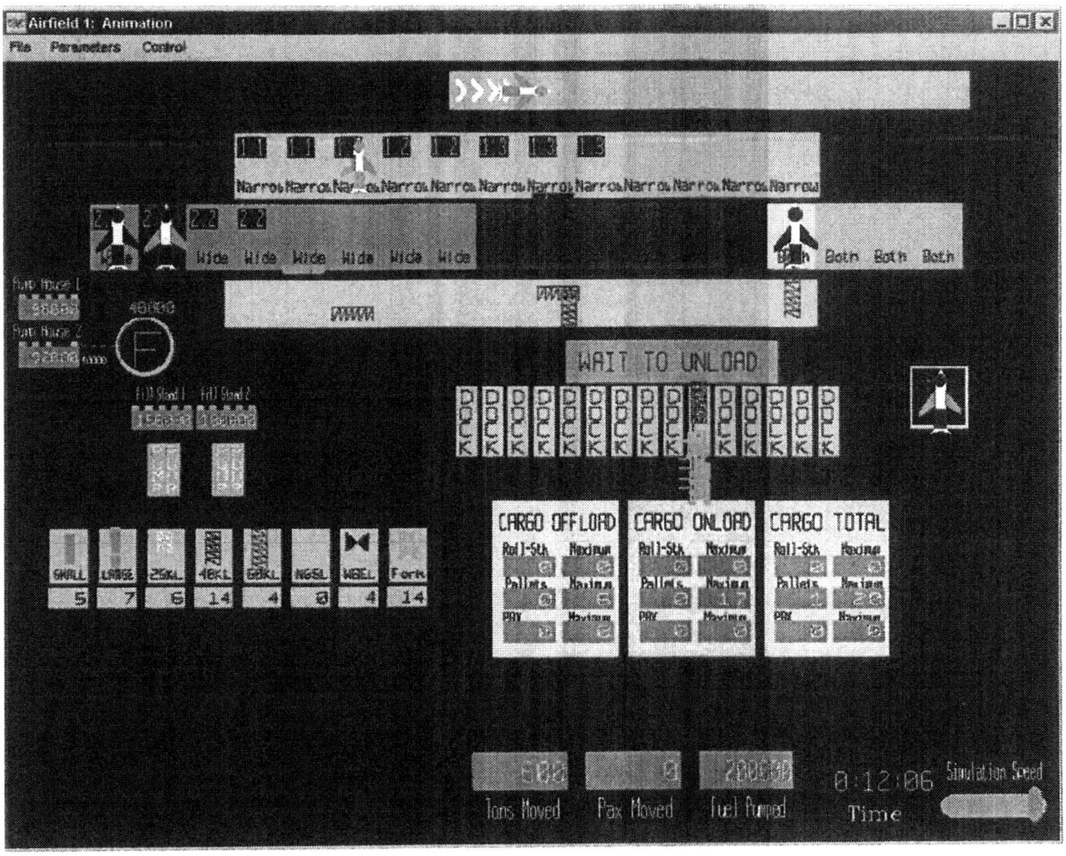

Figure 2. BRACE animation window.

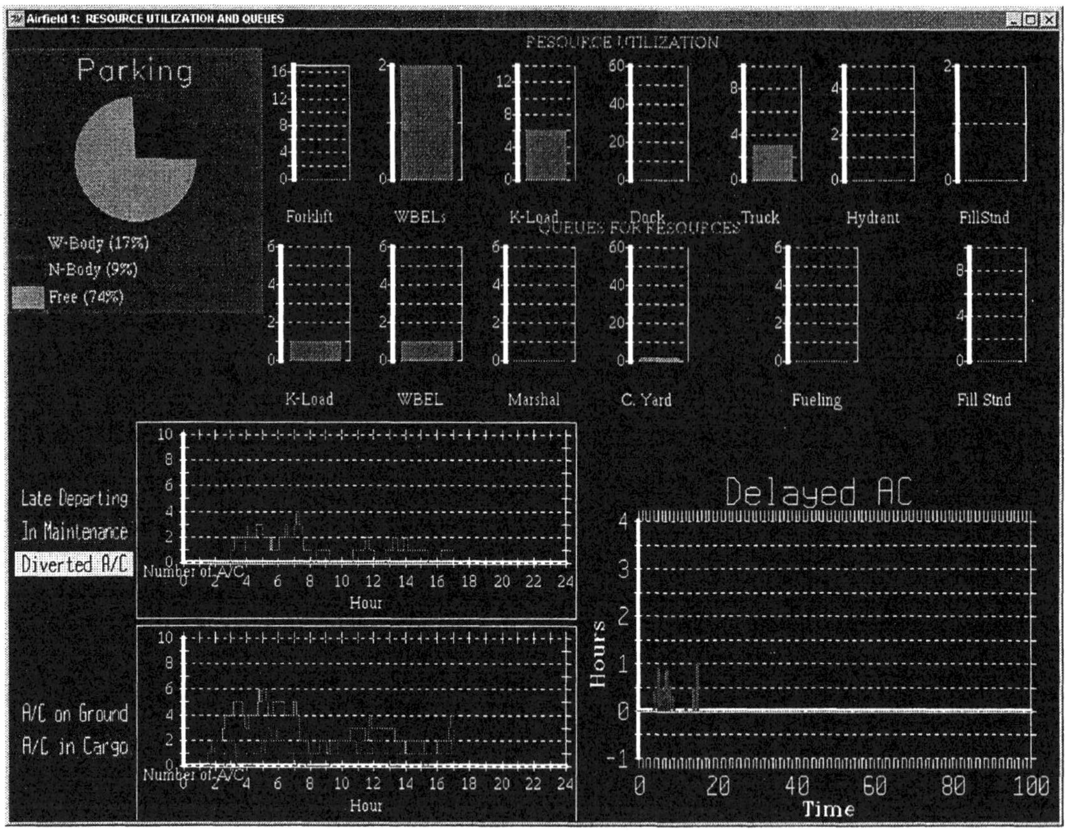

Figure 3. BRACE resource utilization window.

While the program is running, the user has the option of viewing a real-time animation of the activities transpiring during the simulation. The animation is a useful tool for presenting the movement of aircraft and resources around the airfield as well as for showing the interactions between different objects as the appropriate services are performed. Figure 2 shows a snapshot of the animation during a BRACE simulation.

During a simulation, color changes are used in the animation window to indicate the status of aircraft as well as the vehicles servicing the aircraft. The aircrafts themselves have three color zones at the nose, wings, and tail of the plane to indicate passengers, fuel, and cargo, respectively. As the aircraft progresses through its required services, these areas turn red to indicate a status of empty, blue to indicate a transition period, and green to indicate a status of full or complete. The service vehicles also use color changes in a similar way to communicate their status to users of the program.

A second window is used to display the activity levels at the airfield as well as resource utilization and queue length information. Figure 3 shows a snapshot of this window during a BRACE simulation.

2.1. Aircraft Generation

The stimulus that activates an airfield in a BRACE simulation is the arrival stream of aircraft that require space at the airfield as well as service from the airfield's resources. The generation of aircraft for the simulation is generally accomplished by reading a flat file created by a spreadsheet or an airflow model such as MASS. Each line of the file contains a description of the aircraft along with the requirements of the aircraft during its visit to the airfield. The requirements include the number of passengers and amount of cargo to be unloaded from the plane and loaded back onto the plane, as well as fuel requirements and any normally scheduled maintenance. Additional aircraft can be introduced into the simulation with the internally generated aircraft arrival streams. The final type of aircraft generation available to the user creates "bed-down" aircraft that mimic a set of aircraft that are stationed at the airfield. These aircraft run sequential missions from the airfield following user-defined timing parameters and parking constraints.

2.2. Aircraft Service Schedule

Each aircraft simulated in BRACE follows a schedule of activities that require interaction between the various resources provided by the airfield. From the aircraft point of view, every activity during the simulation is analogous to waiting in a queue for an available server and subsequently obtaining service from an airfield resource. The flow diagram in Figure 4 outlines the possible service requirements in the proper sequence.

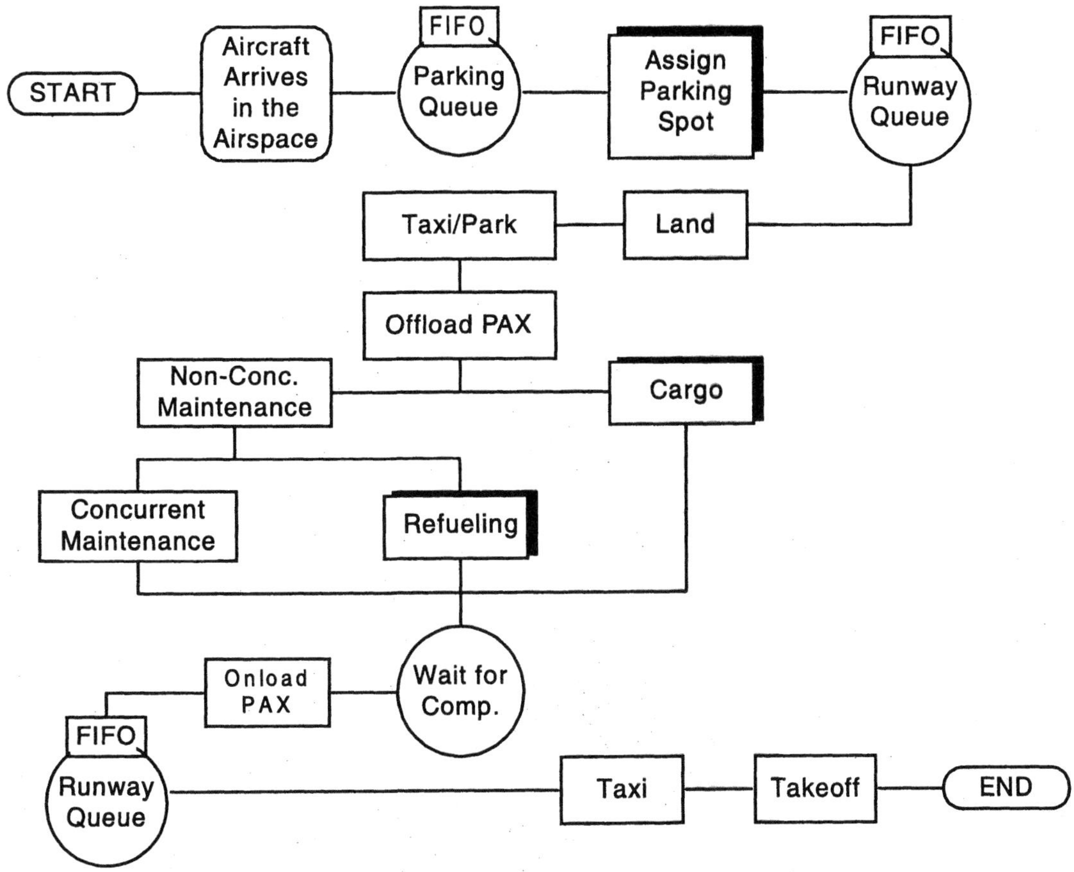

Figure 4. Aircraft service schedule.

The remainder of this section describes the development of mathematical equations that give the length of time required to accomplish some of the aircraft services included in the model. Some of these equations were incorporated into the BRACE simulation as an option to complete simulation in order to reduce computation time.

2.2.1. Pallet off-load operation

The following notation is used to describe the parameters needed to model the operation of removing pallets from an aircraft. The goal is to derive a time delay function as seen from the aircraft point of view.

- p_u = number of pallets to unload from plane
- n = number of k-loaders captured by plane, $n \in \{1, 2, 3\}$
- k_u = number of k-loader pallet loads required to unload plane

- c_i = pallet capacity of k-loader i, $c_i \in \{1,2,3,4,5,6\}$
- p_i = pallets on k-loader i, $p_i \in \{1,2,3,4,5,6\}$
- t_k = one-way travel time for a k-loader
- $t_l(p_i)$ = time required to load pallets onto k-loader i
- $t_d(p_i)$ = time required for k-loader to deliver pallets to the docks and return to plane

Each aircraft is allowed to capture up to three k-loaders for the cargo moving operation. k-loaders are the pieces of material handling equipment used at air bases to transport palletized cargo from the aircraft to the docks or cargo yard. If these loaders have the same capacity c, then the total number of k-loader loads required to complete the operation can be calculated exactly as $k_u = \text{ceil}(p_u/c)$. The round trip k-loader delay ($t_d(p_i)$) equals the k-loader travel time plus the time required to set up and unload the pallets at the docks. Assuming that the capacity of the docks is great enough such that the k-loaders do not have to enter a queue, this time is also deterministic.

During the pallet off-load operation, the aircraft captures the k-loaders simultaneously. When the k-loaders arrive at the aircraft, they form a queue behind the plane's door to await their turn to remove pallets. Upon receiving their load of pallets, the k-loaders perform the round trip operation to the docks to deliver the pallets and then return to the aircraft if their capacity is still needed. Depending upon the number of k-loaders being utilized by the plane and the time required to deposit pallets at the docks, the plane may experience some idle time while waiting for the k-loaders to return to continue service. Taking this into account, the equation describing the total delay time experienced by the aircraft during pallet unloading (T_p^u) is as follows.

$$\begin{aligned} T_p^u &= t_t + (k_u - 1) \times t_l(c) + \text{trunc}\left(\frac{k_u - 1}{n}\right) \times t_I(c) + t_l(p_j), \\ t_I(c) &= \max\{0, t_d(c) - (n-1) \times t_l(c)\}. \end{aligned} \tag{1}$$

The first term (t_t) of the delay equation indicates the time between obtaining the k-loaders and the time when the k-loaders arrive at the plane and set up for the first time. There are a total of $(k_u - 1)$ full pallet loads during the operation, each of which utilizes the full capacity of the k-loader. If the aircraft obtains more than one k-loader, then after all of the k-loaders remove the first set of pallets from the plane, the plane may sit idle for $t_I(c)$ time units while they deliver the pallets to the docks. This will happen when the round trip time to the dock is greater than the pallet pickup time times the number of loaders left at the plane. The final term in the time delay equation indicates the service time of the last k-loader while it removes the final pallets from the aircraft.

This can also be generalized to the case where the capacities of the captured k-loaders are not equal. The k-loader with the largest capacity will be utilized first due to the priority scheme used to capture k-loaders. The number of group round trips as well as the requirements for the final trip to the plane for each k-loader can be computed from the capacities of the k-loaders and the total pallet requirement of the aircraft. The round trip to the docks will take different amounts of time for the k-loaders, thus the delay between subsequent sets of k-loader missions t_I, if any, will have to be calculated appropriately. A complication may occur if due to differences in delay times, two k-loaders return for their second mission to the plane in the opposite order in which they serviced the plane during the first mission. This can only occur if the difference in time required at the docks is greater than the total time required for the second k-loader to remove a full load of pallets from the aircraft, an unlikely occurrence.

The loaders captured by the aircraft for the off-load operation will not be available for service until after they deposit the last load of pallets at the docks and return to the k-loader holding area of the airfield. Therefore, the resource remains unavailable for a longer time than was required for the aircraft to obtain the service. When BRACE is used with the time delay equations in

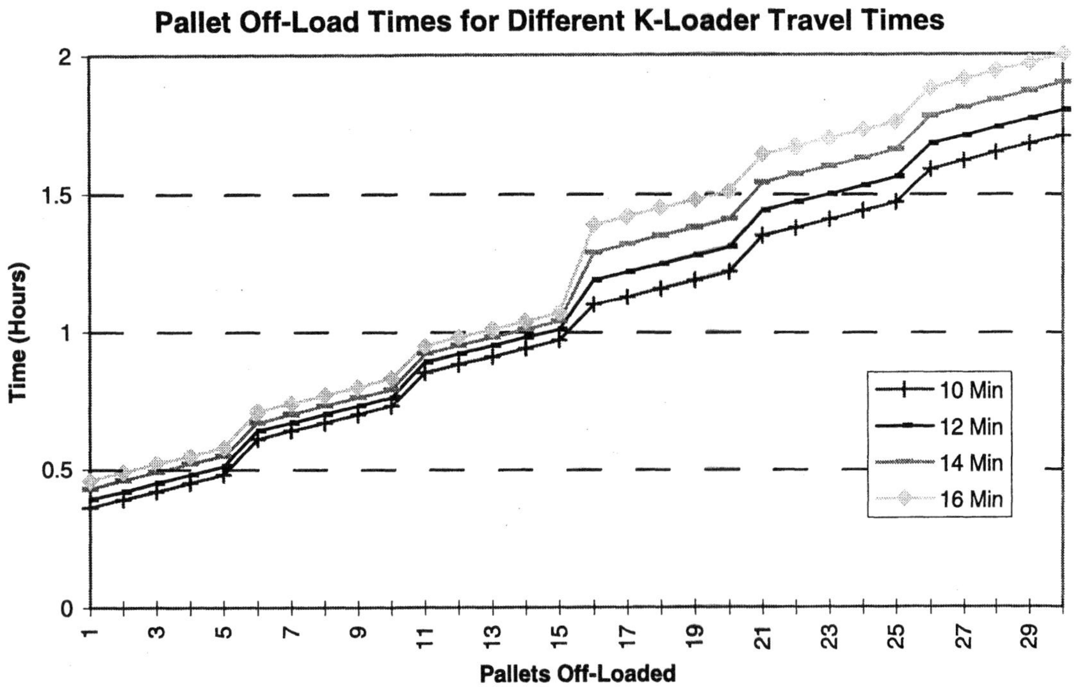

Figure 5. Offload service times.

place of complete simulation, the k-loaders are removed from the pool of available resources for the appropriate amount of time.

Implementing the equations in place of the off-load operations in BRACE resulted in an exact match of off-load delay times as seen by the aircraft in the case of unconstrained cargo resources (k-loaders, dock space, and forklifts). The graph in Figure 5 shows the delay time as a function of the number of pallets being off-loaded from the aircraft for four different travel times between the docks and the aircraft parking spots.

The jump in delay times between a requirement of five and six pallets is caused by the need for a second k-loader. The second k-loader must position itself at the aircraft door before removing the sixth pallet, thus causing the extra time delay as seen by the aircraft. For a requirement of 16 pallets, the three k-loaders captured do not have the capacity to remove all of the pallets in one mission, and thus, one k-loader must return to the aircraft to remove the final pallet. Here, the extra delay is a function of the travel time of the k-loaders, with a longer idle time delay ($t_I(5)$) for the cases with longer travel times for the loaders. For the shortest travel times, the first k-loader returns to the aircraft quickly enough such that the idle time is zero and only the normal setup time is experienced.

2.2.2. Pallet on-load operation

The time delay required to load pallets onto an aircraft (T_l^p) can be developed in a similar manner. In the on-load case, the k-loaders travel to the docks to pick up pallets before traveling to the aircraft to load the pallets. Therefore, the aircraft experiences a delay before service equal to the travel time of the k-loaders plus the time required to load the k-loaders at the docks. The k-loader that picks up the least amount of pallets at the docks will require the least amount of time, and thus, reach the aircraft first. The graph in Figure 6 shows the delay time as a function of the number of pallets being loaded onto the aircraft for four different k-loader travel times.

Notice the nearly identical delay times in the cases of on-load requirements of five and six pallets. In the five pallet case, a second k-loader is required to pick up just one pallet from the docks and deliver it to the plane. This loader is able to deliver the pallet to the plane and get

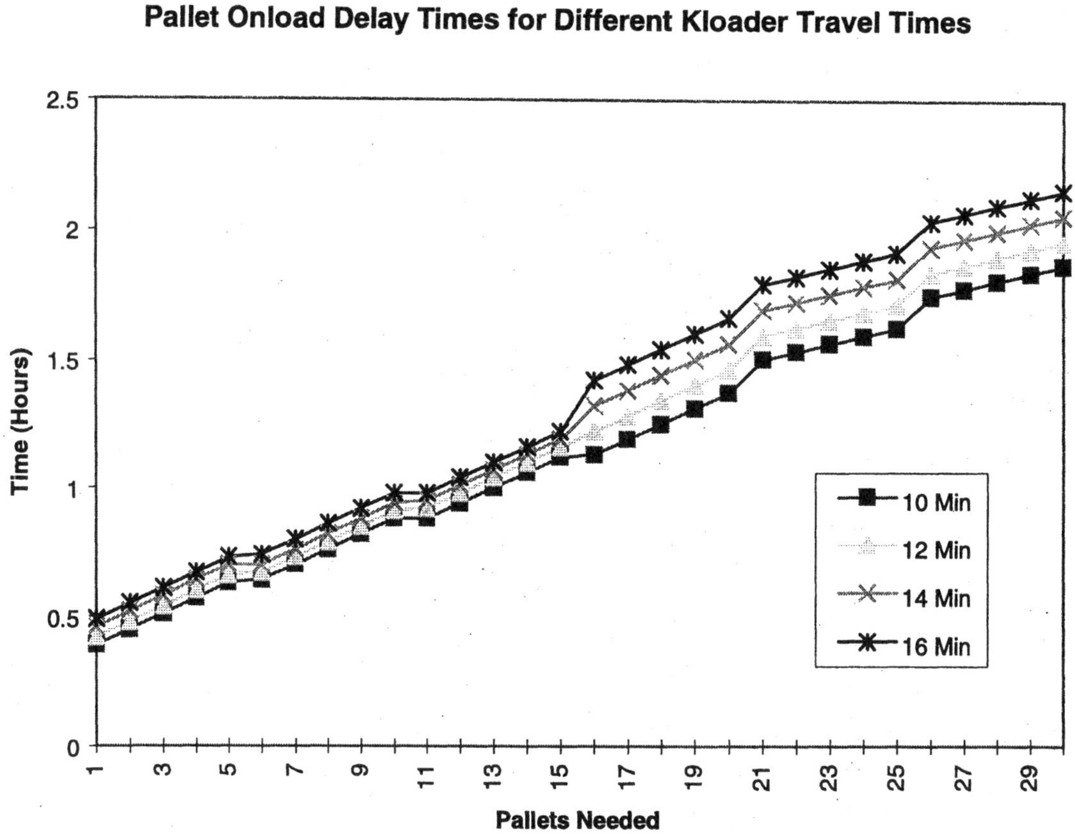

Figure 6. Onload service times.

out of the way before the first k-loader retrieving a full five pallet load has received its pallets and traveled to the plane, thus creating no additional delay as seen by the aircraft.

2.2.3. Refueling operation

For the refueling operation, each aircraft has the opportunity to use either the in-ground hydrant refueling system or fuel trucks that deliver fuel to the aircraft. When the hydrant system is used, the time delay is a function of the fuel flow rate and any delays required to wait for adequate capacity of the fueling system. When using fuel trucks, the delay experienced by the aircraft becomes dependent upon the behavior of the fuel trucks.

When refueling by trucks, one available truck is initially assigned to the aircraft. If more fuel is required than can be supplied by this truck, another available truck is assigned to the aircraft as soon as the first truck completes the transfer of fuel. Using notation similar to the cargo loading procedure, the following variables are needed to compute the fueling delay as seen by the aircraft.

- f = total gallons of fuel needed by the plane, $0 \leq f \leq 37000$
- c = fuel capacity of each fuel truck, $4600 \leq c \leq 6000$
- t_t = one-way travel time for a fuel truck
- t_p = time to setup the fuel truck at the plane
- r = fuel delivery rate
- $k = \text{ceil}(f/c)$ = the number of full fuel trucks required to fully fuel the aircraft, $1 \leq k \leq 9$

The aircraft must wait for each required fuel truck to travel to the plane, set up, and then dispense the proper amount of fuel. For the first $(k-1)$ fuel truck loads of fuel, the fueling time is (c/r), the capacity of the truck divided by the fuel delivery rate. For the final fuel truck, the delay time depends upon the amount of fuel still required by the aircraft. Thus, the truck refueling delay, (T_f), is as follows:

$$T_f = t_t + k \times t_p + (k-1) \times \left(\frac{c}{r}\right) + 1 \times \left(\frac{f-(k-1)\times c}{r}\right) = k \times (t_t + t_p) + \left(\frac{f}{r}\right).$$

2.3. Aircraft and Resource Maintenance

In order to capture normal maintenance problems and to include real world stochastic variances in the results, the BRACE simulation includes the ability to simulate the breakdown and subsequent repair of both airfield resource entities and the aircraft themselves.

For the movable servicing resources (fork-lifts, k-loaders, wide-body elevators, fuel trucks, and hose carts), breakdown incidents follow an exponentially distributed probability distribution for mean time between failures. Actual repair times for the movable resources draw from a triangular distribution. The user has the ability to set each of the required parameters separately for each distinct classification of all of the different resource types. Randomly produced maintenance problems with the airfield's fuel hydrant system are realized by making the affected hydrants unavailable to aircraft needing fuel.

Unscheduled aircraft maintenance can also be simulated in BRACE. In order to best utilize the available data on aircraft reliability, the user parameters for controlling aircraft breakdowns are separated by aircraft type and by the expected time for repairs. Default values are drawn from the latest G081 break fix batch report to simplify data entry requirements for the user. The data consists of actual historical percentages of unscheduled maintenance broken down into the following ranges of repair times: 0–4 hours, 4–8 hours, 8–12 hours, 12–16 hours, 16–24 hours, 24–48 hours, 48–72 hours, and 72–X hours, where the extent of the final range is user adjustable.

In addition to creating unscheduled aircraft maintenance occurrences, the BRACE simulation allows the user to optionally instruct the system to move certain aircraft from the parking ramps to a maintenance facility for the duration of the repair in order to free the parking spot for other aircraft. The parameters for controlling this are adjustable separately for each parking ramp and include a minimum time for repair that would result in the aircraft being moved to the maintenance facility. In addition, the maintenance facility has a user-adjustable capacity of aircraft that can be accommodated.

In order to control the stochastic nature of a study using BRACE, the program provides two random number streams each with 1000 user-adjustable random number seeds. One of the streams is used for the generation of aircraft arrivals and aircraft maintenance incidents while the other is used for the maintenance incidents of all of the airfield resources. This measure of flexibility allows the user to set the aircraft stream with subsequent breakdowns while varying the reliability response of the airfield, or vice versa. During a multiple iteration setup, one or both of the random number seeds can be varied automatically from one run to the next.

2.4. Simulating Chemical Attacks

When a chemical attack on an airfield is simulated using BRACE, the service rates used for moving cargo and refueling aircraft are slowed down as specified by adjustable parameters. All operations are also halted for a short amount of time just after the attack as they would in a real scenario. As the airfield comes back online, all other activities take place as normal. From the outputs of the model, an analyst can compare the behavior of the airfield recovering from an attack to the same airfield working under no adversities. The result is an increased understanding of the ramifications that would result in case of a catastrophic event such as a chemical attack on an airfield. This can be a powerful tool in helping the Air Force prepare for the unexpected, with the aircraft experiencing the most diverts getting top priority.

3. STUDIES USING BRACE

BRACE has already proven itself to be a valuable tool for conducting studies by the Air Force as well as other institutions. The Air Mobility Command at Scott Air Force Base in

Illinois uses BRACE as one of its primary analysis tools. It is used along with the global model MASS (Mobility Analysis Support System, also known as the Air Flow Model) to analyze the capability of the global Air Force system. BRACE has been used in course work and for academic studies [1,2] by graduate students at the Air Force Institute of Technology. Scientific Applications International Corporation (SAIC) has utilized BRACE to conduct a study for the Air Force on the consequences of a chemical attack on a military airfield. In addition to doing general analysis on airfields in the Air Force system, the analysts at the Air Mobility Command are occasionally called upon to conduct more detailed studies using the BRACE simulation.

During 1996, BRACE was used as the primary analysis tool for a study on the Air Force's airfield at Ramstein, Germany [3]. The study was concerned with the effectiveness of the airfield for supporting Operation Joint Endeavor (OJE), the redeployment out of Bosnia. The study was completed before the operation in order to assist Air Force officers in the planning and scheduling of aircraft for the operation.

The Air Force owns an airfield near Elmendorf, AK that is used primarily as an en-route refueling stop for cargo aircraft flying across the Pacific Ocean. The airfield is aging and in 1997 the government decided that improvements to the airfield were in order. The Elmendorf airfield was experiencing reliability problems with the underground refueling systems as well as deterioration of the parking ramps. The Air Mobility Command at Scott Air Force Base was asked to conduct a study to determine the best alternative from three proposed plans of improving the airfield. The study [4] was conducted using BRACE as the primary analysis tool for estimating the benefits of the three proposed infrastructure improvement plans.

4. SYSTEM IMPROVEMENT BY DECOMPOSITION

The airfield system simulated in BRACE is a hybrid system with complex interactions between resources, customers, and other related objects. A hybrid system is a system that contains both continuously varying and discretely varying components working in conjunction.

The continuous components of the airfield system govern the dynamics of the moving objects and characterize the state of continuously depleted resources. The aircraft move dynamically from the landing area to the parking area of the airfield, while movable resources such as the cargo loaders and fuel trucks travel from staging and refilling areas to the aircraft to complete the appropriate service. The central bulk fuel storage unit along with the pump house storage tanks and underground fuel pipes comprise a continuously changing fuel system.

The discrete components of the airfield system control the many instantaneous changes in the state of the system. The refueling system contains many switches that change the flow of fuel at discrete points in time in order to refill storage tanks and service aircraft. The aircraft flowing through the system are cycled through several different queues that dictate how the airfield's resources are allocated among the customers. These queues handle the use of the runway as well as the allocation of cargo loaders, fuel trucks, and underground fueling capacity to the aircraft requiring service. Because all groups of moving objects are divided into individuals, aircraft population levels and resource usage levels all change by discrete values.

Because the airfield system is made up of both continuous and discrete parts, applying classical optimization methods to help improve performance cannot be done in a straightforward fashion. Specialized methods for optimizing hybrid systems may be applied, but would result in extremely large computational complexity. For example, formulating the airfield system into a linear programming model with time windows could be used to optimize the parameters. This, however, would result in an unmanageably large state space representation of the system if a reasonable fidelity level is to be maintained.

Because of the challenges presented in the optimization of complex hybrid systems, there has recently been an increasing amount of research initiated in the area.

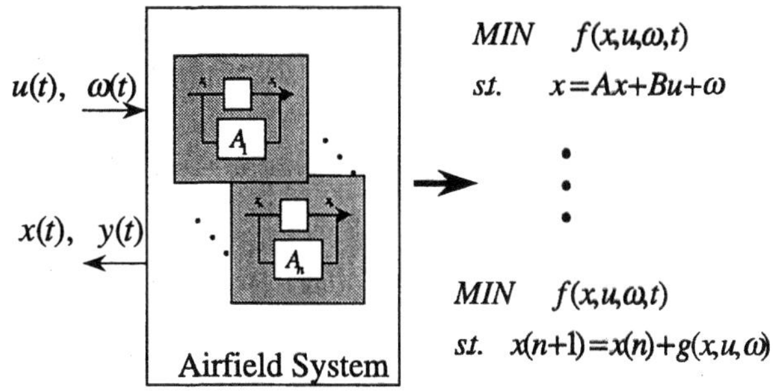

Figure 7. Decomposition of a hybrid system.

4.1. System Decomposition

The method explored here to improve the performance of the airfield system is a hybrid decomposition method [5]. An airfield is made up of many subsystems that work together in complex relationships to form a complete hybrid system as shown in Figure 7. Many of these subsystems have a structure that can be modeled as a pure continuous or discrete system that can be optimized by classical techniques. The decomposition method attempts to identify appropriate subsystems that can be modeled, optimized, and then reconfigured into the larger hybrid system to improve the overall performance of the airfield.

The subsystems that are identified for individual optimization must adhere to several required characteristics. In order to be able to apply proven optimization techniques, the subsystem cannot be a hybrid system, rather it must be modeled as a purely continuous or discrete system. Continuous systems include the systems that control motion dynamics of the objects at the airfield. Discrete systems include the queuing systems that regulate the allocation of resources and the valves that control the underground flow of fuel. Each subsystem being studied must have an accessible and controllable parameter that can be manipulated in order to improve the performance of the system. And the subsystem must be modeled within a manageable size constraint so that the computational complexity is not insurmountable.

Some other desired characteristics should be kept in mind when exploring the airfield system for candidate subsystems. For subsystems that can be modeled as a continuous dynamic system or formulated into a linear programming model, a mathematically definable cost function must be developed. The cost function is required to evaluate the performance of the system under different sets of parameters. For many real world problems, defining a cost function mathematically can be extremely difficult. In the case of an airfield, many of the cost functions can be defined in terms of delay times experienced by the customers and resource utilization. In order to maximize the benefits of conducting a decomposition study, the subsystems explored should also exhibit a noninsignificant effect on the overall system such that optimizing them provides real system improvements. Following is a brief description of the optimizing of some airfield subsystems, with more detail available in [5].

4.2. Subsystem Improvements

A military airfield includes several resource allocation systems, one of which is the underground aircraft refueling system. In this subsystem, capacity is limited by the safe flow capability of the pipes and fuel pumps. The flow of fuel into an aircraft is also limited by the maximum acceptance rate of that aircraft. Within these constraints, the flow to any individual aircraft can be adjusted to either speed the delivery of fuel to that aircraft or to service more aircraft simultaneously. To minimize the overall system time for a queue of customers that can be allocated a percentage of a total resource level, no more than one customer that is receiving service may be assigned a resource level less than its maximum resource acceptance level [5]. The total available resource should be allocated as long as enough customers are present to accept the service. In the airfield system, this means that as many aircraft as possible should be hooked up to the hydrant system and refueled at their maximum receiving rate. Any remaining capacity in the hydrant system should be used to begin the refueling of the next aircraft in the queue.

During the cargo operation in BRACE, each aircraft attempts to capture three k-loaders to move the required number of pallets on and off the plane. From the aircraft's point of view, this provides the fastest possible service under the constraint of using no more than three k-loaders. From the airfield point of view, this procedure may not provide the best utilization of the resources or the best throughput capability for the system.

The discrete data points in Figure 8 show the time required to execute the off-load operation for different pallet requirements while using one, two, and three k-loaders. The two highest lines indicate the resource usage in units of k-loader-hours for the two and three k-loader cases. Notice that for a 50 pallet operation, using two loaders instead of three increases the service time by 0.68 hours while decreasing the resource usage level by 1.31 k-loader-hours. Reducing the service to a one loader operation nearly doubles the service time while only slightly increasing the resource efficiency as compared to the two loader case. The improved resource utilization that results by using less k-loaders per aircraft is due to a reduction in k-loader idle time spent waiting in a queue to service the aircraft. This may be offset by long travel times between the aircraft and the loading docks while fewer k-loaders take more trips to service an aircraft's needs.

When there are plenty of k-loaders available at an airfield, it is generally beneficial to assign up to three k-loaders to each aircraft if needed. This will insure the fastest cargo service possible and will help minimize the number of late departing aircraft. When the pool of k-loaders becomes fully utilized, aircraft must enter a queue and wait for available k-loaders. The BRACE simulation allows for either depth-first or breadth-first heuristics for allocating recently freed k-loaders to

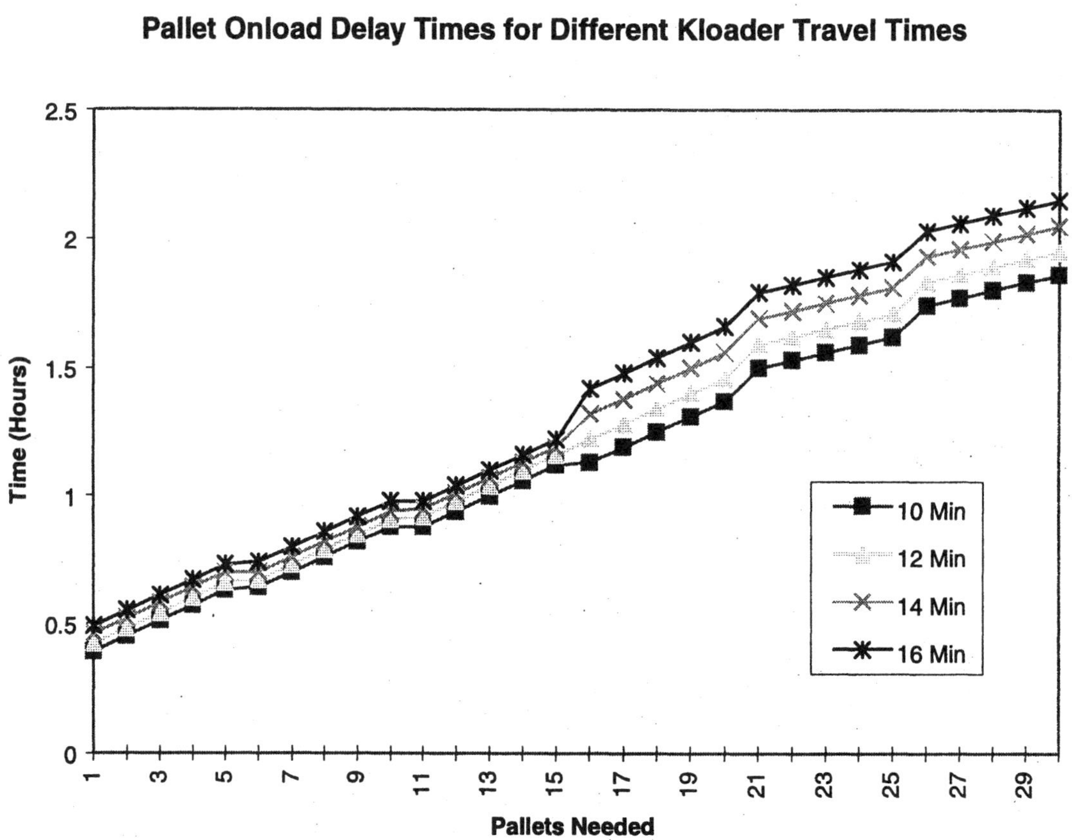

Figure 8. k-loader utilization.

the aircraft waiting in the queue. Deciding upon a rule for allocating the pool of available k-loaders to the aircraft is a compromise between different goals. If the resources are adequate and maximum throughput is desired, breadth-first k-loader allocation creates a more capable airfield system. If cargo moving personnel are limited or it is desired to keep coordination efforts simpler, depth-first k-loader allocation may make sense. These factors help explain why the Air Force has traditionally used maximum sized k-loader teams along with depth-first allocation rules at currently operating airfields.

The BRACE model incorporates an optional control on the arrival of aircraft in an attempt to reduce the number of bottlenecks experienced at an airfield. An optimizing function is used to compute a delay time for each aircraft within a tolerance window with the expectation that the delay can be enforced by slowing the aircraft cruising speed or delaying its departure from a previous airfield. In simulations, the method proved very beneficial during periods of heavy traffic at a constrained airfield.

In order to manage the optional heuristics for improving subsystem performance, a control system was developed and built into the BRACE simulation model. The control system uses a system monitor to track the state and output variables of the airfield system while aircraft are being processed. When the variables indicate that there exists a bottleneck or possible future bottleneck in the airfield, the limited resource is identified. The subsystem that controls the limited resource is then instructed to adjust its parameters according to its new heuristics and the current state of the system. By doing this, the efficiency of the subsystem is increased as needed and the health of the entire airfield improves.

5. SUMMARY

Transportation infrastructures play an extremely important role in the health and well-being of the world's population. Our reliance on transportation has grown tremendously along with capacity expansion and the development of new transportation systems. It is very important that the transportation systems already in place and the new systems to be built are utilized in an intelligent manner, with efficiency, capability, and safety as primary goals.

To help assess the capability of the system and to help plan for contingencies, the Air Force constantly conducts research using sophisticated computer based models and analysis tools. The computer simulation BRACE was started as a project to fulfill the role of airfield capability analysis tool for the Air Mobility Command at Scott Air Force Base, IL. The BRACE (Base Resource and Capabilities Estimator) simulation has been used by the Air Force and by others for many different purposes. It is used to analyze the capability of many of the airfields in the Air Force system under different operating conditions and with varying requirements for the aircraft using the airfields. BRACE is used to determine the feasibility of schedules produced by global scheduling programs such as MASS and to point out slack airfield resources that could be better used elsewhere in the system. In addition, some major studies conducted by the Air Force and private industry have helped to enhance the capabilities of BRACE.

An airfield, like many other transportation systems, is a complex system of customers and resources that must interact in order to accomplish a set of goals. This system is hybrid in nature, containing within both continuous and discrete dynamics that follow generally nonlinear transfer functions. As such, the parameters of the airfield system cannot be optimized using classical optimization techniques without losing fidelity due to simplifications or linear estimations.

In order to attempt to optimize the complex hybrid system that makes up an airfield, a new decomposition method was developed. The hybrid airfield system was decomposed into smaller nonhybrid subsystems that could be correctly modeled and optimized using queuing theory, optimal control, and other proven methods. The analysis and optimization resulted in improved heuristics for many of the airfield's major subsystems. To realize the benefits of the new heuristics, a feedback control paradigm was used to control the parameters of the airfield system.

Using an airfield simulated in BRACE, the decomposition method for improving the performance of a system is shown to be effective. In the case of an airfield, the overall goal of a particular system cannot be known by one researcher or by one officer in command. For that reason, the control system developed with the decomposition method is presented as a set of heuristics. The heuristics are divided among the subsystems on which they operate and they are presented along with the associated effects on system performance. With the aid of the system monitor, the user of the system can intelligently select the best heuristics according the state of the airfield system and the goals of the decision makers.

REFERENCES

1. S. Bellamy and D. Williams, Analysis of the BRACE simulation model, Technical Report, Air Force Institute of Technology, (1999).
2. T.H. Irish, Reducing simulation study times using an external analytical model, Ph.D. Thesis, Air Force Institute of Technology, (1999).
3. K. Schubert and B. Lloyd, Operation joint endeavor redeployment analysis, Technical Report, Air Force Air Mobility Command, Analysis Division, Scott Air Force Base, IL, (1996).
4. T. White and K. Schubert, Elmendorf en route capacity analysis, Technical Report, Air Force Air Mobility Command, Analysis Division, Scott Air Force Base, IL, (1997).
5. T.W. Cusick, Simulation and optimization of a military airfield, Ph.D. Thesis, Washington University, St. Louis, MO, (2000).

Available online at www.sciencedirect.com

SCIENCE DIRECT

Mathematical and Computer Modelling 39 (2004) 759–772

MATHEMATICAL AND COMPUTER MODELLING

www.elsevier.com/locate/mcm

Mathematically Modeling Munitions Prepositioning and Movement

D. P. JOHNSTONE
Air Force Logistics Management Agency
Maxwell AFB, Gunter Annex, AL 36114, U.S.A.

R. R. HILL
Department of Biomedical, Industrial, and Human Factors Engineering
Wright State University
Dayton, OH 45435, U.S.A.

J. T. MOORE
Department of Operational Sciences
Air Force Institute of Technology
Wright-Patterson AFB, OH 45433, U.S.A.

Abstract—The Air Force's ability to deploy, employ, and sustain operations in forward operating locations is a key to mission success. An integral part of this new strategy involving forward operating locations is equipment prepositioning, to include: vehicles, aircraft support, consumable inventory, and munitions. Proper prepositioning strategies provide a means to deploy forces rapidly without resorting to an increased overseas presence. This research focuses on defining and developing a mathematical model to aid decision makers with a strategy for positioning and configuring prepositioned assets. This research places particular emphasis on the strategic, global prepositioning of the afloat prepositioning fleet (APF), the configuration of these ships with respect to precision guided weaponry, the development of a transportation plan in response to modeled contingencies, and a port selection and distribution strategy once the APF ship is tasked to support a contingency. In addition to the APF assets, the model considers U.S.-based supply points used to augment on-hand and APF-provided munitions assets. The primary objective is to minimize the overall response time involved with offloading these ships and transporting their cargo (the munitions) to the intended point of use.

The Pre-Po model developed is a mixed integer program, implemented using the general algebraic modeling system (GAMS), solved using the XA solver package, and tested against a realistically stressing planning scenario. Analytical results and insights are presented along with avenues for further work. © 2004 Elsevier Ltd. All rights reserved.

Keywords—Prepositioning, Mathematical modeling, Optimization, Logistics.

INTRODUCTION

Any military deployment involves a tremendous amount of materiel—materiel that must be transported from various storage locations to the deployed locations where that materiel is then used to generate military power. The United States Air Force (USAF) employs an agile combat

This research was sponsored and partially funded by the Air Force Studies and Analyses Agency. Additional support was provided by the Air Force Logistics Management Agency.

 Typeset by $\mathcal{AMS}$-TEX

doi:10.1016/j.mcm.2004.02.013

support (ACS) system to move materiel and ensure USAF forces respond to global challenges with flexibility, rapidity, and a decisive use of air power [1]. The ACS system is the logistical backbone of the USAF. There are three logistics components, or hubs, within the ACS network: forward operating locations, forward support locations, and continental United States (CONUS) support locations. These are augmented by a transportation network and a command and control system. However, the full system requires the augmentation of prepositioned assets to ensure response flexibility [2]. We define and prototype a mathematical model to aid in prepositioning analyses, and use the model to conduct an analysis based on a realistic scenario.

Munitions are a key component moved within the ACS system as munitions are critical to USAF combat mission success. A substantial amount of munitions is stockpiled at various logistic locations, as well as aboard ships strategically positioned around the world [3]. As needed, these ships, comprising the afloat prepositioning fleet (APF), travel to a port, dock, and have their munitions unloaded and distributed to requesting locations. Lack of timely distribution of munitions can severely hamper Air Force combat operations, and the APF facilitates the timely delivery of munitions and materiel.

Challenges facing munitions force planners include how to load the APF ships, where to position the ships, and how to employ the APF in particular contingencies. Planners employ mathematical optimization tools to plan munitions procurement [4] and to plan airlift (see [5]). There are, however, no tools for planning the prepositioning of munitions. Our work defines and builds a mathematical model for planning the prepositioning and constitution of the APF component of the ACS system. Our initial case study using the mathematical model focuses on precision munitions and is based on a notional, yet realistic, planning scenario.

BACKGROUND AND PROBLEM STATEMENT

As the USAF's overseas presence shrinks, and its global commitments increase, new strategies are needed to ensure the success of military contingency operations. These strategies will necessarily include equipment prepositioning, and in particular, the proper positioning of munitions required to meet particular theater operational needs. We review military prepositioning, some of its advantages and disadvantages, discuss the munitions planning process our model supports, and discuss past use of mathematical modeling for military force planning.

Prepositioning

The Department of Defense utilizes a mobility triad for deployment: strategic airlift, sealift, and prepositioning (see Figure 1) [6]. Strategic airlift is the fastest, most flexible, and most expensive deployment option. Airlift's ability to deliver assets very close to their required destination is militarily prudent, but reduced inventories of airlift assets prohibit sole reliance on airlift. Strategic sealift is relatively inexpensive, compared to airlift, and can haul large assets and greater tonnage. However, sealift is not very fast and is limited in movement to properly equipped seaports. The third leg, strategically located prepositioned assets, can reduce delivery time and potential losses due to enemy attack, but it requires a distribution and maintenance infrastructure.

Prepositioning is the "stockpiling of equipment and supplies at, or near the point of planned use (or point of debarkation)" [7]. Prepositioning helps ensure the timely support of forces during the initial phases of a military operation [8]. Without prepositioned assets, deployments become overly reliant on airlift and sealift. However, the USAF clearly cannot preposition all required assets. The USAF thus maintains a balance; starter stock at, or near the point of intended use, and swing stock munitions to decrease the burden on the transportation network and provide quick access to these vital assets. Starter stock is maintained at operational locations and can be considered those munitions loaded on aircraft when a conflict starts. Swing stock involves the APF and the standard air munitions package/standard tanks, racks, adapters, and pylons packages (STAMP/STRAPP) assets. STAMP/STRAPP assets are palletized, maintained at

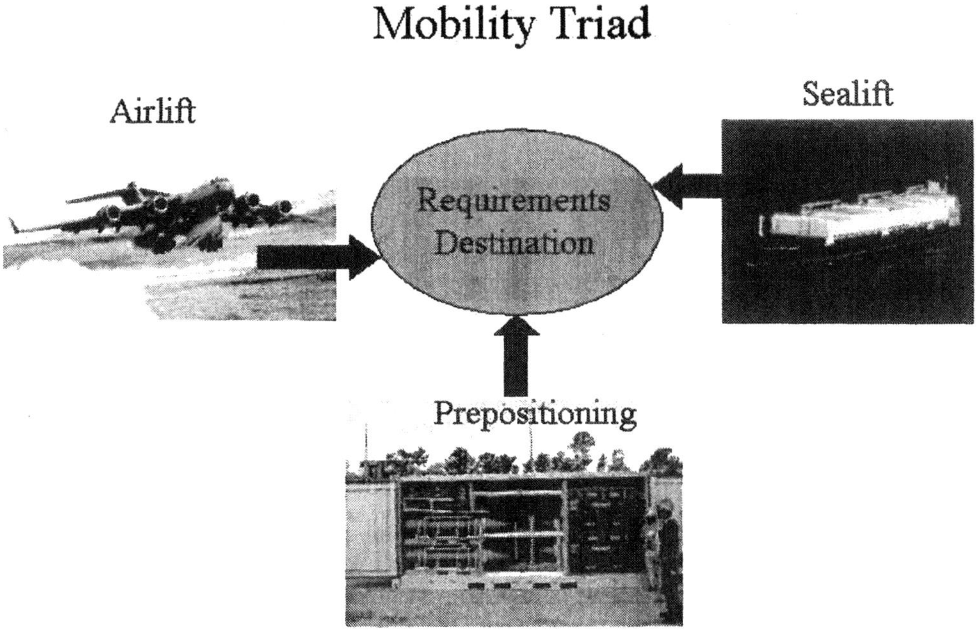

Figure 1. Mobility triad: airlift, sealift, and prepositioning.

stateside locations, and readied for immediate airlift deployment. This balance enables a military response before longer-term, logistical lines of communication are established. Our model also addresses swing stock positioning and planned usage.

The concept of afloat prepositioning fleet stemmed from Congressional concerns over force projection capability and a lack of progress in acquiring basing rights in the Persian Gulf region [9]. The DoD response to these concerns paid immediate dividends during the Gulf War in 1990. Afloat and ashore prepositioning of equipment and munitions helped sustain military forces saving an estimated 1,800 airlift missions and providing direct support to 21 principal airfields [10]. A 1992 Mobility Requirements Study (MRS) noted the considerable risk facing initial deployed troops. This study recommended establishing a "gap filler" force to provide essential assets and equipment during the early stages of a conflict [11]. Prepositioned assets are now a major component of this "gap filler"; the DoD spends over one billion dollars annually to manage prepositioning programs [12]. APF assets are the most deployable assets [9].

Prepositioning has its disadvantages. Prepositioned stocks require duplicate equipment and supplies, as well as additional training and maintenance to maintain materiel in operational condition. Prepositioned sites are not invulnerable to attack; however, some argue that afloat prepositioned assets are safer and easier to defend than their land-based counterparts [13]. Thus, the prepositioned sites require security. Finally, fiscal constraints come into play as prepositioning requires additional funding [8].

Munitions

The USAF munitions inventory comprises a variety of weapons ranging from gravity bombs to advanced precision-guided munitions. Munitions procurement levels are based on targeting requirements established by the Joint Chiefs of Staff. Analysis provides munitions levels required to successfully engage assigned targets. Once procured, munitions are moved into storage locations (to include the APF ships). Planning ensures that the USAF maintains the proper stocks of munitions, that these munitions are properly positioned, and that the munitions are operationally ready for service.

Munitions movement planning is largely a manual process with planning documents produced primarily via planning conferences. An analytical model can facilitate movement plan development while providing analytical insight into movement plan viability in support of any number of operational planning scenarios.

Related Studies and Optimization Modeling Efforts

Prepositioning strategies have been examined using both simulation and mathematical optimization models. The Air Force Logistics Management Agency studied prepositioning munitions using the joint integrated contingency model [14]. Their study focused on a Southwest Asia (SWA) scenario and produced a number of recommendations: reduce war reserve materiel munitions on the ground in SWA, increase the size of the APF, alter the composition of the APF, investigate the possibility of positioning a mix of materiel on fast, smaller, high speed sealifts, and investigate the possibility of strategic prepositioning at forward operating locations. Synergy Corporation developed a simulation model to evaluate current munitions prepositioning practice and provide alternative strategies for prepositioning preferred munitions inventories. The Synergy model did not investigate alternative inventory mixes for the current APF [15].

Sentlinger developed a mixed-integer program to look at the optimal weapons prepositioning mix for established U.S. Naval weapon stations with a focus on minimizing demand shortfalls during a myriad of conflicts [16]. Anderson developed an optimization model that utilizes available shipping assets to redistribute weapons based on a predetermined positioning plan for the Pacific Fleet. However, Anderson's optimization model only examined the redistribution of weapons based on routine, scheduled deployments and is not tied to any wartime scenario [17].

Despite the lack of prepositioning models, mathematical modeling has been successfully applied to both munitions and mobility planning. Might [18] describes the Theater Attack Model, a large-scale linear program long used for munitions force planning. Yost [4] describes USAF efforts to consolidate various munitions planning models. This effort resulted in the Combat Forces Analysis Model, the current USAF standard munitions planning model. A related work is [19] and their discussion of the use of mathematical modeling in munitions planning. Recent works on the use of large-scale mathematical modeling for mobility applications include [20–22]. These optimization models provide a prescriptive solution for input and insight into the complex decisions facing military planners.

METHODOLOGY

We developed a prepositioning model called Pre-Po. The Pre-Po model is a mixed integer program model of munitions flow. A mixed integer program contains both integer and continuous decision variables. We address APF ship(s) munitions stock levels and movement to ports where cargo is offloaded. We consider ship water depth (draft) requirements and net explosive weight (NEW) restrictions for each port. NEW restrictions can prevent ships from offloading in otherwise capable ports and has been overlooked in past studies and models. We also model off-load times on a ship-by-ship basis based on port capabilities and ship configurations.

Once off-loaded, munitions are transported to air bases requiring the munitions via available intratheater transport assets. Finally, we model STAMP/STRAPP and theater hub munitions inventories as these complement APF-supplied munitions to support air base munitions requests reducing occasions where demand levels are not met and a munitions shortage at the requesting air base is experienced.

Model Assumptions

Any model contains inherent assumptions regarding the actual system represented. The following are the key assumptions in Pre-Po. First, APF ships are available for the duration of the scenario; we do not currently model breakdowns or ship damage due to enemy action. Ship transit times and intratheater asset transport times are a function of distance. Munitions requests (by air bases) represent a fixed and known demand of a particular munitions type; we do not currently consider suitable substitute munitions. We assume ports are always open, intratheater transportation infrastructures remain intact, port off-load times are deterministic, and munitions packing containers are fully loaded. We focus on the movement of munitions to requesting air bases versus the allocation of those munitions to aircraft, such as the case in target servicing models used to determine aggregate munitions procurement levels.

Model Formulation

This section discusses the model formulation to include all applicable indices, variables, and parameters.

Indices

l starting location of APF ship
d destinations (requesting air bases)
a APF ship
c conflict
p ports of debarkation
t modes of intratheater transportation (e.g., rail, truck)
m type of precision guided munitions considered in the scenario(s)
h theater munitions hubs
s STAMP locations
k type of airlifters used to transport munitions from STAMP locations

Variables

- X_{mpdc} = number of munitions m moved through port p to destination d for conflict c
- F_{mhdc} = number of munitions m moved from hub h to destination d for conflict c
- ST_{msdc} = number of munitions m moved from STAMP location s to d for conflict c
- SHORT_{mdc} = shortage of munitions m at destination d in conflict c
- W_{ap} = binary variable indicating APF ship a moved to port p
- Y_{alp} = binary variable indicating APF ship a moving munitions from location l to port p
- N_p = binary variable indicating whether or not NEW restrictions violated at port p
- INV_{ma} = number of munitions m stored on APF ship a
- TRAN_{tpd} = number of trips using transportation mode t between port p and destination d
- MOVE_{thd} = number of trips using transportation mode t between hub h and destination d
- AIRLIFT_{ksd} = number of trips using airlifter k between STAMP location s and destination d

Parameters

- AirTime_{ksd} = time to move munitions via airlifter k from STAMP location s to destination d
- APFCap_a = capacity of APF ship a in terms of munitions containers (volume)
- APFWt_a = capacity of APF ship a in terms of weight in pounds
- CanTx_{mpd} = flag with one indicating munition m transportable from port p to destination d
- Dem_{mdc} = demand for munitions type m at destination d in conflict c
- HubInv_{mhd} = flag with one indicating munition m transportable from hub h to designation d
- HubInv_{mh}= inventory of munition type m at hub h
- M = large constant
- MaxNEW_p = Max NEW restriction for port p

- MoveCap_{thd} = number of pallets moved using mode t (per trip) from hub h to destination d
- MoveWt_{thd} = weight moved using mode t (per trip) from hub h to destination d
- Mper463L_m = number of each munition type m on each pallet
- MperISO_m = total number of each munition type m fitted into each munitions container
- MunWt_m = weight of each munition type m (pounds)
- NEWPen_p = time penalty assessed for exceeding NEW restrictions in port p
- NEWperISO_m = NEW value associated with munitions container of munition type m
- Offld_{ap} = time to offload ship a at port p
- Pen_{mdc} = time penalty for shortage of munitions m at destination d for conflict c
- STAMPInv_{ms}= inventory of munition type m at STAMP location s
- Steam_{alp} = transit time of APF ship a from location l to port p
- TotInv_m = total inventory of each munition m
- Tx_{tpd} = transit time of transportation mode t from port p to destination d
- TxCap_{tpd} = munitions containers moved using mode t (per trip) from port p to destination d
- TxTime_{thd} = transportation mode t transit time from hub h to destination d
- TxWt_{tpd} = weight capacity of transportation mode t from port p to destination d
- Wtper463L_m = weight of pallet when loaded with munition m

Formulation

Pre-Po employs an objective function, (1) below, to minimize the total response time to meet the munitions demands of the various air bases.

Min (response time)

$$\begin{aligned}&\sum_{alp}\text{Steam}_{alp} * Y_{alp} + \sum_{mdc}\text{Pen}_{mdc} * \text{SHORT}_{mdc} + \sum_{tpd}\text{Tx}_{tpd} * \text{TRAN}_{tpd} + \sum_{ap}\text{Offld}_{ap} * W_{ap}\\ &+ \sum_{p}\text{NEWPen}_p * N_p + \sum_{ksd}\text{AirTime}_{ksd} * \text{AIRLIFT}_{ksd} + \sum_{thd}\text{TxTime}_{thd} * \text{MOVE}_{thd}.\end{aligned} \tag{1}$$

Response time includes APF ship transit times, port offload times, any time penalty for violating NEW restrictions at the port, inland transportation times from the ports to the requesting air bases, transportation times from overseas hubs to requesting air bases, airlift times from STAMP locations to requesting airbases, and a penalty for any munitions shortages (unmet demands) at the air bases requesting munitions.

The following equations, (2)–(24), capture the model constraints. A brief description of each constraint follows the complete formulation.

$$\begin{aligned}&\sum_{p}\text{CanTx}_{mpd} * X_{mpdc} + \sum_{h}\text{HubAOR}_{mhd} * F_{mhdc}\\ &+ \sum_{s}\text{ST}_{msdc} + \text{SHORT}_{mdc} = \text{Dem}_{mdc}, \qquad \forall m, d, c,\end{aligned} \tag{2}$$

$$\sum_{mdc} X_{mpdc} \le \sum_{mad}\text{CanTx}_{mpd} * W_{ap} * M, \qquad \forall p, \tag{3}$$

$$\sum_{mpc}(X_{mpdc} \div \text{MperIso}_m) \le \sum_{tp}(\text{TxCap}_{tpd} * \text{TRAN}_{tpd}), \qquad \forall d, \tag{4}$$

$$\sum_{mpc}(X_{mpdc} \div \text{MunWt}_m) \le \sum_{tp}(\text{TxWt}_{tpd} * \text{TRAN}_{tpd}), \qquad \forall d, \tag{5}$$

$$\sum_{c} X_{mpdc} \le \text{CanTx}_{mpd} * \text{INV}_{ma}, \qquad \forall a, m, p, d, \tag{6}$$

$$\sum_{a} \mathrm{INV}_{ma} + \sum_{hdc} F_{mhdc} * \mathrm{HubAOR}_{mhd} + \sum_{sdc} \mathrm{ST}_{msdc} + \sum_{dc} \mathrm{SHORT}_{mdc} \geq \sum_{dc} \mathrm{Dem}_{mdc}, \qquad \forall m, \tag{7}$$

$$\sum_{a} \mathrm{INV}_{ma} = \mathrm{TotInv}_{m}, \qquad \forall m, \tag{8}$$

$$\sum_{dc} \mathrm{ST}_{msdc} \leq \mathrm{STAMPInv}_{ms}, \qquad \forall m, s, \tag{9}$$

$$\sum_{dc} F_{mhdc} \leq \mathrm{HubInv}_{mh}, \qquad \forall m, h, \tag{10}$$

$$\sum_{c} (F_{mhdc} \div \mathrm{Mper\,463L}_{m}) \leq \sum_{t} (\mathrm{MoveCap}_{thd} * \mathrm{MOVE}_{thd} * \mathrm{HubAOR}_{mhd}), \quad \forall m, h, d, \tag{11}$$

$$\sum_{c} (F_{mhdc} \div \mathrm{Wtper\,463L}_{m}) \leq \sum_{t} (\mathrm{MoveWt}_{thd} * \mathrm{MOVE}_{thd} * \mathrm{HubAOR}_{mhd}), \quad \forall m, h, d, \tag{12}$$

$$\sum_{msc} (\mathrm{ST}_{msdc} \div \mathrm{Mper\,463L}_{m}) \leq \sum_{ks} (\mathrm{AirVol}_{ksd} * \mathrm{AIRLIFT}_{ksd}), \qquad \forall d, \tag{13}$$

$$\sum_{msc} (\mathrm{ST}_{msdc} \div \mathrm{Wtper\,463L}_{m}) \leq \sum_{ks} (\mathrm{AirWt}_{ksd} * \mathrm{AIRLIFT}_{ksd}), \qquad \forall d, \tag{14}$$

$$\sum_{m} (\mathrm{INV}_{ma} \div \mathrm{MperISO}_{m}) \leq \sum_{p} (\mathrm{APFCap}_{a} * W_{ap}), \qquad \forall a, \tag{15}$$

$$\sum_{m} (\mathrm{INV}_{ma} * \mathrm{MunWt}_{m} \div \mathrm{MperISO}_{m}) \leq \mathrm{APFWt}_{a}, \qquad \forall a, \tag{16}$$

$$\sum_{a} Y_{alp} = 1, \qquad \forall l, p, \tag{17}$$

$$\sum_{l} Y_{alp} = 1, \qquad \forall a, p, \tag{18}$$

$$\sum_{p} W_{ap} \leq 1, \qquad \forall a, \tag{19}$$

$$\sum_{l} Y_{alp} = W_{ap}, \qquad \forall a, p, \tag{20}$$

$$\sum_{t} \mathrm{TRAN}_{tpd} \leq \sum_{ma} \mathrm{CanTx}_{mpd} * W_{ap} * M, \qquad \forall p, d, \tag{21}$$

$$\sum_{mdc} (X_{mpdc} \div \mathrm{MperISO}_{m}) * \mathrm{NEWperISO}_{m} \leq \mathrm{MaxNEW}_{p} + N_{p} * M, \qquad \forall p, \tag{22}$$

$$X_{mpdc}, F_{mhdc}, \mathrm{ST}_{msdc}, \mathrm{SHORT}_{mdc}, \mathrm{TRAN}_{tpd}, \mathrm{MOVE}_{thd}, \mathrm{AIRLIFT}_{ksd}, \mathrm{Inv}_{ma} \geq 0, \tag{23}$$

$$W_{ap}, Y_{alp}, N_{p} = 0 \text{ or } 1. \tag{24}$$

Equation (2) ensures that the model captures munitions demand by destination and conflict. Munitions are moved from a port to a destination using available transportation modes while requested munitions not supplied are considered shortages. Equation (3) indicates whether or not a particular APF ship travels to a particular port. Equations (4) and (5) determine the number of trips required by each transportation mode to move requested munitions from a given port to a requesting air base within a particular conflict.

Equations (6)–(8) determine the proper inventory mix by munitions type assigned to each APF ship. Equation (6) ensures that if an APF ship carries a certain weapon to support a conflict, inland transportation is available to move the munitions from the port to the final destination. Equation (7) calculates munitions demand shortages. Equation (8) forces the total munitions allocated to APF ships to agree with the munitions inventory available to the APF ships.

Equations (9) and (10) capture munitions inventories at each of the STAMP locations and overseas munitions hubs, respectively. Equations (11) and (12) enforce transportation mode volume and weight restrictions, respectively, for each hub while equations (13) and (14) enforce volume and weight restrictions, respectively, for the aircraft used to transport munitions from each STAMP location. Equations (15) and (16) ensure that each APF ship's volume and weight capacities, respectively, are not exceeded. Equations (17) and (18) combine to uniquely preposition each APF ship. Equation (19) ensures each APF ship travels to a single port while equation (20) links the destination port to the ship's initial prepositioned location. Equation (21) ensures that munitions are only carried inland from a port if adequate transportation means and infrastructure are in place. Equation (22) models (and enforces) port NEW restrictions. Finally, equations (23) and (24) define each variable's context: noninteger variables in equation (23) and binary integer variables in equation (24).

The Pre-Po model was implemented in the GAMS (general algebraic modeling system) mathematical modeling language. GAMS provides a front-end to a general purpose mixed integer program solution package; we used the XA solver package in our implementation of the Pre-Po model. GAMS takes as input a general mathematical formulation that is specified with specific problem data, translates the resulting model into a form read by the solver, and outputs the solution obtained by the solver package. The specific problem data for the model was read into GAMS using an Excel-based front-end. These components were implemented on a Dell Latitude laptop system running at 650 Mhz. All subsequent experiments and case study results were derived using an implementation of the Pre-Po model.

CASE STUDY AND RESULTS

The purpose of Pre-Po is to augment existing munitions requirements models and to fill the current void in prepositioning planning and analyses. The following case study was derived from actual planning scenarios (and data), notionalized for security purposes, and limited for demonstration purposes. We considered three planning scenarios, combined into a three-theater simultaneous conflict scenario, and focused on the precision guided munitions portion of the complete military munitions picture.

Scenario Inputs

In recent years, military planning has shifted to planning for simultaneous contingencies to answer questions pertaining to sizing and supporting such scenarios. We model three contingencies located within three separate theaters. These contingencies are a major theater of war in Southwest Asia (MTWS), a small-scale scenario in Europe (SSCE), and a small-scale scenario in Northeast Asia (SSCA). Each theater has differing support structures in the form of demand air bases, ports, munitions hubs, and intratheater distribution modes. We model three APF ships and consider eight different precision-guided munitions. Specific munition types and numbers are not provided in detail. Table 1 lists the air bases demanding munitions by theater.

Table 1. Demand air bases by theater.

Theater	Air Base (Destination)
Europe (SSCE)	RAF Lakenheath Ramstein AB Aviano AB Incirlik AB
Southwest Asia (MTWS)	Prince Sultan Air Base (PSAB) Dhahran AB Al Jaber King Khalid Military City (KKMC)
Northeast Asia (SSCA)	Kadena AB Andersen AB Kunsan AB

Table 2. Ports used in each theater.

Theater	Ports
Europe (SSCE)	Nordenham, Germany Livorno, Italy Iskenderun, Turkey
Southwest Asia (MTWS)	Ad Dammam, Saudi Arabia Aal Jabail, Saudi Arabia
Northeast Asia (SSCA)	Apra, Guam Naha, Guam Chin Hae, South Korea

Table 3. Theater, munitions hubs, and bases served by hubs.

Theater	Munitions Hubs	Bases Served by Hub
Europe (SSCE)	Ramstein, Germany Darby, Italy Welford, United Kingdom	Ramstein AB, Incirlik AB Aviano AB, Incirlik AB RAF Lakenheath
Southwest Asia (MTWS)	None	None
Northeast Asia (SSCA)	Naha, Okinawa	Kadena AB

Table 2 lists the ports servicing each theater, and Table 3 lists the various munitions hubs and the air bases included in each theater.

Data employed to complete each model include: specific munitions quantity demanded by air base, transportation mode by port and hub, and transit times between air base locations by mode of transportation.

Results

A model objective function guides the numerical search process. We next discuss model results and ensure Pre-Po produces reasonable results.

APF Movement

We first assess model recommendations regarding APF ship movement. This includes ship initial location assignment and destination port selection in support of particular theater requirements. Figure 2 displays the result of using objective function (1) to minimize the time required

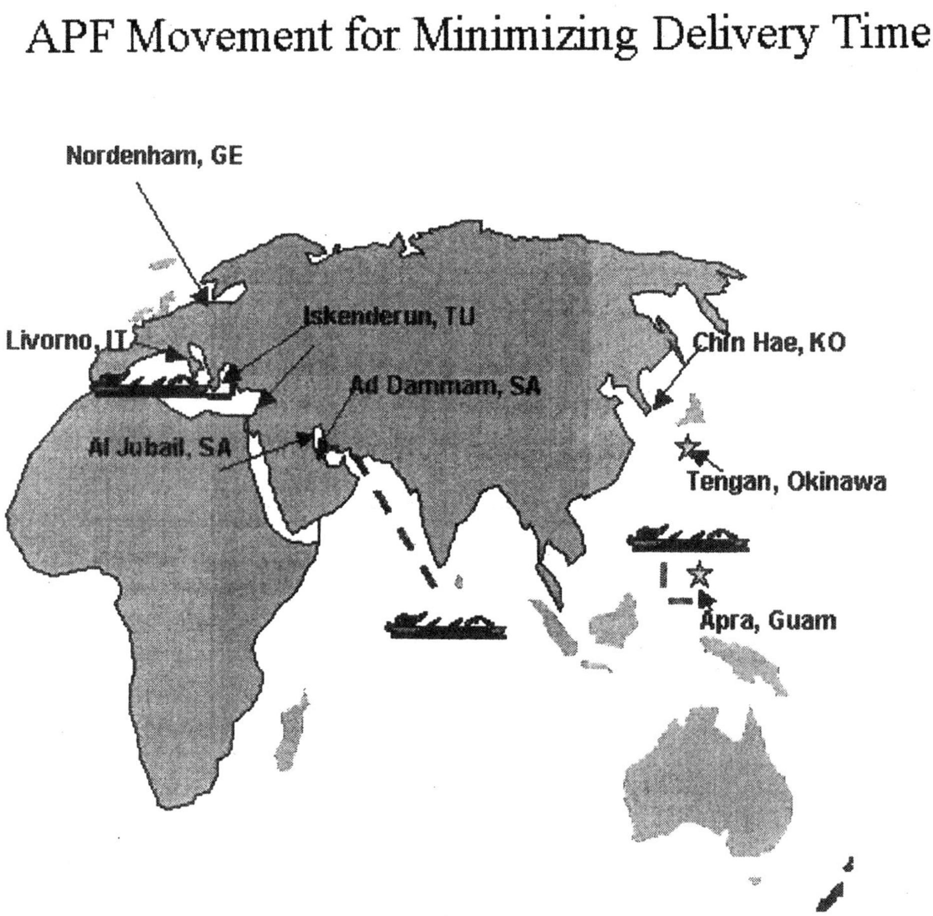

Figure 2. APF movement to minimize munitions delivery time.

to meet munitions demand. These results provide a logical flow of munitions. The first APF ship travels from the Mediterranean to Iskenderun, another travels from Diego Garcia to the Persian Gulf, and the final ship travels from Saipan to Guam. Even though objective function (1) focuses on delivery time, the level of munitions shortages appears reasonable.

Volume of Munitions Provided by Each Source

We next examine the munitions supply pattern prescribed by the Pre-Po model. Table 4 summarizes the level of demand satisfaction by munitions source for each of the theater contingencies modeled. Despite variations due to theater differences, the APF plays a key role in each theater by supplying at least 26% of the munitions demand. This represents a significant amount of the overall munitions movement for the USAF and supports the fundamental rationale for the APF—provide combat response in a timely manner.

The MTWS relies heavily on the APF. This is the largest scenario and the theater has the least amount of infrastructure munitions supply capability. Munitions demand shortages are of

Table 4. Aggregate level of theater demand satisfaction by munitions source.

Theater	APF	Hub	STAMP	Shortage
MTWS	74%	0%	1%	25%
SSCE	26%	61%	1%	12%
SSCA	40%	24%	16%	20%

concern, but they actually point to the need for some level of munitions hub support for the area. Unlike the MTWS, the SSCE scenario has a reasonable level of in-theater munitions hub inventory, and these assets are put to use as demonstrated by the 61% demand satisfaction level from the hubs. As we discuss below, the SSCE requires APF support primarily for Incirlik munitions demands.

The final scenario, SSCA, has the best balance of munitions sources. This is reasonable given the geography of the region—all of the air bases are separated by water negating land-based intratheater transportation modes. Thus, Andersen AB demand is satisfied largely from the APF ship, Kadena AB relied on both hub and STAMP support, and Kunsan AB relied solely on STAMP support to offset the lack of a munitions hub.

Munitions Flow from Port to Final Destination

Our final concern was the prescribed munitions movement from port to requesting air base for APF munitions delivery. Figures 3–5 summarize pictorially the volume of munitions flow from the port utilized by an APF ship to the air bases in each scenario (the arrows represent relative

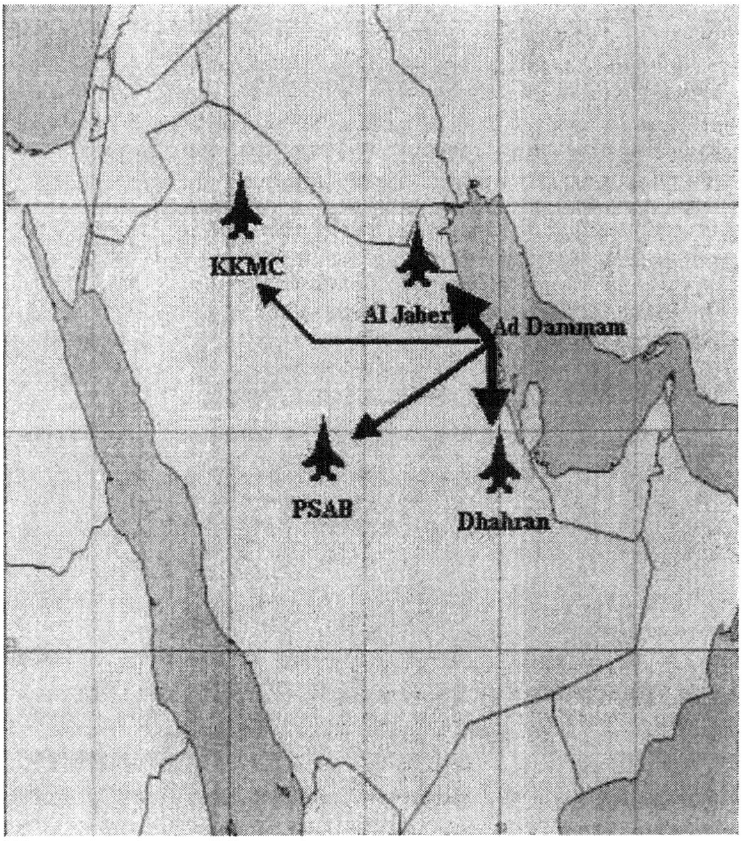

Figure 3. Munitions flow from port to MTWS air bases.

Table 5. Munitions flow from port to air bases in MTWS scenario.

Theater	Port	Destination	Aggregated Munitions Volume
SWA	Ad Dammam	Al Jaber	6951
		Dhahran	5401
		KKMC	2501
		PSAB	3305

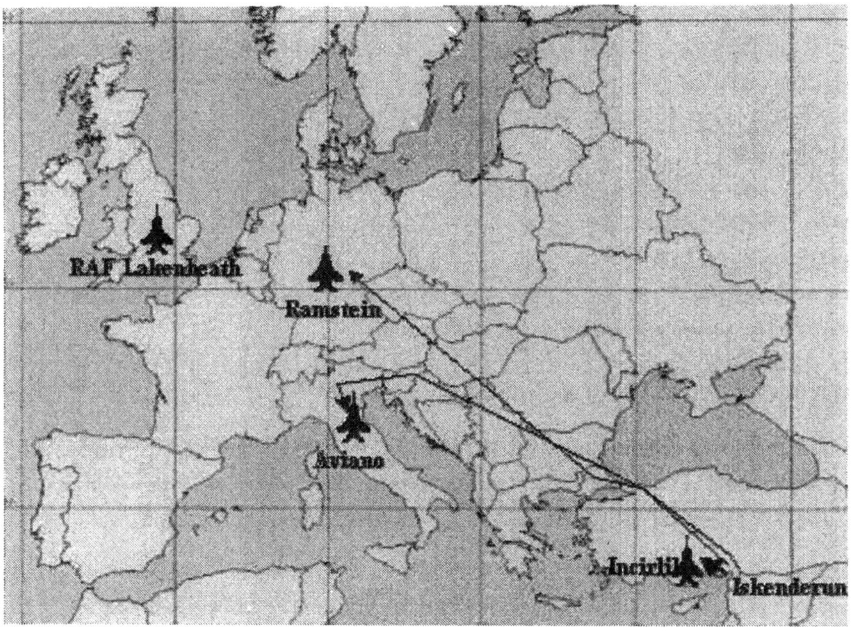

Figure 4. Munitions flow from port to SSCE air bases.

Table 6. Munitions flow from port to air bases in SSCE scenario.

Theater	Port	Destination	Aggregated Munitions Volume
Europe	Iskenderun	Incirlik	2216
		Aviano	467
		Ramstein	100
		RAF Lakenheath	0

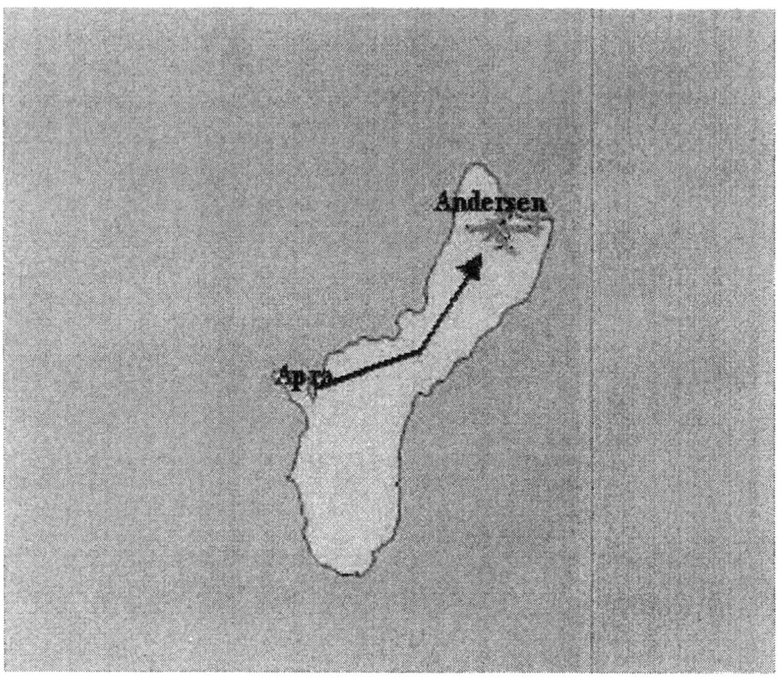

Figure 5. Munitions flow from port to an SSCA air base.

Table 7. Munitions flow from port to air bases in SSCA scenario.

Theater	Port	Destination	Aggregated Munitions Volume
Asia	Apra	Andersen	2336
		Kadena	0
		Kunsan	0

volume of munitions flow). The actual volume levels are listed in Tables 5–7, respectively. All volumes are provided in tons of munitions.

The values in Table 5 indicate how important an APF is in theaters lacking munitions hubs. STAMP inventories supplied the remainder of satisfied demand at each air base.

Unlike MTWS, the SSCE scenario displayed in Figure 4 and summarized in Table 6 involves large munitions hubs located near the three air bases in this theater. Thus, the majority of APF inventory is off-loaded in Iskenderun to support Incirlik demand. The remaining three air bases rely heavily on supply from munitions hub inventories.

Finally, Figure 5 and Table 7 summarize the SSCA scenario in which the APF is used to satisfy Andersen's munitions demand. Neither Kadena nor Kunsan are supplied by the APF. Kadena employs its munitions hub and STAMP support while Kunsan relies solely on STAMP supply. These results suggest the need to consider munitions support areas located near the Kunsan demand location.

CONCLUSIONS AND FUTURE WORK

We defined and prototyped a prepositioning mathematical programming model, Pre-Po. The model was implemented in an algebraic modeling environment, employed a standard general purpose solution routine, and was exercised against a realistic planning scenario. Thus, in addition to providing a new model, we demonstrated an analysis methodology using that model. Initial results depict reasonable movement plans in support of simultaneous military contingencies. Our experiences also demonstrated the viability of using Pre-Po to gain insight into planning theater supply assets (such as munitions hubs).

This initial model was necessarily limited, but the design facilitates expansion. For instance, APF ships can be modeled to support multiple ports if the Pre-Po model is expanded into a time-phased model. Ship vulnerability can be modeled to capture those risks inherent when there is enemy action. Finally, goal programming techniques can be used to accommodate multiple objective functions or to examine changes to initial solutions when scenario details are changed.

Future efforts with the Pre-Po model will implement the previously noted changes. In addition, future efforts will add usability features such as a scenario database, a graphical user interface, analytical tool support, and a link to current munitions planning models.

REFERENCES

1. Department of the Air Force, *Ammo Vision 2010: United States Air Force Agile Combat Support (ACS) for Munitions*, Washington, DC, (2000).
2. R. Tripp, E. Peltz, R. Roll, L. Galway, T. Ramey, M. Amouzegar, C. Grammich and J. Drew, A vision for agile combat support, In *Expeditionary Logistics. Issues & Strategy for the New Millennium*, Montgomery, AL, (July 2000).
3. C.A. Seydel, Discreet fleet, *Airman* **46** (7), 42–47, (2002).
4. K.A. Yost, Consolidating the USAF's conventional munitions models, *Military Operations Research* **2** (4), 53–72, (1996).
5. M.G. Mattock, J.F. Schank, J.P. Stucker and J. Rothenberg, *New Capabilities for Strategic Mobility Analysis Using Mathematical Programming*, National Defense Research Institute, RAND, (1995).
6. B.H. Anderson, The mobility triad and challenges for the operational commander, Research Report submitted to Naval War College, Newport, RI, (1999).
7. Department of the Air Force, *Compendium of Authenticated Systems and Logistics Terms, Definitions and Acronyms*, Air Force Institute of Technology, (1981).

8. J.E. King, Jr., War reserve materiel pre-positioning. Its history, its significance, and its future, MS Thesis, AFIT/GLM/LS/91S-38, School of Systems and Logistics, Air Force Institute of Technology (AU), Wright-Patterson AFB, OH, (August 1991).
9. J.F. Pasquarette, The Army global pre-positioning strategy: A critical review, Research Report submitted to U.S. Army Command and General Staff College, Fort Leavenworth, KS, (1995).
10. White Paper, *Air Force Performance in Desert Storm*, Department of the Air Force, Washington, DC, (1991).
11. M. Kampsen, Army and Marine Corps afloat pre-positioning: Providing full spectrum capability through complementary programs, Report submitted to U.S. Army War College, Carlisle Barracks, PA, (1998).
12. United States General Accounting Office, *Military Pre-Positioning: Army and Air Force Programs Need to Be Reassessed*, Washington, DC, (November 1998).
13. Department of the Navy, MPF 2010 and beyond, *The Marine Corps Gazette* **82**, (February 1998).
14. C.M. McMillon, AFLMA/LGM, Maxwell AFB, Gunter Annex, AL, Interview, (July 2001).
15. Synergy, Inc., Munitions pre-positioning study, Final Report, Research submitted to HQ USAF/ILMW, (2001).
16. B.K. Sentlinger, Optimal positioning of naval precision guided munitions, Master's Thesis in Operations Research, Naval Postgraduate School, (2000).
17. E.B. Anderson, Optimizing ammunition movement in support of the U.S. Pacific fleet's positioning plan, Master's Thesis in Operations Research, Naval Postgraduate School, (1998).
18. R. Might, Decision support for aircraft and munitions procurement, *Interfaces* **17** (5), 55–62, (1987).
19. G.G. Brown, D.M. Coulter and A.R. Washburn, Sortie optimization and munitions planning, *Military Operations Research* **1** (1), 13–18, (1994).
20. D.P. Morton, R.E. Rosenthal and L.T. Wang, Optimization modeling for airlift mobility, *Military Operations Research* **1** (x), 49–68, (1996).
21. R.E. Rosenthal, S.F. Baker, L.T. Wang, D.F. Fuller, D. Goggins, A.O. Toy, Y. Turker, D. Horton, D. Briand and D.P. Morton, Application and extension of the thruput II optimization model for airlift mobility, *Military Operations Research* **3** (4), 55–74, (1997).
22. S.F. Baker, D.P. Morton, R.E. Rosenthal and L.M. Williams, Optimizing military airlift, *Operations Research* **50** (4), 582–602, (2002).

Available online at www.sciencedirect.com
SCIENCE DIRECT•
ELSEVIER
Mathematical and Computer Modelling 39 (2004) 773–797
MATHEMATICAL AND COMPUTER MODELLING
www.elsevier.com/locate/mcm

A Multimethod Approach to the Combat Air Forces Mix and Deployment Problem

S. M. SWARTZ
Department of Operational Sciences, Air Force Institute of Technology
Wright-Patterson AFB, OH 45433-7765, U.S.A.
Stephen.Swartz@afit.edu

A. W. JOHNSON
Department of Mathematical Sciences, United States Military Academy
West Point, NY 10996-5000, U.S.A.
Alan.Johnson@usma.edu

Abstract—The purpose of military logistics is to ensure that the material elements of combat capability come together at the right place and time and in the right configuration to be useful to the supported commander. These material elements are constrained in both quantity and location. The usefulness of any element to a commander is dependent upon both its extrinsic (qualitative; situation dependent) and intrinsic (quantitative; inherent) characteristics. Our research provides a methodology for rationally assigning relative value to material resources over time, in order to improve the linkage between what arrives (becomes available for use) in theater at any given time, and what is actually needed at that time. A blend of qualitative (value focused thinking and hierarchical weighting) and quantitative (a greedy matching algorithm) methods were used against the lift-constrained combat forces material selection/movement problem. The intent is to provide a decision support tool for the formulation of force mixes that best support desired time-phased battlefield objectives, given constraints on available transportation resources. This methodology is applicable to general crisis response planning, such as for disaster relief.

Keywords—Multiattribute decision analysis, Ranking and selection, Heuristics.

1. BACKGROUND

The United States military is faced with global responsibilities that require a global capability to respond. Quite often, military capability is not present at the right time and place prior to need. Therefore, there is a requirement for the ability to transport the elements of combat capability rapidly across global distances. The purpose of military logistics is to ensure that the material elements of combat capability come together at the right place and time and in the right configuration to be useful to the supported commander.

To be useful, the material elements must exist as sets of items. For example, an artillery piece by itself has no value without ammunition and all other ancillary items required for the

This research was supported in part with funds provided by the Defense Advanced Research Projects Agency's Advanced Logistics Project Program Office.
The views expressed are those of the authors, and do not reflect the official policy or positions of the United States Air Force, Department of Defense, or the U.S. Government.

0895-7177/04/$ - see front matter Typeset by $\mathcal{A}_{\mathcal{M}}\mathcal{S}$-TEX
doi:10.1016/j.mcm.2004.02.014

gun to function. A combat aircraft has no value without fuel and munitions. Hence, we define a mission ready resource (MRR) as a fundamental unit of combat capability—a properly configured weapon system with all of its required elements (e.g., fuel, munitions, and operators) in place and ready for use. In order to provide a useful number of MRRs in a battle area, the required MRR elements must typically be moved over large distances. The transportation services needed to provide this movement (called *lift*) are resource constrained. A significant and lasting military logistics problem is to schedule the movement or flow of these material elements into the battle area in order to optimize the availability of the MRRs.

Current planning methods select and flow combat material into theater via a top-down approach, based on two major aggregating assumptions. First of all, current methods start the deployment process by selecting preidentified *force packages*—detailed standardized lists of MRRs, equipment, parts, and people created during deliberate planning in preparation for a specific anticipated mission need. These packages frequently require *paring and tailoring* to scope them for a specific scenario. A force package is pared and tailored by eliminating or adding the equipment the deploying unit deems necessary given the expected location, duration, operating environment, operations tempo, and other factors. Our proposed methodology uses a bottom-up approach that incrementally chooses individual MRRs and their associated required elements for deployment, based on the theater commander's specific mission objectives. Second, current planning methods use rough time scales, measured by milestones called *closure dates* that are set in monthly or weekly increments. Until a closure date is reached, the commander may have minimal capability to satisfy certain mission preferences. Our proposed methodology uses an arbitrary (such as daily) timeline, based on the commander's needs. The arbitrary timeline, coupled with the selection and deployment of complete MRRs, enables combatant commanders to quickly establish initial mission operations that more smoothly progress to full capability as additional MRRs arrive in theater.

Our proposed method differs from the current approach in one additional major characteristic. Currently, the force package selection, force deployment, and force employment aspects of the overall problem are solved as individual subproblems. While close coordination and integration between the three subproblems are currently achieved manually and serially, it is believed that a single integrated approach to the overall problem could yield some benefits. Our proposed approach represents a significant, while incomplete, step in the direction of treating the problem as a single, globally optimizable problem.

Finally, it should be noted that while the current methods are employed successfully in modern warfare, they were developed to overcome limitations in computational and analytical power that are only recently being challenged. Our proposed approach represents a significant departure from existing planning methods, as noted by the subject matter experts (air combat planning staff members) contacted during this research. Our approach was met with a mixture of both skepticism ("computers cannot handle the problem complexity") and enthusiasm ("if it works, it could shorten closure timelines considerably").

Our paper is organized as follows. Section 2 provides a general context of the problem and an overview of our methodology. Section 3 discusses our optimization of *inherent* MRR set utility, while Section 4 shows how we implemented a value-focused thinking approach to optimize *extrinsic* MRR set utility. Section 5 introduces an application of our methodology, and Section 6 presents our summary and research conclusions.

2. MODEL OVERVIEW

Our research provides a methodology for rationally assigning relative value to material resources over time, in order to improve the linkage between what *arrives* (becomes available for use) in theater at any given time, and what is actually *needed* at that time. Our methodology proceeds as follows: the combat commander first states his or her time-phased mission objectives, the best-suited MRRs are matched to those preferences, lift constraints are applied, and tradeoff choices are finally made.

Over the course of a given campaign, commanders have preferences for certain missions over others; these preferences represent the relative value of one mission type over another. For example, suppose that on any given day, a commander has the choice of conducting three types of air missions: air-to-air (AA), suppression of enemy air defenses (SEAD), and close air support (CAS). Two aspects are of interest: the commander's *preference* for one mission type relative to another, and the *total number* of air missions (of any mix of the three mission types) that the commander can conduct per day, as a function of the total resources available. Note that the relative priority and numbers of preferred missions could be different for different days of the campaign. Furthermore, the relative preference will probably not remain constant over varying levels of total resource availability. At any given level of resources available, the actual relative balance or share of mission type out of total missions may or may not remain constant. A certain mission type may be critical at a low level of total resources available, but as resources increase, this mission's marginal value may taper and another mission type becomes paramount. For example, as the total number of missions possible grows, the increase in the number of SEAD and AA missions may taper (diminishing returns), while the value of CAS missions may increase. Conversely, if the total number of missions possible decreases, the CAS missions desired may decrease rapidly, and the commander may be more reluctant to reduce the SEAD missions than the AA missions. At varying levels of total resource availability, the relative marginal utility of one sortie or mission type over another may change. The inflection points of the diminishing/increasing utility curves would be captured using the expert knowledge of the campaign commanders and planners. The commander would be asked to determine relative utility, given various levels of available resources. For example, by identifying the preferred sortie/mission mix for a nominal case and then providing alternative mixes representing points where the relative priorities change as resource levels go up or down, we could represent shifts in relative marginal utility or priority. A graph showing a representative piecewise linear curve of notional preferences for AA, CAS, and SEAD missions is shown in Figure 1.

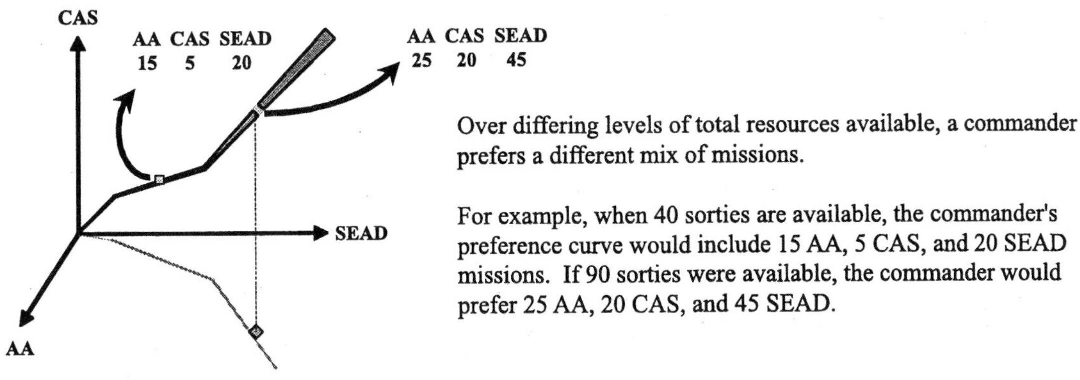

Figure 1. A commander's notional task preference matrix.

The next step is to determine the MRR sets that can best satisfy the commander's desired tasks. Each asset (e.g., an F-16 aircraft in our air campaign example) may be configurable for different mission types, and hence, represent different MRRs. Once committed, an MRR is consumed, but the associated asset may be reused—possibly as a different MRR for a subsequent mission. Certain MRR types can provide higher or lower levels of intrinsic effectiveness in accomplishing a single mission. The favorite (intrinsically best) MRR to apply to a particular mission is assigned a value of unity, and the effectiveness of alternative MRRs are weighted accordingly. For example, the Air Force AC-130H Gunship is arguably the most suitable resource for CAS missions (and thus, is rated a "1" for CAS), but is poorly suited for AA missions (and thus, is rated low—

possibly a "0.2", for AA). MRR-task ratings would be accomplished by subject matter experts, and would not change until the MRRs are modified or replaced. The ratings would be represented by an asset-mission task preference matrix (A-M TPM). A notional A-M TPM showing how five MRR types BA, BB, FA, FB, and FC rank for SEAD, AA, and CAS missions, is shown in Table 1.

Table 1. A-M TPM.

	SEAD	AA	CAS
BA	0.8	0	0.2
BB	0.8	0	0.6
FA	0.3	1	0.2
FB	0.5	0.1	1
FC	1	0.1	0.3

In some cases, there is no way an asset could create the same battlefield effect as another; in those instances, the nonpreferred asset is assigned a value of 0.

Thus, the task is to translate the commander's campaign-specific task preference curve into a corresponding curve of the best-suited MRR sets, as shown in Figure 2. Note from Figure 2 that each point on the task preference curve might map to alternative choices of equally preferable MRR sets. Points farther from the origin on the task preference curve represent more desired missions per day, and thus, should translate into larger sets of MRRs. Finally, points lying on the curve would dominate (be preferable to) any points not on the curve, because they most closely represent the commander's desires. Figure 2 represents a daily preference ratio of 25 AA, 20 CAS, and 45 SEAD missions that could best be met by any of four alternative mixes of BA, BB, and FA, FB, and FC MRRs.

To rank any equally desirable (along the preference curve) alternative MRR mixes, we use a value-focused thinking method based on all extrinsic factors pertaining to the problem. Finally, we base the selected MRR set's transportation requirements and movement order on the commander's task preference matrix.

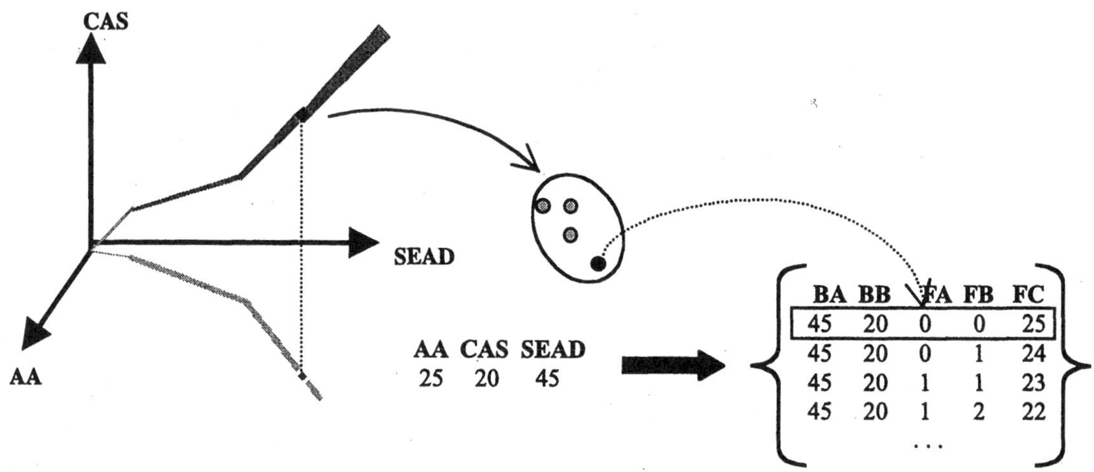

Figure 2. The commander's daily preference ratio.

3. OPTIMIZATION OF INHERENT SUITABILITY

We wish to allocate MRRs to the commander's preferred tasks one at a time, to establish a priority order for transportation scheduling. Since the MRRs are assumed to be integer-valued, the first requirement is to discretize the task preference curve into a series of integer coordinates, each a unit distance apart. (We define the distance between any two r-dimensional coordinates x and y as $\|x - y\| = \sum_{i=1}^{r} |x_i - y_i|$.) Suppose that the commander wishes to perform three SEAD tasks for every two CAS tasks. Figure 3 illustrates a preference curve based on these two competing missions.

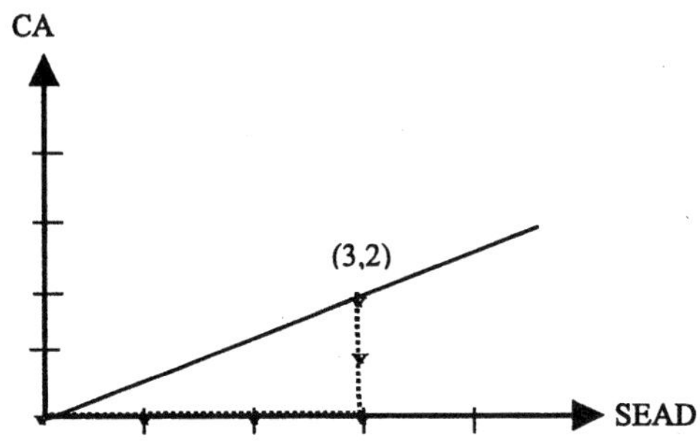

Figure 3. Preference curve with MRR assignments.

The point $(3, 2)$ is the first integer-valued coordinate on the curve. To assign resources, we could sequentially allocate MRRs first to the three SEAD missions and then to the two CAS missions, as shown in Figure 3. However, nine other sequences can be constructed from the origin to the coordinate $(3, 2)$. (If the first integer coordinate on the preference curve has k SEAD missions and $(n-k)$ CAS missions, then there are $\binom{n}{k}$ unique sequences of integer coordinates that can be constructed from the origin to the on-curve coordinate $(k, n-k)$.) A problem with three or more mission types has even more solutions. In general, for a problem with r mission types such that the first integer coordinate on the preference curve is reached after k_j moves for mission j, for $j = 1, 2, \ldots, r$, then there are a total of $n!/(k_1!k_2! \cdots k_r!)$ unique sequences of integer coordinates that can be constructed from the origin to the first on-curve integer coordinate $(k_1, k_2, \ldots, k_r)$. (Note that $n = k_1 + k_2 + \cdots + k_r$.)

Hence, which sequence best preserves the commander's desired task ratio? In other words, which sequence of integer coordinates best approximates the real-valued task preference curve? We seek a sequence identification method that would converge to all integer points along the preference curve, compute quickly, be scalable to seven or more dimensions, and that would control the minimum average and maximum distance between the preference curve and all off-curve integer points (in terms of a line passing through an integer point and perpendicular to the curve). Two methods from the literature were identified [1,2], and we developed two candidate methods of our own. The best overall method proved to be our candidate method we call the relative slope algorithm [3].

The relative slope algorithm (RSA) is based on a form of slope comparison. The difference between the start point and end point in each dimension (i.e., Δx_j, for $j = 1, 2, \ldots, r$) is calculated. The largest delta value is used as the denominator for slope calculations in all directions. The RSA is depicted in the following pseudocode.

INITIALIZATION. Specify initial $(x_1, x_2, \ldots, x_r)$ and final $(y_1, y_2, \ldots, y_r)$ on-curve integer coordinates, and set index $z = 0$.

MAIN STEPS.

(1) compute $\Delta_j = (y_j - x_j)$ for $j = 1, 2, \ldots, r$

(2) sort Δ_j, $j = 1, 2, \ldots, r$, from largest to smallest, and let $n = \sum_{j=1}^{r} \Delta_j$ (we assume without loss of generality that the subscripts reflect this sorted order)

(3) let $\Delta = \max_{j=1 \ldots r}(\Delta_j)$, and compute $m_j = \Delta_j / \Delta$ for $j = 1, 2, \ldots, r$

(4) let $P_0 = \mathrm{TEMP}_0 = (x_1, x_2, \ldots, x_r)$

for $i = 1$ to Δ by 1 do:

$$\mathrm{TEMP}_i = (x_1 + \mathrm{RND}(i \cdot m_1),\ x_2 + \mathrm{RND}(i \cdot m_2), \ldots,\ x_r + \mathrm{RND}(i \cdot m_r))$$

Let $k = \|\text{TEMP}_i - \text{TEMP}_{i-1}\|$
for $p = 1$ to k by 1 do:
let $q =$ (dimension p of $\text{TEMP}_i -$ dimension p of TEMP_{i-1})
for $j = 1$ to q by 1 do:
$z \equiv z + 1$
$P_z =$ (the coordinate P_{z-1}, with its pth element incremented by 1)

Figure 4 shows how the RSA would compute the sequence from $(0,0)$ to $(3,2)$. This sequence would be repeated for as long as the preference curve slope remains constant.

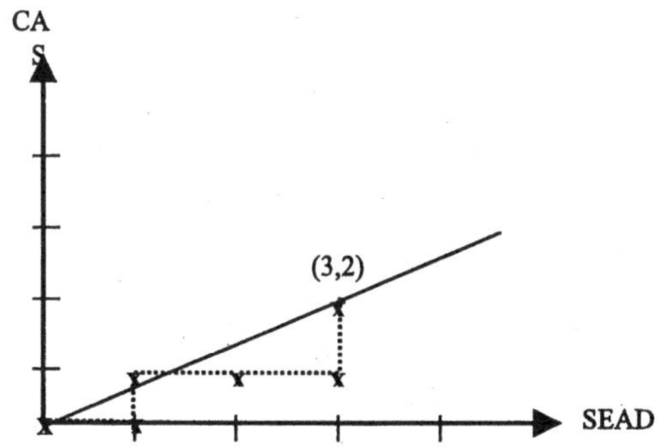

Figure 4. RSA approximation.

Note that each coordinate differs from the previous one by a unit distance in a single dimension. The next step is to assign MRRs to tasks, in order to determine which specific MRR resources to deploy. We use a greedy approach as follows: we consider the first task (the first integer task coordinate), and assign it the MRR with the highest intrinsic suitability for that task. We repeat this process of assigning the most-suitable unassigned MRR to the next task, one task at a time, until either all tasks are satisfied or all candidate MRRs are assigned.

Note that if we have unlimited availability of each MRR type and if no MRR type-task preference ties exist, then the greedy algorithm would provide a single optimal *intrinsic* solution (a unique set of MRRs), since at each step the algorithm chooses the best-suited MRR for the next most-preferred task. In this case, the *extrinsic* portion of our methodology would only be necessary to determine the *go-no go* deployment feasibility of this solution. On the other hand, if multiple MRR types are equally preferable for a given task, then alternate optimal final solutions (final MRR sets) are possible, and the extrinsic portion of our methodology would then be used to rank these solutions. A final case might exist where we have limited MRR-type availability, with or without preference ties. In this case, the greedy algorithm could result in one or more suboptimal solutions, which might then require extrinsic value ranking.

After one or more "optimal" MRR sets are identified, we then use a set of logistics business rules to determine the associated deployment requirement for each selected MRR set. For example, a representative set of rules for F-16 aircraft was consolidated by Goddard [4] from rule sets in the literature [5–7]. Goddard justified the consolidated F-16 rules by comparing his rule-based predictions for a representative set of parts and equipment to the actual records from three historical deployments. He also developed a regression model [4:60] that would estimate the airlift footprint required to deploy F-16-based MRR spare parts and equipment. We did not consider personnel, fuel, or munitions requirements, and we assumed no knowledge about what parts or equipment might already be available at the deployed location. Note that validated logistics business rules are lacking for many weapon systems, and thus, their acquisition will represent a significant obstacle to the implementation of our overall method.

The logistics business rules partition the MRR deployment footprint into two classes: *renewable* resources—those which can be used over and over again for many missions, such as people, aircraft, and support equipment; versus *consumable* resources—e.g., spare parts, munitions, and fuel. Constrained lift resources can then be rationally allocated: the first day's lift would be assigned to those MRRs and associated resources that best address the commander's task preference curve, within available lift capacity. Each subsequent day's lift is allocated first to the consumable resources needed to produce MRRs from assets already deployed. Any residual capacity available that day is then allocated to deploying the resources needed to produce additional MRRs. This approach ensures that materiel arrives to the deployed location in priority order and is complete—the commander's most urgent missions can immediately be accomplished.

4. EXTRINSIC SUITABILITY—VALUE FOCUSED THINKING

In the preceding section, we described how the model approach could develop and search possible MRR combinations for *inherent* suitability, in order to satisfy a commander's preferences for missions and tasks. There are, however, situation-specific or *extrinsic* criteria that would make a given MRR set either more or less desirable in the eyes of the commander [8,9]. In the course of this research, it became clear from interviews with combat mission planners that these extrinsic factors were often ignored by those seeking to solve the mission-resource assignment problem, and that the extrinsic factors could frequently override the intrinsic factors in importance [8,9]. Overall force mix value must be determined through an assessment and combination of both inherent and extrinsic characteristics. The inherent value can be measured using the A-M TPM. The extrinsic value of a force mix includes all factors that are *external to* the set's inherent operational capabilities, such as beddown location, fuels support, and political considerations. A key concern of this research was how to properly identify, analyze, and incorporate these extrinsic factors into a measure of the value of an asset set.

Note that in the current planning process, these extrinsic factors are often considered *post hoc* by tailoring or modifying the standard aggregate force packages discussed earlier. For example, a set of typical capabilities is needed to prosecute a campaign, and typical aggregate MRR sets are identified. The basing decision(s) is then considered, in order to establish destinations for the MRR types to be used. Finally, political, economic, or other extrinsic factors are considered, which may render certain MRRs unsuitable for some bases. The MRR sets must then be modified, and the basing options perhaps also changed, until a reasonable solution is found. Our proposed methodology allows the interaction between intrinsic and extrinsic factors to be considered explicitly. For example, a given set of basing choices could be analyzed according to how quickly the commander's preferences could be met with the best set of MRRs for those bases. This choice could be compared to an alternative set of bases, until a satisfactory response time for capability could be achieved. The capability "cost" of various extrinsic factors could then be measured, at least in a relative sense.

Selection of VFT

Interviews with subject matter experts (air campaign planners) early on in the research validated the separability of intrinsic and extrinsic factors [9]. This phase of the research also identified two general categories of extrinsic factors: *go-no go* and *variable* criteria. *Go-no go* criteria are factors which, by their presence or absence, limit or restrict the types of MRRs that are eligible for consideration in the force mix. For example, a certain platform might not be acceptable to the host nation at the beddown location, so this platform would be prohibited from consideration in the deployed force. *Variable* criteria are considerations that do not limit or restrict an MRR per se, but could make one MRR more or less preferable over another. For example, limited fuel at the operating location might make a more fuel efficient MRR desirable over a platform that consumes fuel at a higher rate. Details about how these factors were identified and categorized are presented in the next section.

The two types of criteria were treated differently by the overall model. *Go-no go* criteria were used up front in the model, to reduce the feasible region from which MRR sets were selected. The elimination of a particular MRR from consideration in the optimization model reduced the combinatorial complexity of the problem, speeding algorithm execution. This was a straightforward application of these types of factors.

The *variable* criteria affected the desirability of proposed MRR sets in somewhat more complex ways. In order to account for these effects, Buzo [8] and Filcek [9] first surveyed the literature of decision theory for rational approaches. The subdiscipline of multiattribute utility theory (MAUT) was identified as the most appropriate area for potential methods. MAUT is recognized as a prominent family of methods in decision analysis, providing a "rigorous technique for combining attributes multiplicatively (thereby incorporating nonlinearity), and for handling uncertainty in the attribute values" [10]. This made MAUT a good fit to the extrinsic factors discovered during this research.

Value focused thinking (VFT) is an application of MAUT developed by Keeney [11]. It modifies classical MAUT techniques in two primary ways: its treatment of nonlinearity of model inputs (discussed later), and its focus on problem objectives rather than candidate alternatives. The purpose of the VFT model is to create a single, composite *value* rating for alternative solutions or choices. The model achieves this by calculating a linear sum of all relevant factors, weighted by their importance. Each factor is assessed individually, according to the response in factor value according to the different aspects of the specific alternative being rated. The VFT method is further discussed by Shepetukha [12].

VFT incorporates nonlinearity through specific functions applied to individual evaluation measures. The expert decision makers-subject matter experts (SMEs) provide the objectives and their respective evaluation measures. They also provide single-dimension response functions that convert some measurable level of achievement (e.g., dollar value of salary) into the model value that represents level of objective achievement (e.g., standard of living), which can then be converted into a normalized level of objective attainment. These single-dimension values are typically exponential, piecewise linear, or discrete functions [13,14].

The single-dimension value functions convert the original evaluation measure values into normalized objective attainment values, using an inverse transformation of a value graph of the objectives. The value graph could take any form (e.g., an exponential curve) as long as the form can be represented as a function. The x-axis represents the evaluation measure, over its entire range. The y-axis represents the normalized relative percent of objective achievement. Commonly, the scales for the objective attainment values are normalized between 0 and 1 [14].

The VFT model now is complete except for a multiobjective value function. The most common multiobjective value function used with VFT takes the additive form

$$v(x_1, \dots, x_n) = \sum_{i=1}^{n} w_i * v_i(x_i), \tag{1}$$

where x_i is the raw score of attribute i, v_i is the single-dimension value function for x_i, w_i is the importance weighting of attribute i, and n is the total number of evaluation measures. The sum represents the overall value across all competing objectives achieved by implementing this particular decision or set of choices.

Research supporting the use of additivity in a VFT model has been established [11,13,14]. The prerequisite condition for an additive value function is that of mutual preferential independence among attributes. This can be established through careful, proper selection and arrangement of objectives within a value hierarchy. This is supported by Kirkwood's Theorems 9.19 and 9.20, in addition to Theorem 3.7 of Keeney and Raiffa [13,15]. Clemen suggests formal testing procedures as well [13].

VFT is certainly an appropriate decision analysis (DA) method for our resource constrained force mix selection problem. It provides a single, integrated value for relative achievement against multiple objectives in a subjective setting, and combines them in a manner that accounts for the nonlinearity of responses. The method achieves this while keeping the values and objectives of the decision maker as the highest priority. This *value focused* approach is preferable to an *alternatives focused* approach because an alternatives-focused method limits potential solutions to a predetermined and finite set of choices. VFT provides the decision maker with a (potentially infinite) wider range of choices that meet the requirements contained in the value model. Following a background review and comparison of many candidate DA theories and methodologies, VFT was selected as the method for modeling this decision situation.

Identification and Treatment of Factors

The value hierarchy was constructed in two major phases. First, the factors (objectives) and their hierarchical relationships and weights were developed from existing literature and subject matter experts. Next, the representative functions for converting objective criteria achievement into measures of objective satisfaction were determined. Each phase will be covered in detail.

Once the initial list of factors was complete, interviews with the SMEs were conducted following the critical decision method (CDM; discussed below). Interview subjects (SMEs) included 34 campaign planning experts from HQ USAF, Air Combat Command, Air Force Southern Command, Air Force Special Operations Command, Air Force Central Command (CentAF), Joint Forces Command, USAF Fighter Weapons School, RED FLAG, USAF Air Expeditionary Forces Center (AEFC), USAF College of Aerospace Doctrine (CADRE), and the AFSOC Command and Control School. The USAF Reserves were included as representatives within the AEFC. The pool of experts included a wide range of diversity in operational experience. The subject pool had 26 members with operational pilot experience spanning a variety of military aircraft, including: F-15, F-16, F-4, F-111, A-10, C-130, KC-10, KC-135, and B-52. Of the 34 total SMEs, eight were career logisticians. Each subject met the following experience requirements: minimum grade of O-4 (or civilian equivalent), minimum of 12 years USAF operational experience, and a minimum of two years of campaign planning experience. This highly diversified subject pool provided a broad range of perspectives and issues, enhancing external validity and generalizability.

CDM is a method of semistructured interviewing developed by Klein, Calderwood and MacGregor [16]. It emphasizes the study of nonobservable skills and expert thinking [17]. CDM applies cognitive probes to the critical decision points that require expert-level decisions or judgements that put the focus on those *most critical* cognitive points or tasks of a job [16]. Using CDM, "issues can be described as points in the campaign planning process where critical decisions, decisions that a novice would have sufficient difficulty overcoming, may be required" [8]. *Critical issues* for this research are those that could hinder selection of the best force mix.

CDM interviews were conducted using directed questioning to elicit "critical decision points" from the SME [18,19]. This research asked each SME to apply their own direct experience to the following question. "What are the critical extrinsic factors in determining the value of a candidate campaign asset (MRR) set?" This approach, coupled with the diverse respondent sample, ensured a high degree of diversity of opinion and increased generalizability. In addition, each participant was exposed to the factors extracted from the literature using content analysis only after they had exhausted their own contributions, and given additional opportunity to expand their list of factors. Each participant was required to provide a specific definition for each factor they provided. In addition, they were asked to comment upon and make corrections to factors provided by the researcher (from the literature). Finally, the participants performed an evaluation of and provided corrections to Buzo's factors from his initial research [8].

The specific factors and their definitions are provided. *Constraints* represent the *go-no go* criteria previously discussed, which were used for filtering the solution space for the intrinsic optimization portion of the model. They are as follows.

(1) Politics—desired force mix allowed?

(2) Operating location—runway length and width adequate?
(3) Operating location—ramp space sufficient?
(4) Operating location—runway and ramp weight capacity sufficient?
(5) Operating location—no IFR, distance less than 700 (fighters) and 3000 (bombers) miles from targets?
(6) Desired force mix available?

The remaining extrinsic factors identified were carried forward into the hierarchical VFT model (all from [9]). A complete list of factors can be seen with the weighting values provided by the SMEs in Table 2.

Table 2. Relative weights of hierarchical value function factors.

Factor	Low	Avg.	High
Host Nation Support	0.025831	0.097000	0.120301
Multi-N Compatibility	0.018786	0.049763	0.090226
Ability to Resupply	0.007380	0.049823	0.174000
Basing	0.215061	0.366000	0.625002
POL Storage	0.067007	0.080772	0.098626
Fighter Distance	0.019145	0.030507	0.049313
Bomber Distance	0.006382	0.026225	0.030000
MSA: Fighter	0.024657	0.063280	0.179999
MSA: Bomber	0.012328	0.056241	0.179999
Climate	0.003522	0.018234	0.030000
Topography	0.015000	0.031175	0.067000
Tanker Support	0.022336	0.062375	0.090226
Force Mix Usage	0.078901	0.137000	0.180451
Force Mix Flexibility	0.011272	0.036324	0.067000
Force Mix Utilization	0.011272	0.031337	0.051000
Mission Capable Rate	0.045000	0.072559	0.1072110
Enemy Capability	0.209999	0.400000	0.624633
Enemy vs. USAF Capability	0.090000	0.210197	0.394505
Enemy ISR	0.030000	0.095283	0.178685
Enemy Interference	0.090000	0.096773	0.134014

Once the factors were identified, they had to be scored by the SMEs in order to establish their relative weight in the VFT hierarchy. Respondents to the survey first classified the factors onto four *parent* categories: host nation, force mix usage, enemy capabilities, and basing. The host nation category included issues directly related to the political considerations of the campaign, multinational compatibility and resupply capability. Force mix usage refers to the ability of the asset set to achieve steady state capability during the campaign, to include inter-mission flexibility, force mix utilization rate, and mission capable status. Enemy capabilities include

USAF vs. enemy capability ratio, enemy intelligence, surveillance, and reconnaissance impact, and enemy interference impact. The basing category included issues specific to the operating location, which covers the remaining issues. Respondents were then asked to provide *weights* or measures of relative importance to achieving campaign objectives, allocating weights that sum to 1.0 among the categories. This was repeated within the broad categories among the specific subfactors. The result is a comprehensive list of weights for all extrinsic factors. The final calculation distributed the category and subcategory weights to determine the global individual category weights. The results are included in Table 2.

Before selecting final (rounded) values for the individual global factor weights, a sensitivity analysis was performed on the effect of high versus low values on the overall outcome. Due to the sensitivity of results on individual values selected for some factors, we decided to retain the high, low, and average values in the decision model to present to the decision maker.

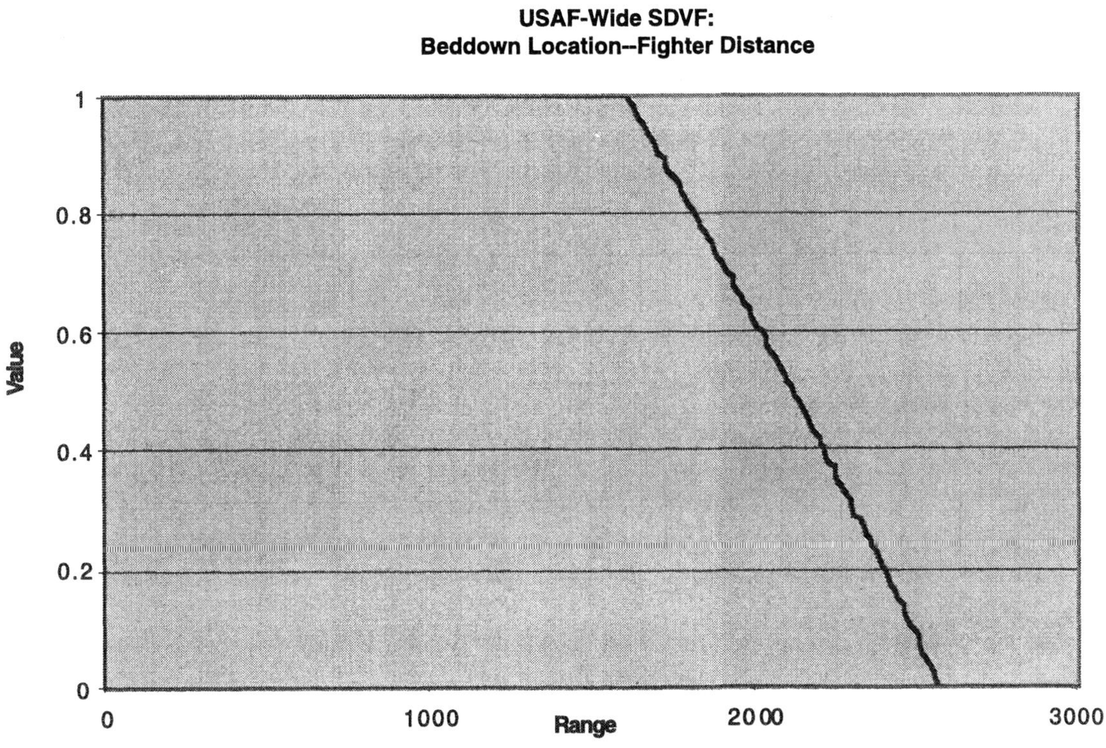

Figure 5. Single dimension value function.

After the individual factor (objective) weights were calculated, single-dimension value functions (SDVFs) were constructed, relating how achievement against an individual objective would translate into an achievement value for that objective. The importance of the SDVFs cannot be overemphasized.

> "The developed single-dimension value functions (SDVFs) are the heart of the VFT decision support tool. It is these values that reflect the subjective judgements of the participating experts in a quantitative fashion, allowing for quantification of the entire decision situation" [9].

In Figure 5, we see one of the SDVFs (beddown location-fighter distance) used to convert the nautical miles of the distance from the operating location for a generic fighter aircraft base into an objective satisfaction measure between 0 and 1. For this example, the objective is fully satisfied until the operating location is approximately 1600 nm away. At this point, the objective satisfaction drops off following a linear curve until the location is approximately 2500 nm away. At this point the objective is no longer being satisfied.

SDVFs were elicited from the same pool of SMEs, and included the CentAF respondents from Buzo's [8] research. This resulted in five different SDVFs for each of the 16 extrinsic factors (80 total). These SDVFs (five per factor) needed to be successfully consolidated into one per factor in order to provide generalizability across potential users. The approach used was to create a composite representation of each of the five response functions into a single function. From Filcek's [9] study we have the following.

> For each factor, the individual SDVFs were analyzed to determine which involved the highest number of functions in its makeup. For example, one SDVF might have a piecewise linear function for the first third of its range, then an exponential function for the next third, and finally either full (1) or zero value for the final third, with no function. If this SDVF had more of these components than any of the others (for this factor) then the final USAF-wide SDVF must possess at least that many components. Once the number of required components had been established, average midpoints among all five SDVFs—for each of the component ranges—were determined. Finally, the appropriate functions, either exponential or piecewise linear, were input for each component range, producing an overall USAF-wide SDVF that accurately represents the preferences of the decision makers.

This process was repeated for all 16 factors. As a result, each factor could now be represented by six different functions—one for each of the original inputs, and a generalized composite. This allowed a decision maker to select from among a library of SDVFs, choosing the most applicable function for their specific scenario. The composite model (USAF-wide) could therefore be used as a default model for computing the extrinsic values of candidate force mixes. The composite functions are included in Appendix B. The final model included all 96 SDVFs (five specific and one composite for each of the 16 factors), in addition to all of the parent and average factor weights. This allows decision makers to choose from among the captured opinions of the group of experts singly, or in composite, depending upon their individual circumstances. The result is a family of VFT models in one model, enhancing the usability and applicability of the decision support tool.

At this point, the content analysis of the literature and SME interviews have given us a list of multiple objectives to be satisfied. The Delphi interviews provided us with relative weights in a hierarchical model. Finally, additional SME interviews provided us with the SDVFs that could be used to translate measurable levels of performance against definite criteria into relative satisfaction values for the individual objectives. The end result is a hierarchical VFT model that calculates a single measure of value in satisfying multiple objectives, according to the decision performance against definite measurable criteria. We can now apply our model against competing asset sets of approximately equal intrinsic value in order to determine overall value.

Buzo [8] and Filcek [9] both validated the individual SDVF and composite SDVFs with the subject matter experts at the conclusion of their research. In most cases, agreement was reached as to the representation of the individual and composite SDVFs, as well as the overall scoring of the "total value" represented by each force mix. Indeed, even when differing SDVFs were used, the respondents generally agreed with the overall result. Filcek [9] explicitly investigated the sensitivity of the overall VFT model result to differences in SDVF composition. At the extrema (using the "most different" combinations of SDVFs compared against the composite VFT model), Filcek found the ranking of alternatives to exchange no more than five positions in the top 30 ranked force mix preferences; and to exchange no alternative more than two positions in the ranking. While this seemed to be a satisfactory result, the model retains a full library of SDVFs to allow individual decision-makers the latitude to select the SDVF that most closely matches his or her perception of the situation.

Use of the Hierarchical VFT Model

The completed VFT model was programmed into a Microsoft Excel spreadsheet for testing, and integrated into the full model using visual basic functions. The basic model input is the force mix (specific asset set) to be scored, from the intrinsic portion of the meta model (previously discussed). These asset sets have been selected by finding those MRRs that achieve the greatest performance against the commander's preferences for tasks, according to their capabilities, constrained by their availabilities. The decision maker interacts with the model on the selection of which SDVFs to use for the specific scenario, and reviews and validates the ability of each MRR type to satisfy the objective represented by the SDVF. The model then calculates the total extrinsic value (modified from equation (1)) according to

$$V_e = \sum_{i=1}^{m} \sum_{j=1}^{n} \mathrm{FW}_j * T_j\left(\mathrm{MRR}_i\right), \tag{2}$$

where i increments across the total number m of different MRRs included in the asset set, j increments across the total number n of extrinsic factors (in this case, 16); T_j represents the transformation function of the jth SDVF, MRR_i is the MRR type i being scored against SDVF j, and FW_j is the global factor weight of factor j in the hierarchy. The resulting V_e is the scored *extrinsic* value in the range $[0,1]$ of the asset set.

This V_e can now be applied against the *intrinsic* score V_i to provide a single overall asset set value V_o. It should be noted at this point that while the intrinsic score rank structure is linear, scalar, and bounded by 0 and some arbitrary large number, the extrinsic scores are nonlinear, nonscalar, and bound by 0 and 1. Indeed, intrinsic and extrinsic value represent very different value concepts or dimensions of value. The greedy intrinsic-valued model in Section 3 and Filcek [9] were, in effect, addressing different questions. Therefore, many methods could be used to combine V_i and V_e into an overall V_o number.

However, a likely method suggests itself from the interviews conducted with the SMEs in the conduct of this investigation. Many interview respondents suggested that V_i represents a *hard* or primary consideration, while V_e is a *soft* or secondary consideration. If we assume that the concept of value represented by V_i dominates or takes precedence over the concept of value represented by V_e, then the solution is readily apparent. The force mixes selected by the greedy intrinsic-valued algorithm represent an "optimal" set where all members are approximately equal with respect to V_i. A simple multiplicative approach

$$V_o = V_i V_e \tag{3}$$

would then represent a logical method for combining intrinsic and extrinsic value. The issue of how to best to combine V_i and V_e is an open research question.

5. APPLICATION

The final decision support tool was developed at the Air Force Institute of Technology during 2001 with the assistance of several contributors: the Air Force Research Laboratory Human Effectiveness office, the Defense Advanced Research Projects Agency, and the TASC Corporation. The completed model uses a visual basic shell for data input and presentation, integrated into a Microsoft Access database and Excel spreadsheet applications. While the model is not ready for implementation in a real-world application environment (much of the data is notional), the majority of functionality is in place. Our beta version of the overall model was then tested (verified and validated), mainly for functionality and reasonableness. Funding was not available for full-scale development or testing; however, initial results show promise. The model was run against a small set of notional data involving several scenarios requiring the deployment of various MRR sets. The test "commanders" were stepped through the model by the designers, who assisted with the model execution. Results were generally positive; but certainly inconclusive, given the data set we used. No full scale development or testing has yet been completed.

The following narrative provides a brief description of how the model would be used. Assume a situation develops requiring the application of combat airpower. The decision making team would initialize the tool by describing the situation in terms of the task preference curve (desired sortie or task mix). This preference curve would represent the slopes of the individual objective function coefficients, giving the relative desirability of achieving any task relative to any other task, as a vector of increasing overall value. The criteria for the extrinsic *go-no go* VFT factors would also be updated at this time. These factors provide an immediate screening of potential MRRs that might not be suitable for inclusion. The decision makers then review the library of SDVFs, selecting those which are most appropriate for the specific scenario (or modifying existing SDVFs if none are suitable). At this point, the model would engage the various databases and begin seeking the MRR sets with the highest possible intrinsic value, as follows.

> The model filters all unsuitable MRRs from consideration, and creates the updated A-M TPM for those MRRs still in contention. The intrinsic optimization algorithm begins selecting the best MRRs (according to their task suitability) to satisfy the preference curve, tracing a vector of MRR sets of increasing intrinsic value along the curve which are resource feasible. The intrinsic algorithm concludes by recording those MRR sets which provide equally satisfactory results at the farthest feasible point along the preference curve.

After these candidate MRR sets of approximately equal intrinsic value are identified, the user is prompted for VFT weighting or SDVF mapping if not previously accomplished. The MRR sets are scored according to the VFT model, and their new overall score is calculated. The VFT scoring applies the range of overall score values according to the high, average, and low factor weightings retained from the value hierarchy. This provides the decision makers with a range of overall scores and degree of overlap between MRR sets to choose from.

Note that at this point, when the decision maker selects the final force mix, the vector of increasingly valuable MRR sets (from zero to best) is retained. The vector itself represents the best series of MRRs to be phased into the operating location over time, in order to generate the most combat capability, in the most desirable form, over time. The model has constructed a list of materials, required to create the most desired MRRs, as defined by the commander, subject to constrained lift, according to temporal precedence. In this way, combat capability is generated in the best time sequence of its resource constrained form, considering a variety of factors both intrinsic and extrinsic.

6. SUMMARY AND CONCLUSIONS

Our research provides a methodology for rationally assigning relative value to material resources over time, in order to improve the linkage between what *arrives* in theater on any given day and what is *needed* on any given day. An immediate benefit is that deploying resources are clearly traceable to the commander's prioritized mission needs. Second, this methodology helps ensure that we use constrained lift wisely by deploying *only* what is needed.

A third, less obvious benefit accrues as well. Research by DARPA's Advanced Logistics Project [20] demonstrated that agent computing technology and the internet can be used to radically improve the Department of Defense's capability to develop and monitor the execution of the logistics plans associated with major military deployments. One gain is that the time needed to develop such plans can be reduced from weeks or months to a few hours. Given this capability, it is now possible to develop several competing plans. Our methodology can then be used to discriminate among alternative logistic plans, by providing a measure of the relative intrinsic and extrinsic utilities of these plans.

Successful implementation of our methodology must overcome several obstacles. A key challenge is the ability to acquire the logistics business rules needed to reasonably map selected mission-ready resources into pallet positions. These rules are typically derived from prior deployment records and from interviews with experts, and can be difficult to obtain. A secondary challenge may arise when seeking agreement from experts on the relative rankings for the asset-mission task preference matrix. For example, Air Force and Army planners may disagree with each other on the relative suitability of each service's respective airborne platforms for the close air support mission. A final challenge (to military application) is that our *bottom-up* methodology represents a much different way of logistics planning for deployment than the *top-down* approach used today—cultural resistance to change could prove to be a significant issue. Current planning methods relying on assumptions of standardized, aggregated combat capability provided by critical closure dates, would become irrelevant.

Our current research is investigating alternative approaches of assigning MRRs to missions, that will guarantee that the MRR sets identified during the intrinsic optimization stage are indeed optimal. One approach employs a large-scale linear integer program [21], while the other uses a multiobjective, evolutionary algorithm [22]. Additional research is addressing the ability to optimize MRR combinations from "on-hand" resources [21] and to assign costs and value to materials in transit. A promising area of research would investigate how interactions between candidate MRRs might best be captured in the A-M TPM (our current matrix assumes that MRRs are mutually independent, however, synergies can result from packaging certain combinations of different MRRs).

APPENDIX A
VALUE FUNCTION FACTORS

MULTI-NATIONAL COMPATIBILITY. The extent to which host nation assets, to include combat aircraft, equipment, spares, and ground support equipment can be incorporated along side and into USAF combat aircraft [8].

BEDDOWN LOCATION—FIGHTER DISTANCE FROM TARGETS, REFUELED. The effectiveness of an individual aircraft type within a candidate force mix is dependent upon its distance from the operating location to its primary mission targets.

BEDDOWN LOCATION—BOMBER DISTANCE FROM TARGETS, REFUELED. The effectiveness of an individual bomber aircraft type within a candidate force mix is dependent upon its distance from the operating location to its primary mission targets.

ABILITY TO RESUPPLY. Continuation of aerospace missions from the operating location is dependent upon the ability of USAF forces to resupply equipment, materials, and spares as necessary. The candidate operating location can impact resupply capability and combine with individual aircraft resupply requirements to affect overall mission accomplishment. Aircraft that require smaller amounts of POL, munitions, and other equipment and spares will have a higher independent value than aircraft that require more resources, especially if resources are difficult to come by at the candidate operating location.

MUNITIONS STORAGE AREA—FIGHTER. Continued combat fighter operations depend on the operating location's ability to store and deliver adequate munitions in a timely manner. Fighters can bring to theater only one load of munitions each. Additional aerospace missions require the operating location to store and deliver munitions.

MUNITIONS STORAGE AREA—BOMBER. Same as Munitions Storage Area—Fighter.

PETROLEUM, OIL, AND LUBRICANTS (POL) STORAGE AND DELIVERY. The operating location's POL system includes storage and supply from both military and host nation contracted sources. POL capability for a particular force mix must take into consideration the per-sortie POL requirements of each individual aircraft in the force mix as well as the daily sortie requirements for each type of aircraft [8].

TANKER SUPPORT PROVIDED. Depending upon the operating location's distance from enemy targets and the requirements of individual aircraft and aircraft types within a force mix, tanker support may be required or highly desirable.

OPERATING LOCATION—TOPOGRAPHY. The extent to which natural and man-made land formations in and around the operating location affect the ability of individual aircraft within a force mix to take-off, land, and conduct operations.

OPERATING LOCATION—CLIMATE. The extent to which heat, humidity, wind, and adverse weather conditions affect the ability of force mixes to conduct operations at or around the operating location.

MISSION CAPABLE RATE OF FORCE MIX. Extent to which aircraft in a candidate force mix are operationally capable of performing aerospace missions as designated by the theater or component commander.

INTER-MISSION FLEXIBILITY. Extent to which individual aircraft types within a candidate force mix can perform all of the aerospace missions defined in AFM 1-1 and AFDD 2-1. The relative worth of the force mix would be highest if it could perform all of the missions required by the theater or component commander [8].

USAF VERSUS ENEMY CAPABILITY. The comparison of enemy assets to USAF combat aircraft assets as contained in the candidate force mix. Assuming U.S. forces' intelligence can discern the extent of the enemy's capability, this measure shows the relative worth of the amount of aircraft assets sent to the operating location. One issue addressed within the function is the number of USAF combat aircraft sent. The second issue is the capabilities of the enemy to counter the USAF force mix [8].

ENEMY INTELLIGENCE, SURVEILLANCE, AND RECONNAISSANCE (ISR) IMPACT. Addresses the enemy's ability to see or obtain information on U.S. activity at the operating location. Enemy ISR could be obtained through aerial or satellite photography, local sympathizers monitoring U.S. activity, or spies within the host nation working within or around the operating location [8]. Also necessarily addressed by this factor is the sensitivity to ISR of certain aircraft types within candidate force mixes, and the tradeoffs of such sensitivity with the enemy's ISR capabilities at the candidate operating location.

ENEMY INTERFERENCE. Addresses the enemy's ability to interfere with U.S. operations at the operating location. Interference is any action on the part of the enemy that could hamper U.S. combat operations. The interference could range from relatively harmless demonstrations and propaganda to bomb threats and actual sabotage upon USAF assets and harm to personnel. This necessarily includes defensibility of the operating location from all-out attack upon the base, considering the strength of opposing forces in the vicinity of the operating location as well as the projected defense forces in place and/or to be sent.

APPENDIX B

SINGLE DIMENSION VALUE FUNCTIONS

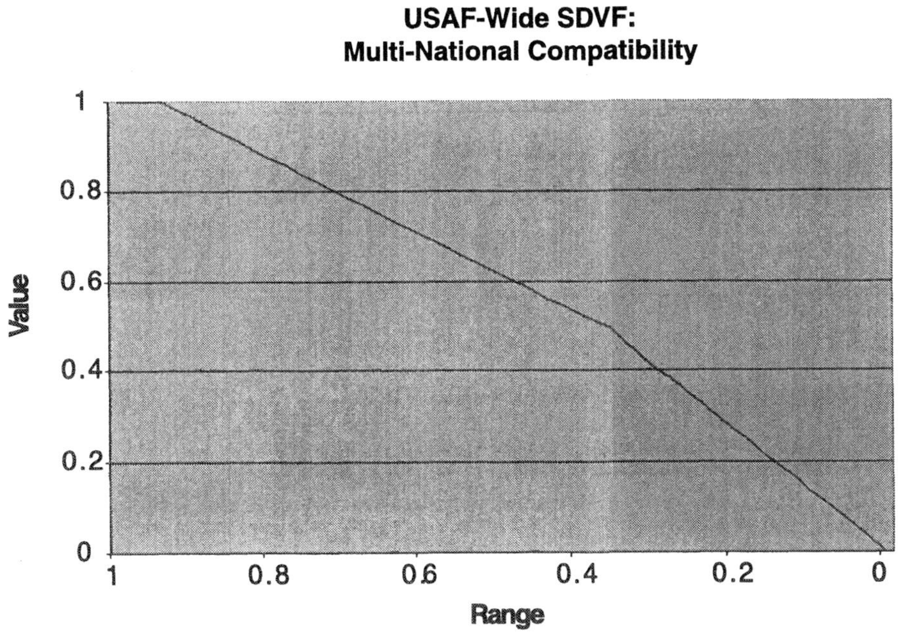

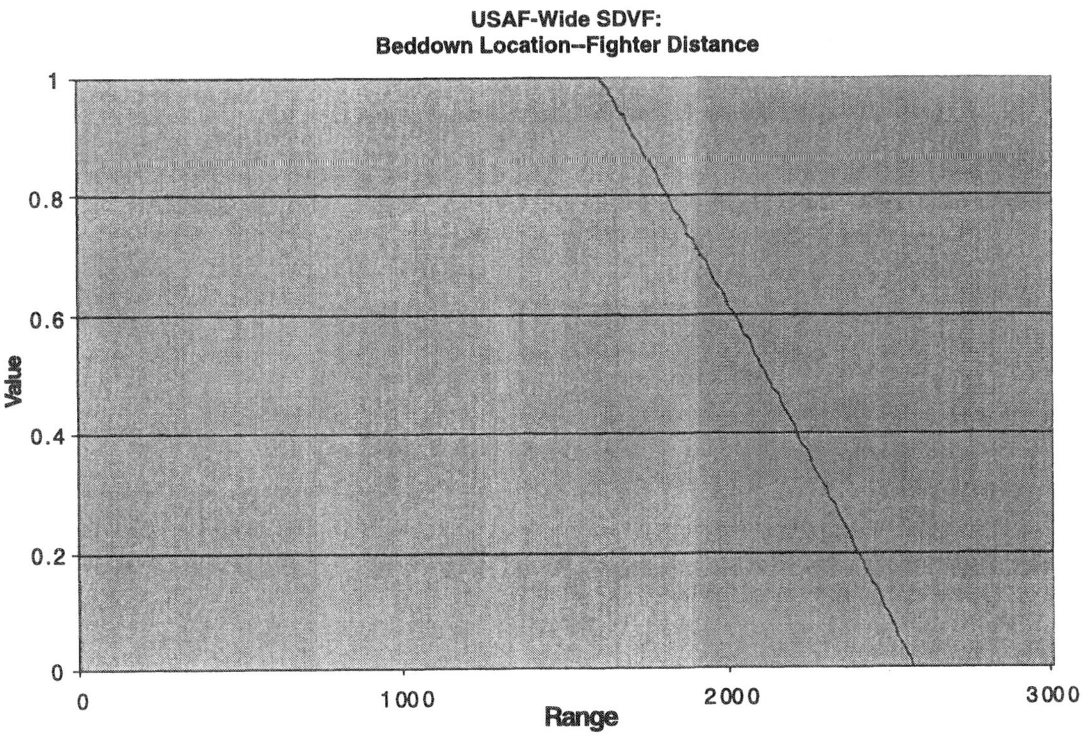

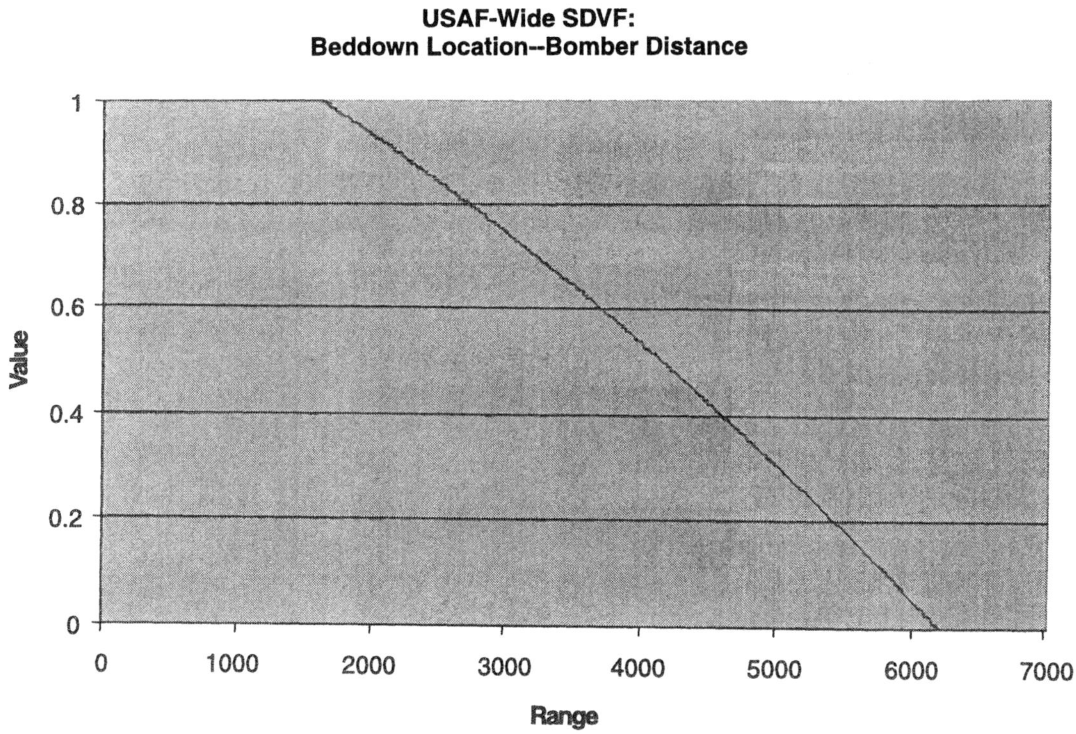
USAF-Wide SDVF:
Beddown Location--Bomber Distance
Value
1
0.8
0.6
0.4
0.2
0
0
1000
2000
3000
4000
5000
6000
7000
Range

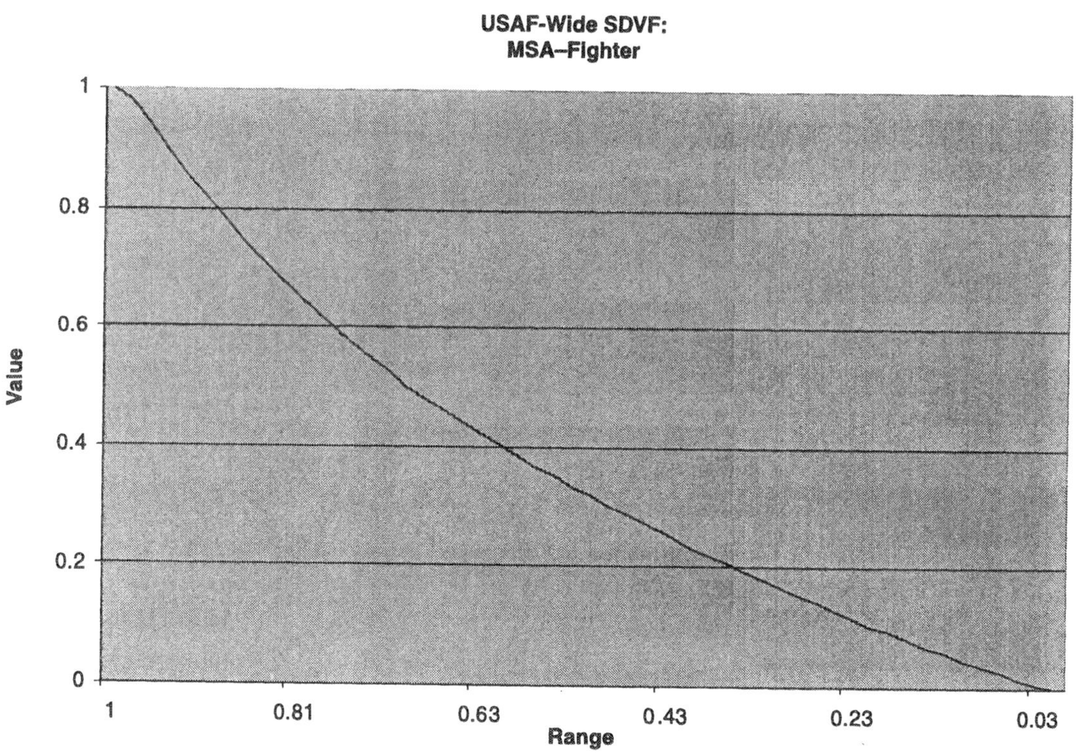
USAF-Wide SDVF:
MSA--Fighter
Value
1
0.8
0.6
0.4
0.2
0
1
0.81
0.63
0.43
0.23
0.03
Range

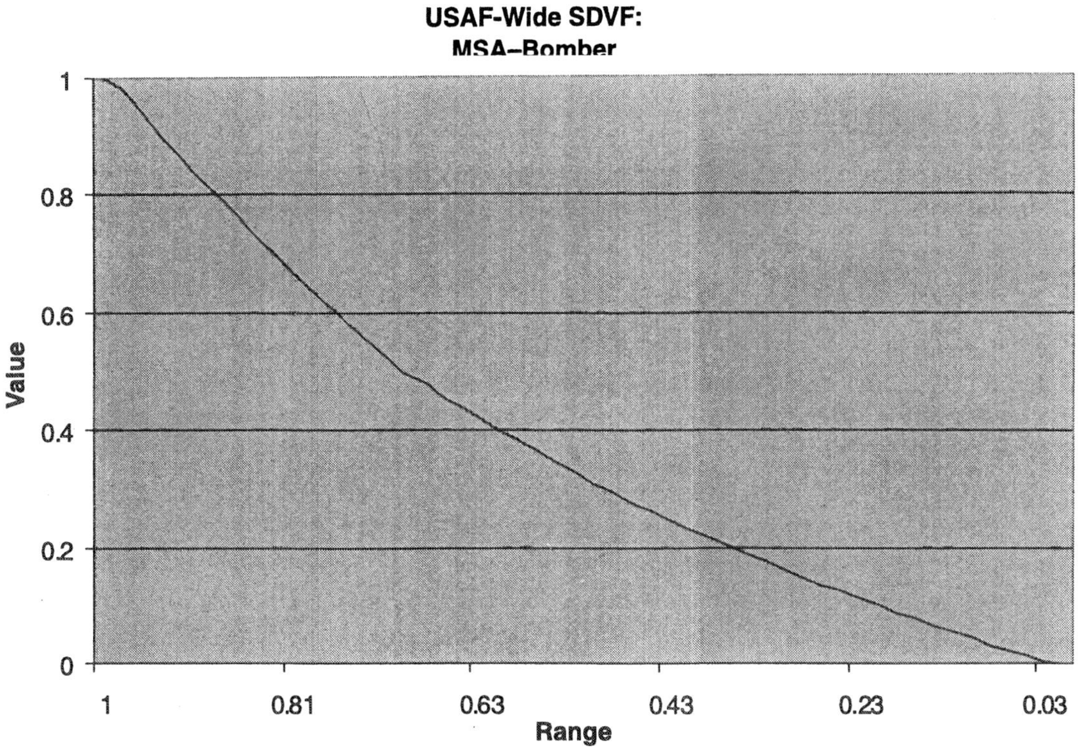
USAF-Wide SDVF:
MSA–Bomber
Value
1
0.8
0.6
0.4
0.2
0
Range
1
0.81
0.63
0.43
0.23
0.03

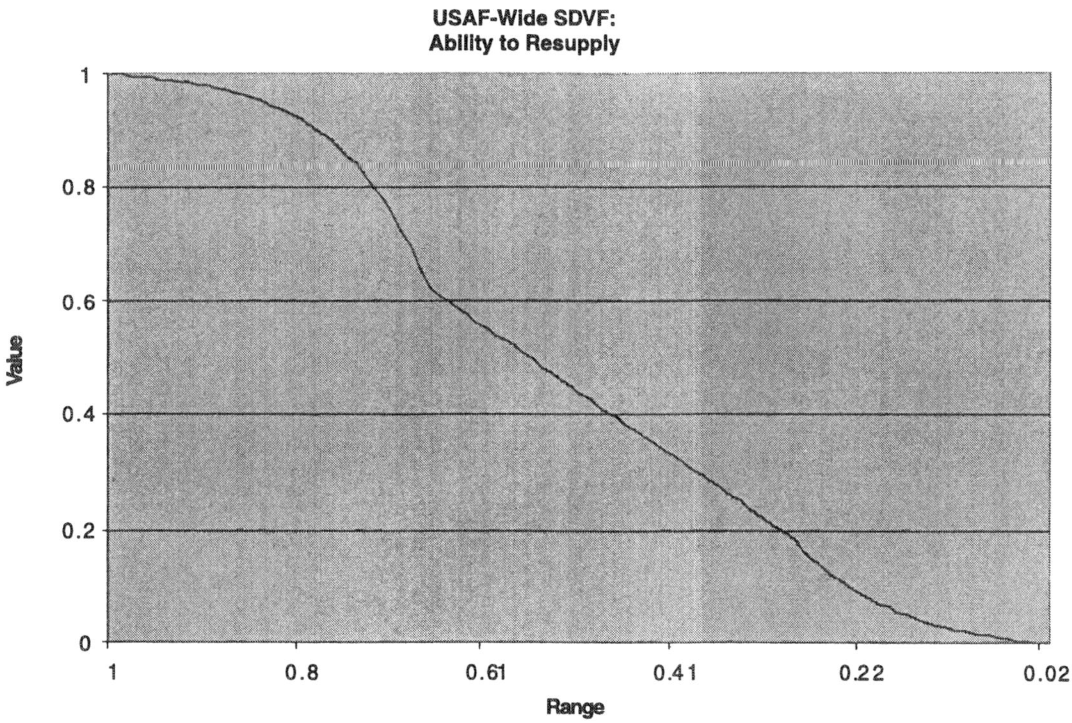
USAF-Wide SDVF:
Ability to Resupply
Value
1
0.8
0.6
0.4
0.2
0
Range
1
0.8
0.61
0.41
0.22
0.02

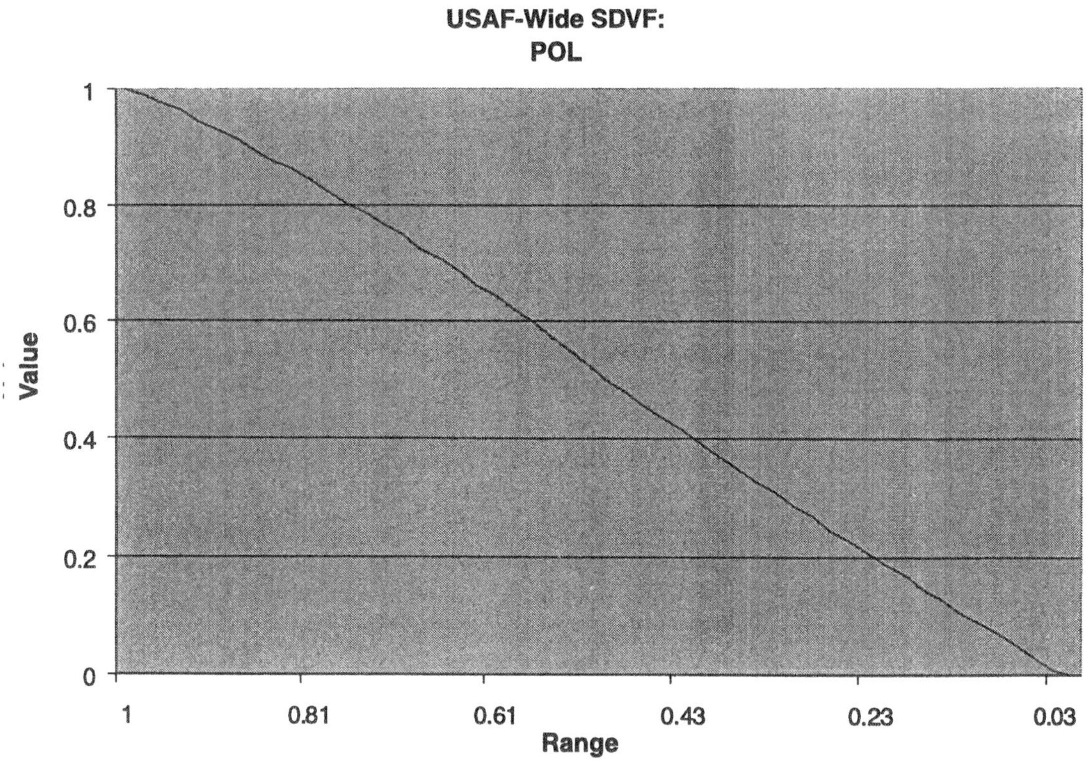
USAF-Wide SDVF:
POL
Value
1
0.8
0.6
0.4
0.2
0
1
0.81
0.61
0.43
0.23
0.03
Range

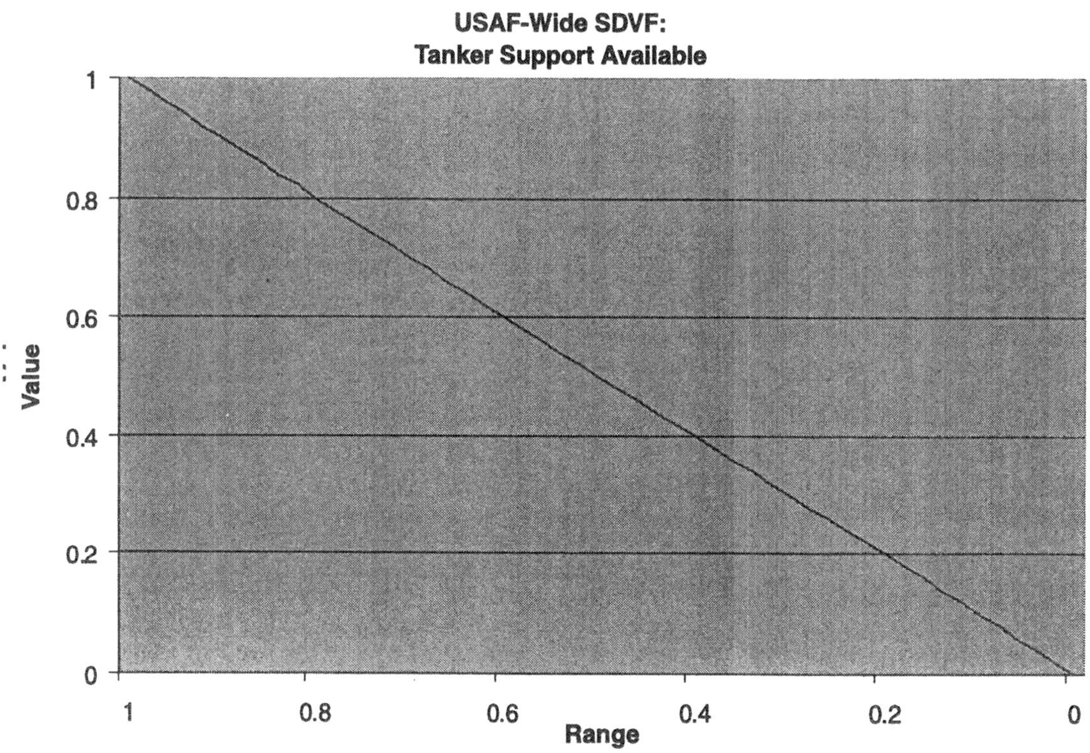
USAF-Wide SDVF:
Tanker Support Available
Value
1
0.8
0.6
0.4
0.2
0
1
0.8
0.6
0.4
0.2
0
Range

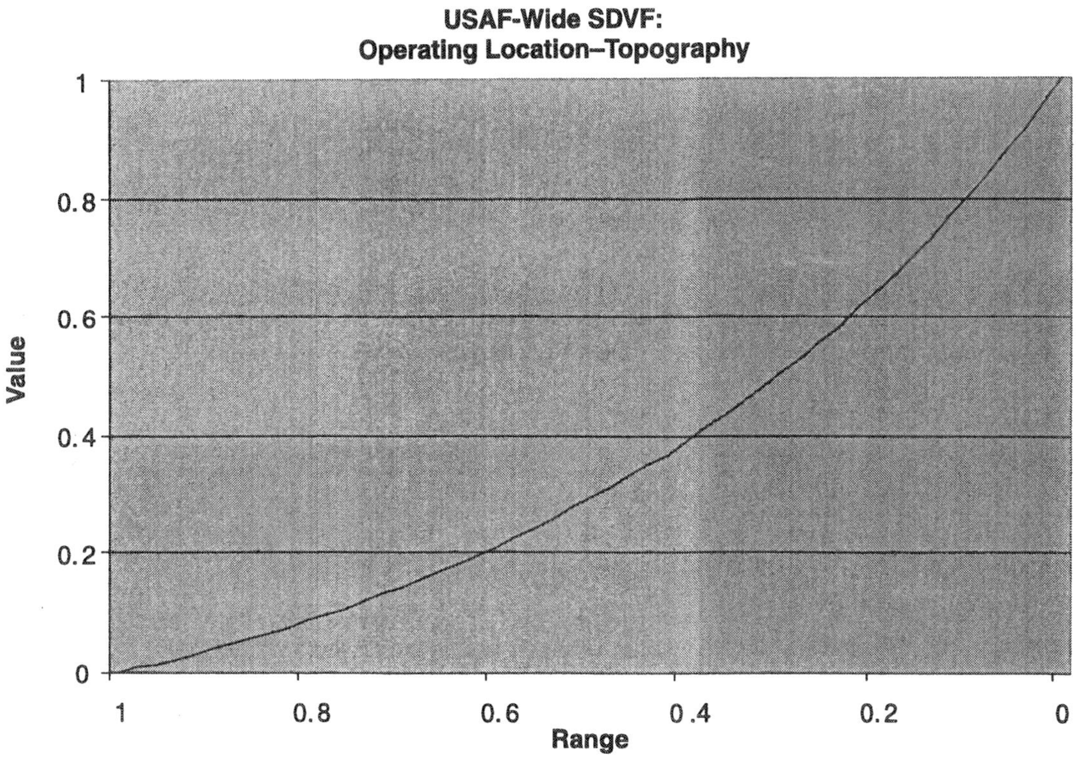
USAF-Wide SDVF:
Operating Location–Topography
Value
Range
1
0.8
0.6
0.4
0.2
0

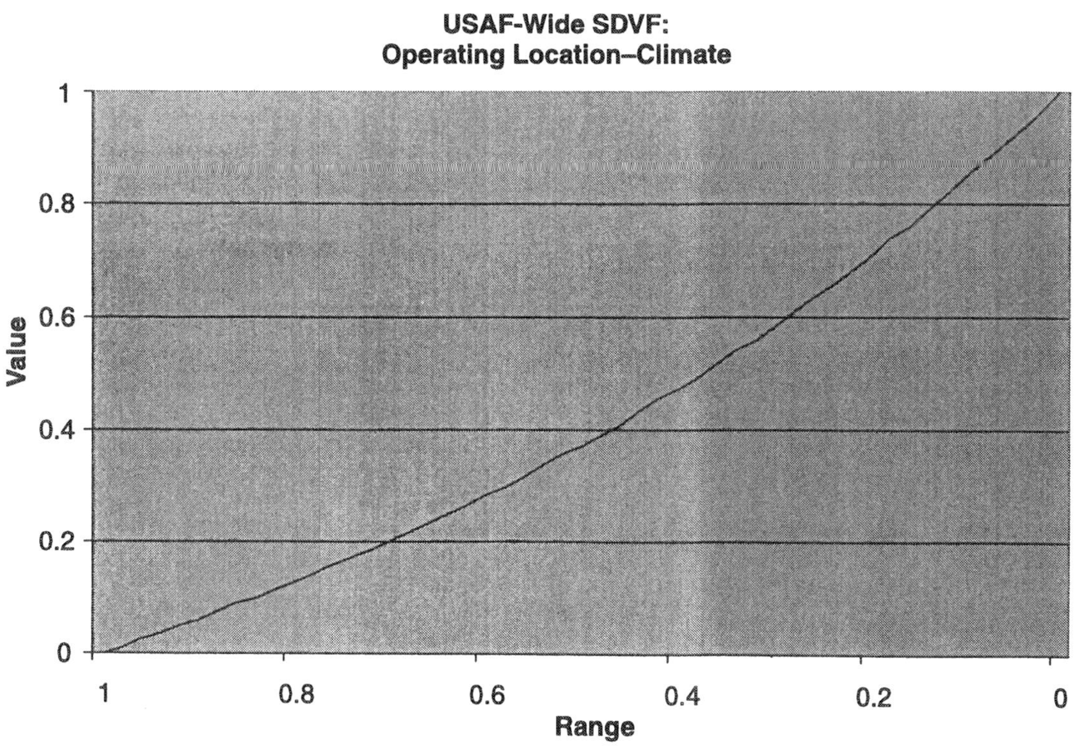
USAF-Wide SDVF:
Operating Location–Climate
Value
Range
1
0.8
0.6
0.4
0.2
0

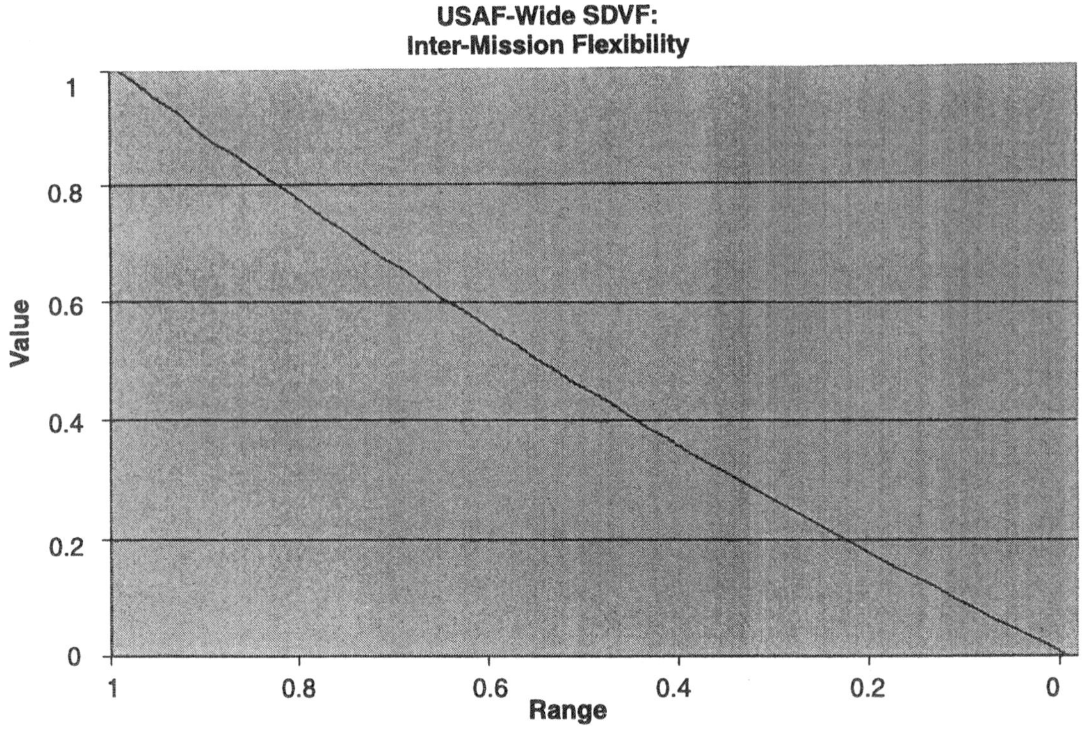
USAF-Wide SDVF:
Inter-Mission Flexibility
Value
1
0.8
0.6
0.4
0.2
0
1
0.8
0.6
0.4
0.2
0
Range

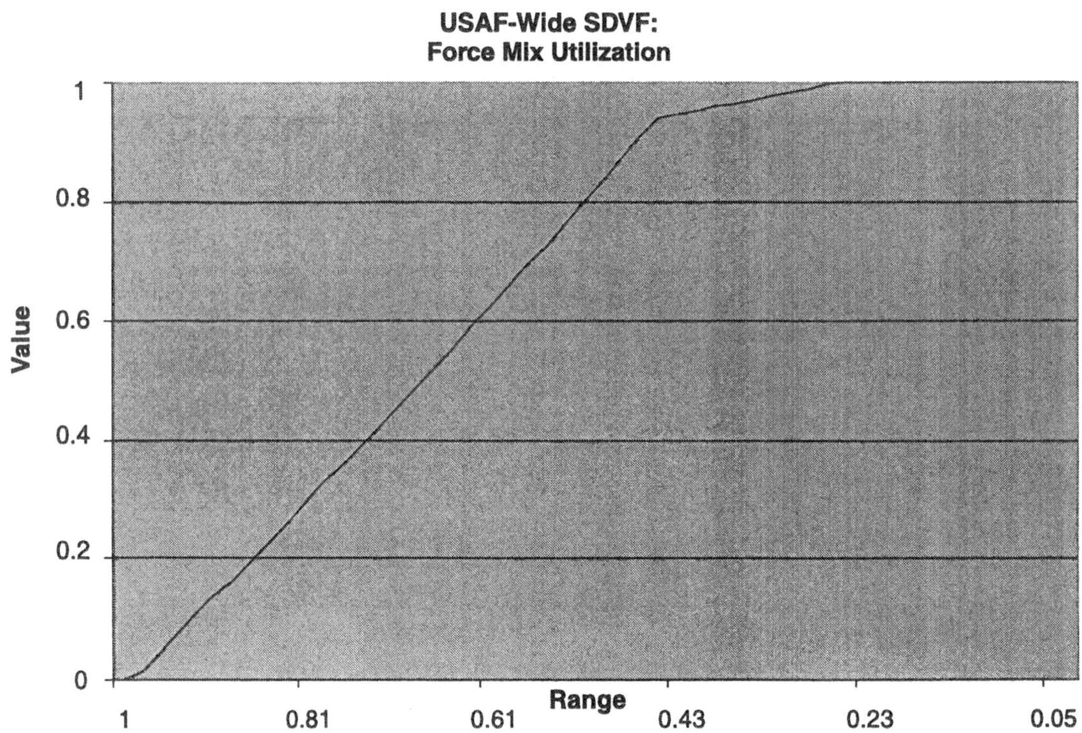
USAF-Wide SDVF:
Force Mix Utilization
Value
1
0.8
0.6
0.4
0.2
0
Range
1
0.81
0.61
0.43
0.23
0.05

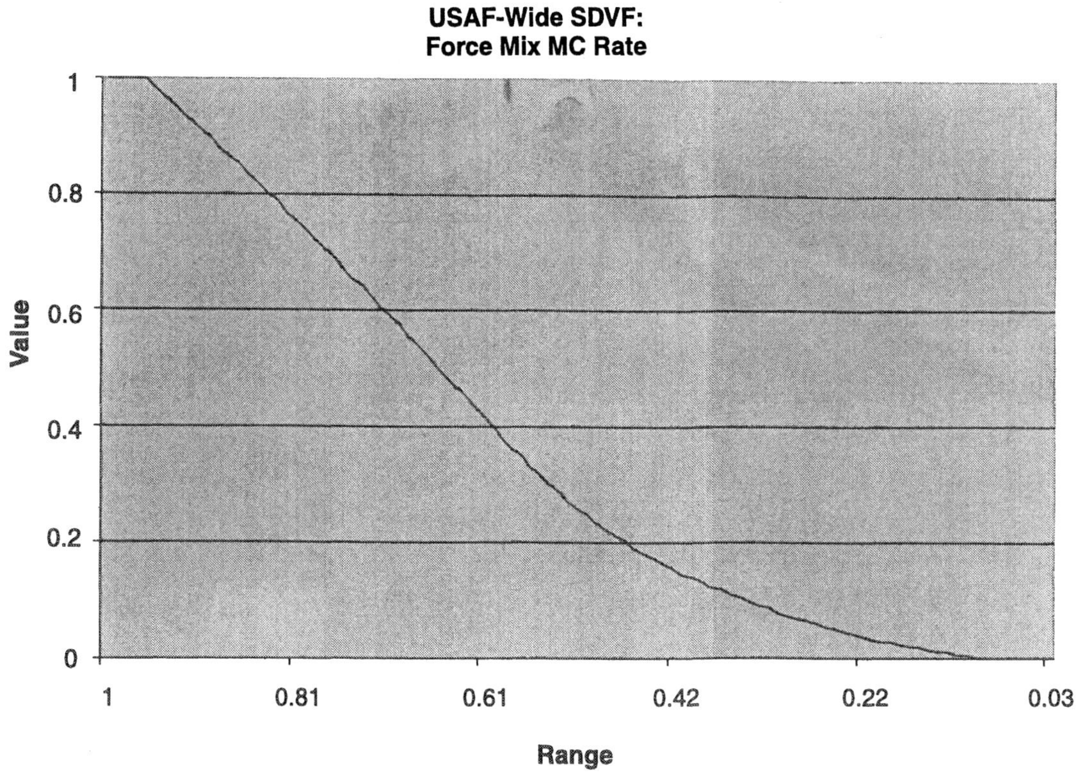
USAF-Wide SDVF:
Force Mix MC Rate
Value
1
0.8
0.6
0.4
0.2
0
1
0.81
0.61
0.42
0.22
0.03
Range

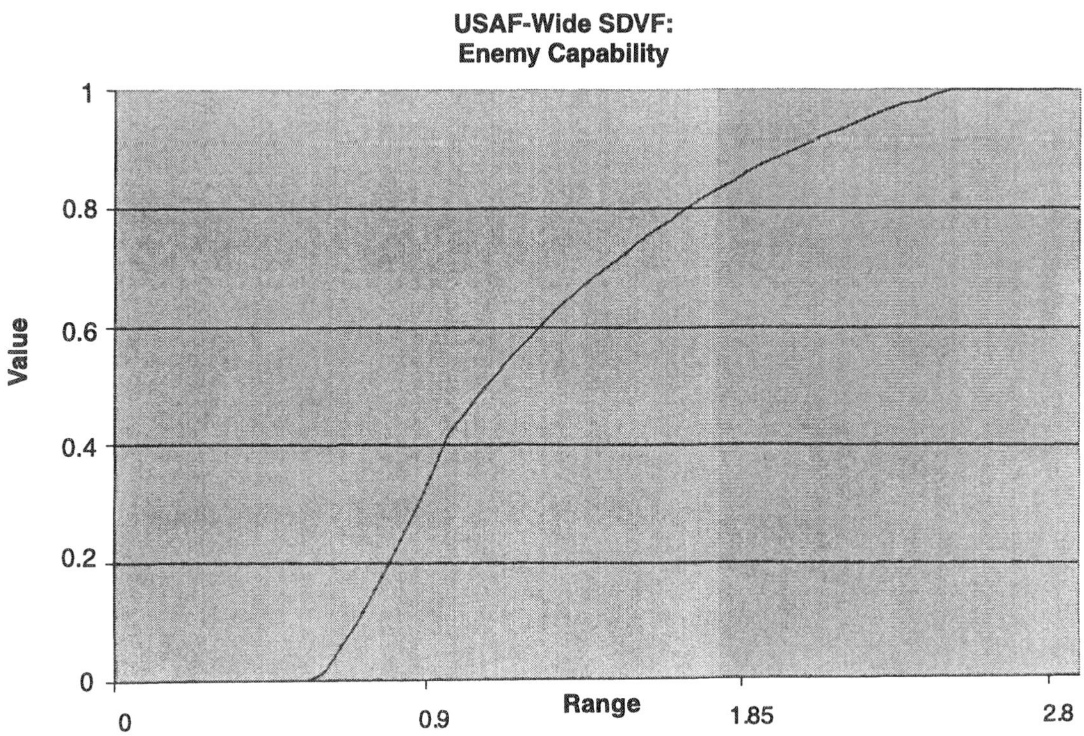
USAF-Wide SDVF:
Enemy Capability
Value
1
0.8
0.6
0.4
0.2
0
0
0.9
1.85
2.8
Range

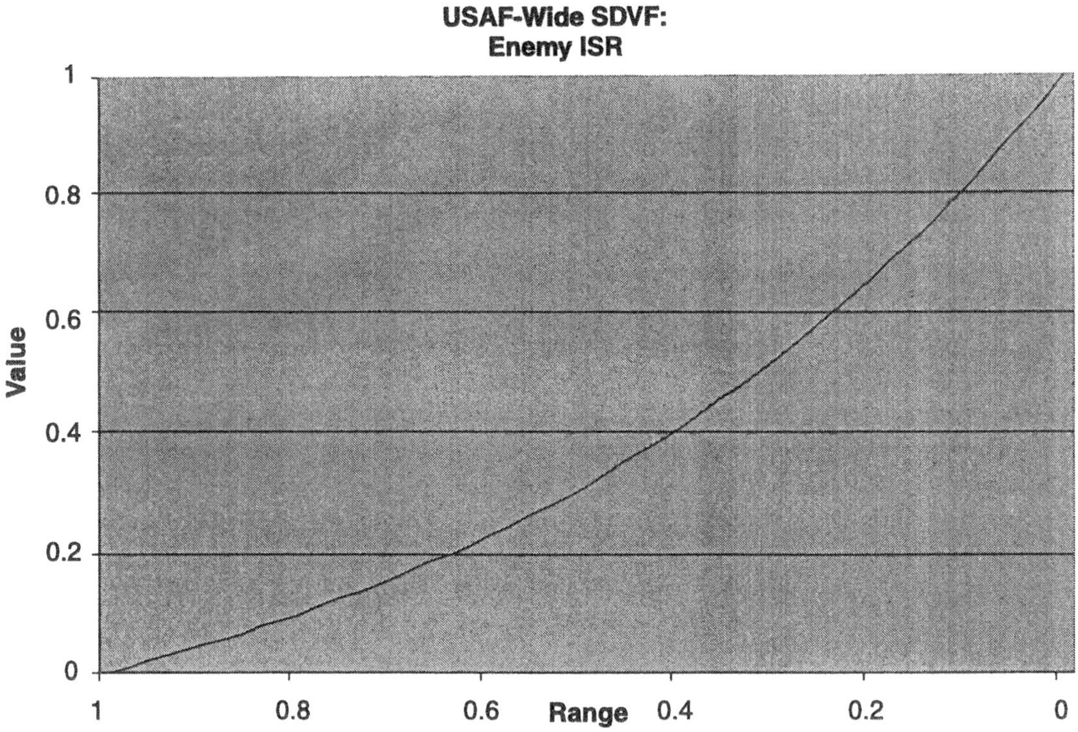
USAF-Wide SDVF:
Enemy ISR
Value
1
0.8
0.6
0.4
0.2
0
1
0.8
0.6
Range
0.4
0.2
0

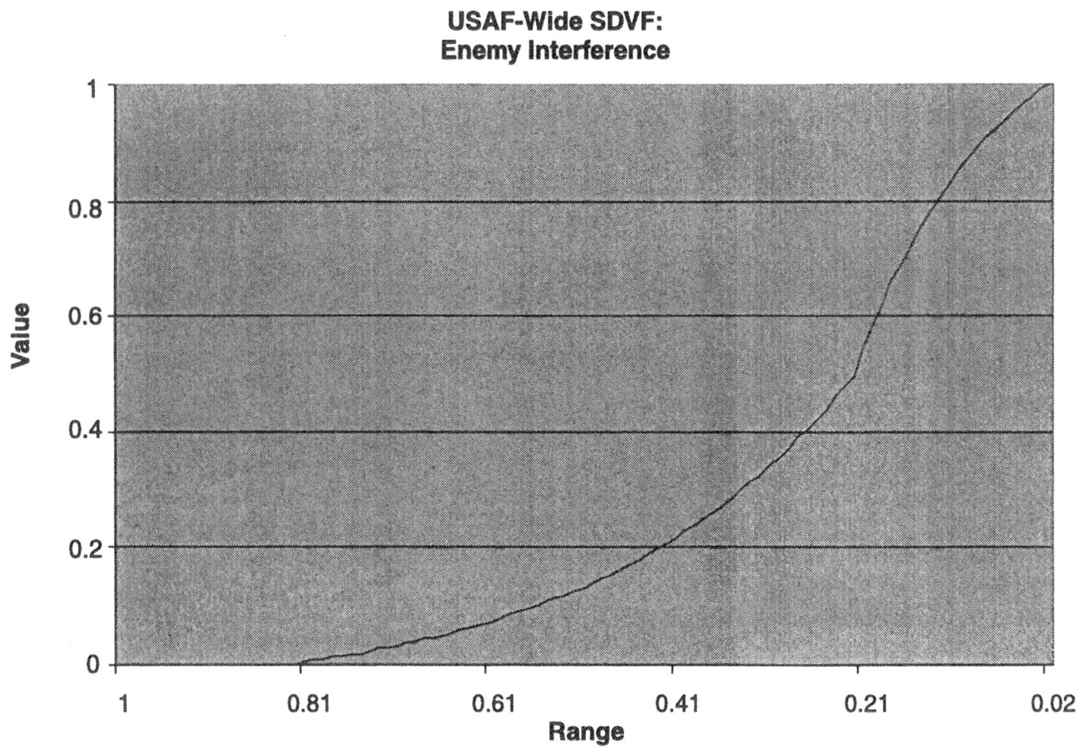
USAF-Wide SDVF:
Enemy Interference
Value
1
0.8
0.6
0.4
0.2
0
1
0.81
0.61
0.41
0.21
0.02
Range

REFERENCES

1. W.M. Newman and R.F. Sproull, *Principles of Interactive Computer Graphics*, Second Edition, McGraw-Hill, New York, (1979).
2. D. Hearn and M.P. Baker, *Computer Graphics*, Prentice Hall, Englewood Cliffs, NJ, (1997).
3. R.M. Antoine, Integer approximation of real valued preference curves, M.S. Thesis, AFIT/GLM/ENS/01J-01, School of Engineering and Management, Air Force Institute of Technology (AU), Wright-Patterson AFB, OH, (May 2001).
4. M.W. Goddard, Estimating deployed airlift and equipment requirements for F-16 aircraft in support of the advanced logistics project, M.S. Thesis, AFIT/GLM/ENS/01M-11, School of Engineering and Management, Air Force Institute of Technology (AU), Wright-Patterson AFB, OH, (March 2001).
5. F.M. Slay *et al.*, *Optimizing Spares Support: The Aircraft Sustainability Model*, Logistics Management Institute (LMI), McLean, VA, (1996).
6. J. Leftwich and M. Shaw, Final Technical Report/Study services for unit type code-development and tailoring (UTC-DT), Synergy Inc., Washington, DC, (1997).
7. R.S. Tripp *et al.*, *Supporting Expeditionary Aerospace Forces: An Integrated Strategic Agile Combat Support Planning Framework*, Rand, Santa Monica, CA, (1999).
8. C.D. Buzo, A decision support tool to aid campaign planners in selecting combat aircraft for theater crisis, M.S. Thesis, AFIT/GEE/ENS/00M-02, School of Engineering and Management, Air Force Institute of Technology (AU), Wright-Patterson AFB, OH, (March 2000).
9. P.G. Filcek, A quantitative decision support model to aid selection of combat aircraft force mixes for contingency deployment, M.S. Thesis, AFIT/GLM/ENS/01M-10, School of Engineering and Management, Air Force Institute of Technology (AU), Wright-Patterson AFB, OH, (March 2001).
10. J. Horn and N. Nafpliotis, Multiobjective optimization using the niched Pareto genetic algorithm, In *Proceedings of the First IEEE Conference on Evolutionary Computation, IEEE World Congress on Computational Intelligence, ICEC '94, Volume 1*, Piscataway, NJ, (1994).
11. R.L. Keeney, *Value Focused Thinking: A Path to Creative Decisionmaking*, Harvard University Press, Cambridge, MA, (1992).
12. Y. Shepetukha and D.L. Olson, Comparative analysis of multiattribute techniques based on cardinal and ordinal inputs, *Mathl. Comput. Modelling* **34** (1/2), 229–241, (2001).
13. R.T. Clemen, *Making Hard Decisions: An Introduction to Decision Analysis*, Duxbury Press, Belmont, CA, (1991).
14. C.W. Kirkwood, *Strategic Decision Making: Multiobjective Decision Analysis with Spreadsheets*, Wadsworth Publishing, Belmont, CA, (1997).
15. R.L. Keeney and H. Raiffa, *Decisions with Multiple Objectives: Preferences and Value Tradeoffs*, John Wiley & Sons, New York, (1976).
16. G. Klein, R. Calderwood and D. MacGregor, Critical decision method for eliciting knowledge, *IEEE Transactions on Systems, Man, and Cybernetics* **19**, 462–472, (1994).
17. T.L. Seamster, R.E. Redding and G.L. Kaempf, *Applied Cognitive Task Analysis in Aviation*, Ashgate Publishing, Brookfield, VT, (1997).
18. M.R. Klein and L.B. Methlie, *Knowledge-Based Decision Support Systems with Applications in Business*, John Wiley & Sons, New York, (1995).
19. L.G. Militello and R.J.B. Hutton, Applied cognitive task analysis (ACTA): A practitioner's toolkit for understanding cognitive task demands, *Ergonomics* **41** (11), 1619–1641, (1998).
20. M. Greaves, Advanced logistics project, Excerpt from unpublished article, `http://dtsn.darpa.mil/ixo/alp.asp`, (November 2002).
21. C.A. Punches, A large scale integer linear program as a decision support tool for force mix selection, M.S. Thesis, AFIT/GLM/ENS/02-15, School of Engineering and Management, Air Force Institute of Technology (AU), Wright-Patterson AFB, OH, (March 2002).
22. D.J. Wakefield, Jr., Identification of preferred operational plan force mixes using a multiobjective methodology to optimize resource suitability and lift cost, M.S. Thesis, AFIT/GLM/ENS/01-M24, School of Engineering and Management, Air Force Institute of Technology (AU), Wright-Patterson AFB, OH, (March 2001).

Available online at www.sciencedirect.com
SCIENCE @ DIRECT•
ELSEVIER
Mathematical and Computer Modelling 39 (2004) 799–815
MATHEMATICAL AND COMPUTER MODELLING
www.elsevier.com/locate/mcm

Analytical Modeling of Joint Reception, Staging, Onward Movement, and Integration

N. P. SHERMAN AND J. P. KHAROUFEH*
Department of Operational Sciences
Air Force Institute of Technology
AFIT/ENS, Bldg. 640, 2950 Hobson Way
Wright Patterson AFB, OH 45433, U.S.A.
Jeffrey.Kharoufeh@afit.edu

Abstract—We present a stochastic model for the performance evaluation of a key phase in the military deployment process, joint reception, staging, onward movement, and integration (JRSOI). The process is modeled as an open, multiclass queueing network, wherein personnel and various classes of cargo are modeled as the flow entities and the phases of the process constitute individual queueing stations. We present low and high resolution models that provide a quick look at key aggregate performance measures such as system throughput and closure.

Keywords—Deployment, Stochastic models, Queueing networks.

1. INTRODUCTION

When the U.S. military responds to a contingency, it must assemble the necessary personnel, equipment, and materiel and move them to the area of operations (AO). This process is commonly referred to as deployment. The U.S. military conducts deployment in four phases: preparation activities, movement to ports of embarkation (POEs), movement from POEs to ports of debarkation (PODs), and movement from PODs to tactical assembly areas (TAAs). The fourth and final phase of deployment, referred to as reception, staging, onward movement, and integration (RSOI), is the focus of this research. Because deployment typically involves a joint effort of the military services, this phase is often referred to as *joint* reception, staging, onward movement, and integration (JRSOI).

JRSOI is the essential process that transitions deploying personnel (pax), and equipment and materiel (cargo) into combat-ready forces in the AO. It comprises four stages: receiving pax and cargo at PODs (reception), assembling them into units at designated staging areas (staging), moving these units to destinations within the area of conflict (onward movement), and integrating them into combat-ready, joint fighting forces (integration). One of the primary goals of JRSOI is to achieve flow balance, i.e., pax and cargo are directed at a rate that can be accommodated

The views expressed in this paper are those of the authors and do not reflect the official policy or position of the United States Air Force, Department of Defense, or the U.S. Government.

This research was partially funded by United States Transportation Command.

*Author to whom all correspondence should be addressed.

0895-7177/04/$ - see front matter Typeset by $\mathcal{A}\mathcal{M}\mathcal{S}$-TEX
doi:10.1016/j.mcm.2004.02.015

at every stage of the process from arrival at PODs to final integration within combat units [1]. However, this goal is seldom realized in military exercises and real world conflicts [2]. Saturation often occurs at various points within the phases of JRSOI because flow is not directed at an appropriate rate or because resources used to process pax and cargo become constrained [1]. Congestion that persists for an extended period of time provides adversarial forces a vulnerable target. For this reason, it is imperative that personnel and cargo flow through the respective stages of the process and reach their ultimate destination in an expedient manner. Thus, the modeling and analysis of this phase of the deployment process is of great importance to military decision makers. This paper presents an analytical, stochastic model of the JRSOI process to obtain computationally expedient estimates of critical performance measures such as congestion and throughput for activities within JRSOI and for the process as a whole. Such estimates can provide insight to aid decision makers in the planning and execution of impending military deployments.

To the authors' knowledge, no analytical models capturing the aggregate features of the JRSOI process exist. The literature does reveal, however, a host of simulation tools that have been developed for the purpose of enhancing force projection planning and execution and we review a few of those here. For a more thorough description of current deployment simulation tools, their interaction, and ongoing development efforts, the reader is referred to the survey by Drummer [3].

The most prevalent JRSOI simulation tool is the enhanced logistics intra-theater support tool (ELIST). It is designed to evaluate the feasibility of surface transportation movement plans, to simulate the joining of unit equipment and troops in staging areas, and to estimate closure trends [3]. Other simulation tools developed to model JRSOI, or various aspects of it, include TRANSCAP, SMARTBRIDGE, MATT, CITM, and FASTALS [3]. However, these tools address only certain aspects of JRSOI and have only limited capability to interact and share data [4]. Furthermore, due to extensive run times, often only a single replication is performed in practice, precluding any ability to provide statistically verified results. These extensive run times can significantly affect a combatant commander's ability to expediently evaluate the feasibility of operational plans related to JRSOI [5]. For these reasons, it is desirable to develop analytical tools that can efficiently and effectively aid in the planning and execution of this phase of the deployment process.

The main contributions of this work can be summarized as follows. First, we provide a novel approach for modeling the JRSOI process. The process is modeled as an open, multiclass queueing network wherein personnel and various classes of cargo represent the flow entities and the phases of the process are represented by individual queueing stations. We present low and high resolution models that provide a quick look at key aggregate performance measures such as system throughput (the rate at which pax and cargo are "pushed" through the system) and closure (the average time required for entities to reach their ultimate destination at the integration phase of the process). We view the JRSOI process as originating at a single APOD even though there may be other PODs in the area of operations. Although queueing network models are commonly employed in a variety of settings (e.g., telecommunication systems, transportation systems, etc.), our model captures some detailed features of the JRSOI process by using a fork-join queueing station which is discussed in Section 4. The relevant approximation equations enable the computation of key performance metrics in a computationally expedient manner (as compared with discrete-event simulation). The model can be used to identify potential bottlenecks in the JRSOI process and to what extent they affect the overall process throughput and closure. This information can substantially aid decision makers in regulating process flow. Moreover, the network topology can be easily adapted to any potential area of operations with appropriate modifications.

The remainder of this paper is organized as follows. In Section 2, we present the formal mathematical model for the JRSOI process and review some well-known results for analyzing the model. In Sections 3 and 4, we, respectively, present low and high resolution models for the performance evaluation of the JRSOI process. Section 5 provides two example problems using the analytical approximations and compares numerical results with discrete-event simulation. In Section 6, we provide our concluding remarks and directions for future research.

2. FORMAL MODEL DESCRIPTION

We model the JRSOI process as an open, multiclass queueing network. Such a network may be described as a directed graph $G(\mathcal{N}, \mathcal{A})$ where $\mathcal{N}$ and $\mathcal{A}$, respectively, denote the set of all nodes and arcs in the network. Each node represents an individual queueing station with its own stochastic characteristics. An arc $(i, j) \in \mathcal{A}$ exists only if it is possible for an entity to proceed from node $i \in \mathcal{N}$ to node $j \in \mathcal{N}$. In queueing network models, it is conventional to assume that no time elapses as an entity moves between nodes of the network, though this assumption may be relaxed. Our model is open, meaning that entities may enter the network at various locations. For example, not all pax and cargo necessarily join the process at the reception phase. Some entities may join the network at a downstream phase such as staging. This is particularly important as it permits assets, originating at PODs other than the single APOD used in the model, to enter the network. Moreover, in the terminology of queueing networks, our model is a multiclass model, as pax and cargo have distinct characteristics and, consequently, distinct processing requirements. Due to the sequential flow of activities through the JRSOI process, the topology of the network may be described as a feed-forward (or tandem) topology as depicted in Figure 1. Although entities may not have the same origin node, their common destination is the integration node.

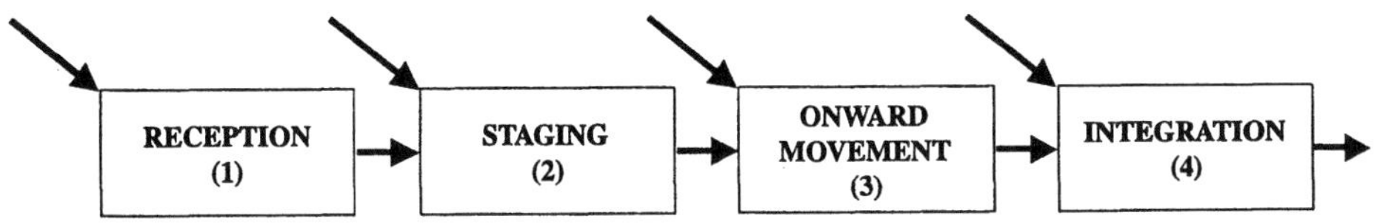

Figure 1. A graphical depiction of the JRSOI process.

In this paper, we present queueing network models at two levels of resolution: low and high. The queueing network for the low resolution model consists of four nodes, one for each stage of the process. In the high resolution model, we replace each of the four nodes of the lower resolution model with a subnetwork of nodes detailing the process within that node's respective JRSOI stage. We separate the flow entities into four classes: pax, bulk cargo, oversize cargo, and outsize cargo. Each cargo classification is based on how the cargo is packaged and which aircraft is appropriate for its transport. Bulk cargo is assembled and transported on a single pallet that can fit on any aircraft. Oversize cargo is too large to fit on a single pallet but can fit on any aircraft. Some pieces of oversize cargo can be assembled onto a train of pallets for transport. The final cargo class is outsize which can only be carried on C-17 or C-5 aircraft due to its size and dimensions. It is assumed that there are no capacity constraints on the number of entities in the network and that each node has unlimited waiting space. The algorithm can, however, be modified to account for finite-capacity queues. The primary performance metrics of interest are throughput, closure, and queue length. Throughput indicates the rate at which entities are processed, closure indicates how long it takes assets to move through the entire JRSOI process, and queue length indicates the number of entities waiting to be processed.

With regard to the individual nodes of the network, each is modeled as a GI/G/m queue. The first component in the node description (GI) indicates that the interarrival times of entities are general, independent, and identically distributed (i.i.d.) random variables for each class (i.e, the stochastic process of entity arrivals forms a renewal process), the second component (G) indicates that the service times are also i.i.d. for each class, and m denotes the finite number of resources (or servers) available for processing entities at the queueing station. Each node operates according to the first come, first served (FCFS) queueing discipline and is assumed to have a single server (i.e.,

$m = 1$). The mean arrival and service rates at each node are dependent upon the route where each possible path through the network for each entity class defines a distinct route. Entities are neither created nor combined at the nodes, meaning bulk arrivals and departures are not considered. One major advantage of using the GI/G/1 queue at each node is that we do not require full characterization of the interarrival and service time probability distributions, just the lower moments (i.e., the mean and variance).

Due to the relatively simplistic network topology, we analyze the queueing network model via parametric decomposition which assumes that each node of the network behaves in a manner that is statistically independent of the other nodes (i.e., we assume the network admits a product-form solution). In particular, the well-known queueing network analyzer (QNA) due to Whitt [6] is applied to approximate the desired performance metrics. The internal flow parameters attempt to capture dependencies that exist among the nodes. The decomposition approximation provides more accurate results for non-Markovian networks than would be acquired by assuming that the network is Markovian. A Markovian network is one in which all interarrival and service time distributions are exponential. In such case, the equations yield exact results [6]. In what follows, we review the basic analysis of the general queueing network model. This discussion follows, in large part, from [6].

Define N as the number of nodes in the network ($|\mathcal{N}| = N$). Each node of the network is labelled by one of the integers in $\mathcal{N} = \{1, 2, \ldots, N\}$. Moreover, we define Node 0 to represent the "universe" external to the network. For multiclass networks, each possible processing path for each entity class forms a distinct route. We shall denote the total number of distinct routes by R. The number of nodes on route k, $k = 1, 2, \ldots, R$, is denoted by n_k. Let n_{kj} indicate the jth node visited along route k.

One required input is the external arrival rate of route k entities, denoted by $\hat{\lambda}_k$, $k = 1, 2, \ldots, R$. These rates are used to compute aggregate external arrival rates for each node using the following equation:

$$\lambda_{0,j} = \sum_{k=1}^{R} \hat{\lambda}_k I_{\{k:n_{k,1}=j\}}, \qquad j \in \mathcal{N}, \tag{1}$$

where I is the indicator function (i.e., $I_A = 1$ when $k \in A$ and $I_A = 0$ otherwise). This means the external arrival rate to Node j is the sum of all external arrival rates of routes that have Node j as their entry node to the network. Similarly, the rate of flow from Node i to Node j is obtained by

$$\lambda_{ij} = \sum_{k=1}^{R} \sum_{l=1}^{n_k-1} \hat{\lambda}_k I_{\{(k,l):n_{kl}=i,\, n_{k,l+1}=j\}}, \qquad i, j \in \mathcal{N}. \tag{2}$$

Equation (2) merely sums the external arrival rates $\{\hat{\lambda}_k\}$ for all routes that include arc (i,j). If an arc (i,j) is traversed n times on Route k (indicating rework), then $\hat{\lambda}_k$ is added n times when calculating λ_{ij}. Note that, in our models, this does not occur (i.e., the probability of traversing an arc multiple times is zero). The rate of departures from the network out of Node i is calculated in a similar manner as

$$d_i = \lambda_{i,0} = \sum_{k=1}^{R} \hat{\lambda}_k I_{\{k:n_{kn_k}=i\}}, \qquad i \in \mathcal{N}. \tag{3}$$

This means the departure rate from Node i is the sum of all external arrival rates of routes that have Node i as the last node in their route. This performance measure indicates the rate of flow of pax and cargo completing service at each JRSOI service activity.

The proportion of entities at Node i that proceeds directly to Node j is

$$r_{ij} = \lambda_{ij} \left(\lambda_{i,0} + \sum_{h=1}^{N} \lambda_{i,h} \right)^{-1}, \qquad i, j \in \mathcal{N}. \tag{4}$$

These values are used to populate the network's routing matrix which is assumed to be state-independent. The overall arrival rate to Node $j \in \mathcal{N}$ can now be calculated using the well-known traffic-rate equations (cf. [7])

$$\lambda_j = \lambda_{0,j} + \sum_{i=1}^{N} \lambda_i r_{ij}, \qquad j \in \mathcal{N}, \tag{5}$$

or in matrix notation,

$$\Lambda = \Lambda_0 (\mathbf{I} - \mathbf{R})^{-1}, \tag{6}$$

where $\Lambda_0 := [\lambda_{0,j}]$ is the external arrival-rate vector, $\mathbf{R}$ is the routing matrix, and $\mathbf{I}$ denotes the identity matrix. The proportion of arrivals to Node j originating from Node i is given by

$$p_{ij} = \frac{\lambda_{ij}}{\lambda_j}. \tag{7}$$

The next required input is the mean service rate for the lth node of Route k which shall be denoted by $\hat{\mu}_{kl}$. This value is used to obtain the aggregate service rate at each node by averaging the route-specific service rates as

$$\mu_j = \frac{\sum_{k=1}^{R} \sum_{l=1}^{n_k} \hat{\lambda}_k I_{\{(k,l):n_{kl}=j\}}}{\sum_{k=1}^{R} \sum_{l=1}^{n_k} \left(\hat{\lambda}_k / \hat{\mu}_{kl} \right) I_{\{(k,l):n_{kl}=j\}}}, \qquad j \in \mathcal{N}. \tag{8}$$

The numerator of equation (8) sums the external arrival rates for the routes that include Node j. If a node is visited n times on a given route (indicating rework), then the external arrival rate for that route is included n times in the sum. Note that, in our models, this does not occur (i.e., the probability of returning to a node that has been visited is zero). The denominator of equation (8) is equivalent to the numerator with the exception that each summand is divided by the service rate at Node j according to the occurrence of Node j on the corresponding route. The traffic intensities, $\{\rho_j\}$, may now be computed for each node by

$$\rho_j = \frac{\lambda_j}{m_j \mu_j}, \qquad j \in \mathcal{N}, \tag{9}$$

where m_j denotes the number of servers at Node j. In the language of queueing systems, the stability condition, $\rho_j < 1$, $j \in \mathcal{N}$, is assumed throughout this paper. This implies that the mean service rate is greater than the mean arrival rate of entities at each of the nodes. This assumption is initially needed to ensure mathematical tractability. However, by using some modifications (e.g., time-varying arrival rates) it is possible to allow for arrival rates that, at times, exceed the mean service rate for a given node.

Next, the squared coefficient of variation of the service-time distribution at the lth node of Route k, denoted by $\hat{c}^2_{skl}$, is required. The coefficient of variation is the ratio of the mean to the standard deviation. The aggregate service-time squared coefficients of variation $\{c^2_{sj}\}$ are computed by

$$c^2_{sj} = \frac{\mu_j^2 \sum_{k=1}^{R} \sum_{l=1}^{n_k} \left(\hat{\lambda}_k / \hat{\mu}^2_{kl} \right) \left(\hat{c}^2_{skl} + 1 \right) I_{\{(k,l):n_{kl}=j\}}}{\sum_{k=1}^{R} \sum_{l=1}^{n_k} \hat{\lambda}_k I_{\{(k,l):n_{kl}=j\}}} - 1, \qquad j \in \mathcal{N}. \tag{10}$$

The final inputs required are the squared coefficients of variation for the external arrival process for each route, denoted $\{\hat{c}_{0k}^2\}$. These values are used to calculate the aggregate external arrival process squared coefficients of variation, $\{c_{0j}^2\}$, at Node $j \in \mathcal{N}$ by

$$c_{0j}^2 = (1 - \hat{w}_j) + \hat{w}_j \sum_{k=1}^{R} \hat{c}_{0k}^2 \left(\frac{\hat{\lambda}_k I_{\{k:n_{k1}=j\}}}{\sum_{l=1}^{r} \hat{\lambda}_l I_{\{l:n_{l1}=j\}}} \right), \qquad j \in \mathcal{N}, \tag{11}$$

where $\hat{w}_j$ is defined as

$$\hat{w}_j = \left\{ 1 + 4 (1 - \rho_j)^2 (\hat{v}_j - 1) \right\}^{-1}, \qquad j \in \mathcal{N}, \tag{12}$$

and $\hat{v}_j$ is given by

$$\hat{v}_j = \left[\sum_{k=1}^{R} \left(\frac{\hat{\lambda}_k I_{\{k:n_{k1}=j\}}}{\sum_{l=1}^{R} \hat{\lambda}_l I_{\{l:n_{l1}=j\}}} \right)^2 \right]^{-1}, \qquad j \in \mathcal{N}. \tag{13}$$

Finally, the arrival process squared coefficient of variation for each node is computed by the system of equations

$$c_{aj}^2 = a_j + \sum_{i=1}^{N} c_{ai}^2 b_{ij}, \qquad j \in \mathcal{N}, \tag{14}$$

where a_j and b_{ij} are constants given by

$$a_j = 1 + w_j \left\{ \left(p_{0,j} c_{0j}^2 - 1 \right) + \sum_{i=1}^{N} p_{ij} \left[(1 - r_{ij}) + (1 - v_{ij}) r_{ij} \rho_i^2 x_i \right] \right\} \tag{15}$$

and

$$b_{ij} = w_j p_{ij} r_{ij} \left[v_{ij} + (1 - v_{ij}) \left(1 - \rho_i^2 \right) \right], \tag{16}$$

x_i and w_j are defined as

$$x_i = 1 + m_i^{-0.5} \left(\max \left\{ c_{si}^2, 0.2 \right\} - 1 \right), \tag{17}$$

and

$$w_j = \left[1 + N (1 - \rho_j)^2 (v_j - 1) \right]^{-1}, \tag{18}$$

with

$$v_j = \left(\sum_{i=0}^{N} p_{ij}^2 \right)^{-1}. \tag{19}$$

The values $\{v_{ij}\}$ of equations (15) and (16) are adjustable values used to approximate departure processes.

Using the traffic intensities, the mean arrival rates, and variability parameters for the internal arrival processes, the performance measures for the individual nodes of the network can be computed. The aggregate network performance measures are obtained assuming the network nodes are stochastically independent (i.e., assuming a product-form network).

The long-run average waiting time in queue for an entity at Node j is

$$W_{q_j} = \frac{\rho_j \left(c_{aj}^2 + c_{sj}^2 \right) g_j}{2 \mu_j (1 - \rho_j)}, \qquad j \in \mathcal{N}, \tag{20}$$

where $g_j \equiv g_j(\rho_j, c_{aj}^2, c_{sj}^2)$ is defined in [6] as

$$g_j\left(\rho_j, c_{aj}^2, c_{sj}^2\right) = \begin{cases} \exp\left(\dfrac{-2\left(1-\rho_j\right)\left(1-c_{aj}^2\right)^2}{3\rho_j\left(c_{aj}^2+c_{sj}^2\right)}\right), & c_{aj}^2 < 1, \\ 1, & c_{aj}^2 \geq 1. \end{cases} \tag{21}$$

Applying Little's Law, the long-run average time spent by entities at Node j, denoted by W_j, the average number of entities in each queue, L_{q_j}, and the average number of entities at each node, L_j, can be computed for $j \in \mathcal{N}$, respectively, as

$$W_j = \frac{1}{\mu_j} + W_{q_j}, \tag{22}$$

$$L_{q_j} = \lambda_j W_{q_j}, \tag{23}$$

$$L_j = \rho_j + \lambda_j W_{q_j}. \tag{24}$$

The measure W_j is the average time required to completely move assets through service activity (or phase) j of the JRSOI process. The measures L_{q_j} and L_j indicate the level of congestion (i.e., the number of pax and cargo occupying space, waiting to be serviced) at service activity j.

Finally, the aggregate performance measures for the network may be computed. The overall network throughput is given by

$$d = \sum_{i=1}^{N} d_i. \tag{25}$$

Throughput indicates the rate at which pax and cargo complete the JRSOI process (i.e., the rate at which assets are integrated with their respective combat units in the area of operations). The overall long-run average time spent in the network for an arbitrary entity is

$$W = \sum_{j=1}^{N} W_j. \tag{26}$$

The other three overall steady-state performance measures for the network are computed as

$$W_q = \sum_{j=1}^{N} W_{q_j}, \tag{27}$$

$$L = \sum_{j=1}^{N} L_j, \tag{28}$$

$$L_q = \sum_{j=1}^{N} L_{q_j}. \tag{29}$$

The measure W corresponds to the overall JRSOI performance measure called closure, the average time it takes to completely move a given set of pax and cargo through the JRSOI process. The measure L_q indicates the overall average level of congestion of the process. These two measures, combined with the throughput, are the primary measures used by planners and warfighters to evaluate the JRSOI process during the planning and execution of military operations [1].

The equations provided in this section follow from the parametric decomposition procedure outlined in [6]. The main advantage of modeling the JRSOI process in this way is that we require only the lower moments (mean and variance) of the interarrival and service time distributions. Such values can be directly observed in training exercises or in actual deployments. In Sections 3 and 4, low and high resolution models are, respectively, presented for the JRSOI process.

3. LOW RESOLUTION MODEL

We term the first model "low resolution" because it aggregates all JRSOI activities into four tandem nodes. This model provides the broadest view of the process. The reception, staging, onward movement, and integration nodes are indexed as Nodes 1, 2, 3, and 4, respectively (as in Figure 1). Once an entity enters the network, it remains in the network until service completion at the integration node. The four entity classes each have four distinct routes depending on their inception node into the network. Consequently, there are 16 total routes. Let Routes 1, 2, 3, and 4 be the respective routes for the four entity classes, pax, outsize cargo, oversize cargo, and bulk cargo, entering the network at Node 1 in Figure 1. Similarly, let Routes 5–8, 9–12, and 13–16 indicate the routes for entities entering the network at Nodes 2, 3, and 4, respectively, in Figure 1.

The number of nodes on Route k, n_k, for this model indicate that entities entering the network at Nodes 1, 2, 3, and 4 have, respectively, four, three, two, and one node on their route. The aggregate external arrival rates for each node are given by

$$\lambda_{0,j} = \sum_{k=1}^{16} \hat{\lambda}_k I_{\{k:n_{k,1}=j\}}, \qquad j = 1,2,3,4. \tag{30}$$

The total flow rate from Node i to Node j is

$$\lambda_{ij} = \begin{cases} \sum_{k\in\mathcal{R}_{ij}} \hat{\lambda}_k, & 1 \le i \le 3, \quad j = i+1, \\ 0, & \text{otherwise}, \end{cases} \tag{31}$$

where the set $\mathcal{R}_{ij} \equiv \{k : (i,j) \in k\}$ is the set of all routes that contain arc $(i,j) \in \mathcal{A}$. The departure rates are

$$d_i = \begin{cases} \sum_{j=1}^{i} \lambda_{0,j}, & i = 4, \\ 0, & i = 1,2,3. \end{cases} \tag{32}$$

The routing matrix is given by

$$\mathbf{R} = \begin{pmatrix} 0 & 1 & 0 & 0 \\ 0 & 0 & 1 & 0 \\ 0 & 0 & 0 & 1 \\ 0 & 0 & 0 & 0 \end{pmatrix}. \tag{33}$$

The simplistic structure of the routing matrix is due to the tandem configuration of the feed-forward network. Using equation (5), the arrival rates to each node are

$$\lambda_j = \sum_{i=1}^{j} \lambda_{0,i}, \qquad j = 1,2,3,4. \tag{34}$$

The proportion of Node j arrivals from Node i is computed by equation (7) as

$$p_{ij} = \begin{cases} 1, & i = 0, \quad j = 1, \\ \dfrac{\lambda_{0,j}}{\lambda_j}, & i = 0, \quad j = 2,3,4, \\ \dfrac{\lambda_{ij}}{\lambda_j}, & 1 \le i \le 3, \quad j = i+1, \\ 0, & \text{otherwise}. \end{cases} \tag{35}$$

The aggregate service rates are computed by equation (8). The traffic intensities are then $\rho_j = \lambda_j/\mu_j$, $j = 1,2,3,4$. The aggregate service-time squared coefficients of variation are computed by equation (10) and the aggregate external arrival process square coefficients of variation are computed by equations (11) through (13). The approximated squared coefficients of variation for the arrival processes to each node are thereby computed using equations (14) through (19) as

$$c_{a1}^2 = a_1 + \sum_{i=1}^{4} c_{ai}^2 b_{i,1} = a_1,$$

$$c_{aj}^2 = a_j + \sum_{i=1}^{4} c_{ai}^2 b_{ij} = a_j + c_{a(j-1)}^2 b_{(j-1)j}, \qquad j = 2,3,4,$$

where the variability constants a_j and b_{ij}, defined in equations (15) and (16), are

$$a_1 = 1 + w_1 \left(c_{01}^2 - 1\right).$$

For $j = 2,3,4$, we have that

$$a_j = 1 + w_j \left\{ \left[\left(\frac{\lambda_{0,j}}{\sum\limits_{h=1}^{j} \lambda_{0,h}} \right) c_{0j}^2 - 1 \right] + \sum_{i=1}^{4} \left[\left(\frac{\sum\limits_{h=1}^{i} \lambda_{0,h}}{\sum\limits_{h=1}^{j} \lambda_{0,h}} \right) \left(\frac{\sum\limits_{h=1}^{i} \lambda_{0,h}}{\mu_i} \right)^2 x_i \right] \right\},$$

and

$$b_{ij} = \begin{cases} w_j \left(\frac{\sum\limits_{h=1}^{i} \lambda_{0,h}}{\sum\limits_{h=1}^{j} \lambda_{0,h}} \right) \left(1 - \left(\frac{\sum\limits_{h=1}^{i} \lambda_{0,h}}{\mu_i} \right)^2 \right), & 1 \le i \le 3, \quad j = i+1, \\ 0, & \text{otherwise.} \end{cases} \tag{36}$$

The total throughput for the network is given by

$$d = \sum_{i=1}^{4} d_i = \sum_{j=1}^{4} \lambda_{0,j}. \tag{37}$$

The remaining performance measures of interest for each node and the network as a whole can be calculated using equations (20) through (24) and (26) through (29).

4. HIGH RESOLUTION MODEL

The high resolution queueing network model consists of 21 nodes comprising four subnetworks representing the four stages of JRSOI (see Table 1 and Figure 2). Each partition of the network in Figure 2 corresponds to a single node in Figure 1. This notional model is based on information from multiple sources including Joint Publication 4-01.8 [1] and the Defense Transportation Regulation [8]. The model is designed to capture the salient features and network constructs of the generalized JRSOI process. In reality, the specific details of JRSOI are classified, and their configurations are situation- and operating-location specific. However, the approximation equations can be used to analyze the network topology of a specific operating location with the appropriate modifications.

In the high resolution model, flow is directed sequentially, and once an entity enters the network, it remains in the network until service completion at the integration node. We allow entities to enter the network at Nodes 1 and 10. We define 12 routes based on the four entity classes described in Section 3 and an additional route to account for combat units that enter JRSOI already intact at Node 1. In total, there are 13 routes for this model. The number of nodes along Route k (n_k), is given in Table 2. In addition, the values $\{n_{kj}\}$, indicating the jth node visited

Table 1. Network node descriptions.

Node	Description
1	Offload pax and cargo at APOD
2	Clear pax and cargo
3	Move pax and cargo to holding area
4	In-process pax (reception phase)
5	Inspect vehicles and perform maintenance
6	Breakdown and reorganize pallets
7	Hold sensitive cargo
8	Move pax and cargo to marshalling area
9	Marshall pax and cargo
10	Move pax and cargo to staging area
11	Receive and inspect cargo
12	In-process pax (staging phase)
13	Conduct operability checks on cargo
14	Conduct training of pax as required
15	Prepare pax and cargo for onward movement
16	Plane
17	Train
18	Convoy
19	Receive and inspect cargo
20	In-process pax (integration phase)
21	Conduct integration

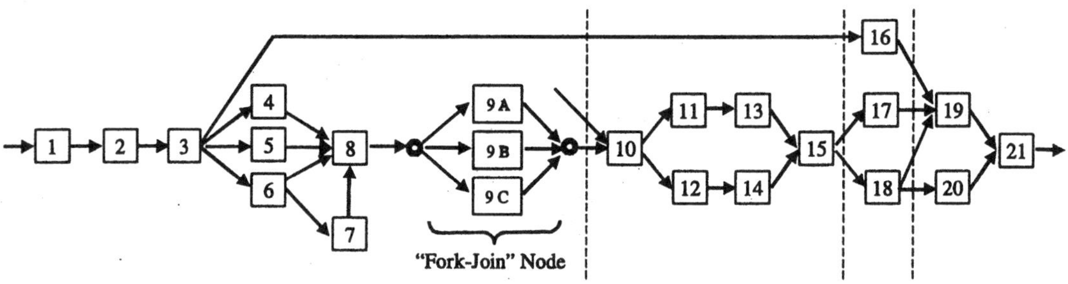

Figure 2. Graphical depiction of high resolution JRSOI network.

Table 2. Enumeration of routes for the high resolution model.

k	Label	Path	n_k
1	Pax1	1,2,3,4,8,9,10,12,14,15,18,20,21	13
2	Pax2	10,12,14,15,18,20,21	7
3	Outsize1	1,2,3,5,8,9,10,11,13,15,17,19,21	13
4	Outsize2	10,11,13,15,18,19,21	7
5	Oversize1	1,2,3,6,8,9,10,11,13,15,17,19,21	13
6	Oversize2	1,2,3,6,7,8,9,10,11,13,15,18,19,21	14
7	Oversize3	1,2,3,5,8,9,10,11,13,15,18,19,21	13
8	Bulk1	1,2,3,6,8,9,10,11,13,15,17,19,21	13
9	Bulk2	1,2,3,6,8,9,10,11,13,15,18,19,21	13
10	Bulk3	1,2,3,6,7,8,9,10,11,13,15,17,19,21	14
11	Bulk4	1,2,3,6,7,8,9,10,11,13,15,18,19,21	14
12	Bulk5	10,11,13,15,18,20,21	7
13	Unit	1,2,3,16,19,21	6

by Route k, can easily be determined using the information in Table 2. It is assumed that the routing matrix is state-independent; however, the service rates at each node are dependent upon the route (i.e., distinct entity types carry with them unique service requirements).

A unique feature of this model is the incorporation of a fork-join queueing station (Node 9 of Figure 2). A fork-join queueing station is one in which, upon entering service, an entity awaits multiple, concurrent service activities. Service for that entity is complete only when all of the required activities are complete, or equivalently at the completion time of the activity whose duration is the longest.

The external arrival rate to Node $j \in \mathcal{N}$ is the sum of all external arrival rates of routes that have Node j as their first node. These are computed by expanding equation (1) as

$$\lambda_{0,j} = \begin{cases} \hat{\lambda}_1 + \hat{\lambda}_3 + \hat{\lambda}_5 + \hat{\lambda}_6 + \hat{\lambda}_7 + \hat{\lambda}_8 + \hat{\lambda}_9 + \hat{\lambda}_{10} + \hat{\lambda}_{11} + \hat{\lambda}_{13}, & j = 1, \\ \hat{\lambda}_2 + \hat{\lambda}_4 + \hat{\lambda}_{12}, & j = 10, \\ 0, & \text{otherwise}. \end{cases} \tag{38}$$

As before let $\mathcal{R}_{ij} \equiv \{k : (i,j) \in k\}$ denote the set of all routes in the network containing arc $(i,j) \in \mathcal{A}$. The total rate of flow from Node $i \in \mathcal{N}$ to Node $j \in \mathcal{N}$ is obtained by equation (2) as

$$\lambda_{ij} = \sum_{k \in \mathcal{R}_{ij}} \hat{\lambda}_k. \tag{39}$$

The departure rate from the network out of Node i is given by equation (3)

$$d_i = \lambda_{i,0} = 0, \qquad i = 1, 2, \ldots, 20,$$

$$d_{21} = \lambda_{4,0} = \sum_{i=1}^{13} \hat{\lambda}_i.$$

The proportion of entities at Node i that proceed to Node j for this model are

$$r_{3,j} = \frac{\lambda_{3,j}}{(\lambda_{3,4} + \lambda_{3,5} + \lambda_{3,6} + \lambda_{3,16})}, \qquad j = 4, 5, 6, 16,$$

$$r_{6,j} = \frac{\lambda_{6,j}}{(\lambda_{6,7} + \lambda_{6,8})}, \qquad j = 7, 8,$$

$$r_{10,j} = \frac{\lambda_{10,j}}{(\lambda_{10,11} + \lambda_{10,12})}, \qquad j = 11, 12,$$

$$r_{15,j} = \frac{\lambda_{15,j}}{(\lambda_{15,17} + \lambda_{15,18})}, \qquad j = 17, 18,$$

$$r_{18,j} = \frac{\lambda_{18,j}}{(\lambda_{18,19} + \lambda_{18,20})}, \qquad j = 19, 20,$$

where $r_{ij} = 1$ for $(i,j) \in \{(1,2), (2,3), (4,8), (5,8), (7,8), (8,9), (9,10), (11,13), (12,14), (13,15), (14,15), (16,19), (17,19), (19,21), (20,21)\}$ and $r_{ij} = 0$ otherwise. Since the network contains a total of 21 nodes, the routing matrix contains 441 entries. For the sake of brevity, we do not display the matrix.

By equation (5), the mean arrival rate to each node is

$$\lambda_1 = \lambda_{0,1} = \hat{\lambda}_1 + \hat{\lambda}_3 + \hat{\lambda}_5 + \hat{\lambda}_6 + \hat{\lambda}_7 + \hat{\lambda}_8 + \hat{\lambda}_9 + \hat{\lambda}_{10} + \hat{\lambda}_{11} + \hat{\lambda}_{13},$$

$$\lambda_8 = \lambda_4 r_{4,8} + \lambda_5 r_{5,8} + \lambda_6 r_{6,8} + \lambda_7 r_{7,8},$$

$$\lambda_{10} = \lambda_{0,10} + \lambda_9 r_{9,10} = \hat{\lambda}_2 + \hat{\lambda}_4 + \hat{\lambda}_{12} + \lambda_9 r_{9,10},$$

$$\lambda_{15} = \lambda_{13} r_{13,15} + \lambda_{14} r_{14,15},$$

$$\lambda_{19} = \lambda_{16} r_{16,19} + \lambda_{17} r_{17,19} + \lambda_{18} r_{18,19},$$

$$\lambda_{21} = \lambda_{19} r_{19,21} + \lambda_{20} r_{20,21},$$

and $\lambda_j = \lambda_i r_{ij}$ for $(i,j) \in \{(1,2),(2,3),(3,4),(3,5),(3,6),(3,16),(6,7),(8,9),(10,11),(10,12),(11,13),(12,14),(15,17),(15,18),(18,20)\}$.

The proportion of arrivals to Node j from Node i is computed by equation (7) as

$$p_{ij} = \begin{cases} 1, & i=0, \quad j=1, \\ \dfrac{\lambda_{0,j}}{\lambda_j}, & i=0, \quad j=10, \\ \dfrac{\lambda_{ij}}{\lambda_j}, & (i,j) \in \mathcal{A}, \\ 0, & \text{otherwise}. \end{cases} \tag{40}$$

The aggregate service rates at each node are found by averaging the route specific service rates according to equation (8)

$$\mu_j = \lambda_j \left(\sum_{k \in \mathcal{R}_j} \frac{\hat{\lambda}_k}{\mu_{kj}} \right)^{-1}, \qquad j \in \mathcal{N}, \tag{41}$$

where $\mathcal{R}_j$ denotes the set of all routes that contain Node $j \in \mathcal{N}$ and μ_{kj} denotes the service rate for Route k at Node j. The traffic intensities are then computed by

$$\rho_j = \frac{\lambda_j}{\mu_j}, \qquad j \in \mathcal{N}. \tag{42}$$

The aggregate service squared coefficients of variation, $\{c_{sj}^2\}$, are found by equation (10)

$$\begin{aligned} c_{sj}^2 &= \frac{\mu_j^2 \sum_{k=1}^{13} \sum_{l=1}^{n_k} \left(\hat{\lambda}_k / \hat{\mu}_{kl}^2\right) \left(\hat{c}_{skl}^2 + 1\right) I_{\{(k,l):n_{kl}=j\}}}{\sum_{k=1}^{13} \sum_{l=1}^{n_k} \hat{\lambda}_k I_{\{(k,l):n_{kl}=j\}}} - 1 \\ &= \frac{\mu_j^2}{\lambda_j} \left(\sum_{k \in \mathcal{R}_j} \left(\frac{\hat{\lambda}_k}{\mu_{kj}^2} \right) \left(c_{skj}^2 + 1 \right) \right) - 1, \qquad j \in \mathcal{N}, \end{aligned} \tag{43}$$

where c_{skj}^2 is the service squared coefficient of variation for Route k at Node j. The aggregate external arrival square coefficients of variation are found using equation (11)

$$c_{01}^2 = 1 - \hat{w}_1 + \frac{\hat{w}_1}{\lambda_{0,1}} \sum_{i \in \mathcal{R}_1} \hat{c}_{0i}^2 \hat{\lambda}_i,$$

$$c_{010}^2 = 1 - \hat{w}_{10} + \frac{\hat{w}_{10}}{\lambda_{0,10}} \left(\hat{c}_{02}^2 \hat{\lambda}_2 + \hat{c}_{04}^2 \hat{\lambda}_4 + \hat{c}_{012}^2 \hat{\lambda}_{12} \right),$$

and $c_{0j} = 0$ otherwise. The values $\{\hat{w}_j\}$ are computed by equations (12) and (13) in which the only nonzero $\{\hat{v}_j\}$ values, $\hat{v}_1$ and $\hat{v}_{10}$, are given by

$$\hat{v}_1 = \frac{\lambda_{0,1}^2}{\hat{\lambda}_1^2 + \hat{\lambda}_3^2 + \hat{\lambda}_5^2 + \hat{\lambda}_6^2 + \hat{\lambda}_7^2 + \hat{\lambda}_8^2 + \hat{\lambda}_9^2 + \hat{\lambda}_{10}^2 + \hat{\lambda}_{11}^2 + \hat{\lambda}_{13}^2},$$

$$\hat{v}_{10} = \frac{\lambda_{0,10}^2}{\hat{\lambda}_2^2 + \hat{\lambda}_4^2 + \hat{\lambda}_{12}^2}.$$

The primary measures may be computed for each node and for the entire network by applying equations (14) through (29). We demonstrate numerical examples for the low and high resolution models in the next section.

5. NUMERICAL EXAMPLES

In this section, we demonstrate the performance of the analytical models developed in Sections 3 and 4. The analytical performance metrics for the JRSOI queueing network were computed using computer codes created in the MATLAB computing environment and executed on a personal computer. Corresponding discrete-event simulations were also developed for comparison of steady-state performance measures. Though extensive empirical testing was done, we present one example for the low and high resolution models each for the sake of brevity.

With regard to the simulation model, one long replication of one million 24-hour days was used in all tests to approximate steady-state results. A 10,000 day warm-up period was used to overcome the effect of initial conditions. The relevant statistics were initialized upon completion of the warm-up period. Each arrival and service process in the network utilized a unique random number generating stream and we used 95% confidence intervals for the simulated performance measures at each node.

A fixed set of input parameters was prescribed for the low and high resolution models. The data were chosen within a reasonable range of values. More specifically, the stability condition was satisfied at every node, implying that the traffic intensity was less than unity. If this condition is not satisfied, the approximation equations are invalid and the computer simulations will experience an overload of queued entities. Though the stability condition is satisfied, the selected traffic intensities were moderately high (between 0.8 and 0.99) as one might expect in real-world operations.

While the input data remained fixed, the specified probability distributions for arrival and service processes, and their corresponding squared coefficients of variation, were varied from test to test. However, each arrival or service was assumed to use the same distribution, though this is not a necessary assumption. This was done to observe the effect of the selected parametric distributions and their associated squared coefficients of variation on model performance. In practice, any distribution can be specified since only the lower moments (mean and variance) are required.

The measures L_q, W, and d were the performance metrics used for testing. The measure L_q corresponds to the congestion experienced at the different stations in the network. The average time spent at each station for an arbitrary entity is captured in the value W while the measure d corresponds to throughput. The category in each table labelled "overall" aggregates the individual results of each node in the network. In case overall network performance measures are desired for specific entity types, they can be obtained by summing the performance measures for only those nodes along the routes of such entities.

The external arrival and service rates for the low resolution model, in number of entities per hour, are provided in Table 3. These model inputs are arbitrarily chosen. Each of the 16 defined routes for the four entity classes, pax, outsize cargo, oversize cargo, and bulk cargo, had a route-specific service rate at each node.

This numerical experiment utilized Weibull distributed interarrival and service times with shape parameter, 0.8, and scale parameter γ (calculated using the input values). Henceforth, we shall denote this distribution by $W(0.8, \gamma)$. All nodes represent GI/G/1 queueing stations. The $W(0.8, \gamma)$ has a squared coefficient of variation of $8\Gamma(2.5)/5\Gamma(1.25)^2 - 1 \approx 1.5889$ where Γ denotes the gamma function. (By comparison, the exponential distribution has a squared coefficient of variation of unity.) The numerical results of this test are provided in Table 4.

The relative error rates for this model were at most 9.6%. However, the throughput measure had a maximum error of 1.5%. The elevated error rates occurred at nodes with larger confidence interval half-widths relative to the size of the performance measure, indicating some contribution by the simulation to these errors. It should be noted that the simulation run time was 14 hours and 43 minutes as compared to approximately 0.5 seconds for the analytical solutions.

The external interarrival and service rates for the high resolution model are given in Tables 5 and 6. These model inputs are arbitrarily chosen. The service rates are rounded to the nearest tenth. Each of the 13 defined routes had a route-specific service rate at each node along its path.

Table 3. External arrival and service rates for low resolution model (1/hr).

Route (k)	External Arrival	$\mu_{k,1}$	$\mu_{k,2}$	$\mu_{k,3}$	$\mu_{k,4}$
1	4.5	20	30	30	32
2	0.5	2	20	20	24
3	0.5	2	20	20	24
4	0.5	2	20	20	24
5	2.0	–	30	30	32
6	4.0	–	20	20	24
7	4.0	–	20	20	24
8	4.0	–	20	20	24
9	0.5	–	–	30	32
10	0.5	–	–	20	24
11	0.5	–	–	20	24
12	0.5	–	–	20	24
13	0.5	–	–	–	32
14	0.5	–	–	–	24
15	0.5	–	–	–	24
16	0.5	–	–	–	24

Table 4. Low resolution measures using $W(4/5, \gamma)$ interarrival and service times.

Node	Analytical			Simulated		
	L_q	W	d	L_q	W	d
1	131.1516	21.8586	6.0449	143.0600	24.1950	5.9528
2	14.9970	0.7499	21.2628	14.6120	0.7303	21.3091
3	100.5134	4.5688	22.2173	106.0000	4.8199	22.1980
4	17.6540	0.7356	25.3217	18.0860	0.7535	25.2906
Overall	264.3160	27.9129	74.8467	281.7580	30.4987	74.7504

Table 5. External arrival and service rates for high resolution model (1/hr).

Route (k)	External Arrival	$\mu_{k,1}$	$\mu_{k,2}$	$\mu_{k,3}$	$\mu_{k,4}$	$\mu_{k,5}$	$\mu_{k,6}$	$\mu_{k,7}$	$\mu_{k,8}$	$\mu_{k,9}$	$\mu_{k,10}$
1	16	64.8	68.4	67.5	18.0	–	–	–	66.6	62.1	124.2
2	4	57.6	60.8	60.0	–	9.6	–	–	59.2	55.2	110.4
3	10	57.6	60.8	60.0	–	–	38.4	–	59.2	55.2	110.4
4	2	36.0	38.0	37.5	–	–	24.0	4.5	37.0	34.5	69.0
5	4	57.6	60.8	60.0	–	9.6	–	–	59.2	55.2	110.4
6	7	50.4	53.2	52.5	–	–	33.6	–	51.8	48.3	96.6
7	7	50.4	53.2	52.5	–	–	33.6	–	51.8	48.3	96.6
8	1	36.0	38.0	37.5	–	–	24.0	4.5	37.0	34.5	69.0
9	1	36.0	38.0	37.5	–	–	24.0	4.5	37.0	34.5	69.0
10	2	72.0	76.0	75.0	–	–	–	–	–	–	138.0
11	16	64.8	68.4	67.5	–	–	–	–	–	–	124.2
12	2	72.0	76.0	75.0	–	–	–	–	–	–	138.0
13	30	50.4	53.2	52.5	–	–	–	–	–	–	96.6

This test utilized a lognormal distribution for all interarrival and service times, hereafter denoted by LN$(\mu, 0.5625)$, where the scale parameter μ is calculated using the problem inputs and the shape parameter is fixed at 0.5625. The mean and variance for this distribution are given by

Table 6. External arrival and service rates for high resolution model (1/hr).

Route (k)	$\mu_{k,11}$	$\mu_{k,12}$	$\mu_{k,13}$	$\mu_{k,14}$	$\mu_{k,15}$	$\mu_{k,16}$	$\mu_{k,17}$	$\mu_{k,18}$	$\mu_{k,19}$	$\mu_{k,20}$	$\mu_{k,21}$
1	–	20.3	–	18.9	119.7	–	–	105.8	–	21.6	126.0
2	100.0	–	95.2	–	106.4	–	24.8	–	96.0	–	112.0
3	100.0	–	95.2	–	106.4	–	24.8	–	96.0	–	112.0
4	62.5	–	59.5	–	66.5	–	–	58.8	60.0	–	70.0
5	100.0	–	95.2	–	106.4	–	–	94.0	96.0	–	112.0
6	87.5	–	83.3	–	93.1	–	21.7	–	84.0	–	98.0
7	87.5	–	83.3	–	93.1	–	–	82.3	84.0	–	98.0
8	62.5	–	59.5	–	66.5	–	15.5	–	60.0	–	70.0
9	62.5	–	59.5	–	66.5	–	–	58.8	60.0	–	70.0
10	125.0	–	119.0	–	–	2.7	–	–	120.0	–	140.0
11	112.5	–	107.1	–	119.7	–	–	105.8	108.0	–	126.0
12	–	22.5	–	21.0	133.0	–	–	117.5	–	24.0	140.0
13	87.5	–	83.3	–	93.1	–	–	82.3	84.0	–	98.0

Table 7. High resolution results using LN(μ, 0.5625) interarrival and service times.

Node	Analytical			Simulated		
	L_q	W	d	L_q	W	d
1	31.2504	0.5787	55.7421	30.7960	0.5704	55.7611
2	9.2002	0.1704	60.0238	8.7384	0.1618	60.3832
3	11.3152	0.2095	58.8881	11.0260	0.2042	59.0044
4	6.0416	0.3776	18.7601	5.5251	0.3453	19.0689
5	3.5982	0.4498	10.4105	3.0126	0.3768	11.0520
6	3.8842	0.1387	35.7773	3.2693	0.1168	37.7273
7	6.1547	1.5387	4.6751	4.8917	1.2240	4.8830
8	9.0482	0.1740	57.9061	8.8461	0.1701	58.0467
9	59.4707	1.1437	52.8783	56.5460	1.0876	52.9174
10	12.2901	0.1229	108.3653	11.8680	0.1187	108.6678
11	5.7218	0.0698	97.0495	5.1972	0.0634	98.9047
12	5.4817	0.3045	21.4409	4.9293	0.2738	21.9084
13	10.4581	0.1275	90.0699	9.9503	0.1214	90.4812
14	11.8739	0.6597	19.5494	11.6890	0.6494	19.5783
15	48.8370	0.4884	102.0506	45.3640	0.4537	102.2064
16	1.8498	0.9249	3.3358	1.4683	0.7333	4.0456
17	16.2534	0.7388	23.3679	13.7860	0.6268	23.6250
18	4.4583	0.0572	96.6364	4.0931	0.0525	98.8319
19	12.6896	0.1511	90.7202	11.7830	0.1403	91.2871
20	3.3060	0.1837	23.9707	2.9830	0.1657	24.8732
21	14.2415	0.1396	109.3042	13.8710	0.1360	109.4770
Overall	287.4246	8.7492	1140.9223	269.6334	6.5983	1152.7306

$$e^{\mu+\sigma^2/2}$$

and

$$e^{2\mu+\sigma^2}\left(e^{\sigma^2}-1\right),$$

respectively. All nodes were assumed to be GI/G/1 queues. The LN(μ, 0.5625) distribution has a squared coefficient of variation of $(e^{0.5625}-1) \approx 0.7551$. The results for this test are summarized in Table 7.

As evidenced by Table 7, the analytical approximations closely match the simulated results for each of the performance measures. However, as with the low resolution model, the computational effort required to obtain these mean-value measures is drastically different. The simulation results were obtained in 11 hours and ten minutes as compared to approximately 0.5 seconds for the analytical approximations.

6. CONCLUSIONS

In this paper, we have presented an analytical, stochastic model of the JRSOI process to obtain computationally expedient estimates for critical performance measures such as congestion, throughput, and closure for activities within JRSOI and for the process as a whole. Such estimates can provide insight to aid decision makers in the planning and execution of impending military deployments. To the authors' knowledge, no purely analytical models exist that capture the aggregate features of the JRSOI process; however, the literature does reveal a number of simulation models for the enhancement of force projection planning and execution.

By modeling the JRSOI process as an open, multiclass queueing network, we are able to capture the aggregate features of the process by utilizing the well-known queueing network analyzer (QNA) due to Whitt [6]. Using parametric decomposition, this approach provides the appropriate approximation equations for performance measures. This approach assumes that a network of GI/G/m queues admits a product-form solution, which is not the case in general. The high resolution model of our network extends the basic network by incorporating a fork-join node that allows for concurrent processing within one phase of the process. Though the models presented here are notional, they lay a foundation for a more realistic and complex analytical model for the JRSOI process.

The performance of the analytical equations were compared with simulated values on two example problems. The first problem was a low resolution model while the second was a high resolution model. The numerical comparisons of Section 5 demonstrate that we are able to obtain accurate measures using the analytical approximations in a fraction of the time required for discrete-event simulation. The computation time for discrete-event simulation ranged from five to 16 hours, whereas those for the analytical approach were on the order of 0.5 seconds. Furthermore, the simulation run times, despite being extensive, were only long enough to ensure that the half-widths for the 95% confidence intervals were less than 5% of the size of the confidence interval means. Longer run lengths would be required to reduce the confidence interval half-widths significantly. There was a noticeable variance in relative error between the analytical approach and the simulation depending on the queue structure, network dependency, squared coefficients of variation, parametric probability distributions, and traffic intensity specific to each node. In general, the analytical approach performed reasonably well for individual nodes and the entire system for the models tested. Most relative errors were at or below 10%.

As expected, the approximation equations tend to perform better when squared coefficients of variation are close to a value of 1.0. As noted by Whitt [9], the accuracy of the approximations does not necessarily decrease as the complexity of the network increases. In fact, extensive empirical testing on a number of examples indicated that some of the most accurate results occurred on the largest and most complex networks. It should be noted that our analytical approximations can be improved by incorporating higher-order moments.

There are many potential extensions to the proposed analytical model for the JRSOI process. This work did not consider bulk arrival or service processes. It would be beneficial to consider these cases since they are likely to prevail in real-world operations. It may also be useful to consider the optimal selection of processing rates at each queueing station for the purpose of maximizing throughput or minimizing closure. In future work, it will be important to better account for superposition and departure processes at queueing stations. Whitt [6] utilized parameters in his algorithms (the values $\{v_{ij}\}$) that can be adjusted to account for the impact of these processes on performance. In this paper, these parameters were set to zero, though the values can be chosen on the interval $[0,1]$ to improve the approximations.

The main contribution of this paper is a novel approach for modeling JRSOI that is computationally expedient and produces accurate results for a few critical performance measures. It lays the groundwork for the development of a comprehensive queueing network analysis tool specifically tailored for JRSOI. The base model developed here can be readily adapted to any potential area of conflict with appropriate modifications. The capability to expediently compute network performance measures can greatly enhance a combatant commander's ability to properly regulate entity flow and obtain other useful information to aid the efficient build up of combat capability.

REFERENCES

1. Department of Defense, *Joint Tactics, Techniques, and Procedures for Joint Reception, Staging, Onward Movement, and Integration*, Joint Publication 4-01.8, GPO, Washington, D.C., (2000).
2. Department of the Army, *Reception, Staging, Onward Movement, and Integration*, Field Manual 100-17.3, HQ USA, Washington, D.C., (1999).
3. D.G. Drummer, An assessment of modelling and simulation tools for force projection, 20000526 074, U.S. Army War College, USAWC Class of 2000, (2000).
4. M.A. Lidy, D.P. Baird, J.M. Cook and W.J. Sheleski, Force deployment rock drill after action report, Document D-1954, Institute for Defense Analyses, Alexandria, VA, (1996).
5. D.A. Meyer, Transportation Strategy, Military Review, Command & General Staff College, `http://www.cgsc.army.mil/milrev/english/JanFeb01/meyer.asp`, (2001).
6. W. Whitt, The queueing network analyzer, *The Bell System Technical Journal* **62.9**, 2779–2815, (1983).
7. G. Bolch, S. Greiner, H. de Meer and K.S. Trivedi, *Queueing Networks and Markov Chains*, John Wiley & Sons, New York, (1998).
8. Defense Transportation Regulation (DTR) DOD Regulation 4500.9-R-Part III Mobility, (November 2001).
9. W. Whitt, Performance of the queueing network analyzer, *The Bell System Technical Journal* **62.9**, 2817–2843, (1983).
10. L. Kleinrock, *Queueing Systems, Volume I: Theory*, John Wiley & Sons, New York, (1975).

ELSEVIER

Available online at www.sciencedirect.com

SCIENCE @ DIRECT•

Mathematical and Computer Modelling 39 (2004) 817–838

MATHEMATICAL AND COMPUTER MODELLING

www.elsevier.com/locate/mcm

A Simulation Architecture to Support Intratheater Sealift Operations

J. F. LEATHRUM, JR., R. R. MIELKE, S. MAZUMDAR,
R. MATHEW, Y. MANEPALLI, V. PILLAI AND R. N. MALLADI
Department of Electrical and Computer Engineering
Old Dominion University, Norfolk, VA 23529, U.S.A.
leathrum@ece.odu.edu
rmielke@odu.edu
<saurav_m><reejo_mathew><ymane001><vinayrajp>@hotmail.com
nmall003@odu.edu

J. JOINES
Military Traffic Management Command
Transportation Engineering Agency (MTMCTEA)
720 Thimble Shoales Blvd., Suite 130
Newport News, VA 23606-2574, U.S.A.
Joseph.Joines@tea.army.mil

Abstract—A new architecture for simulating intratheater sealift operations is presented. Intratheater sealift operations refer to new strategies proposed for quickly deploying a military force to a theater of war when major seaports are not available. In this strategy, a self-deployable force is transported to a sea-based intermediate staging base (SISB) by conventional cargo transport ships. The SISB is a world-class seaport generally located within 800 miles of the theater of war. At the SISB, cargo is transferred to a new ship platform called the theater support vessel (TSV). TSVs are to be designed to access very small ports located at or near the theater of war. Simulation provides an efficient and cost-effective method for testing these strategies and for evaluating the required new logistics technologies. Should intratheater sealift operations prove viable, the simulation also provides a means to plan and rehearse an exercise. The new simulation architecture is described and example simulation case studies are conducted to demonstrate the capabilities and potential benefits of the approach.

Keywords—Port simulation, Intratheater sealift, Cargo logistics, Nodal networks.

1. INTRODUCTION

In order for the military to strategically deploy worldwide, it is necessary to deliver and then sustain forces, potentially without the benefit of a world-class seaport through which to move cargo. Therefore, alternative scenarios such as joint logistics over the shore (JLOTS) have been investigated, where cargo is moved over a bare beach or by temporary port infrastructure [1,2]. JLOTS operations require the transfer of cargo from a ship to a lighter (a small craft designed

Supported by the Military Traffic Management Command Transportation Engineering Agency through the contract "Cargo Logistics Modeling and Simulation".

0895-7177/04/$ - see front matter Typeset by $\mathcal{A}\mathcal{M}\mathcal{S}$-TEX
doi:10.1016/j.mcm.2004.02.016

to transfer cargo or personnel from ship to shore) while in-stream. For this reason, these scenarios are extremely slow, have low throughput capabilities, and can be dangerous to personnel and equipment. The result is that other options, such as intratheater sealift operations, are being considered. In intratheater sealift operations, cargo is first offloaded at a large seaport of debarkation (SPOD) relatively near the theater of operation, but not within range to surface deploy the cargo by road or rail. The cargo is then transported to numerous smaller ports or protected harbors within the theater of operation where it can be deployed over land routes. A full description of army watercraft operations is found in [3]. Intratheater airlift operations are similar in nature and an integrated air-sea model is presented in this paper. Operations of this type require the development of new technologies, force structures, and equipment characteristics to enable such a deployment [4]. A simulation is used in the initial planning phases as a means to assess technology requirements and to estimate potential cargo throughput capabilities. As this new technology matures, the same simulation can be used to support tactical and operational planning/replanning should the intratheater sealift operation prove viable through the initial simulation effort.

The objective of this paper is to describe the development of a new simulation model for intratheater sealift operations. The simulation is constructed as a network of cargo terminal nodes, that is, seaports, airports, and destination staging bases. Each cargo terminal is modeled using the configurable port simulation (CPortS) constructed in support of the port simulation (PORTSIM) project conducted for the Military Traffic Management Command Transportation Engineering Agency (MTMCTEA) [5]. CPortS is designed to analyze port capabilities for handling military cargo. The simulation is a discrete event simulation performed at the entity cargo level, thus, supporting the analysis of how various cargo types move through constrained port environments. Infrastructure, resources, and transports are parameterized to allow the study of new technologies and their impacts on port operations. An example of the use of this capability is an investigation of how the capabilities of theater support vessels, such as speed and berthing capabilities, affect cargo throughput.

In Section 2, intratheater sealift operations are described in terms of a network of cargo terminals. Potential applications for this model are explored and operational bounds, based on a high-level queuing model, are developed. In Section 3, a fictitious example scenario based in Japan and South Korea is presented to illustrate the use of the intratheater sealift operations simulation. Then, in Section 4, the detailed model for the intratheater sealift operations simulation is presented. The cargo terminal models are derived from the CPortS model and the system model is formulated as an interconnection of cargo terminals. The conclusion is presented in Section 5.

2. INTRATHEATER SEALIFT OPERATIONS

Intratheater sealift operations support the movement of military cargo into areas where there is insufficient access to world-class seaports to support a standard military deployment as was done in Desert Storm. An intratheater sealift operation utilizes a large, world-class seaport of debarkation, located a safe distance from the region of conflict, to transfer cargo from large cargo transport ships to smaller and faster vessels that are capable of utilizing the small or reduced capacity ports in the region. These smaller vessels, called theater support vessels (TSVs), are anticipated to achieve a maximum speed of 40 knots under fully loaded conditions, a range of 400 nautical miles, and a maximum draft of 13–15 feet. Therefore, TSVs should be capable of rapidly shuttling cargo to ports as small as commercial fishing ports. The potential exists to go into extremely small ports utilizing new technologies for port enhancement where the port could be improved to accept the TSVs by adding piers and breakwaters [6].

The forces anticipated for use in this scenario must be self-sustaining in that they must organically move themselves. The cargo for the force will not have transportation resources such as trucks or railcars nor the infrastructure to move the cargo once reaching the final leg in the transportation network. Therefore, all cargo will be configured as convoy (self-propelled wheeled and tracked vehicles) or self-deployed (helicopters and small watercraft). This approach works well for the initial surge as the force is made fighting capable. However, issues still remain over how to later sustain the force, an activity that generally requires containerized cargo be transported.

The basic structure of the joint operation encompassing both intratheater sealift operations and intratheater airlift operations is displayed in Figure 1. The operation utilizes a world-class seaport as the sea-based intermediate staging base (SISB) and a world-class airport as the air-based intermediate staging base (AISB). In the SISB, ships arrive with cargo that is offloaded to staging areas to await an appropriate TSV for transport.

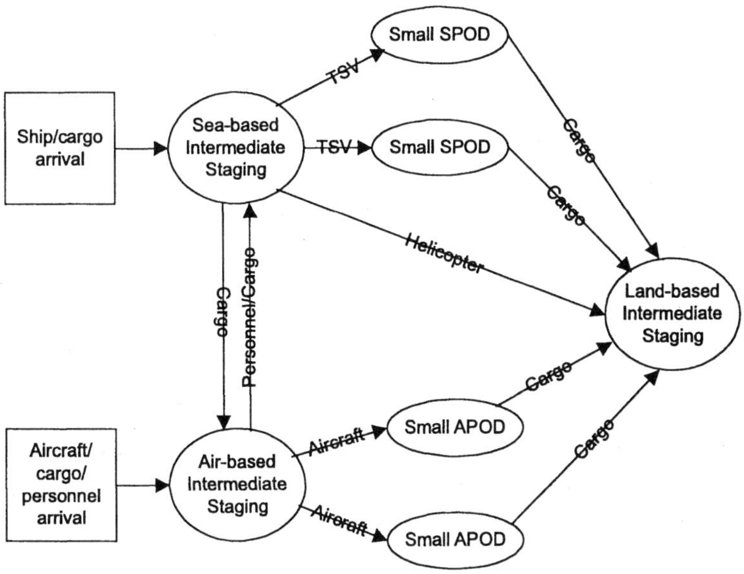

Figure 1. Joint intratheater sealift and airlift model.

Once a TSV-size load is made ready at the SISB, and unit drivers and an empty TSV are available for the cargo (vehicles), the cargo is loaded on the TSV for transport to a small or reduced capacity SPOD. The unit drivers generally are flown to the AISB; from there they are transported to the SISB to marry up with their vehicles on the TSVs. At the reduced SPOD, the TSVs berth and the vehicles are driven off by the unit drivers. The vehicles may or may not be staged in the reduced SPOD before rolling out for transit to a large land-based intermediate staging base (LISB) for deployment in the theater of war.

For air cargo, the reduced airports of debarkation (APOD) are limited as to the types of aircraft that can land. Therefore, the AISB is used in a manner similar to the SISB; cargo is reconfigured for loading on smaller aircraft having the required characteristics. Besides unit drivers, the possibility is left open for cargo to be transferred between the SISB and the AISB should the need arise.

Initial work on this project has focused on the sea-based component of the operation, although the air component can be integrated at a future time with relative ease due to the architecture presented here. Therefore, the remainder of the paper will focus solely on the intratheater sealift operations.

2.1. Model Requirements

Simulation offers a means to study operational requirements for the intratheater sealift operation prior to complete commitment to this strategy. This presents the opportunity to perform feasibility studies based on the TSV characteristics and availability of compatible ports for the

TSV. The TSV characteristics are of primary concern. While research and development are ongoing to develop a vessel capable of meeting the desired requirements [7], there is a need to test and validate the requirements. It is impractical to develop a sufficient number of TSVs to conduct live testing of the requirements, only to discover the design to be flawed.

The primary question is how fast a fleet of TSVs can shuttle the cargo based on the rate of availability of the cargo at the SISB. The rate of availability of cargo is limited by ship arrivals and the capability of the SISB to handle the cargo, given that the military is unlikely to gain access to the whole port due to ongoing commercial activities. The initial set of parameters identified for studying the capabilities of the TSV fleet to shuttle cargo includes the following.

- *TSV Capacity.* Obviously, the more cargo that a TSV can carry, the fewer TSV trips required to transport the complete set of cargo, thus improving throughput. However, a larger capacity adversely impacts other TSV characteristics.
- *TSV Loading/Offloading Rate.* The loading/offloading rate of the TSV dictates how long the TSV must spend in port. For instance, should the TSV have two side loading ramps, theoretically (not practically) the load/offload rate should double, thus improving the throughput of the system.
- *TSV Speed/Range.* The range and speed of a TSV dictate its efficiency in cycling to transport cargo. A larger range opens the possibility for more and/or larger reduced SPODs to be utilized. A faster speed reduces the cycle time, allowing a single TSV to complete more trips in a given time period.
- *Number of TSVs.* If the current number of TSVs does not fully utilize the available capabilities of the intermediate seabase and the reduced SPODs, then adding more TSVs allows more trips to be completed in a given time period.
- *Reduced SPOD Capacities/Rates/Quantities.* The more TSVs that the reduced SPODs can handle and the faster they can handle them, the more TSVs that can be effectively applied to the problem.
- *Proximity of Potential SISBs to Regions of Interest.* The closer the SISB is to the region of interest, the shorter the cycle time required by the TSVs, enabling more trips in a given time frame.
- *Force Characteristics.* By reconfiguring a force to be lighter, more mobile, and self-deployable, it is easier to transport the force by TSV, and then by land within the theater of war [4].

2.2. Intratheater Sealift Performance Bounds

The cycling of TSVs to shuttle cargo from the SISB to the reduced SPODs can be viewed as a simple queuing model and some simple bounds can be derived. Two performance bounds are derived prior to simulation to determine the capability of the TSVs to support the scenario. The first is to determine an upper bound on the number of TSVs that can be applied to a scenario without saturating the cargo terminal system. When a port reaches saturation, TSVs start queueing up while waiting for the necessary loading/unloading resources. Then, knowing the number of TSVs appropriate for the scenario, a lower bound on the closure time for the scenario can be derived, where the closure time is the time the last piece of cargo reaches its final destination.

Upper bound on the number of TSVs before saturation

To focus on the requirements for the number of TSVs, the TSV processes are simplified to the loading time (T_L), the travel time under load (T_{TL}), the unloading time (T_U), and the travel time under no load (T_{TU}). Then the total cycle time for a single TSV with no contention for port infrastructure and resources is

$$T = (T_L + T_{TL} + T_U + T_{TU}). \tag{1}$$

If the nodes of the system are considered to have an infinite capacity of holding TSVs and the intermediate seabase can provide available cargo for the TSVs faster than they can shuttle it (based on the ship arrival profile, port resources, and port infrastructure), then the upper limit on the number of TSVs that can be served by a single loading site at the SISB without saturation is bounded by $\lceil T/T_L \rceil$. Likewise, the upper limit served by a single unloading site is bounded by $\lceil T/T_U \rceil$. The upper limit on the number of TSVs before saturation for a system with a single loading and a single unloading site is then

$$N_{\text{bound}} = \min\left(\left\lceil \frac{T}{T_L} \right\rceil, \left\lceil \frac{T}{T_U} \right\rceil\right). \tag{2}$$

Taking into account that as the number of TSVs approaches the theoretical bound, TSVs are more likely to have to wait on other TSVs, it may be desirable to add a waiting factor to T_L and T_U for a more realistic result.

When taking into account that an SISB probably has more than one loading site (N_L loading sites) and the reduced SPODs probably have more than one unloading site (N_U unloading sites), equation (2) becomes

$$N_{\text{bound}} = \min\left(N_L \cdot \left\lceil \frac{T}{T_L} \right\rceil, N_U \cdot \left\lceil \frac{T}{T_U} \right\rceil\right). \tag{3}$$

Lower bound on closure time

A theoretical lower bound for the time required for TSVs to transport cargo can be derived as an initial step in studying scenario requirements. If this lower bound satisfies operational requirements, simulation study is warranted to determine more accurate operational capabilities. The lower bound is obtained by again assuming that the intermediate seabase can provide available cargo for the TSVs faster than they can shuttle it (based on the ship arrival profile, port resources, and port infrastructure).

The minimum number of required TSV loads is computed as

$$\#\text{ of loads} = \max\left(\left\lceil \frac{\text{SQFT(cargo)}}{\text{SQFT(TSV)}} \right\rceil, \left\lceil \frac{\text{STON(cargo)}}{\text{STON(TSV)}} \right\rceil\right), \tag{4}$$

where SQFT(cargo) and STON(cargo) indicate the square feet and short tons, respectively, of the total amount of cargo requiring transfer, and SQFT(TSV) and STON(TSV) indicate the square feet and short ton capabilities, respectively, of a single TSV. If the scenario has a number N_{TSV} of TSVs available, the number of effective TSVs $N_{\text{effective}}$ is defined by $\min(N_{\text{bound}}, N_{\text{TSV}})$. Then assuming no conflict for infrastructure or resources at either the SISB or the reduced SPODs, the time to transport all of the cargo is defined by

$$T_C = \left(\left\lceil \frac{\#\text{ of loads}}{N_{\text{effective}}} \right\rceil \cdot T\right) - T_{TU}, \tag{5}$$

where T_C is the time to closure when all cargo has been transferred. The actual time will be larger than T_C as resource contention and realistic loading of TSVs reduce throughput. Therefore, if the lower bound does not meet operational requirements, operational parameters must be modified before generating more realistic scenario results via simulation.

3. EXAMPLE INTRATHEATER SEALIFT OPERATION SCENARIO

In this section, an example simulation study is described to demonstrate the application and potential benefits of a simulation capability for intratheater sealift operations. In this fictitious scenario, it becomes necessary to deploy a United States mechanized division from bases in Europe to south-central South Korea. The mechanized division is moved via an intratheater sealift operation. Large cargo transport ships move the division to SISB located at Naha, Japan. Here the division is loaded onto TSVs for transport to four reduced SPODs located on the southern and eastern coasts of South Korea. Finally, the division moves by road to an inland staging area. The focus of the study is to determine the number of TSV resources necessary to conduct the intratheater sealift operation, and then to investigate the impact of different TSV designs on the port usage profile. In addition, the effects of introducing additional berthing capabilities for the TSVs at the SISB, provided through either berth reallocation or port enhancements that take place during sealift operations, are also investigated.

First, the intratheater sealift operation scenario is described. Then the model characteristics used to represent the SISB, the set of reduced SPODs, and network interconnection of these ports are defined. Next, three different simulation experiments are described. In the first experiment, simulation runs using different numbers of TSVs are conducted. The objective is to determine the number of TSVs required to achieve a reasonable port usage profile and to investigate the constraints that limit throughput. In the second experiment, two different sizes of TSVs are used to transport cargo between the SISB and the reduced SPODs. The effects of TSV design characteristics on the port usage profile are investigated. In the third experiment, the effects of adding additional TSV berthing to the SISB, after the start of an exercise, are investigated. This experiment is similar to a host of studies that could be conducted to explore the value of developing rapid port reallocation strategies and port enhancement capabilities.

It is important to note that this scenario is fictional and is not based on any past or contemplated military activities. The scenario was invented primarily because detailed port data for the included ports were readily available to the authors.

3.1. Scenario Description

The fictitious scenario is based on a newspaper article, written by James A. Baker III, U.S. Secretary of State from 1989 to 1992, that appeared originally in The Washington Post and was reprinted in The Virginian-Pilot on October 25, 2002. In response to the revelation that North Korea had escalated its nuclear weapons development program, the United Nations Security Council issued political and economic sanctions. As a result, the United States Army was asked to expand quickly its military force in South Korea by the addition of one mechanized division. Due to the perceived urgency of the situation, it was decided to move the mechanized division using an intratheater sealift operation.

The scenario calls for U.S. forces stationed in locations throughout Europe, corresponding to one mechanized division, to be sent by cargo transport ships to an SISB at Naha, Japan. At Naha, the force is loaded aboard a small fleet of TSVs for transit to South Korea. Because of the desire to sustain scheduled commercial activity at the South Korean ports and the need to maintain a low political profile, it is decided to use only very limited components of four commercial ports: Pusan, Pohang, Masan, and Chinhae. From these ports, division units will move by road to an inland staging area located approximately 100 kilometers due west of Pohang. The ports of Pusan, Masan, and Chinhae are located in relatively close proximity and are approximately 720 miles from the ISB at Naha. The port of Pohang is 80 miles further north. All port data are derived from GIS data provided by MTMCTEA's System Integration Division.

The intratheater sealift operation concept is still in its infancy. Simulation studies as proposed here appear to be an inexpensive and efficient method to investigate the many possible system configurations that could be used. The example simulation study has three objectives, to determine the number of TSVs necessary to conduct such an intratheater sealift operation, to explore the effects of TSV design on cargo throughput, and to investigate the effects of port resources and infrastructure at the SISB on port usage profiles.

A new class of ships, called theater support vessels, is proposed for transporting fighting-ready units from the SISB to the reduced SPOD. At this time, several different sizes have been

Table 1. TSV characteristics. These characteristics are derived from MTMCTEA's Deployability Division and are projected ship characteristics, not to reflect any particular design.

TSV Size / TSV Characteristics	Small TSV	Large TSV
Payload Area	12,000 Sq. Ft.	25,000 Sq. Ft.
Payload Weight	600 STons	1,250 STons
Speed	35 Knots	42 Knots
Length	300 Ft.	420 Ft.
Beam	87 Ft.	89 Ft.
Draft	12 Ft.	15 Ft.

proposed for these ships. In this example, port usage profiles for cargo transport from Naha to the destinations in South Korea are compared for two differently sized TSVs. The objective of the experiment is to determine if a larger fleet of small TSVs performs better than a smaller fleet of larger TSVs. The characteristics of the two TSVs are presented in Table 1.

Another technology thought to be of importance in an intratheater sealift operation is the capability to enhance or improve very quickly port infrastructure at the seaports. These ports could be as small as a commercial fishing port that may not have the pier or road facilities required by the unit vehicles. In addition, since these ports are selected as close as possible to the theater of war, it may be that port capabilities have been reduced because of hostile action. Thus, even when a world-class port is selected as the reduced SPOD, enhancements might be required just to make small portions of the port operational. In this example, studies are conducted to determine the effects on the port usage profile of increasing the berthing capacity of the intermediate staging base midway through a sealift exercise.

3.2. Simulation Model

The example simulation model captures the process of transporting one mechanized division from bases in Europe to an inland destination in south-central South Korea. Division equipment is transported to the SISB at Naha, Japan aboard large cargo transport ships. The example mechanized division consists of 8,686 vehicles having a storage area requirement of 1,060,834 square feet and a payload weight of approximately 79,676 short tons. The vehicles arrive on nine cargo ships that reach Naha over a six day period. At Naha, the vehicles are unloaded and organized in staging areas by destination and by unit. Divisional forces are transported to Naha by air, and marry up with their respective equipment for loading on the TSVs. The TSVs are loaded to capacity, limited either by storage area (square feet) or payload weight (short tons (STons)) for a particular destination, so as to preserve unit integrity. When fully loaded, the TSVs depart for their assigned reduced SPOD. At the reduced SPOD, the TSVs are unloaded and vehicle convoys are formed for movement to the inland staging area designated as the destination. As soon as a TSV is unloaded, it returns to the SISB at Naha to receive another load.

The port models used in the simulation are quite detailed and accurately represent constraints imposed by port geometry and size, port infrastructure, and the availability of port resources necessary to operate the port. The sea transport model is much less detailed and is modeled simply by a random delay having mean equal to distance traveled divided by ship speed. Of course, this delay can be changed to represent different ship loading and different weather conditions. The port models are described in more detail in the remainder of this section.

Sea-based intermediate staging base

The SISB used in this example is the Port of Naha, Japan. Naha is located approximate 720 miles due south of South Korea. Although classified as a world-class commercial port, Naha is

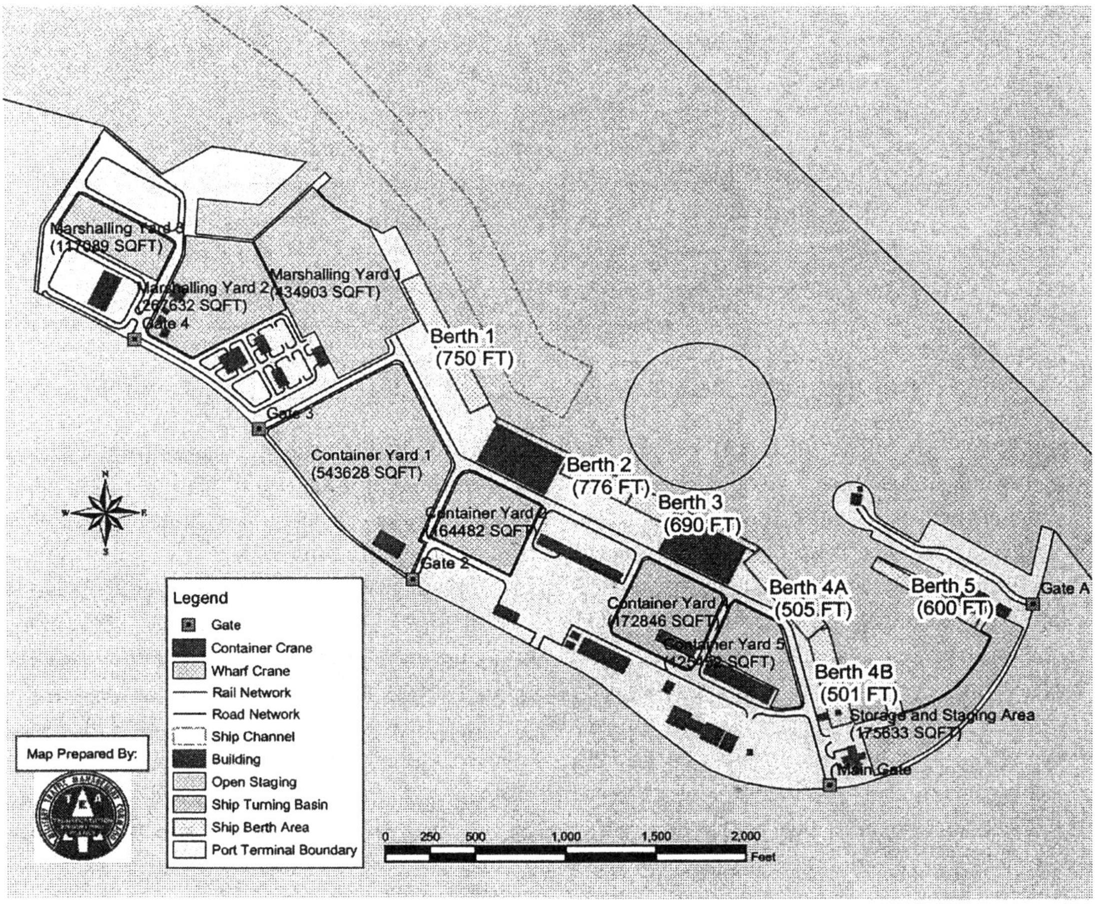

Figure 2. The Port of Naha, Japan.

considered a relatively small port and is just large enough to be viable for use as a SISB. Even for this relatively small exercise, it is necessary to utilize most of the available port resources. The Port of Naha is shown in Figure 2.

As cargo ships arrive, they are placed in anchorage just out of view in the upper left of Figure 2. When an appropriate berthing space becomes free and the necessary port resources are available, the ship is moved to berth with the assistance of two harbor tugs, a harbor pilot, and other port berthing resources such as line handlers. At Naha, Berth 1 and an adjacent undeveloped shoreline can berth one large cargo ship, and the combined adjacent berths, Berth 2 and Berth 3, can accommodate a second large cargo ship. As the ships are unloaded, cargo is moved and sorted by destination and unit to nearby staging areas. Three areas, Marshalling Yard 1 with 434,903 sq. ft., Marshalling Yard 2 with 267,632 sq. ft., and Container Yard 1 with 543,628 sq. ft., are used for this purpose. A 65% parking factor is applied to these areas. Container Yard 2, consisting of a covered area of 45,789 sq. ft. and an open area of 164,482 sq. ft., is used for helicopter reassembly, staging, and takeoff.

As empty TSVs arrive at Naha, they also are placed in anchorage. As dedicated TSV berths become available, TSVs transit from anchorage to berth. The TSVs are self berthing/deberthing in that they do not require tugs. Berth 4A with a length of 580 ft., Berth 4B with a length of 550 ft., and Berth 5 with a length of 600 ft. are used as the TSV berths at Naha. All three berths have a depth at mean low water (MLW) of greater than 30 ft., well exceeding TSV requirements. When a complete TSV load is assembled in staging, that load is moved to the TSV berth area and then loaded aboard a TSV. Loaded TSVs then exit the port and begin the trip to a specified reduced SPOD.

Reduced SPODs

Four reduced SPODs located along the southern and eastern coastlines of South Korea are used in this example as unloading nodes for the TSVs. These ports, Pohang, Pusan, Masan, and Chinhae, are world-class commercial seaports of varying sizes; however, only a very small subset of the available infrastructure is utilized in this scenario. As TSVs arrive at one of the reduced SPODs, they are placed in anchorage until a TSV berth becomes available. When a berth is ready, a TSV moves to the berth and unloads. All cargo consists of self-deployable vehicles that roll-off the TSV via a side-ramp located near the stern of the ship. The cargo is directed first to a staging area for final preparation for insertion to the theater of war, and then to a convoy construction area in preparation for exiting the port. When ready, small convoys consisting of ten vehicles each exit the port by passing through a port gate and then drive by existing roads to the destination. In this example, the destination is a large inland assembly area located approximately 100 kilometers due west of Pohang. The restricted port resources are shown in Table 2. Note that depths are recorded for mean low water (MLW).

Table 2. Reduced POD characteristics.

Ports	Berth		Staging Area (sq. ft.)
	Length (ft.)	Depth (ft.)	
Pohang	550	30	342,904
Chinhae	570	30	624,476
Masan	580	20	1,474,757
Pusan (Two Berths)	600	40	147,155
	580	30	6,646,210

3.3. Example Case Studies

In this section, three example simulation case studies are described to illustrate the application of the intratheater sealift operation simulation. In the first case study, the number of available TSVs is varied to determine how many TSVs are required to transport the mechanized division. In the second case study, the intratheater sealift operation is conducted using two different TSV fleets, one consisting of large TSVs and the other consisting of small TSVs. The objective is to determine if one of the TSV fleets is able to deliver the mechanized division faster than the other. In the third case study, reallocation of port infrastructure is conducted during the sealift operation to increase the number of TSV berths available at the SISB. The objective is to investigate how much faster the mechanized division can be delivered because of the availability of these additional berths.

The intratheater sealift operation toolset includes several output user interfaces to gather performance data useful in these case studies. One of these interfaces gathers data that indicate performance of the overall port network. In this interface, an event is defined as the occurrence of one or more cargo entities entering or departing a port. When an event occurs, information concerning the event is written to an event list. This information includes: event time, port ID, transporter ID, event type (cargo arrival or departure), and cargo information including number of cargo entities, cargo area, and cargo weight. The event list then is used to develop several graphical displays, the port usage profile and the TSV activity profile. The port usage profile is a plot of the number of cargo items in a specific port displayed as a function of time. The TSV activity profile displays the state of each TSV as a function of time; possible TSV states are loading cargo, transit to reduced SPOD, unloading cargo, and transit to SISB. Together, these plots produce a high level view of the performance of the overall port network.

A second output user interface gathers data that indicate how cargo items move through a single port. The port is partitioned into major activity areas through which cargo moves as it passes through the port. For example, at the SISB the major port activity areas are: ship anchorage, ship berth, staging, TSV berth, and TSV anchorage. An event is defined as a cargo item entering or departing one of these activity areas or a process being performed on the cargo. When an event occurs, information concerning that event is written to an event list. This information includes: event time, activity area ID, cargo ID, event type, and other more detailed information concerning associated resource utilization. The event list then is used to develop several graphical displays, the port area usage profile and the cargo item activity profile. The port area usage profile is a plot of the number of cargo items in a specific port activity area displayed as a function of time. The cargo item activity profile displays the cargo location within the port as a function of time. Together, these plots produce a low level view of the performance of individual ports.

Investigation of TSV fleet size

The first case study is designed to investigate the relationship between TSV fleet size and the time required to deliver all cargo to the reduced SPODs. The intratheater sealift scenario is run using a fleet of large TSVs, and the number of TSVs in the fleet is varied from four to 13. For each fleet size, the closure time is measured and the results are displayed in Figure 3.

The results indicate that the closure time decreases as the number of ships in the TSV fleet increases. The closure time continues to improve until the number of TSVs reaches approximately 12; increasing the number of TSVs further results in little additional improvement in system performance. The reasons for this system behavior can be explained by observing system operation at a more detailed level as provided by the port usage profile and the TSV activity diagram. The port usage profile for eight TSVs is shown in Figure 4. The port usage profile shows the number of pieces of cargo in the port as a function of time. Similar port usage profiles

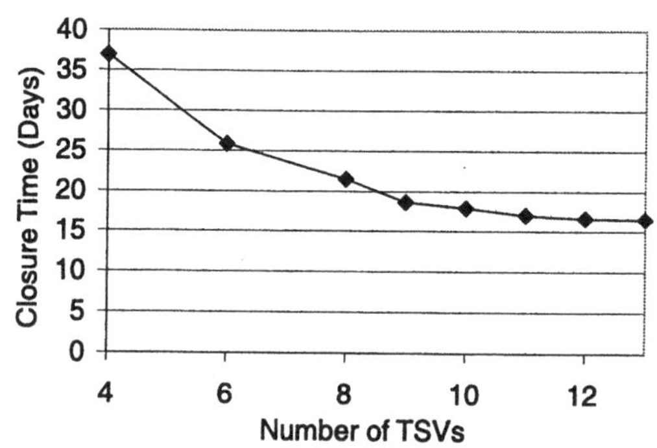

Figure 3. Closure time for varying fleet sizes for large TSVs.

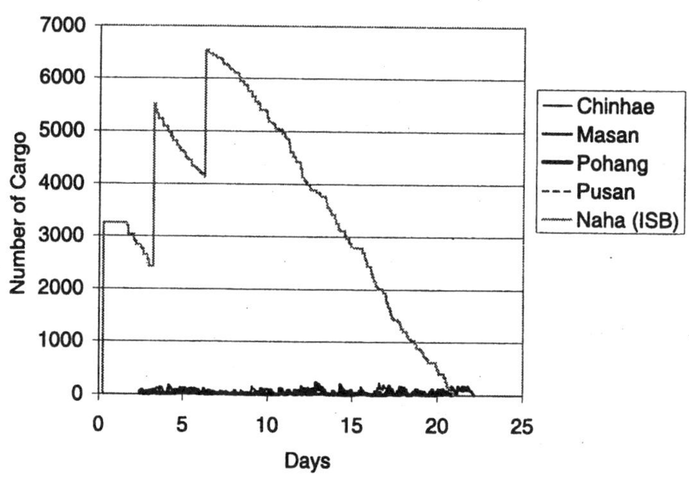

Figure 4. Port usage profile for eight large TSVs.

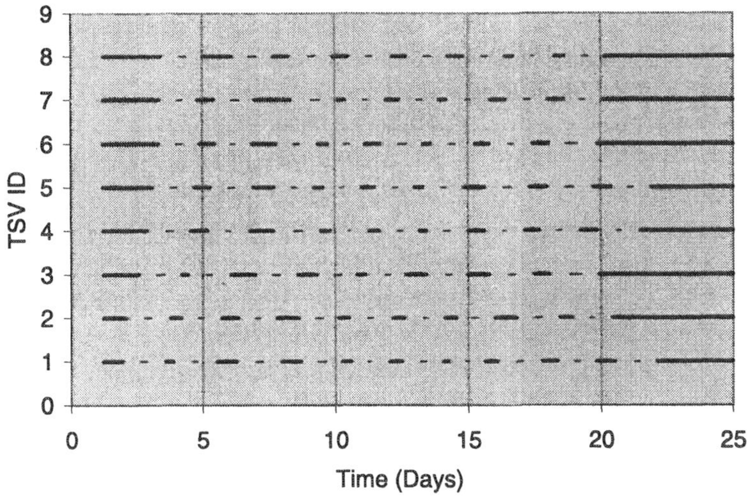

Figure 5. TSV activity diagram for eight large TSVs.

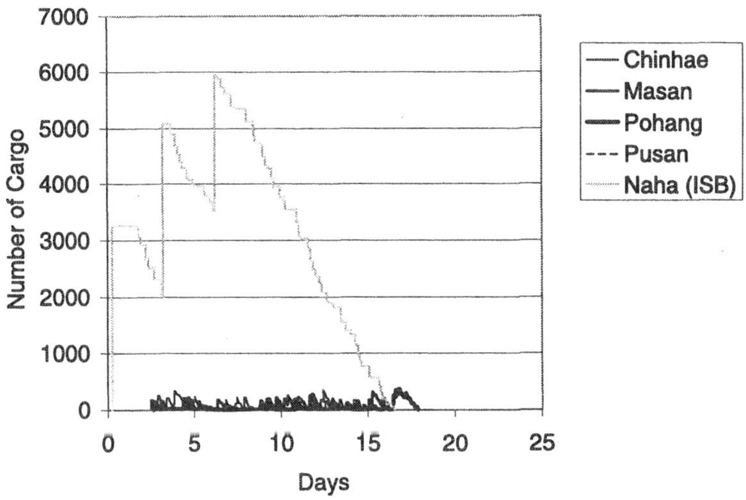

Figure 6. Port usage profile for 12 large TSVs.

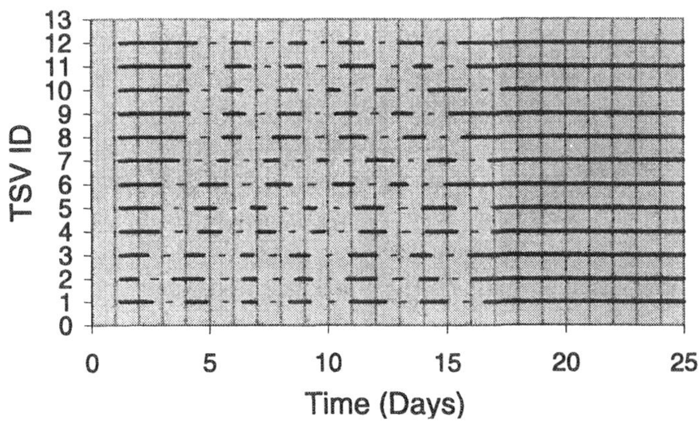

Figure 7. TSV activity diagram for 12 TSVs.

are available in terms of square feet and short tons of cargo. The ISB (Naha) dominates the graph with the individual reduced PODs peaking at less than 250 pieces of cargo, a relatively inconsequential level of activity. The corresponding TSV activity diagram for eight TSVs is shown in Figure 5. The port usage profile and the TSV activity diagram for 12 TSVs are presented in Figures 6 and 7, respectively. The peak usage for reduced PODs is close to 400 pieces of cargo.

The distance from the SISB to the reduced SPODs is approximately 720 nautical miles and the average TSV speed is approximately 42 knots; therefore, the one-way travel time for a TSV is approximately 17 hours. The simulation data suggest that on average a TSV requires approximately nine hours for loading at the ISB and five hours for unloading at the reduced SPOD. Thus, the round-trip cycle time for a TSV is approximately 48 hours. The SISB has three TSV loading berths while there are a total of five TSV unloading berths at the reduced SPODs. This indicates that system performance likely is limited by the ability to load TSVs at the SISB. Thus, the ratio of TSV cycle time to TSV loading time is an upper limit on the number of TSVs that can be loaded at an ISB berth in one cycle time. In addition, as the number of TSVs increases, the load time will increase because TSVs will be required to wait in anchorage until a berth becomes available. Approximating this wait time at two to three hours on average, it is apparent that each TSV loading berth can accommodate approximately four TSVs during any single cycle time. This suggests that the ability to load TSVs saturates when the total number of TSVs reaches approximately 12.

The saturation effects predicted above are clearly visible in the TSV activity diagrams shown in Figures 5 and 7. In Figure 5 for eight TSVs, it is apparent that there are many time intervals when fewer than three TSVs are located at the SISB; these time intervals are indicative of excess loading capacity available at the SISB. However, in Figure 7 for 12 TSVs, there is almost no time when fewer than three TSVs are located at the SISB. This indicates that the SISB loading berths are being utilized nearly continuously; the addition of more TSVs does not improve system performance because the additional TSVs cannot gain access to a loading berth. The addition of more TSVs will improve system performance only if additional TSV loading berths are established at the SISB.

Investigation of TSV characteristics

The second case study is designed to investigate the effects of different TSV design characteristics on the time required to deliver all cargo to the reduced SPODs. The theater support ship is still in the concept stage of development and several different sets of design specifications are being considered. The purpose of this example is to illustrate how the intratheater sealift simulation tools can be used to evaluate the merits and shortcomings of different designs. Here, the relative performance of two different TSV designs, a large TSV and a small TSV, are compared. The characteristics of each TSV are shown in Table 1. In this scenario, the size of the smaller TSV does not create opportunities for greater port access as might be the case in other scenarios. All ports in this scenario are deep enough to accommodate the draft requirements of both ship designs. In addition, the berth lengths at the ports used in this scenario accommodate equal numbers of large TSVs and small TSVs. However, it is not difficult to imagine other scenarios where the smaller draft requirements and the shorter length of the small TSV would allow more small TSVs to berth than large TSVs. The payload capacity of the small TSV design, measured in both payload area and payload weight, is approximately half that of the large TSV design. In addition, the cruising speed of the small TSV is 35 knots compared to a cruising speed of 42 knots for the large TSV. Therefore, it is clear that in this example the small TSV is at a disadvantage compared to the large TSV. However, it is interesting to investigate if this disadvantage can be offset in part by utilizing a larger fleet of small TSVs.

The scenario described in the first case study was repeated using a fleet of small TSVs. The number of TSVs in the fleet was varied from ten TSVs to 30 TSVs in steps of four TSVs. The results of this experiment are presented in Figure 8. As expected, the fleet of small TSVs does not perform as well as the fleet of large TSVs for this scenario. As in the first case study, system performance improves with increasing numbers of TSVs; however, increasing the number of small TSVs beyond approximately 22 ships does not produce increasingly better performance. This is caused by the saturation of the loading facilities at the SISB. However, since the SISB can

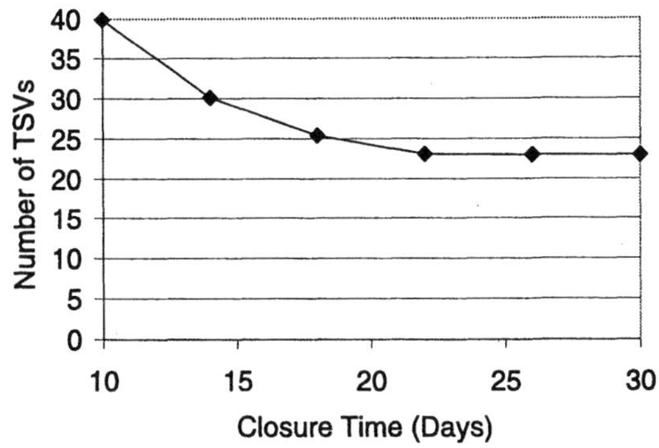

Figure 8. Closure time for varying fleet sizes of small TSVs.

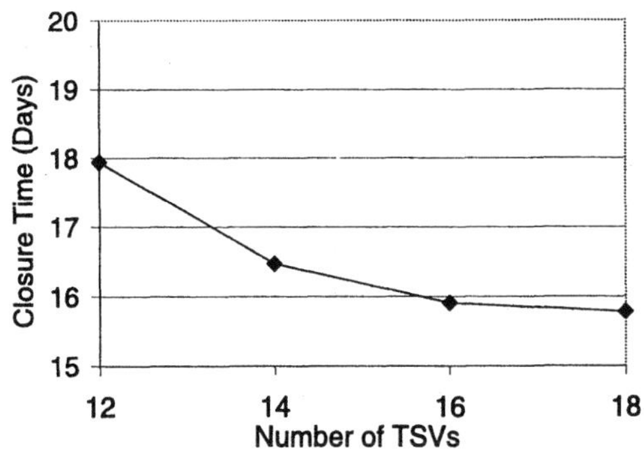

Figure 9. Closure time for varying numbers of large TSVs with additional berthing.

load only three small TSVs simultaneously, the surprising result is that saturation does not occur at 12 TSVs, as in the first case study. Again, a more detailed look at the results is necessary to explain this behavior.

The small TSVs travel at 35 knots, increasing the one-way travel time between the SISB and the reduced SPODs to approximately 21 hours. Because of the smaller deck space that is available, the small TSVs require more time per vehicle to load and unload; however, each TSV can carry a smaller number of vehicles. The simulation data suggest that on average a small TSV requires approximately six hours for loading at the SISB and four hours for unloading at the reduced POD. Thus, the round-trip cycle time for a small TSV is approximately 52 hours. System performance is still limited by the number of TSV loading berths available at the SISB, so that the ratio of total cycle time divided by the SISB loading time identifies the number of TSVs that can be loaded in one cycle time at each SISB berth. Again, allowing two to three hours of wait time as the SISB nears saturation, it is apparent that each SISB berth can accommodate approximately six TSVs during any single cycle time. This suggests that the ability to load small TSVs will saturate when the total number of TSVs reaches approximately 18. The data shown in Figure 8 show that saturation actually occurs between 18–22 TSVs.

Investigation of port enhancements

In the first two case studies, the number of TSV berths available at the SISB was the limiting factor in system performance. In the third case study, the berths that were dedicated to unloading the cargo transport ships at the ISB are reallocated during the intratheater sealift operation. As soon as the cargo ships are unloaded and moved from berth back to anchorage, the berths that were used to unload these ships are reconfigured to load TSVs. Thus, at approximately 300 hours into the sealift operation, three additional TSV loading berths are reallocated to TSV loading, bringing the total number of TSVs capable of loading simultaneously at the SISB to six. The experimental results for the third case study are shown in Figure 9.

Without the additional berths, the ISB was limited to supporting approximately 12 TSVs before saturation of the loading facilities occurred. Now with six TSV loading berths available, increasing the number of large TSVs above 12 again improves system performance. Since there are six loading berths at the SISB and five unloading berths at the reduced SPODs, extending the previous analysis suggests that system performance should improve until 20 or more TSVs are in use. However, the experimental data indicate that little additional performance improvement occurs beyond 16 TSVs. The cause of this behavior can be determined by observing the internal port activity at the SISB. While additional berth areas were allocated to loading TSVs, the port resources available at these berths were not increased. At approximately 16 TSVs, the number of port resources needed to actually load berthed TSVs becomes the limiting factor. Thus, in order to achieve the expected gains of adding TSV berthing, it is necessary to increase the port resources available to operate this additional infrastructure.

4. INTRATHEATER SEALIFT MODEL

The model described here is the result of the evolution of a model built to simulate the flow of military cargo through a commercial seaport called the configurable port simulation (CPortS). This model currently is capable of simulating SPOD operations, and a prototype recently was built to demonstrate concurrent SPOD/SPOE operations in the same port [8]. The model is configurable; that is, routes are defined through the various port areas to define the sequences of port operations. An example of the importance of this capability is demonstrated by the following situation. One scenario may actually stage cargo outside the physical port boundaries, requiring cargo to pass through a gate while transiting from a berth to a staging area. Another port may have staging located within the physical boundaries, therefore, requiring cargo to pass through a gate after staging. In the former scenario, the ability to offload ships is decreased because it takes longer to cycle port resources (drivers, container handlers, chassis, etc.) required for offloading. In the latter scenario, the time to clear the port is decreased because transports and convoys must pass through the gate after loading. Depending on where the bottleneck in the system is located, this minor difference in routing can have a dramatic impact on system performance. The movement of cargo between physical areas within the port involves the use of a transit infrastructure that includes the transit times and routes.

It was observed that the software architecture developed to support transferring cargo between physical areas within the port also would support transferring cargo between cargo terminals at the next higher level. The result is a hierarchical structure, still in development, to support an end-to-end logistics model focusing on the cargo terminals as bottlenecks rather than the transportation infrastructure. This model is shown in Figure 10. While this model was still in development, ongoing work on a joint logistics over the shore (JLOTS) simulation [2] resulted in the identification of the intratheater sealift as an excellent example of the network structure already being developed. With relatively little effort, a model was developed to satisfy the

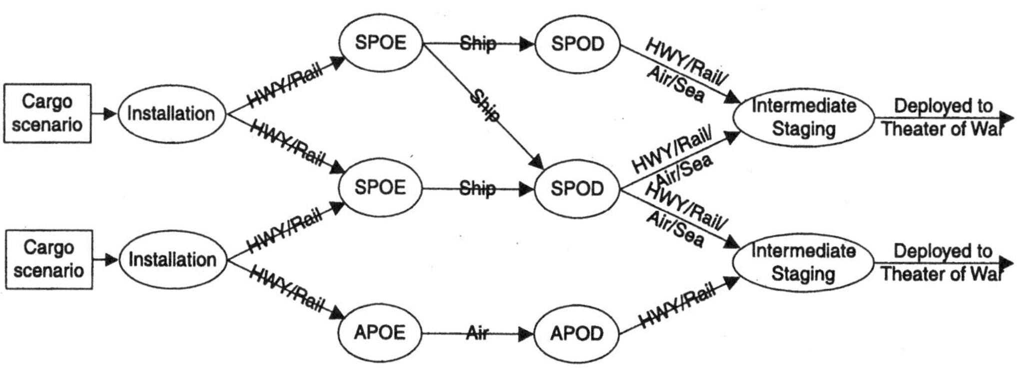

Figure 10. Model for a network of cargo terminals.

seabased component of Figure 1. The development effort required some modification of the SPOD model in CPortS to handle SISBs (required the loading of TSVs) and minor modifications to support operations in a reduced SPOD (operational changes due to the reduced resources). The simulation requirements and resulting model are described in this section.

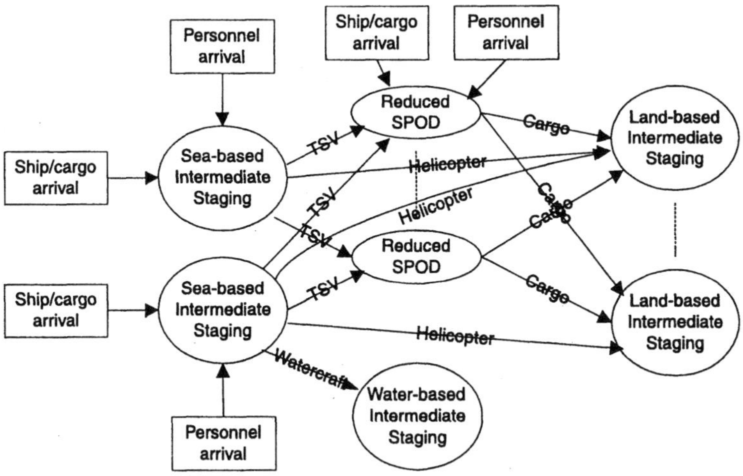

Figure 11. Intratheater sealift model.

4.1. Model Description

The initial model focuses on sea-based operations and omits air-based operations until a future date. The managed components are shown in Figure 11. The focus of the model is to demonstrate cargo terminal capabilities at the transportation network nodes, and the resource requirements to transport cargo between cargo terminals on the transportation links. It is important to note that the model does not analyze the capacities of the transportation links; rather, other simulations such as ELIST [9], MIDAS [10], and JFAST [11] should be utilized to determine expected delays on the links, and these data are used as inputs to this model. These models focus more on the restrictions of the transportation links than the nodes (cargo terminals). The AMP model [12] acts as a shell to interconnect these models into an end-to-end logistics model, but again at a lower level of fidelity, focusing more on the links than the nodes in the network.

The discussion of the model focuses on the following main features.

- *Cargo terminal interface/interconnection architecture* defines the software structure used to manage the movement of cargo between cargo terminals.
- *Cargo terminal model* defines the inner operational structure of the cargo terminals.
- *Programmatic events* define a model for modification of operational and infrastructure characteristics of the simulation.

Cargo terminal interface/interconnect

The cargo terminals shown in Figure 11 are interconnected using a *transit object* to manage the communication [5]. The transit object manages routing, travel time, and physically passing the cargo to the next cargo terminal. At this level, the model considers the cargo terminal objects as black boxes where transports enter either empty or carrying cargo, cargo is removed from transports and reconfigured for loading on other transports, and transports leave either empty or carrying cargo.

Each cargo terminal object has an associated transit object. All communication between cargo terminals is performed using the transit object. This layered communication model is demonstrated in Figure 12. To simplify the interface between the cargo terminal and the transit object, all calls within the cargo terminal object to/from the transit object are managed through

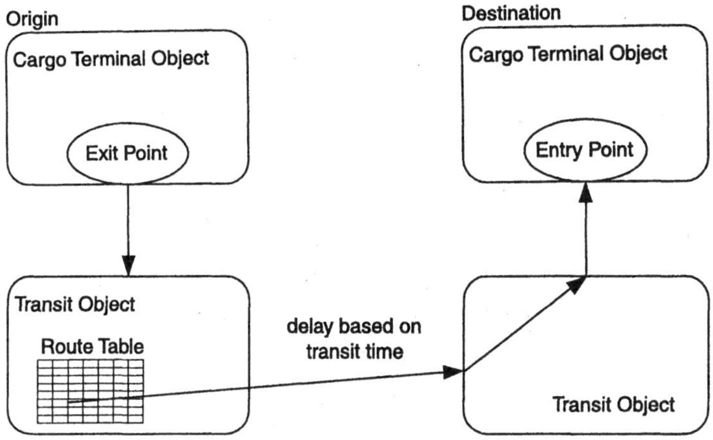

Figure 12. Communication between cargo terminals utilizing the transit object.

two methods. The *exit point* method is the only place where the transit object is referenced from the cargo terminal object, passing a transport carrying cargo for transit. The transit object is limited to calling only the method entry point at the destination cargo terminal object to physically pass the transport and cargo on for processing.

The selection of an appropriate destination is based on a route table. A series of potential routes through the system is defined. Each piece of cargo is assigned to a particular route (military practice). Generally, route assignments are based on unit, cargo type, and required delivery date. Within a cargo terminal, cargo is batched on a transport based on the next cargo terminal on each cargo entity's route.

The route table is then defined based on the current cargo terminal and the route being taken. A route is defined by a row in the table. Each entry of the row corresponds to a cargo terminal, and holds the address of the transit object of the cargo terminal object that is the next node in the route sequence (the transit object is denoted in the sample table by the corresponding cargo terminal ID). Each transit object holds a single column of the table, that column associated with the corresponding cargo terminal, such that the complete route table is defined by the union of the route tables in individual transit objects.

Another table, the transit time table, references a random variate object corresponding to the current cargo terminal and the next cargo terminal in route. The random variate object is used to determine an appropriate time before the transport carrying the cargo arrives at the destination. Again, each transit object only maintains a single column of the table, that corresponding with its corresponding originating cargo terminal.

Cargo terminal model

The cargo terminal model defines the operations associated with each cargo terminal. The model is based on the configurable port simulation (CPortS) [5] that defines the operations at a SPOD. The model partitions the cargo terminal into objects associated with physical operational areas termed cargo terminal areas. Cargo is routed between the cargo terminal areas using the same transit object structure defined to route cargo between cargo terminals. Each cargo terminal area then has the associated operational processes captured within its object. The operational processes include acquiring the necessary infrastructure and resources to complete the tasks.

The intratheater sealift model has three basic types of cargo terminals, sea-based intermediate staging bases, reduced PODs, and destinations. The general model for each is briefly explained.

Sea-based intermediate staging base

The intermediate staging base acts as a transfer point to move cargo from large ships to the smaller TSVs for shuttling to the reduced SPODs. The SISB is the most complicated cargo

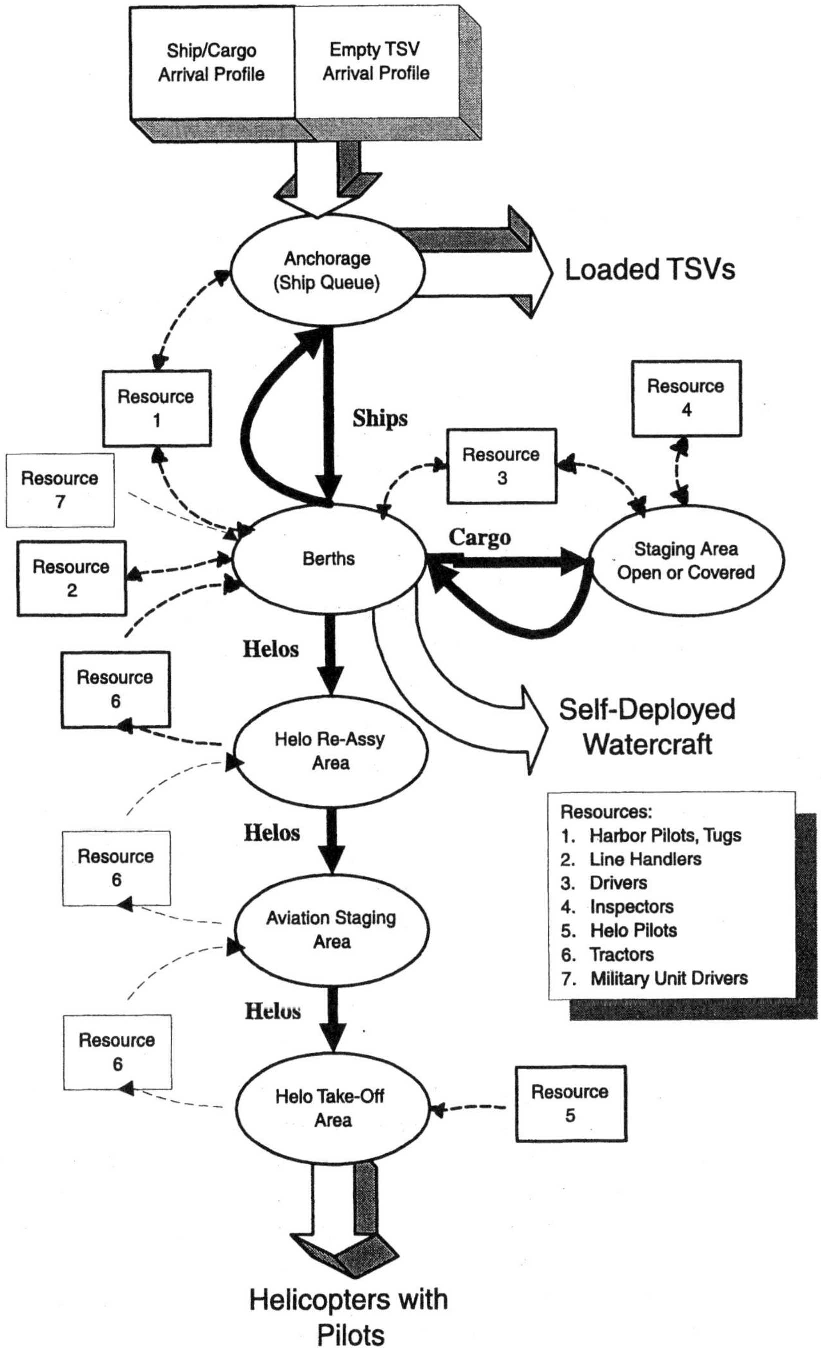

Figure 13. Macro flow for a sea-based intermediate staging base.

terminal in the model, though not as complicated as the original CPortS from which the model was derived due to the reduction in cargo types handled. The majority of processes are actually a subset of the CPortS SPOD model; in fact, the models are actually integrated such that a single simulation can handle either case.

The macro level flow of cargo and resources in the SISB is shown in Figure 13. Cargo is partitioned into two categories: helicopters and watercraft that self-deploy to the theater of war, and convoy vehicles that are transported out of the port by TSV. The convoy vehicles are the important component of this model as they constitute the largest percentage of overall cargo and are the hardest to move to the theater of war. In Figure 13, the process starts with a ship carrying cargo arriving at the port. The ship waits in anchorage for an available berth capable

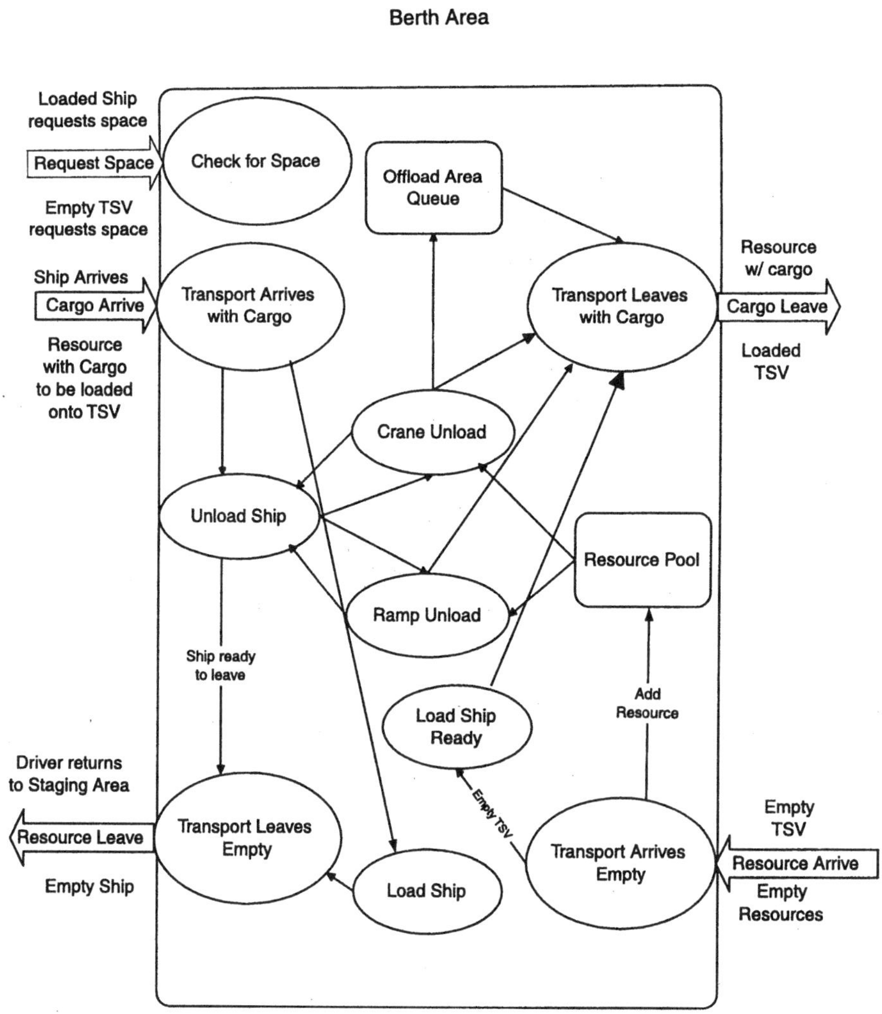

Figure 14. Berth area model.

of handling the ship and the resources to move it to the berth (tugs and harbor pilots). Once on berth, all helicopters and watercraft are first offloaded from the ship. Convoy vehicles are then offloaded and moved to a staging area. While in staging, TSV loads are constructed, primarily based on the destination reduced SPOD port through which the cargo will move. When a TSV load is completed for a particular TSV on berth, the cargo is transported to the TSV and loaded. Each port area has specific operations involved in processing the cargo. The structure of the berth area is shown in Figure 14 where rounded rectangles are objects and ovals are methods operating on the objects. Transports arrive either carrying cargo or empty. A transport carrying cargo is immediately partitioned based on the activity performed on the cargo, either loading onto a ship or offloading from a ship. Activities can then be further subdivided; for instance, the offloading of a ship spawns a separate process for each crane and each ramp in order to model the increased offloading throughput based on the increase in available offloading mechanisms. Within each activity, specific processes are defined. As an example, the processes associated with unloading by ramp are illustrated in Figure 15. It is important to note that all processes are performed at the cargo entity level, allowing for modeling to include realistic constraints in terms of the necessary resources and process times.

Reduced PODs

The reduced SPODs act similarly to the original CPortS POD model, except that they are largely constrained by the physical characteristics of the port and only handle convoy cargo that

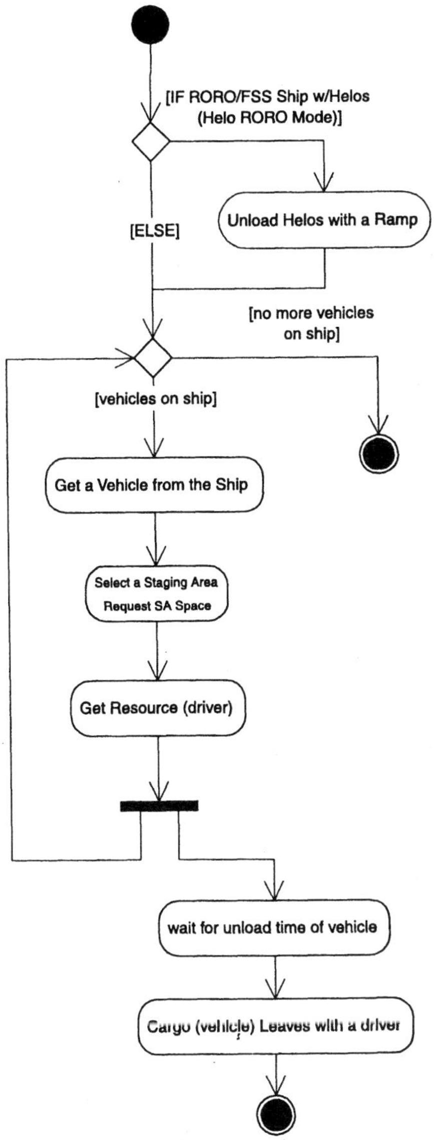

Figure 15. Ramp unload process.

is organic in nature (roadable and organized to move on its own, towed pieces are married to prime movers, such that no external resources are required).

The majority of processes in the reduced SPODs are a subset of the CPortS POD model, as was the case with the SISB model. Again, the models are actually integrated such that a single simulation handles all types of cargo terminals. The berth processes are actually a subset of the SISB model as shown in Figure 16. The model includes loaded TSVs entering the port and going through the same berthing process that occurs at any other port. The TSVs are then unloaded using a ramp with no port resources being required because the unit drivers are aboard the TSVs with their vehicles. On exiting the berth, vehicles may either exit the port directly (potentially through a gate) or may go to a staging area where they wait to join a convoy before leaving. The processes reflect the military's goal of moving the cargo through the port as quickly as possible to enable more cargo to come in.

Destinations

Destinations in this model are the land-based intermediate staging areas where cargo is staged prior to moving into the theater of war. The model used for the destinations is extremely simple.

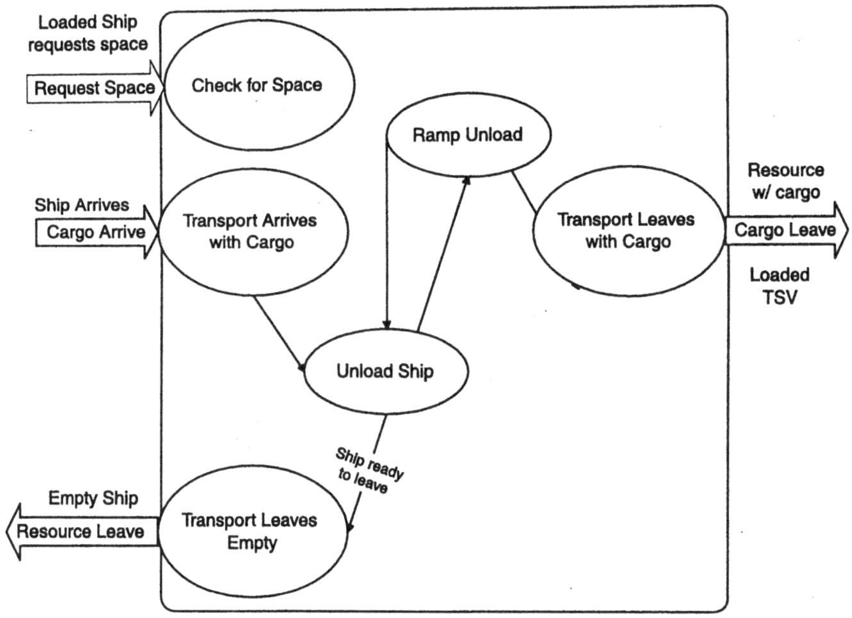

Figure 16. Reduced SPOD berth model.

The destinations act as a sink in the network. All transports and cargo that enter a destination are consumed. There is no recycling of transports to retrieve more cargo and this point currently constitutes the limit of interest in the observable results of the simulation. There is assumed to be no physical limitation to the amount of cargo that can be accepted at the destination as there is no knowledge of the processes to send the cargo on, thus freeing space.

Programmatic events

Programmatic events are an interesting feature inherited from the CPortS project. Programmatic events provide the ability to schedule changes in the behavior of the simulation. The events provide the ability to modify the following.

- *Infrastructure.* The available infrastructure in the cargo terminal can be increased or decreased. For instance, the available square feet in staging can be modified and berths can be made available or unavailable.
- *Resources.* The resources available to support operations within a cargo terminal can be increased or decreased. This includes the resources available to offload and load ships (cranes, drivers, etc.).
- *Process times.* The time required for various activities in the cargo terminal is adjustable. The times are managed by a random variate object capable of handling complex situations such as multimodal distributions. The programmatic events support changing the parameters to a given distribution as well as totally redefining a distribution.

Programmatic events are crucial in studying intratheater sealift operations since it is anticipated that many of the reduced SPODs may originally be incapable of supporting TSVs or have limited capabilities. However, the Army Corps of Engineers has an ongoing port enhancement program to improve a port through operations such as adding temporary berths, dredging, and adding breakwaters [6]. Thus, at some time after exercise initiation, it may be desirable to increase the capabilities of a reduced SPOD. Similarly, it may be of interest to represent the impact of enemy activities by reducing the capabilities of a reduced SPOD.

4.2. Simulation Output Capabilities

The final simulation is structured to support several levels of analysis. The first partitioning of the analysis is based on whether detailed results are desired for a single simulation run or aggregate results are desired from multiple runs [13]. For a single run, data are captured at a high level of detail, tracking detailed activity for each individual piece of cargo. For multiple runs, data are captured at an aggregate level, sampling the data periodically either based on event occurrences or simulation time.

Within these partitions, the analysis can focus on the movement through the network (as performed within this paper), or on the movement through a single cargo terminal. Analysis begins at the network level, measuring overall system performance and identifying cargo terminals that become bottlenecks. Should more detail on a particular cargo terminal be required, output analysis is available for tracking various system behaviors within individual port areas such as the berths or staging areas utilizing output analysis tools developed to support CPortS [14]. Analysis of results are appropriately performed in a spreadsheet application such as MS Excel as demonstrated in Section 3.

5. CONCLUSION

A new simulation architecture for simulating intratheater sealift operations is presented. The model is useful for investigating the viability of this logistics strategy and for evaluating the many new technologies that must be developed to support the strategy. Should the intratheater sealift strategy prove feasible, the simulation also is useful for planning and rehearsing exercises at an entity level of detail. The simulation provides insight into the bottlenecks resulting from constrained port resources, infrastructure, and processes at an entity level. It supports studying proposed technology characteristics and force reconfigurations. This was achieved with a minimal amount of effort and cost due to the availability of an existing simulation architecture supporting SPOD operations that proved flexible and reusable. The simulation is extremely fast while maintaining a high level of detail, executing a single run in less than ten seconds on a PC system for the example force under study. Future analyses will include collaborating with the work done in [4], a study on the impact of force characteristics on SPOD operations using the CPortS model, to contrast the impact of force characteristics between standard SPOD operations and intratheater sealift operations to identify if a single force characterization can meet both needs.

A future objective is to develop an end-to-end logistics simulation model for deploying military forces world-wide. Model flexibility will allow studying numerous strategies under varying constraints and conditions. The architecture is easily scalable to much larger exercise models and data sets. The original CPortS simulation has proven robust and fast at simulating upwards of 500,000 pieces of cargo moving through a single seaport. While a properly configured force of similar size has not been constructed for study with the intratheater sealift model, results at lower cargo counts indicate similar scalability. For this reason, further performance enhancements will focus on distributing sets of simulation runs to get statistical data rather than look for parallelism within a single run. Further cargo terminal processes for installations, SPOEs, APOEs, and APODs can easily be developed with similar levels of effort. The JLOTS model presented in [2] can also be integrated, supporting future analyses of operations requiring multiple modes including intratheater sealift, JLOTS, and classical SPOD. The current results lead us to believe that the architecture presented here forms the foundation for a more universal logistics modeling and simulation strategy for military logistics exercises.

REFERENCES

1. Joint Chiefs of Staff, *Joint Tactics, Techniques, and Procedures for Joint Logistics Over-the-Shore (JLOTS)*, Joint Pub 4-01.6, (November 1998).
2. J. Leathrum, R. Mielke, T. Frith and J. Joines, Modeling new technologies in a joint logistics over the shore (JLOTS) operations, In *Proceeding of the Summer Computer Simulation Conference*, (July 2002).
3. U.S. Army Combined Arms Support Command, Army watercraft master plan, `http://www.cascom.army.mil/transportation/Army_Watercraft_Master_Plan-Draft_May-99/`.
4. M.F. Cochrane, Improving deployment velocity at the SPOD: A force mobility characteristics analysis, *MORS Journal*, (submitted).

5. J. Leathrum and T. Frith, A reconfigurable object model for port operations, In *Proceeding of the Summer Computer Simulation Conference*, pp. 603–608, (July 2000).
6. Rapidly Installed Breakwater System (RIBS), `http://chl.wes.army.mil/research/projects/ribs`.
7. US evaluates joint venture, *Ships Monthly* **37** (3), 9, (2002).
8. R. Mathew, An object-oriented architecture for concurrent processes in a port simulation, Masters Thesis, Department of Electrical and Computer Engineering, Old Dominion University, (December 2002).
9. Model for Intertheater Deployment by Air/Sea (MIDAS), OSD-PA&E (Projection Forces), Pentagon, Washington, DC.
10. M.D. Braun, G.R. Lurie, K.L. Simunich, C. Van Groningen, H.J. Vander Zee and M.A. Widing, ELIST8: A simulation system for transportation logistics planning support, In *Proceeding of the Summer Computer Simulation Conference*, pp. 693–698, (July 2000).
11. JFAST: Joint flow and analysis system for transportation, `http://www.jfast.org`.
12. Analysis Mobility Platform (AMP), USTRANSCOM TCJ5-SC, Scott AFB, IL.
13. S. Mazumdar, Support for statistical analysis of the configurable port simulation (CPortS), Masters Thesis, Department of Electrical and Computer Engineering, Old Dominion University, (December 2002).
14. J.R. Kiran, Output analysis of the configurable port simulation (CPortS), Masters Thesis, Department of Electrical and Computer Engineering, Old Dominion University, (May 2003).

Available online at www.sciencedirect.com
SCIENCE DIRECT
Mathematical and Computer Modelling 39 (2004) 839–868
MATHEMATICAL AND COMPUTER MODELLING
www.elsevier.com/locate/mcm

A Review of Strategic Mobility Models Supporting the Defense Transportation System

K. McKinzie and J. W. Barnes
ETC 5.128, Graduate Program in OR/IE
The University of Texas at Austin
Austin, TX 78712-1063, U.S.A.
kaye.mckinzie@us.army.mil   wbarnes@mail.utexas.edu

Abstract—The complexity of military logistics and force deployment modeling requires the use of advanced computer models for analysis. The last 20 years have not only seen a concerted effort to improve the fidelity of these models, but development to improve their interconnectivity. The area of strategic mobility has received greater interest in the last decade as the U.S. Military has become more reliant on a force projection posture rather than prepositioning its forces outside the continental United States. Strategic mobility describes how forces within the continental U.S. are deployed in support missions outside the continental U.S. This posture combined with the ever shrinking military budget and force size has placed increased emphasis on the capability to efficiently deploy personnel, equipment, and support materiel. Mobility modeling is conducted at various levels of the mobility planning process. The result is a myriad of models addressing different aspects of the process. Current models addressing strategic mobility use aggregate network flow models, one-pass greedy approaches, and simple bounding techniques. This paper presents an overview of these models, their operating characteristics, and their advantages and disadvantages for mobility modeling applications.

Keywords—Strategic mobility models, GDAS, JFAST, MIDAS, MobSim.

1. INTRODUCTION

The United States Military has insufficient personnel and equipment to place resident forces everywhere they may be needed. Consequently, the military employs a "capability based force projection platform" (FPP) [1]. This force structure allows the military to "rapidly alert, mobilize, deploy, and operate anywhere in the world" [2]. This enables the military to achieve the national military strategy with limited personnel, equipment, and support material. (For the reader's convenience, a glossary of acronyms and abbreviations is given in the Appendix.)

When forces within a given region are insufficient to complete an operation, additional forces must be deployed. Such forces cannot originate from a location outside the continental United States (OCONUS) without compromising the security of the donor. Therefore, forces from within the continental United States (CONUS) must be deployed to the theater and sustained during the operation. This deployment capability is critical to our national military strategy. The airlift

This paper has benefited greatly from the support and input of persons in the modeling community. We specifically acknowledge from the assistance of: Maj. J. Hoover, B. Jones, B. Key, C. Keyfauver, T. Kowalsky, P. Loudin, J. Riveta, LTC J. Sees, and S. Young.

0895-7177/04/$ - see front matter Typeset by AMS-TEX
doi:10.1016/j.mcm.2004.02.017

and sealift assets used to transport forces (cargo and passengers) are procured and operated by the military or by commercial firms under contract to the military.

In order to clarify the links between the military's strategic and tactical operations, the military defines three levels of war:

(1) tactical: employment of small combat units for a brief duration of time;
(2) operational: employment, design, and organization of forces in campaigns, major operations and battles; and
(3) strategic: highest level where a nation uses its resources to achieve its national objectives [3] (involves movement of cargo (outsize, oversize, bulk, and total cargo) and passengers (PAX) to and from CONUS and OCONUS.

The focus of this paper is on strategic mobility models (SMMs). As detailed below, strategic mobility is critical to force projection (FP) addressing six of its eight elements. SMMs enable analysts and planners to determine the methods and sequences for cargo and PAX movement at the strategic level of war by analyzing and comparing a variety of scenarios. Activities not requiring movement between CONUS and OCONUS are not the concern of SMMs because they are not at the strategic level of war. The two most recent analyses of SMMs are the Rand corporation study published in 1991 [4] and the U.S. TRANSCOM decision report published in 1998 [5]. Significant changes and developments have occurred since these studies. This paper details the current relevant strategic mobility models and also describes several supporting models in use today.

This paper is organized as follows: Section 1 introduces SMMs; Section 2 presents some historical/legacy models that are no longer in use today but were critical to the development of today's models; Section 3 describes and compares current SMMs; Section 4 discusses several supporting models that can augment the SMMs; and concluding remarks are given in Section 5.

1.1. Overview of Strategic Mobility

Strategic mobility is a subset of both strategic logistics and force projection. Strategic logistics is broadly defined as "the art and science of harnessing the economic and societal strengths of a nation for national defense" (Basic National Defense Doctrine [6]). Force projection is "the ability to project the military element of national power from the continental United States (CONUS)

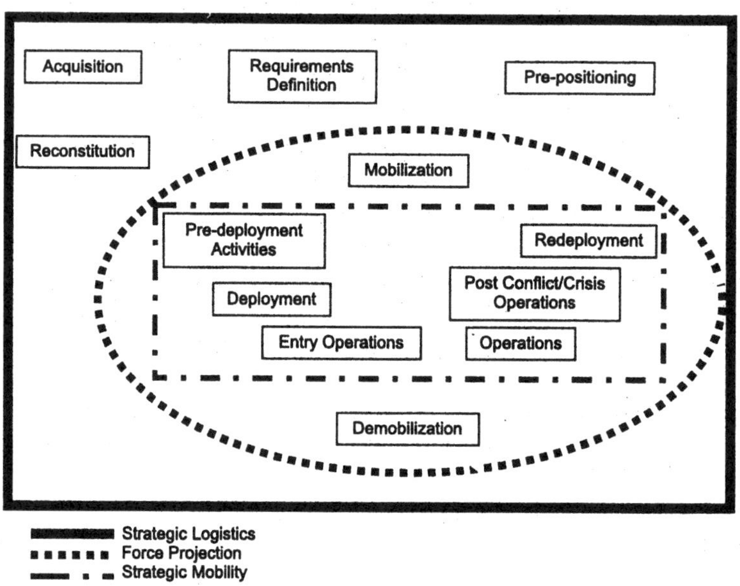

Figure 1. Strategic logistics, force projection, and strategic mobility hierarchy.

or another theater, in response to requirements for military operations" [7]. Strategic logistics, FP, and strategic mobility have a hierarchical relationship depicted in Figure 1.

Strategic mobility consists of six of the eight components of force projection and six of the twelve components of strategic logistics.

1.2. Overview of Strategic Mobility Modeling

Strategic mobility models are logistics models which represent the flow of cargo and PAX from CONUS to OCONUS theaters. These models represent the movement of cargo and PAX from their origin through a port of embarkation (POE) (a departure point in CONUS, Alaska, or Hawaii) and a port of debarkation (POD) (an arrival point in theater), to the designated destination/employment location. Utilizing prescribed resource parameters (e.g., number of aircraft and ships) and associated routes, such models attempt to deliver all cargo and PAX within prescribed time windows. To successfully utilize these routes, various transportation methods may be used and numerous "waypoints" (temporary holding locations) may be required between any of the four previously-mentioned points (origin, POE, POD, destination). Graham and Dowdy [8] depict this process with the following diagram (Figure 2).

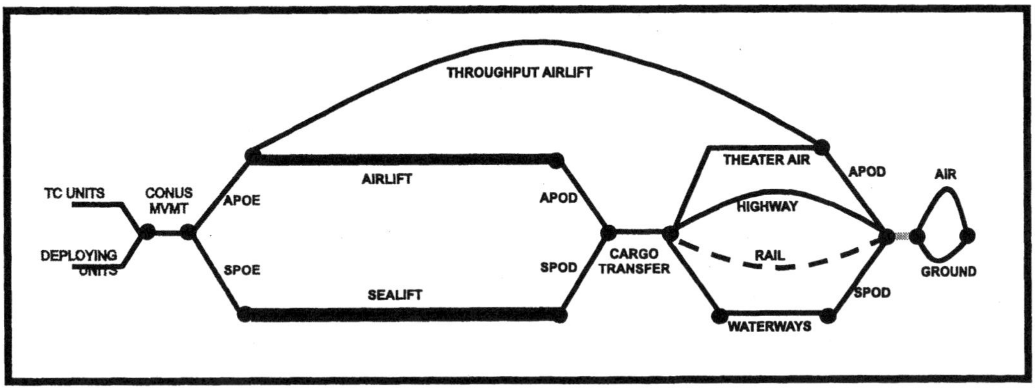

Figure 2. End-to-end strategic mobility model [8].

This diagram shows units mobilizing at a CONUS origin location and transitioning by ground to a POE (air or sea). From there cargo and PAX moves across ocean by the designated transportation method (air or sea) to a POD. Items are then moved again by selected transportation methods to their final destinations. In this latter stage, there can be several changes of transportation mode prior to arriving at their destination in theater.

This process from origin to destination (end-to-end) and actions at each of the stages pictured in Figure 2 are represented in SMMs in a variety of ways. This paper will describe and compare the current SMMs. Each model is evaluated in regard to the following features: operating platform (UNIX or PC and software requirements), ease of use by analysts and planners, ability to interface with other models and doctrinal formats, level of tracking detail for both cargo and PAX and transportation assets, whether it can model multiple port pickup (p/u) and drop-off (d/o) locations for each airplane/ship modeled, and its ability to accurately model the strategic mobility environment and meet force closure times requirements.

1.2.1. Types of strategic mobility planning

There are three types of strategic mobility planning: resource, deliberate, and crisis planning. As described below, the differing emphases of the three types of strategic mobility planning have led to the development of several different models.

Resource planning, largely synonymous with long term planning, is used to support long term budget planning and resource allocation. Resource planning focuses on improving the strategic mobility process by improving the flow of cargo and PAX via changes in force structure and policy to include the development of new equipment and implementation procedures. Resource planning is accomplished through two primary activities—capability assessments and requirement studies. A capability assessment analysis with a given set of transportation assets and determines the deployment capabilities of those assets under different scenarios. A requirements study seeks to determine the appropriate set of transportation assets for use in a given scenario or set of scenarios.

Deliberate planning, or midrange planning, addresses the requirements and capabilities to support a specific deployment scenario, but does not focus on the details of a specific deployment. Deliberate planning assesses the feasibility of a plan and provides estimates and expectations of a deployment schedule in its support of the plan. If and when the plan needs to be employed, specific scenario dependent criteria will need to be considered prior to implementation. This is conducted in the next level of planning.

Crisis action planning, or near term planning, focuses on the actual implementation of a deployment plan. While higher-level planning may be conducted over a period of months or years, crisis action planning takes place on the order of weeks or days and will be executed at the end of the planning horizon. This process can be significantly accelerated by the deliberate planning phase. In crisis action planning, the plan is reassessed for any changes either in force structure or policy that may have occurred since the deliberate plan was assessed. Specific criteria are considered such as changes due to weather, natural or man-made disaster, and international agreements. Completion of these activities leads directly to final implementation and force deployment.

1.2.2. Input files

For each of the SMMs, there are typically three types of inputs: requirements prepositioned, transportation resources, and a scenario. The requirements file is provided in the form of a time phased force deployment data (TPFDD). Portions of a TPFDD are extracted (or constructed) for use in the SMMs.

The TPFDD contains time-phased force data, cargo and PAX data, and movement data [9]. In short, the TPFDD defines when and where cargo and PAX need to be picked up and when and where they need to be delivered. TPFDD data includes (see Figure 3) a latest arrival time (LAD) which imposes a desired sequence of arrival at the POD. Other time constraints such as ready to load date at the origin (RLD), available to load date at the POE (ALD), earliest arrival date at the POD (EAD), and required delivery date to the destination (RDD) are also present. The pairing of the EAD and LAD establishes an arrival time window at the POD. Violations of these constraints may significantly affect the safety of the mission and of cargo and PAX in general. In many types of analysis, an early completion of a schedule may be the dominant consideration. However, in SMMs, early completion is not dominant but rather one of several considerations in achieving a multicriteria objective.

The standard descriptions for modeling level of detail for military logistics simulations are those used in joint operation planning and execution system (JOPES). The JOPES level of detail can

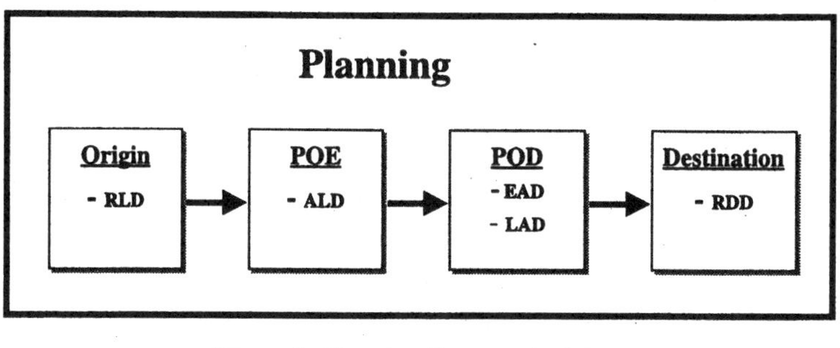

Figure 3. Planning time constraints.

be an aggregation of items such as in Levels 1, 2, or 3 or finer detail such as in Levels 4 or 5. Level 1 aggregates items as total number of passengers and total short tons, total measurement tons, total square feet, and/or total hundreds of barrels. Level 2 is the summary level and expresses total number of passengers, short tons, measurement tons (including barrels), total square feet of bulk, oversize, outsize, and nonair-transportable cargo and PAX. Level 3 is detailed by cargo and PAX category and is expressed as total number of passengers, short tons and/or measurement tons (including barrels), and total square feet of cargo. Level 4 details passengers by service specialty code and considers individual dimensional data (expressed in length, width, and height in number of inches) of cargo by equipment type (as defined by individual national stock number) by unit line number (ULN). Finally, Level 5 considers priority of shipments and expresses passengers by service specialty code in deployment sequence by ULN, plus individual weight (in pounds) and dimensional data (expressed in length, width, and height in number of inches) of equipment in deployment sequence by ULN [10].

The TPFDD lists items by ULN which may contain multiple quantities of a given item. A ULN may be composed of multiple pallets of material, unpalletized materiel, or multiple personnel. Other ULN restrictions such as size and weight restrictions may also be present.

The primary classifications for aircraft are PAX and cargo where cargo is further classified as bulk, oversize, outsize, and nonair transportable. PAX must be assigned to aircraft. Bulk cargo is palletized and fits on a "pallet of 88 inches by 108 inches, or with tie-down devices that occupies a space not greater than 84 inches by 104 inches" [11]. Oversize cargo is larger than bulk and is "loaded to a design height of 96 inches but is equal to or less than 1,090 inches in length, 117 inches in width, and 105 inches in height" and is nonpalletized rolling stock [11]. Outsize cargo, the largest cargo category, is not palletized and less than "1,453 inches in length, 144 inches in width, and 156 inches in height" or less than "1,453 inches in length, 216 inches in width, and 114 inches in height" [11]. Nonair transportable cargo is any single item that exceeds the dimensions of outsize cargo. Ships also use these cargo categories, but due to the larger capacity of a ship it is more common to use the larger load measurements of 20 foot containers (TEUs), breakbulk (roll on roll off—RORO), or square feet rather than inches.

Table 1 presents a small portion of a TPFDD [12].

The military has prepositioned equipment and support material around the world on land and sea for deployment use. This reduces the distance the equipment and support material must be

Table 1. TPFDD sample.

Line ID	Onload	Offload	Load	Required	Bulk	Oversize	Outsize	Passengers	Owner Type
UNIT1486	KBLV	RKPS	10	24	292	1009	59	0	9
UNIT1487	KWRI	RKPS	10	24	116	349	35	0	23
UNIT1488	KTIK	RKPS	10	24	6	9	2	0	2
UNIT1489	KTCM	RKPK	10	24	0	0	15	0	5
UNIT1490	KTIK	RKPS	10	24	0	41	85	0	5
UNIT1491	PAEI	RKPS	11	24	0	110	5	19	2
UNIT1492	KSUU	RKPK	11	24	133	32	7	59	18
UNIT1493	KTIK	RKPS	11	24	29	764	9	0	18
UNIT1494	PHIK	RKPS	11	25	63	182	7	0	18
UNIT1495	KSUU	RKTY	11	25	634	562	880	0	4
UNIT1496	KDOV	RKJK	11	25	220	208	212	0	1
UNIT1497	KTIK	RKSO	11	25	0	190	83	402	1
UNIT1498	KHOP	RODN	11	25	47	44	12	44	1
UNIT1499	KLFI	PHIK	11	25	0	0	0	1876	2
UNIT1500	KOFF	PHIK	11	25	0	0	0	814	2

transported. If there are prepositioned stocks available, their locations and quantities are also provided as inputs.

Transportation resources input includes availability and constraints on transportation vehicles, ports, and routes. Among these restrictions are constraints associated with fuel usage, cargo and PAX capacities, loading practices, and maintenance.

The scenario file includes any additional data for a particular version of a scenario, such as availability of ports and canals and varying time driven constraints.

1.2.3. Node and link coverage

As depicted in Figure 2, the modeling process is performed in a network environment with nodes and arcs. Each node may require the completion of several activities. Transport of cargo and PAX occurs on the arcs. All but one of the current models implement activities by conducting deterministic activity simulations. The primary nodes of interest include: home station, POD, POE, and destination.

1.2.4. Task coverage

In [4], nine tasks were addressed for the SMMs: merge files, aggregate records, prioritize records, select modes, schedule cargo and PAX, simulate movements, prepare textual output, prepare graphical output, and check and correct. For comparison purposes, we will consider the same nine tasks. In [4] all of the SMMs were deterministic simulations, with most tasks taking place within the models. In the last 11 years the models have evolved to interfacing with other models. This leverages the capabilities of supporting models so that many SMM tasks are performed by calling these models. The models also allow some probabilistic considerations. However, these are usually specified deterministic failure rates. All of the current models are characterized as a "simulation models" since they simulate (emulate) movement of cargo and PAX, even if they are not stochastic in nature.

1.2.5. Solution characteristics

The solutions provided by an SMMs are multitiered and comprise the item level schedule of the cargo and PAX, to include the transportation asset schedule and force closure profiles. Many criteria are considered including: time constraints, cargo and PAX delivered (on time, late, not delivered), cargo type (bulk, oversize, outsize) to include PAX, transportation assets used (type, number, distance traveled), and ports usage frequency. The objective is a cost driven function that is measured in terms of monetary costs, time, cargo and PAX delivery, and/or asset usage.

1.3. Strategic Modeling

The above discussion gives only an overview of the more important factors that analysts and planners consider when choosing an SMM to use. Military analysts would prefer that models depict every aspect of their modeled environment. The size and scope of the scenarios associated with an SMM precludes this preference with the modeling capabilities currently available. As a consequence, many of the detailed aspects of strategic mobility are represented, but not fully modeled. Many such aspects are discussed in more detail in supporting models. A selected set of such supporting models are addressed later in this paper. This additional capability for detailed analysis supports enhanced interoperability and further development of supporting models and SMMs.

2. LEGACY MODELS

Many of the defense transportation system (DTS) SMMs that were developed and used by the Department of Defense (DoD) are no longer in use. This section provides a brief description of some of the more important of these legacy models.

Some models have become obsolete due to a change in operating strategies, others have been replaced by more capable models, and others have been replaced due to their failure to meet COE standards. This ongoing, dynamic improvement process will continue in the future. As part of this process, the DoD has implemented guidelines to ensure new and developing models comply with interoperability standards (COE). This has led to the development of a system for integrating models into one command and control (C2) system and for insuring the interoperability of transportation/logistical systems.

"The end of the Cold War combined with a maturing simulation technology environment created an environment for change" [13]. This dynamic was enhanced by a draw down of the military forces and funding which resulted in a modified DoD simulation acquisition strategy. Stand alone models and simulation models were identified for replacement by models that were COE compliant. Today, most standalone models are legacy systems and the models in use today are interoperable with many other models [14].

2.1. Rapid Intertheater Deployment Simulation Model (RAPIDSIM)

This transportation flow model is the predecessor of the model for intertheater deployment by air and sea (MIDAS). RAPIDSIM does not model specific items; rather it aggregates all items and capacities into common units of flow. RAPIDSIM only modeled the movement of cargo and PAX from POE to POD. The cargo and PAX records required a priority sorting by the analyst prior to the model execution. This very cumbersome model required an expert to operate [4,15].

2.2. Transportation Feasibility Estimator (TFE)

TFE, a transportation flow model, was the predecessor of the joint flow and analysis system for transportation (JFAST). TFE was used to determine the gross feasibility of a TPFDD's transportation requirement. It had the capability to model ten times as many requirements as the MIDAS of that era in a typical run because of the flow nature of the model rather than performing a detailed simulation [4,15].

2.3. World Wide Military Command and Control System (WWMCCS)

WWMCCS provided "the means for operational direction and technical administrative support involved in the function" of C2 of U.S. Military Forces [16]. In 1996, this system was replaced by the global command and control system (GCCS) as part of the initiative towards interoperability of military models and systems [17]. Although neither WWMCCS nor GCCS simulate a specific aspect of military operations, they integrate models and systems to improve the information flow and decision making capabilities for military leaders.

2.4. Computer Aided Load Manifesting (CALM)

Primarily used by the U.S. Air Force (USAF), CALM was replaced by automated air load planning system (AALPS) [18]. CALM was an automated air load planner that printed manifests and produced load plans to support aircraft loading [19].

2.5. Strategic Sealift Analysis System (SEASTRAT)

SEASTRAT was replaced by JFAST 7. It was designed for sealift analysis contingency planning. Consisting of two primary functional modules, ship file and route generation, it revolutionized the methods for calculating ship routes [20].

2.6. Air Mobility Command (AMC) Deployment Analysis System (ADANS)

ADANS, used by deliberate planners, managed information on cargo and PAX, scheduled air missions, and analyzed schedules. Prior to ADANS, air flow planners were limited to planning their missions by hand and typing them into the existing command and control system [21]. ADANS was replaced by the consolidated air mobility planning system (CAMPS) which joined two models, ADANS and the combined mating and ranging planning system (CMARPS), adding a tanker refueling capability to ADANS [22] in February 2002 [23].

2.7. Combined Mating and Ranging Planning System (CMARPS)

CMARPS was the second of the two models replaced by CAMPS as a part of the suite of GCCS models. CMARPS was used to schedule specific tanker aircraft to refueling points. The model takes a given mission for aircraft then determines the fuel that mission will need. Next, it determines where the mission aircraft will need to be refueled and schedules refueling points consistent with other parameters such as "minimizing use of tankers, minimizing tanker fuel consumption, using air refuelable tankers, regenerating tankers for tanker reuse and satisfying abort base requirements" [24].

3. STRATEGIC MOBILITY MODELS

All of the SMMs in use today are COE compliant and are under continual development. Some SMMs improvements are designed to provide greater fidelity in modeling capability and algorithms. Other SMM developments attempt to improve interfaces and transitions to more deployable platforms.

Although there are many models which interface with SMMs, none are used throughout the DoD. Each of the SMMs is used by one or more organizations that find an SMM's capabilities uniquely suited to their required level of planning. In the descriptions presented below, the SMMs are described in regard to their task coverage, node and link coverage, and solution characteristics. Following a separate description of each SMM, they are compared.

Only one of the models being used today, MIDAS, was covered by Shank *et al.* [4]. For this reason, an additional discussion is provided on the changes in MIDAS since that study.

The four major SMMs in current use today are the global deployment analysis system (GDAS), JFAST, MIDAS, and the mobility simulation model (MobSim©). Each section is prefaced with a short description of the model provided by the model user/developer. This is followed by our assessment of the model.

3.1. Global Deployment Analysis System (GDAS)

GDAS was developed by Noetics, Inc. in cooperation with the Center for Army Analysis (CAA), the U.S. Transportation Command (USTRANSCOM), Stanley Associates Inc., and the U.S. Department of Transportation's John A. Volpe National Transportation Systems Center (Volpe Center). GDAS is used to perform analyses of transportation policy issues and operational planning tasks for large or small scale force deployments. The transportation requirements represented by these deployments may be aggregated or may be very specific. The latest version of GDAS runs on standard personal computers (PCs) running Microsoft Windows and Office 2000 [25].

3.1.1. Data preparation

GDAS allows users to model new technology, define new units of measure, as well as add new ports and capabilities, all without programmer support. This ability significantly assists in resource planning by providing the means to analyze future capabilities prior to their development and acquisition. Results from this analysis may be used to influence future production and acquisition decisions and policy decisions.

GDAS allows the user to import the TPFDD in JOPES Menu B Level 8 formatted file (the standard for DOD models), the associated type unit characteristics (TUCHA) file, and the geographic location file (Geoloc) directly from the JOPES system to build movement requirements.

The model merges the TPFDD (both unit and nonunit requirements) with the TUCHA to develop individual unit requirements (ULN level) at JOPES Levels 3 (default), 4, or 5 detail if available. GDAS then translates the requirement types, Geoloc, and cargo and PAX category codes to GDAS formatted nodes and requirements. These table driven mappings allow the analyst flexibility in aggregating and representing the requirements at any desired level. An audit trail is maintained throughout this process to allow the analyst to backtrack to the original TPFDD ULN.

Movement requirements can also be imported from other sources and formats (e.g., Dbase, Excel, ASCII text) and easily mapped into GDAS tables. These requirements can also be defined, translated, and aggregated by the analyst [26].

3.1.2. Prioritize records

GDAS uses a multitiered structure for determining cargo and PAX prioritization. Included among many other factors are lateness penalties on the RDD. In addition, GDAS uses the RLD to determine the initiating movement time and considers the EAD and LAD to establish a time window of arrival at the POD. The time between the LAD and the RDD can be obtained by either a mathematical calculation or simulation. If mathematical calculations are used to calculate this time window, nothing is added by using both time constraints since it is a constant. However, when simulation is used, there can be a difference between these times. GDAS simulates all legs and a delay is possible. Due to this possible delay, both the RDD and the LAD are considered.

3.1.3. Select modes

Models that select modes of transportation must be able to change the POE and POD because most ports serve only aircraft or only ships. If a POE or POD is changed, this can have an effect on the ground travel time as well as the ability to implement the mission plan (due to ground travel and security constraints). GDAS can either input the modes of transportation and the ports provided in a TPFDD or it can select modes and ports using a constrained dynamic programming formulation.

3.1.4. Schedule cargo

GDAS inputs define the location of cargo and PAX and their required destination along with many other limiting criteria on the cargo and PAX such as time constraints, weight, dimension, and transportation restrictions (hazardous cargo) consistent with those in standard TPFDD descriptions (Figure 4 depicts a GDAS screenshot editing transportation assets). In addition, many penalties are evaluated as cargo and PAX are assigned to vehicles. Some of the penalties are cargo and PAX lateness penalties, first time vehicle use penalties, penalties for each port the cargo and PAX visit, stow factor penalties for specified cargo and PAX loading combinations, and movement horizons. GDAS uses alternating greedy cargo and greedy vehicle heuristics combined with route insertion techniques to attempt to minimize both the number of vehicles used and the transportation time. These penalties direct GDAS as it performs both the assignment of cargo and PAX to modes of transportation and schedules cargo and PAX from origin to destination through POE and POD and required intermediate stops. Thus, GDAS is an end-to-end strategic mobility model.

All inputs are from databases that require the user to specify the desired level of modeling detail. These databases are open database connectivity (ODBC) compliant, thereby enabling interfaces with MS Access, Oracle, Sybase, or any other ODBC compliant database. Due to the user-defined level of detail, cargo and PAX can be tracked at the ULN or in aggregated form. GDAS can aggregate data or specify the detail down to the "tail number" scheduling of all aircraft and the tracking of individual ULNs if needed to track individual materiel items.

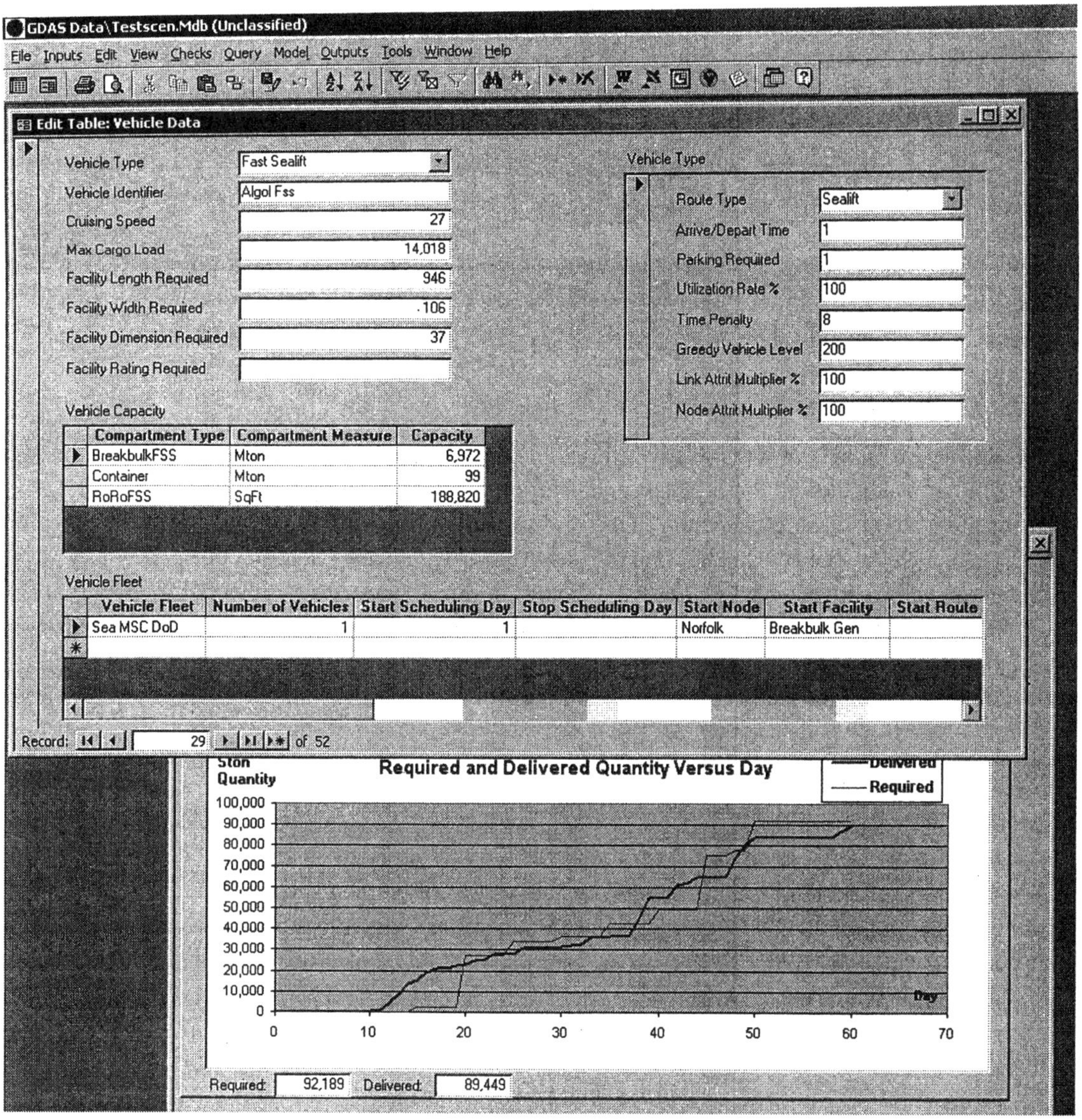

Figure 4. Editing vehicle, compartment, and fleet availability in GDAS (all modes are treated similarly), with deliver profile in background.

Unlike many models, GDAS can identify and reconfigure cargo and PAX that are not optimally organized. If desired, GDAS can model individual ships, aircraft, and ULN to provide a detailed assignment and schedule of transport.

GDAS uses a variety of algorithms to assign cargo and PAX to specific vehicles. Depending on the type of analysis desired, one of the following four algorithms can be selected: travel time, vehicle flow, pickup/delivery, or multiport. Travel time provides a quick estimate of delivery with unconstrained vehicle availability. Vehicle flow allocates cargo and PAX based on roundtrip calculations for aircraft and ships. Pickup/delivery is a more detailed algorithm tracking discrete locations of vehicles. The most detailed of the algorithms, the multiport algorithm, allows multiple pickup and deliveries on each vehicle trip.

3.1.5. Simulate movements

The user can set the boundary of the deployment (origin to destination, POE to POD, POE to destination, or any combination) and incorporate the TPFDD designated modes and ports into the requirements.

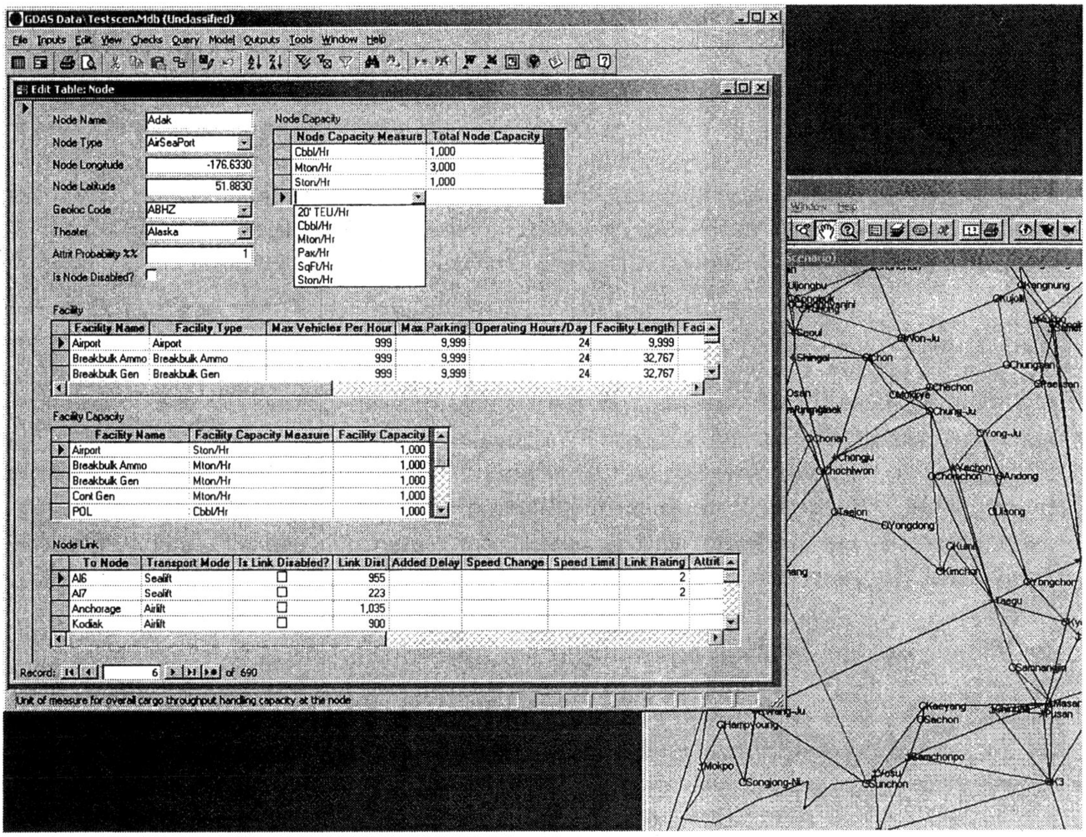

Figure 5. Editing node, facility, and link data in GDAS with map display in the background.

In scheduling transportation assets and assigning cargo and PAX, GDAS implements user stipulations and RDD requirements to assign priorities. GDAS uses a five phase cyclical process of planning, assigning, scheduling, simulating, and updating. In planning, GDAS selects nodes, ports, cargo, and PAX configurations using a dynamic programming cargo flow formulation to minimize various penalty factors. It then performs scheduling and assigns the cargo and PAX to transportation vehicles using route insertion techniques over a rolling time horizon. Once the schedule and assignments are complete, it performs a deterministic "simulation" to determine the actual arrival, departure, loading, unloading, and queuing events at each facility. It concludes by performing an update and creating the plans and schedules.

In attempting to model reality, GDAS can define ports with multiple vehicle types. This allows transloading across different vehicle types. It also allows any vehicle to conduct multiple pickups and drop-offs of cargo and PAX at multiple locations during one trip. This capability enables the modeling of small scale contingencies (SSC) where aircraft may have multiple origins and/or destinations requiring small quantities to be picked up or delivered. Without the ability to conduct multiple pickups and drop-offs during one trip, the model would have to schedule excessive trips. This multiple transshipment capability and its ability to model predefined cyclical routing timetables increases the efficiency of transport and allows it to model voluntary intermodal sealift agreements (VISA). GDAS uses an intermodal network of nodes and links that may be aggregated or considered in great detail with thousands of nodes and links within and between any SMM leg (Figure 5 depicts a node editing screen shot from GDAS).

3.1.6. Prepare output/graphics

The output formats are quite versatile and can be displayed graphically, superimposed on a world map with capabilities such as zoom, pan, layer display, and print/plot. Finally, there are several charts and graphs of model results available including cargo and PAX flow, throughput, and time analysis.

3.1.7. Check and correct

GDAS uses relational databases for all input data. This minimizes input errors. The tracker located within the GDAS TPFDD editor checks data consistency and allows return to a previously edited TPFDD. Many other checks on the input data are performed.

3.1.8. Other

GDAS, a PC-based HLA compliant model written in C/C++ running Microsoft Windows and Office, is available with permission from CAA. Because of its near exclusive use by CAA, other DoD entities are largely unaware of its capabilities. GDAS is designed to be tailored to each scenario. This structure is both an enhancement to the design and a challenge to users. It provides extensive capabilities for analysis, but also can require a significant amount of time and effort to tailor it to a specific model.

3.2. Joint Flow and Analysis System for Transportation (JFAST)

JFAST is a multimodal transportation analysis model designed for USTRANSCOM and the joint planning and execution community (JPEC). JFAST forecasts transportation requirements, performs course of action analysis, evaluates "what-if" scenarios, and builds delivery profiles of troops and equipment. JFAST assesses the transportation feasibility of contingency, deliberate, and exercise plans. It is a Windows NT/Windows 2000-based, transportation-planning tool that provides an "end-to-end" transportation analysis capability to model the movement of forces from origin to the tactical assembly area. JFAST routes trucks, trains, buses, convoys, aircraft, and ships over selected lines of communication to identify transportation network bottlenecks, determine lift requirements, and project force closures. JFAST is also capable of simultaneously analyzing multiple plans to optimize the use of DTS resources [27]. This was the model recommended by the TAMS report to model the POE to POD leg of strategic mobility.

3.2.1. Data preparation

JFAST uses a JOPES B8 TPFDD format as its requirements input file. In the event that a JOPES B8 TPFDD is not available, JFAST can be used to build a "notional" TPFDD as defined by the user. This TPFDD can then be used in JFAST for transportation analysis and, if warranted, as an execution TPFDD.

3.2.2. Prioritize records

The primary measure for prioritizing items for JFAST is the RDD. However, JFAST also uses the EAD-LAD time window, the RLD and the ALD.

3.2.3. Select modes

JFAST does not perform mode selection. Placing operational necessity before theoretical mode optimization, JFAST accepts the transportation modes as determined by combatant commanders to fully analyze a specific concept of operations. This methodology allows USTRANSCOM transportation analysts to provide meaningful feedback (i.e., TPFDD refinement) to combatant commanders on the strategic transportation feasibility of their concept of operations.

3.2.4. Schedule cargo

JFAST's TPFDD editor allows quick modifications to a TPFDD which enhances the capability to perform comparison analysis. JFAST Version 8 (summer 2002) significantly enhances Version 7.2.56. In Version 7, JFAST could model from origin through POE to POD. JFAST Version 8 can also model from the POD to the destination (Figure 6 depicts this.) This is accomplished by interfacing with enhanced logistics intra-theater support tool (ELIST) for the simulation of the POD to destination leg [28].

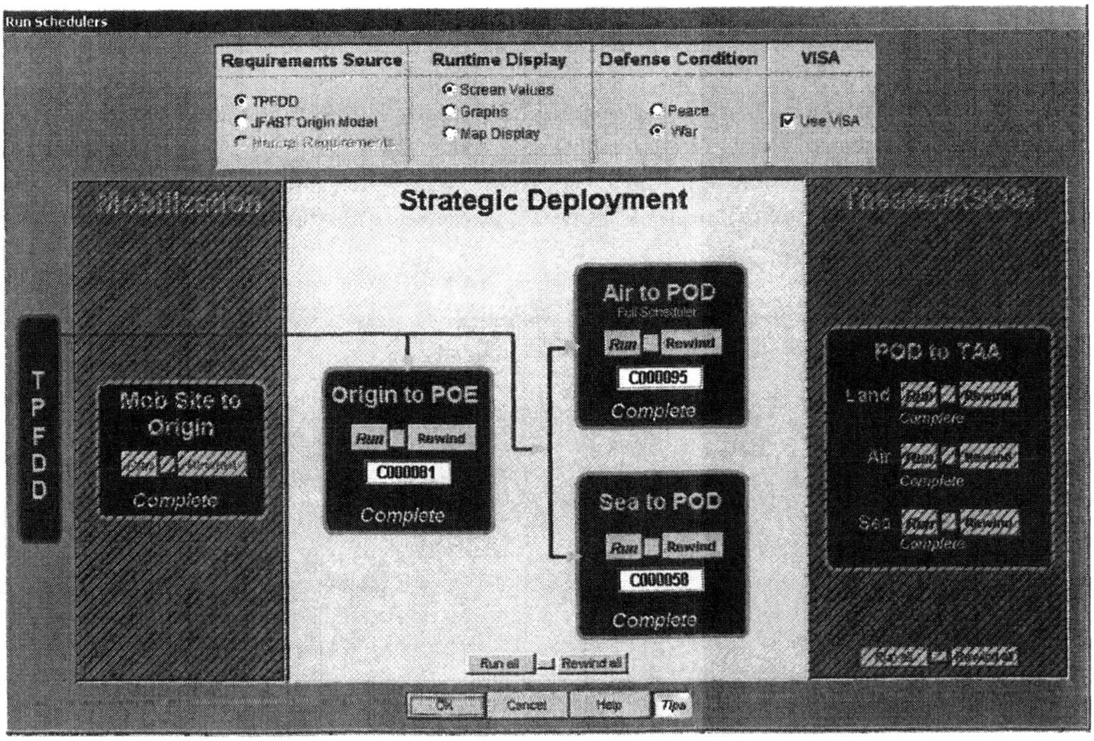

Figure 6. Run scheduler in JFAST.

3.2.5. Simulate movements

JFAST can run in scheduler or flow mode. These enhancements yield, respectively, more realistic transportation schedules (ULN and tail number schedules) or quick runs to obtain lower bounds and identify bottleneck points. When creating the schedule, JFAST cannot schedule multiple aircraft pickups or drop-offs. JFAST can perform multiple pickups for ships, but not multiple drop-offs.

The airlift scheduler affords the user a range of options from the basic, capacitated flow model through a quick tail number scheduler to a detailed dynamic routing tail number scheduler. The objective functions of the scheduler are to minimize lateness and overall mission time via automatic network load balancing. The critical mission leg is governed by aircraft loading times as well as cargo manifesting factors using a weight and cubic displacement evaluation. Flow through the nodes of the airlift network is constrained by user-defined port characteristics such as: maximum on ground, throughput, operating hours, event-driven permissions, hazardous cargo restrictions, port management policy, and special port attributes. The global routing network supports use of mode specific exclusion areas with a temporal aspect to add consideration for such things as time-dependent diplomatic over-flight constraints while imposing no constraint on the ground network during that same period in the same area when appropriate.

JFAST's sealift scheduler is similar to the heuristic (nonoptimizing) option in SEASTRAT (used by the Military Sealift Command (MSC)). Since the MSC is the proponent for all sealift issues, JFAST's use of the techniques in SEASTRAT adds to the validity of the model.

All JFAST schedulers use only a simple greedy heuristic to generate solutions. JFAST assesses cargo and PAX based on priorities and schedules the cargo and PAX from highest priority down. No process is considered that would optimize the scenario.

3.2.6. Prepare output/graphics

JFAST uses of the Microsoft (MS) Office suite for output (Word, Excel, and PowerPoint). JFAST easily produces graphs, documents, and briefing slides in one step and graphically displays the simulation on a color world map.

Unique to JFAST is its ability to create executable formatted airlift and sealift schedules. Airlift output is transmitted to global decision support system (GDSS) for actual departure and arrival times for each mission. For sealift, JFAST transmits to the integrated command, control, and communications system which produces the sealift schedule. An example of a JFAST execution is depicted in Figure 7.

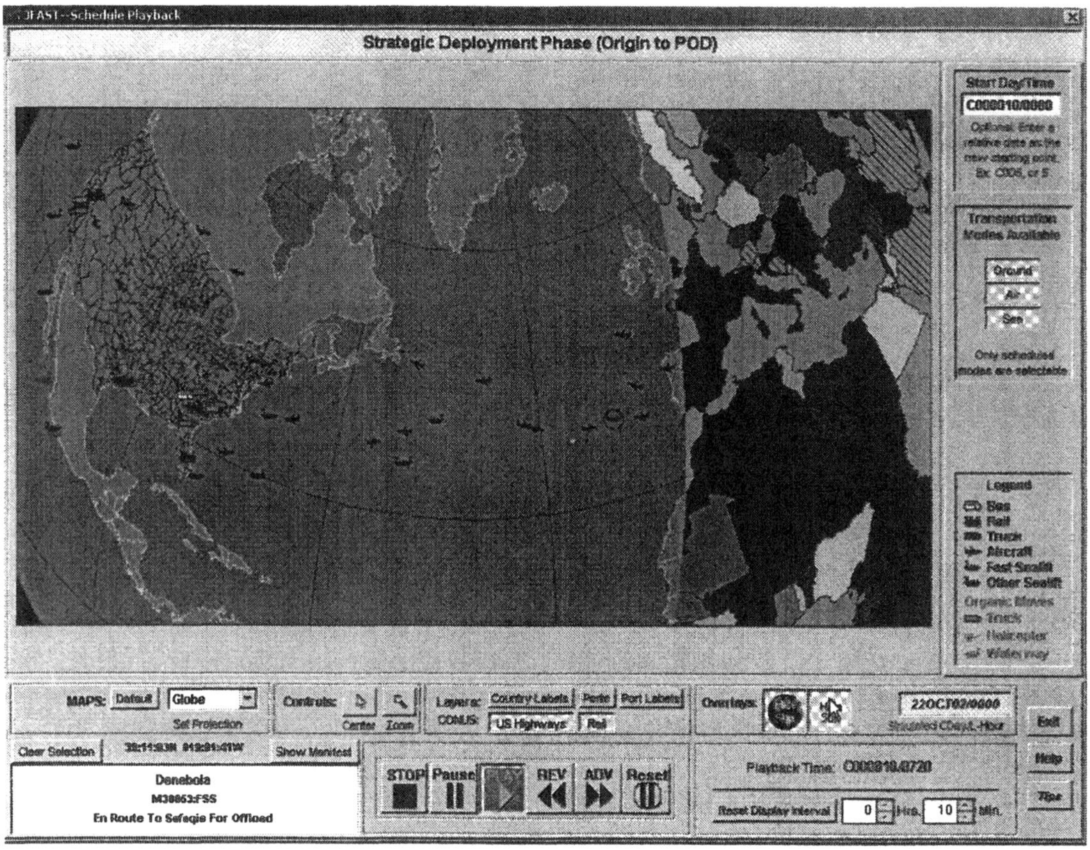

Figure 7. JFAST playback.

3.2.7. Check and correct

Several user screens may be used to verify input data. These screens, designed for easy editing, separate data into different categories such as ground, air, sea, canals, and VISA. These categories are further broken down to allow the user to edit constraints down to JOPES Level 5. The JFAST TPFDD editor supports quick changes in TPFDDs supporting comparison analysis. A graphical representation of the TPFDD is also available. When a particular requirement line number (RLN) is selected, the map will display the path for that RLN. (An RLN is a TPFDD line that has not split the personnel from the materiel to create a ULN.)

3.2.8. Other

Although initially designed for use by USTRANSCOM, JFAST has many users, primarily in the planning community, throughout the DoD. It is PC based (Windows NT/Windows 2000) with output capabilities through Microsoft Office 2000. USTRANSCOM has made several scenario libraries available through a remote server to enhance the speed and ease of preparing modeling runs.

3.3. Model for Intertheater Deployment by Air and Sea (MIDAS)

MIDAS is a strategic sealift and airlift model which can simulate multiple strategic deployment scenarios. The model was developed by GRC International, Inc. (now AT&T Government Solutions) for the Office of the Director of Program Analysis and Evaluation within the Office of the Secretary of Defense. Improvements have been performed for USTRANSCOM. The model is designed to measure the capability of a given set of strategic transportation assets to deploy a specified force. MIDAS projects schedules over a planning period, makes mode selection based on required delivery date, and adapts scenarios to expected and unexpected events [29].

3.3.1. Data and record preparation

MIDAS requires many input files including the TPFDD, requirements file, aircraft file, ship file, ship cargo and PAX file, ramp file, berth file, VISA file, scenario file, and event file. The

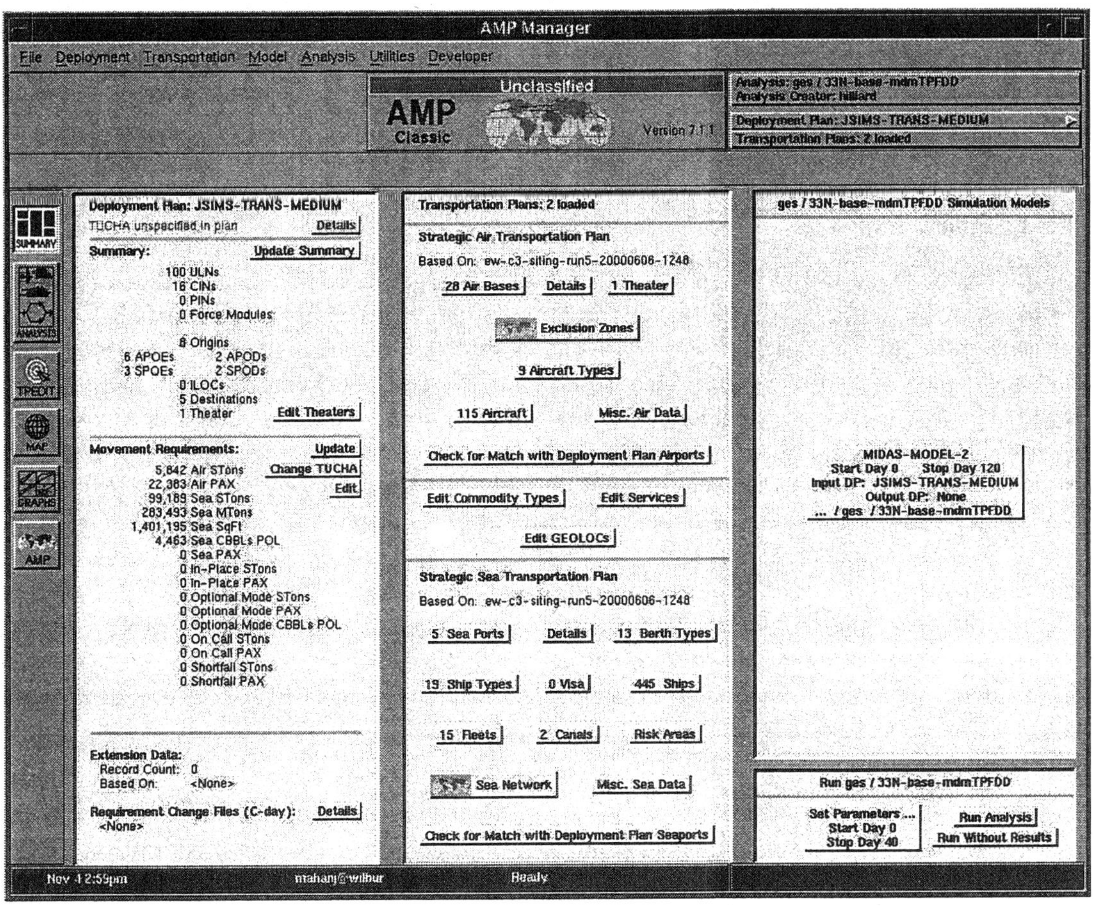

Figure 8. AMP manager screen.

requirements file can be input in standard TPFDD format. However, by itself, MIDAS lacks key aspects common to other models such as a TPFDD editor and a detailed ground transportation modeler. The editing of flat TPFDD files (often more than 80 lines and 100 columns of data) is very error prone, cumbersome, and time consuming, so direct editing of the files is rarely done. MIDAS has overcome many of its previous shortcomings by using an interface with the analysis of mobility platform (AMP) to provide data manipulation and input tools for the user (see Figure 8). AMP, an end-to-end transportation modeling shell, provides interfaces with numerous models and is discussed in Section 4. This platform was recommended by the TAMS report [5] to be the platform for all other transportation models to interface trough. One of the many advantages of this interface is a graphical TPFDD editor.

3.3.2. Prioritize records

MIDAS does not establish an explicit time window for cargo and PAX arrival. Instead this model uses RDD to estimate an expected arrival time for the cargo at its POE on one of the most preferred (usually shortest) routes. This estimate is used to establish the loading priority of cargo and PAX at the POE. Items that have the earliest loading priority are loaded first, subject to their arriving at the POD no earlier than their EAD. The scheduling algorithm for MIDAS uses the preferred route to attempt to establish an upperbound on the latest delivery time for the cargo. The assignment of the preferred route is made randomly in cases of ties so that all candidate routes are given equal consideration.

Scheduling of cargo and PAX within a mode of transportation in MIDAS evaluates sets of transportation resources over all routes subject to the constraint that each new route must improve on the delivery time of the best route so far discovered. The preferred route is considered first, followed by other routes in random order. Two random route sequences will produce either the same result or mathematically equivalent results. MIDAS uses this scheduling approach because there is no expectation of time-window feasibility in the types of studies for which MIDAS is most often used. These future program analyses do not have the benefit of having been subjected to the contingency planning process that resolves infeasibilities in the plan.

3.3.3. Select modes

MIDAS's mode selection capability starts with all cargo assigned to aircraft (except cargo restricted to be on ships). When considering cargo for sealift scheduling, the airlift delivery date of the cargo is applied as a bound to the sealift schedule. If ships can schedule the cargo within the bound constraint, the cargo is assigned to a set of ships. (Materiel that will miss delivery requirements regardless of travel mode remain assigned to aircraft.) The switch of this cargo to a ship creates a hole in the airlift schedule that may be filled by delivering later scheduled cargo earlier. When the size of the holes created in the airlift schedule reaches a threshold level, a replanning of the airlift schedule occurs during sealift scheduling.

The need to optimally assign modes of transport arises from the cost/time relationships of aircraft and ships. An aircraft delivers a small amount of cargo on a single mission relative to the amount that a ship delivers. Airlift operations overcome this shortcoming with far greater speed, shorter turn around times, and often shorter routes. However, aircraft are both expensive and limited in quantity. Consequently, a ship will be the more timely delivery platform for some cargo with a sufficiently large delivery requirement.

3.3.4. Schedule cargo

The level of detail MIDAS can model is sufficient to produce schedules with individual aircraft tail numbers and ULN level detail. Each aircraft is limited to one POE and one POD per trip. Government-owned ships and commercial ships under government charter or requisition ships can have multiport delivery capability but are limited to one POE. Commercial ships operating under the VISA program may operate on planned itineraries along designated routes. These ships have predetermined port stops and by definition have multiple pickup and drop-off locations.

Once transportation modes are determined and the route established, scheduling ULNs to specific craft on that route follow a similar assignment process for both airports and seaports. The model determines what vehicles are available. Then each ULN is tracked by its priority. All items that can feasibly meet the schedule are greedily assigned in priority order to a specific craft. Once a specific craft cannot take the next item on the list reaches a threshold load level, the craft is scheduled for departure. Items on the list are skipped to allow smaller items to be loaded on a craft that is not completely full. This practice significantly decreases the number of craft needed in most scenarios and reduces the estimated force closure time. A more robust loading heuristic could significantly improve MIDAS's closure time estimates.

3.3.5. Simulate movements

MIDAS has the capability to model ground transportation assets; however, it does not explicitly deal with road, rail, or waterway routes. It relies on ELIST for detailed modeling of the POD to destination leg. Although ELIST is a cargo flow model, it does perform vehicle routing of integer numbers of vehicles at Level 4 cargo detail. Individually-identified theater transports are not modeled.

MIDAS' sea scheduler simulates POE berthing and loading, ship transit, POD berthing and unloading by the individual ship name. It can incorporate multiple ship drop-off locations.

3.3.6. Prepare output and graphics

Through the interface with AMP, MIDAS's reports can be displayed graphically, viewed as flat files and printed. The outputs are produced in tables, graphs, charts, and global maps. The outputs are in standard format and can be exported in various formats. Several standard outputs are available and outputs and graphs can be customized.

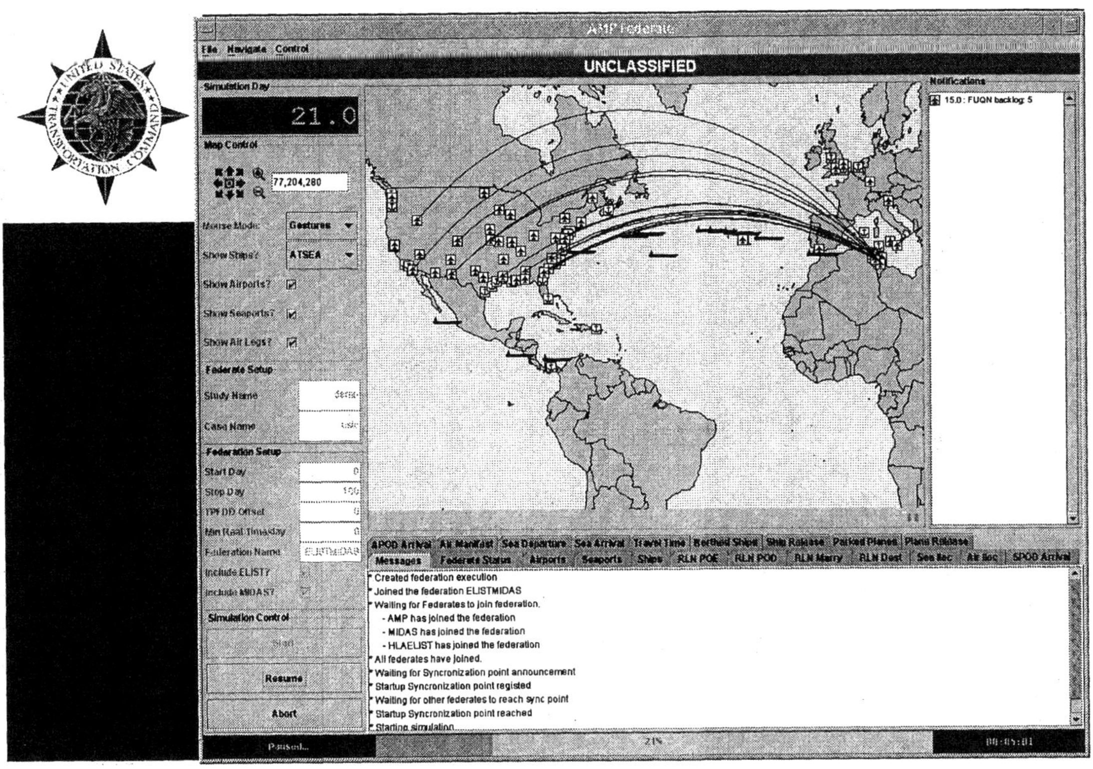

Figure 9. AMP graphical display.

3.3.7. Check and correct

There are extensive check methods within MIDAS. As in the other models, checks exist for the TPFDD not only for consistency but completeness.

3.3.8. Other

Like GDAS, MIDAS is used mostly by the resource planning communities. Its primary users are the Office of the Director of Program Analysis and Evaluation within the Office of the Secretary of Defense, the Logistics Directorate of the Joint Staff, and the J5 (plans and policy) in USTRANSCOM. MIDAS is the only strategic mobility model used by DoD that was designed for a Unix operating system. MIDAS operates on Unix because Unix workstations provide the high-capacity rapid-response computing environment needed to make dozens of MIDAS runs per day during the intensive analysis phase of DOD studies. The model can run on a PC, but AMP provided data viewing and editing are not yet available for the PC. All other strategic mobility models have graphical user interface (GUI) data entry and editing in the PC environment. The intense complexity of MIDAS presents a significant roadblock for many planners who have little experience and education in modeling.

3.4. Mobility Simulation Model (MobSim)

MOBSIM (mobility simulation model) is a network-based discrete event stochastic model employing state-of-the-art programming concepts that have the capability of dealing with large mobility simulation problems and questions and yet can be run on a PC computer. It is a simulation tool that deals with multiple modes of transportation to include (but not limited to) airlift,

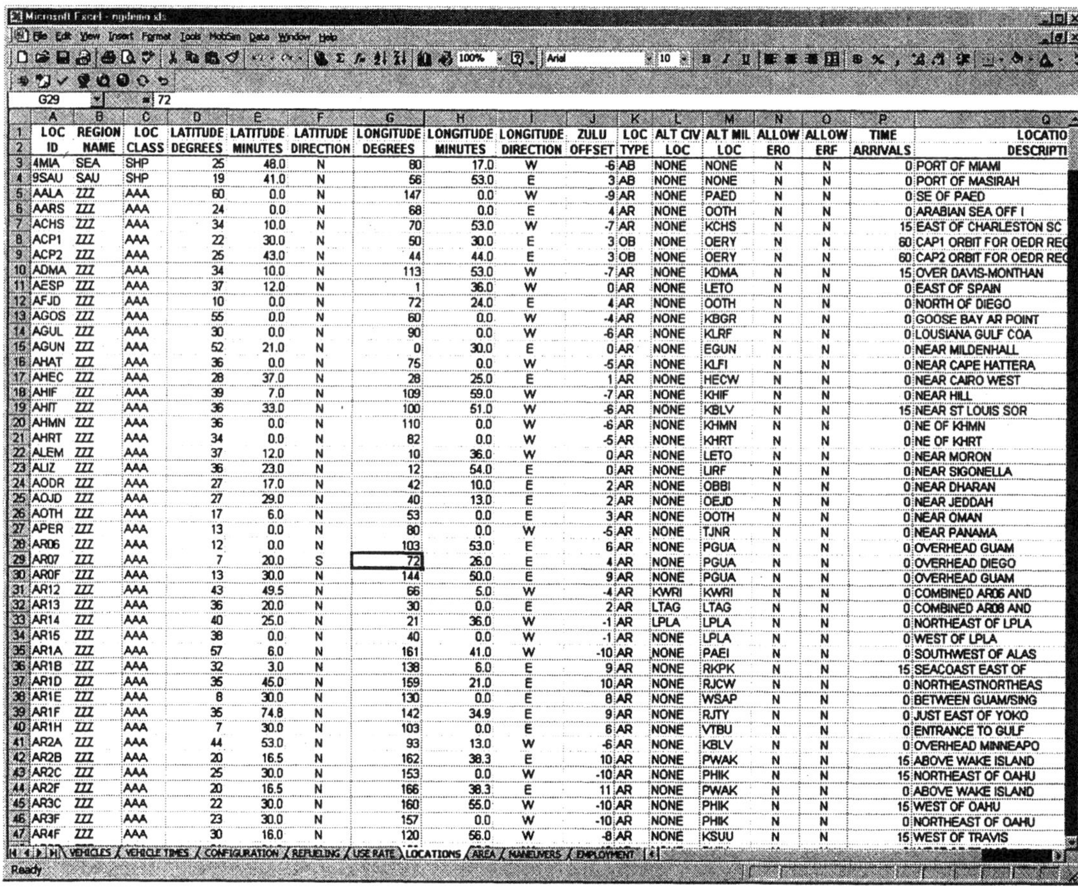

LOC ID	REGION NAME	LOC CLASS	LATITUDE DEGREES	LATITUDE MINUTES	LATITUDE DIRECTION	LONGITUDE DEGREES	LONGITUDE MINUTES	LONGITUDE DIRECTION	ZULU OFFSET	LOC TYPE	ALT CIV LOC	ALT MIL LOC	ALLOW ERO	ALLOW ERF	TIME ARRIVALS	LOCATIO DESCRIPTI
4MIA	SEA	SHP	25	48.0	N	80	17.0	W	-6	AB	NONE	NONE	N	N	0	PORT OF MIAMI
9SAU	SAU	SHP	19	41.0	N	56	53.0	E	3	AB	NONE	NONE	N	N	0	PORT OF MASIRAH
AALA	ZZZ	AAA	60	0.0	N	147	0.0	W	-9	AR	NONE	PAED	N	N	0	SE OF PAED
AARS	ZZZ	AAA	24	0.0	N	68	0.0	E	4	AR	NONE	OOTH	N	N	0	ARABIAN SEA OFF I
ACHS	ZZZ	AAA	34	10.0	N	70	53.0	W	-7	AR	NONE	KCHS	N	N	15	EAST OF CHARLESTON SC
ACP1	ZZZ	AAA	22	30.0	N	50	30.0	E	3	OB	NONE	OERY	N	N	60	CAP1 ORBIT FOR OEDR REC
ACP2	ZZZ	AAA	25	43.0	N	44	44.0	E	3	OB	NONE	OERY	N	N	60	CAP2 ORBIT FOR OEDR REC
ADMA	ZZZ	AAA	34	10.0	N	113	53.0	W	-7	AR	NONE	KDMA	N	N	15	OVER DAVIS-MONTHAN
AESP	ZZZ	AAA	37	12.0	N	1	36.0	W	0	AR	NONE	LETO	N	N	0	EAST OF SPAIN
AFJD	ZZZ	AAA	10	0.0	N	72	24.0	E	4	AR	NONE	OOTH	N	N	0	NORTH OF DIEGO
AGOS	ZZZ	AAA	55	0.0	N	60	0.0	W	-4	AR	NONE	KBGR	N	N	0	GOOSE BAY AR POINT
AGUL	ZZZ	AAA	30	0.0	N	90	0.0	W	-6	AR	NONE	KLRF	N	N	0	LOUSIANA GULF COA
AGUN	ZZZ	AAA	52	21.0	N	0	30.0	E	0	AR	NONE	EGUN	N	N	0	NEAR MILDENHALL
AHAT	ZZZ	AAA	36	0.0	N	75	0.0	W	-5	AR	NONE	KLFI	N	N	0	NEAR CAPE HATTERA
AHEC	ZZZ	AAA	28	37.0	N	28	25.0	E	1	AR	NONE	HECW	N	N	0	NEAR CAIRO WEST
AHIF	ZZZ	AAA	39	7.0	N	109	59.0	W	-7	AR	NONE	KHIF	N	N	0	NEAR HILL
AHIT	ZZZ	AAA	36	33.0	N	100	51.0	W	-6	AR	NONE	KBLV	N	N	15	NEAR ST LOUIS SOR
AHMN	ZZZ	AAA	36	0.0	N	110	0.0	W	-6	AR	NONE	KHMN	N	N	0	NE OF KHMN
AHRT	ZZZ	AAA	34	0.0	N	82	0.0	W	-5	AR	NONE	KHRT	N	N	0	NE OF KHRT
ALEM	ZZZ	AAA	37	12.0	N	10	36.0	W	0	AR	NONE	LETO	N	N	0	NEAR MORON
ALIZ	ZZZ	AAA	36	23.0	N	12	54.0	E	0	AR	NONE	LIRF	N	N	0	NEAR SIGONELLA
AODR	ZZZ	AAA	27	17.0	N	42	10.0	E	2	AR	NONE	OBBI	N	N	0	NEAR DHARAN
AOJD	ZZZ	AAA	27	29.0	N	40	13.0	E	2	AR	NONE	OEJD	N	N	0	NEAR JEDDAH
AOTH	ZZZ	AAA	17	6.0	N	53	0.0	E	3	AR	NONE	OOTH	N	N	0	NEAR OMAN
APER	ZZZ	AAA	13	0.0	N	80	0.0	W	-5	AR	NONE	TJNR	N	N	0	NEAR PANAMA
AR06	ZZZ	AAA	12	0.0	N	103	53.0	E	6	AR	NONE	PGUA	N	N	0	OVERHEAD GUAM
AR07	ZZZ	AAA	7	20.0	S	72	26.0	E	4	AR	NONE	PGUA	N	N	0	OVERHEAD DIEGO
AR0F	ZZZ	AAA	13	30.0	N	144	50.0	E	9	AR	NONE	PGUA	N	N	0	OVERHEAD GUAM
AR12	ZZZ	AAA	43	49.5	N	66	5.0	W	-4	AR	KWRI	KWRI	N	N	0	COMBINED AR06 AND
AR13	ZZZ	AAA	36	20.0	N	30	0.0	E	2	AR	LTAG	LTAG	N	N	0	COMBINED AR08 AND
AR14	ZZZ	AAA	40	25.0	N	21	36.0	W	-1	AR	LPLA	LPLA	N	N	0	NORTHEAST OF LPLA
AR15	ZZZ	AAA	38	0.0	N	40	0.0	W	-1	AR	NONE	LPLA	N	N	0	WEST OF LPLA
AR1A	ZZZ	AAA	57	6.0	N	161	41.0	W	-10	AR	NONE	PAEI	N	N	0	SOUTHWEST OF ALAS
AR1B	ZZZ	AAA	32	3.0	N	138	6.0	E	9	AR	NONE	RKPK	N	N	15	SEACOAST EAST OF
AR1D	ZZZ	AAA	35	45.0	N	159	21.0	E	10	AR	NONE	RJCW	N	N	0	NORTHEASTNORTHEAS
AR1E	ZZZ	AAA	8	30.0	N	130	0.0	E	8	AR	NONE	WSAP	N	N	0	BETWEEN GUAM/SING
AR1F	ZZZ	AAA	35	74.8	N	142	34.9	E	9	AR	NONE	RJTY	N	N	0	JUST EAST OF YOKO
AR1H	ZZZ	AAA	7	30.0	N	103	0.0	E	6	AR	NONE	VTBU	N	N	0	ENTRANCE TO GULF
AR2A	ZZZ	AAA	44	53.0	N	93	13.0	W	-6	AR	NONE	KBLV	N	N	0	OVERHEAD MINNEAPO
AR2B	ZZZ	AAA	20	16.5	N	162	38.3	E	10	AR	NONE	PWAK	N	N	15	ABOVE WAKE ISLAND
AR2C	ZZZ	AAA	25	30.0	N	153	0.0	W	-10	AR	NONE	PHIK	N	N	15	NORTHEAST OF OAHU
AR2F	ZZZ	AAA	20	16.5	N	166	38.3	E	11	AR	NONE	PWAK	N	N	0	ABOVE WAKE ISLAND
AR3C	ZZZ	AAA	22	30.0	N	160	55.0	W	-10	AR	NONE	PHIK	N	N	15	WEST OF OAHU
AR3F	ZZZ	AAA	23	30.0	N	157	0.0	W	-10	AR	NONE	PHIK	N	N	0	NORTHEAST OF OAHU
AR4F	ZZZ	AAA	30	16.0	N	120	56.0	W	-8	AR	NONE	KSUU	N	N	15	WEST OF TRAVIS

Figure 10. Location configuration definitions input.

sealift, rail, and truck operations and any combination of those modes. It employs the concept of in-transit visibility where the user can track a piece of cargo and PAX from its origin to the final destination as it travels through a complicated network of processing and shipping locations via those various modes of transportation that have been chosen [30].

3.4.1. Data preparation (merge files and aggregate records)

MobSim gives the user direct control over the input process with an GUI. This GUI allows the user to create, merge, and aggregate and otherwise manipulate all inputs with a Microsoft Excel Workbook as depicted in Figure 10. This workbook provides separate worksheets (20) for each input area, a worksheet for the scenario file, and a worksheet for the random number seeds. The input files can be saved as an Excel Workbook and edited as needed. The model also has extensive cross-checking capability to test the Worksheets for logic and format consistency. The input utilities include a JOPES B8 TPFDD converter.

3.4.2. Prioritize records

MobSim employs user-defined priorities for assigning and scheduling the cargo and PAX. Priorities can be set by any of the time requirements, such as RDD, EAD, or LAD, or they can be defined by unit integrity considerations. Once priorities are set, the search algorithm evaluates these priorities and searches priorities of equal measure based on a radial distance from the location of the item currently in consideration.

3.4.3. Select modes

MobSim is an end-to-end mobility model that allows mixed modes of transport for any given requirement. Each requirement is allowed up to three transshipment points. For each requirement the user must specify the allowable transshipment points. The user also specifies up to 11 possible combinations of the shipment mission types through or avoiding the specified transshipment points. The search algorithm is then restricted to these 11 possible mission types (each with unlimited routings possible) per requirement. In this fashion, the model can select the mode of transportation from the possible routes provided.

3.4.4. Schedule cargo

For each vehicle, items are loaded in priority order. When all feasible cargo and PAX are loaded on a vehicle, the model searches all PAX to see if any available space can be used by PAX that are available for movement.

MobSim can represent cargo and PAX down to the ULN level, modeling items as outsize, oversize, bulk, and PAX. It can also schedule aircraft down to the unique tail number. MobSim can model POEs/PODs with characteristics such as parking, cargo or PAX throughput, fuel outtake per day, daily operating hours, arrivals per day, and interarrival time. MobSim limits transshipments to four.

A shortfall noted by the 1991 study [4], was the inability of SMMs to optimize transportation assets. Although MobSim does not find the optimal assets, it attempts to a find good transportation asset mix within MobSims scheduling algorithm. When cargo and PAX are ready to move, MobSim randomly looks for vehicles by type by first looking at existing idle vehicles. If no vehicle exists, it creates a new vehicle subject to constraints on total number of vehicles to be used.

3.4.5. Simulate movements

MobSim is the only current SMM that emulates movements, but also incorporates probabilistic occurrences of events. MobSim can run a deterministic (expected value) simulation or a probabilistic simulation. To further enhance the stochastic aspect, the random number seed can be changed so that additional runs of the scenario yield independent results. MobSim also simulates air crew scheduling and tanker refueling operations.

3.4.6. Prepare output and graphics

MobSim uses a Microsoft Excel interface allowing all output files to be presented directly in Excel. Raw data can also be presented in space-delimited files for input by any ODBC compliant software. Output of each scheduled itinerary may be provided in global decision support system (GDSS) formats. A graphical depiction of the simulation results is provided by SimViewer as seen in Figure 11. SimViewer allows the display to pause, reverse, fast forward, summarize, and zoom at any level of detail.

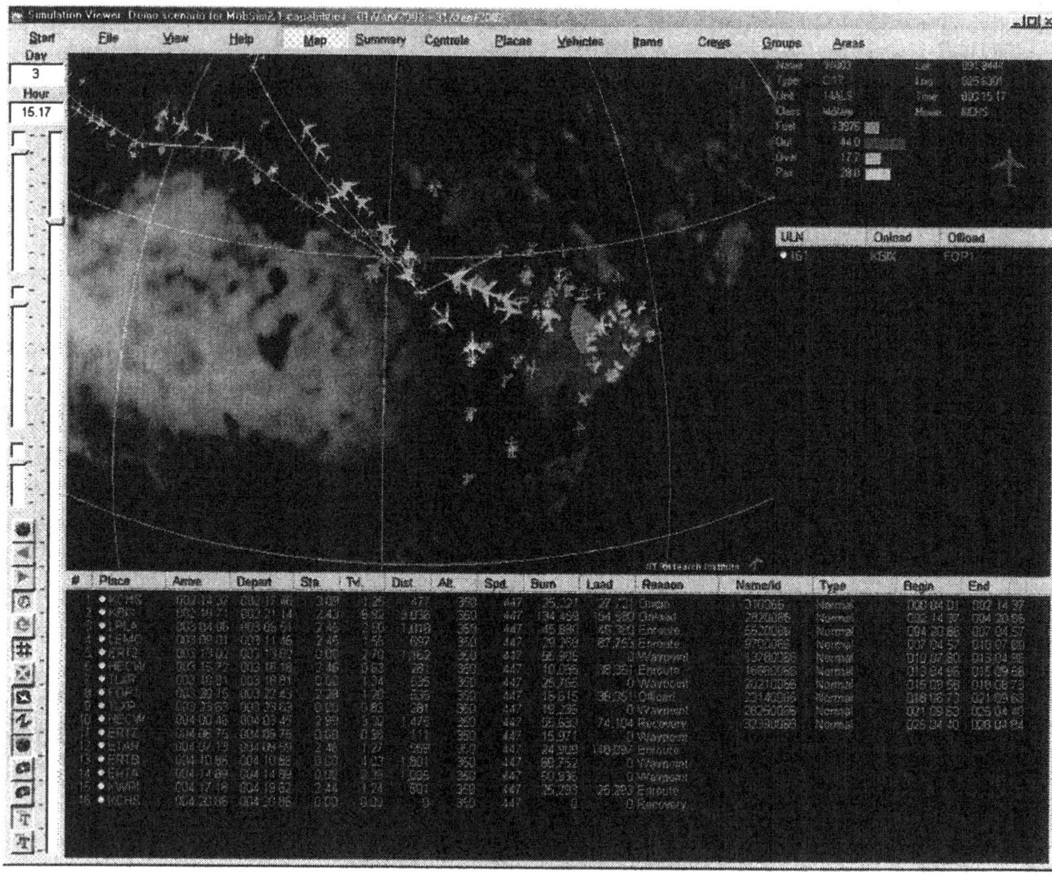

Figure 11. MobSim simulation map.

3.4.7. Check and correct

Several data validation checks are present in MobSim. Vehicle load quantities are verified. If a vehicle is underloaded by user-defined values, it will attempt to place that vehicle's load onto another vehicle. Unique to MobSim is a verification of crew and tanker availability prior to any aircraft scheduling.

3.4.8. Other

MobSim and its companion SimViewer, both proprietary and not government sponsored, are challenging and expensive systems to acquire for individual organizations. However, the expense of maintenance and development are not born by the government. Its Windows environment and GUIs make this model extremely portable, adaptable, and easy to use. Its users include civilian corporations and both U.S. and foreign countries. It is defense information infrastructure common operating environment (COE) compliant and can export and import directly from the common JOPES B8 TPFDD format files. This suite of tools has been verified, validated, and accredited by AMC.

MobSim's dependence on a user-defined rule-based hierarchy for scheduling decisions allow users to control which mobility policies and procedures are implemented. This along with its heuristic rule for ending the search, once a feasible solution is found, significantly reduces its run time. Since MobSim honors all the user's rules as it builds an itinerary, the first itinerary found to be feasible is the user-preferred itinerary. The solution found may or may not be optimal, however the time required to search the entire solution space for real world scheduling and dispatching problems is severely limiting. Thus, MobSim takes the approach of trading off slow performance and limited-use optimality for very fast solutions and feasible missions.

3.5. Strategic Mobility Model Comparison

Each of the current strategic mobility SMMs was designed to primarily support a specific type of planning and/or resource capability assessment analysis. This has driven their development and capabilities in similar, yet different directions. Of the three levels of planning, current SMMs are targeted towards only resource and deliberate planning. No model is specifically designed to be used in crisis action planning. Both GDAS and MIDAS are primarily designed and used for resource planning. MobSim© and JFAST are designed and used for deliberate planning. When comparing these four models it is important to not only compare them against models within their planning domain, but also with models in other planning domains. Many similarities are apparent in MIDAS and GDAS and many similarities are apparent in JFAST and MobSim©. GDAS and MIDAS are more difficult to use, but provide a level of analytical detail that is necessary for resource planning. JFAST and MobSim© lack this detailed level of analytical capability, but are easy to use and provide the quick run times necessary for deliberate planning in a significantly shorter planning horizon. None of the existing models combine both this detailed analytical capability and quick response times.

3.5.1. Input files

All four models can input standard TPFDD files in JOPES format. They also use standard codes for locations of ports. They differ in the format of constraint data input. Much of this is performed manually, a time-consuming and error-prone process. However, once input for any study, this data can be reused and easily modified for any SMM.

3.5.2. Task coverage

Table 2 summarizes task coverage of the different SMMs. When the model addresses the tasks completely within its own framework, an X is placed in this chart. If the model obtains the process or part of the process from another model, an O is present. If the task is not available when using the model, the chart is blank.

In the previous study, a significant number of the cells in this table were empty indicating the function could not be modeled with the SMMs in existence. This table is indicative of significant progress in the breadth of the models used today. For the current SMMs, only JFAST and MIDAS do not cover the entire set of tasks. In addition, JFAST is limited to modeling predetermined modes of transportation. MIDAS previously could not merge files, aggregate records, or check and correct. In addition, MIDAS' calculation of ground movement times has been improved by calling the ELIST model.

3.5.3. Node and link coverage

Calculations for each of the stages within the strategic mobility process are performed either by simulation or by a simplified mathematical calculation. Table 3 details whether the model

Table 2. Task coverage.

	GDAS	JFAST	MIDAS	MobSim©
Merge Files	X	X	X	X
Aggregate Records	X	X	X	X
Prioritize Records	X	X	X	X
Select Modes	X		X	X
Schedule Cargos	X	X	X	X
Simulate Movements	X	X	O	X
Multiport PU & DO				
Airlift POE & POD	X			X
Sealift POE	X			X
Sealift POD	X	X	X	X
# Transshipment Points	Unlimited	1	Unlimited	4
VISA Modeling	X		X	X
Prepare Textual Output	X	X	X	X
Prepare Graphical Output	X	X	X	X
Check and Correct	X	X	X	X

Table 3. Node and link coverage.

	GDAS	JFAST	MIDAS	MobSim©
Home Station to POE	S	S	C	S
Sealift				
POE Berthing	S	S	S	S
POE Loading	S	S	C	S
Movement to Convoy Point	S	S	S	S
Convoy Assembly	S	S	S	S
Movement to POC	S	S	S	S
POD Berthing	S	S	S	S
POD Unloading	S	S	C	S
Airlift				
POE Berthing/Ferry	S	S	C	S
POE Loading	S	S	C	S
En Route Stop Operations			S	S
Movement to POD	S	S	C	S
POD Ground Operations	S	S	C	S
POD Unloading	S	S	C	S
Movement to Recovery Area	S		S	S
Recovery Ground Operations	S		S	S
POD to Destination				
Movement to Marshalling Area	S	S	C	S
Marshalling	S	S	C	S
Movement to Destination	S	S	C	S

simulates the process (S) or provides the simplified calculation (C). A blank indicates that the model does not address this stage.

Previously, five models were used for comparison. Of those five models, none of them addressed all areas in this chart. MIDAS came the closest, but did not address recovery ground operations. Today's SMMs have matured significantly from those ten years ago. Now, only JFAST does not address all areas mentioned in the chart.

3.5.4. Solution characteristics

The time characteristics which each model uses are presented in Table 4. These are used to assign priorities to cargo and PAX for scheduling and assignment and to evaluate the model objective functions.

Table 4. Solution characteristics.

	GDAS	JFAST	MIDAS	MobSim©
First	RDD	RDD	RDD	RDD
Second	EAD, LAD	RLD, ALD, EAD, LAD	RLD, EAD	EAD, LAD
Third	RLD			

Each model uses time delivery as one of the factors in determining the priority of assigning and scheduling cargo and PAX. Even when the models consider other criteria and use associated penalties, they use a simple first pass greedy heuristic. They do not consider lateness of cargo and PAX that have the same priority. Further, if cargo or PAX are late and there is an associated supporting cargo/PAX, no consideration is given to that supporting cargo/PAX. Each of these models could gain from the use of more advanced heuristic search methods.

Each SMM uses the RDD and EAD as their primary time constraints. However, JFAST and GDAS also consider the LAD and RLD and use EAD and LAD to provide a time window for cargo and PAX to arrive at the POD. No change to the solution characteristics of MIDAS has been performed since the 1991 study.

3.5.5. Model summary

The SMMs used today have a wide range of user support from several different agencies within DoD. Each of the SMMs has unique strengths and weaknesses. With the current trend of constant development and interfacing of these models, many weaknesses are being corrected, leading to even more overlap among the SMMs. For example, when MIDAS is interfaced with AMP, one must also consider the advanced AMP components to truly represent the analysis that is performed using MIDAS.

Table 5 gives a brief comparison of the four SMMs. While there are numerous aspects that could be compared, these were chosen based on the volume of interest by the user communities. When interviewed regarding what the users liked about their model of choice and why they were not

Table 5. Strategic mobility model comparison.

	GDAS	JFAST	MIDAS/AMP	MobSim
Operating Platform	PC	PC	Unix	PC
Tail Number Aircraft Scheduling	X	X	X	X
Line Item Number Tracking	X	X	X	X
Multiple Pickup Locations by Mode	A & S	S	S	A & S
Multiple Drop-Off Locations by Mode	A & S	S	S	A & S
Government Owned Software	X	X	X	NO
Avg. Model Setup Time (large problem) 85,000 TPFDD records	30 days	7 days	14 days	14 days
Avg. Model Run Time (large problem) 85,000 TPFDD records	4 hours	2 hours	2 hours	30 min
Avg. Model Setup Time (small problem) 45 TPFDD records	3 hours	10 min	15 min	15 min
Avg. Model Run Time (small problem) 45 TPFDD records	1 min	1 min	1 min	5 min
Data Entry/Complexity of Use	Hard	Easy	Hard	Easy

using one of the other three models, the categories in Table 5 were repeated consistently [31–37]. The chief complaints from the deliberate planning community were directed at ease of use. Such users are often military personnel with little experience with modeling. Any system they use must be transportable, operate on a laptop with a Microsoft Windows operating environment, and be simple to learn. Only JFAST meets these criteria. JFAST is the model of choice for most strategic mobility analysts in the planning arena, despite its inability to perform mode source selection.

GDAS has more user-preferred capabilities (as noted in Tables 2 and 3) than other models but requires significantly longer setup times. Time sensitive environments, like deliberate/crisis planning, discourage GDAS use. MIDAS's interface with AMP restricts it to the UNIX environment and its mode selection feature uses a greedy feasible solution obtained by a one-pass greedy algorithm. JFAST has the most limited capability of the four models. Its strengths lie in its portability, ease of use, and fast run times.

4. SUPPORTING MODELS

In addition to the end-to-end SMMs, there are many models that focus on finer detail than the SMMs address. These models are often used by organizations responsible for those more detailed aspects. Many of these organizations would prefer that their specific interests be included in the SMMs. Unfortunately, including all of these details would cause the SMMs to grow to unmanageable size requiring impractical execution times.

The supporting models described below were chosen for numerous reasons. The first model was chosen due to its significant role in integrating transportation information systems. The next three are directly interfaced with the current SMMs previously discussed or they are used in establishing feasibility bounds for SMMs. The next four models are used for detailed modeling of air, port, and ground activities within the strategic mobility spectrum. The final three are included due to their use of modern metaheuristic search methodologies which fill the gap between feasible solutions and exhaustive search procedures yielding excellent near optimal solutions in a remarkably short amount of time.

4.1. Transportation Coordinators Automated Information for Movement Systems II (TC-AIMS II)

There are several transportation models used within DoD. One transportation model type is transportation information systems (TIS). These are used for the gathering, tracking, and relaying of information about transportation assets and items being transported. There are three TIS models in current use: TC-AIMS II, transportation coordinator-automated command and control information system (TC-ACCIS), and DA movements management system-redesign (DAMMS-R). Currently in its testing phase of acquisition, TC-AIMS II is scheduled to replace all TIS models [19], the cargo movement operating system (CMOS), and Marine Air Ground Task Force (MAGTF) deployment support system II (MDSS) [18].

TC-AIMS II is a joint information management system that facilities the movement of unit cargo and PAX during peace and war and provides visibility of that cargo and PAX throughout the deployment. Its primary mission is to support the warfighter in the planning and execution of deployment, sustainment, and redeployment of forces. Some of the activities it models are planning convoys, requesting convoy clearances, and conducting load planning. TC-AIMS will integrate current DoD transportation systems supporting installation and unit movement requirements into a single system [18,38].

4.2. Deployment Network Tool Extended (DANTE)

DANTE is a network flow model that was developed to perform quick deployment analysis. Since it is a flow model and does not model actual items, DANTE is not considered a strategic mobility model since it does not analyze TPFDD data, but rather it aggregates cargo and PAX into short tons (STon). It then flows these through a predefined network to provide a lower bound on force closure and identify possible bottlenecks in the network [39]. Interested persons are also directed to the COMFLOW and deployment scheduling analysis tool (DSAT) models [40].

4.3. Analysis of Mobility Platform (AMP)

AMP is a system for analyzing logistics and is sponsored by USTRANSCOM. AMP provides end-to-end strategic mobility analysis through the integration of MIDAS and ELIST combined with a TPFDD editor that imports and exports in the standard JOPES B8 TPFDD file format. AMP can also provide inputs for other simulation platforms which enhances its interoperability.

Recently, AMP was remodeled to integrate even more models into the high-level architecture (HLA) federate of models. While the HLA is an architecture, not software, use of a runtime infrastructure (RTI) software is required to support operations of a federation execution. The RTI software provides a set of services which are used by federates to coordinate their operations and data exchange during a runtime execution [41]. This HLA significantly increases the capabilities of AMP. The current operating system limitations of AMP, UNIX, may be quickly overcome when a new JAVA based system, AMP 21, completes development. Although currently in prototype, once proven and verified, AMP and MIDAS should be able to run on a PC and be available to a larger number of planners and analysts.

4.4. Enhanced Logistics Intratheater Support Tool (ELIST)

ELIST is an intratheater transportation network model developed by Argon National Labs. Although normally used to evaluate the theater portion of a course of action, it can also simulate the CONUS portion of a course of action. ELIST is often used in conjunction with MIDAS to evaluate the ground portion (origin to POE and POD to destination) of the strategic mobility end-to-end model. As such, it can input a TPFDD file in the standard JOPES B8 format and assess capabilities of assets at origin, POE, POC, and destination to support the ground movement of TPFDD items including the linking of cargo and PAX at the POD prior to movement to the destination [17].

4.5. Airlift Flow Model (AFM)

AFM was written in C/C++ and operates on a SPARC workstation. This legacy system is not HLA compliant, but it is one of the few models that provide a stochastic representation of events. It is still in use today awaiting completion of its successor model (AMOS). AFM models a fleet of aircraft from a given location (POE) along with a listing of cargo and PAX, through multiple "way" points, to a given destination (POD). It then recovers and returns the aircraft for reuse [42].

4.6. Automated Air Load Planning System (AALPS)

This model is one of the many interface models to TC-AIMS II. Given a list of equipment and passengers (TPFDD) AALPS provides air load planners the capability to estimate airlift requirements, plan force packages, modify aircraft loads, and save these force package models for future use [19].

4.7. Port Simulation (PORTSIM)

Under current development, PORTSIM is part of a force projection modeling (FPM) development program of deployment and transportation modeling and simulation tools. It will used by Military Sealift Command (MSC) and Military Traffic Management Command (MTMC). FPM tools will provide detailed transportability characteristics of the force and throughput capability of ports and installations [43]. FPM tools includes PORTSIM, ELIST, TRANSCAP, and Transportability Analysis Report Generator (TARGET).

PORTSIM is a port of embarkation/debarkation model simulating activities at a seaport during a force deployment. When complete, the model will evaluate in detail, operations and activities that occur at specific ports of embarkation and debarkation. The model provides planners a capability to determine a port's reception, staging, cargo, and PAX clearance, throughput capabilities, and force clearance profiles. It also identifies port constraints and the utilization of port assets. PORTSIM is being developed to provide answers to deployment related questions such as: "how long does it take to move a force through a port, what and where the port bottlenecks are and what specific port facilities are needed to support a deployment" [44].

4.8. Transportation Capability (TRANSCAP)

TRANSCAP simulates installation (reception, staging, onward movement, and integration (RSO&I): home station, in-theater staging bases (ISB), and tactical assembly areas (TAA)) operations for planning, training, analysis, and execution at the cargo and PAX item level of detail and operates in a Windows or UNIX environment. Some of the activities that are represented in the model are: motor pool, marshalling, convoy, commercial truck and rail, and container. The sponsor is MTMCTEA. Its proponent is DA DCSLOG [45]. This model was recommended by the TAMS report to address modeling of activities that occur at origin locations.

4.9. Supporting Models Conclusion

Discussed in the above sections are just a few of the models currently in use by Department of Defense organizations for different aspects of strategic mobility. Currently, there are many new developments and ongoing enhancements to these models. In addition to these models, there are many more models for varying aspects of the strategic mobility model such as those that support the sustainment portions of deployment (logistical simulation (LOGSIM), simulation of logistics systems (SIMULOGS), combat service support training simulation (CSS-TS), independent logistic assessment tool (ILA), and integrated consumable item support model (ICIS)). There is also an entire suite of models not mentioned in this paper that interface with AMP HLA, GCCS, and/or TC-AIMS II. A discussion of these models is beyond the scope of this paper.

5. CONCLUSION

There are many transportation models in use today throughout DoD which support the defense transportation system. A significant number of these models are under continual development. Those models that are not currently HLA/COE compliant are being upgraded to be HLA compliant or are being replaced. There is also a trend towards interoperability with either GCCS or TC-AIMS II.

Although most models operate on a PC platform, there are still several models operating in a UNIX environment. This prevents wider use of the models as the PC is standard platform in most military units. There is a trend, however, to develop new models on the PC platform and for models to be able to connect to a network or server for the larger storage requirements.

The significant changes since the previous report on SMMs are evident in all models in use today. They address a wider range of tasks while making both the input and output more user friendly. Each model includes a GUI for inputs and changes to the model as wel! as displaying the outputs in multiple formats to include global depictions of the results.

The major aspect that is lacking in the models today is the use of advanced optimization techniques for estimating force closure. Each SMM described in this paper either uses cumbersome ineffective classical optimization algorithms or simplistic and ineffective greedy approaches to find solutions. This aspect was addressed as a shortcoming in the models 11 years ago and remains the major shortcoming today.

APPENDIX
GLOSSARY

- AALPS: automated air load planning system
- ADANS: airlift deployment analysis system
- AFM: airlift flow model
- ALD: available for load date—a day, relative to C-day (commencement date), that unit and nonunit equipment and forces can begin loading on an aircraft or ship at the POE
- ALP: aircraft loading practices
- AMC XPY: Air Mobility Command XPY
- AMEP: aerial medical evacuation problem
- AMOS: air mobility operations simulator
- AMP: analysis of mobility platform
- B8: (flat file used for JOPES TPFDD reader)
- C2: command and control
- CAA: Center for Army Analysis (formerly the Concepts Analysis Agency)
- CALM: computer aided load manifesting
- CAMPS: consolidated air mobility planning system
- Cargo: equipment and support material identified as bulk, oversize and outsize cargo
- CMARPS: combined mating and ranging planning system
- CMOS: cargo movement operating system
- CSS-TS: combat service support training simulation
- COE: common operating environment
- CONUS: Continental United States
- DA DCSLOG: Department of the Army (DA) Deputy Chief of Staff for Logistics (DCSLOG)
- DAMMS-R: DA movements management system-redesign
- DANTE: deployment network tool extended
- d/o: drop off
- DoD: Department of Defense
- DSAT: deployment scheduling analysis tool
- DTS: defense transportation system
- EAD: earliest arrival date—a day, relative to C-day, that is specified by a planner as the earliest date when a unit, a resupply shipment, or replacement personnel can be accepted at a POD during deployment (used with the LAD, it defines a delivery time window for transportation planning)
- EDD: earliest delivery date
- end-to-end SMM: the modeling from origin through POE and POD to destination of SMMs, including tasks in Table 2 and coverages in Table 3
- ELIST: enhanced logistics intratheater support tool
- FLOGEN: flow generator
- FP: force protection
- FPP: force projection platform
- GCCS: global command and control system
- GDAS: global deployment analysis system
- Geoloc: geographic location
- HLA: high level architecture
- ICIS: integrated consumable item support model
- ILA: independent logistics assessment tool
- ISB: in-theater staging bases
- JFAST: joint flow and analysis system for transportation
- JOPES: joint operations planning and execution system
- JPEC: joint planning and execution community
- LAD: latest arrival date—a day, relative to C-day, that is specified by a planner as the latest date when a unit, a resupply shipment, or replacement personnel can arrive and

complete unloading at the POD (used with the EAD, it defines a delivery time window for transportation planning)

- LOGSIM: logistical simulation
- NIMA: National Institute of Mapping Agency
- MAGTF: Marine Air Ground Task Force
- MDSS: MAGTF deployment support system II
- MIDAS: model for intertheater deployment by air and sea
- MobSim©: mobility simulation
- MSC: military sealift command
- MTMCTEA: Military Traffic Management Command (MTMC) Transportation Engineering Agency (TEA)
- OCONUS: outside of the continental United States
- ODBC: open database connectivity
- OOP: object oriented programming
- OPLAN: operational plan
- PC: personal computer
- POC: point of contact
- POD: point of debarkation
- POE: point of embarkation
- PORTSIM: port simulation
- PRI: movement priority of cargo having the same LAD
- p/u: pick up
- RAPIDSIM: rapid intertheater deployment simulator
- RDD: required delivery date—a day, relative to C-day, when a unit must arrive at its destination and complete offloading
- RLD: is the ready to load date—a day, relative to C-day, when the unit, nonunit equipment, and forces are prepared to depart their origin on organic transportation or are prepared to begin loading on provided transportation
- RLN: requirement line number
- RORO: roll on roll off
- RSO&I: reception, staging, onward movement, and integration
- RTI: runtime infrastructure
- SAP: strategic intertheater airlift problem
- SEASTRAT: strategic sealift analysis system
- SIMULOGS: simulation of logistics systems
- SMM: strategic mobility model
- SMMSP: strategic mobility mode selection problem
- SSC: small scale contingencies
- TAA: tactical assembly areas
- TC-ACCIS: transportation coordinator—automated command and control information system
- TC-AIMS II: transportation coordinators automated information for movement systems II
- TC Units: transportation corps units
- TEUs: 20 foot container unit of measurement
- TFE: transportation feasibility estimator
- TIS: transportation information systems
- TRANSCAP: transportation capability
- TPFDD: time phase force deployment data
- TUCHA: type unit characteristic
- ULN: unit line number
- USAF: United States Air Force
- USAREUR: United States Army Europe
- USCENTCOM: United States Central Command
- USEUCOM: United States European Command
- USFK: United States Forces Korea

- USJFCOM: United States Joint Forces Command
- USTRANSCOM: United States Transportation Command
- VISA: voluntary intermodal sealift agreement
- WWMCCS: world wide military command and control system

REFERENCES

1. Reception, staging, onward movement and integration (RSOI) (n.d.), Retrieved July 22, 2002 from http://call.army.mil/products/newsltrs/99-17/intro.htm.
2. Force projection, In *Field Manual 100-5, Operations*, (1993).
3. Levels of war, In *Joint Publication 3-0 (JP 3-0) Doctrine for Joint Operations*, (Chapter 2), (2001).
4. J. Shank, M. Mattock, G. Sumner, I. Greenberg, J. Rothenberg and J. Stucker, A review of strategic mobility models and analysis, (R-3926-JS), Rand's National Defense Research Institute, Santa Monica, CA, (1991).
5. USTRANSCOM/TCJ5 and Joint Transportation Corporate Information Management Center, Transportation analysis, modeling and simulation (TAMS) transportation systems decision report, USTRANSCOM, Scott Air Force Base, IL, (February 1998).
6. Basic national defense doctrine (n.d.), In *Joint Pub 0-1.*
7. Department of Defense dictionary of military and associated terms, In *Joint Publication 1-02*, (2002).
8. D. Graham and M. Dowdy, Briefing to the JLOTS R&D Symposium, Retrieved July 2002 from http://chl.wes.army.mil/research/projects/ribs/JLOTS%20Symposium/presentations02.htm, (Jan. 2002).
9. TPFDD. (n.d.), Retrieved August 1, 2002 from http://www.jfast.org/jfast/html/Terms/TPFDD.htm.
10. JOPES Functional Manager Orientation Guide, (February 1996); Retrieved September 2002 from http://www.fas.org/nuke/guide/usa/c3i/jopes/index.html.
11. Air Mobility Command (AMC), Analysis of alternatives (AOA) study plan for AMC outsize and oversize airlift capability, Studies and analysis flight, USTRANSCOM, Scott Air Force Base, IL, (November 1998).
12. S. Baker, D. Morton, R. Rosenthal and L. Williams, Optimizing military airlift, *Operations Research* **50** (4), 582–602, (2002).
13. W.H. Lunceford, Jr., Army model and simulation organizational overview briefing for MG Kensinger, ADCSOPS. Retrieved July 28, 2002 from http://www.amso.army.mil/library/bfgs/amso-info.ppt, (October 2000).
14. Advanced concepts and requirements (ACR) model and simulation (M&S) domain management plan, Retrieved July 28, 2002 from http://www.amso.army.mil/structure/domains/acr/plan2001.doc, (May 2001).
15. Department of Defense dictionary of military and associated terms, In *Joint Publication 1-02*, (1994).
16. World-Wide Military Command and Control System (WWMCCS), In *Department of Defense Directive Number 5100.30 (DoDD 5100.30)*, (1971).
17. Transportation related automated C2 and information systems. (n.d.). (Chapter 6). Retrieved July 27, 2002 from http://www.transchool.eusstis.army.mil/DTO/.
18. Logistics automation systems and enablers, In *Theater Logistics Handbook*, Fifth Edition, Chapter 4, (2001); Retrieved July 27, 2002, from http://www.almc.army.mil/LEDD/8A-F17/TLogHBChaps.html.
19. PM, Transportation Information Systems (TIS). (n.d.) Retrieved July 2002, from http://www.tcaimsii.belvoir.army.mil/interfaces.htm.
20. Sealift scheduler port throughput model. (n.d.). Retrieved July 25, 2002, from http://www.jfast.org/jfast/Html/WhitePapers/SeaPortThroughput.htm.
21. M. Hilliard, R. Solanki, C. Liu, I. Busch, G. Harrison and R. Kraemer, *Transportation-Air Decision Analysis-Applications Military*, The Institute of Management Sciences, (1992).
22. Air mobility command deployment analysis system (ADANS). (n.d.) Retrieved July 28, 2002 from http://www.globalsecurity.org./intll/library/reports/2001/compendium/adans.htm.
23. Global command and control system (GCCS) consolidated air mobility planning system (CAMPS). (n.d.). Retrieved July 10, 2002, from http://jitc.fhu.disa.mil/gccsiop/interfaces/camps.htm.
24. Logicon, *Combined Mating and Ranging Planning System Overview*, Briefing, (1996).
25. S.K. Young, GDAS abstract, (n.d.). GDAS global deployment analysis system overview, Noetics.
26. P. Loudin, Personal communication. CAA, (2002).
27. J. Hoover, JFAST statement of work for 2003, U.S. TRANSCOM, (2002).
28. R. Hazdra, Operational requirements document (ORD) for the joint flow and analysis system for transportation (JFAST). United States Transportation Command document, (April 2002).
29. U.S. Army Transportation School, *DTO Defense Transportation Officer's Guide*, Reference Number 01-01, Fort Eustis, VA, (June 2001).
30. MOBSIM©. (n.d.), Retrieved July 27, 2002, from http://www.daedalic.com/software.html, IIT Research Institute, O'Fallon, IL.
31. W. Key, Personal communication. USTRANSCOM, J5. william.key@hq.transcom.mil, (2002).
32. C. Keyfauver, Personal communication. AT&T Government Solutions. ckeyfauver@grci.com, (2002).
33. J. Sees, Personal communication. Concepts Analysis Agency. sees@caa.army.mil, (2002).
34. S. Young, Personal communication. Noetics, Inc. S.Young@stanleyassociates.com, (2002).
35. J. Hoover, Personal communication. USTRANSCOM, J3. John.Hoover@hq.transcom.mil, (2002).

36. B. Jones, Personal communication. DPRA. Brian.Jones@dpra.com, (2002).
37. T. Kowalsky and J. Riveta, Personal communication. IITRI Software Development Team. tomk@ikarik.com, jrevetta@iitri.org, (2002).
38. TC-AIMS II Description, Retrieved June 27, 2002, from http://www.deploy.eustis.army.mil/Info-Fusion/TCAIMSII.htm, (May 2002).
39. DANTE. The deployment network tool extended, Retrieved July 31, 2002, from http://www.tea.army.mil/tools/dante.htm, (June 19, 2002).
40. B. Melendez, On scheduling delivery in a military deployment scenario. Powerpoint presentation received from author, (2002).
41. Models. (n.d.), Retrieved July 10, 2002, from the JTC Page from http://www.usafe.af.mil/direct/wpc/Products/JTCContent.htm.
42. Airlift flow model (AFM). (n.d.), Retrieved July 29, 2002, from the Air Force Modeling & Simulation Resource Repository from http://afmsrr.afams.af.mil/bookmark_link.cfm?RID=SMN_AF_1000001.
43. ACR M&S domain management plan (n.d.), Retrieved July 28, 2002 from http://www.amso.army.mil/structure/domains/acr/annex_a.htm.
44. J. Joines and M. Cassada, PORTSIM. Presented at the *JLOTS R&D Symposium V*, Retrieved July 22, 2002, from http://chl.wes.army.mil/research/projects/ribs/JLOTSSymposium/JLOTSR&DSymposiumV/MTMCTEAModels.ppt, (February 2000).

Available online at www.sciencedirect.com
SCIENCE @ DIRECT•
ELSEVIER
Mathematical and Computer Modelling 39 (2004) 869–883
MATHEMATICAL AND COMPUTER MODELLING
www.elsevier.com/locate/mcm

The NATO Strategic Commanders' Assessment of Requirements for Strategic Sea and Airlift

J. J. DE NIJS
Operations Analysis Branch
Future Capabilities Research and Technology Division
Supreme Allied Command Transformation
7857 Blandy Rd., Suite 100, Norfolk, VA 23551-2490, U.S.A.

Abstract—With the end of the Cold War and the adoption of a new NATO strategic concept, NATO nations now emphasize the use of mobile, flexible, and multinational military forces to be deployed for a myriad of crisis response operations outside the normal NATO treaty area. One critical shortfall for a number of NATO members has been the ready availability of strategic sea and airlift assets. Most NATO nations rely on the civilian transport market to provide dry cargo vessels and wide-body cargo aircraft. The two NATO strategic commands, Supreme Headquarters Allied Powers Europe (SHAPE) and Headquarter Supreme Allied Command Atlantic (SACLANT), have been assessing the requirements for sea and airlift and have proposed to nations a variety of measures to improve their movement and transport capability. SACLANT staff has been developing the operations research methods to assist in this assessment. The current paper conveys the methodology and the mathematical programming model used in this analysis, using ship, aircraft, and port availability constraints. Furthermore, the paper presents a framework of the modeling and simulation capability of the NATO commands and agencies in the movement and transportation area. Additionally, the paper provides an example of the use of simulation models in follow-up activities such as high-level seminars in which national military force planners and movement and transport staff participate. During these events, participants are provided with the results from a number of transportation simulation models, in an attempt to steer the decision making process in NATO.

Keywords—Strategic lift, NATO, Requirement, Optimization, Force planning.

1. INTRODUCTION

With the end of the Cold War and the adoption of the new strategic concept by NATO at the London Summit in 1990, a new era for the Atlantic Alliance began. The strategic concept emphasized the use of flexible, multinational, mobile, and deployable forces to cope with the emerging threats, risks, and responsibilities that the new Europe was confronted with. The introduction of the notion of immediate and rapid reaction forces for the high readiness forces of the alliance stressed the idea that nations may have to deploy their military forces out of the NATO area of responsibility. This became clear when the NATO nations were called upon for the peacekeeping missions in the Balkans, beginning with the deployment of forces in Bosnia-Herzegovina in 1995 and in 1999 in Kosovo. Both deployments demonstrated the necessity of having ready access to strategic lift assets to transport the forces to the theater of operation. While the United States can rely on organic military lift assets and call upon the services of the

0895-7177/04/$ - see front matter Typeset by $\mathcal{AMS}$-TEX
doi:10.1016/j.mcm.2004.02.018

U.S. Transportation Command (TRANSCOM) with its subordinate commands such as the Air Mobility Command (AMC) and the Military Sealift Command (MSC), the European allies rely heavily on the commercial markets for the provision of their lift demands. While in the Cold War era, those nations could use legislation for the requisition of lift, those measures are not deemed applicable or desirable during peacetime conditions in the home countries. Therefore, lift assets needed to be sought through normal commercial means, and in times, those markets may be tight, and readily available lift with the commercial shipping brokers or the national aviation companies may not be available. Various initiatives had identified that problem, however, no solutions were at hand. In the mean time, the problem became more and more prominent. At the Washington summit in 1999, the Defense Capability Initiative (DCI) was accepted by the heads of states. The DCI is an instrument to nations to identify the high priority shortfall areas in the NATO military capability. In the area of deployability and mobility, strategic sea and airlift were seen as those areas that needed immediate improvements. The question remained, however, how much needed to be done to alleviate the shortfall, since that shortfall was never quantified.

2. ASSESSMENTS OF STRATEGIC LIFT CAPABILITY

During the 1990s the NATO strategic commands, various committees within the NATO structure, and the NATO nations have been discussing and studying the strategic lift needs of the alliance. While the emphasis before the end of the Cold War was on the timely reinforcement of the European theater by American and Canadian troops, the emphasis in the 1990s was shifted towards the capability for all NATO nations to be capable of transporting their own national forces. In order to understand the interactions that were taking place, it is necessary to understand the way in which the military commands and the nations cooperate in NATO. The highest political body within NATO is the North Atlantic Council (NAC) which may convene at the heads of state level, but mostly the secretaries of state and ministers of defense are representing their nation. The NAC gives guidance to the Military Committee (MC) where each nation is represented by their Chief of Defense, and to the Defense Planning Committee (DPC), the Political Committee (PC), the Conference of National Armaments Directors (CNAD), and the Senior Civil Emergency Planning Committee (SCEPC). Under the SCEPC, three civil transport planning boards are assisting the military in measures concerning the acquisition of transport means, transport infrastructure, transport legislation, etc. The NATO civil transport planning boards, such as the Planning Board for Ocean Shipping (PBOS), the Civil Aviation Planning Committee (CAPC), and the Planning Board for Inland Surface Transport (PBIST), have been assisting the two strategic commands in assessing the need for reinforcement and resupply. However, what had formerly been an allocation problem since nations could requisition shipping and aircraft from the commercial market in times of crisis during the Cold War era, now became a market demand and supply problem. As was demonstrated during Desert Storm, commercial freight rates and insurance rates skyrocketed. In order to manage the commercial markets, the nations thus had to approach the civilian shipping and air freight markets in a more cautious way. Thus, it was advised that nations would prioritize their request for shipping in the marketplace. During the PBOS Symposium in 1996 in Hamburg, Germany, it became apparent that shortages in the marketplace still would exist, but it was not clear which nation would be confronted with what kind of shortage in transport. Additionally, nations were not considering what to do about the shortage in shipping and cargo aircraft. It was time to quantify the NATO and national requirements for strategic lift.

3. DEFENSE PLANNING AND REQUIREMENTS ANALYSIS

Within the planning staffs in NATO, the understanding grew that to ensure that nations were including into their national defense plans any acquisition of lift assets, legal action, or civil arrangements for making lift available, proposals from NATO should provide the first initiative. Within NATO's two-yearly force planning cycle, nations are requested to improve their defense posture by proposing to include new acquisition plans, direct research, enhance or decrease readiness of the forces, etc. This process takes into account the economic and political situation in the particular country. It attempts to modify the military spending in such a way that the common goals of the NATO alliance are served. Official NATO force goals are thus developed and nations are requested to commit their forces in a yearly questionnaire called the defense planning questionnaire (DPQ). With respect to strategic lift, nations can be requested to take action and commit themselves to acquire appropriate lift assets. That process, however, asks for a quantitative input and the formulation of a NATO requirement for strategic lift. A major NATO study, called the defense requirement review (DRR), provides the rationale for requesting forces. Thus, it was decided in 1999 to formulate strategic lift requirements as part of the DRR. The DRR bases the requirements on a number of planning situations that provide geographic backdrops for developing a scenario, mission, timelines, and force employment for NATO forces. Taking into account threat, risks, and a level of ambition of NATO to be involved in peace support operations, it is possible to derive quantitative results on the number of frigates, destroyers, army divisions, and air force squadrons that need to be deployed to perform the formulated missions. Thus, it also became necessary to develop criteria for quantification of the strategic deployment of the NATO forces and the assessment of the number of lift assets. For that purpose, a model, the strategic lift requirement model (SLRM), was developed at HQ SACLANT. The model was subsequently used to calculate requirements for each of the planning situations representative for large scale deployment operations, which include peace support operations such as currently are conducted in the Balkans, and Article 5 situations based on the perceived threat estimate.

In the DRR 1999, this model was used to assess the requirement for national lift and quantify this requirement in the NATO force goals [1]. Results from the DRR 99 educated the nations on two counts: first that the strategic lift requirements numbers were reasonable, and second, that in-depth analysis on overall lift requirements had been conducted for the first time since the adoption of the new NATO strategy in 1990. Nations came to realize that signing up to the reaction forces also meant that those forces may have to be moved to a contingency area far away from the home base, and that such a movement will require the forces to be ready to be moved according to their readiness category by any strategic movement asset that will have to be made available.

The DRR 99 analysis on lift focused mainly on the strategic part of the lift. Port considerations such as number of berths, vehicle parking space, port throughput, and aircraft parking slots were used to restrict the flow of ships and aircraft. These parameters were chosen in such a way that they did not impact on the requirements if they were shown to heavily restrict transportation. They were treated as required throughput and capability measures rather than reflecting the existing infrastructure.

Lift requirements were determined based on the available cargo, i.e., units and supplies that were delivered at the port of embarkation (POE), after a notional two day road or rail movement from the home base. Equally, the required timely delivery of the cargo in the theater was used as the other constraint by which it was determined how many ships and aircraft were needed. Again, a notional two day period for the movement from the port of debarkation (POD) to the final destination was inserted. Thus, cargo time availability and delivery profiles were determined for each planning situation. Based on these constraints, the optimal number of ships and aircraft was calculated taking into account the fact that those transportation assets could make multiple trips when time allowed that.

While these computations provided a good minimum military requirement for strategic lift, it was noted that there is probably a need to understand the transportation processes in the ports and in the theater much better, especially when DRR is requested to determine requirements for port reception and onward movement. Additionally, this may have an impact on the usage of strategic lift. Thus, it was recognized that for DRR 2001, some more detailed models than the SLRM may have to be used to assess requirements and provide better rationale for input to the force proposals. The following analytical approach for the strategic lift problem within the DRR context was adopted. The DRR process in determining the force structure provided information on the number and type of force required, their readiness, the final destination of those forces, and the commander's required date (CRD). To calculate lift requirements, additional information such as force holdings, home bases, mode of transportation, infrastructure of air and seaports, lines of communications, lift assets characteristics, and supply factors had to be gathered. Information from the allied deployment and movement system (ADAMS) database on generic force holdings and consumption rates for all classes of supply were taken as the basis for the amount of cargo to be transported.

The most important assumption that has great impact on lift requirements is the assumption that the initial deployment for any planning situation is not overlapping with the initial deployment of another planning situation. This ensures that strategic lift assets used for the transport of troops and unit equipment can be reused in another deployment, thereby avoiding the requirement to double or triple. However, it was assessed that sustainment of the operations, by resupplying the troops, must be done for all planning situations considered concurrently at the same time. Because it is impossible to determine beforehand which forces will be offered up by the nations in the planning situations, it is equally impossible to determine the home base of the forces that should be used in the calculations. The assumption was made that there were three main areas from which military units would be drawn, and would embark in ships and aircraft to be moved to the area of operations. Minor differences in distance and timing would be lost in the fog of the uncertainties that accompany a general assessment. A general North-American home base on the U.S. east coast, a north-European home base around the North Sea, and a south-European home base on the French/Italian Mediterranean coast was assumed to represent the various air and seaports in the NATO nations.

The assumption was made that all rolling stock within a military unit was loaded on roll-on-roll-off (RoRo) ships. This was done to ensure unit integrity and minimum load and unload of unit equipment. Smaller items were believed to be loaded inside vehicles. Containerized equipment, equipment on pallets, supplies, and ammunition were assumed to be loaded on break bulk and container ships. The study considered RoRos with a capacity of 1000, 1500, 2500, 5000, 8000, and 14,000 lane meters, break bulk ships with a capacity of 11,000 M3, 13,500 M3, and 18,000 M3, and container shipping with a capacity of carrying 600 and 1500 20 feet equivalent (TEU) containers. It was also assumed that a limited number of berths were available in the seaport of debarkation (SPOD), as well as restrictions on parking space or storage area.

Ground forces' unit equipment, that was airlifted, is assumed to be time critical to the operation. Especially, the airborne units need to have a large portion of their equipment with them, when they are committed to the operation. Assumptions were made on the percentage of unit equipment that would be airlifted and that assumption depended on the phase of the operation. All army and airforce personnel were flown into theater by commercial type of aircraft. Aircraft types considered were the C-130, the C-17, the C-5 for cargo aircraft, and an Airbus/Boeing type of passenger aircraft capable of carrying 200 personnel. Sortie rates were dependent on the distances. At the airports of debarkation (APOD), there is a limit on the number of missions on the ground, and restrictions are placed on the amount of storage area, and the throughput capacity of the airbase. This is done to simulate workload, unit integrity, and nonconcurrent arrival on unit personnel.

The DRR 2001 report [2] emphasized the validity of the rationale for strategic lift requirements, and with the conclusions derived from NATO's DCI under the deployability and mobility chapter [3], nations are even more aware of the requirement for lift, especially for wide-body air lift assets to carry outsized cargo.

4. THE STRATEGIC LIFT REQUIREMENT MODEL (SLRM)

The model used to calculate the lift requirements is based on an integer programming formulation of the lift problem. The algorithm applied seeks to formulate the minimum military requirement, and thus, does not resolve detailed items such as port loads, differences in shipping, delays, congestion, and unavailability of lift assets. The objective of the algorithm is to minimize either the number of ship sailings and aircraft sorties, or to minimize the number of ships and aircraft allocated to the deployment. Since the allocation of the transport assets can be made for the whole deployment and the ships and aircraft return to their original port of departure because they are owned by the nation, we can calculate when a ship or aircraft becomes available again for a new voyage or sortie.

4.1. Objective Function

In order to formulate our objective function, we first introduce our main variables to be used throughout this section.

(i) Let Index j indicate Day j after the start of the decision to deploy.
(ii) Let Index i be the type of lift asset to be used.
(iii) Define $x_{i,j}$ as the number of ship sailings or aircraft sorties of Type i, required at Day j.
(iv) Let T be the total number of asset types.
(v) Let J be the total number of days in the deployment.
(vi) Finally, let r_i be the number of days a lift asset of Type i needs to make a roundtrip. x_{ij} is a nonnegative integer by definition.

Our aim is to minimize either the number of ship sailings or aircraft sorties for the whole deployment, thus ensuring that ships and aircraft are loaded efficiently, or to minimize the number of ships or aircraft allocated to the deployment, with the understanding that ships and aircraft will be used multiple times. The first case represents the policy of NATO nations to minimize variable costs. When nations are acquiring commercial ships on the market, they want to ensure that the costs of the voyage itself is minimized or that the ship is used to its maximum capacity. In that case, it is not important to use the ship in multiple voyages, as the nation will reason that another ship may come available when needed. The latter case represents the case that ships and aircraft are owned by NATO nations, or at least that there is an incentive to use a ship or aircraft efficiently during the whole deployment. It may be that the nation has invested in acquiring lift assets and wants to ensure that they are used to the maximum extent. If we translate that in economic terms, one can interpret the first case as the case where variable costs are the driving factor, and in the last case where investment or sunken costs are determining the nation's decision how to deploy most economically. We can formulate an objective function for both cases. Our model clearly should be classified as a minimization problem, and it can be even of the class of linear programming problems, even if we consider that most cost minimization problems are of a quadratic type [4]. Our model should consider the number of voyages in total, which clearly can be formulated as a summation. The variable costs model attempts to minimize

$$\min_{i,j} \sum_{i=1}^{T} \sum_{j=0}^{J} x_{i,j}. \tag{1}$$

The number of sailings or sorties is the sum of all sailings or sorties that begin at Day j for ship or aircraft Type i. It is obvious that we should not mix ships of a certain type with ships of another type, and it is even more obvious that we should not mix them with aircraft. RoRo ships of different size should be used to model the deployment of rolling cargo, such as tracked and wheeled vehicles, whereas containers and palletized cargo should be transported by containerships with different capacity. Thus RoRo Type 1 could be a small typical European RoRo with a capacity of 25,000 sq. ft., while a medium type of RoRo vessel of 50,000 sq.ft. or a larger one of 100,000 sq. ft. would be other possibilities. It is understood that U.S. lift assets such as the large medium speed RoRo (LMSR) and the fast sealift ships (FSS) are extremely more capable (350,000 sq. ft. and 200,000 sq. ft., respectively).

The sunken cost model can be formulated as

$$\min_{i,j} \sum_{i=1}^{T} \left(\sum_{j=0}^{J} x_{i,j} - \sum_{j=r_i}^{J} x_{i,j-r_i} \right). \tag{2}$$

This case attempts to minimize the number of voyages of Type i departed from the POE as of Day j while taking into account the ships or aircraft returned to the POE before or on Day j.

We can now introduce the constraints for our model. All constraints are linear, ensuring that our model can be solved by standard linear programming methods. However, since our variables represent number of sailings or sorties and this number can only be integers, our problem becomes an integer programming problem. Standard techniques for solving such a problem are available.

4.2. Readiness Profile

Equipment and personnel may not be ready to be lifted into theater immediately after Day 0, and may be ready at different times. Let

- c_i = capacity of lift asset of Type i;
- b_j = cargo in tons or square feet, number of containers or number of personnel (PAX) ready to embark at the POE on Day j;
- $c_{\min} = 0.99 \min_i\{c_i\}$.

Then the set of equations that ensures that the carrying capacity of all sailings or sorties up to Day j does not exceed the amount of equipment or personnel that is ready to embark at Day j is as follows:

$$\sum_{i=1}^{T} \sum_{k=0}^{j} c_i x_{i,k} \leq \sum_{k=0}^{j} b_k + c_{\min}, \qquad \text{for } j = 0, 1, \ldots, J. \tag{3}$$

This equation represents the fact that ships and aircraft should be loaded to the maximum extent possible and reflects also the notion that they can only carry cargo and personnel available at the port of embarkation. The first fact is modeled in the double summation on the left side of the equation, ensuring that lift assets available on Day j will load cargo and personnel ready both on Day j *and* before Day j. The second fact is modeled on the right side of the equation, where the factor $c_{\min}$ represents the fact that one of the ships and aircraft may have to leave not fully loaded to ensure that all cargo will be loaded on one of the ships or aircraft. The factor 0.99 in the definition of $c_{\min}$ ensures that that last ship or aircraft is not leaving empty. The readiness constraints are a set of $J+1$ equations with $T*(J+1)$ variables.

4.3. Delivery Profile

Cargo and personnel are required to be delivered in theater at different times. Basically, this is to ensure that the joint force commander has available to him those units that enable the initial entry into theater, support the employment of follow-up forces, and provide him the bulk of the forces at a later time. The CRD is defined for each of the units as the time to be in place in theater. The CRD determines the flow of cargo and personnel to the final destination, thus also the amount of cargo and personnel to be delivered at the POD. Let

- a_j = cargo in tons or square feet, number of containers or number of PAX required to be delivered at the POD on Day j;
- q_i = number of days it takes for a ship or aircraft of Type i to deliver cargo from the POE to the POD;
- l_i = number of days it takes to load cargo at the POE on a ship or aircraft of Type i;

- t_i = number of days it takes to travel between the POE and the POD with ship or aircraft of Type i;
- u_i = number of days it takes to unload cargo at the POD for a ship or aircraft of Type i.

Then the set of constraints for the delivery of cargo and personnel at the POD is

$$\sum_{i=1}^{T} \sum_{k=q_i}^{j} c_i x_{i,k-q_i} \geq \sum_{k=q_i}^{j} a_k, \qquad \text{for } j = q_i, q_i+1, \ldots, J, \tag{4}$$

where $q_i = l_i + t_i + u_i$. The constraints will ensure that the lift assets will take at least the amount of cargo or personnel that has be delivered to the port of debarkation on Day j. The double summation represents the fact that the total cargo of the ships and aircraft used up to Day j is at least the amount of cargo to be delivered by Day j, and the right-hand side of the equation represents the amount of cargo to be delivered at Day j. The set of constraints on the delivery of cargo adds another $J - q_i + 1$ constraints with $T * (J - q_i + 1)$ variables. The two basic sets of constraints, the readiness and the delivery profiles, represent the requirement to deliver cargo and personnel once they are ready to be transported. The feasibility of the problem is determined by these two basic sets, as they determine whether it is possible to transport the cargo with the types of lift assets and the time it takes to deliver cargo from the POE to the POD. If, e.g., q_i is larger than time between the required delivery date and the availability at the POE, then the transportation problem is not feasible.

4.4. Number of Lift Assets Available

We can extend the model further by incorporating a set of constraints representing the number of lift assets that are available for the deployment. It is possible that a certain type of ship or aircraft is unavailable in large quantities or limited on the market, thus forcing to look for alternatives. Let

- s_i = the number of available lift assets of Type i.

Then, the constraint set

$$\sum_{k=0}^{j} x_{i,k} - \sum_{k=r_i}^{j} x_{i,k-r_i} \leq s_i, \qquad \text{for } j = 0, 1, \ldots, J \quad \text{and} \quad i = 1, \ldots, T, \tag{5}$$

with $r_i = l_i + t_i + u_i + t_i$ the number of days for a roundtrip voyage, and l_i, t_i, and u_i are as defined above, models the number of available lift assets. The constraint first sums the number of lift assets that have left the POE at and before Day j and subtracts the number of assets that have returned to the POE at and before Day j (or actually left at Day $k - r_i$, and thus, are back at Day k). The variable $x_{i,k-r_i}$ is the number of sailings or sorties that have returned to the POE on Day k, which can never be before Day r_i and later than Day j to contribute.

4.5. Number of Available Shipping Berths or Missions on Ground

At the port of debarkation, the number of berths for ships or parking space for aircraft may be limited due to a number of factors, such as limited space allocated because the mission concerns a mission under peacetime conditions and commercial traffic may continue, or due to the fact that shipping or aircraft can only use a certain type of berth or parking space. The number of parking spaces on an air force base is called maximum on ground (MOG) and may be further limited by the notion working MOG, since that represents the number of aircraft that can be worked on simultaneously. Obviously, the MOG or berths available depend on the type of lift assets, but for convenience, it is assumed that that is independent of type. Let

- z = the number of available berths or MOG at the POD;
- p_i = the number of days a lift asset of Type i takes to arrive at the POD.

Then, the set of constraints

$$\sum_{i=1}^{T}\left(\sum_{k=p_i}^{j} x_{i,k-p_i} - \sum_{k=p_i+u_i}^{j} x_{i,k-p_i-u_i}\right) \leq z, \qquad \text{for } j = 0, 1, \ldots, J, \tag{6}$$

where $p_i = l_i + t_i$ and l_i, t_i, and u_i as defined above, models the number of available berths or MOG at the POD. The first summation is for all types of lift assets that share the same berth or MOG. The second summation represents the number of lift assets that arrive between Day p_i and Day j, while the third summation models the number of lift assets that leave between Day $p_i + u_i$ and Day j. Day p_i can be interpreted as the day that a ship or aircraft arrives at the POD, and Day $p_i + u_i$ as the day a ship or aircraft leaves the POD.

4.6. Availability of Staging Area at the POD

At the POD there may be limited area available for staging cargo. The space used for parking vehicles, containers, and pallets ensures a swift unloading operation of the ship or the aircraft.

From the staging area, columns of vehicles may be formed, or containers and pallets may be picked for onward movement. Military personnel thus can marry up with their vehicles and move to the final destination. It can be assumed that on average the equipment will be a number of days in the staging area before it is moved to the final destination. The staging time can vary by the type of cargo. Let

- $y =$ the amount of available parking space at the POD measured in square feet or tons of cargo;
- $v =$ the number of days that the cargo will be in the staging area.

Then the set of constraints

$$\sum_{i=1}^{T}\sum_{\hat{j}=j-v+1}^{j}\left(\sum_{k=p_i}^{\hat{j}} \frac{c_i}{u_i} x_{i,k-p_i} - \sum_{k=p_i+u_i}^{\hat{j}} \frac{c_i}{u_i} x_{i,k-p_i-u_i}\right) \leq y, \qquad \text{for } j = 0, 1, \ldots, J, \tag{7}$$

with p_i, u_i, and c_i as defined above, models the time spent the cargo amount that is unloaded on average per day, i.e., $c_i/u_i\, x_{i,k-p_i}$, spends in the staging area for v days. The inner-bracket two summations reflect the amount of cargo unloaded per day for ships and aircraft that stay in the POD for u_i days. Summation follows over the v days, and that is also taken for all types of ships or aircraft.

4.7. Example

An example may illustrate the method better. Suppose we have three types of RoRo ships, as defined in Section 3.

- RoRo small: capacity 2500 sq. ft., speed 15 knots, load and unload time of five hours each, a one-way travel (with load and unload) time of 12 days, and a roundtrip voyage time of 23 days.
- RoRo medium: capacity 3750 sq. ft., speed 16 knots, load and unload time of seven hours each, a one-way travel (with load and unload) time of 11 days, and a roundtrip voyage time of 21 days.
- RoRo large: capacity 6250 sq. ft., speed 21 knots, load and unload time of 12 hours each, a one-way travel (with load and unload) time of 10 days, and a roundtrip voyage time of 18 days.

This means that the amount of cargo space that can be left empty is $c_{\min} = 2475$. Assume that we have to deploy within 60 days, and that cargo comes available on Days 10, 20, 25, and 30 in the amounts of 5,000, 12,000, 25,000, and 75,000 sq. ft., and that the delivery of cargo at the POD is required at Days 30, 40, 50, and 60 with amount of 9,000, 15,000, 35,000, and 58,000 sq. ft. Assume we can contract at most four small RoRos, three medium RoRos, and two large RoRos. In this example, we do not explicitly formulate the constraints for number of berths and the amount of staging area available.

Let $x_{i,j}$ be the number of ships of Type i that depart from the POE at Day j. Assume we want to minimize the number of sailings:

$$\min_{j} \sum_{j=0}^{60} (x_{1,j} + x_{2,j} + x_{3,j}),$$

then the cargo readiness profile and delivery profile can be formulated as constraints in the following way:

$$\begin{aligned}
2500x_{1,k} + 3750x_{2,k} + 6250x_{3,k} &\leq 2475, && \text{for } k = 0,\ldots,9;\\
2500x_{1,k} + 3750x_{2,k} + 6250x_{3,k} &\leq 7475, && \text{for } k = 10,\ldots,19;\\
2500x_{1,k} + 3750x_{2,k} + 6250x_{3,k} &\leq 19475, && \text{for } k = 20,\ldots,25;\\
2500x_{1,k} + 3750x_{2,k} + 6250x_{3,k} &\leq 44475, && \text{for } k = 25,\ldots,29;\\
2500x_{1,k} + 3750x_{2,k} + 6250x_{3,k} &\leq 119475, && \text{for } k = 30,\ldots,59;\\
6250x_{3,k-10} &\geq 9000, && \text{for } k = 10;\\
3750x_{2,k-11} + 6250x_{3,k-10} &\geq 9000, && \text{for } k = 11;\\
2500x_{1,k-12} + 3750x_{2,k-11} + 6250x_{3,k-10} &\geq 9000, && \text{for } k = 12,\ldots,30;\\
2500x_{1,k-12} + 3750x_{2,k-11} + 6250x_{3,k-10} &\geq 24000, && \text{for } k = 31,\ldots,40;\\
2500x_{1,k-12} + 3750x_{2,k-11} + 6250x_{3,k-10} &\geq 59000, && \text{for } k = 41,\ldots,50;\\
2500x_{1,k-12} + 3750x_{2,k-11} + 6250x_{3,k-10} &\geq 117000, && \text{for } k = 51,\ldots,60.
\end{aligned}$$

The constraints for the number of ships that can be used at any one time depends on the number that departed and that have returned after their roundtrip voyage, giving each ship type an additional eight days to return to the port of origin after possible delivery on Day 60,

$$\begin{aligned}
x_{1,0} + x_{1,1} + \cdots + x_{1,23} - x_{1,0} + x_{1,24} - x_{1,1} + x_{1,25} - x_{1,2} + \cdots + x_{1,68} - x_{1,45} &\leq 4;\\
x_{2,0} + x_{2,1} + \cdots + x_{2,21} - x_{2,0} + x_{2,22} - x_{2,1} + x_{2,23} - x_{2,2} + \cdots + x_{2,68} - x_{2,47} &\leq 3;\\
x_{3,0} + x_{3,1} + \cdots + x_{3,18} - x_{3,0} + x_{3,19} - x_{3,1} + x_{3,20} - x_{3,2} + \cdots + x_{3,68} - x_{3,50} &\leq 2.
\end{aligned}$$

In a similar way, the constraints for the available berths and staging area can be formulated.

4.8. Software

The software for solving the integer programming problem was selected based on compatibility with other standard office software. What's Best! [5] is an all-purpose solver that is installed as an add-in to Microsoft Excel. It will model and solve smaller type problems with a maximum of 16,000 variables and 8,000 constraints. It is possible to model integer problems but with an added cost. In solving a problem, the software first attempts to find a feasible solution, from which What's Best! jumps from feasible point to feasible point to find the optimum solution.

The run time can be restricted by specifying time or number of tries before which either What's Best! must have found the optimum value or admits failure.

The integration of What's Best! in Excel enabled us to develop the formulation of the constraints automatically through the use of macros in Excel filling the sheet with the right number of variables and coefficients for the constraints. Automation of this process enabled us to formulate for each strategic lift pair of POE and POD in each planning situation the requirement for RoRo, breakbulk/container combination, wide-body aircraft, and passenger aircraft requirements. For each planning situation, we thus would formulate for each of the four pairs of POE and POD, four calculations. For the seven planning situations considered to be relevant for the strategic lift requirements (there are other planning situations that drive other requirements), we performed in total 112 optimization problems. Additionally, the embedding of the formulation in the spreadsheet enabled the easy postprocessing of the results in graphs and tables.

During the analysis phase, it became apparent that although the programming problem was feasible, the software was using considerable runtime to find an integer optimal solution. In a number of cases, it was evident that feasibility of the problem and not optimization was a desired result, since there were only a few points in the solution space that would provide an integer solution. Therefore, in some cases the objective function was dropped and only constraint analysis was performed.

5. RESULTS

A graphical representation of a typical requirement for moving cargo is provided in Figure 1, where the profiles of readiness of cargo and required delivery of that cargo are given over time. The solution that the model provided shows a delivery of cargo over time as the curve in between the two constraint profiles.

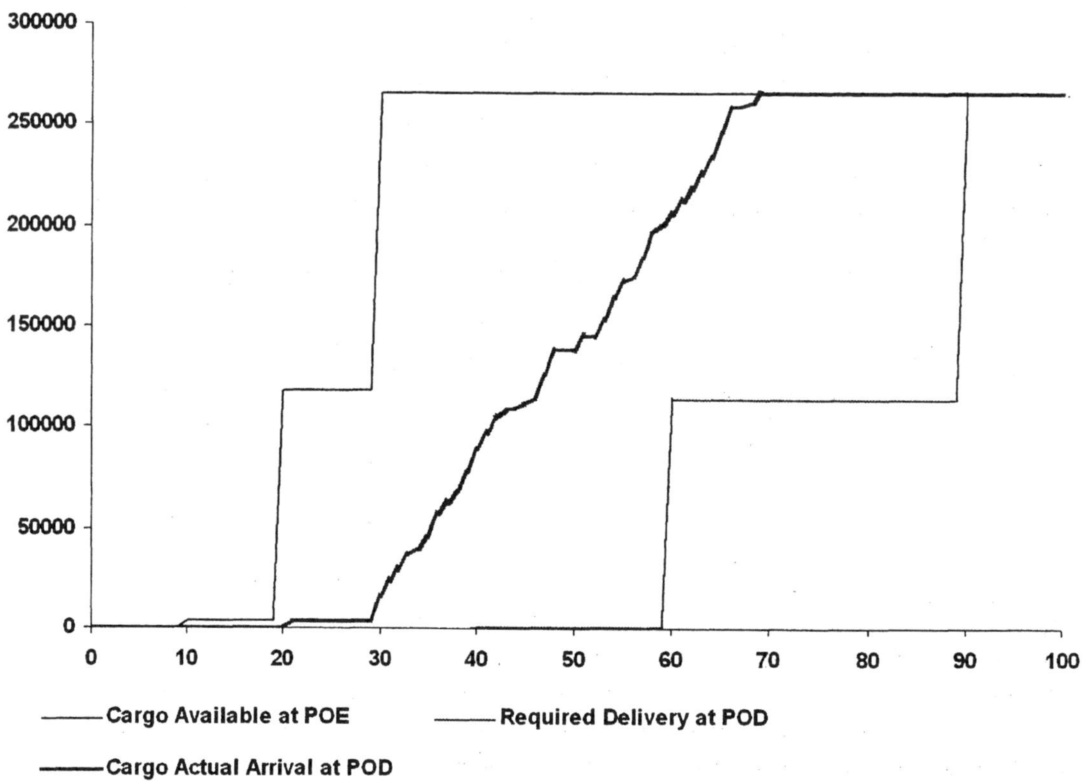

Figure 1. Readiness and delivery profiles with actual cargo delivery.

A typical result from the model is provided in Figure 2, which details the number of RoRo ships required for the initial deployment of unit equipment for a typical planning situation. The third (Figure 3) graph provides a typical run of the requirement for cargo aircraft and passenger aircraft.

The ports of debarkation in the theater of operations are likely to be congested due to the high traffic, the demand for unloading of equipment, the limited amount of staging area, and the

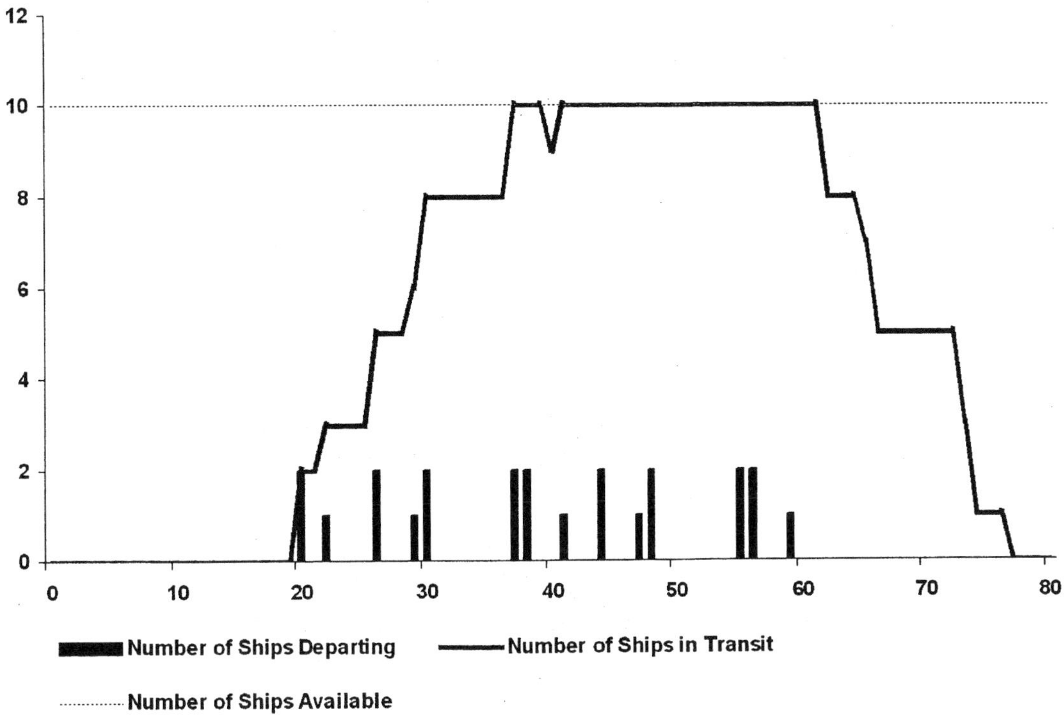

Figure 2. Number of RoRos used.

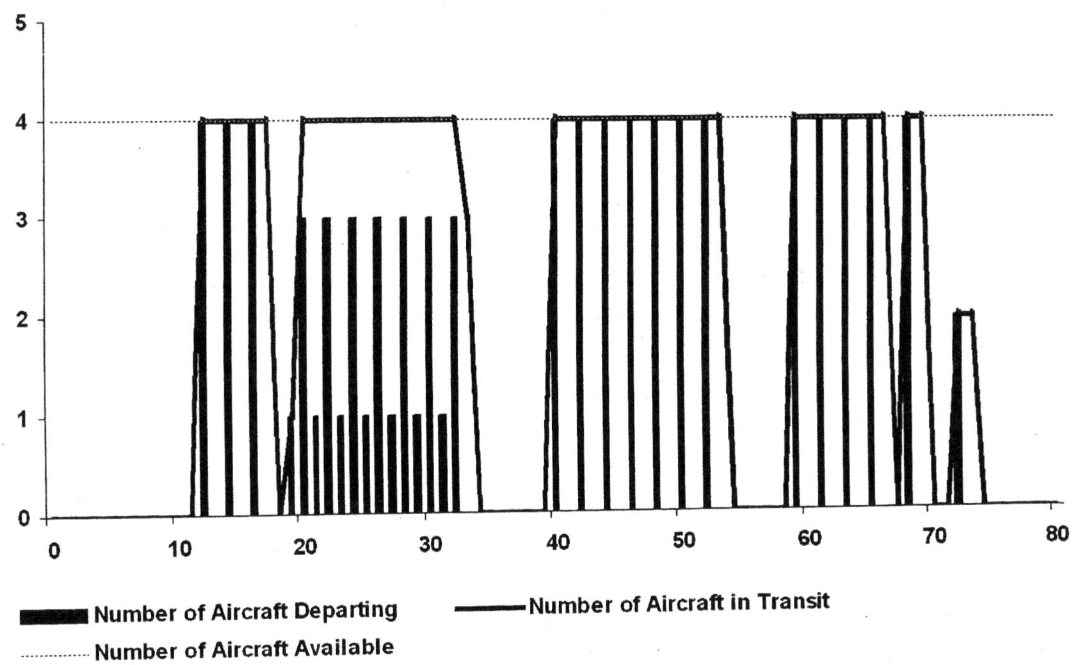

Figure 3. Number of aircraft used.

capacity of the road and rail network leading out of the port. Typically, seaports in the areas that were considered do not generally have the infrastructure to support the arrival of a surge of military unit equipment and cargo. Additionally, the mission that is conducted is typically geared toward the establishment of peace (peacekeeping or peace enforcement), and thus, the country is assumed to be in turmoil. Economic shipping for normal trade and humanitarian aid is likely to further contribute to the nonavailability of port services in the theater of operations. Thus, it is of importance to calculate the required number of berths by type (RoRo or break bulk/container) and the amount of staging area in square feet, that should be available within the theater. That required capacity may be subdivided over a number of ports (typically two to three). One of the RoRo berths has to be able to receive a LMSR/FSS type of RoRo and must, therefore, have a length of at least 350 M and a draft of 11 M. Other RoRo berths may be smaller, but typically should be about 130–160 M in length and have 8–10 M draft. For break bulk and container berths, the requirement is for cranes that can handle up to 40 metric tons of cargo, and container crane capacity should be about 35 MT. The length of those berths should be 100–150 M, and draft of 8–10 M. Figure 4 provides the results of a typical run for the required number of berths that should be available in theater.

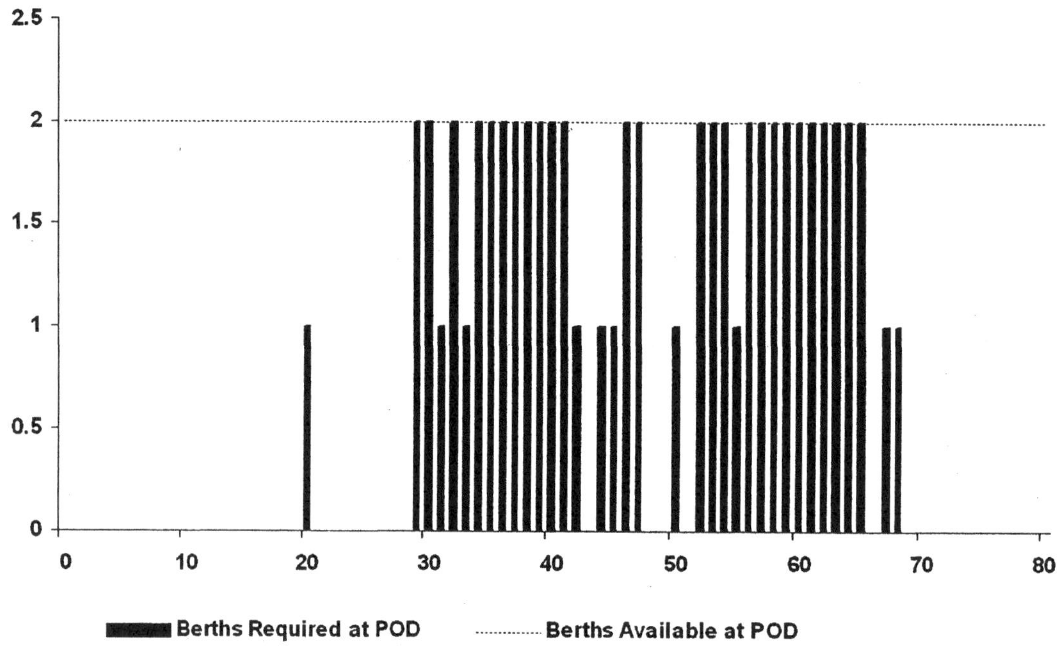

Figure 4. Number of berths used.

A similar requirement for the APOD exists. The requirement is for a so-called working MOG, which is a parking spot on the airport from which the aircraft can be unloaded. Typically, the unloading times for C-130 type of aircraft is one hour, so one MOG can sustain 24 C-130 per day for an airport that works day and night.

The results of the analysis for each planning situation provides a requirement for lift. As it is possible that requirements for different types of ships and aircraft differ from planning situation to planning situation, the maximum number of required assets is taken as the total NATO requirement, as to cover any possible planning scenario. This requirement is then fed to the NATO force planning process. The appropriate number of assets are allocated to the nations based on the contribution of forces to the operation.

While it is understood that the analysis does not describe a revolutionary method for solving the optimization problem, it must be stressed that the application of this method enabled the formulation of proposals to nations in a comprehensive manner and laid a foundation for a rationale for the requirements for strategic lift in the NATO alliance.

6. FURTHER ANALYSIS

At the conclusion and presentation of the DRR lift study results, the consensus grew to use more tools and models to ensure more robust results and higher acceptability of the results at the national level. A request was made to validate the outcome of the analysis in a hypothetical deployment of NATO forces to East Africa. It was possible to plan that deployment in more depth, and therefore, it was decided to use the NATO ADAMS system for that purpose. ADAMS is the widely accepted NATO tool for the planning of strategic deployments. This system, which has been developed by the NATO Consultation, Command and Control Agency (NC3A) in the Hague, The Netherlands, enables the planner to construct a force structure, let nations fill in the details of force commitment, provide the movement path and timings, and source the movement of units and supplies by allocating transportation assets to the plan. A full multinational detailed deployment plan (MNDDP) is in a common format for all NATO nations and NATO commands, enabling easy update and transfer of data. The ADAMS system is installed at all NATO nations and the major NATO commands. ADAMS consists of a number of modules to represent accurate geography, plan unit deployment, provide for supplies, animate movements, and keep track of transport assets. ADAMS contains a module that enables the user and planner to simulate the transportation allocation process. This module is the general deployment model (GDM) and is intended for operational analysis of deployment plans, or to provide the operational planner with a first cut of a feasible transportation plan.

It was understood that models and tools such as ADAMS have a wide acceptance level, and therefore, should be used instead or in a complementary fashion to the national deployment and movement information systems. Additionally, using a variety of tools would enhance the credibility and the accuracy of the results.

Since the U.S. has a wide experience in modeling and simulation within the movement and transportation area, contacts between HQ SACLANT staff and U.S. agencies were established to explore the opportunities of using selected U.S. tools in the analysis phase of a next DRR. And when the U.S. kindly offered to assist officially during a NATO meeting in May 1999, the SACLANT staff initiated a study to assess the feasibility of using U.S. models in concert with the ADAMS tools and the SLRM optimization model. U.S. models could provide the detailed information on, e.g., port throughput, in-theater transport, and those parameters could be fed into a higher-level model such as GDM within the ADAMS system to derive the required results. Invitations to other nations have been extended to request other models and tools nations may have available, and they wished to be used in the analytical process of determining the movement parameters. Inclusion of a variety of national models would enhance the results from any analysis and will increase the confidence and fidelity that NATO can put into the results. As a consequence, a study on how to incorporate current U.S. models with the NATO models was done with the assistance of the Military Traffic Management Command (MTMC) Traffic Engineering Agency (TEA) in Newport News and TRANSCOM J5 division at Scott Air Force Base. The U.S. models that were considered were for port simulation (PORTSIM), intratheater movement (ELIST), air movement (Air Flow Model—AFM), and strategic lift (MIDAS). Conclusions of the study [6] were that for NATO, ADAMS should be considered the primary system for planning movement, while requirements analysis could be better performed by the SLRM model. Additionally, U.S. models can enhance the analytical effort for detailed analysis as appropriate. Continued effort should be put in fostering cooperation with the U.S. agencies to improve the bridging of ADAMS related movement plans with U.S. formats and vice versa.

In the autumn of 2000, a continuation of the U.S.-NATO cooperation was visible during the Unified Spirit 2000 Mobility Seminar which focused on the further progress of the DCI in deployability and mobility and attempted to further increase the acceptance of nations of the NATO proposals for enhancing strategic lift plans in the NATO force proposals. Basing the mission and forces on the original scenario for the unified spirit exercise, the geography was changed from the eastern U.S. to the coast of East Africa. This was to ensure a challenging situation for lift, host nation support, and infrastructure. The seminar discussed four hypotheses as follows.

(1) Improvements in strategic lift that would result from the implementation of the nationally agreed NATO force goals 2000, will significantly reduce the closing time of the deployed units at the final destination.
(2) Improvements in reception, staging, and onward movement (RSOM), including transportation networks, port infrastructure, and organizational concepts, will significantly reduce closing time.
(3) The adoption of collective responsibility for movement and transportation (M&T) by alliance members will provide better utilization of scarce transport resources and reduce closing times.
(4) The application of new technology in the design of transport vehicles, ships and aircraft, transportation networks, material handling, organization, and information systems will improve M&T capability and facilitate more effective planning for future operations and exercises.

The discussion and analysis during the seminar were conducted by first examining the mobility aspects of the illustrative scenario using estimates of current movement and transport capability. This "baseline" was presented in ADAMS format and was based upon present estimates of available military useful sea and airlift and predicted RSOM capabilities for the East African coast. The deliberations were assisted by the use of modeling and analysis conducted prior to and during the event by staff from NC3A, HQ SACLANT, and U.S. TRANSCOM. The ADAMS was used to develop the baseline movement plan, and TRANSCOM assisted in the modeling effort by examining specific movement aspect such as port handling with PORTSIM, air flow with AFM, and intratheater movement with ELIST. Based upon the models, analysis results were used to show delivery and throughput statistics for the baseline and to quantify the impact of the improvement measures outlined in the hypotheses. The impact of the seminar was such that the program of work for NATO and the strategic commands were influenced by the outcome and conclusions for the last two years. Considerable understanding of the transportation problem was created with the senior national logisticians. The seminar assisted in the acceptance of the NATO requirements and paved the way for nations to be more responsible for strategic lift and think about sharing resources, and have jumpstarted the doctrinal process for RSOM measures in NATO.

7. CURRENT STATUS

In November 2002, the follow-up of the Unified Spirit 2000 Seminar was held in Istanbul, Turkey, where topics such as multinational logistics, sharing lift assets, and RSOM were main topics of discussion. In the same month, the Prague summit dealt with the Prague capability commitments (PCC). Strategic lift was high on the agenda of the national commitments, and especially wide-body cargo aircraft were a point of discussion. Furthermore, it is planned to use the concept, development, and experimentation (CDE) process to further the development of RSOM doctrine, procedures, and arrangements to create a true NATO capability in this field.

8. SUMMARY AND CONCLUSIONS

In a new era that emphasizes deployment of multinational forces beyond the traditional NATO area of responsibility, it became apparent that it was necessary to define strategic lift requirements from which proposals to NATO nations could be formulated for the acquisition of organic and commercial lift assets. A requirement that searches for the minimum of ships or aircraft for strategic lift is more acceptable to NATO nations. The requirement should be based on simple equations. Additionally, a framework of modeling and simulation in the transportation area will enable the NATO nations to understand the strategic transportation problem and accept its results.

REFERENCES

1. NATO Confidential, *The 1999 Bi-MNC Defence Requirements Review*, (June 1999).
2. NATO Confidential, *The 2001 Bi-SC Defence Requirements Review*, (July 2001).
3. NATO Unclassified, Defense capability initiative deployability and mobility decision 5, AC/305(MAG) D(2001), (May 2001).
4. D.P. Bertsekas, *Nonlinear Programming*, Athena Scientific, Belmont, MA, (1995).
5. Lindo Systems, *What's Best! User's Manual*, Chicago, IL, (1996).
6. HQ SACLANT, NATO Restricted, ACLANT mobility study, (January 2000).
7. HQ SACLANT, NATO Restricted, *Proceeding of the Unified Spirit 2000 DCI Mobility Seminar*, (April 2001).

ELSEVIER

Available online at www.sciencedirect.com
SCIENCE @ DIRECT•

Mathematical and Computer Modelling 39 (2004) 885–896

MATHEMATICAL AND COMPUTER MODELLING

www.elsevier.com/locate/mcm

A Multiagent Framework for Collaborative Airlift Planning using Commercial Air Assets

G. A. Godfrey, C. Hellings and A. Knutsen
Metron, Inc.
11911 Freedom Drive, Suite 800
Reston, VA 20190-5602, U.S.A.
<godfrey><hellings><knutsen>@metsci.com

Abstract—Future operations by the U.S. military services will require greater collaboration within the government and with the private sector. Commercial enterprises that normally compete with one another will have to cooperate to satisfy the goals of the operation. For example, the military uses commercial airlift assets to support the movement of soldiers and cargo to the theater. Ideally, the military would like to receive adequate commercial airlift capacity at a reasonable cost, while the commercial air carriers would like to balance their workload and minimize the disruption to their daily operations. We present a distributed optimization approach that uses software agents—representing the interests of the military and commercial carriers—to collaboratively plan the airlift. By auctioning the missions and allowing carriers to swap missions when mutually beneficial, this approach cuts the controllable operating costs and schedule disruption costs by more than half compared with a centralized planning approach currently used.

Keywords—Strategic airlift, Commercial aviation, Multiagent systems, Game theory, Auctions.

1. BACKGROUND

Future operations by the U.S. military services will require intense collaboration within each service, across the services, with other departments and agencies (e.g., the State Department and the CIA), and with its allies. Successful collaboration will also need to occur between the government and the private sector. Within the private sector, enterprises that normally compete with one another will have to cooperate to satisfy the goals of the operation. In fact, it will often be the case that, while the parties agree on the basic goals of the operation, each party may have its own subagenda and operating constraints. Furthermore, all of the collaborating parties may not fully trust each other, and some may be in competition, economic or otherwise.

Consequently, these dynamic resource allocation problems cannot be formulated as a traditional, centralized optimization problem because the players involved have a greater degree of autonomy and potentially conflicting goals. Instead, we consider a distributed optimization approach to what are semiautonomous agents negotiating the division of tasks and resources. The disadvantage of this agent approach, however, is that there is no guarantee that solutions based

This research has been supported by the contract F30602-00-C-0175 from the Defense Advanced Research Projects Agency (Taskable Agent Software Kit program). The authors would also like to thank Mr. S.D. Draper for his assistance in developing the military demand data sets used in this paper and Dr. T. Mifflin for introducing the concept and potential benefits of collaborative airlift planning to the authors.

0895-7177/04/$ - see front matter Typeset by $\mathcal{A}_{\mathcal{M}}\mathcal{S}$-TEX
doi:10.1016/j.mcm.2004.02.019

on agents pursuing local goals have desirable system-level characteristics, such as efficiency (no wasted utility) or stability (no incentive to cheat). The research problem is to develop appropriate protocols (rules) of agent interactions that induce agents to behave in a manner that satisfies the system goals.

In this paper, we apply negotiation protocols to the distributed optimization problem of commercial air carriers supporting military airlifts, a problem area that:

(1) is extremely relevant, timely, and has huge potential military payoff, and
(2) has a rich environment for testing multiagent systems.

The operational goal is to make next-generation airlift procurement agreements more flexible and mutually beneficial without relying on centralized mechanisms that ensure convergence but reduce efficiency. We begin with a brief review of the negotiating protocol literature and then follow with a description of the commercial airlift problem. In Section 2, we describe the protocols and distributed optimization applied to the collaborative airlift planning problem and in Section 3, we present experimental results for a sample airlift scenario.

1.1. Negotiation Protocols for Multiagent Systems

In the vast literature of multiagent system research (see recent reviews in [1–3]), we are interested in designing mechanisms for modifying the rules of agent interaction to achieve desirable system results. Rosenschein and Zlotkin call this "*social engineering for machines*" [4]. They describe these negotiating protocols, the public rules by which agents can come to agreements, to include the kinds of deals that can be made, the sequence of offers and counteroffers that are allowed, and the threats, promises, and concessions that can be made. A proper set of negotiating protocols, along with the requisite incentives and punishment mechanisms, can encourage individual designers to build a self-interested agent whose behavior also has desirable system attributes. This behavior is not forced or altruistic; rather it is that the strategies that evolve or that the agent chooses—those that maximize self-interest under a given set of negotiating protocols—also promote desirable system behavior.

Binmore and Vulkan [5] apply game theory to autonomous agent negotiation as part of the advanced decision environment for process tasks (ADEPT) project, which uses negotiating agents to provide quotes to design custom British Telecom networks for customers. Faratin *et al.* [6] construct a mathematical model of contract scoring functions, and define a negotiating thread to represent the sequence of offers and counteroffers between two negotiating agents. Matos *et al.* [7] use an evolutionary genetic algorithm to determine successful negotiating strategies.

Rosenschein and Zlotkin describe attributes that would be important to system designers: efficiency, stability, simplicity, distribution, and symmetry. However, negotiating protocols do not need to include all of these attributes. In particular, the notion of stability may change meaning as agent strategies evolve to maximize self-interest. In that case, stability may be linked more closely to efficiency, in that strategies that evolve and increase system efficiency will dominate those that decrease system efficiency.

One of the most important considerations in the multiagent system that we investigate is that agents are direct competitors, so agents must be able to keep specific information private during public negotiations. Agent cooperation cannot be expected unless its vulnerability to its competition is minimized.

1.2. Civil Reserve Air Fleet (CRAF)

Department of Defense (DoD) plans call for commercial air carriers to airlift 93% of all soldiers and 41% of all airlifted cargo during crises. This airlift capacity would cost the military $50B to procure and about $3B per year to operate and maintain as part of its organic fleet [8]. To support these airlifts, the military created the Civil Reserve Air Fleet (CRAF) program. CRAF is a voluntary program in which commercial air carriers contractually agree to provide a fixed set of aircraft and crews to the military in times of crisis in return for the opportunity to bid on peacetime business. Essentially, CRAF is an insurance policy for the military in which the peacetime premiums paid to the carriers guarantee the availability of airlift capacity during crises.

Although this peacetime business is attractive to many carriers, activation of the CRAF fleet (such as during the 1990–91 Gulf War) can be extremely disruptive to the air carriers' domestic schedules, especially during peak holiday seasons. Some effects are short term, such as having fewer aircraft available to satisfy the carrier's domestic schedule, and some are long term, such as losing market share to a competitor who is not a CRAF participant. In fact, some airlines have concluded that the potential peacetime business is not worth the risk of CRAF activation and have dropped out. Consequently, the premiums paid for this airlift capacity have increased significantly over the past 15 years.

One reason why CRAF activation is so disruptive to the carriers is the "mission-by-mission" basis by which it is assigned tasking. The air component of large military airlifts goes through the Air Mobility Command (AMC) based at Scott Air Force Base. In the planning stage, AMC identifies individual missions that are then assigned to an organic asset (e.g., a C17) or contracted out to the commercial sector (e.g., a United Airlines 747). These assignments are made according to CRAF obligation (or volunteered assets) without accounting for carrier preferences (such as proximity to a hub or available aircraft). Using the carriers in this manner fails to take advantage of their primary strengths—their command and control systems and air operations personnel. Carriers have the tools and personnel to schedule and execute large, dynamic air operations, but they lack the autonomy and flexibility to manage their share of the airlift more efficiently.

In the next section, we describe an alternative concept for airlift procurement, called the Virtual Transportation Company (VTC), that allows each carrier some autonomy in deciding which missions will constitute its share of the airlift obligation. Furthermore, allowing each carrier to plan its missions in collaboration with the other carriers (as part of a multiagent system) means that the entire commercial sector acts as a single VTC for purposes of the airlift.

2. MULTIAGENT VIRTUAL TRANSPORTATION COMPANY

We propose an airlift procurement approach that uses software agents representing the commercial and military parties to collaboratively plan the airlift. Rather than have the military assign the missions arbitrarily according to obligation, the missions are auctioned to the highest bidder subject to a reserve price. Carriers can also exchange missions with one another when there is mutual benefit.

This collaborative approach provides more flexible planning, more reliable missions, and uses commercial "best practices" without integrating those practices into military planning systems or having to share those practices with the other carriers. This multiagent approach satisfies the following properties:

- allows a commercial carrier to assert its private, competitive interests through negotiation agents rather than having to make those interests explicit and public (as would be the case for classical, centralized optimization approaches);
- provides incentives to carriers to volunteer assets early in the planning process;
- enables the military agents to enforce airlift constraints such as delivery time windows and airfield congestion when evaluating offers from carrier agents;
- enforces fairness in that no carrier can be forced to provide more than its airlift obligation, but carriers who want additional business may request it; and
- guarantees that each mission is assigned to one of the carriers.

The remainder of this section describes the process by which a carrier optimizes its missions, the auction framework for allocating missions, and the process by which carriers swap missions.

2.1. Mission Planning by Individual Carriers

Describing how carriers optimize the missions for which they are responsible requires details regarding the characteristics of airlift missions and the economic models used to represent carriers. In this paper, we summarize these features and refer interested readers to the more detailed description in [9].

Airlift demand

We represent the military contingency demand with a stripped-down version of a time-phased force deployment database (TPFDD). This modified TPFDD is a set M of individual movement requirements. Associated with movement $m \in M$, we define

- PAY_m = the payload vector (passengers, bulk cargo) for the movement;
- POE_m = the origin or point of embarkation (POE) of the movement;
- POD_m = the destination or point of debarkation (POD) of the movement;
- TT_m = the expected travel time between the POE and POD of the movement;
- EAD_m = the earliest arrival date (EAD) of the movement at the POD; and
- LAD_m = the latest arrival date (LAD) of the movement at the POD.

The payload consists of either the number of personnel or amount of bulk cargo (expressed in short tons). Due to commercial aircraft configuration (such as door size and floor strength), we assume that commercial carriers cannot move oversized and outsized cargo. We also assume that each movement will be ready to load at the POE at a date consistent with the EAD and LAD (typically, the EAD and LAD are about three days apart). To simplify matters, we assume that movement requirements have been aggregated or broken into either passenger or cargo missions, roughly the size of a wide-body commercial aircraft for each payload type when possible.

Carrier economic model

We assume that the cost for a carrier to assign an aircraft to satisfy a mission depends on two factors:

(1) the location of the aircraft when it is pulled from service, and
(2) the time interval during which the aircraft is unavailable for normal commercial flights.

For simplicity, we assume that each carrier has a set of hubs with available aircraft and that the aircraft must be returned to its original hub upon completing the mission.

As shown in Figure 1, there are two components to the mission cost for the carrier:

(1) the operating cost, which is the cost to operate the aircraft for that mission (carrier hub to POE to POD and back to hub), and
(2) the opportunity cost, which is the potential profit lost by not having the aircraft available for commercial demand.

The opportunity cost requires more explanation. Assume that each carrier's fleet is spread out over a relatively small number of hub locations. Each day, assets leave the hub at a given time, are unavailable for a certain amount of time, and then return to the hub. This out-and-back shuttle may repeat several times during a day. Figure 2 illustrates the fleet inventory on the ground at a particular hub for a set of arrivals and departures over the course of a day. The inventory decreases by one for each departure and increases by one for each arrival.

In order to model the impact of adding a military mission, we add a new departure when the asset leaves the hub and a new arrival when the asset returns to the hub. As long as the inventory never dips below zero, the asset can be "borrowed" with no impact on the remainder of the schedule (assuming no delays or maintenance problems). However, if the inventory dips below

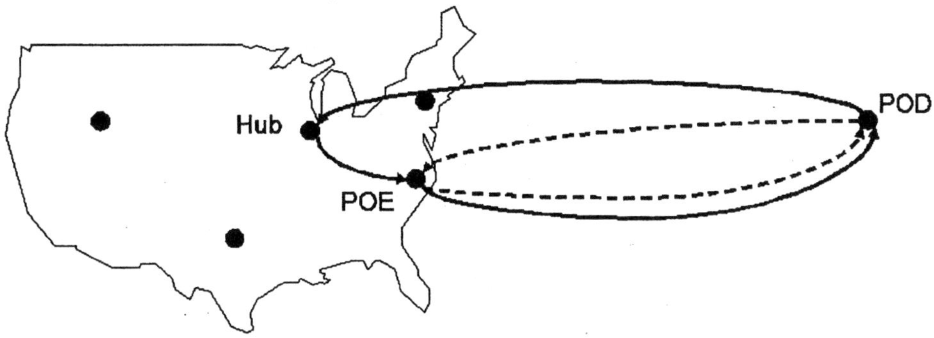

- **Revenue** (broken line) is paid by the military per passenger-mile or short ton-mile based on the round-trip distance between the POE and POD
- **Operating Cost** is proportional to the total distance traveled by the aircraft (Hub to POE to POD back to Hub)
- **Opportunity Cost** is the potential profit lost by satisfying military missions rather than commercial customers (cost of delays, etc.)
- **Profit = Revenue - Operating Cost - Opportunity Cost**

Figure 1. Components of mission profit for carrier.

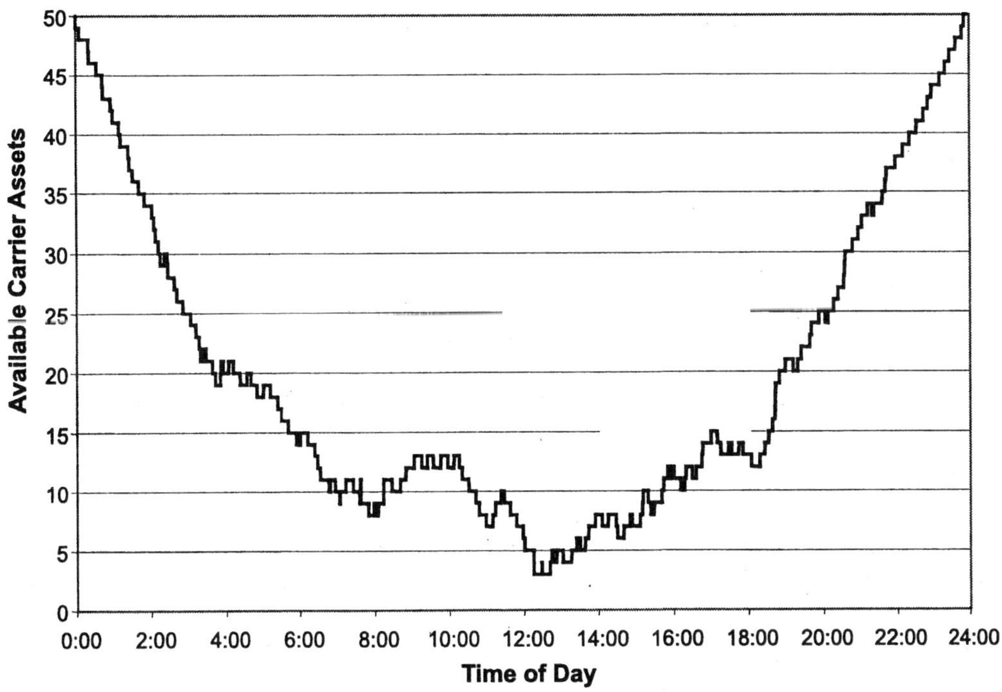

Figure 2. Typical carrier inventory at a single hub by time.

zero, then a departure is scheduled at a time when no assets are available. Consequently, that departure will have to be delayed until a new asset arrives. As additional assets are dedicated to military missions, the delay imposed on the commercially scheduled flights escalates. To model the financial impact, the carrier converts the delay into a cost that is proportional to the delay.

When a carrier is assigned a mission, it attempts to minimize the sum of the mission operating and opportunity costs through two choices:

(1) which hub to use, and
(2) what time the aircraft will depart the hub and return, subject to the mission EAD and LAD constraints.

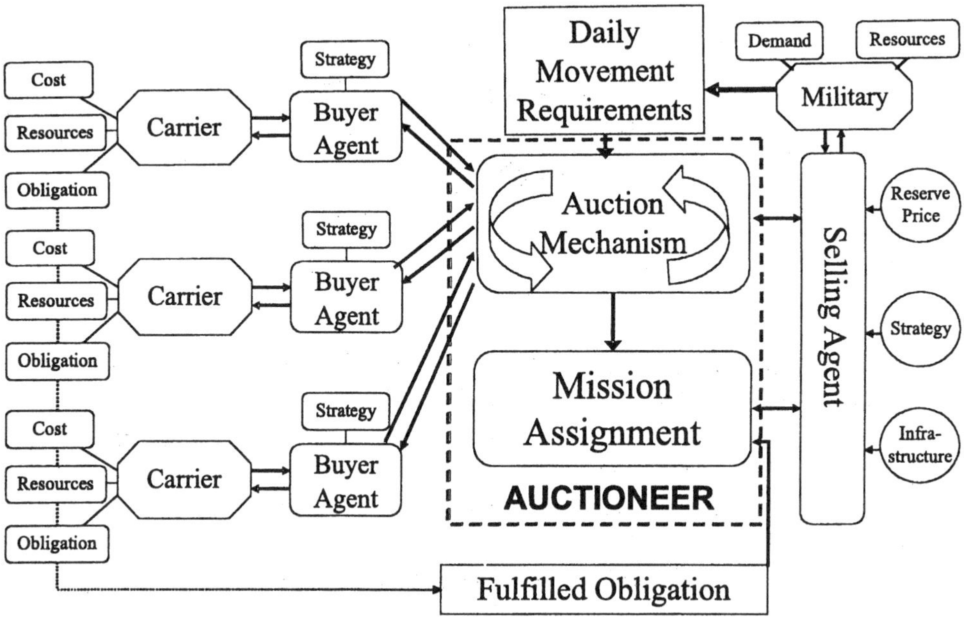

Figure 3. Description of airlift auction simulation.

2.2. Auction Framework for Mission Allocation

Figure 3 illustrates the different entities and the interactions between the entities in the airlift auction simulation. The simulation was written in Java and implemented to be multithreaded. Each buyer agent (representing one of the commercial carriers) and the seller agent (representing the military) acts on its own processing thread. Frequently, we refer to the buyer and seller agents as carrier agents and military agents, respectively. The agents communicate with each other and with the auction and assignment modules via a messaging protocol.

Given a set of airlift missions to be performed, the auction module puts each mission up for bid sequentially by sending a message to each carrier agent specifying the details of the mission. To reduce profiteering, the military agent sends to the auction module a reserve price for the mission (that is not made public) to limit how much the military will pay. In the experiments, the reserve price for a mission is set to be a multiple of the price that the military would pay if the mission was assigned (a fixed per-mile rate times the round-trip distance from POE to POD). If the reserve price is equal to the assignment price, then the military is guaranteed not to pay more for the airlift under the auction approach than it would under the assignment approach.

Each carrier agent represents a single carrier and has access to that carrier's fleet information, operating and opportunity cost functions, and CRAF obligation that specifies what fraction of the airlift the carrier is obligated to provide. As an incentive to volunteer assets early in the planning process, once a carrier has fulfilled its fraction of the airlift voluntarily, it has no residual military obligation. Under this protocol, a carrier benefits from negotiating its airlift assignments early in the planning process. The alternative is waiting until the attractive movements have been satisfied by other carriers and having to fulfill its obligation with the remaining missions.

For a given mission, each carrier agent computes an appropriate bid based on its private bidding strategy module. A bid consists of a price to perform the mission and the time at which the mission will be completed. In the experiments, the bid is based solely on the cost to the carrier of satisfying that mission. However, a carrier could make its bidding strategy more sophisticated by taking into account CRAF obligation or estimates of other agents' bids.

The auction mechanism module uses a Vickrey auction format with simultaneous sealed bids and a reserve price specified by the military agent. Under the Vickrey format, the lowest bidder wins, but receives the second-lowest bid amount. Although the military pays more than the lowest bid, the military benefits because the Vickrey format has desirable theoretical properties that encourage accurate bids [10]. The winning carrier receives more than its bid, and each bidder benefits by not wasting effort trying to outguess its opponents.

The following condition ensures fairness and encourages realistic bidding: *if all bids exceed the reserve price, then assign the mission to the carrier who has satisfied the smallest percentage of its CRAF obligation.* In other words, the reserve price caps what the military is willing to pay for a mission. If no carrier is willing to accept that price, then the mission goes to the carrier who has satisfied proportionately the least. This encourages carriers to bid aggressively, even taking small losses on some missions to protect against large losses on missions that no carrier wants.

Ultimately, the military has final control over the airlift assignments. For example, the military agent may reject a bid due to excess congestion at the POD airfield on the day that the bidder proposed. This increases the cost to the military, but the military has that discretion.

2.3. Mission Swapping among Carriers

Carriers will occasionally "regret" winning a mission when a more suitable mission appears later in the auction. To remedy this, we allow carrier agents to swap missions with one another, as long as both carriers benefit from the swap. Figure 4 describes an algorithm for performing one-to-one (pairwise) swaps between carriers. A similar approach is used for one-way swaps in which both carriers benefit by one carrier giving the other a mission without receiving one in return.

---

1. All carriers generate a list of potential swaps of missions it owns with missions it does not own, sorted by the profitability of each swap.
2. The system selects a carrier to propose a set of swap requests using a random permutation.
3. The selected carrier proposes its most profitable swap to the carrier who owns the other mission. The other carrier responds in one of two ways depending on swap profitability.
   a. The other carrier rejects the swap if it does not satisfy the carrier's minimum profitability threshold. The first carrier then returns to Step 3 using the next-highest profitable swap. If no other profitable swaps exist, then return to Step 2.
   b. The other carrier accepts the swap, and both carriers exchange missions and update schedules. Since the selected carrier has had a swap accepted, return to Step 2 to select the next carrier to propose a swap.

- The one-for-one swapping procedure ends when all carriers have proposed all profitable swaps and no swaps are accepted.

Figure 4. One-for-one mission swapping algorithm from the perspective of one carrier.

3. EXPERIMENTS

Data set characteristics

Table 1 lists several key characteristics of the data sets used in the following experiments, broken down into bulk cargo and passenger components. The modified TPFDD is based on a Desert Shield/Desert Storm-type scenario generated by the United States Transportation Command for the Defense Advanced Research Projects Agency (DARPA) Advanced Logistics Program. Additional guidance regarding rough parameters for airlift planning (such as turnaround times for refueling, unloading, etc.) was provided by the Air Force *Air Mobility Planning Factors* pamphlet [11].

The base revenue rate specifies how much the military would pay for a mission under an assignment solution. In these experiments, the auction reserve price is set to a multiple of the base revenue rate. In practice, the military likely would choose the reserve price during the planning of the airlift. In Section 3.2, we show that large reserve prices have little effect on the total revenue paid by the military when carriers are bidding truthfully.

Table 1. Airlift parameters for experiments.

	Bulk Cargo Missions	Passenger Missions
Total Commercial Payload	182,944	436,676
Number of Days for Airlift	90	90
Number of Carriers	14	11
Total Fleet Size	1143	1852
Number of Carrier Hubs	24	21
Aircraft Payload Capacity	70	262
Number of Missions	2753	1857
Base Revenue Rate	$0.2725/short-ton-mile	$0.0672/pax-mile
Operating Cost Rate	$15.29/mile	$13.07/mile
Opportunity Cost of Delay	$75/minute of delay	$75/minute of delay

To simplify the planning process, all carriers use the same type of generic wide-body aircraft for each payload type, and TPFDD movement requirements were preaggregated into missions compatible with the wide-body payload capacity when possible. The carriers, fleet sizes, and CRAF obligations are based on those of the 1999 CRAF carriers. The set of hubs used by each carrier, as well as the opportunity cost functions, were constructed by hand by the authors.

If this concept of operations was adopted to plan actual airlifts, then the fleet characteristics and economic factors would be specific to each carrier and kept private from the other entities, including the military. The list of airlift missions and duration of the airlift would be maintained by the military and shared with the carriers only at the time of the auction. The software agents would be distributed across a private communications network across which messages regarding mission information, carrier bids, and auction results would be exchanged. The goal is to preserve the greatest amount of autonomy for each agent, while ensuring that the mission allocation process is fair to all players and guarantees a feasible, reasonably priced solution for the military.

3.1. Cost Comparison of Auction versus Assignment

In the first set of experiments, we compare the assignment results with those of the reserve price auction and the auction plus swapping. For the assignment run, each mission is assigned in sequence to a single carrier accordingly to CRAF obligation. This assignment is equivalent to a reserve price auction with a reserve price of zero. The carrier then chooses the hub and departure time that minimizes the cost to satisfy the mission. The reserve price auction run uses a reserve price equal to 0.9 times the base revenue rate (other multiples are considered in Section 3.2). Missions that do not satisfy the reserve price are assigned to the carrier who has satisfied the smallest percentage of its CRAF obligation. After the auction ends, carriers may perform one-way or two-way mission swaps when mutually beneficial.

Even an optimal solution (in which every aircraft starts at and returns to the POE, rather than the carrier hub) has a large operating cost, so we want to measure the amount of excess operating cost above this optimal bound because that is what the carrier can control. We define the *controllable operating cost* to be the difference between the operating cost for a given run and the optimal operating cost.

Figure 5 breaks down the results of the three runs (assignment, auction, and auction plus swapping) by passenger and bulk cargo missions. In each case, the auction reduces both the operating and opportunity costs by at least 30%. Furthermore, allowing the carriers to swap

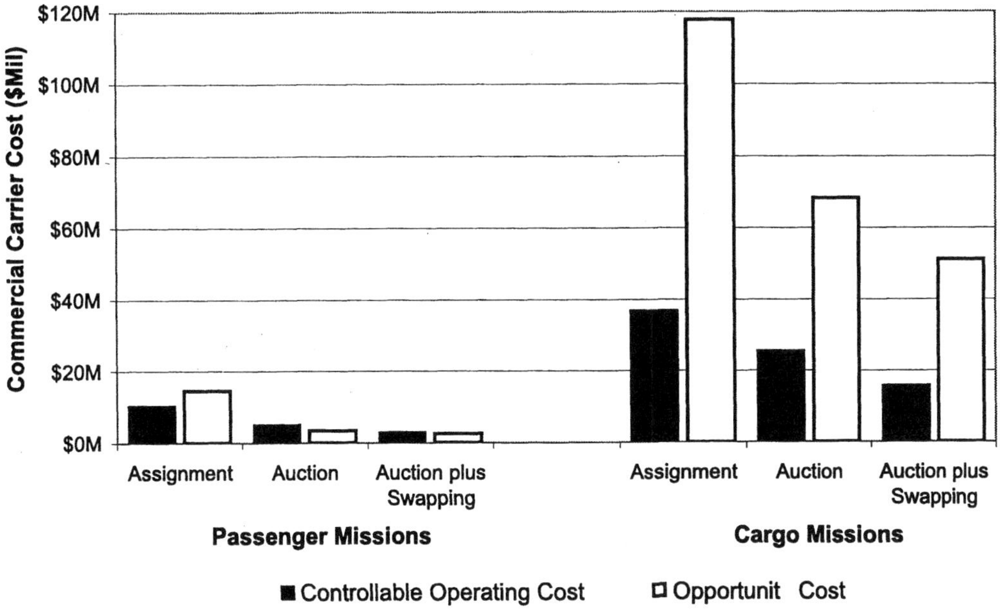

Figure 5. Carrier cost breakdown by technique.

missions drops the costs by another 30%, leading to a total cost reduction of over 50% compared with the assignment solution for both cost categories and both payload types.

3.2. Effects of Reserve Prices on Cost and Revenue

The sole focus of the remaining experiments is on cargo missions because that is the harder problem of the two in this airlift scenario. This experiment measures the effect of the reserve prices on the airlift solution using two pairs of runs. The first pair contains the assignment and the assignment plus swapping results for a series of five multipliers to the base revenue rate (0.6, 0.7, 0.8, 0.9, and 1.0). The second pair contains the reserve auction and the reserve auction plus swapping results for seven different reserve price multipliers to the base revenue rate (0.6, 0.7, 0.8, 0.9, 1.0, 1.2, and 1.5).

Figure 6 illustrates the four data series corresponding to the two pairs of runs. Starting with the assignment results, the revenue multiplier does not affect the cost of the assignment-only solution because the carriers try to minimize the cost of the same assigned missions. Swapping the assigned missions decreases the carriers' airlift cost, but does not affect the revenue (which is fixed). Notice that the swaps become more attractive and effective as the revenue multiplier increases because the potential profit for carriers who have available capacity also increases.

The auction solutions show a different pattern. Up to a reserve multiplier of 0.8, almost no bids satisfy the reserve price, so the auction solution is essentially the same as the assigned solution. As the reserve multiplier increases, so does the number of carriers who can satisfy the missions efficiently; consequently, the airlift cost drops. However, the rate of cost improvement slows as the multiplier increases because once one carrier bids less than the reserve price, increasing the reserve price will not lower the cost any further. Similarly, the revenue increases slowly as the reserve multiplier increases because of the Vickrey mechanism (the military only has to pay the lesser of the reserve price and the second-lowest bid).

The Vickrey mechanism also caps the profit that a carrier receives for a particular mission. If all carriers have roughly the same cost structure with primary differences of hub locations and opportunity costs, then the bids will tend to cluster over a relatively small range. Consequently, the small gap between the lowest bid (the lowest cost to perform the mission) and the second-lowest bid (the revenue that the military will pay) means a small profit for the winning carrier.

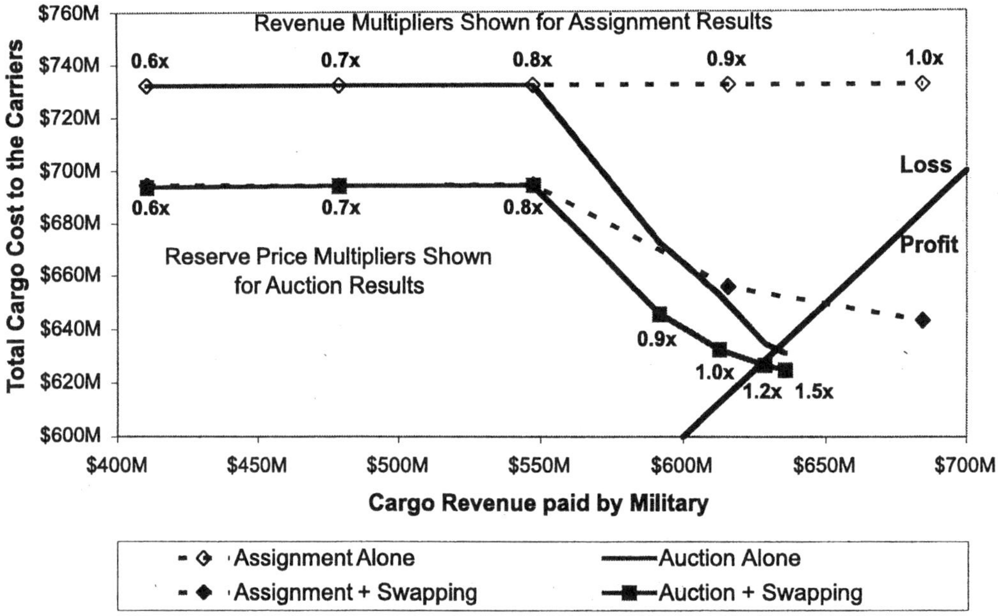

Figure 6. Cost versus revenue for different reserve prices.

However, when bids do not satisfy the reserve price, then there can be a large gap between the reserve price the military will pay and the cost to the carrier who is assigned the mission.

Unlike the assignment results, postauction swapping becomes less effective as the reserve multiplier increases. The reason is that a carrier who wins an auction with the lowest bid tends to be the carrier best-suited to perform the mission, so there is no incentive to swap.

One obvious question is what reserve price should the military choose in a given instance. The answer is that the reserve price should be set low enough to induce active, accurate bidding from the carriers, but no lower. If the reserve price is set too low, then a higher proportion of missions will be assigned. This leads to unprofitable missions and discourages carriers from CRAF participation in the future. On the other hand, if carriers are bidding reasonably, then the reserve price can be set high because the Vickrey format limits the price that the military pays.

The potential for abuse occurs when carriers exploit a reserve price that is set too high by collectively agreeing to bid artificially high. If all carriers agree to inflate their bids by 20% above actual cost, then the same carriers will win as before, but the revenue received will be 20% higher. However, there is an incentive for one carrier to violate this collusion by bidding accurately. If it wins the auction, then the Vickrey format pays the carrier based on the second-lowest bid (which is inflated). As happens in prisoner's dilemma problems, this high bidding exploit fails if more than one carrier violates this agreement. To discourage "gaming the system," we recommend not sharing the reserve price with the carriers.

3.3. Computational Effort and Unfair Swapping

Figure 6 raises two other interesting points. The first is that swapping the assigned missions produces a relatively low-cost solution without the overhead and infrastructure of an auction. The second is that the results assume swapping when there is mutual benefit. What would be the impact of considering an unfair swapping approach in which swaps are accepted as long as there is a net benefit (one carrier could be slightly worse off, but the other carrier much better off)? Although impractical, this result would provide a useful bound on the fair swapping solution.

To address the first point, swapping does alleviate much of the burden associated with the assignment, but there are two primary disadvantages. The first is that the amount of improvement is sensitive to the revenue rate that the military chooses. Ideally, the military would like to pay only enough to allow the carriers to break even or make a small profit. However, under the assignment, the revenue paid increases linearly with the revenue rate, while the cost decreases due to swapping. Conversely, the auction results are not as sensitive to the reserve price, especially for high values, because the Vickrey mechanism acts as a natural cap on profits.

The other disadvantage of swapping assigned missions is the greater computational effort (number of swaps) required to reach the final solution, compared with the auction approach. There are three reasons why this effort is required:

(1) there is a large list of potential swaps that would be attractive to a particular carrier;
(2) most proposed swaps are rejected as unprofitable by the other carrier; and
(3) after a number of swaps are accepted and executed, the profitability of the remaining list of potential swaps must be re-evaluated.

The left-hand side of Figure 7 (up to where the data series are marked "start unfair swapping") shows the consequences of this computational effort. Using a reserve multiplier of 0.88 (and a revenue multiplier such that the assigned revenue would be the same as the auction revenue), we plot the total airlift cost as a function of cumulative CPU time.

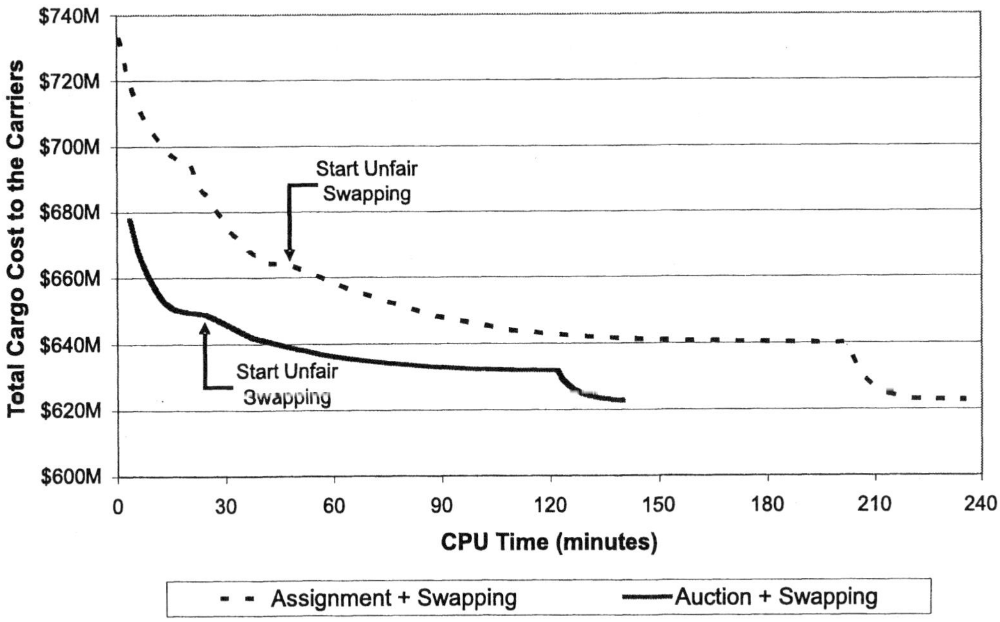

Figure 7. Effect of unfair swapping on auction and assignment solutions.

Although the initial assignment is nearly instantaneous, another 30 minutes of swapping is required to lower the cost to be equal to what the auction reaches in less than four CPU minutes. In fact, the assigned swap solution converges after about 45 minutes at a cost comparable to the auction plus swap after seven minutes. Note that the computational burden is distributed across fourteen carriers, so a total CPU time of 15 minutes corresponds to about one minute of real time.

To address the latter issue of the unfair swapping bound, we start with the fair swapping solutions and perform unfair swapping in which there only needs to be a net benefit to the system in order to accept a swap. The reason that this is unfair is that each mission tends to end up with the carrier who can satisfy the mission at minimal cost, regardless of profit or obligation.

Figure 7 shows that both solutions converge to roughly the same cost through unfair swapping. The drop at 120 minutes for the auction solution and 200 minutes for the assigned solution is due to a switch between considering two-way swaps and one-way swaps. Although roughly the same solution is reached in the limit, the assigned solution requires nearly double the CPU time (and double the number of swaps) to converge to the auction solution.

4. CONCLUSIONS

In this paper, we presented a distributed optimization approach that uses software agents—representing the interests of the military and commercial carriers—to collaboratively plan an airlift using commercial aircraft. By auctioning the missions subject to a reserve price and allowing carriers to swap missions when mutually beneficial, this approach cut the controllable operating costs and schedule disruption costs by more than half compared with a centralized assignment approach. Furthermore, this new approach to airlift procurement protects the military by capping mission profit potential using a Vickrey auction mechanism, and protects the carriers from being forced to share information or cooperate with its economic competitors. In the future, we would like to investigate more sophisticated bidding strategies for the carriers and expand the auction to allow concurrent auctions and bids on bundles of more than one mission.

REFERENCES

1. N.R. Jennings, K. Sycara and M. Wooldridge, A roadmap of agent research and development, *Int. Journal of Auto. Agents and Multi-Agent Systems* **1** (1), 7–38, (1998).
2. N.R. Jennings and M. Wooldridge, Agent-oriented software engineering, In *Handbook of Agent Technology*, (Edited by J. Bradshaw), AAAI/MIT Press, (2000).
3. H.S. Nwana, Software agents: An overview, *Knowledge Engineering Review* **11** (3), 205–244, (October/November 1996).
4. J.S. Rosenschein and G. Zlotkin, *Rules of Encounter: Designing Conventions for Automated Negotiation among Computers*, MIT Press, Cambridge, MA, (1994).
5. K. Binmore and N. Vulkan, Applying game theory to automated negotiation, In *DIMACS Workshop on Economics, Game Theory and the Internet*, Rutgers University, (April 1997).
6. P. Faratin, C. Sierra and N.R. Jennings, Negotiation decision functions for autonomous agents, *International Journal of Robotics and Autonomous Systems* **24** (3–4), 159–182, (1998).
7. N. Matos, C. Sierra and N.R. Jennings, Determining successful negotiation strategies: An evolutionary approach, In *Proc. of 3rd International Conference on Multi-Agent Systems (ICMAS-98)*, Paris, France, 1998, pp. 182–189.
8. C.T. Robertson, Jr., USAF Commander in Chief, U.S. Transportation Command, Statement to the Senate Armed Services Committee, (March 1999).
9. G. Godfrey and T. Mifflin, Virtual transportation company REF white paper, `http://www.metsci.com/abc/`, Metron, Inc., (March 2001).
10. W. Vickrey, Counterspeculation, auctions, and competitive sealed tenders, *Journal of Finance* **16**, 8–37, (March 1961).
11. Air Force, Air mobility planning factors, Pamphlet 10-1403, (March 1998).

Available online at www.sciencedirect.com
SCIENCE @ DIRECT®
Mathematical and Computer Modelling 39 (2004) 897–904
MATHEMATICAL AND COMPUTER MODELLING
www.elsevier.com/locate/mcm

Deploying the Army Interim Brigade Combat Team. A Quick-Look Approach for Strategic Force Closure Assessments

J. M. MAHAN AND W. H. KEY II
Northrop Grumman Information Technology Government Solutions
United States Transportation Command (USTRANSCOM), TCJ5-SC
Joint Analytical Support Program
508 Scott Drive, Scott AFB, IL 62225, U.S.A.
<jean.mahan><william.key>@hq.transcom.mil

K. RECKAMP AND R. T. BRIGANTIC
United States Transportation Command, TCJ5-AI
508 Scott Drive, Scott AFB, IL 62225, U.S.A.
<karyl.Reckamp><robert.brigantic>@hq.transcom.mil

Abstract—The United States Transportation Command (USTRANSCOM) recently examined the U.S. Army's Vision for future small-scale contingency deployments with a focus on airlift transportation. The main objective was to provide feedback to the Army on initial concept feasibility. When evaluating transportation scenarios for future concepts, many of the key parameters impacting force closure are not yet well defined, such as the size, location, and time phasing of the deploying force, the level of hazardous cargo processing required, the size and composition of the dedicated airlift fleet, the location of the conflict, the available en route infrastructure, etc. To assess the essence of future transportation challenges, closure estimates and constraints were examined for a number of representative future scenarios. This paper provides details of the development and use of a strategic airlift quick-look tool to support USTRANSCOM's study effort. The tool supports rapid closure assessments and constraint identification for up to 42 different scenarios simultaneously. It is especially useful for evaluating best available future data and planning assumptions when time phased force deployment data is unavailable or of poor quality for making more detailed assessments.

Keywords—Strategic airlift, Closure estimates, Maximum on the ground (MOG), Army transformation, Quick-look tool, Hot cargo parking, Airfield constraints, Interim Brigade Combat Team (IBCT).

1. INTRODUCTION

In October 1999, the Chief of Staff of the Army issued an Army vision statement for army transformation including deployment goals of putting a combat force anywhere in the world within 96 hours after liftoff [1]. To make the Army's vision for transformation a reality, the Army must reduce its transportation requirements while working with U.S. Transportation Command (USTRANSCOM) and the services to improve force closure using limited airlift assets. In early 2001, USTRANSCOM analysts were tasked to assess the force closure of a light interim brigade

0895-7177/04/$ - see front matter Typeset by $\mathcal{A}_{\mathcal{M}}\mathcal{S}$-TEX
doi:10.1016/j.mcm.2004.02.020

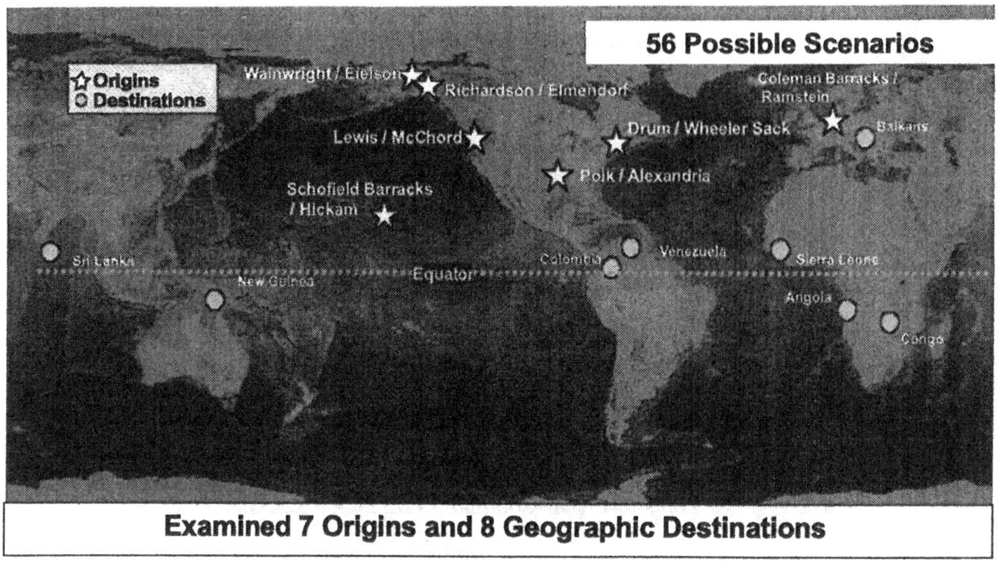

Figure 1. IBCT origins and destinations.

combat team (IBCT) from seven candidate home station locations referred to as origins to eight destinations around the world representing potential geographic regions for future conflict for a total of 56 different scenarios (reference Figure 1) [1].

Two high fidelity simulations were available to conduct this assessment: the U.S. Air Force Air Mobility Command's (AMC's) airlift flow model (AFM) and the USTRANSCOM's model for intertheater deployment for air and sea (MIDAS). Both these tools are data intensive, requiring significant manpower to set-up, run, and analyze the results for a single excursion of a single scenario. Early analysis results for this study focused on a single scenario (consisting of one origin to destination scenario pair). Analysis using the first scenario was still ongoing after several months due to the iterative "what-if" questions from USTRANSCOM and Army leadership. Despite an approaching study completion deadline, the challenge of assessing the remaining 55 scenarios remained untouched. To help focus the effort, USTRANSCOM analysts developed a strategic airlift quick-look tool that was easy and quick to set-up and do initial analysis. The quick-look tool estimates the number of days to achieve force closure assuming a maximum steady flow of aircraft through a simple transportation system. The tool's visual presentation of results was invaluable to facilitate real-time leadership "what-if" sessions where the force closure impact from changing scenario parameters such as fleet size was examined across several scenarios simultaneously. Results from the quick-look tool were used to address the impact of key transportation constraints for the scenarios and to focus the detailed analysis using the AFM and MIDAS simulation models on selected scenarios. The overarching results and findings for the study, documented in the USTRANSCOM study report, were consistent using both the detailed models and the quick-look tool [1]. This consistency in large part is a result of the rapid closure goals (maximum flow) and a simplified transportation infrastructure associated with deploying forces from a single origin to a single destination, rather than from many origins to many destinations.

The remainder of the paper is organized as follows: Section 2 provides an overview of the quick-look tool, Section 3 decomposes the problem, Section 4 presents the quick-look tool graphical user interface, and lastly, Section 5 presents conclusions.

2. OVERVIEW

The strategic airlift quick-look tool input parameters include the defined force size (i.e., weight) to be deployed, the percentage of aircraft cargo loads with hazardous cargo requiring special handling and parking, the available number of C-5 and C-17 strategic airlift aircraft for deploying the force, and the aircraft planning factors for payloads, USE rates, and ground times. USE rate is a planning factor used to represent the average flying hours per day an aircraft can fly after maintenance, crews, routing, etc., are taken into account. For aircraft payloads, USE rates, and ground times, standard AMC planning factors are provided as an option for the analyst [2]. Additional input parameters include origins (onload locations), destinations (offload locations), origin to destination routing distance matrix, airfield processing capacities (onload, en route, and offload airfields) for standard loads and for hazardous cargo loads. With these parameters defined, calculating closure estimates is possible using airlift cycle analysis for a single origin to destination pair. The associated closure calculations are reviewed in Section 3.

Indeed, the quick-look tool is an automated implementation of airlift throughput formulas. The parameter input and output graphics were customized allowing the USTRANSCOM study team the capability to rapidly investigate relevant issues and respond consistently to new inquiries made almost daily by the leadership, when detailed model runs would not have been possible. The initial prototype of the tool was used to educate U.S. Transportation Command leadership on the impact of key parameters on force closure. Microsoft Excel was selected for the tool taking advantage of in-house expertise to quickly prototype a user-friendly tool utilizing the many built-in features such as drop down lists, buttons, checkboxes, and the capability for integrated graphics.

The fundamental equations used to compute closure results remain constant within the tool, but input parameters and assumptions can be interactively changed. The power of the strategic airlift quick-look tool is its ability to quickly and consistently calculate and depict force closure estimates for multiple scenarios, to identify for each scenario which parameter must be changed first to improve force closure, and to provide estimates of the airfield infrastructure required to maximize scenario throughput for a defined airlift fleet. A unique feature of this tool is the graphical presentation facilitating comparison and comprehension of related results across multiple scenarios.

3. DECOMPOSING THE PROBLEM

The quick-look tool methodology includes defining relevant scenario parameters, calculating fleet force closure potential for a given airlift fleet assuming unconstrained airfield infrastructure, determining the level of airfield infrastructure required to support the force closure potential, calculating actual force closure supported by defined actual airfield infrastructure (or hypothetical improved airfield infrastructure), and then displaying results for the user. Fleet force closure potential represents how quickly a dedicated airlift fleet could close a given force without any airfield infrastructure constraints (ramp/aircraft parking space, fuel availability, and delivery system, etc.). Identifying the difference between potential fleet closure and actual fleet closure is important for determining the marginal benefit of additional infrastructure resources. If the potential fleet closure and the actual fleet closures were equal then the only way to improve closure is to increase the fleet capability (since airfield infrastructure is not constraining in this case).

For the quick-look tool and many other strategic mobility models, airfield infrastructure is represented by an airfield throughput parameter referred to as maximum on ground (MOG). MOG is defined as the maximum number of aircraft an airfield location can process, within an aircraft's ground time, simultaneously. For example, if an aircraft ground time is three hours and the MOG is three, then the airfield can process a maximum of 24 aircraft a day assuming a perfect steady flow schedule without queueing inefficiencies. In the quick-look tool, the airfield MOG was defined in general terms representing an overall MOG for the airfield, and also in more restrictive terms specific to the processing of hazardous cargo.

The quick-look tool was designed to allow for simultaneous comparison of up to 42 scenarios. Limited computer display space made expansion beyond 42 scenarios impractical, but such adaptations could be easily made. Fortunately, for this analytical effort, the six onload origins or aerial port of embarkations (APOEs) and seven off-load destinations or aerial port of debarkation (APODs) were sufficient to cover general geographic locations of interest. Quick-look tool results are available in the form of an integrated graphic with mouse-over capability to get actual values displayed in the graph. These results include: fleet force closure potential (in days), actual closure (in days constrained by airfield infrastructure), and MOG required to maximize fleet closure potential at origin/APOE, en route, and offload airfields. Hot cargo MOG is only calculated for APOEs and en route airfields since the study effort assumed there were no hot cargo constraints at the APODs. A constraint matrix identifying the limiting factor for up to 42 scenarios is also available.

3.1. Computing Fleet Force Closure Potential

The following steps were performed to compute fleet force closure potential for the different scenarios.

(1) Define total force deployment requirement, R, in tons, to be moved.

(2) Define airlift fleet parameters, which include the type and number of airlift aircraft, the average aircraft payloads (tons), and the aircraft USE rates. Let A be the set of all aircraft types $i \in A$. Let n_i, p_i, and u_i be the number of aircraft of type $i \in A$, the payload of aircraft of type $i \in A$, and the USE rate of aircraft of type $i \in A$, respectively.

(3) Let S be the set of all scenarios $s \in S$. Define scenario roundtrip flying distance, D_s, for each onload to offload scenario pair.

(4) For each aircraft type $i \in A$, determine number of en route stops and aircraft average flying speeds to associate with a matrix of roundtrip flying distances from 2,000 to 28,000 nautical miles (NM). This range was chosen as a matter of practicality.

(5) Define the roundtrip flying time associated with an aircraft type $i \in A$ and a scenario $s \in S$ as F_{is} which is equal to the roundtrip flying distance, D_s, divided by the average aircraft flying speed for aircraft type $i \in A$.

(6) Define ground times for each aircraft type $i \in A$ for onload, en route, and offload stops as g_i^{onload}, g_i^{enroute}, and g_i^{offload}.

(7) Define the roundtrip ground time, G_{is}, for each scenario $s \in S$ and aircraft type $i \in A$ as the sum of the g_i^{onload}, g_i^{offload}, and g_i^{enroute} multiplied by the number of round trip en route stops.

(8) Define the roundtrip airlift cycles per day associated with each aircraft type $i \in A$ and scenario $s \in S$ as c_{is}, where

$$c_{is} = \min\left\{\frac{24}{(F_{is} + G_{is})}, \frac{u_i}{F_{is}}\right\}.$$

(9) Define the average throughput per day (in tons) associated with each aircraft type $i \in A$ and scenario $s \in S$ as t_{is}, where $t_{is} = c_{is}p_i$.

(10) Compute average daily fleet throughput potential $T_s^{\text{potential}}$ tons per day, where

$$T_s^{\text{potential}} = \sum_{i \in A} t_{is} n_i, \qquad \text{for each scenario } s \in S.$$

(11) Compute fleet force closure potential (in days) $C_s^{\text{potential}}$ for each scenario $s \in S$ where

$$C_s^{\text{potential}} = \frac{R}{T_s^{\text{potential}}}.$$

3.2. Computing Infrastructure Requirements to Support Fleet Closure Potential

Unless a relatively small airlift fleet is used, scenarios will often be limited by infrastructure constraints that prevent the aircraft fleet from maximizing throughput potential at one or more airfields associated with a scenario's roundtrip cycle. The infrastructure requirements to support maximizing the fleet potential are computed using the following steps.

(1) Define queuing efficiency as q. Queueing efficiency is an AMC planning factor used to represent inefficiencies in aircraft scheduling into the parking at an airfield. This planning factor must be less than or equal to 1.0. For AMC standard planning, q has been defined as 0.85 [2].

(2) Define the onload MOG requirement to support maximizing the fleet potential for scenario $s \in S$ as M_s^{onload}, where

$$M_s^{\text{onload}} = \sum_{i \in A} \frac{c_{is} n_i \left(g_i^{\text{onload}}/24\right)}{q}.$$

(3) Define en route MOG requirement to support maximizing the fleet potential for scenario $s \in S$ as M_s^{enroute}, where

$$M_s^{\text{enroute}} = \sum_{i \in A} \frac{c_{is} n_i \left(g_i^{\text{enroute}}/24\right)}{q}.$$

If the en route airport is used inbound and outbound M_s^{enroute} should be doubled.

(4) Define offload MOG requirement to support maximizing the fleet potential for scenario $s \in S$ as M_s^{offload}, where

$$M_s^{\text{offload}} = \sum_{i \in A} \frac{c_{is} n_i \left(g_i^{\text{offload}}/24\right)}{q}.$$

(5) Define percentage of aircraft loads carrying hot cargo requiring special handling as h.

(6) Define onload hot cargo MOG requirement to support maximizing the fleet potential for scenario $s \in S$ as H_s^{onload}, where

$$H_s^{\text{onload}} = h M_s^{\text{onload}}.$$

(7) Define en route hot cargo MOG requirement to support maximizing the fleet potential for scenario $s \in S$ as H_s^{enroute}, where

$$H_s^{\text{enroute}} = h M_s^{\text{enroute}}.$$

En route hot cargo parking is only required on the inbound leg to the APOD.

3.3. Identifying Airfield Throughput and Force Closure Supportable by Actual Airfield Infrastructure

Understanding the closure capacity of an origin to destination pair requires an evaluation of each airfield associated with the roundtrip cycle to determine what level of throughput each node can support. An airfield throughput capacity equation is evaluated for each airfield to determine the throughput capacity at onloads, en routes, and off-loads.

$$T_s^{\text{onload}} = \min\left\{\left(\frac{\text{actual MOG}^{\text{onload}}}{M_s^{\text{onload}}}\right) T_s^{\text{potential}}, \left(\frac{\text{actual hot cargo MOG}^{\text{onload}}}{H_s^{\text{onload}}}\right) T_s^{\text{potential}}\right\},$$

$$T_s^{\text{enroute}} = \min\left\{\left(\frac{\text{actual MOG}^{\text{enroute}}}{M_s^{\text{enroute}}}\right) T_s^{\text{potential}}, \left(\frac{\text{actual hot cargo MOG}^{\text{enroute}}}{H_s^{\text{enroute}}}\right) T_s^{\text{potential}}\right\},$$

$$T_s^{\text{offload}} = \left(\frac{\text{actual MOG}^{\text{offload}}}{M_s^{\text{offload}}}\right) T_s^{\text{potential}}.$$

If $T_s^{\text{onload}} < T_s^{\text{potential}}$, $T_s^{\text{enroute}} < T_s^{\text{potential}}$, or $T_s^{\text{offload}} < T_s^{\text{potential}}$, then the fleet's throughput potential is constrained by the airfield's actual MOG. When one or more airfields constrain the fleet's throughput potential, the airfield with the minimum throughput capacity defines the actual scenario throughput, T_s^{actual}. The same airfield's infrastructure is also identified as the scenario's primary constraint. If none of the airfields limit the fleet's throughput potential, $T_s^{\text{potential}}$, then the actual scenario throughput, T_s^{actual}, will be equal to the fleet throughput potential, $T_s^{\text{potential}}$. In either case, the actual scenario closure, C_s^{actual} (days), is defined as

$$C_s^{\text{actual}} = \frac{R}{T_s^{\text{actual}}}.$$

4. STRATEGIC AIRLIFT QUICK-LOOK TOOL GRAPHICAL USER INTERFACE

The quick-look tool main screen is shown in Figure 2, with estimated closure time results displayed. The graphical interface allows a user to compare all origin (APOE) to destination (APOD) pairs for a selected metric, such as fleet closure potential, constrained closure, or infrastructure requirements to quickly identify the best options to meet the desired objective. Many of the user-defined scenario parameters are available from the main screen such as the airlift fleet, the size (weight) of the deploying force, the percentage of cargo requiring a hot cargo pad, and airfield MOGs as defined on the far right of Figure 2. Additional screens for setting payloads, USE rates, and ground times are also available from the main screen by clicking on the appropriate button. These parameters can be set up using standard planning factors or they can be user-defined.

Check boxes at the bottom of the main screen just below the graph provide the user with the ability to select or fine-tune which APOE and APOD scenario pairs are displayed on output graphs. The user may select no scenario, in which case the graph will be empty, one scenario pair, or up to all 42 scenarios. The setup is flexible enough to allow for the display of all destinations

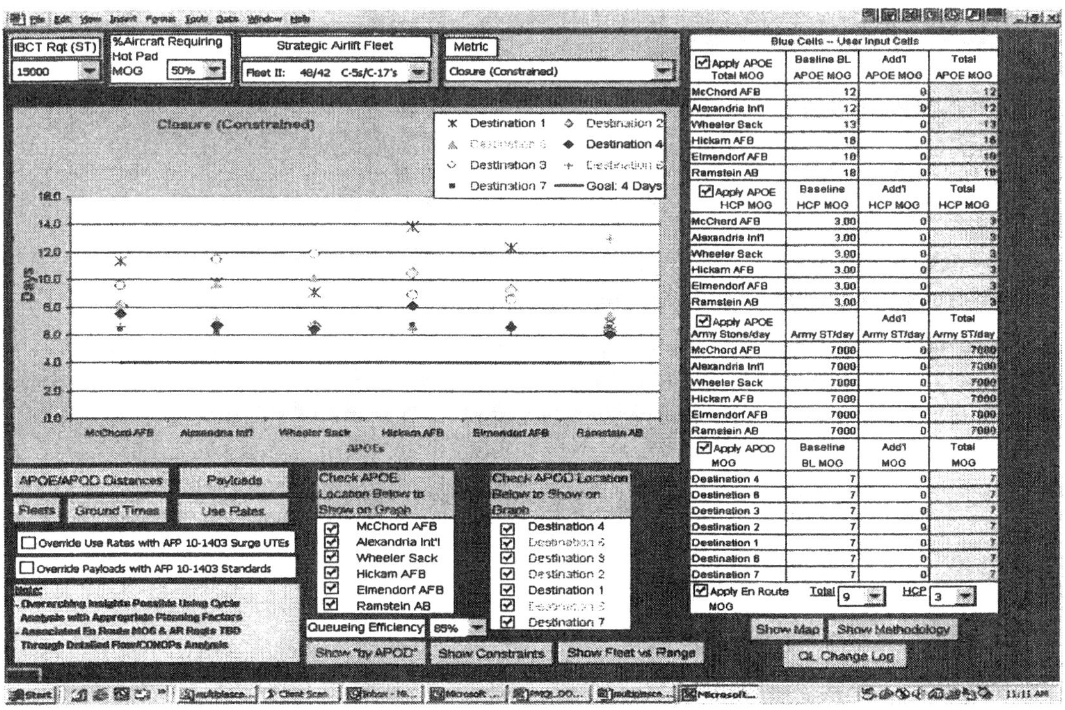

Figure 2. Main user input screen with parameter inputs.

Fleet Label	C-5	C-17	WB Pax	User Defined Fleets
Fleet I:	14	20	0	Fleet I: 14/20 C-5s/C-17's
Fleet II:	48	42	0	Fleet II: 48/42 C-5s/C-17's
Fleet III:	60	84	0	Fleet III: 60/84 C-5s/C-17's
Fleet IV:	0	144	0	Fleet IV: 0/144 C-5s/C-17's

Figure 3. User screen for user-defined air fleets.

1/2 Round Trip Flying Distance or approx "Onload-Offload Flying Distance"	Destination 4	Destination 6	Destination 3	Destination 2	Destination 1	Destination 6	Destination 7
McChord AFB	6554	4599	8500	7000	10000	7000	3650
Alexandria Int'l	5099	6175	10100	5600	8700	8600	2162
Wheeler Sack	3998	5860	10500	5100	8000	9000	2180
Hickam AFB	7003	3870	7800	9300	12300	4680	5450
Elmendorf AFB	4593	3337	7500	8150	10900	5800	4875
Ramstein AB	1000	11500	5000	2700	5900	6500	4550

Figure 4. User input screen for origins, destinations, and distances.

Constraint LEGEND

Symbol	Description
HCP	APOE Hot Cargo MOG
APOE	APOE Total MOG
APOD	APOD MOG
ER MOG	Total En Route MOG
ER HCP	En Route Hot Cargo MOG
Army	Army ST/day
Fleet	Fleet

CONSTRAINT MATRIX	Destination 4	Destination 6	Destination 3	Destination 2	Destination 1	Destination 6	Destination 7
McChord AFB	FLEET	APOE HCP	FLEET	FLEET	FLEET	FLEET	APOE HCP
Alexandria Int'l	APOE HCP	FLEET	FLEET	APOE HCP	FLEET	FLEET	APOE HCP
Wheeler Sack	APOE HCP	FLEET	FLEET	APOE HCP	FLEET	FLEET	APOE HCP
Hickam AFB	FLEET	APOE HCP	FLEET	FLEET	FLEET	APOE HCP	APOE HCP
Elmendorf AFB	APOE HCP	APOE HCP	FLEET	FLEET	FLEET	FLEET	APOE HCP
Ramstein AB	APOE HCP	FLEET	APOE HCP	APOE HCP	FLEET	FLEET	APOE HCP

Figure 5. Constraint matrix.

associated with a single APOE or all onloads associated with a single APOD, depending on what is desired by the user.

The quick-look tool was designed to evaluate up to four user-defined airlift fleets of just three aircraft types: C-5, C-17, and widebody passenger (WB PAX) aircraft (e.g., Boeing 747). The different levels can be used to represent either different aircraft withhold/mobilization rates or even future aircraft procurement levels. The input screen shown in Figure 3 is used for defining the airlift fleet and can be accessed by pressing the button labeled *fleets* on the main screen shown in Figure 2.

The quick-look tool provides the user with flexibility to define the set of APOE and APOD pairs to be evaluated by selecting the button labeled *APOE/APOD distances* on the main display. The origins, destinations, and distance are all user definable in the matrix shown in Figure 4. The distance in the matrix should represent approximately one-half the roundtrip flying distance for each scenario pair, and ideally, this distance should include all necessary routing deviations required for flight plans.

The output constraint matrix shown in Figure 5 identifies the specific constraint associated with each scenario evaluated. The fleet will be identified as the limiting constraint only if the infrastructure at all required airfields is able to support the potential fleet force closure. Otherwise, one of the airfields will be identified as a scenario infrastructure constraint.

5. CONCLUSION

The strategic airlift quick-look tool incorporates relatively straightforward mobility formulas, but allows for quite powerful, comprehensive analysis for ascertaining force closure across a wide range of potential deployment scenarios and input parameter conditions and assumptions. This quick-look tool was successfully used by the U.S. Transportation Command to identify critical factors associated with meeting the Army vision to rapidly deploy future forces. In short, the tool was used to demonstrate the demanding nature of the initial Army vision and the challenges that must be tackled to make it viable. For instance, the quick-look tool demonstrated the significant impact that hot cargo parking requirements has on overall force closure. Reducing the hot cargo requirement (i.e., decreasing the percentage of aircraft required to carry hazardous or explosive munitions) can greatly reduce force closure time as many airfields have limited hazardous cargo infrastructure. Likewise, the tool vividly demonstrated the importance of reducing the overall weight of the envisioned Army brigade to be deployed. Lastly, the tool was used to show the huge impact that overall distance to the destination has on overall force closure. Ultimately, these insights and results were used to brief the highest leadership levels of the U.S. Transportation Command and the U.S. Army and are being used by senior level DoD leaders to implement more efficient and deployable fighting forces.

REFERENCES

1. Interim Brigade Combat Team Air Mobility Deployment Analysis, (Prepared by K. Reckamp, Approved by Lieutenant General Daniel G. Brown, U.S.A.), United States Transportation Command, (2002).
2. Air Force Pamphlet 10-1403, Air Mobility Planning Factors, (1998).

Available online at www.sciencedirect.com
SCIENCE DIRECT•
Mathematical and Computer Modelling 39 (2004) 905–924
MATHEMATICAL AND COMPUTER MODELLING
www.elsevier.com/locate/mcm

The Deployment Scheduling Analysis Tool (DSAT)

T. J. HODGSON
Industrial Engineering Department, North Carolina State University
Raleigh, NC 27695-7906, U.S.A.
hodgson@eos.ncsu.edu

B. MELENDEZ
Department of Mathematical Sciences, United States Military Academy
West Point, NY 10996-1779, U.S.A.
ab7596@exmail.usma.army.mil

K. A. THONEY
Textile and Apparel, Technology and Management Department, North Carolina State University
Raleigh, NC 27695, U.S.A.
kathoney@unity.ncsu.edu

T. TRAINOR
Department of Systems Engineering, United States Military Academy
West Point, NY 10996-1779, U.S.A.
ft5890@exmail.usma.army.mil

Abstract—The deployment scheduling analysis tool is an analysis tool for studying military deployment scenarios. The tool has a user interface through which the user selects the deploying units, equipment, and their required delivery dates. The user also selects the ports (air, rail, and sea) through which the units will travel to get to the final destination. Finally, the user selects the transportation assets on which the units will travel and assigns those assets to the routes in the deployment network. The system schedules the equipment for deployment by creating individual equipment routings and then repetitively simulating the deployment to determine the deployment closure time and the maximum lateness ($L_{\max}$) of any unit. The equipment is scheduled to minimize the maximum lateness of all deploying units. Deployment information is formatted into various graphs and reports. Finally, the user can modify various aspects of the deployment scenario to conduct sensitivity analysis. A valuable option is a heuristic procedure to reassign transportation assets in an attempt to further reduce the deployment closure time and $L_{\max}$.

Keywords—Military deployment, Analysis tool, Equipment routing, Deployment network, Equipment scheduling.

1. INTRODUCTION

When asked about the secret of his many successful military operations, Confederate Cavalry General Nathan Bedford Forrest answered that victory often goes to " ... whoever gets there

This research was supported, in part, by the Office of Naval Research, Contract #N00014-90-J-1009, and the Military Traffic Management Command-Transportation Engineering Agency.

0895-7177/04/$ - see front matter Typeset by AMS-TEX
doi:10.1016/j.mcm.2004.02.021

firstest with the mostest ...". The simple logic of this statement underscores the fact that military victories are critically dependent upon the military transportation system. The military must be able to effectively plan, analyze, schedule, and execute force deployment operations. Many deployments are short-notice contingency operations that require rapid planning and scheduling.

Currently, deployment planners have few software tools available to assist them. One tool, the Joint Flow and Analysis System for Transportation (JFAST) [1], is a simulation model that provides detailed estimates for strategic force movement by air and sealift assets. JFAST requires a rigid input structure involving considerable time to prepare, and is not a good tool for sensitivity analysis. Another tool, the Deployment Analysis Network Tool Enhanced (DANTE) [2], is a valuable tool for deployment planning sensitivity analysis. DANTE is extremely fast to use, but lacks the detail necessary to construct a usable deployment schedule.

The need for computational speed and detailed estimates drove the development of a PC-based tool for deployment scheduling and analysis. Illingworth [3], then Trainor [4] initially developed the Deployment Scheduling Analysis Tool (DSAT). DSAT provides a flexible and rapid means for analysis of deployments. It is quick and flexible enough to be used for sensitivity analysis of various aspects of the deployment scenario. At the same time, enough information concerning the deploying forces is retained that detailed equipment schedules (what equipment moves over which routes at which time) can also be analyzed. A Visual Basic (VB) graphic user interface (GUI) facilitates modeling of deployment scenarios and viewing of key outputs for analysis. User inputs, coupled with data drawn from military databases, provide the information needed to schedule the movement of equipment and cargo on transportation assets and deployment routes. A specially tailored job shop scheduling procedure [5–7] performs the scheduling. The user can invoke a heuristic procedure to move transportation assets between routes to affect improved schedules. The overall logic used in DSAT is represented in Figure 1 and detailed in the rest of this paper.

Section 2 introduces DSAT and presents the steps used to model a problem. Section 3 describes the heuristics used to create a deployment schedule and to determine an alternate transportation asset to route allocation. Section 4 discusses the various reports provided and the options available for sensitivity analysis. Section 5 presents conclusions.

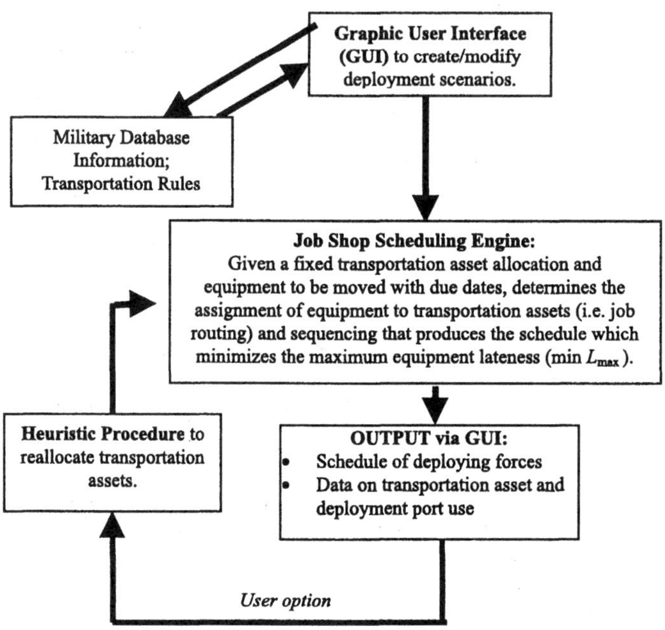

Figure 1. Overall DSAT methodology.

2. MODELING A DEPLOYMENT PROBLEM WITH DSAT

The intended use of DSAT requires ease of use in developing deployment scenarios and speed in calculating the corresponding "optimal" schedule. While DSAT models the deployment problem in a good deal of fidelity, it should not be used as a final scheduling tool for an actual deployment. Rather, DSAT enables planners to quickly develop and analyze schedules for possible deployment courses of action in order to reduce the set of viable alternatives for scheduling using more detailed, less flexible, deployment simulations. DSAT also enables planners to rapidly perform sensitivity analysis to determine the impact on deployment schedules by changing key parameters. To meet the intended use, some assumptions are modeled in DSAT that do not necessarily reflect the many uncertainties that affect a real world deployment. Specifically, DSAT assumes transportation assets are operational 24 hours a day, although standard ground load, unload, and maintenance times are factored into asset availability. Port facility restrictions are known in advance and remain fixed during the deployment, as do asset-operating characteristics. While not explicitly capturing the many uncertainties to which a real world deployment is subject, DSAT retains the level of fidelity necessary to create an "optimal" equipment and asset schedule yet has the speed and flexibility needed to conduct deployment sensitivity analysis.

A deployment problem is built by retrieving and storing information in Microsoft ACCESS© database tables. The DSAT database contains information for several military units and the characteristics of their equipment, global position and capacity data on ports throughout the world, and characteristics of aircraft, railcars, and ships used by the military. Using structured query language (SQL), the appropriate information is retrieved from these tables to formulate the problem. Deployment information is grouped into four areas:

- deploying units and equipment,
- ports through which deploying units are routed,

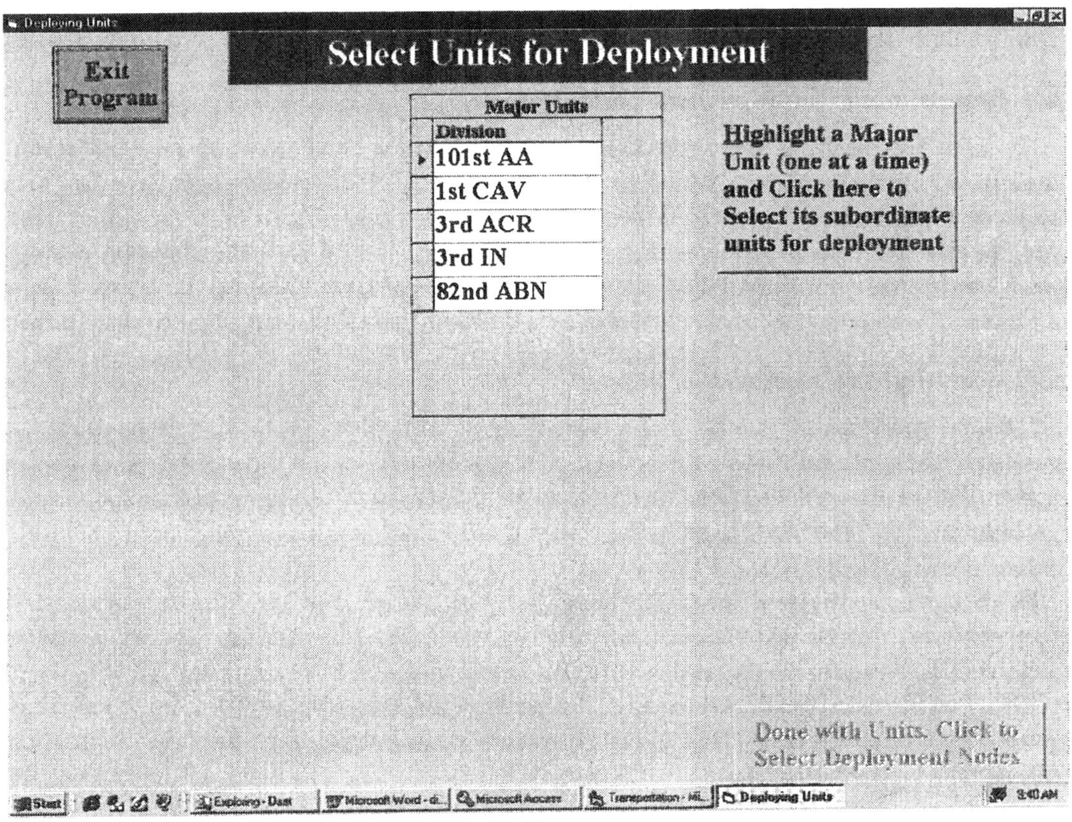

Figure 2. Major units.

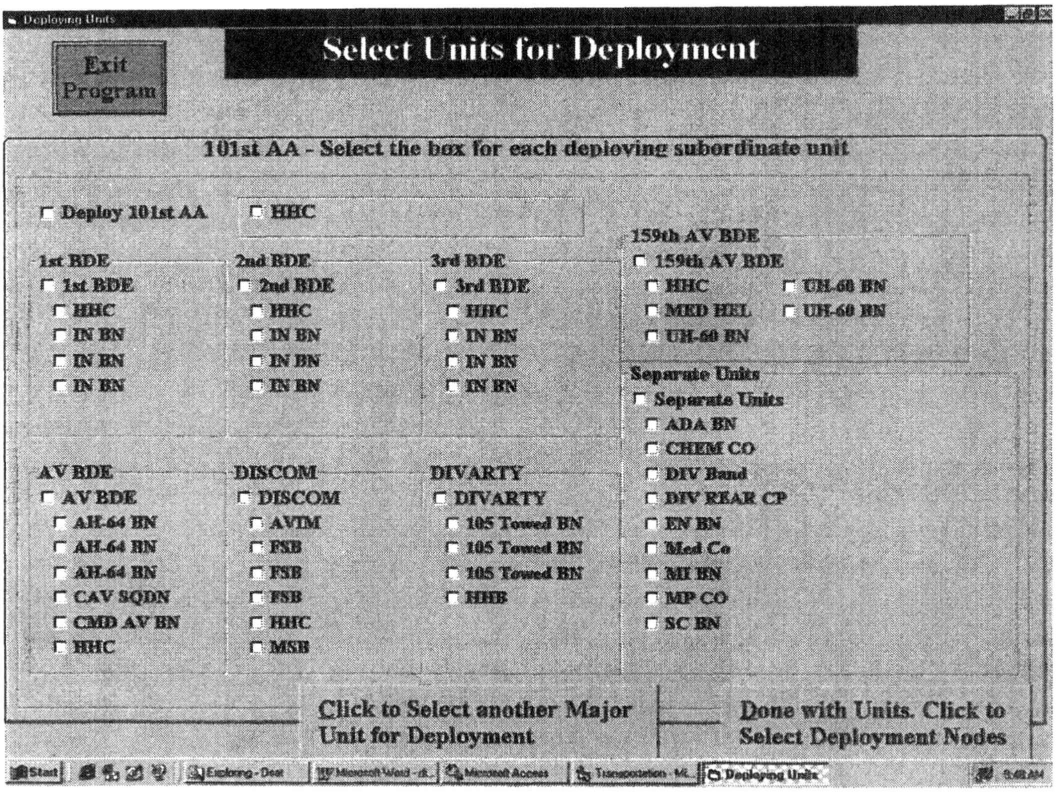

Figure 3. Selecting subordinate units for deployment.

- deployment time windows, and
- characteristics of transportation assets.

DSAT builds the problem in this sequence as the user navigates through a series of GUI screens.

2.1. Determining the Movement Requirement

To build the deploying force, the user first selects a major unit from an interface screen as depicted in Figure 2. Figures 2–10 show the various DSAT GUI screens users navigate through to model a deployment scenario. When the user selects a subordinate unit for deployment by checking the box next to its name, the unit's equipment is added to the deployment equipment list by retrieving it from the DSAT database. The user navigates through the interface screens of Figures 2 and 3 for each major unit desired, and thus, builds the deploying equipment list.

2.2. Selecting the Deployment Ports

The set of ports used is another major component of the deployment network. The chosen ports determine the deployment route distances used to calculate the travel times for the transportation assets. Each port is uniquely identified in the DSAT database by a four-character code termed a geolocation code. The code identifies the port in tables containing geographical position, distance, and any known facility data.

All deploying equipment leaves its home base (or current physical location) by air or rail transportation. In the DSAT database, each unit is linked to a habitual airport of embarkation (APOE), seaport of embarkation (SPOE), and rail depot from which equipment travels to the SPOE. The user verifies and changes, if necessary, these deployment ports using the interface screen depicted in Figure 4. The intent is to allow the user maximum flexibility in developing realistic deployment scenarios.

Based on the desired deployment scenario, the user selects any intermediate staging bases (ISBs) desired and the final destination ports. This selection process is shown in Figure 5. Once

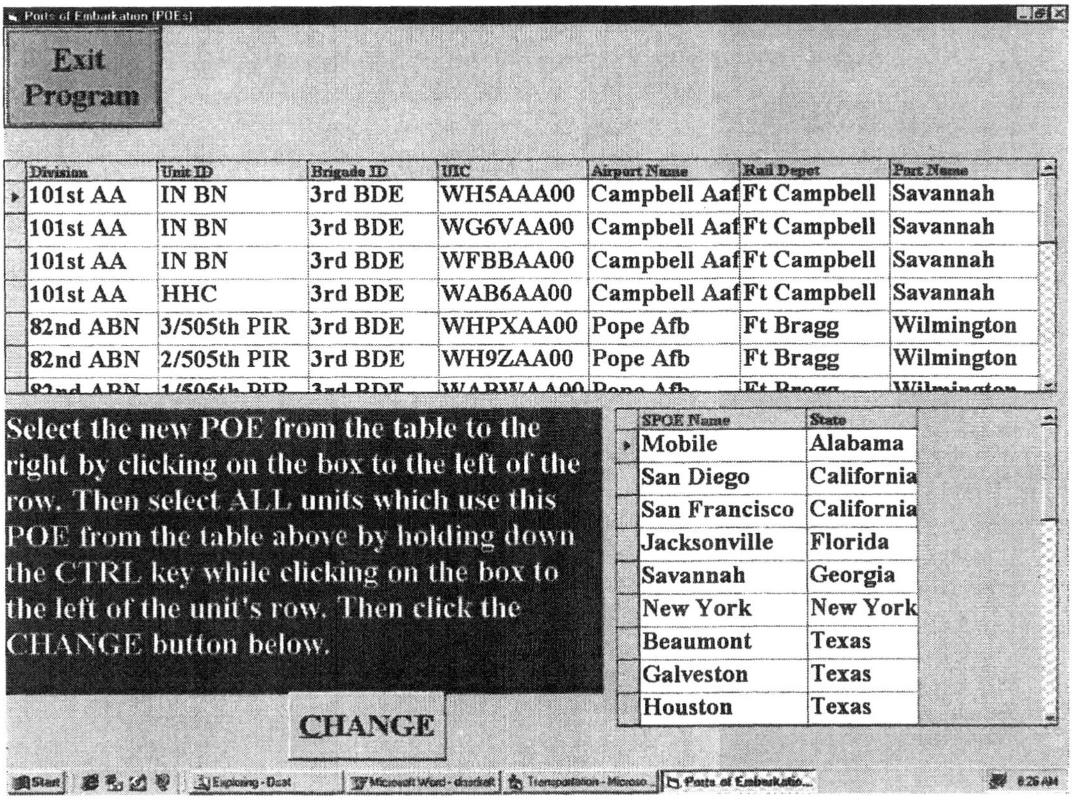

Figure 4. Verifying the ports of embarkation.

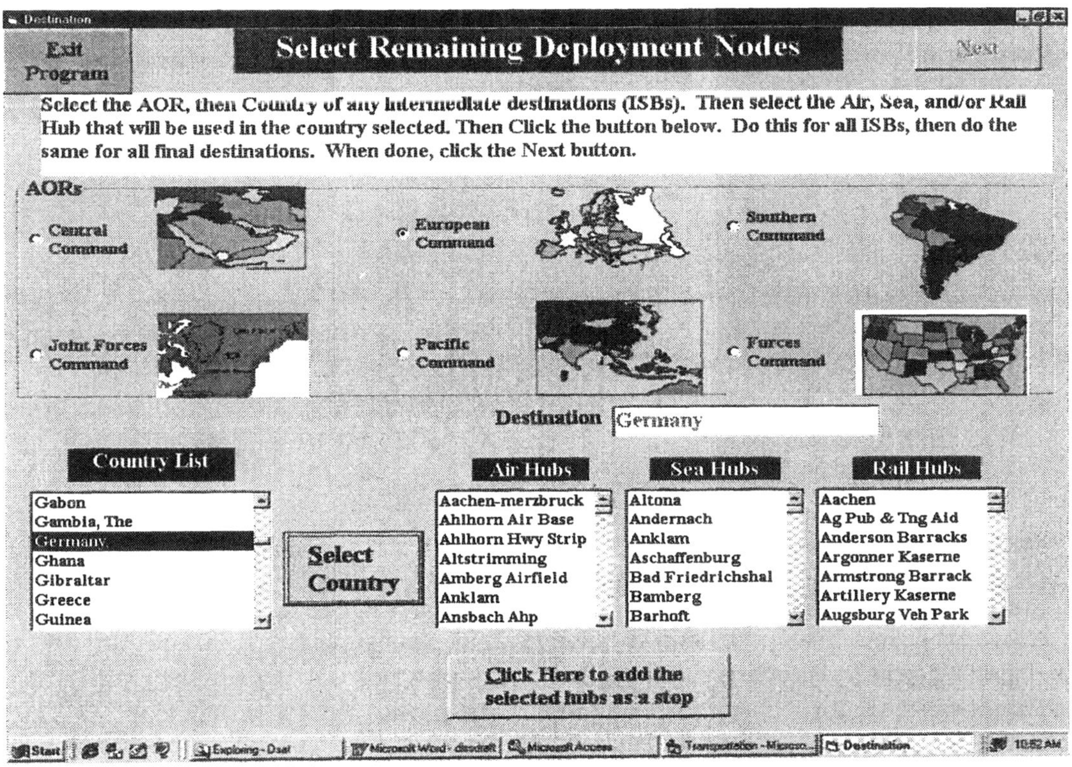

Figure 5. Selecting additional deployment ports.

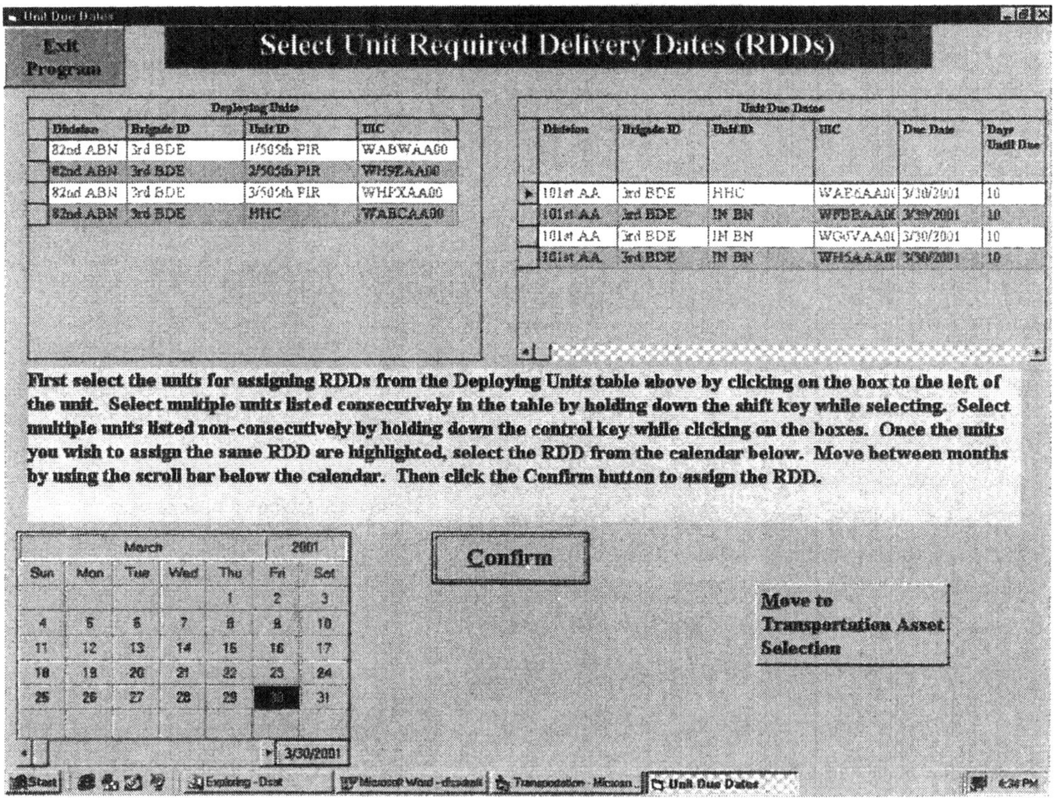

Figure 6. Entering port facility restrictions.

the user selects the countries and the various hubs (ports) to be used, the geolocation codes are used to retrieve distance data. If no distance data exists in the tables for a chosen set of ports, position data is used to calculate the great circle distance between two selected ports. DSAT uses the haversine formula (see [8,9]) to calculate the great circle distance, d, between two points with coordinates $\{\text{lat }1, \text{lon }1\}$ and $\{\text{lat }2, \text{lon }2\}$. The equation is as follows:

$$d = 2 * R * \arcsin\left(\sqrt{\sin^2\left(\frac{(\text{lat }1 - \text{lat }2)}{2}\right) + \cos(\text{lat }1) * \cos(\text{lat }2) * \sin^2\left(\frac{(\text{lon }1 - \text{lon }2)}{2}\right)}\right), \quad (1)$$

where R is the earth's radius. The great circle distance calculator used in DSAT is a modified version of a function developed by North [10], with formulae accredited to Chamberlain [11] and Greer [12]. This is an accurate means for calculating the distance traveled by aircraft between airports, but might not accurately reflect actual travel distances for rail and sea routes. The user has an option to overwrite the great circle distances generated by the program.

Ports have facility characteristics that also affect the deployment problem. Airports have a limited number of runways that limit throughput capacity. The available space for aircraft, fueling capacity, and loading and unloading capability are also limited. These factors are modeled by the maximum-on-ground (MOG) parameter that constrains the number of aircraft on the ground at an airport at a given time. The number and type of berths at a seaport, along with the type of material handling equipment available, determine the number and type of ships that can be loading or unloading. The size of rail depots and the type of loading ramps available dictate the number of cars that can be loading or unloading. These facility restrictions affect the amount of cargo capable of being processed through the port in a specific time period.

DSAT explicitly incorporates the number of runways and MOG restrictions, and the number of berths available as simple numerical parameters. The DSAT database lacks airport MOG data since the USAF Air Mobility Command (AMC) closely guards this information, while berth information is available for many of the major seaports of the world. The user can update available information for seaports and airports using the interface depicted in Figure 6. DSAT does not verify that transportation assets chosen by the user match the capability available at a selected port. Transportation planners have the requisite information available to select assets that can be accommodated at the selected ports. DSAT does not account for facility restrictions in rail depots. While loading and unloading times for railcars are explicitly incorporated, the user must select a realistic number of cars that can efficiently operate between chosen rail depots.

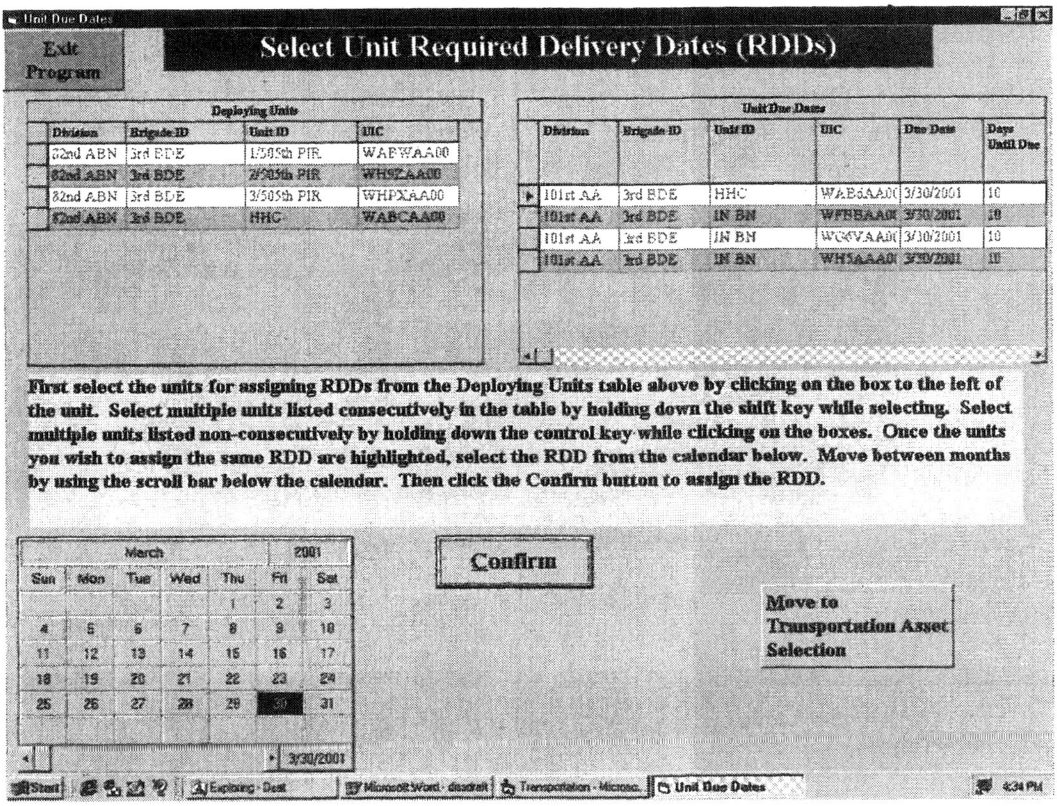

Figure 7. Assigning RDDs.

2.3. Determining the Deployment Time Window

The Unified Combatant Command determines the required delivery date (RDD) for each deploying unit based on the operational plan. Transportation planners are expected to backwards plan the deployment of units to meet these RDDs. Another time constraint is the unit available to load (ALD) date. That is, the time equipment is available to start movement from its home base or current location.

DSAT accepts user-input for the ALD; this ALD applies to all deploying units. The user selects an RDD for each unit as shown in Figure 7. In scheduling terms, the ALD is the release date and the RDD translates to the due date for each item of equipment in the unit. These release and due dates play a significant role in the scheduling methodology employed by DSAT.

2.4. Assigning Transportation Assets

The user assigns transportation assets to specific deployment routes in DSAT that are developed from the user-selected ports. The military uses various types of planes, trains, and ships, each with their own set of operating characteristics. DSAT enables the user to assign multiple types of transportation assets to a route and to vary their operating characteristics. As shown in Figure 8, the user simply follows the onscreen instructions to change any characteristic of interest.

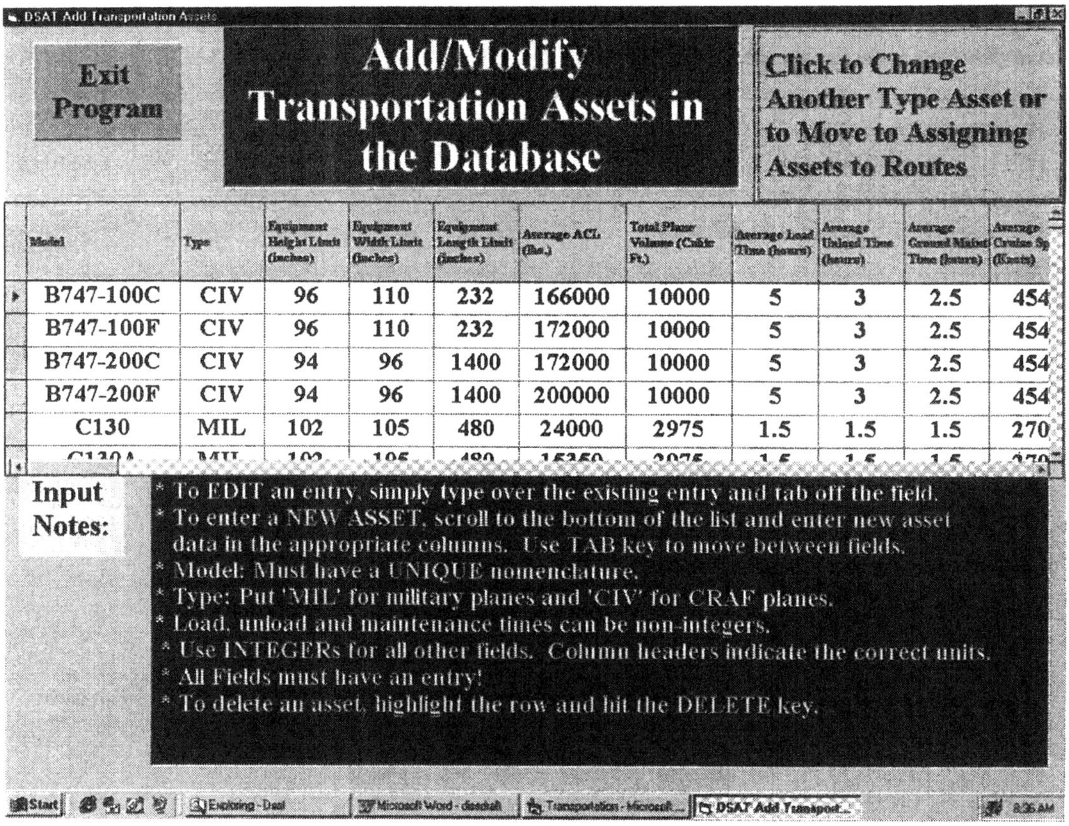

Figure 8. Modifying aircraft operating characteristics.

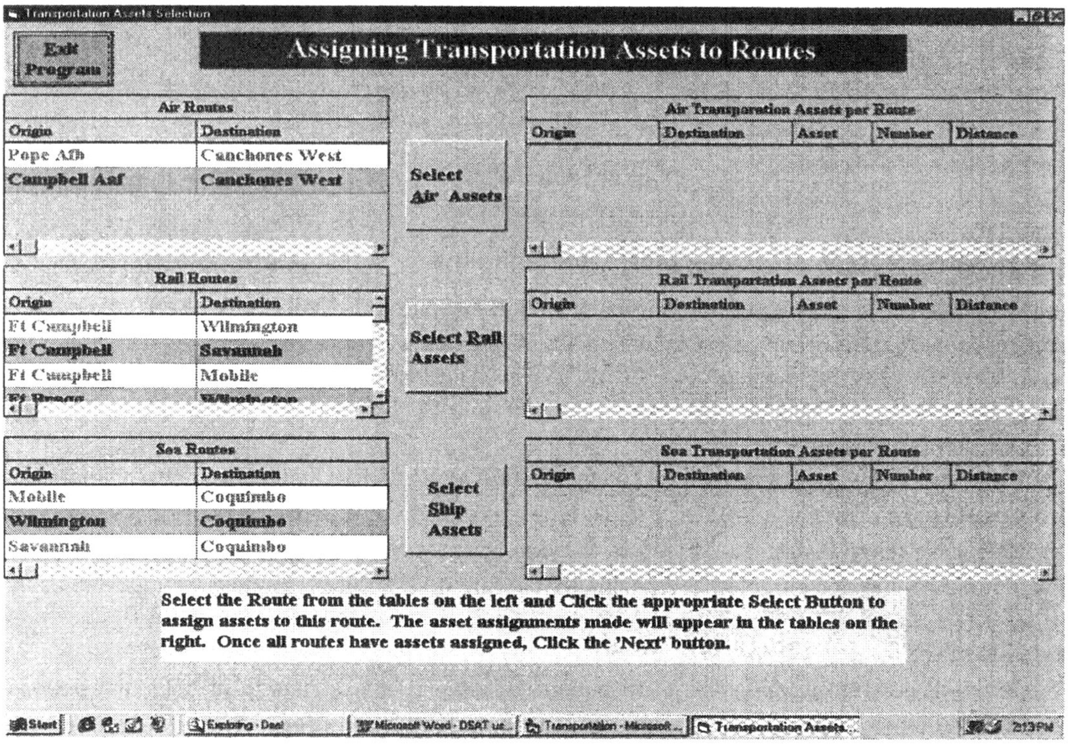

Figure 9. Assigning transportation assets to routes.

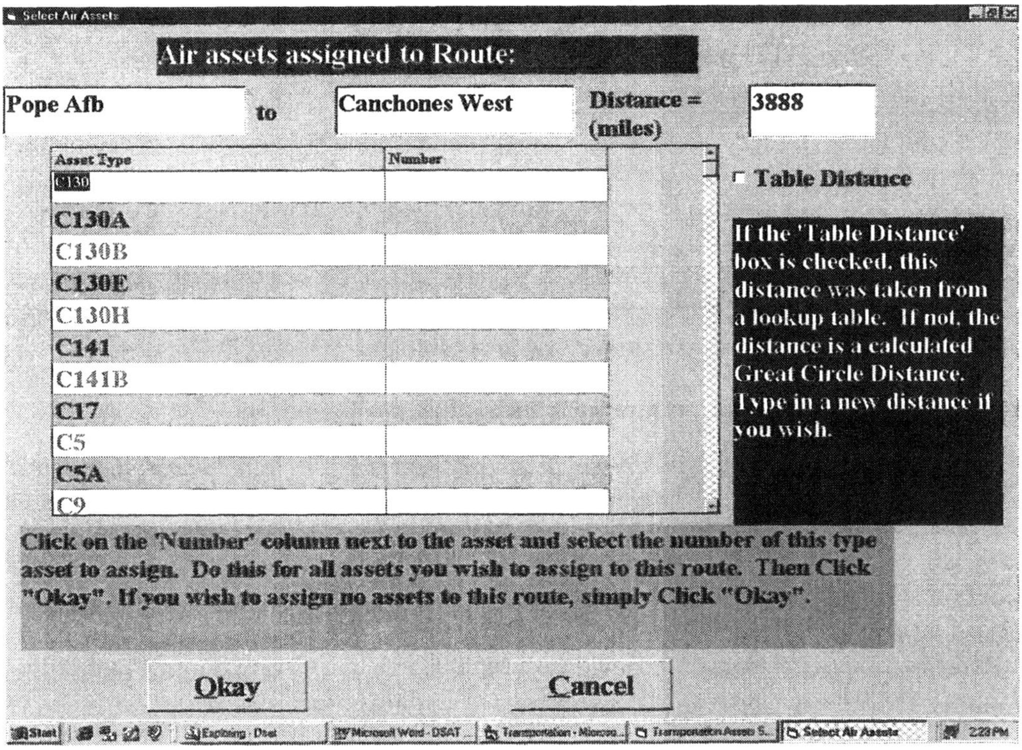

Figure 10. Example assignment of aircraft to a route.

The deployment routes are presented to the user in the screen displayed in Figure 9. The routes are segregated by air, rail, and sea. Assets are assigned to each route by using a screen similar to that in Figure 10. This figure represents an example of assigning aircraft to a deployment route from Pope Air Force Base, NC, to the Canchones West Airfield in Chile. The route distance appears in the top right corner. The user may edit the distance data and follow the onscreen directions to assign assets to the routes. The transportation asset assignment is complete after repeating the process for each route.

2.5. Feasibility Checks of the Deployment Problem

Once the deployment problem is created, DSAT performs a set of feasibility checks, modifies the inputs as required, and builds a text input file used to schedule the deployment.

DSAT performs a check to ensure the user has created a feasible deployment problem with equipment fit on the selected transportation assets being the primary focus. All military equipment will fit on the set of ships and railcars in the DSAT database. Certain items may need overhang clearance to travel on some railcars. DSAT generates a list of items needing overhang rail clearance as an output report.

The most crucial equipment fit checks are for aircraft. Individual pieces of unit equipment are checked to see if they exceed the total weight and volume capacities of the planes used in the deployment asset fleet. Equipment dimensions are also compared to the dimensions of the aircraft-loading doors. From these checks, a list of feasible transportation assets on which each item of equipment can fit is passed to the scheduling procedure.

If the user selects no assets on which a certain deploying item of equipment will fit, DSAT provides a series of options to correct the problem. The user can view this list of equipment and choose to remove the items from the deploying equipment list or return to assigning transportation assets to correct the problem. DSAT prompts the user to the smallest-sized aircraft on which the item of equipment will fit. DSAT provides an output report of any items of equipment removed from the deployment.

3. DSAT SCHEDULING AND ASSET-ROUTE REALLOCATION ROUTINES

The DSAT software package contains two key routines. The interface discussed above is written in VB and allows the planner to develop scenarios and conduct sensitivity analysis. The first routine, the scheduler routine, is written in C++. It creates a (heuristically optimized) detailed equipment deployment schedule by allocating equipment to routes and then sequencing that equipment onto the transportation assets. The scheduler routine attempts to meet the required delivery dates (RDD) for all equipment. The second routine, the asset-route reallocation heuristic, is written in VB. It reallocates transportation assets to alternative routes in the deployment network to reduce the total time to close on the objective.

3.1. Military Application of the Tailored Job Shop Scheduler

DSAT takes the input information from the planner and generates a text file appropriate for the scheduler routine. The information passed includes the deployment routes, the facility restrictions of each port, the number and operating characteristics of each type transportation asset assigned to each route, and unit equipment data. The equipment data includes the delivery time window, start location, dimensions, and a vector listing the types of transportation assets on which the item fits.

Hodgson *et al.* [5] demonstrated that a conceptually simple simulation-based procedure (first proposed by Lawrence and Morton, 1986) is both effective and efficient in providing optimal or near optimal schedules for minimizing the maximum lateness ($L_{\max}$) in large job shops. Thoney [6] and Thoney *et al.* [7] report on the development of the military scheduling procedure based on scheduling networks of factories; this became DSAT's scheduling routine. Each item of unit equipment being deployed represents one "real" job to be scheduled (fake jobs are created as "space fillers" for the various transportation assets). Airports and seaports are "factories" through which a job must process. Transportation assets, "vehicles" operating on routes, are batch processors on which jobs move between "factories". Different asset types operating between the same two ports are considered different asset-routes. The procedure assigns the equipment to transportation asset-routes and then sequences the equipment onto the assets to minimize the worst case difference between the equipment arrival at destination and its required delivery date or RDD (i.e., schedule to minimize $L_{\max}$).

3.2. Scheduler Routine Heuristics

The scheduler routine incorporates two unique heuristics. These heuristics work together to allocate the jobs to the paths (sequence of asset-routes from origin to final destination) in an attempt to minimize the maximum lateness over all jobs. Jobs are presorted by due date. To minimize maximum lateness, the job to path allocation scheme attempts to schedule the jobs' arrival at the final destination by their due date. The initial allocation heuristic constructs the path that each job will travel over based on the average travel time to complete the path. The jobs are initially assigned to the path that is anticipated to be the fastest.

The reallocation heuristic makes use of information gained through simulating the previous allocation. In the simulation, as vehicles arrive and are unloaded at the base(s), arrival times are recorded. Jobs usually do not arrive in exact due-date order. Therefore, based on this information, jobs then are reallocated to paths according to actual arrival at the final destination. This process is repeated a set number of times. The best schedule is saved.

The amount of real time needed to create the equipment schedule varies according to the size and complexity of the deployment scenario. However, DSAT's scheduling engine creates the deployment schedule in minutes. For example, a two-division sized force (17,942 pieces of equipment) deployed by rail, sea, and air was scheduled in slightly over two minutes on a 700-megahertz PC.

3.3. Initial Allocation Heuristic

The initial allocation heuristic builds each job's path based on the structure of the deployment network. To build the paths, multiple passes through the network are required. During the first pass, a backward traverse of the network, the average "remaining time" from each base to the final destination is computed using all possible paths. During the next passes of the network, forward traverses, each job at the current base, Base i, is allocated to a vehicle (deployment transportation asset) that has the earliest anticipated final destination arrival time and can accommodate the job.

At each base, the jobs are sorted in due date order. Once the job reaches the next destination in the path, it is inserted into the list of jobs at that base. Job scheduling at Base i cannot begin until all jobs at bases preceding Base i have been scheduled. Then all jobs scheduled to move through Base i are on Base i's job list, and job allocation at that base can now begin. The anticipated final destination arrival time of jobs allocated on a vehicle is the vehicle's "job time" plus the average remaining time to reach the final destination base from that location. The "job time" is the amount of time needed to load and unload the vehicle in addition to the one-way travel time needed to reach the vehicle's assigned destination. The earliest that subsequent trips for each vehicle can start is after the vehicle returns to its origin base.

In the deployment network, multiple asset types can operate between the same two ports. Each asset type operating on such a route is called a center; each center has a number of vehicles operating on that route. The following additional definitions are necessary for both the initial and the reallocation heuristics.

- N number of jobs
- U_i area of Job i
- W_i weight of Job i
- V_i volume of Job i
- Q_i current path (in terms of centers) of Job i
- B_{il} Boolean value indicating if Job i can be placed on Center l
- M number of centers
- m_j number of vehicles within Center j
- $\mathrm{TU}j$ total area capacity of each vehicle in Center j if j is a ship, otherwise $\mathrm{TU}_j = -1$
- TW_j total weight capacity of each vehicle in Center j
- TV_j total volume capacity of each vehicle in Center j, if j is a not a ship, otherwise $\mathrm{TV}_j = -1$
- K_j vehicle type of Center j
- J_j time job spends on a vehicle from Center j (load time + one way travel time + unload time)
- H_j time to complete return trip of vehicle from Center j (maintenance time + one way travel time + maintenance time)
- T trip number of a vehicle
- R_b average remaining time from Base b to the final destination base
- A_{jm} the anticipated final destination arrival time if a job is scheduled on the mth trip of a vehicle in Center j
- D_j destination base of Center j
- $C(b)$ set of centers originating at Base b
- $L(b)$ set of jobs currently located at Base b
- $F(b)$ set of fake jobs currently located at Base b

Note the conditional definitions of TU_j and TV_j. The scheduler routine maintains information concerning the weight and area capacities for all ships throughout the simulation. The scheduler also maintains information concerning the weight and volume capacities for all other types of transportation assets (trains and planes).

The first trip of a vehicle in Center j is anticipated to arrive at the final destination at time $A_{j1} = J_j + R_{Dj}$. The second trip of a vehicle in Center j is anticipated to arrive at the final destination at time $A_{j2} = J_j + H_j + J_j + R_{Dj}$. Consequently, the Tth trip of a vehicle in Center j is expected to arrive at time $A_{jT} = T(J_j) + (T-1)H_j + R_{Dj}$. The average remaining time from Base b to the final destination base is 0 if b is the final destination base, otherwise it is calculated as

$$R_b = \frac{\sum_{x \in C(b)} m_x \left(J_x + R_{D_x}\right)}{\sum_{x \in C(b)} m_x}.$$

The algorithm for the initial allocation heuristic has three parts; each part is carried out for every base. The first part involves creating a list of vehicle nodes sorted in increasing order of anticipated arrival time at the final destination. There is one vehicle node list created for each base. Let node (s, t, u, v, w) be a vehicle node where s is the anticipated arrival time at the final destination, t is the center number, u is the available area capacity, v is the available volume capacity, and w is the available weight capacity. For each vehicle, one node is placed on the list representing its first arrival at the final destination. The first part of the heuristic (the backward traverse) is detailed as follows.

For each Base b:
- For each $j \in C(b)$: (for each center operating at Base b)
  - Step 1. Calculate A_{j1}
  - Step 2. Set vehicle k within Center j equal to 1
  - Step 3. Insert node $(A_{j1}, j, \mathrm{TU}_j, \mathrm{TV}_j, \mathrm{TW}_j)$ on the vehicle node list
  - Step 4. if $k < m_j$, set k to $k+1$, go to Step 3
- Next Center j

Next Base b

The completion of this part of the initial allocation heuristic results in a vehicle node list at each base sorted in increasing order of anticipated arrival times at the final destination. A node for each vehicle in each center is placed on this list. Each entry details the cargo's first anticipated arrival time at the final destination, the center number, and the vehicle's available capacities. This provides a structure for initially assigning jobs to vehicles based on the job due dates.

The second part of the initial allocation heuristic (a forward pass) allocates the real jobs to the vehicles and adds subsequent vehicle trips on the vehicle node list as necessary. This part's algorithm is as follows.

For each Base b: (starting at origin base)
- For each $i \in \{L(b) - F(b)\}$: (for each real job at Base b)
  - Step 1. Scan vehicle node list from beginning; find the first node (s, t, u, v, w) simultaneously satisfying the following conditions:
    - $Ui \le u$ (if $u \ne -1$) (job area fits into remaining vehicle area capacity)
    - $Vi \le v$ (if $v \ne -1$) (job volume fits into remaining vehicle volume capacity)
    - $Wi \le w$ (job weight fits into remaining vehicle weight capacity)
    - $B_{it} = \text{True}$ (Job i fits on Center t)

    If no such node exists, go to the next real job.
  - Step 2. If $u = \mathrm{TU}_j$, and $v = \mathrm{TV}_j$, and $w = \mathrm{TW}_j$, insert node $(s + J_t + H_t, t, \mathrm{TU}_t, \mathrm{TV}_t, \mathrm{TW}_t)$ on list (create next trip)
  - Step 3. For the node found in Step 1, let $u = u - U_i$ (if $u \ne -1$), $v = v - V_i$ (if $v \ne -1$) and $w = w - W_i$. (decrement remaining capacities)
  - Step 4. Let $Q_i = Q_i + \{t\}$ (augment current path with Center t)

Step 5. Set $L(D_t) = L(D_t) + \{i\}$ (insert job on job list at next destination)
Next i
Next b

This part of the initial allocation heuristic assigns each job to move on a specific center vehicle. If the job fits into the remaining volume (or area) and weight capacities of the vehicle and is compatible with the center, then that job is allocated to that vehicle. If the vehicle is empty, a subsequent trip for that vehicle is added to the vehicle node list (Step 2), while the remaining capacities of the vehicle for its current trip are decremented (Step 3). The path of the job is updated to indicate job travel on that center (Step 4). Finally, the job is added to the job list at the center's destination base (Step 5). Any job that does not fit into any vehicle originating at that base is essentially removed from that base's job list. These jobs are assigned a path at the end of the initial allocation heuristic. This results in each job having a specific path built for it. The path is expressed as the sequence of centers the job travels on to get from its origin to its final destination.

In creating the initial job to path allocation, the initial allocation heuristic could over- or under-utilize a particular path. This situation, in turn, reduces the options available to the reallocation procedure that shifts jobs to alternate paths. To alleviate this problem, *fake jobs* are created for each path. These fake jobs have very low priority (i.e., their due dates are much later than real job due dates). Allocating these fake jobs to paths creates additional path arrival times at the final destination. Thus, the reallocation procedure has more options available for all paths in considering job rerouting. Consequently, the third part of the initial allocation heuristic creates the fake jobs and their paths. Once again, the bases are treated individually, traversing in a forward manner. One fake job, i, is initially placed at each origin base with $U_i = V_i = W_i = \infty$. The procedure is as follows.

for each Base b:
  for each $i \in F(b)$: (for each fake job)
    Step 1. Let temp = 0
    for each $j \in C(b)$: (for each center)
      Step 2. set temp = temp + 1
      If temp $\neq |C(b)|$ (if temp $\neq$ number of centers at base)
        Step 3. Create a fake job, d
        Step 4. Let $Q_d = Q_i + \{j\}$
        Step 5. If $\text{TU}_j \neq -1$, let $U_d = \min\{U_i, \text{TU}_j\}$,
          If $\text{TV}_j \neq -1$, let $V_d = \min\{V_i, \text{TV}_j\}$,
          Let $W_d = \min\{W_i, \text{TW}_j\}$
        Step 6. Let $L(D_j) = L(D_j) + \{d\}$
      Else
        Step 7. Let $Q_i = Q_i + \{j\}$
        Step 8. If $\text{TU}_j \neq -1$, let $U_i = \min\{U_i, \text{TU}_j\}$,
          If $\text{TV}_j \neq -1$, let $V_i = \min\{V_i, \text{TV}_j\}$,
          Let $W_i = \min\{W_i, \text{TW}_j\}$
        Step 9. Let $L(D_j) = L(D_j) + \{i\}$
      End if
    Next j
  Next i
Next b

When this procedure is complete, each path has one fake job assigned to it that has the maximum possible weight and volume a job can have if it is allocated to that path. The assignment of fake jobs to paths is done in both Steps 3–6 and Steps 7–9. Steps 3–6 basically clone each fake job that is currently at the base. The cloned jobs are assigned to the same path taken by the current fake job in arriving at the current base. Then each of the cloned jobs is designated for transport by a unique center at the current base. Steps 7–9 assign the last fake job for transport by the remaining center.

After this procedure is complete, the smallest possible area, volume, and weight over all of the paths are found. Each fake job is then cloned 50 times and the clones' area, volume, and weight are set equal to these smallest values. The purpose for having 50 smaller jobs and one large job on each path is to help ensure that at least one extra trip is created for each vehicle on the path and that remaining capacity on partially filled "final" trips of vehicles in all centers are completely filled with fake jobs. The purpose of this is to produce additional arrival times at the destination for each path; this provides the reallocation procedure more options in rescheduling jobs. In forming the reallocation list, blocks are created from aggregating job capacity regardless if a job is real or fake. In contrast, only the real jobs are rescheduled into the blocks. The fake jobs have a fixed path.

The final part of this heuristic creates paths for real jobs that have not yet been allocated. Each remaining real job is compared with the fake jobs (each fake job has a fixed path) until a compatible path is found. The real job is then allocated to that path.

3.4. The Reallocation Heuristic

Once the jobs are scheduled by the initial allocation heuristic, that job allocation is simulated by the scheduler routine. Information is gathered on the actual arrival times of each job to the final destination. Each time a job arrives at the final destination, its area, volume, and weight are added to the aggregate area, volume, and weight of jobs that already arrived by way of the same path at the same time. The arrival time information is thus used to create blocks of used capacity that arrive at the final destination at given times. The reallocation heuristic reschedules the jobs (sorted in order of increasing due dates) to these blocks of used capacity sorted in increasing order of final destination arrival time.

The reallocation heuristic has two parts. Each part is performed once. The first part involves developing a list of used capacity blocks during the simulation sorted in increasing order of final destination arrival times. The second part of the heuristic entails the actual reallocation of the jobs to the vehicles. The reallocation heuristic uses many of the terms defined for the initial allocation heuristic, but several additional terms are defined next. Let block (s, t, u, v, w) be a used-capacity block where s is the final destination arrival time, t is the tth arrival at time s, u is the current used area capacity, v is the current used volume capacity, and w is the current used weight capacity for the block. The following additional definitions are also necessary.

P_{qr} current path (in terms of centers) of the rth block arriving at time q
$E(s)$ set of jobs arriving at the final destination at time s
NB_s total number of blocks arrived at time s

The first part of this heuristic records the final destination arrival times and aggregates certain used capacities into blocks of used-capacities. It is detailed as follows:

Step 1. Let x be the first time in which at least one job arrives at the final destination.
Step 2. Set NB_x equal to 1. (initialize total number of blocks arriving at time x)
Step 3. For each $i \in E(x)$: (for each job that arrives at the final destination at time x)
- a. Search list of all blocks (s, t, u, v, w), where $s = x$ to see if $P_{st} = Q_i$ for any t (find a block arriving at time x with the same path as Job i).
- b. If a block exists at some t (number of arrival, not time), let $u = u + U_i$ (if $u \neq -1$), let $v = v + V_i$ (if $v \neq -1$) and let $w = w + W_i$. Otherwise increment NB_x by 1 and add block $(x, \text{NB}_x, U_i, V_i, W_i)$ to the list.

next i

Step 4. If all jobs are not at the final destination, let x be the next time at least one job arrives at the final destination and go to Step 2.

The result of this first part of the reallocation heuristic is a list of used capacity blocks sorted in increasing arrival time at the final destination. Each used capacity block is then inflated by 20%; i.e., the used area, volume, and weight are increased by 20%. The purpose of this inflation is to reduce the amount of unused capacity on the blocks' path in preparation for the eventual job rescheduling.

The second part of the algorithm performs the rescheduling of the real jobs (sorted in increasing due date order) onto the identified used-capacity blocks. If a real job cannot be rescheduled, it remains on its current path. The fake jobs always keep their initial path. The second part of the heuristic is as follows.

Step 1. Set the job, i, equal to 1. (current job to be scheduled)

Step 2. Search the list of blocks to find the first block (s, t, u, v, w) that simultaneously satisfies the following conditions:

block has same origin base as Job i

$U_i \leq u$ (if $u \neq -1$) (job fits into remaining used area capacity)

$V_i \leq v$ (if $v \neq -1$) (job fits into remaining used volume capacity)

$W_i \leq w$ (job fits into remaining used weight capacity)

$B_{ik} =$ True $\forall\, k$ in P_{st} (job fits onto all centers in path)

Step 3. If no such block exists, go to Step 6, otherwise, go to Step 4.

Step 4. If $u \neq -1$, let $u = u - U_i$. If $v \neq -1$, let $v = v - V_i$. Let $w = w - W_i$ (decrement remaining block capacities)

Step 5. Let $Q_i = P_{st}$ (redesignate path for Job i)

Step 6. If $i < N$, increment i by 1 and go to Step 2.

This results in jobs being reassigned to paths based on previously demonstrated performance, i.e., final destination arrival time established by the previous deployment simulation. Note, during the simulation, vehicles are loaded and unloaded at bases. No vehicle is loaded beyond its user-defined capacities for weight and volume or area.

3.5. Redefining the Asset-Route Allocation

The assignment of jobs (equipment) to assets produced by the scheduling routine is limited by the fixed allocation of transportation assets to routes used in DSAT. The transportation asset-

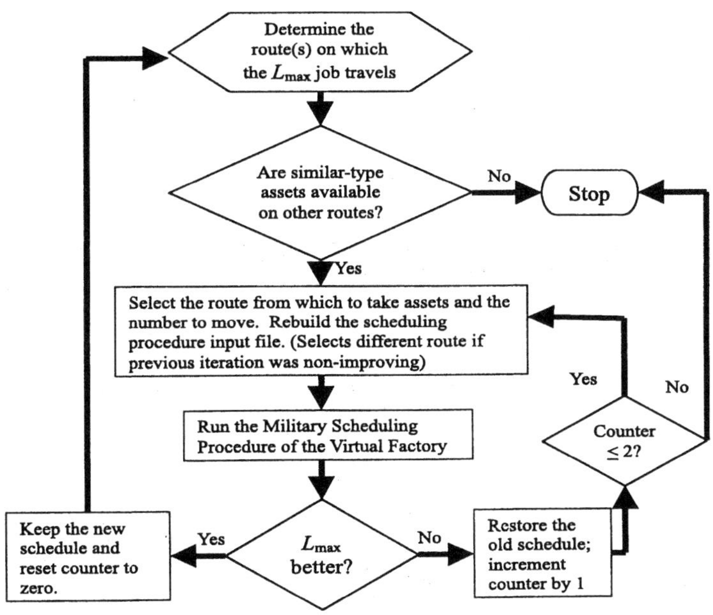

Figure 11. Asset-route reallocation heuristic.

route allocation, input by the planner, may not necessarily be the best possible. The user has the option to activate a heuristic procedure that reallocates assets seeking to find an improved schedule.

The basic concept of this procedure is to shift underutilized transportation assets to the route(s) on which the latest pieces of equipment move. By adding capacity to these "late job" route(s), congestion and possible queuing experienced by the equipment may be reduced, leading to an improved schedule in terms of better satisfying the RDDs (i.e., a lower $L_{\max}$ value). It can be time-consuming (approximately five minutes for a two brigade-sized deploying force) due to the supporting calculations needed; this heuristic is limited to a maximum of three iterations. The logic of this heuristic is shown in the flowchart depicted in Figure 11.

4. OUTPUT AND SENSITIVITY ANALYSIS

The interface screen displayed in Figure 12 provides information on deploying unit closure at the final destination and transportation asset use on each route. The top part of the screen provides unit closure results. The bottom table provides data concerning transportation asset-route utilization. The top right portion of the screen shows the aggregate closure information. In this example, the deployment of 40 units with a total of 9,762 items of equipment was completed in $C + 47$ days (C day is the ALD) with 26 units arriving beyond their specified RDD. The top table provides a row for each unit with its actual closure date. If a unit did not close by its RDD, the information is presented in red.

The user can choose to look at detailed results of the current schedule or can conduct sensitivity analysis by modifying the scenario and rescheduling the deployment. To analyze the results of the current schedule, the user can look at various graphs depicting the weight or volume utilization history for a specific asset-route couple or view various reports concerning asset schedules, unit

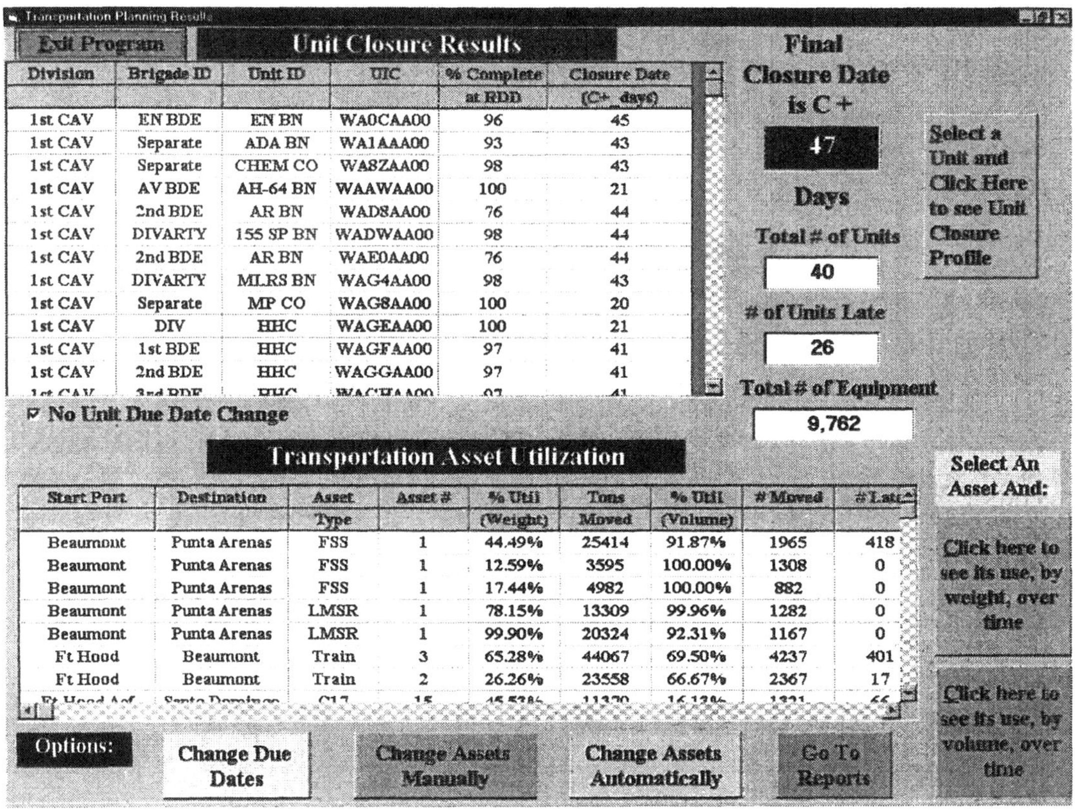

Figure 12. Output of DSAT scheduling results.

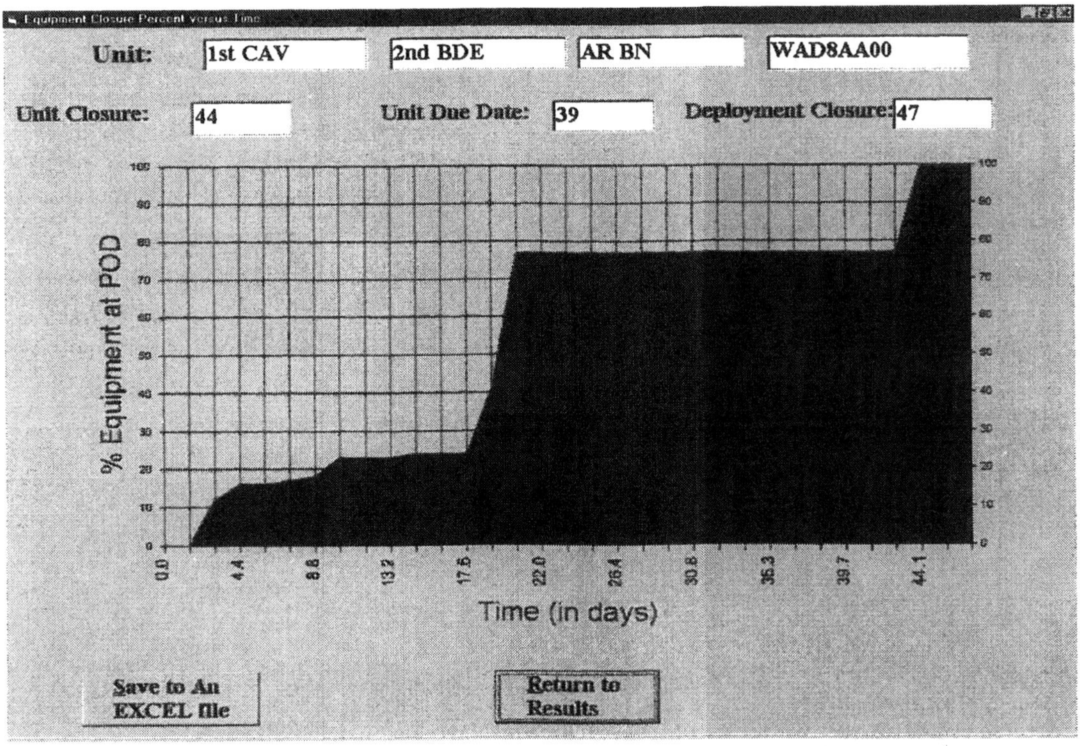

Figure 13. Example unit closure graph.

closure profiles, etc. To perform sensitivity analysis, the user can modify the scenario by changing unit due dates or the transportation asset-route allocation and reschedule the deployment to determine the impact of the change(s).

DSAT graphically represents the arrival of units to the final destination over time. A unit's closure profile can be generated for any unit selected from the top table in Figure 12. An example is provided in Figure 13. The graph is calculated simply by summing the weight of unit equipment delivered to the port of debarkation (POD) at specific time intervals. The graph displays the timing of unit equipment arrival to the POD along with pertinent unit and closure information. All graphs may be saved for future use in a Microsoft EXCEL© file.

4.1. Utilization of Transportation Assets

The bottom table in Figure 12 provides key information on the use of transportation assets. Each row represents the assets assigned to a particular route. For example, row one of the table represents one fast sealift ship moving cargo from Beaumont, TX, to Punta Arenas, Chile. Each ship sailing between the same origin and destination represents one route since each ship tends to have unique operating characteristics. Figure 12 shows five ships sailing between Beaumont and Punta Arenas. Planes and railcars of the same type have the same operating characteristics; multiple assets of the same type moving between the same origin and destination represent one route. Rows six and seven of Figure 12 show a total of five trains hauling cargo from Fort Hood, TX, to the seaport at Beaumont; the different listings indicate different types of railcars used for each group of trains.

A key measure of effectiveness for the deployment schedule is the utilization of the transportation assets. After the scheduling procedure is complete, DSAT calculates the utilization of all assets on each route. First, the total amount of weight moved over a specific route is computed and displayed as depicted in Figure 12. Next, based on the operating characteristics of each asset type operating on a route, the possible number of roundtrips completed by a single asset is computed. The asset-route weight utilization percentage reflects the average percentage of asset

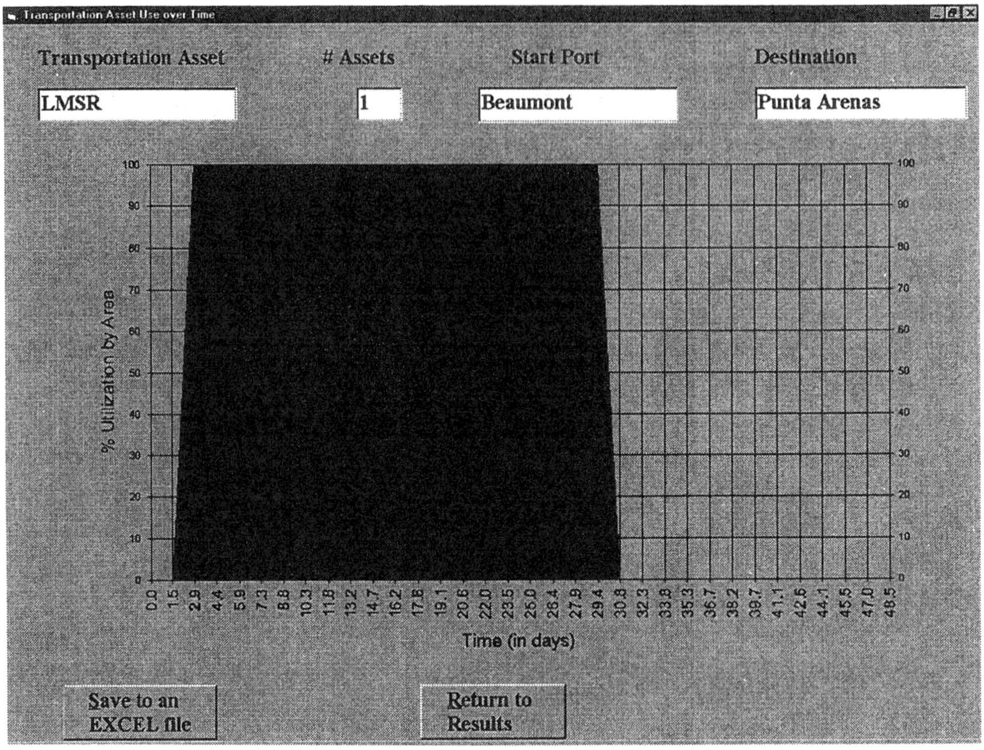

Figure 14. Example graph of ship loading area utilization.

weight capacity utilized in each trip, assuming that all assets assigned to the route completed the maximum possible number of roundtrips. The volume utilization percentage is computed similarly. The "volume" utilization for ships is actually the utilization of the ship's loading area since the capacity of ships used for moving military equipment is normally expressed in terms of surface loading area. The weight and volume (area for ships) utilization of assets on each route is listed in the bottom table of Figure 12. Graphs are generated for the user to view the utilization of assets on a route over time. An example is provided in Figure 14. This graph represents the utilization of the surface loading area of one light-medium ship, roll-on, roll-off (LMSR). The surface area, adjusted for necessary tie-down equipment, was effectively 100% utilized by the equipment loaded on this ship from the scheduling procedure.

4.2. Data Reports of Deployment Information

Deployment planners need information on the schedule of unit equipment movement and transportation asset use in an understandable format. DSAT generates several reports that planners can view, print, and/or save. The data displayed in these reports is generated through database queries and by using the output information from the scheduling routine. A sample of the deploying unit information report is provided in Figure 15. A brief description of each report is provided below.

- *Deployment schedule by unit* details how a unit moved from its start base to the POD(s). If any items of equipment were on a particular transportation asset, the unit's UIC is listed along with the C-date/time the asset started loading and when the asset completed unloading at its destination. The asset name and number are also provided.
- *Deployment schedule by unit and item of equipment* details how each item of equipment in each unit moved from its start base to the POD(s). The C-date/time when loading begins, the origin, destination, C-date/time when unloading is complete, and the transportation asset name and number are provided for each movement an item of equipment makes.

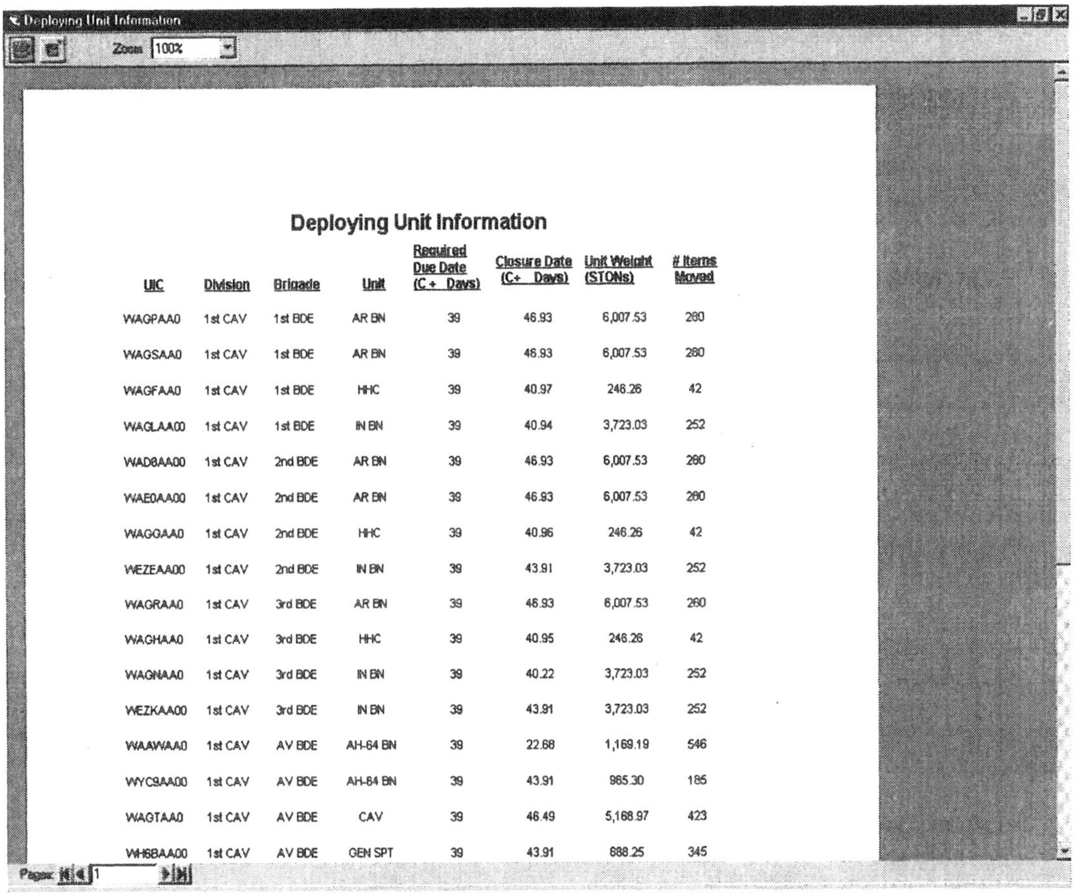

Deploying Unit Information

UIC	Division	Brigade	Unit	Required Due Date (C+ Days)	Closure Date (C+ Days)	Unit Weight (STONs)	# Items Moved
WAGPAA0	1st CAV	1st BDE	AR BN	39	46.93	6,007.53	280
WAGSAA0	1st CAV	1st BDE	AR BN	39	46.93	6,007.53	280
WAGFAA0	1st CAV	1st BDE	HHC	39	40.97	246.26	42
WAGLAA00	1st CAV	1st BDE	IN BN	39	40.94	3,723.03	252
WAD8AA00	1st CAV	2nd BDE	AR BN	39	46.93	6,007.53	280
WAE0AA00	1st CAV	2nd BDE	AR BN	39	46.93	6,007.53	280
WAGGAA0	1st CAV	2nd BDE	HHC	39	40.96	246.26	42
WEZEAA00	1st CAV	2nd BDE	IN BN	39	43.91	3,723.03	252
WAGRAA0	1st CAV	3rd BDE	AR BN	39	46.93	6,007.53	280
WAGHAA0	1st CAV	3rd BDE	HHC	39	40.95	246.26	42
WAGNAA0	1st CAV	3rd BDE	IN BN	39	40.22	3,723.03	252
WEZKAA00	1st CAV	3rd BDE	IN BN	39	43.91	3,723.03	252
WAAWAA0	1st CAV	AV BDE	AH-64 BN	39	22.68	1,169.19	546
WYC9AA00	1st CAV	AV BDE	AH-64 BN	39	43.91	965.30	185
WAGTAA0	1st CAV	AV BDE	CAV	39	46.49	5,168.97	423
WH6BAA00	1st CAV	AV BDE	GEN SPT	39	43.91	888.25	345

Figure 15. Sample deploying unit information report.

- *Transportation asset schedule* chronologically lists the C-date/time of each load and unload activity for each transportation asset used in the deployment.
- *Transportation asset input and use information* lists the key operating characteristics for each type of transportation asset used in the deployment as well as the total weight carried by each asset type and its percent utilization by both volume and weight.
- *Deploying unit information* details the required delivery date (RDD), actual closure date, total weight of unit equipment (in STons), and number of equipment items for each unit.
- *Port information* lists the port facility input characteristics, e.g., the MOG and number of runways for an airport and the amount of cargo processed through the port (STons).
- *Items needing special rail clearance* lists any items of equipment detected as exceeding the dimensions of railcars chosen during the feasibility checks.
- *Equipment removed from deployment.* If the feasibility checks identify equipment not fitting on any transportation asset selected, the user can elect to remove those items from the deploying equipment list. Details on these items are in this report.

5. CONCLUSIONS

DSAT is a personal computer-based deployment planning tool that provides maximum flexibility to deployment planners. Deployment planners can model various deployment scenarios and rapidly create readable "optimal" deployment schedules and conduct valuable sensitivity analysis of various aspects of the deployment problem. DSAT occupies an important niche in the realm of existing deployment planning tools. It quickly provides the detailed information needed to create a deployment schedule. DSAT also provides the processing speed necessary for sensitivity analysis not provided by more detailed scheduling models.

REFERENCES

1. MTMCTEA, Modeling and simulation, `http://www.tea.army.mil/dpe/modeling.html`, (2000).
2. T.J. Hodgson, O. Spivey, T.E. Trainor and M.K. Williams, The deployment analysis network tool enhanced (DANTE), *Military Operations Research* **6** (3), (2001).
3. J. Illingworth, A simulation based modeling of military transportation applications: A combat logistics and scheduling system for deployment of United States Armed Forces worldwide, Unpublished Masters' Thesis, North Carolina State University, (1999).
4. T.E. Trainor, Scheduling military deployments, Unpublished Ph.D. Dissertation, North Carolina State University, (2001).
5. T.J. Hodgson, D. Cormier, A.J. Weintraub and A. Zozom, Satisfying due dates in large job shops, *Management Science* **44** (10), 1442–1446, (1998).
6. K.A. Thoney, Scheduling batch processing machines in job shop scenarios, Unpublished Ph.D. Dissertation, North Carolina State University, (2000).
7. K.A. Thoney, T.J. Hodgson, R.E. King, M. Taner and A. Wilson, Satisfying due-dates in large multi-factory supply chains, *IIE Transactions* **34** (9), (2002).
8. R.W. Sinnott, Virtues of the haversine, *Sky and Telescope* **68** (2), (1984).
9. E. Williams, Aviation formulary V1.30, `http://www.best.com/~williams/avform.htm#GCF`, (2001).
10. C. North, Lat/lon to distance!, `http://home.eol.ca/~cnorth/frame_11.html`, (2001).
11. R.G. Chamberlain, Calculating distances on the surface of the Earth, `http://www.census.gov/cgi-bin/geo/gisfaq?Q5.1`, (1996).
12. A. Greer and D. Hancox, *Tables, Data and Formulae for Engineers and Mathematicians*, Stanley Thornes, (1991).
13. Department of Defense Almanac, Unified combatant commands, `http://www.defenselink.mil/pubs/almanac/unified.html`, (2001).
14. B.S. Melendez, On scheduling delivery in a military deployment scenario, Unpublished Ph.D. Dissertation, North Carolina State University, (2002).

Available online at www.sciencedirect.com
SCIENCE @ DIRECT®
Mathematical and Computer Modelling 39 (2004) 925–943
MATHEMATICAL AND COMPUTER MODELLING
www.elsevier.com/locate/mcm

Network Design Formulations for Scheduling U.S. Air Force Channel Route Missions

C. A. NIELSEN*
Air Force Studies and Analyses Agency
1570 Air Force Pentagon
Washington, DC 20330-1570, U.S.A.
cnielsen@alum.mit.edu

A. P. ARMACOST*
United States Air Force Academy, Department of Management
2354 Fairchild Drive, Rm. 6H128, USAF Academy, CO 80840, U.S.A.
andy.armacost@usafa.edu

C. BARNHART
Massachusetts Institute of Technology
Center for Transportation and Logistics
77 Massachusetts Avenue, Bldg. E40-149, Cambridge, MA 02139, U.S.A.
cbarnhar@mit.edu

S. E. KOLITZ
The Charles Stark Draper Laboratory, Inc.
555 Technology Square, Cambridge, MA 02139, U.S.A.
kolitz@draper.com

Abstract—Each month, the United States Air Force's Air Mobility Command is responsible for designing a large-scale air mobility network—called the *channel route network*—that is used to transport military personnel and cargo throughout the world. Traditionally, planning the channel route network has been a manual process, requiring numerous hours to generate a monthly channel route schedule. We formulate the monthly channel route scheduling problem using a traditional network design formulation, and we use price-directive decomposition to overcome tractability issues. The resulting linear programming bounds on the optimal integer solution are weak. To overcome these challenges, we apply a variable redefinition technique known as *composite variable* modelling. Using this technique, we alleviate the need to explicitly include cargo flow decisions by implicitly capturing them in the design variables. The resulting formulation is computationally superior to the traditional network design formulation because it achieves tighter bounds, allowing excellent integer solutions to be found quickly.

Keywords—Composite variables, Airlift, Large-scale optimization, Mixed-integer programming, Network design.

*As members of the Air Force, we acknowledge that the views expressed in this paper are ours and do not reflect the official policy or position of the United States Air Force, the Department of Defense, or the United States Government.

0895-7177/04/$ - see front matter Typeset by AMS-TEX
doi:10.1016/j.mcm.2004.02.022

1. INTRODUCTION

The United States military logistics system is crucial for success during contingency operations and times of conflict. Equally important, the posture of the military logistics system during peacetime ensures that military personnel around the world have the resources required to maintain a high level of readiness.

Attaining a superior peacetime logistics system is a daunting task. The logistics system is a large-scale, complex system that involves many detailed, interrelated decisions, processes, and organizations. A critical component of the military logistics system is the defense transportation system (DTS), which includes air, land, and sea modes of transportation. The United States Air Mobility Command (AMC)—one of three transportation component commands (TCCs) within the United States Transportation Command (USTRANSCOM)—is responsible for air transportation, or air mobility. To fulfill its mission, AMC—namely, the Tanker Airlift Control Center (TACC)—must manage a large, complex air mobility network.

A key component of the air mobility network is the *channel route network*. This network is used to move cargo and personnel between military installations located throughout the world on a predictable, recurring basis. For each calendar month, channel route schedulers are responsible for determining the set of aircraft missions that will fly during the month so that all demanded cargo and personnel are delivered. We refer to this as the *monthly channel route scheduling problem*, which has historically been a manual process requiring many time-consuming iterations to generate a single channel route schedule.

In this paper, we introduce optimization models to quickly and effectively design the channel route network (i.e., generate a monthly channel route schedule) and to provide a method by which channel route schedulers can generate and evaluate several, rather than a single, candidate channel route structures. The major contributions of this paper are as follows.

- We derive a mixed-integer network design formulation for the channel route scheduling problem and explore its computational benefits and pitfalls.
- We recast the network design formulation as a pure integer program using a variable redefinition approach known as *composite variable modelling*.
- We demonstrate the computational superiority of the composite variable formulation across a variety of planning scenarios.

2. CHANNEL ROUTES AND THE CURRENT PLANNING SYSTEM

The *channel route network* consists of *cargo items*, *aerial ports*, *aircraft*, and *aircrews*. In this paper, we focus on the portion of the channel route network used to transport cargo. The term *channel route* refers to the purpose and the general sequence of stops made by an aircraft. There are two types of channel routes, *requirements channel routes* and *frequency channel routes*. Requirements channel routes are demand driven, initiated when enough cargo exists to warrant an aircraft mission be flown. Frequency channel routes, on the other hand, are driven by a frequency-of-service requirement (e.g., an aircraft must visit location A twice per month). Frequency channel routes are often created to service out-of-the-way locations for which the amount of cargo demanded would never trigger a requirements channel route. When a specific aircraft type and timing (i.e., takeoff and landing times at each aerial in the sequence of stops) are assigned to a channel route we refer to it as a *channel route mission*.

2.1. Cargo Items

Nearly all cargo moved via channel route missions can be loaded on standard cargo pallets. All cargo items with a common origin and destination can be aggregated into a single *cargo commodity* to determine the total number of short tons that must be moved between the two locations.

Channel route cargo can follow various paths as it flows through the channel route network. In this paper, we focus on the movement of cargo from its origin aerial port—the aerial port of embarkation (APOE)—to its destination aerial port—the aerial port of debarkation (APOD). At the APOE, cargo is palletized, and onloaded to an aircraft. The cargo is flown either directly to the APOD, or through one or more enroute aerial ports prior to reaching the APOD, located outside the continental United States (OCONUS). At enroute aerial ports, additional cargo—whose destination is a downstream aerial port—can be onloaded to an aircraft.

2.2. Aerial Ports

Aerial ports are the physical locations where cargo is consolidated from distribution warehouses and where aircraft land, take off, onload/offload cargo, and refuel. Aerial ports contain runways, ramp space for aircraft parking and servicing, cargo holding facilities, cargo loading equipment, fuel storage, and aircraft fuel trucks. The number of servicing resources available at an aerial port determines the number of aircraft that can be serviced, referred to as the maximum on ground (MOG). Aerial port capacity is an important planning consideration. There are, however, aircraft missions other than channel route missions that share aerial port facilities. Consequently, MOG is not rigorously considered in the context of the monthly channel route scheduling problem we consider in this paper. Rather, channel route planners consider MOG limitations three or four days prior to the start of a channel route mission.

Cargo warehouses located at aerial ports have extremely large capacity and rarely ever approach maximum capacity during peacetime. As a result, channel route planners do not consider aerial port warehouse capacity when creating a channel route schedule.

Some aerial ports also serve as the squadron base (i.e., home base) for one or more aircraft types and aircrews. Aircraft and aircrews must start and end all aircraft missions at their assigned squadron base. In addition, each aerial port has time windows which limit the times aircraft can arrive and depart from the aerial port.

2.3. Aircraft

The aircraft used to operate channel route missions come from four sources: Air Force active duty, Air Force Reserves, Air National Guard, and commercial carriers that are *Civil Reserve Air Fleet* (CRAF) participants.

Active duty, Reserve, and Air National Guard aircraft and aircrews are organized into aircraft wings. An aircraft wing consists of one or more aircraft squadrons, each consisting of a single aircraft type and associated aircrews. Thirty days prior to a given calendar month, the aircraft wings will allocate a portion of the aircraft and aircrews in each aircraft squadron for the TACC's use. These aircraft and aircrews provide an upper limit on the number of aircraft and aircrews that can be assigned by the TACC to fly channel route missions, as well as other AMC missions.

Each aircraft has different capabilities, including cargo capacity, maximum flying range, and cruising speed. We use the average flight time for a specific aircraft type between two locations, calculated from a database consisting of actual flight times from all past AMC missions. Additionally, each aircraft has an associated minimum ground time, reflecting the minimum allowed turn-time between aircraft missions.

President Truman established the Civil Reserve Air Fleet (CRAF) in 1951 to augment military airlift capabilities in wartime and national mobilization efforts. In the CRAF program, commercial carriers pledge a certain percentage of their aircraft fleet and aircrews for military use when the President activates the CRAF program.

Although commercial carriers do not receive money for the aircraft they commit unless CRAF is activated, the number of aircraft that a carrier commits also earns the carrier peacetime bid points. These bid points can then be used to procure two types of peacetime contracts—*fixed-buy contracts* and *expansion-buy contracts*—which are offered exclusively to CRAF participants.

Fixed-buy contracts are offered annually and span an entire year (e.g., an aircraft flying the same route every Tuesday for an entire year), whereas expansion-buy contracts are offered at a moment's notice on a one-time basis.

2.4. Aircrews

Aircrews, like aircraft, have operating restrictions. Specifically, aircrews must not exceed the crew duty day (CDD) limit, which is the number of consecutive hours an aircrew can fly. It is typical for an aircrew to remain with an aircraft for an entire channel route mission.

There are two types of crews, basic aircrews and augmented aircrews. An augmented crew is a combination of two basic crews, which extends the aircrew's allowable CDD. There are a few select locations where aircrews have been prepositioned in order to quick-turn an aircraft. We leave the consideration of augmented and prepositioned crews for further research.

2.5. Current Scheduling Process

Currently, planning and scheduling channel route missions is a labor intensive, manual process that undergoes many time-consuming iterations before an implementable schedule is created. To deal with the overwhelming amount of information that must be incorporated into the channel route schedule, the scheduling process has traditionally disaggregated many highly related decisions. Specifically, *organic channel schedulers* determine the routing of channel route missions, *cargo bookies* assign cargo to channel route missions, and the *barrelmaster* determines the aircraft types that should operate the channel route missions. As a result of this disaggregated approach, the system-wide interactions and impact of tightly coupled planning decisions can only be evaluated on a limited scope, relying on planners' intuition and experience. In a system of this magnitude, intuition and experience do not always yield the optimal use of resources.

2.6. Research Motivation

Two key ideas motivate this research. First, manually creating and maintaining a channel route schedule is time consuming, leaving little or no time to analyze alternate channel route network structures. An automated approach can drastically reduce the time and effort required to generate a channel route schedule, allowing channel route planners to evaluate the system-wide effects of various solutions. Second, an optimization-based approach can simultaneously—rather than sequentially—consider all relevant inputs. Consequently, highly related decisions remain coupled during the scheduling process, yielding increased performance of the channel route network.

3. CONVENTIONAL NETWORK DESIGN APPROACHES

To represent the channel route network mathematically, we first represent the physical channel route network using a *time-space graph* (see [1,2] for examples of time-space graphs).

The time-space graph is constructed by creating a node for each aerial port during every time period in the planning horizon (see Figure 1). The planning horizon is the entire time period of interest, which is 30 days for the channel route scheduling problem. Each node in the time-space graph is indexed by an aerial port and a time period. For instance, the index (A, t) corresponds to aerial port A in time t. Directed arcs connect the nodes and represent cargo flows and aircraft movements through time and space. Specifically, *ground arcs* (represented by the dashed arcs in Figure 1) represent cargo and/or aircraft that remain at a given aerial port from time t to time $t+1$. Similarly, *flight arcs* (represented by solid arcs in Figure 1) represent cargo flows and aircraft movements through time between two different aerial ports. Finally, *wrap-around arcs* (represented by the dotted arcs in Figure 1) are used to ensure aircraft balance of flow.

The formulations in this paper use a time-space graph on which to design the *channel route schedule*, which specifies an initial sense of timing rather than precise timing, routing information

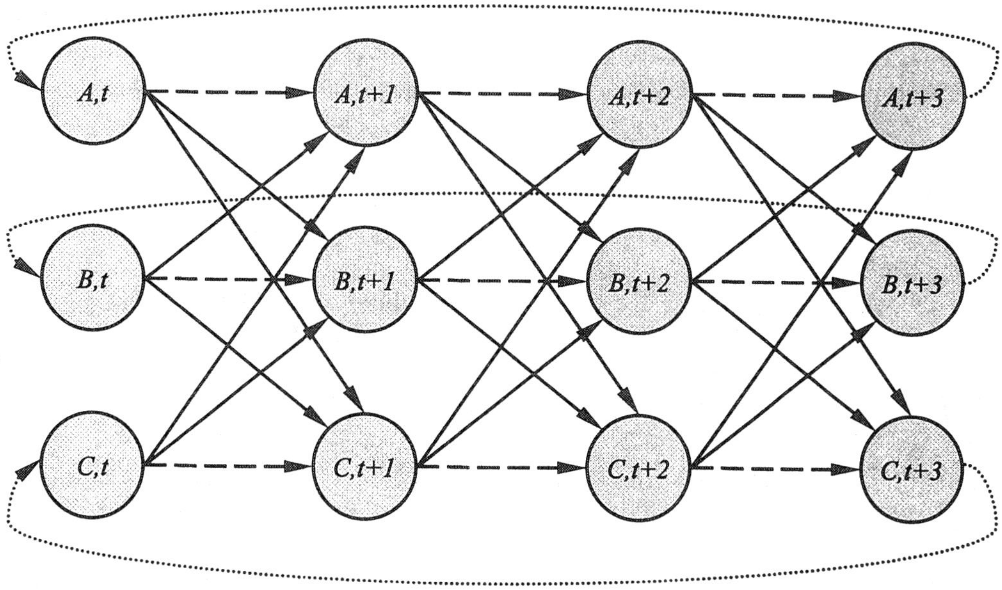

Figure 1. Example of a time-space graph.

for the cargo flows, and routing and execution details (e.g., onload/offload cargo, refuel, crew rest) for the aircraft movements.

3.1. Network Design Literature Review

At its core, the channel route scheduling problem is a *network design* problem. In network design problems, design decisions are made about on which arcs in the time-space graph to install aircraft capacity, thereby allowing flow of the cargo commodities. The use of network design problems to model transportation systems is common in the literature. Rather than providing an exhaustive literature review of network design problems, we point the reader to [3–5]. Magnanti and Wong [3] provide an extensive overview of network design problems, with an emphasis on transportation problems. Their research includes optimization models, heuristic methods, and algorithms. Gendron *et al.* [4] provide a comprehensive survey of models and algorithms for network design problems, with an emphasis on telecommunications and transportation applications. Armacost *et al.* [5] provide an overview of network design problems, express shipment service network design, and solution strategies.

3.2. Conventional Network Design Formulation and Decomposition

Initially, our approached focused on conventional network design formulations using path variables (for examples of traditional network design formulations, see [3–6]). Specifically, we investigated the use of two sets of path variables to formulate the problem. Cargo path variables represent the flow of cargo through the time-space graph. Aircraft route path variables represent the flow of aircraft through the time-space graph and are the design decisions that allocate capacity to arcs throughout the time-space graph. The drawback of path variables, however, is that there are many feasible cargo paths and aircraft routes, which results in an extremely large number of variables (i.e., columns). The large number of columns can be addressed, however, using price-directive decomposition and column generation.

We investigated a decomposition approach, based on price-directive decomposition (see [6,7]), aimed at improving the tractability of the traditional network design formulation (i.e., addressing the large number of variables).

In such a decomposition, *subproblems* identify candidate cargo paths and aircraft missions to be considered by a *master level scheduler*. Cargo path subproblems are formulated as pure shortest path problems (see [6]) and aircraft route subproblems are formulated as multilabel shortest path problems (see [8,9]). In general, multilabel shortest path problems take longer to solve than pure shortest path problems. For the channel route scheduling problem, however, the structure of the channel route network allows the multilabel shortest path subproblems to be solved quickly and efficiently.

We use a set of channel route missions from an existing real-world channel route schedule as an initial feasible solution to the master level scheduler. New columns are generated in the root node linear program (LP) until a predetermined stopping criterion is met (e.g., maximum time, maximum number of restricted master level scheduler iterations). To obtain an optimal integer solution, we apply a heuristic technique presented by Barnhart *et al.* [10] in which column generation is used only at the root node in the branch-and-bound tree and the remainder of the branch-and-bound tree is solved using a standard branch-and-bound algorithm with the set of columns determined at the root node.

To illustrate the drawbacks of conventional network design approaches and to motivate the following section, we test such a decomposition approach using a small data set. The small data set consists of 30 aerial ports, five aircraft types, 254 cargo commodities, 19 frequency requirements, and eight commercial fixed-buy missions. The data set spans a seven-day planning horizon and each day is split into two, 12-hour time periods.

The decomposition procedure was terminated after a maximum number of master level scheduler iterations, and the branch-and-bound algorithm was terminated at the first integer solution. The problem was solved using a Pentium-III 550 MHZ processor and 256 megabytes of random access memory (RAM). The shortest path algorithms were coded as separate functions in C++ and the commercial optimization software XPress-MP [11] was used to solve the master level scheduler. Additionally, the presolve, automatic cut generation, and auto perturbation optimization solver options were turned on. The results are summarized in Table 1.

Table 1. Computational results for small data set using decomposition.

Max Iterations Allowed	175	200	275
Rows	11,694	11,694	11,694
Initial Columns	7,403	7,403	7,403
Additional Columns	32,888	37,588	49,620
Time to First Integer Solution (secs)	5,239	5,386	29,820
Integer Solution—Number of Aircraft	82	67	65
Best Bound	47.289	46.005	41.799
LP-IP Gap	42%	31%	36%

Table 1 illustrates the weak LP-relaxations, especially given the cut generation employed by the optimization solver. In addition to a weak LP-relaxation, the traditional network design formulation does not accurately capture the real-world channel route system. A more accurate representation of the real-world system requires more time periods per day and the consideration of the complex operational rules and regulations that govern the aircraft and aircrews (e.g., crew rest, minimum ground time). However, increasing the fidelity of the formulation yields a larger, more complex time-space graph as well as more complicated subproblems.

Although the decomposition approach improves the tractability of the traditional network design formulation, the associated LP-relaxation is weak. The weak LP-relaxation results in long solve times, which, in turn, prohibit the ability to increase the fidelity of the model to accurately capture the real-world channel route system. Thus, we turn to a new formulation that has a stronger LP-relaxation and the ability to better capture the real-world system.

4. COMPOSITE VARIABLE FORMULATION

Conventional network design approaches to the channel route scheduling problem pose computational problems that cannot be overcome for realistic instances of the channel route network. In this section, we develop a *composite variable formulation* (CVF) that overcomes these computational challenges. The CVF has a stronger LP-relaxation, which dramatically decreases the time required to obtain an integer solution. Additionally, the CVF is able to handle complex operational rules and regulations that constrain aircraft movements and cargo flows through the channel route network.

The traditional network design approach explored in the previous section is stated in terms of cargo flow variables and aircraft route variables. This formulation strategy yields forcing constraints (see [5,6]) that typically cause fractional aircraft usage in the solution to the LP-relaxation. Furthermore, balance-of-flow constraints (see [5,6]) propagate fractional aircraft throughout the network, increasing the fractionality of the solution to the LP-relaxation. The result of a large number of fractional variables is a weak LP-relaxation, which provides a poor lower bound on the optimal integer solution. Consequently, significant effort is spent in the branch-and-bound tree to find the optimal integer solution.

The key idea of *composite variables* is to create a formulation that is stated solely in terms of the aircraft route variables (i.e., the design variables) and to implicitly capture feasible cargo flows within the aircraft route variables. Combining several variables to create a single variable is a common reformulation strategy. Transitioning from an arc-based formulation to a path-based formulation is one such example (see [6]). The key difference between this type of reformulation strategy and composite variables is that composite variables are based on the combination of different variable types—cargo flow variables and aircraft route variables—into a single variable. The purpose of the variable redefinition is to achieve a problem structure that is computationally superior to the traditional network design formulation approached investigated in the previous section.

A formulation stated in terms of composite variables yields an equivalent formulation that is computationally more attractive than a traditional network design formulation because of its tighter LP-relaxation and shorter solve times (see [5]). These benefits, in theory, come at the expense of an increased number of integer variables. In practice, however, the number of variables can be limited using complex operational constraints from the real-world system, dominance, and branch-and-price techniques (see [12]). In general, by formulating the channel route scheduling problem using a CVF we are able to balance the effort between solving the mixed-integer programming (MIP) formulation and constructing composite variables.

Further, using the composite variable formulation, we focus on cargo flow decisions, aircraft route design, and the assignment of fleet types. Although an initial sense of timing is considered, postprocessing is required to generate a channel route schedule with precise timing and proper sequencing. The literature provides examples of such postprocessing (see [6,13]) and is the subject of ongoing research.

4.1. Composite Variable Example

This section illustrates that a composite variable formulation has a stronger LP-relaxation because the forcing constraints associated with the traditional network design formulation can be replaced with *cover constraints.* Consider the channel route network in Figure 2 that consists of two aerial ports, A and B, and two aircraft types, $f1$ and $f2$ with capacities of 16 tons and 50 tons, respectively. Each aircraft type flies the same channel route mission, (A, B). There are 15 tons of cargo at Aerial Port A that must be delivered to Aerial Port B, indicated by $b_{A,B} = 15$.

There is no need to explicitly model the cargo flow variables for this channel route network because the cargo tonnage is less than the capacity of each available aircraft. Rather, we use

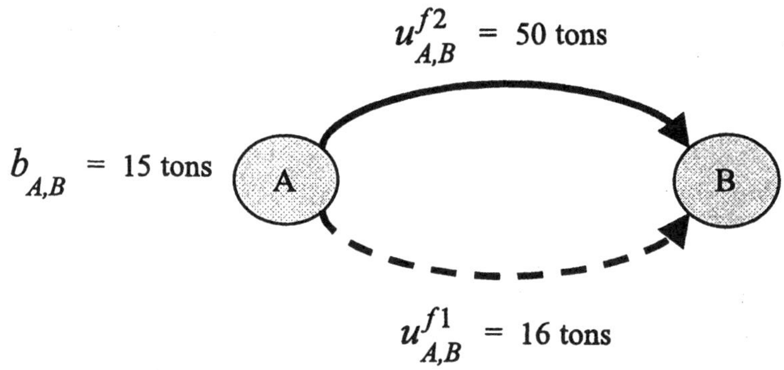

Figure 2. Notional channel route network with one cargo commodity.

capacity-demand constraints to model the aircraft capacity available to cover the cargo commodities. The following is such a constraint.

$$16y^{f1} + 50y^{f2} \geq 15. \tag{1}$$

The capacity-demand constraint (1) ensures that the total amount of aircraft capacity assigned to cover the cargo commodity is greater than the cargo commodity's tonnage requirement. The **y** variables are aircraft route variables, and $y^{f1} = 1$, for example, indicates that aircraft type $f1$ flies the channel route mission (A, B). Relaxing the integrality restriction on the aircraft route variables and minimizing the number of aircraft will yield a fractional solution, either $y^{f1} = 15/16$ or $y^{f2} = 15/50$. Using coefficient reduction (see [14]), the capacity-demand constraint (1) is equivalently written as the *cover constraint*

$$y^{f1} + y^{f2} \geq 1, \tag{2}$$

which removes the fractionality from the solution.

Because the cargo commodity's tonnage is less than the capacity of each available aircraft, we are guaranteed that by choosing either $y^{f1} = 1$ or $y^{f2} = 1$ that a feasible cargo flow for $b_{A,B}$ exists. A feasible cargo flow is not guaranteed, however, when the tonnage of the cargo commodity is greater than the capacity of at least one aircraft in the constraint. For instance, consider $b_{A,B} = 30$. The capacity-demand constraint is written as

$$16y^{f1} + 50y^{f2} \geq 30. \tag{3}$$

Applying coefficient reduction to this constraint does not yield a cover constraint that guarantees a feasible cargo flow (i.e., $y^{f1} = 1$ does not guarantee a feasible cargo flow). Using two $f1$ aircraft, however, will cover the tonnage. Thus, we create a new variable, $y^{f1,f1}$, representing the combination of two $f1$ aircraft flying the channel route mission (A, B). The new capacity-demand constraint is stated as

$$32y^{f1,f1} + 50y^{f2} \geq 30, \tag{4}$$

which can be transformed into a cover constraint using coefficient reduction, as done in transforming constraint (1) to constraint (2). The variable $y^{f1,f1}$ is a composite variable, and $y^{f1,f1} = 1$ indicates that two $f1$ aircraft are assigned to fly the channel route mission (A, B). While this example is simple, it can be extended to cargo flows and aircraft movements in our time-space graph.

Composite variables are not limited to combinations of aircraft of the same type flying the same channel route mission. For instance, consider the channel route network in Figure 3.

The channel route network contains four aerial ports, A, B, C, and D. There are two channel route missions. Channel Route Mission 1—represented by the dashed arcs in Figure 3—is one $f1$

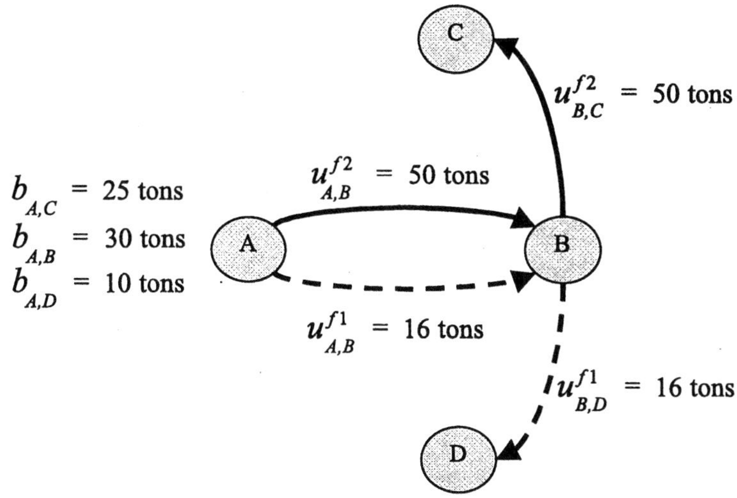

Figure 3. Notional channel route network with three cargo commodities.

aircraft flying the channel route mission (A, B, D), and Channel Route Mission 2—represented by the solid arcs in Figure 3—is one $f2$ aircraft flying the Channel Route Mission (A, B, C). Independently, neither Channel Route Mission 1 nor Channel Route Mission 2 can completely cover all the cargo commodities incident to the mission. For instance, Channel Route Mission 1 can only completely cover $b_{A,D}$. Similarly, Channel Route Mission 2 can completely cover either $b_{A,B}$ or $b_{A,C}$, but not both. Combining the two missions, however, yields a composite variable $y^{f1,f2}$ that completely covers all the cargo commodities because the cargo commodity $b_{A,B}$ can be split among the residual aircraft capacities on the two channel route missions.

We only consider composite variables that *minimally cover* a set of cargo commodities incident to the channel route missions contained in the composite variable. Minimally covering a set of cargo commodities implies that a composite variable has the following two properties.

PROPERTY 1. The composite variable completely covers a set of cargo commodities incident to the channel route missions contained in the composite variable, ensuring that feasible cargo flows exist for each cargo commodity.

PROPERTY 2. Removing one channel route mission from the composite variable does not allow the remaining channel route missions to completely cover the set of cargo commodities.

The composite variable $y^{f2,f2,f2}$ (representing three $f2$ aircraft assigned to fly Channel Route Mission 2 in Figure 3) is not a minimal cover of $b_{A,B}$ and $b_{A,C}$ because after removing one $f2$ aircraft, the remaining channel route missions in the composite variable can still completely cover $b_{A,B}$ and $b_{A,C}$. Property 2 prevents dominated composite variables (i.e., composite variables that will not be in the optimal solution) from being considered. For example, when the objective is to minimize the number of aircraft used, the composite variable $y^{f2,f2}$ dominates $y^{f2,f2,f2}$ because it contains fewer aircraft and completely covers the same set of cargo commodities.

Two key observations lead to the use of composite variables for the channel route scheduling problem. First, assuming that cargo is not permitted to transfer between aircraft at intermediate locations, cargo flow variables need not be explicitly modelled in the formulation when capacity-demand constraints are used. Second, aircraft routes can be combined so that the capacity-demand constraints can be restated as cover constraints, which yield tighter LP-relaxations with superior computational behavior compared to models with capacity-demand constraints.

4.2. Composite Variable Literature Review

Although the literature focuses solely on the use of composite variables to model transportation and logistics problems, current research is exploring the use of composite variables in a variety of settings, including general network design and fixed-charge problems.

Armacost et al. [5] introduce and provide an extensive development of composite variables in the context of designing the air network for an express shipment service problem. They show the equivalence of CVFs with traditional network design formulations within this context, and they prove that CVFs achieve stronger LP-bounds on the optimal integer solution. Additionally, they show that CVFs have the ability to incorporate difficult operational constraints that render traditional network design formulations intractable. They formulate a major commercial carrier's next day air network using a CVF, reducing the number of required aircraft by 11% and decreasing the total annual cost by nearly 25%. Armacost [15] presents composite variables in a more general setting, presenting a CVF as a Dantzig-Wolfe decomposition of a traditional network design formulation and relating composite variables to Chvátal-Gomory cuts.

Barth [16] uses the work of Armacost [15] to formulate a real-time mission planning problem in terms of composite variables that implicitly capture numerous decisions and several complex constraints, allowing them to be removed from the formulation. The formulation using composite mission variables has a stronger LP-relaxation compared to conventional models used to generate air operations plans. The solution methodology employs a price-coordinated decomposition that generates composite mission variables dynamically.

Barnhart et al. [17] formulate the fleet assignment problem using composite variables that represent the simultaneous assignment of fleet types to subnetworks consisting of one or more flight legs. Their use of composite variables, which accurately capture spill costs, yields a formulation with an LP-relaxation that is stronger than that of traditional fleet assignment formulations.

Cohn and Barnhart [12] use composite variables to integrate the crew pairing and maintenance routing problems. Their formulation—the extended crew pairing (ECP) model—successfully handles realistic instances and has a tighter LP-relaxation than that of other integrated approaches.

Cohn and Barnhart [18] use composite variables to formulate a service parts logistics problem. They consider a specific problem, referred to as the high-cost, low-demand stocking problem. For large instances of the problem, employing the use of composite variables reduces the number of constraints from over a half of a million to fewer than one thousand. Reducing the number of constraints, however, comes at the price of an exponential number of composite variables. Cohn and Barnhart [18] provide insights into techniques that can be used to limit the number of composite variables, and illustrate the importance of defining composite variables such that efficient pricing problems can be constructed to identify cost-improving columns.

4.3. Formulation

We introduce the following notation, which is used to construct a composite variable formulation for the channel route scheduling problem. Let B be a set of all aerial ports. We define M to be the set of all aircraft models (e.g., Boeing C-5 Galaxy), and F to be the set of aircraft types. Each aircraft type $f \in F$ is indexed by $\{m, i\}$, indicating the model type $m \in M$ and the squadron Aerial Port $i \in B$ from which the aircraft must originate and conclude all channel route mission.

Let $G(N, A)$ denote the time-space graph. Each node $n \in N$ is indexed by $\{i, t\}$, indicating the Aerial Port $i \in B$ and time period $t \in T$. Each arc $a \in A$ is indexed by $\{i, j, t\}$, indicating that a originates at Aerial Port $i \in B$ in time $t \in T$, and terminates at Aerial Port $j \in B$.

Let K be the set of all cargo commodities. Each cargo commodity $k \in K$ is indexed by $\{i, j, t\}$, indicating that the cargo must move from Aerial Port $i \in B$ to the destination Aerial Port $j \in B$ and that the cargo is available-to-load at the origin Aerial Port $i \in B$ starting in time period $t \in T$. Similarly, we define W to be the set of all frequency channel commodities. Each frequency channel commodity is indexed by $\{i, j, t, t'\}$, indicating the origin Aerial Port $i \in B$, the destination Aerial Port $j \in B$, and the time window—starting at $t \in T$ and ending in $t' \in T$—during which the frequency requirement must be satisfied.

We define the *cutset*, $\tilde{A}$, to be the set of all arcs that cross a predetermined time period, called the *cutset time* (e.g., all flight arcs, ground arcs, and wrap around arcs that pass through time period zero). We define the set F^n to be the set of aircraft types whose squadron base is the aerial port corresponding to node $n \in N$. Let N^S be the set of nodes that correspond to a squadron aerial port and let $\tilde{N}$ be the set of all nodes whose outgoing ground arc crosses the cutset time period.

Let C be the set of candidate composite missions, which we partition into two disjoint sets: C^O is the set of composite missions that can be flown by military aircraft and C^R is the set of composite missions for commercial aircraft. Let $f' \in FB$ be the set of all fixed-buy commercial aircraft missions.

Let η_c^f be the number of aircraft type $f \in F$ from composite mission $c \in C$ that cross the cutset time period on a flight arc. The number of aircraft type $f \in F$ that are flying into node $n \in N$ from composite mission $c \in C^O$ is represented by $\phi_c^f(n)^+$. Similarly, $\phi_c^f(n)^-$ is the number of aircraft type $f \in F$ that are flying out of node $n \in N$ from composite mission $c \in C^O$.

We map composite variables to frequency channel commodities by defining indicator β_c^w to equal one if composite mission $c \in C$ covers frequency channel $w \in W$, and zero otherwise. Similarly, we map composite variables to cargo commodities using indicator δ_c^k, which equals one if composite mission $c \in C$ covers cargo commodity $k \in K$, and zero otherwise. Finally, we map various cargo loadings of a commercial fixed-buy mission using indicator $\gamma_c^{f'}$, which equals one if composite mission $c \in C^R$ corresponds to fixed-buy mission $f' \in FB$, and zero otherwise.

We define the decision z_c to be the number of times that composite mission $c \in C$ is flown. There is a subtle, yet important difference in the decision variables z_c when $c \in C^R$ and when $c \in C^0$. When $c \in C^R$, the decision z_c encapsulates a decision about where to allocate aircraft capacity in the time-space graph and a decision about how the aircraft traversing the arcs should be loaded with cargo commodities. When $c \in C^O$, however, the decision z_c represents only how a commercial fixed-buy mission should be loaded with cargo commodities (it is known *a priori* which arcs will have assigned commercial aircraft capacity).

Generating composite variables is computationally intensive compared to solving a shortest path subproblem as we did in the previous section to generate aircraft route variables. As a result, the aircraft missions associated with a composite variable typically span one to five days, rather than the entire planning horizon. Thus, we use ground arc variables to ensure aircraft balance of flow between the completion of the channel route missions in a given composite variable to the start of the channel route missions in another composite variable. Specifically, let the decision $g^f(n)^+$ be the number of aircraft type $f \in F$ assigned to the ground arc incoming to $n \in N$ and the decision $g^f(n)^-$ be the number of aircraft type $f \in F$ assigned to the ground arc outgoing from $n \in N$.

The composite variable formulation is given by CRCF,

$$\text{CRCF} = \min \sum_{c \in C^O} \sum_{f \in F} \eta_c^f z_c + \sum_{n \in \tilde{N}} \sum_{f \in F} g^f(n)^-, \tag{5}$$

$$\text{s.t.} \sum_{c \in C^O} \delta_c^k z_c + \sum_{c \in C^R} \delta_c^k z_c \geq 1, \qquad \forall k \in K, \tag{6}$$

$$\sum_{c \in C^O} \beta_c^w z_c + \sum_{c \in C^R} \beta_c^w z_c \geq \xi^w, \qquad \forall w \in W, \tag{7}$$

$$\sum_{c \in C^O} \eta_c^f z_c + \sum_{n \in \tilde{N}} g^f(n)^- \leq \rho^f, \qquad \forall f \in F, \tag{8}$$

$$\sum_{c \in C^O} \phi_c^f(n)^+ z_c + g^f(n)^+ - \sum_{c \in C^O} \phi_c^f(n)^- z_c - g^f(n)^- = 0, \qquad \forall n \in N^S, \quad f \in F^n, \tag{9}$$

$$\sum_{c \in C^R} \gamma_c^{f'} z_c = 1, \qquad \forall f' \in FB, \tag{10}$$

$$g^f(n)^+ \geq 0, \qquad \forall n \in N, \quad f \in F, \tag{11}$$

$$g^f(n)^- \geq 0, \qquad \forall n \in N, \quad f \in F, \tag{12}$$

$$z_c \in Z^+, \qquad \forall c \in C. \tag{13}$$

The objective function (5) minimizes the number of military aircraft that cross the cutset time period on either a flight arc or a ground arc. We investigate other objective functions in later sections, demonstrating the flexibility provided by composite variables. Cover constraints (6)—which replace the computationally burdensome forcing constraints—ensure that all cargo commodities are covered (i.e., flown) by either a military aircraft or a commercial aircraft. Similarly, using cover constraints (7), we ensure that all frequency channels are serviced by either a military aircraft or a commercial aircraft.

Constraints (9) ensure balance of flow for military aircraft, connecting aircraft movements from the completion of the channel route missions in a given composite variable to the start of the channel route missions in another composite variable. Balance-of-flow is only enforced at squadron aerial ports because operational rules require that an aircraft starts a channel route mission from its squadron base and returns to its squadron base at the conclusion of the channel route mission. We consider only the composite variables that satisfy this rule. As a result, aircraft balance of flow at nonsquadron aerial ports will be satisfied without explicitly stating the associated balance of flow constraints in the formulation. Balance of flow is not required for commercial aircraft because the fixed-buy contracts only specify the routing and timing that commercial aircraft must follow, leaving the task of positioning and depositioning commercial aircraft to the commercial carriers.

There are potentially many composite variables that correspond to a single commercial fixed-buy mission because the same aircraft route could potentially cover a different set of cargo commodities (i.e., an aircraft could be loaded many different ways and fly the same routing). Constraints (10) ensure that only one of these composite variables is in the solution, capturing the fact that the fixed-buy contract is for a single commercial aircraft mission.

Aircraft count constraints (8) enforce an upper bound on the number of aircraft that can be used in an optimal solution. Finally, the composite variables must be integral (13). We only enforce that the aircraft assigned to each ground arc be nonnegative with constraints (11) and constraints (12) because constraints (13) and constraints (9) will ensure that the ground arc variables are integral in the optimal solution.

4.4. Composite Variable Generation Procedure

There are four steps in constructing a composite variable for the channel route network. First, we identify a list of *flight sequences*. Second, *generic missions* are generated from the list of flight sequences. In the third step, we use the generic missions to create *single-route composite missions*. Finally, in the fourth step, we combine single-route composite missions to create *multiroute composite missions*. We create *single-route composite variables* (i.e., columns in CRCF) after the third step and *multiroute composite variables* (again, columns in CRCF) after the fourth step, as illustrated in Figure 4. In the following sections, we describe each of the four steps.

The composite variable formulation relies on having a set of composite variables. Currently, no generalized method exists to generate composite variables. As a result, constructing composite variables is problem specific, incorporating operational constraints and other unique characteristics of the given problem. There are many possible composite variables. Experience has illustrated, however, that in some instances real-world operational rules and regulations significantly limit the number of feasible composite variables. Consequently, the entire set of composite variables for certain problems can be enumerated (see [5,12]). Additionally, real-world scheduling knowledge can be built into the composite variable generation procedure to make an initial estimate of the composite variables likely to be in an optimal solution, which further reduces the

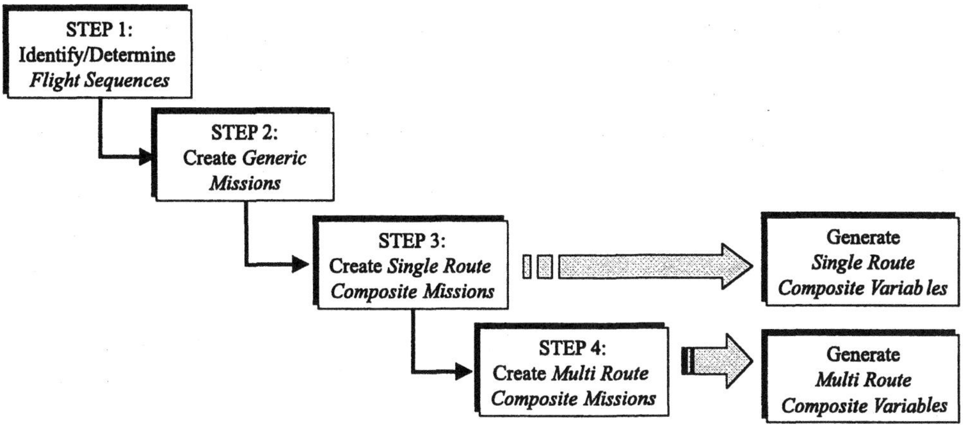

Figure 4. Composite variable generation procedure.

number of composite variables. In other instances, the set of composite variables is too large for all composite variables to be enumerated. In these situations, carefully constructed pricing problems and decomposition methods have been used to generate composite variables on the fly (see [12,16]).

4.4.1. Step 1: Flight sequences

The first step toward identifying the set of composite variables is to generate a set of *flight sequences.* A flight sequence is simply an ordered list of aerial ports that an aircraft will visit during a channel route mission. Two techniques can be used to identify flight sequences. In the first technique, the set of flight sequences is taken from an actual schedule implemented in the real-world channel route network. Because the composite variable formulation has a strong LP-relaxation and can be solved quickly, channel route schedulers would be able to manually create new flight sequences and iteratively solve the formulation, gaining insights about flight sequences that might improve the solution at each iteration.

The second technique enumerates a complete list of feasible flight sequences. Although the complete list of feasible flight sequences is large, heuristic scheduling rules—such as limiting the total number of aerial ports permitted in a flight sequence and political routing instructions—and operational rules and regulations reduces the number of feasible flight sequences. These constraints would be algebraically cumbersome to include in a traditional network design formulation and would increase the effort required to solve the LP-relaxation. In a composite variable approach, however, these types of constraints are easily incorporated in the composite variable construction procedures and, in fact, help reduce the number of composite variables that must be included in the formulation.

When the complete list of flight sequences is not used, the optimal solution to the original problem might not be found. However, an optimization-based approach is still attractive because the model returns an optimal solution for the given set of flight sequences. This allows, for example, channel route planners to determine the system-wide impact of introducing a limited set of new flight sequences (e.g., redesigning a limited portion of the channel route network).

4.4.2. Step 2: Generic missions

After the set of flight sequences is identified, we create a set of *generic missions.* A generic mission specifies an aircraft type and a flight sequence with generic arrival and departure times assigned to each aerial port in the flight sequence. We assign the generic timing to each aerial port in the flight sequence, considering aircraft and aircrew operating characteristics and regulations (e.g., flight times, minimum crew rest times, minimum ground times). Consequently, all composite variables, which are constructed from generic missions (discussed in the next section), are feasible with respect to the complex operating rules and regulations governing aircraft movements and cargo flows through the channel route network.

To generate the feasible generic missions, we begin by looping through all combinations of flight sequences and aircraft types. If the aircraft type's squadron base is the first aerial port in the flight sequence, then the combination of aircraft type and flight sequence is feasible and we continue checking the feasibility of the generic mission with respect to operational rules and regulations (e.g., crew rest, crew duty day) as well as aircraft capabilities (e.g., range, minimum ground times).

The arrival and departure days of an aircraft at each aerial port in the flight sequence of a generic mission determines the cargo commodities and the frequency channel commodities that the single-route composite mission can cover (discussed in the next section). We provide an example of a generic mission in Figure 5.

```
Startday = t
Acft = Type B, Capacity = 50 tons, Squadron Aerial Port = A
Flight Sequence = (A,B,C,D,A)
```

Aerial Port	ArriveDay	ArriveTime	CrewRest	DepartDay	DepartTime
A	--	--	--	t	0000
B	t	1300	yes	t+1	0500
C	t+1	1230	no	t+1	1545
D	t+1	2045	yes	t+2	1330
A	t+2	2300	--	--	--

Figure 5. An example generic mission.

4.4.3. Step 3: Single-route composite missions

The set of generic missions created in Step 2 is used to generate the set of *single-route composite (SRC) missions.* An SRC mission consists of a generic mission, a specific start day in the planning horizon, a set of *potential cargo commodities* that can be covered, a set of *actual cargo commodities* covered, and a set of frequency channel commodities covered.

We begin generating SRC missions by looping through all combinations of generic missions and days in the planning horizon. The generic timing assigned to the flight sequence in the generic mission is updated to reflect the specific starting day of the SRC mission. We maintain a list of times that each aerial port is open for aircraft takeoffs and landings during each day in the planning horizon. The list is used to test the feasibility of each generic mission/day combination, ensuring that each aerial port in the flight sequence (which has been updated to reflect specific, rather than generic timing) is open for operation. If each aerial port is open, we scan the SRC mission's flight sequence to determine the cargo commodities and frequency channels that can potentially be covered by the SRC mission. A cargo commodity is added to the potential cargo commodity list of the SRC mission if both the origin and destination of the cargo commodity are contained in the flight sequence, and if the aircraft departs the cargo commodity's origin within a predetermined window after the cargo commodity's available-to-load time. It should be noted that this predetermined window is a reflection of a desired level of customer service. For instance, planners might enforce that all cargo be moved from its origin within 48 hours of the available-to-load time. By incorporating this constraint into the composite variable generation procedure, we are guaranteed that an optimal solution will satisfy the desired customer service. Similarly, a frequency channel commodity is added to the list of frequency channel commodities covered by the SRC mission if both the origin and destination of the frequency channel are contained in the flight sequence, and if the aircraft arrives at the frequency channel commodity's destination within the frequency of service requirement (i.e., between $t \in T$ and $t' \in T$).

Next, we determine which of the potential cargo commodities can be completely covered by the SRC mission, given the capacity of the assigned aircraft type. There are four possible outcomes, which we describe below.

CASE 1. Sufficient aircraft capacity exists to completely cover all potential cargo commodities.

In this case, each cargo commodity is removed from the potential list of cargo commodities and added to the list of actual cargo commodities covered. We create an SRC variable (i.e., a column in CRCF) from the SRC mission. We use the list of actual cargo commodities covered, the list of frequency channels covered, and the departure and arrival times at the squadron aerial port of the assigned aircraft to determine the column's constraint coefficients (e.g., β_c^w, δ_c^k, ϕ_c^f).

CASE 2. After each cargo commodity with a tonnage requirement greater than the aircraft capacity is removed from the list of potential cargo commodities, sufficient aircraft capacity exists to completely cover all of the cargo commodities in the list of potential cargo commodities.

If the aircraft capacity cannot completely cover all the cargo commodities in the potential cargo commodity list of an SRC mission, the list of potential cargo commodities is scanned. Each cargo commodity with a tonnage requirement greater than the aircraft capacity is removed from the potential list and added to a list of *noncovered cargo commodities.* After removing a cargo commodity from the list of potential cargo commodities, we refer to the list as the *updated potential cargo commodity list.* Information is kept indicating that the SRC mission has residual aircraft capacity that can possibly be used to transport a fraction of the cargo commodity added to the noncovered cargo commodity list. If all of the cargo commodities in the updated potential cargo commodity list can be completely covered, a single-route composite variable—covering the cargo commodities in the updated potential cargo commodity list—is created, as described in Case 1 above.

CASE 3. After each cargo commodity with a tonnage requirement greater than the aircraft capacity is removed from the list of potential cargo commodities, sufficient aircraft capacity exists to completely cover only some of the cargo commodities in the list of potential cargo commodities.

Case 3 is similar to Case 2, except that after removing all the cargo commodities with a tonnage requirement greater than the aircraft capacity from the list of potential cargo commodities, the aircraft capacity is not sufficient to cover all the cargo commodities in the updated potential cargo commodity list. As in Case 2, we keep track of the residual aircraft capacity available for the cargo commodities removed from the list of potential cargo commodities.

We use the updated potential cargo commodity list to identify the set of *maximal cover cargo loadings.* A cargo loading is simply a subset of the cargo commodities in the updated potential cargo commodity list that can be completely covered by the aircraft capacity. A cargo loading is a maximal cover if adding one more cargo commodity will exceed the aircraft capacity on at least one flight leg in the flight sequence. We only consider maximal cover cargo loadings to prevent dominated SRC missions from being considered. There is, however, a potential drawback—which we discuss in the next section—of considering only maximal cover cargo loadings. An SRC variable is generated—as described in Case 1 above—for each maximal cover cargo loading.

CASE 4. Sufficient aircraft capacity does not exist to completely cover any of the cargo commodities in the list of potential cargo commodities.

In this case, each of the cargo commodities in the list of potential cargo commodities has a tonnage requirement greater than the aircraft capacity. Each cargo commodity is removed from the list of potential cargo commodities and added to the list of noncovered cargo commodities, noting that the SRC mission has residual aircraft capacity to cover a fraction of the cargo commodity added to the noncovered cargo commodity list. The residual capacity available is the entire aircraft capacity and will be used—in combinations with residual aircraft capacities from other SRC missions—to cover the noncovered cargo commodities. No SRC variable is generated for the formulation.

4.4.4. Step 4: Multiroute composite missions

For each cargo commodity in the noncovered cargo commodity list, we create *minimal cover multiroute composite (MRC) missions.* An MRC mission is composed of two or more SRC missions, a list of actual cargo commodities covered, and a list of covered frequency channel commodities. Specifically, an MRC mission is the combination of two or more SRC missions such that the collective residual aircraft capacities from the SRC missions completely cover a cargo commodity in the list of noncovered cargo commodities.

An MRC variable (i.e., a column in CRCF) is generated for each MRC mission. We use the list of actual cargo commodities covered, the list of frequency channels covered, and the departure and arrival times at the squadron aerial port of the assigned aircraft from each SRC mission in the MRC mission to determine the correct constraint coefficients of the column (e.g., β_c^w, δ_c^k, ϕ_c^f).

As described in the Step 3, we only consider maximal cover cargo loadings. This has an impact on our ability to successfully construct MRC missions that completely cover the cargo commodities in the noncovered cargo commodity list because considering only maximal cover cargo loadings might prevent SRC missions with relatively large residual aircraft capacity from being generated. As a result, cargo commodities with large tonnage requirements would have to be split among many different channel route missions, which might not be operationally feasible.

4.5. CRCF Computational Results

This section presents the computational results of the composite variable formulation applied to the small set of aerial ports and aircraft used for the traditional network design approach explored in the previous section. As a result of the composite variable formulation's superior computational behavior, however, we are able to increase the planning horizon from seven days to 30 days. The increased planning horizon, in turn, increases the number of cargo commodities considered to 1,106, the frequency channel commodities considered to 67, and fixed-buy missions considered to 32.

We use the same set of flight sequences—taken from an existing real-world channel route schedule—used to initialize the decomposition explored in the previous section. We require that cargo be moved from its origin aerial port within 48 hours of its available-to-load time and we require that an SRC mission have at least 20% of a cargo commodity's tonnage of residual capacity available to be considered as a candidate for an MRC mission. For instance, for a 120-ton cargo commodity, we require that an SRC mission have at least 24 tons of available residual capacity for it to be used in constructing MRC missions. Furthermore, we require that each aircraft in an MRC mission depart the origin aerial port of the cargo commodity that the MRC mission is constructed to cover within one day of the other aircraft in the MRC mission. Finally, we only allow each SRC mission to start one time during each day in the planning horizon.

The computational results—which we refer to as the baseline CRCF results—are summarized in Table 2.

It should be noted that we report the time required to find the first integer solution. We justify using the first integer solution from theoretical standpoint based on the tight LP-IP gaps associated with CRCF. From a practical standpoint, we justify using the first integer solution because given the tight LP-IP gaps it is unlikely that channel route schedulers would invest the time to solve the problem to optimality. Rather, they would capitalize on the excellent integer solutions that are produced quickly by CRCF.

Further, the run time presented in Table 2 does not include the time required to generate the set of composite mission variables. For the data sets considered in this research, generating the set of

Table 2. Baseline computational results of CRCF using small data set.

Composites	Flight Sequences	139
	Fixed-Buy	3,314
	Single-Route	7,654
	Multiroute	5,534
Problem Size	Columns	16,982
	Rows	1301
	Nonzeroes	197,596
Objective Value	LP Relaxation	21.96879
	First Integer	23
	LP-IP Gap	0.046
Run Time (sec)	LP Relaxation	317
	First Integer	1,596

composite mission variables required between one and five minutes of processing time. Generating the set of composite mission variables is not required, however, each time the formulation is solved. In the case of changes to the objective function, we can reuse the set of previously generated composite variables. Changes to parameters related to operational rules and regulations requires the set of composite mission variables be regenerated. Each set of composite mission variables can be stored in an oracle of composite mission variables, which, over time, reduces the required set-up time.

In addition to the fast run time illustrated in Table 2, CRCF yields attractive solve times across a variety of problem instances. Table 3 illustrates the results of CRCF, solved under different objective functions. Specifically, we test three additional objective functions: minimize the total operating cost (Cost), minimize the total number of channel route missions flown (Msns), and minimize the unused aircraft capacity across all flight legs originating in CONUS and terminating OCONUS (Ute).

Table 3. Computational results for CRCF under various objective functions.

Objective Function	Cost	Msns	Ute
Rows	1301	1301	1301
Columns	16982	16982	16982
Nonzeroes	197596	197596	197596
LP (sec)	154	202	255
First Int. Sol'n (sec)	116	260	322
LP-IP Gap	0.022	0.028	0.031

In addition to testing the computational performance of CRCF across various objective functions, we also test the performance of CRCF under various parameter changes to the composite variable generation procedure. Each scenario differs in only one aspect from the original small data set used to obtain the baseline CRCF results. The objective function for each scenario is to minimize the total operating cost (Cost). While each scenario reflects a real-world change of interest to channel route planners, the thrust behind the set of scenarios we present is to illustrate the computational performance of the composite variable approach across a wide-range of problem instances. Below we describe how each scenario differs from the original small data set and provide general comments regarding the real-world relevance each scenario might have to a channel route planner.

- 24hrs: We require that all cargo be picked up from its origin within 24 hours of its available-to-load time. This scenario reflects increased customer service in the channel route network.
- 10%: In order for an SRC mission to be considered for inclusion in an MRC mission, we require that each SRC mission have residual capacity that is at least 10% of a cargo commodity's tonnage requirement. Fewer available aircraft in the real-world channel route network might warrant such a reduction in this parameter. Similarly, the desire to deliver cargo quicker would also motivate a reduction in this parameter.
- Rgnl: We add a set of flight sequences that includes direct flight sequences as well as flight sequences that visit multiple aerial ports within a given geographic region (e.g., central Europe). Similar to the above scenario, a reduction in available aircraft might provoke this type of route structure change. Such a change in route structure might also be motivated by the desire to introduce hub-and-spoke operations only in a limited portion of the channel route network.
- H&S: We add hub-and-spoke flight sequences, designating only two OCONUS aerial ports as hubs which all channel route mission must pass through as the first OCONUS enroute stop. This type of route structure change might be motivated, for example, by the desire to switch to a hub-and-spoke network or to investigate the impact of overseas aerial port closures.
- 3/day: We allow each SRC mission to start up to three times per day in the planning horizon. This scenario is focused primarily on computational testing, which results from an increased number of columns. Increasing this parameter, however, also provides the channel route planner more flexibility.
- 4/day: We allow each SRC mission to start up to four times per day in the planning horizon.

The results of the scenarios described above are presented in Table 4.

Table 4. Computational results of CRCF across various scenarios.

	Baseline	24hrs	10%	Rgnl	H&S	3/day	4/day
Rows	1301	1301	1301	1301	1301	1301	1301
Columns	16982	11307	19691	73106	81903	86735	142767
Nonzeroes	197596	94722	256918	1816220	2382102	1258700	2137261
LP (sec)	154	61	187	1533	987	269	458
First Int (sec)	116	17	107	2023	1030	720	895
LP-IP Gap	0.022	0.010	0.024	0.031	0.0314	0.018	0.019

5. CONCLUSION

The results in the above tables illustrate the strength of the composite variable formulation's LP-relaxation, especially considering the increased size of the data set resulting from the longer planning horizon. Furthermore, by carefully constructing the composite variables, we ensure that all the composite variables in the solution satisfy the complex operational rules and regulations that the traditional network design formulation could not easily capture.

We use composite variables to model the channel route network for two reasons. First, the LP-relaxation of the traditional network design formulation is weak, making realistic instances of the channel route scheduling problem difficult to solve. Second, complex rules and regulations that constrain aircraft movements and cargo flows through the channel route network are difficult to enforce in the traditional network design formulation. Composite variables overcome both of these shortcomings because the forcing constraints that cause the poor LP-relaxations in traditional network design formulations can be replaced by cover constraints, and the composite variable generation procedures enforce complex operational rules and regulations. We formulate the channel route scheduling problem using a composite variable formulation, and implement the formulation using a small data set. The results illustrate the improved computational behavior of the composite variable formulation compared to the traditional network design formulation. The price of improved computational behavior is increased effort required to generate the set of composite variables. Although current research seeks a generalized method for composite variable generation, techniques ranging from careful enumeration to optimization formulations have proved useful (see [5] for enumeration and [12] for optimization formulations).

From a channel route scheduler's perspective, the ability to quickly generate a 30-day channel route schedule allows the scheduler to generate multiple schedules, each under a different planning priority. Specifically, the channel route scheduler would be able to change the objective function of the formulation and parameters of the composite variable generation procedure without changing the formulation's structure that yields short solution times. As a result, the scheduler would be able to quantify the differences between various schedules for the decision maker.

The transition of the methods presented in this paper to the desk of a channel route planner is the subject of current research. Specifically, graphical displays that present meaningful ranges for the input parameters are being explored. Another approach being explored relies less on the user-defined input values, but rather on the ability of CRCF to quickly generate many solutions. In this approach, a set of solutions is generated via an input perturbator. Graphical displays then guide the user through the solution space, allowing differences between solutions to be quantified and explored.

REFERENCES

1. C. Barnhart and K. Talluri, Airline operations research, In *Design and Operation of Civil and Environmental Engineering Systems*, (Edited by A. McGarity and C. ReVelle), pp. 435–469, (1997).
2. C. Hane, C. Barnhart, E. Johnson, R. Martsen, G. Nemhauser and G. Sigismondi, The fleet assignment problem: Solving a large-scale integer program, *Mathematical Programming* **70** (2), 211–232, (1995).
3. T. Magnanti and R. Wong, Network design and transportation planning: Models and algorithms, *Transportation Science* **18** (1), 1–49, (1984).
4. B. Gendron, T. Crainic and A. Frangioni, Telecommunications and network planning, In *Multicommodity Capacitated Network Design*, (Edited by B. Sanso and P. Soriano), Kluwer Academic, Dordrecht, (1999).
5. A.P. Armacost, C. Barnhart and K. Ware, Composite variables formulations for express shipment service network design, *Transportation Science* **36** (1), 1–20, (2002).
6. R. Ahuja, T. Magnanti and J. Orlin, *Network Flows: Theory, Algorithms, and Applications*, Prentice-Hall, Upper Saddle River, NJ, (1993).
7. D. Bertsimas and J.N. Tsitsiklis, *Introduction to Linear Optimization*, Athena Scientific, Belmont, MA, (1998).
8. C. Barnhart, E. Johnson, G. Nemhauser and P. Vance, Crew scheduling, In *Handbook of Transportation Science*, (Edited by R.W. Hall), pp. 493–521, Kluwer Academic, Norwell, MA, (1999).
9. M. Desrochers and F. Soumis, A generalized permanent labeling algorithm for the shortest path problem with time windows, *INFOR* **26**, 191–212, (1988).
10. C. Barnhart, E. Johnson, G. Nemhauser, M. Savelsbergh and P. Vance, Branch-and-price: Column generation for huge integer problems, *Operations Research* **46** (3), 316–329, (May–June 1998).
11. Dash Optimization, *XPress-MP User's Manual, Version 12*, Englewood Cliffs, NJ, (2000).
12. A. Cohn and C. Barnhart, Improving crew scheduling by incorporating key maintenance routing decisions, *Operations Research* (to appear).
13. D. Kim, C. Barnhart, G. Reinhardt and K. Ware, Multimodal express package delivery: A service network design application, *Transportation Science* **33** (4), 391–407, (November 1999).
14. G. Nemhauser and L. Wolsey, *Integer Programming and Combinatorial Optimization*, John Wiley & Sons, New York, (1999).
15. A. Armacost, Composite variable formulations for express shipment service network design, Massachusetts Institute of Technology, Cambridge, MA, (2000).
16. C. Barth, Composite mission variable formulation for real-time mission planning, Massachusetts Institute of Technology, Cambridge, MA, (2001).
17. C. Barnhart, A. Farahat and M. Lahatepont, Airline fleet assignment: An alternative model and solution approach based on composite variables, *Operations Research*, (submitted).
18. A. Cohn and C. Barnhart, Composite-variable modeling for service parts logistics, *Annals of Operations Research*, (submitted).

Available online at www.sciencedirect.com
SCIENCE @ DIRECT•
Mathematical and Computer Modelling 39 (2004) 945–961
MATHEMATICAL AND COMPUTER MODELLING
www.elsevier.com/locate/mcm

Performing Comprehensive Reception, Staging, Onward Movement, and Integration Analysis in a Theater of Operations

C. VAN GRONINGEN, D. BLACHOWICZ, M. BRAUN AND M. WIDING
Argonne National Laboratory
Decision and Information Sciences Division
9700 S. Cass Ave., Building 900
Argonne, IL 60439, U.S.A.
vang@anl.gov <blach><duffy><widing>@dis.anl.gov

Abstract—The enhanced logistics support tool (ELIST) is a comprehensive information management and discrete event simulation program for analyzing the deployment of military units into a theater of operations. ELIST performs a detailed vehicle-level simulation of the reception, staging, onward movement, and integration of forces. This simulation receives loaded ships and planes at the ports, unloads them, and transports the personnel and cargo using air, water, rail, road, and pipeline modes of transportation. ELIST then generates a variety of reports and graphs that are structured to be multilevel, allowing the users to navigate through the results to determine the problems or constraints of the scenario. © 2004 Elsevier Ltd. All rights reserved.

Keywords—Military, Deployment, Simulation, Transportation, Java.

1. INTRODUCTION

Upon arrival in a theater of operations, military units must undergo extensive operations before they can be employed to perform their primary mission. Formerly, military planners had no tools for analyzing the complex deployment once the units and resupply arrived in theater. A deployment analysis tool called ELIST (enhanced logistics intratheater support tool) was created to fill this void. It uses a discrete event simulation to model a deployment plan in a constrained transportation infrastructure, identify problems with the plan, and test alternatives. The ELIST design is based on the experiences, observations, and requirements of many military logisticians, as well as military doctrine. ELIST provides facilities for analyzing questions such as:

- Can the seaports handle the required volume of ships and cargo?
- Does the road infrastructure need to be improved to handle the required amount of traffic?

This work was supported under a military interdepartmental purchase request from the U.S. Department of Defense, Military Traffic Management Command Transportation Engineering Agency (MTMCTEA), through the U.S. Department of Energy contract W-31-109-ENG-109.
The submitted manuscript has been created by the University of Chicago as Operator of Argonne National Laboratory ("Argonne") under Contract No. W-31-109-ENG-38 with the U.S. Department of Energy. The U.S. Government retains for itself, and others acting on its behalf, a paid-up, nonexclusive, irrevocable worldwide license in said article to reproduce, prepare derivative works, distribute copies to the public, and perform publicly and display publicly, by or on behalf of the Government.

0895-7177/04/$ - see front matter © 2004 Elsevier Ltd. All rights reserved.
doi:10.1016/j.mcm.2004.02.023
Typeset by AMS-TEX

- Are there enough transportation assets in the theater to move the supplies?
- Are military assets scheduled for the correct time periods?
- Are the transportation assets located where they can best be utilized?
- Are the personnel and equipment for the same units scheduled to arrive at the same time?

This paper describes intratheater deployment, discusses the scenario data used, details the simulation engine developed, summarizes the types of analysis performed, and concludes with some possible avenues for further work.

2. INTRATHEATER DEPLOYMENT

During a deployment, each military unit in the plan must travel from its home base to its destination in the foreign theater and be ready for its primary mission by a certain date. Supplies must also be delivered to the units at various times and locations.

Unit personnel, equipment, and supplies travel to the foreign theater on strategic assets. Once in the theater, equipment must be assembled and readied during staging. In a process called "marry-up," personnel and equipment that belong to associated units must join together at a specified location. En route to their in-theater destinations, units may perform additional activities at other locations as shown in Figure 1. All of these movements occur before the primary mission begins and are referred to as reception, staging, onward movement, and integration (RSO&I). ELIST models the intratheater deployment from the arrival of the loaded strategic assets through the completion of RSO&I.

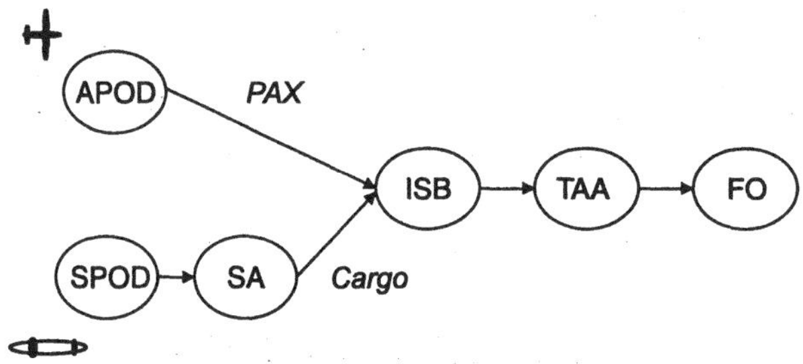

Figure 1. Typical unit deployment.

In a typical unit deployment, cargo and personnel (PAX) arrive via plane at the airport of debarkation (APOD). The plane must land and park, and the people must disembark. The unit equipment arrives via ship at a seaport of debarkation (SPOD). The ship must be berthed, and its cargo off-loaded, documented, and moved to a storage area at the port. Often the unit equipment must then be moved to a staging area (SA) not far from the port where units are integrated. This integration may include unwrapping and reconfiguring cargo, marrying personnel with their equipment, filling units with their basic load of supplies and ammunition, and performing basic training.

In some cases, marry-up may be required at an in-theater staging base (ISB). ISBs are locations near the tactical assembly areas where units perform final training and integration before being employed as an integrated unit. A tactical assembly area (TAA) is usually considered the destination of a unit in the theater. This is the location where the unit begins its assigned mission. Some units also have one or more follow-on locations (FO). Follow-on locations are further destinations to which units must move as the plan progresses.

Within the theater, movement can be via road, rail, helicopter, fixed-wing aircraft, watercraft, or pipeline. Some movements require assets (e.g., military or commercial vehicles) to transport them to their final destination. Other movements occur with "organic" equipment, using the trucks or other vehicles belonging to the unit being moved.

The U.S. military maintains an extensive set of manuals documenting various components of RSO&I [1]. Processes, heuristics, and factors from many of these documents have been used in the development of the ELIST model. (See Section 7.) Other documents we used in developing our methodology include *Deployment Planning Guide, Transportation Assets Required for Deployment* [2], *Logistics Handbook for Strategic Mobility Planning* [3], and *Air Mobility Planning Factors* [4].

Other systems exist for analyzing and planning deployments. SUMMITS, scenario unrestricted mobility model for intra-theater simulation, evaluates the logistical feasibility of a proposed theater transportation course of action at a very detailed level. It does not model the full RSO&I, and it requires extensive setup. AMP, analysis of mobility platform, is a shell for integrating deployment systems that are modeling different pieces of a deployment. ELIST is one of the systems incorporated in AMP.

Most other work in deployment planning systems focuses on different parts of the whole deployment.

- JFAST: Joint flow and analysis system for transportation. JFAST is a strategic deployment tool used primarily for contingency planning. ELIST can use JFAST output directly for the initial unit movements into a theater. Additional information can be found at `www.jfast.org`.
- MIDAS: Model for inter-theater deployment by air and sea. MIDAS is a strategic deployment tool used primarily to analyze future force structures [5]. ELIST can also read MIDAS output directly.
- PORTSIM: Port simulation model. PORTSIM models the deployment of units through specified ports of embarkation (POEs) or ports of debarkation (PODs) at a detailed level. Additional information can be found at `www.dis.anl.gov/msv/PORTSIM.pdf`.
- TRANSCAP: Transportation capability model. TRANSCAP models the deployment of units from their power projection platform forts. Additional information can be found at `www.dis.anl.gov/msv/TRANSCAP.pdf`.

3. SIMULATION DATA

To analyze the feasibility and other aspects of an intratheater deployment, ELIST uses a discrete event simulation. All the data required by the simulation are grouped into an ELIST scenario [6]. A scenario includes the four major data sets as shown in Figure 2: network, requirements, vehicles, and movement rules. (A detailed description of these items can be found in [7].)

To represent the infrastructure of the theater of operation, the scenario uses a network of nodes, links, and features with associated data. The requirements include all the military units from

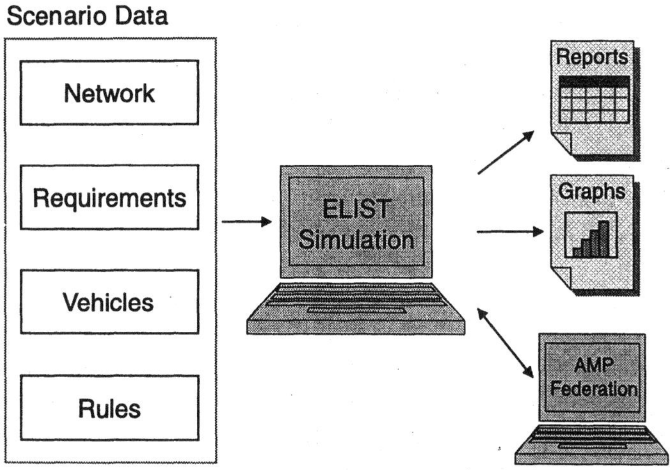

Figure 2. Scenario data.

the deployment plan with schedules of required tasks, locations, and times. Tasks include travel through the network, delays, and marry-up of related units. Vehicles available to the scenario must be specified so the cargo can be transported over the network. Finally, a set of movement rules specifies preferences about how each type of cargo can be moved.

These data sources are represented internally using objects in memory. A deterministic simulation is then performed using these objects. As the simulation runs, it translates the movement requirements into activities based on the preferences the user has made in the rules, as well as the current utilization of vehicles and network resources. Each activity is executed as a series of events. After performing the simulation, the user can view a wide range of reports and graphs that detail what occurred or send the results to presentation graphics programs for developing briefing materials.

In performing different types of studies, users focus on various parts of the analysis. Users can specify the level of model detail based on how the scenario is defined. Most significantly, users can select the level of detail at which to model the forces being deployed. The size of a plan can be considerable, involving tens of thousands of units with hundreds of thousands of people and millions of short tons of equipment and supplies. At times, the analyst wants to model the plan at a high level to get a quick idea of its feasibility, whereas at other times, a detailed analysis is required, such as to verify that all the heavy and oversized equipment can reach their destinations.

The following sections describe in more detail these components of an ELIST scenario which the user defines.

3.1. Network

The network contains nodes and links with attributes. Node types include airports, seaports, and intersections. Links are roads, railways, pipelines, or waterways. Air links are assumed to exist between any two airports and are not explicitly defined. Users can create networks built with external tools using data from military map products and other sources. They can import and tailor these networks to fit the scenario or define a network from scratch using the network editing functionality provided in ELIST. All of the locations referenced in the movement requirements must be represented in the network.

The quantity, availability, accuracy, and stability of data about the network are all vastly variable for different theaters. Decisions regarding the modeling of various capabilities of the infrastructure were based on how constraining that component would generally be to a deployment plan, and whether accurate data would usually be available. Berths, for example, are modeled on an individual basis at each seaport, with length, depth, apron width, and cranes. Most of a force arrives via ship, and if a ship cannot berth or be unloaded for some reason, that will have a large impact on the plan. On the other hand, resources that are somewhat subjective or imprecise, such as the capability of available personnel to load cargo on railcars, are modeled at a higher level, as a short-ton per day capability. Capability values that are not available or not critical can be set to a default value with little user effort.

Each node and link has a set of resources based on its class. Network resources are modeled in three ways within ELIST: as rate resources, gate resources, or capacity resources.

3.1.1. Rate resource

A rate resource is characterized by its ability to process a given amount of cargo or PAX in a given time. The personnel and equipment used to load containers on railcars are modeled as a rate resource. The capability of this consumable resource is expressed in containers per hour. The duration of an activity that requires a rate resource is at least the amount processed divided by the rate. However, the duration may be longer than the time dictated by one resource, in the case where multiple resources are required. The end time of an activity using rate resources is determined by

$$t_{\text{end}} = t_{\text{start}} + \max\left(\frac{A}{r_1}, \frac{A}{r_2}, \ldots, \frac{A}{r_i}\right),$$

where t_{end} is the end time, t_{start} is the start time, A is the total amount to be processed in the activity, and r_i is the processing rate of resource i required by the activity.

3.1.2. Gate resource

A gate resource also represents a capability described by a rate. However, no duration is associated with the use of this type of resource. Road capacities, for example, are modeled using gate resources; some number of vehicles may travel onto the road link each day. This rate, however, will not affect how long the trip takes to complete.

An activity requiring a gate or rate resource cannot start until a time at which *some* capability is available. Rate and gate resources model capabilities that are usually defined as some amount *per day* that can be moved, loaded, or otherwise processed. However, it is not necessarily true that this capability is evenly distributed over the day. To allow the analyst some flexibility in selecting how resource capabilities are distributed, a time interval smaller than 24 hours may be used to segment the capability. For instance, if an interval of six hours is selected, one-quarter of the daily capability is available during each six-hour interval. The smaller the interval, the more evenly distributed the capability becomes. This distribution does not affect overall capability of the resource or the duration of individual activities. It may, however, affect the start times of activities using a resource. Figure 3 shows a resource that processes 120 short tons per day using a 24 hour interval and a 12 hour interval.

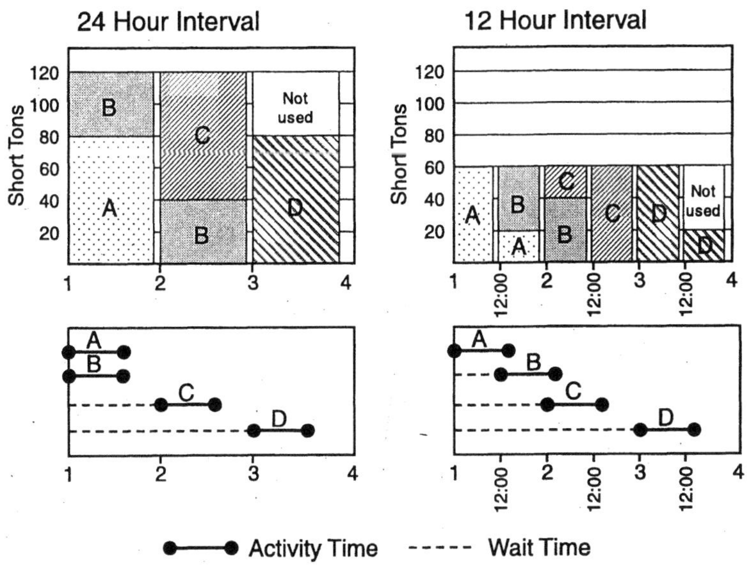

Figure 3. Resource availability and use for different intervals.

The resource is required for four events, each of which has 80 short tons of cargo, and each of which is scheduled for Time 1. The events all have the same duration, but Event B starts later when a smaller interval distributes the resource availability; it cannot begin until some resource capability is available for it. One might think that more intervals per day would extend the overall time of a scenario run as fewer activities requiring the same resource execute in parallel, and start time delays in these activities lead to further delays in subsequent activities. However, in ELIST scenarios where the numbers of activities and resources are large and their interactions are complex, no such trends have been observed.

Some infrastructure resources are modeled using variations of the rate, gate, or capacity resources. For instance, a four-rate resource is used to model crane capability. This means there is one resource, in this case the crane, that can perform four different types of operations at four different rates, specifically, on-loading bulk cargo, off-loading bulk cargo, on-loading containers, and off-loading containers.

3.1.3. Capacity resource

A capacity resource is a nonconsumable resource used for the duration of an activity. Its use has no impact on the activity duration. An example is a storage area at a port. A storage area is modeled as a resource with a capacity of some amount of square feet. An activity that requires storage area can commence when the required area is free. The required amount is held in use by the activity until it finishes; that portion of the capacity resource is then freed for another use.

3.2. Requirements

The requirements data contain the focus of an analysis: the deployment plan with all the units involved. A military unit includes personnel and their associated equipment and supplies. These cargo components, as well as attribute data and an ordered list of tasks for each unit, compose the requirements data. Figure 4 is a sample task schedule for a unit identified as 0ZHFC. The diagram shows its complete deployment, whereas ELIST usually models only the movements at the POD and beyond. This requirement shows that the unit must move from the origin (ORG) and through the port of embarkation (POE) before arriving at the port of debarkation (POD) with an earliest arrival date (EAD) of $C + 20$ and latest arrival date (LAD) of $C + 25$ (where $C + 20$ refers to 20 days after the commencement of the deployment). The unit must then unload from the strategic asset and perform staging activities such as unpacking and reassembling equipment through day $C + 26$. At the intermediate staging base (ISB), the linked rings indicate a marry-up requirement for the cargo and PAX as well as four days of integration activities such as acclimation, maintenance, and training. Finally, the unit must move to the destination (DST) by the required delivery date (RDD) of $C + 35$.

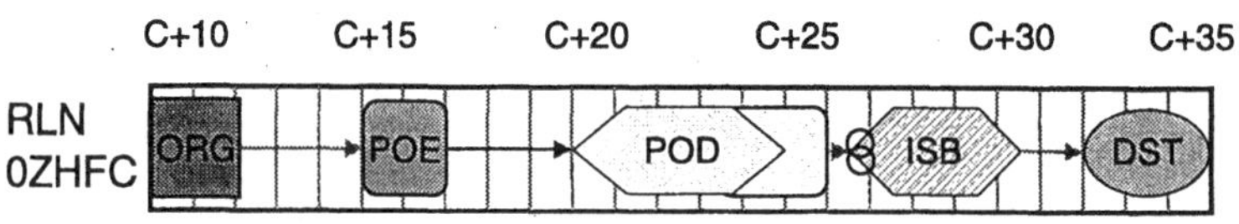

Figure 4. Sample unit schedule.

Each unit is composed of a number of cargo components. These components can be defined at multiple levels of detail. At the highest level, cargo components are defined by a commodity type and a number of people, short tons, or gallons. This level of component detail can be divided into multiple items with area specified as well. At the most detailed level, the components can be described as a set of items, each with a serial number, weight, and size dimensions. The analyst can select the level of detail to use for each unit in the simulation.

Movement requirements are usually generated by importing time-phased force deployment data (TPFDD) files. Unfortunately, the standard TPFDD format can only represent basic movement within a theater. To perform a substantive RSO&I analysis, a simulation needs more detailed information. To meet this need, Argonne developed a tool, ETEdit (expanded TPFDD editor) [8] for editing and augmenting a TPFDD to produce an expanded TPFDD (ETPFDD).

Three major modifications can be made to a TPFDD. In the standard TPFDD, unit cargo can only be specified in aggregate (up to Level 3) [9]. In the ETPFDD, however, more detailed items (Levels 4–6) can replace these aggregate quantities, providing a more accurate representation of the cargo, focusing on large, hard-to-move items, and stuffing containers with cargo. ELIST can model equipment and supplies as either aggregations of cargo with a specified weight and a generic weight-to-size ratio, or as discrete pieces of equipment with specified identifier, weight, and dimensions. Second, relationships between items can be modeled in the ETPFDD. This capability enables us to model associations between units for marry-up requirements. Built-in tools are provided in ETEdit to identify and associate groups of units as part of this modeling. Third, the ETPFDD allows additional movements to be specified for units, rather than limiting the unit to traveling to three locations in the theater. Often, marry-up, training, and other activities are required at intermediate locations, which are not represented in the standard TPFDD. An additional attribute that is added to each cargo component for the ELIST simulation is a commodity type.

3.2.1. Cargo categories

Five basic categories of cargo have been defined for ELIST and need to be moved in a military deployment:

- people (PAX);
- containers;
- breakbulk;
- roll on, roll off (RORO); and
- petroleum, oil, and lubricants (POL).

These categories are important to the simulation because they determine

(1) how the cargo should be handled during loading on and off vehicles,
(2) which attributes are important for fitting the cargo on vehicles (e.g., area, weight, volume), and
(3) how the cargo should be reported (e.g., weight, amount).

These categories are straightforward to assign to an amount of cargo. To accurately model how each piece should be transported, however, a "commodity type" must also be assigned to each item of cargo.

3.2.2. Commodity types

Each of the cargo categories is made up of one or more commodity types. Commodities allow the analyst to classify cargo into groups that have the same rules of movement. Before running a simulation, a commodity is assigned to each record of cargo by applying a set of commodity rules to the TPFDD data. Figure 5 shows some sample commodity rules with associated priorities and names.

Priority	Name	Rule
1	Water	if Cargo Category Code = "JDD" then Commodity = Water
2	Tanks	if Line Item Number = "T13305" then Commodity = Heavy Equipment Transport Required
3	Unit POL	if Cargo Category Codes = "POL" and Record Type = "U" then Commodity = POL Unit Cargo
4	Bulk RR	if Cargo Category Code starts with "A3", "A7", "AD", "R7", or "RD" then Commodity = Bulk Tonnage RORO
5	Bulk BB	if Cargo Category Code position 1 = "3 ", "7", or "D" then Commodity = Bulk Tonnage Breakbulk
6	Outsized	if Cargo Category Code = "OUT" then Commodity = Outsized Tonnage
7	Oversized	if Cargo Category Code = "OVR" then Commodity = Oversized Tonnage
8	Bulk	if Cargo Category Code = "BLK" then Commodity = Bulk Tonnage

Figure 5. Sample commodity rules.

The highest priority rule whose premise matches a record is fired for that record, and lower priority rules that may also match that record are ignored. This rule ordering allows each rule to be simpler, because fewer conditions are in the premise. The conditions are based on attributes in the TPFDD, such as record type, detail level, and CCC (cargo category code). For example, the first rule in the table assigns the commodity "water". These commodity rules and the commodity types that they create can vary from scenario to scenario depending on the focus of the analysis, the theater, and the types of transport available.

3.3. Vehicles and Assets

An ELIST scenario must include the vehicles available to move cargo and personnel within the theater. Numbers of vehicles are defined to work specific geographic areas, closely modeling the concept of operations utilized by the military. In addition, military transport unit equipment arriving in the theater can be made available to other units.

ELIST stores data on every vehicle type that might be used in a deployment. The model uses information such as payload, cargo area dimensions, curb weight, average speed, and average on-load and off-load times.

For a scenario, a specific collection of vehicles is defined. There are two ways to model vehicles in a scenario: "fully tracked" or "capability asset". A fully tracked vehicle is a discrete entity that makes loaded and empty trips and that always has a current location in the network, whether or not it is in use. A capability asset, on the other hand, is one or more vehicles that are considered to be generally available. Such a vehicle is only specifically modeled when it is being used to transport cargo. When its trip is finished, a vehicle designated as a capability asset returns to the pool, and it can be used immediately in an entirely different location. No empty vehicle trips are modeled for a capability asset.

Through the use of asset pools, analysts specify the geographic area where vehicles can be used. Asset pools are collections of vehicles that serve specific locations within the theater network. An asset can also be designated to serve all locations. Linehaul operations may be set up using asset pools of trailers that can serve a region and asset pools of tractors that can serve pairs of nodes. Asset pools have "home nodes" where all fully tracked vehicles congregate when they are idle.

Finally, the analyst may specify an interval of availability for each vehicle or group of vehicles. By default, an asset is available throughout the scenario. However, initial and/or final times of availability may be specified, if desired.

3.4. Movement Rules

Users must provide rules that specify how movement is to occur. Default sets of rules are provided with the system that can be modified to give the users flexibility to analyze new types of equipment and to focus on special areas of interest.

ELIST simulates five modes of travel: road, rail, air, water, and pipeline. For each of the first four modes, many different vehicles can be used. Some means is needed to specify both the possible and the preferred ways to move various commodity types within the theater. For example, it is possible to move personnel by buses, passenger railcars, and certain helicopters and aircraft. Movement rules are defined to represent these choices. Figure 6 shows a set of rules for transporting personnel.

The movement rules have a preference ordering for each commodity type with conditions based on its current time restriction and its distance to the destination. The time restriction indicates whether or not the unit can be late.

To simplify rule development and reduce the number of rules, the concept of an "asset type" is used. An asset type is a collection of similar vehicles that are used to transport the same type of cargo on the same mode, but with potentially different capacities or dimensions. For

Asset Name	Time Restriction	Distance Restriction	Miles
Buses	Any Time		
Helo	Any Time	<	25.0
Rail, Passengers	Any Time	>	115.0
C-130 PAX Only	Any Time		
ATT	Any Time		

Figure 6. Sample personnel movement rules.

example, one asset type used in Figure 6 is "C-130 PAX only". This asset type includes several configurations of the aircraft such as C-130P, C-130EP, and C-130HP. Movement rules use assets to specify the vehicle selection. Using the rules shown in Figure 6, the second choice for moving personnel is by asset type "Helo" if the distance is less than 25 miles. These movement rules are used during the execution of the simulation described in Section 4.

4. SIMULATION

On the basis of the objects described in the data sets of the scenario, ELIST performs a discrete event-based simulation [10]. In the simulation, the requirements are translated into activities, and the corresponding objects are created. Activities are always scheduled at the earliest possible time. The simulation produces a delivery profile based on this push-forward methodology, and no attempt is made to detain or slow cargo that is arriving early (i.e., before its required arrival date).

Before simulation starts, each initial event will have a time at which to execute (its scheduled time) and be stored in the scheduled-events collection. During the simulation, each active event will either be scheduled at a future time, or will be waiting in one or more queues for currently busy resources or assets. Events waiting in the same queue or scheduled at the same time are executed in priority order.

Activities that involve unit components, such as trips to transport cargo, are assigned priorities based on the due dates of all units involved. Units with the same due date are prioritized in order of arrival or scheduling (i.e., FIFO). These priorities minimize the wait time of most units, while testing the scenario feasibility. Activities that do not involve units, such as return trips of unneeded trucks, are assigned lower priorities.

An activity that cannot successfully execute at its scheduled time because some condition is not met, or some resource or asset is not available, is put into one or more queues. The activity will wait in these queues, until it can acquire the needed resources. Queues are created by the simulation as they are needed—one queue for each constraining network resource, asset, or condition. The events in a queue are not attempted again, until that queue is triggered when its associated object becomes available.

At each simulation cycle, an event is selected and executed. The selection procedure is illustrated in Figure 7. Events are scheduled at Time t while the queues are always at the current time. The next item to be processed is the item with the highest priority (p).

Each active event has a priority, with a value of 1 being the highest priority. When the simulation is ready for an event, it first executes events in queues that have been triggered, marked in gray. The events in the second queue execute first, as it has the highest priority, having inherited the highest priority of its events. Events in that queue execute in order until the resource associated with the queue is no longer available. This method was chosen over selecting the highest priority event from all triggered queues after each event execution, for model runtime performance reasons.

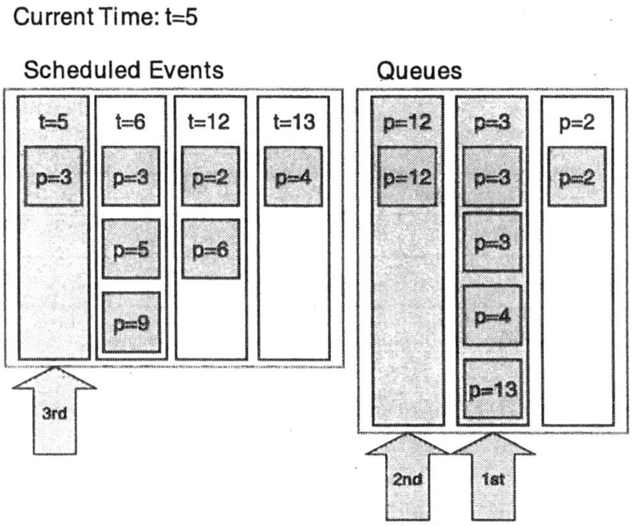

Figure 7. Event priority and execution order.

When no more queues are ready, the first event scheduled at the current time is executed. Before execution of each subsequent scheduled event, the queues are again examined. When there are no more triggered queues, and no more events scheduled at the current time, time is advanced to the time of the next scheduled event.

The simulation of the unit movements begins with their arrival in the theater on strategic ships and aircraft. These data may be generated by another military model, such as JFAST (joint flow and analysis system for transportation), or by a subprogram within ELIST. From these data, ELIST builds and schedules a set of initial events, which model the asset arrivals with their unit cargo. Units may alternately start as "available" at a location within the theater.

During a simulation, a cargo entity completes an activity when it is released by the final event of that activity. At that time, the cargo attempts to implement its next scheduled requirement. If the cargo entity has no more requirements, it is done and is added to the final delivery profile. Final delivery for a unit is achieved when *all* of its components have completed their last movement requirement.

4.1. Activities

Using the options specified for the scenario, the movement requirements in the ETPFDD are translated into the following requirements in the simulation:

- marry-up with one or more other units,
- implement a delay,
- begin operating as asset vehicles,
- begin operating as a resource, and
- move to a location.

Activities model all these tasks in the simulation. Many activities are composed of multiple subactivities, which must be scheduled and executed in order. Each activity checks for the resources and conditions required for successful completion; if all conditions cannot be met, the activity waits in the appropriate queues. If an event succeeds, the next subactivity is scheduled.

Of the five requirement types listed above, the first four are straightforward. No decisions or choices are involved; in fact, to implement a delay, operate as assets, or operate as a resource, no conditions are even required. Movement to a location, however, is much more complex. Fulfilling a move-to requirement can involve initializing a trip, assigning assets, loading vehicles, traveling on routes, and using convoys. The following sections examine some of these activities in more detail.

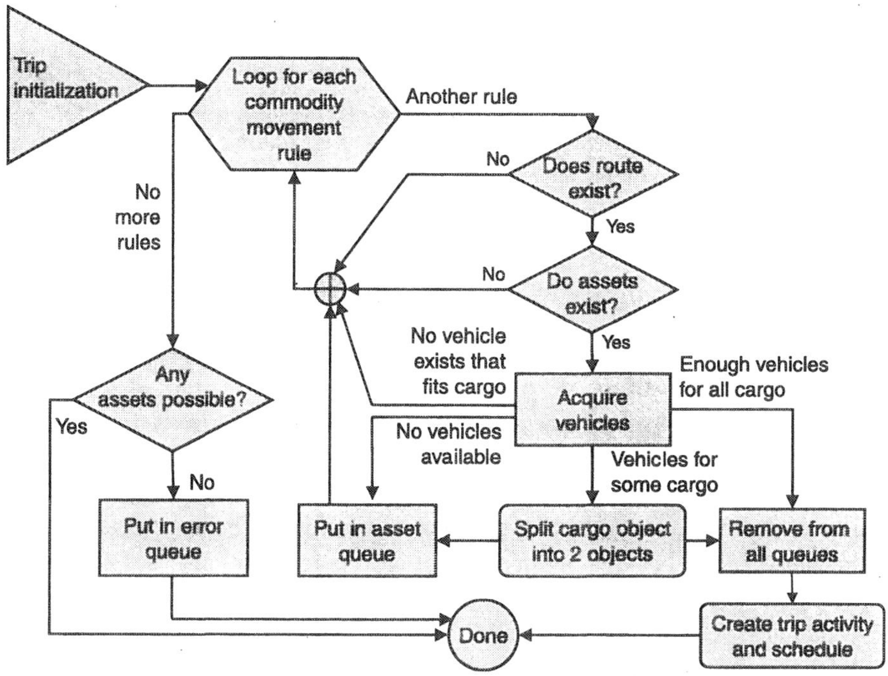

Figure 8. Trip initialization logic diagram.

4.1.1. Trip initialization

A trip initialization is created and scheduled to meet all move-to requirements. Some of these requirements specify the mode to be used, whereas, for others, the movement rules must be used to select both the mode and the asset type. A trip initialization consumes no time (except possibly queue time) as it examines the modes and vehicles possible. Figure 8 is a logic diagram of initializing a trip.

When a trip is initialized, the movement rules for the commodity to be moved are used in priority order. The event with the cargo goes into an error queue if the scenario does not include vehicles that can move the cargo or if an appropriate route does not exist to the destination. The event waits in asset queues if, at that time, no vehicles are available at the location of the cargo. If vehicles are available that can hold some of the cargo, the cargo object is split into two objects: one moves ahead on the vehicle, while the other remains in the trip initialization object, waiting in asset queues. When this activity is completed, it will have ensured that a route exists, selected assets, created a trip activity of the selected mode, and assigned the vehicles or asset capability and cargo to the trip.

4.1.2. Asset queues

A trip initialization activity is put into one or more asset queues if the cargo location does not have appropriate assets. At this time, if this type of asset is available elsewhere in the network, a new activity is created and scheduled to move these assets to the cargo location. These empty assets are not, however, specifically tagged for that cargo. Instead, they are matched with the highest priority event in the queue at the time that they arrive.

When a trip activity that utilizes assets completes its unload subactivity, the vehicles are released. When vehicles are released, and there is an associated asset queue with waiting events, the queue is queried as to whether additional assets might be required. The queue keeps track of the number of expected assets (i.e., the number that has been sent from other locations, but has not yet arrived). If more assets are required than expected, the newly free assets are sent as well.

4.1.3. Vehicle loading

Determining whether assets are available to transport a piece of cargo begins with determining whether a vehicle can accommodate the size or weight of the cargo. There are different constraints for loading each cargo category on various types of vehicles. Loading people and gallons of POL is straightforward because all vehicles specify the amount they can carry. Loading container cargo onto vehicles is also straightforward. Each vehicle has an attribute for the number of 20 foot containers that it can carry. In addition to the number of containers, the weight of the loaded containers must be less than the weight capability of the vehicle. Weight is a limiting factor for all vehicle types and all cargo categories, except people and POL. Some vehicle type/cargo category combinations also use area as a constraint. In addition, the loading of airplanes requires that the cargo fit through the door.

Ideally, only full vehicles would depart for a destination. However, there is not always enough cargo traveling between two nodes to fill a vehicle. Another consideration is the time cargo may spend waiting for additional cargo to fill the vehicle; this wait should not be unlimited. ELIST deals with these factors by having parameters that allow the user to tailor loading to the conditions in the scenario. For each mode, two scenario parameters are used: adequate load and maximum wait. These parameters are used as follows. When an event with a new asset is first created, it is assigned a given amount of cargo. The percent load which that cargo constitutes is calculated by using either weight (for breakbulk and RORO) or amount (for containers, people, and gallons of POL). If the percent load is greater than the adequate load, and if no other cargo is waiting, the vehicle can depart immediately. Otherwise, the activity is put in a special queue where it stays for no more than the maximum wait time. Other appropriate cargo arriving within that time can be added to the waiting activity. Whenever an adequate load is reached, the vehicle can depart.

Air and water travel use an additional parameter—minimum load. This value is used when requesting assets from other locations or when determining if it is time to begin loading cargo on a ship or aircraft. It is necessary to have a minimum load of cargo before an empty ship or plane will be sent to a new location to pick up cargo. In this case, the time cargo waits is not limited, as ships and planes are not used to transport such a small amount of cargo. Instead, small amounts of cargo are usually transported via rail or road.

4.1.4. Routes

After a vehicle has been loaded, the simulation selects a route. ELIST finds routes for all movement requirements before the simulation is run. For each known origin and destination pair, a route of each mode is stored, if one exists. The user can modify the default route set by changing the search criteria from the default of shortest distance to the greatest capacity or shortest travel time. Different criteria can be selected for different paths. Multiple routes can be stored for the same nodes and modes with different priorities. Specific routes can also be assigned to specific purposes. For example, a route can be specified as being required for use by either commercial or military assets.

Nodes and links can have "limits" that constrain the size or weight of vehicles and cargo that can travel over them. A tunnel or bridge, for example, limits the height of the vehicle. Thus, not all cargo can travel over all routes.

When more than one route could be used for a vehicle, the highest priority route is tried first. If it is busy, the trip activity checks the next route. If all routes are busy at the time an activity is ready to depart, it waits in one queue for each route. When it departs, it uses the first available route.

As the ELIST simulation runs, it searches for a new route if it needs a route that it does not have stored and it has not yet tried to find. Because military practice recommends limiting the number of routes, the simulation will not search for another path just because the existing path is busy.

Although a route is composed of a set of links and nodes, the simulation treats it as one entity. When a route is needed, the available capacity of the entire route is checked. This ensures that a vehicle will arrive at its destination without unwanted en route delays, and prevents the simulation from having to schedule and execute multiple events for every route traversal. Intersection capacity must be available for each node, and entrance capacity must be available for each link at the time that the vehicles will reach that section of the route. Both links and vehicles have a speed attribute; a vehicle on a link travels at the slower speed. Using the speed and link length, the time of arrival at the end of each link is calculated. The capacities available at that time of the next node and link are then checked. In this way, the number of vehicles that can depart at a given time (interval) is determined. Any additional vehicles wait in a queue for that route which is triggered at the next time with route capacity available.

4.1.5. Convoys and trains

ELIST gives the option of grouping some types of ground vehicles in convoys. Convoys are created based on the following scenario parameters:

- minimum vehicles per convoy,
- maximum vehicles per convoy,
- maximum wait,
- rate of march, and
- spacing distance.

Activities with road vehicles wanting to make a trip that requires a convoy are put in a convoy queue. Such an activity waits up to the maximum wait time to form a group of at least the minimum vehicles per convoy. If this number is not reached within the wait time, a smaller convoy departs. A convoy never has more than the maximum vehicles per convoy.

Once a convoy departs, the next convoy does not depart until the first convoy has traveled a minimum of the spacing distance. The convoy travels at a speed given by the rate of march, unless a vehicle or link speed is slower. In that case, the slower speed is used for the applicable portion of the route.

Rail travel is always performed using trains (i.e., strings of railcars moving as a group). The movement of trains is controlled in the same way as convoys. Locomotives are not explicitly modeled in ELIST; it is assumed that they are always available.

4.2. Results

When an analyst has completed (or partially completed) a simulation, many reports and graphs become available. Generally, the first chart an analyst examines is the delivery or closure profile. This chart provides an overall view of the success of the deployment plan. The example shown in Figure 9 includes all breakbulk, RORO, and container cargo in the plan. Delivery can also be viewed by cargo category, commodity, or a user-defined set.

The lines in the graph show the total amount of short tons (of breakbulk, RORO, and containers) required at all PODs and all destinations in the plan. The areas are the amounts delivered to the PODs, the SAs, the ILOCs, and the TAAs. The frontmost area shows the short tons "closed", i.e., those whose entire unit has arrived at its TAA (destination). The amounts not delivered can also be determined.

The availability and use of every network resource, every asset pool asset and vehicle type, and every route can be graphed. In addition, all resources, assets, and conditions that constrained movement during the simulation can be listed, and those amounts that are waiting can be graphed over time. Figure 10 shows a constraints report; constraints are listed in order of severity, measured by the number of intervals during which use was over 90% of capacity. The time at

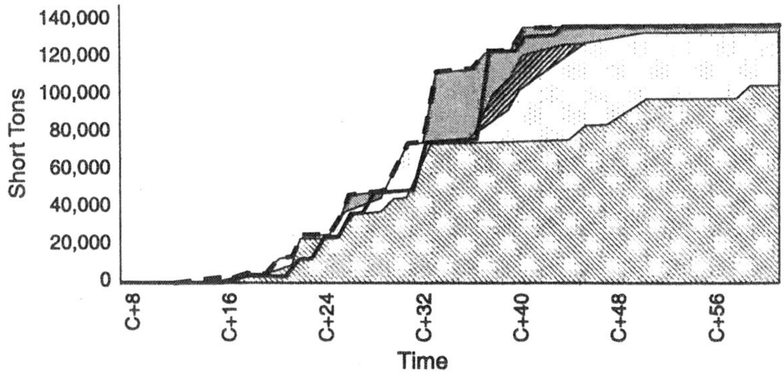

Figure 9. Delivery profile.

All Constrained Assets and Resources

Current Time: 50 11:13

Network: Caspian

Scenario: ARWG02-6May02

Resource	First Queued (Time)	Last Queued (Time)	First Used (Time)	Last Used (Time)	Max Interval Use (%)	#Intervals Used > 90% Capacity	Average Interval Use (%)
Intratheater Air Asset C-130 PAX only	−7 18:00	49 0:00	−4 0:00	49 11:39	100.0	213	97.88
Intratheater Air Asset ATT	−7 18:00	49 0:00	0 0:00	50 10:36	100.0	196	98.25
Azerbaijan Road Link 17 (Road Forward)			4 12:00	14 0:00	100.0	151	81.23
Geo Road Link 1 (Road Reverse)			−8 6:00	47 6:00	100.0	151	72.30
SWA Region Road Link—978 (Road Reverse)			4 18:00	14 0:00	100.00	151	81.30

Figure 10. Constraints report.

which the first event was put in a queue for the resource (or asset) is listed, as well as some other times of interest.

Note that the three road links in the table that are constrained do not have values for first and last queued times. This is because queues are associated with routes, rather than individual links, which do not have their own queues.

The analyst can use the information in the reports to examine each asset and resource more closely, and to consider options for alleviating the bottlenecks.

Higher-level reports give an overview of what is happening in the simulation. The table shown in Figure 11, for example, gives information about the numbers of ships arriving, off-loading, on-loading, and departing at every seaport berth group.

Low-level reports provide complete information about every activity performed by each bit of cargo and details about each convoy and train. Any unit components that could not meet their requirements for some reason are displayed in the error queue report along with the requirement and activity that led to the error.

Seaport Overview
Current Time: 50 11:13
Network: Caspian
Scenario: ARWG02-6May02

Seaport	Berth Group	Arrivals	Departures	Intra Onloads	Intra Offloads	Strat Offloads
BATUMI-AZCY-PRT	BG Batumoi RoRo Berth	13	13	0	0	13
MERSIN-QBAL-PRT	BG Mersin Berth 1	6	6	0	0	6
MERSIN-QBAL-PRT	BG Mersin RoRo Container Berth 1	5	5	0	0	5
NOVOROSSIYSK-SDPM-PRT	BG Novorossiysk-Berth No. 39	5	5	0	0	5
NOVOROSSIYSK-SDPM-PRT	BG Novorossiysk-Berth No. 5	4	4	0	0	4

Figure 11. Overview report.

5. IMPLEMENTATION AND USE

The military logistics community has successfully used the previous version of ELIST (Version 7) in planning and training exercises for a number of years [11]. In the past few years, we have rewritten the original ELIST system to address the military's requests for more detail and more capabilities. The latest version of ELIST is written in the Java language with data stored in an Oracle relational database. To develop this new version, the application was structured into modular layers using object-oriented techniques. The resulting system is more reliable and easier to maintain; it also provides greater modeling flexibility.

ELIST is being used continually for many different types of analyses. A representative set of these analyses includes the following.

- ELIST is routinely used at U.S. Transportation Command TPFDD refinement conferences. Each theater of operation in the world is required to have plans ready to implement for a variety of contingencies. ELIST is used to determine if the plan is transportation feasible based on the commanders' RSO&I concept. Critical units are identified as arriving early at their tactical assembly areas, on time, or late, and to what degree. Lateness can be caused by a lack of assets, constraining infrastructure, a lack of essential personnel, or if the plan itself is too aggressive. ELIST is used to help identify and quantify these constraints. Looking at under-utilized infrastructure like seaports or airports, for instance, the analyst is able to make suggestions to the planners about shifting the late units to other ports.
- ELIST was recently used to support the Joint Staff's advanced mobility concepts study, which is a capabilities-based effort to examine military deployment using strategic and theater future concept transport vehicles. Unit closure times were compared using "high speed shallow draft sealift", "monohull sealift", "theater support vessel", "global reach transport aircraft", "ultra large airlifter", "heavy lift vertical takeoff and landing", and "super short takeoff and landing" concept vehicles. The study measured unit closure times at the tactical assembly areas and utilization of the theater transport vehicles when changing the weights, dimensions, and quantities of the vehicles. The study provided insights into which configurations and combinations of strategic and theater vehicles were the most effective in terms of being utilized and improving closure.
- ELIST has been used in various U.S. Army transformation studies. To support the U.S. Army interim division design analysis, ELIST in conjunction with the joint flow and

analysis system for transportation (JFAST) model evaluated the deployability of different designs for the Army's interim division by comparing legacy heavy and light divisions to the new designs. The study measured strategic responsiveness of the various division designs given three different theaters of operation. ELIST was used to determine how fast units could close at the tactical assembly areas and to identify theater choke points. The airlift and sealift arrival manifests from JFAST were passed electronically to ELIST which then offloaded the ships and aircraft, staged and moved the equipment and soldiers forward to their tactical assembly areas. ELIST was used to assess the interim division's organic composition in regards to self-deployability and reliability on host nation support assets. The study team was awarded the "Department of the Army Dr. Wilbur B. Payne Memorial Award for Excellence in Analysis Group Category 2002" for this study.

6. CONCLUSIONS AND FUTURE DIRECTION

ELIST provides tools for evaluating the transportation portion of military movement planning. Continuous interaction and feedback between the developers and the military logistics experts have led to a system that is viewed as useful and accurate by the users. Several additional initiatives are being considered for inclusion in ELIST.

ELIST has been integrated into the analysis of mobility platform (AMP) system [12]. Within this system, ELIST and the model for inter-theater deployment by air and sea (MIDAS) [5] have historically run serially. New work has begun on a dynamic capability, allowing the strategic arrivals to influence the theater deployment, and the theater deployment to affect the strategic deployment.

We would like to enhance the options for viewing and distributing results by expanding our simulation playback capabilities, by automatically generating presentation graphics, and by publishing the results to web pages.

To broaden the scope of the model, we would like to provide dynamic generation of sustainment throughout the theater. Using a manual process, current tools were used to provide some sustainment requirements for the MRS05 study. Automated tools would greatly simplify this task. In addition, more detailed modeling of the supply and consumption of fuels by all transportation vehicles would improve the accuracy of the results. Furthermore, results would be enhanced by having access to dynamic data from the actual executions. If ELIST had feeds of the current deployment status, planners could identify future problems and address them before they become critical.

Finally, many of the concepts and analysis techniques used in ELIST are applicable beyond the military. These techniques can be applied to other transportation sectors. For example, for the private sector, ELIST could be extended to analyze specialized freight shipments or perform analysis of fleet apportionment and distribution plans. Both private and governmental sectors could extend ELIST to analyze emergency and disaster scenarios, evaluating their effects as well as their contingency plans.

7. MILITARY FIELD MANUALS

(1) FM 5-101 Mobility
(2) FM 10-18 Petroleum Terminal and Pipeline Operations
(3) FM 10-67 Petroleum Supply in Theater of Operations
(4) FM 10-27 General Supply in a Theater of Operations
(5) FM 55-10 Movement Control
(6) FM 55-20 Rail Transport in a Theater of Operations
(7) FM 55-50 Army Water Transport Operations
(8) FM 55-60 Army Terminal Operations, FM 100-5 Operations
(9) FM 100-10 Combat Service Support

(10) FM 100-17 Mobilization, Deployment, Redeployment, Demobilization
(11) FM 100-17-1 Army Pre-Positioned Afloat Operations
(12) FM 100-17-2 Army Pre-Positioned Land
(13) FM 100-17-3 Reception, Staging, On-Ward Movement, & Integration (RSO&I)
(14) FM 100-17-5 Redeployment

REFERENCES

1. D.J. Reimer, Training and doctrine digital library, `http://www.adtdl.army.mil`.
2. *Deployment Planning Guide, Transportation Assets Required for Deployment*, MTMCTEA Reference 97-700-5, (July 1997).
3. *Logistics Handbook for Strategic Mobility Planning*, MTMCTEA Reference 97-700-2, (August 1997).
4. *Air Mobility Planning Factors*, AFPAM 10-1403, (June 1997).
5. C.J. Keyfauver *et al.*, *MIDAS Version 3.1 Users Manual (Draft)*, Vienna, VA, (May 2001).
6. C.N. Van Groningen, M.D. Braun, M.A. Clemmons, G. Lurie, K.L. Simunich, D. Timmerman, H. Vander Zee and M.A. Widing, *ELIST 8.1 User's Manual*, ANL/DIS/TM-62, Argonne National Laboratory, Argonne, IL, (February 2002).
7. M.D. Braun and C.N. Van Groningen, *ELIST 8 Transportation Model*, ANL/DIS/02-1, Argonne National Laboratory, Argonne, IL, (February 2002).
8. C.N. Van Groningen, M.D. Braun, M.A. Clemmons, G. Lurie, K.L. Simunich, D. Timmerman, H. Vander Zee and M.A. Widing, *ETEdit 8.1 User's Manual*, ANL/DIS/TM-63, Argonne National Laboratory, Argonne, IL, (February 2002).
9. *Joint Operation Planning and Execution System Volume II (Planning Formats and Guidance)*, CJCSM 3122.03, (June 1996).
10. M. Braun, G. Lurie, K. Simunich, C. Van Groningen, H. Vander Zee and M. Widing, ELIST8: A simulation system for transportation logistics planning support, In *Proc. 2000 Summer Computer Simulation Conference*, Vancouver, BC, July 16–20, 2000.
11. C. Macal, C. Van Groningen and M. Braun, Simulation of transportation movements over constrained infrastructure networks, In *Proc. 1995 Simulation Multi-Conference, Volume 4*, Phoenix, AZ, pp. 97–102, April 1995.
12. J.P. Tustin *et al.*, Integrating MIDAS and ELIST into the AMP HLA federation, In *Fall 2001 SISO Simulation Interoperability Workshop*, 01F-SIW-057, (September 2001).

9780080444055